Popular Culture in the Ancient World

Popular Culture in the Ancient World is the first book to provide an interdisciplinary study of the subject. Traditionally neglected by classical scholars, popular culture provides a new window through which we can view the ancient world. An international group of scholars tackles a fascinating range of subjects and objects – from dice oracles to dressing up, from toys to theological speculation. Diverse comparative and theoretical approaches are used alongside many different ancient sources to provide a wide-ranging and rigorous approach to ancient popular culture. After a substantive introduction, the book moves from classical Greece through the Roman Empire to end in the late antique world. It enriches our understanding of the ancient world as well as our conception of the legacy of the ancient world in our own.

LUCY GRIG is Senior Lecturer in Roman History in the Department of Classics at the University of Edinburgh where she also directs the MSc in Late Antique, Islamic and Byzantine Studies. She is the author of *Making Martyrs in Late Antiquity* (London, 2004) and co-editor, with Gavin Kelly, of *Two Romes: Rome and Constantinople in Late Antiquity* (New York, 2012) as well as a number of articles and book chapters on the cultural and religious history of Late Antiquity.

Popular Culture in the Ancient World

Edited by LUCY GRIG
University of Edinburgh

CAMBRIDGE
UNIVERSITY PRESS

CAMBRIDGE
UNIVERSITY PRESS

University Printing House, Cambridge CB2 8BS, United Kingdom

One Liberty Plaza, 20th Floor, New York, NY 10006, USA

477 Williamstown Road, Port Melbourne, VIC 3207, Australia

4843/24, 2nd Floor, Ansari Road, Daryaganj, Delhi – 110002, India

79 Anson Road, #06–04/06, Singapore 079906

Cambridge University Press is part of the University of Cambridge.

It furthers the University's mission by disseminating knowledge in the pursuit of education, learning, and research at the highest international levels of excellence.

www.cambridge.org
Information on this title: www.cambridge.org/9781107074897
DOI: 10.1017/9781139871402

© Cambridge University Press 2017

This publication is in copyright. Subject to statutory exception and to the provisions of relevant collective licensing agreements, no reproduction of any part may take place without the written permission of Cambridge University Press.

First published 2017

Printed in the United Kingdom by Clays, St Ives plc

A catalogue record for this publication is available from the British Library.

ISBN 978-1-107-07489-7 Hardback

Cambridge University Press has no responsibility for the persistence or accuracy of URLs for external or third-party Internet Web sites referred to in this publication, and does not guarantee that any content on such Web sites is, or will remain, accurate or appropriate.

Contents

List of Figures [*page* vii]
List of Contributors [viii]
Acknowledgements [ix]
Abbreviations [x]

1 Introduction: Approaching Popular Culture in the Ancient World [1]
   LUCY GRIG

   PART I: CLASSICAL GREECE [37]

2 The Popular Culture of the Athenian Institutions: 'Authorized' Popular Culture and 'Unauthorized' Elite Culture in Classical Athens [39]
   MIRKO CANEVARO

3 Humouring the Masses: The Theatre Audience and the Highs and Lows of Aristophanic Comedy [66]
   JAMES ROBSON

   PART II: ROME [89]

4 Popular Public Opinion in a Nutshell: Nicknames and Non-Elite Political Culture in the Late Republic [91]
   CRISTINA ROSILLO-LÓPEZ

5 Plebeian Culture in the City of Rome, from the Late Republic to the Early Empire [107]
   CYRIL COURRIER

6 Pollio's Paradox: Popular Invective and the Transition to Empire [129]
   TOM HAWKINS

7 The Music of Power and the Power of Music: Studying Popular Auditory Culture in Ancient Rome [149]
ALEXANDRE VINCENT

PART III: THE ROMAN EMPIRE: GREECE, ROME AND BEYOND [165]

8 The Intellectual Life of the Roman Non-Elite [167]
JERRY TONER

9 Divination and Popular Culture [189]
VICTORIA JENNINGS

10 Children's Cultures in Roman Egypt [208]
APRIL PUDSEY

PART IV: LATE ANTIQUITY [235]

11 Interpreting the Kalends of January: A Case Study for Late Antique Popular Culture? [237]
LUCY GRIG

12 Popular Christianity and Lived Religion in Late Antique Rome: Seeing Magic in the Catacombs [257]
NICOLA DENZEY LEWIS

13 Popular Theology in Late Antiquity [277]
JACLYN MAXWELL

14 Communication and Plebeian Sociability in Late Antiquity: The View from North Africa in the Age of Augustine [296]
JULIO CESAR MAGALHÃES DE OLIVEIRA

Bibliography [318]
Index [365]

Figures

11.1. Drawing of DSP plate featuring a stag. Drawn by Belinda Washington, after J. Rigoir, Y. Rigoir and J. F. Meffre 1973: 207–63, at 255, no. 901. [*page* 248]
11.2. Drawing of DSP plate featuring stags and a human figure. Drawn by Belinda Washington, after J. Rigoir, Y. Rigoir and J. F. Meffre 1973: 207–63, at 254, no. 898. [249]
11.3. Man dressed as a stag from the *Roman d'Alexandre*. MS Bodley 264, fol. 70r. Bodleian Libraries, University of Oxford. [250]
11.4. Animal mummers and dancers from the *Roman d'Alexandre*. MS Bodley 264, fol. 21v. Bodleian Libraries, University of Oxford. [251]
12.1. Drawing of bone token from the catacombs featuring a bald sphinx. Vat. Mus. inv. 60628. Drawn by Belinda Washington. [265]
12.2. Drawing of *loculus* closing depicting a rider-god spearing a demon. Drawn by Belinda Washington, after Nuzzo 2000: 249–56, at 250, Fig. 26.1.7. [268]

Contributors

MIRKO CANEVARO, University of Edinburgh

CYRIL COURRIER, Aix-Marseille University

LUCY GRIG, University of Edinburgh

TOM HAWKINS, Ohio State University

VICTORIA JENNINGS, independent scholar

NICOLA DENZEY LEWIS, Brown University

JACLYN MAXWELL, Ohio University

JULIO CESAR MAGALHÃES DE OLIVEIRA, University of São Paulo

APRIL PUDSEY, Manchester Metropolitan University

JAMES ROBSON, Open University

CRISTINA ROSILLO-LÓPEZ, Universidad Pablo de Olavide

JERRY TONER, University of Cambridge

ALEXANDRE VINCENT, University of Poitiers

Acknowledgements

The bulk of the chapters in this volume had their origin as papers delivered at the conference 'Locating Popular Culture in the Ancient World', held at the University of Edinburgh in July 2012. A second conference, 'Locating Popular Culture in the Ancient World 2', organized with Dr Agnieszka Kotlińska-Toma, was held at the University of Wroclaw in September 2014, at which two more of the chapters received helpful feedback. These contributions have in turn been supplemented by two more, following up excellent suggestions from reviewers from Cambridge University Press. All the chapters have been developed and revised in a spirit of collegiality by the volume contributors. The study of ancient popular culture is, if my experience is anything to go by, a lively, open-minded and friendly field, and it is to be hoped that further conferences and collaborations will follow.

I would like to thank the School of History, Classics and Archaeology at the University of Edinburgh for supporting the initial conference. I would also like to thank my colleagues here in the Classics department for their warm support, especially, for more specific help, Judy Barringer, Mirko Canevaro, David Lewis, Calum Maciver, Richard Rawles, Ben Russell and Simon Trépanier. Other friends and colleagues have helped with the preparation of the volume in various ways, particularly Cristina Rosillo-López, Jerry Toner and Ville Vuolanto, but most particularly Victoria Jennings. I am very grateful indeed to Belinda Washington for taking the time to produce the fine drawings. I would also like to thank all the Edinburgh students who have taken my 'Popular Culture in the Ancient World' course over the last few years and have been such lively and thoughtful interlocutors.

Michael Sharp at Cambridge University Press has been an enthusiastic supporter of the project throughout and I am also very grateful for the helpful and constructive comments of the anonymous referees.

Thanks are due to Alan Grig and to Mary and Peter Hayes for family support during related conferences and research trips. The most important acknowledgements (and much more) are nonetheless due to Rosa, Clem, Frieda and, especially, Damian Hayes.

Abbreviations

Abbreviations of classical works, authors and reference works are as in the *Oxford Classical Dictionary*. Journal titles are abbreviated as in *L'année philologique*.

Abbreviations of patristic text editions, reference works and translations not given in the *Oxford Classical Dictionary* are as follows:

AASS:	*Acta sanctorum quotquot toto orbe coluntur*
Aesopica:	Perry, B. E. (ed. and trans.) (1952) *Aesopica: A Series of Texts Relating to Aesop or Ascribed to Him or Closely Connected with the Literary Tradition that Bears his Name.* Collected and critically edited, in part translated from Oriental languages, with a commentary and historical essay. Urbana, IL.
CCL:	*Corpus christianorum, series Latina*
GNO:	*Gregorii Nysseni Opera*
ICUR:	*Inscriptiones christianae urbis Romae septimo saeculo*
MGH Conc.:	*Monumenta Germaniae historica: Concilia*
MGH Epp. sel.:	*Monumenta Germaniae historica: Epistolae selectae*
MGH SRM:	*Monumenta Germaniae historica: Scriptores rerum Merovingicarum*
PG:	*Patrologiae cursus completus. Series graeca*
PL:	*Patrologiae cursus completus. Series latina*
RE:	*Paulys Realencyclopädie der classischen Altertumswissenschaft*, ed. G. Wissowa *et al.*, 33 vols., 15 suppls. (Stuttgart, 1983–1978 (sic))
SC:	*Sources Chrétiennes*

1 | Introduction: Approaching Popular Culture in the Ancient World

LUCY GRIG

Was there such a thing as popular culture in the ancient world? And even if there was, how on earth can we, as scholars, access it? Can we expect to find a single 'popular culture' across the wide chronological and geographical terrain represented by the chapters in this book? The scholars contributing to this volume, a diverse group from across the classical disciplines, and from different scholarly traditions, share a conviction that ancient popular culture is both accessible and worth studying. Moreover, there is a shared conviction that it is *important* to study ancient popular culture, in that it will enrich and broaden our understanding of the ancient world, as well as our conception of the legacy of the ancient world in our own. Although the chapters collected here do not claim to offer a complete picture of ancient popular culture, they represent an important step forward in its study.

Classical scholarship has traditionally been concerned with the elite of the ancient world and their culture. One of the contributors to this book, Jerry Toner, has argued that classicists, tending to derive 'from the upper and upper-middle classes ... have tended to be content to remain in the more comfortable thought-worlds of the Roman elite'.[1] When popular culture does come their way, classicists have tended to look upon it with a considerable degree of condescension. For instance, while discussing the fascinating Mimes of Herodas W. G. Arnott suggests that it might be 'healthy' for classicists 'occasionally to turn away from the ivory towers of scholarly pursuits towards the seamier corners of real life'.[2] Even more strikingly, B. E. Perry famously described the ancient novel as 'a low and disrespectable level of literature, adapted to the taste and understanding of uncultivated or frivolous-minded people'.[3] This volume will take the reader beyond the 'comfortable thought-worlds of the Roman elite', at times into 'the seamier corners of real life', while demonstrating the

---

Thanks are due to a number of friends and colleagues who commented on drafts of this chapter or provided information and suggestions of various kinds: Mirko Canevaro, David Lewis, Cristina Rosillo-López and Ville Vuolanto.

[1] Toner 1995: 22; this applies most fittingly to British-trained classicists, rather than to ancient historians in general.
[2] Arnott 1971: 132.   [3] Perry 1967: 98.

richness of a culture which is far more rounded than the merely 'low and disrespectable'.

The popular culture under examination in this volume will take us from fifth-century BCE Greece to sixth-century CE Gaul. Both unity and diversity[4] will characterize the phenomena we encounter on this journey. Objects and subjects under discussion range from children's toys to theological speculation, from mental arithmetic to dressing up, from nicknames to oracles, from fables to musical instruments. The 'people' are also a diverse bunch. They are the political actors and theatre audiences of classical Athens. They are the urban plebs of the Roman Republic, as well as the subjects of the Roman emperor. They are the oft-chided congregations of late antique preachers. They are children, adults, soldiers, slaves, peasants and urbanites, performers and spectators. In each case, the authors in this book seek to examine this cast of characters in their own terms, to restore their agency. In each case, we show that we can move beyond a 'top-down' view of history, to construct a far more lively picture of the ancient world, making use of a diverse range of historical sources, as well as a variety of methodological approaches, taking inspiration from a rich comparative and theoretical literature.

Nonetheless, this book is not, and does not claim to be, a complete, or indeed a diachronic history of ancient popular culture. As will become clear, the chapters show a notable bias towards the Roman world. While such imbalances are often circumstantial, it is worth pausing to consider whether in fact there is more than sheer chance involved here. Was it ultimately the developments of the Hellenistic period that brought about the conditions for popular culture to flourish? That is, did the smaller, more equal societies of classical Greece allow less space for the development of a specifically popular culture? In any case, it is clear that the evidential basis for the study of ancient popular culture increases massively in the Roman imperial period. Even more so, as we shall see, in Late Antiquity Christianization entailed a new elite interest in the activities of the lower classes, offering both a new ideological approach and a new wealth of evidence for 'popular culture'.

In this introductory chapter I shall lay out the parameters for a study of ancient popular culture. This involves first of all a substantial study of the theoretical and historical literature relating to the investigation of popular culture, ancient and modern. For most of the contributors to this volume, methodological and theoretical discussions are not an optional extra for

---

[4] Taken from a chapter title of Burke 2009, 'Unity and diversity in popular culture'.

the study of ancient popular culture, but an essential aspect. Only at this point does discussion turn to the ancient world, firstly asking the crucial question 'who were "the people?"', before surveying recent scholarship on ancient popular culture, then finally turning to investigate key aspects that constitute ancient popular culture (such as religion, politics, literature and material culture) and its location (urban, rural, public and private).

Approaching Popular Culture

How can we define popular culture?[5] The classicist Holt Parker suggests, not entirely tongue-in-cheek, that 'we may not be able to define it, but we know it when we see it'.[6] Parker also provides one of the neatest, breeziest summaries available of the most important theories in current currency:

Definitions of popular culture as 1) quantitatively superior, 2) qualitatively inferior, 3) mass culture, 4) a product of 'the people', 5) a battlefield for hegemony or 6) a chimera to be deconstructed by Postmodernism, have much to offer, but none is completely satisfying.[7]

Some readers will perhaps prefer to skip this section at this point, but it should already be clear that 'popular culture' (like 'elite culture') is of course a *construct* rather than a self-evident reality, and as such requires methodological and theoretical interrogation, which will take us from Romanticism, through Marxism, to postmodernism, with many permutations in between.

As we shall see, in the definition of *popular* culture the definition of culture itself is at stake, and this turns out to be highly contested. No less a figure than Raymond Williams, founder of the discipline of Cultural Studies, declared that:

Culture is one of the two or three most complicated words in the English language ... mainly because it has now come to be used of important concepts in several distinct intellectual disciplines and in several distinct and incompatible systems of thought.[8]

Indeed we shall see, as this survey progresses, that the definition of 'culture' at play oscillates wildly, from a pluralistic 'way of life' to an elitist 'high'

---

[5] There are a number of useful readers and introductory books to help readers navigate the large body of theoretical work on popular culture, which is only briefly introduced here. See, in particular, Bigsby 1976; Guins and Zaragoza Cruz 2005; Storey 2006, 2008; Strinati 2004.
[6] Parker 2011: 147. [7] Parker 2011: 169. [8] Williams 1976: 76–7.

culture, which can thus be contrasted with a 'popular', 'mass' or other type of 'low' culture, and back again.[9]

The history of the study of popular culture, or, as Peter Burke puts it, 'the discovery of the people', goes back as far as the late eighteenth century, with the development of what was the first serious investigation of 'folk' culture.[10] As Burke has demonstrated, the academic study of popular culture was born, not coincidentally, at precisely the time when traditional popular culture was starting to disappear. The influential poet and critic Johann Herder was a key figure here, motivated not least by a radically pluralistic notion of *Kultur*, rejecting the existing teleological Eurocentric narrative of cultural superiority.[11] Herder made two important collections of *Volkslieder*, and contrasted the *Kultur des Volkes* with the *Kultur der Gelehrten*: popular culture and learned culture. Equally influential were the collections of folk tales made by Jakob and Wilhelm Grimm between 1812 and 1857. Jakob Grimm stressed the idea of communal authorship, of collective creativity, writing 'Das Volk dichtet' ('the people creates'). Elsewhere in Europe folksongs in particular, but also traditional literature, featured in a number of national collections. The key intellectual influences were undoubtedly Romanticism and nationalism, while the impact of industrialization on traditional culture played a crucial role. The popular culture envisaged by its champions was undoubtedly rural, communal rather than individualistic, and largely timeless, or ahistorical. We can see the continuing presence of these characterizations in the scholarship that followed.

If traditional popular culture was discovered 'just in time'[12] by this first generation of scholars, many of their successors strongly believed that this traditional culture had been replaced by a debased and vulgar substitute. While there had been concerns about the threat to traditional culture from mechanized and industrialized civilization, the concern of the 'learned' was now focused on a threat to a much more limited, elitist definition of 'culture'. In the hugely influential *Culture and Anarchy* (1869), Matthew Arnold (who popularized the idea of 'Philistines' as the uncultured opponents of enlightened culture) defined 'culture' as knowledge of 'the best that has been said and thought in the world'.[13] In other words, Arnold influentially limited the definition of 'culture' to what would now be

---

[9] Williams 1976: 77 notes how romantic notions of culture have been 'politically schizoid, swimming between radicals and reaction'.
[10] Burke 2009: 23–48.   [11] As discussed by Williams 1976: 25–32.   [12] Burke 2009: 40.
[13] Arnold 1960: 6. Furthermore, 'Culture is properly defined as the love of perfection; it is a study of perfection': Arnold 1960: 48.

termed 'high culture'. Popular culture itself is not specifically defined by Arnold, and yet it is clearly implied in the 'anarchy' opposed to his (high) 'culture'.[14]

Mechanization brought about a great transformation in people's experience of and participation in culture, as increasingly noted by critics and scholars in the first half of the twentieth century. In a hugely influential essay, the German critic Walter Benjamin welcomed the democratic and participatory opportunities brought about by the mechanical reproduction of art.[15] However, conservative critics contended, equally influentially, that modern civilization had been overly mechanized and that traditional hierarchies of culture were now under threat from new technologies of reproduction. Meanwhile F. R. Leavis took up the mantel of Arnold, in *Mass Civilisation and Minority Culture* (1930), arguing that there was a clear division between minority culture and mass civilization: the influence of the former was under threat and the latter was an object of fear and disapproval.[16] Criticism of this new 'mass culture' came from the left, as well as the right, as with the writings of the prolific social critic Dwight MacDonald, who asserted a clear distinction between mass and *popular* culture, asserting of the former: 'its distinctive mark is that it is solely and directly an article for mass consumption, like chewing gum'.[17] MacDonald contrasted this mass culture with 'folk art', which he saw, like Herder and the Grimms before him, as 'a spontaneous, autochthonous expression of the people, shaped by themselves' while 'Mass Culture is imposed from above. It is fabricated by technicians hired by businessmen; its audiences are passive consumers, their participation limited to the choice between buying and not buying.'[18]

A pessimistic approach to twentieth-century popular culture often has its roots in the Marxist analysis of culture. At the heart of this analysis lies the notion that a society's culture is determined by its economic base, upon

---

[14] Arnold 1960: 176. Furthermore, he refers to the non-elite in highly derogatory terms, writing of the 'raw and uncultivated ... masses' and 'those vast miserable unmanageable masses of sunken people': 193.
[15] Benjamin 2008.
[16] Leavis was concerned about the strength of Americanization, particularly as transmitted through films: Leavis 1930: 35. 'They provide now the main form of recreation in the civilized world; and they involve surrender, under conditions of hypnotic receptivity, to the cheapest emotional appeals, appeals the more insidious because they are associated with a compellingly vivid illusion of actual life.'
[17] MacDonald 1957: 59.
[18] MacDonald 1957: 60. Note that MacDonald specifically criticizes conservative attacks on mass culture for making the error of confusing it with folk art: 69.

which was built an ideological 'superstructure'.[19] It should be noted that almost right from the start the heavily reductive determinism of this concept was being modified.[20] Nonetheless the basic theory perdures: that, as a result of the inequality that is built into the relations of production, the leading ideas in capitalist society, even including popular culture, are those of, and those spread by, the ruling classes.

We can see the scholarly approach to popular culture became even more negative, indeed fatalistic, in twentieth-century thought. Prominent members of what is known as the Frankfurt School, Max Horkheimer and Theodor Adorno, coined the notion of the 'culture industry' in 1944.[21] In this analysis, even the concept of mass culture was inadequate, as in fact the masses had no responsibility for this culture at all, which was a homogeneous, uniform product. The culture industry, it was argued, uses culture to promote a dominant ideology, and by this means it incorporates the people into this ideology, and thus mass conformity, far from the 'anarchy' envisaged by Arnold.[22]

The idea that the capitalist mode of production produced a closed system of 'culture' from which there could be no escape was shared by another influential theorist, Louis Althusser. For Althusser, ideology in the capitalist system 'interpellates' the individual as a subject, representing 'the imaginary relationship of the individual to their real conditions of existence',[23] so that we are bound to ignore, or 'misrecognize' reality.[24] Althusser influentially argued that ideology was a system, a *practice*, with 'a material existence', produced by 'ideological state apparatuses' (ISAs: for instance, mass media churches, schools, the family).[25] This idea of

---

[19] As most classically stated in the famous Preface and Introduction to Marx's *Contribution to the Critique of Political Economy* of 1859: Marx 1976: 3. In *The German Ideology* of 1845–6 (1974), Marx and Engels had already argued that the ruling class, having the means of material production, would inevitably have control of the means of *mental* production.

[20] Even by Engels himself in his letter to Joseph Bloch: 'According to the materialist conception of history, the ultimately determining element in history is the production and reproduction of real life. Neither Marx nor I have ever asserted more than this. Therefore if somebody twists this into saying that the economic factor is the only determining one, he is transforming that proposition into a meaningless, abstract absurd phrase': Marx and Engels 1977: 75.

[21] Adorno and Horkheimer 1979: esp. 120–1.

[22] E.g. Adorno 1991: 104: 'The categorical imperative of the culture industry no longer has anything in common with freedom. It proclaims: you shall conform, without instruction as to what; conform to what exists anyway, and that which everyone thinks anyway as a reflex to power and omnipotence. The power of the culture industry's ideology is such that conformity has replaced consciousness.'

[23] Althusser 1971: 153.   [24] Althusser 1971: 170.

[25] Althusser 1971. For application in the context of the ancient world, discussing the Roman games as an ISA (alongside other theoretical interpretations) see Gunderson 1996: 116–18.

imposing conformity through cultural means rather than through outright coercion[26] is also key to the work of Antonio Gramsci, whose concept of 'cultural hegemony' has been hugely influential in the study of popular culture.[27] Gramsci argued that dominated or subordinate groups (*classi subalterne*) were unable to produce their own autonomous, genuinely popular culture. Rather than understanding this as a version of the rather crude concept of 'false consciousness', the position of these groups is seen rather by Gramsci as one of 'contradictory consciousness' – 'always divided and ambiguous'.[28]

Gramsci's theories have been hugely influential on the Subaltern Studies movement,[29] while the influence of postcolonial scholarship itself has important implications for our study of popular culture. More accessibly, James C. Scott's idea of 'infrapolitics', especially as laid out in *Domination and the Arts of Resistance*[30] has been cited by many scholars of premodern popular culture.[31] Scott's key concept of the '"hidden transcript" that represents a critique of power spoken behind the back of the dominant' is a particularly suggestive idea, tying in nicely with theories of the carnivalesque and its radical potential,[32] as discussed further below. But can popular culture ever seriously challenge dominant, hegemonic culture? The answer surely lies in understanding cultural relations as dynamic, rather than static. Here we can look, most helpfully, to Stuart Hall's seminal essay 'Notes on deconstructing the "popular"' (1981), which clearly stresses the *embeddedness* of popular culture: 'there is *no* whole, authentic, autonomous "popular culture" which lies outside the field of force of the relations of cultural power and domination'.[33] Hall stresses that any proper understanding of popular culture must, by necessity, be political. He argues that the dominant culture will always seek to suppress popular culture, though this is not to say that we need to accept an entirely pessimistic

---

[26] Althusser clearly distinguished between 'repressive' and 'ideological' state apparatuses.
[27] Insofar as Gramsci ever offers a precise definition of this term, it is described as the '"spontaneous" consent given by the great masses of the population to the general direction imposed on social life by the dominant fundamental group; this consent is "historically" caused by the prestige (and consequent confidence) which the dominant group enjoys because of its position and function in the world of production': Gramsci 1971: 12.
[28] Lears 1985: 569, 570.
[29] Note a useful definition of subaltern studies from Bernstein and Byres 2001: 33: 'the desire to write history from the viewpoint of subalterns (peasants and workers) as autonomous agents who create their own forms of oppositional culture and identity, who are not victims and/or followers, and whose ideas and actions are not to be represented (appropriated) by elite agents and discourses that claim to speak on their behalf'.
[30] Scott 1990, building on his earlier fieldwork-based studies: Scott 1976, 1985.
[31] E.g. Forsdyke 2012; Kurke 2011; Toner 2009, all discussed below.   [32] Scott 1990: xii.
[33] Hall 1981: 232.

reading, whereby popular culture is impossible because it is inevitably defeated by hegemonic forces. Hall stresses that popular culture is both *dynamic* and *dialectical* in nature;[34] therefore its position vis-à-vis the dominant culture and ideology is always Janus-like: 'In the study of popular culture, we should always start here: with the double-stake in popular culture, the double movement of containment and resistance, which is always inevitably inside it.'[35] This then gives us a starting point for wrestling an understanding of ancient popular culture from its massively unequal source base. Stuart Hall's contribution thus enables a constructive approach to popular culture, which does not deny Gramscian 'cultural hegemony', but does allow it to be more permeable than a conventionally pessimistic reading of Gramsci would allow.

Hall's insistence on 'the people' as both producers and users of culture can be compared with various poststructuralist approaches which describe popular culture as *bricolage*.[36] The work of Michel de Certeau, who stressed the creativity and powers of invention of ordinary people, examining their '*ré-emploi*' of popular culture, is particularly relevant here.[37] This approach helps break down and through the bald and unhelpful dichotomies which have traditionally beset the subject, as we have already seen: does popular culture come properly up from below (e.g. 'folk culture'), or is it imposed downwards from the top (e.g. 'mass culture')?

Meanwhile Holt Parker has recently suggested that we move our focus away from the 'people' to the objects of the culture itself, to the 'social life of things'.[38] Parker also suggests that while discussions of the subject remain

---

[34] 'what is essential to the definition of popular culture is the relations which define "popular culture" in a continuing tension (relationship, influence and antagonism) to the dominant culture. It is a conception of culture which is polarized around this cultural dialectic': Hall 1981: 235.

[35] Hall 1981: 228. Further, Hall refers to a 'continuous and necessarily uneven struggle' by dominant culture to 'enclose and confine' culture: Hall 1981: 233. Cf. Bennett 1986: xv: 'The field of popular culture is structured by the attempt of the ruling class to win hegemony and by the forms of opposition to this endeavour. As such, it consists not simply of an imposed mass culture that is coincident with dominant ideology, nor simply of spontaneously oppositional cultures, but is rather an area of negotiation between the two within which – in different particular types of popular culture – dominant, subordinate and oppositional cultural and ideological values and elements are "mixed" in different permutations.'

[36] The concept of social bricolage is taken from Lévi-Strauss 1966: esp. 16–23; for its application to the study of popular culture see, for example, Hebdige 1979.

[37] An 'art of doing things': Certeau 1984: esp. xi–xxiii and 15–41. Relevant here too is the growing interest in contemporary cultural studies in the seemingly straightforward concept of 'everyday life'; see Highmore 2002; for the material culture aspect of this in particular, focusing on the study of 'things', see Attfield 2000.

[38] See Parker 2011: 159; the term derives from Appadurai 1985: 45, itself building on Baudrillard's essay 'The system of objects': Baudrillard 1988: 16–17.

tied to an essentially Marxist framework, the framework of class is best replaced by that of 'status' (which is indeed more readily applicable to the ancient world). Parker also takes inspiration from Pierre Bourdieu, and his much-cited notion of 'cultural capital'.[39] In this analysis, Parker suggests, we can define popular culture as that which is produced for and/or consumed by those *without* cultural capital.[40] Most distinctively, Parker suggests that popular culture can in fact best be understood as 'unauthorized culture',[41] the advantage of which is that this definition bears no inherent political or aesthetic status, and implies no value judgement.

This discussion of Parker's contribution draws to a close this admittedly partial survey of theoretical material. As will become clear, some of the definitions and issues under discussion explicitly deal with the issue of popular culture under capitalist modernity and can only with difficulty be applied to a study of premodern popular culture. We shall now look to see how historians of this period have approached the subject.

Historicizing Popular Culture in the Premodern World

The study of popular culture in the premodern world has first of all built upon the huge advances in the study of the non-elite made by social historians. This is not the place for a detailed survey of this huge body of work, including the predominantly Anglo-Saxon social-science-led work from the 1960s onwards (part of a strong strain of Marxist historiography),[42] the pioneering work of the French *Annales* school,[43] and the often fascinating insights brought by the study of 'microhistory'.[44] Overall, however, the most important and relevant work from this period is undoubtedly E. P. Thompson's *The Making of the English Working Class*. The bringing of the cultural dimension to the work of social and economic history was crucial and the key concept contained in the title is that of

---

[39] Again, an extended definition is elusive, but see Bourdieu 1977: esp. 159–97; Parker 2011: 160, n. 69.
[40] Although this definition might be thought too limiting: cultural capital is of course at play among all social groups.
[41] Parker 2011: esp. 165. However, see Canevaro below, who critiques this concept in the case of classical Athens.
[42] See here the special issue of the *Journal of Social History* of 1976: 'Social History Today and Tomorrow?', esp. Stearns 1976.
[43] See, for a useful summary, Clark 1985.
[44] See here Muir 1991. The work of Carlo Ginzburg, who coined the term, is discussed by Canevaro below, notably Ginzburg 1980.

making: 'The working class made itself as much as it was made.'[45] That is, Thompson stressed both the agency of the non-elite and the constructedness of culture – key themes for this project.

Thompson's work is foundational for many of the new cultural historians, whose work first came to prominence in the 1970s. We have already seen that 'culture' is a polyvalent term; in the hands of this new wave of cultural historians, it became markedly *symbolic*. According to an oft-favoured definition from the anthropologists Kroeber and Kluckhorn:

> Culture consists of patterns, explicit and implicit, of and for behavior acquired and transmitted by symbols, constituting the distinctive achievements of human groups, including their embodiment in artifacts.[46]

This concentration on the symbolic has been a marked feature of this new cultural history, as helpfully described by one of its most influential practitioners, Peter Burke:

> cultural historians might usefully define themselves not in terms of a particular area or 'field' such as art, literature and music, but rather by a distinctive concern for values and symbols, wherever these are to be found, in the everyday life of ordinary people as well as in special performances for elites.[47]

This concern for the symbolic is seen in the striking influence of cultural anthropology, particular the work of Clifford Geertz.[48] Geertz' idea, much cited, that 'the culture of a people is an ensemble of texts, themselves ensembles, which the anthropologist strains to read over the shoulders of those to whom they properly belong' has been hugely stimulating for many historians, who recognize, all the same, that their interpretive task is even harder than that of the anthropologist.[49]

This influence has greatly impacted upon cultural historians and the study of popular culture, in a focus on rituals such as religious festivals but also other kinds of culturally stereotyped (or 'ritual') behaviour, including feasting, violence and the activities of groups and organizations.[50] Among

---

[45] Thompson 1963: 194.

[46] Kroeber and Kluckhohn 1952: 181. The symbolic element in this definition is thus more marked than in, for instance, the more traditional anthropological definition of culture as 'civilization', e.g. Tylor 1871: 1: 'Culture ... is that complex whole which includes knowledge, belief, art, morals, law, custom, and any other capabilities and habits acquired by man as a member of society.'

[47] Burke 2009: 18–19.

[48] Geertz' method of 'thick description' has been particularly influential: see Geertz 1973: esp. 3–30 and 412–53.

[49] Geertz 1973: 452.

[50] See, for instance, the now classic articles by Natalie Zemon Davis on 'charivari', 'abbeys of misrule' and ritual violence, collected together in Davis 1975. Davis in her turn was influenced

the festivals studied, none has been as influential as the early modern festival of carnival, particularly as analysed by Mikhail Bakhtin. Bakhtin, a Russian literary critic and philosopher, wrote prolifically in Soviet Russia, but was only 'discovered' by Western scholarship in the 1960s. *Rabelais and his World*, which appeared in English translation in 1968, has had a massive impact on the study of popular culture (or 'folk culture' as Bakhtin himself calls it).[51] Bakhtin argued for the symbolic centrality of carnival to early modern culture: 'carnival' is a place of inversion, of comedy, of the grotesque, where high becomes low, and the 'lower bodily stratum' reigns supreme. Carnival is 'a second world and a second life outside officialdom, a world in which all medieval people participated more or less';[52] it is *the* place where uninhibited, unofficial discourse, could be uttered:[53] 'carnival is the people's second life, organized on the basis of laughter'.[54] It is a place where hierarchical society could, temporarily at least, be infused with its opposite; it is a site of liberation and renewal.[55] For Bakhtin, carnival went beyond the festival itself and he stressed the strength of the 'carnivalesque': 'a potent, populist, crucial inversion of *all* official words and hierarchies in a way that has implications far beyond the specific realm of Rabelais studies'.[56] Bakhtin's notion of carnival as providing a crucial site for opposition and rebellion in 'pre-political' societies has made his work particularly stimulating for scholars of pre-industrial societies.[57] Obviously Bakhtin's work on carnival has been questioned, critiqued and developed. Certain critiques are almost immediately apparent. Is it really so easy to write about folk culture on the basis of an elite text? Is the apparent licence of carnival not just another form of social control (licensed licence)?[58] Should we essentialize carnival

---

  by the great social historian E. P. Thompson; see, in particular, the essays collected in Thompson 1991.
[51] In this volume, the importance of Bakhtin is shown in the chapters by Grig, Hawkins, Jennings and Toner.
[52] Bakhtin 1968: 6.
[53] See Scott 1990: 175, n. 91: 'It doesn't take much in the way of inference to equate the realm of official mendacity and dominated discourse with the Stalinist state and the carnivalesque of Rabelais as an offstage negation and scepticism that will survive repression.'
[54] Bakhtin 1968: 8.
[55] Bakhtin 1968: esp. 10: 'The suspension of all hierarchical precedence during carnival time was of particular significance ... all were considered equal during carnival time ... People were, so to speak, reborn for new, purely human relations.'
[56] Stallybrass and White 1986: 7.
[57] See, for instance, Le Roy Ladurie 1979; Davis 1975: 97–123, esp. 103. See further discussion below.
[58] E.g. Eagleton 1981: 148: 'Carnival, after all, is a *licensed* affair, in every sense, a permissible rupture of hegemony, a contained popular blow-off as disturbing and relatively ineffectual as

in this way, in any case?[59] Nonetheless, its importance for the study of popular culture is almost impossible to overstate.

Bakhtin's influence on the study of popular culture is not limited to his work on Rabelais. In fact, of almost equal prominence is his work on 'heteroglossia' or polyphony in the novel, extrapolated into a broader reading of culture itself as many voiced, of language as inherently 'dialogic'.[60] An important aspect of this dialogue is Bakhtin's argument for the interpenetration of high culture by low culture. Here we can see clear thematic continuity with his work on carnival, when Bakhtin talks about the heteroglossia of folk and street songs, as 'sharply opposed to ... literary language' and as 'parodic'.[61] In a clear anticipation of the later deconstructionist theorists, Bakhtin saw the text 'as an arena for a multiplicity of cultural struggles'.[62] This work has been productively taken up by scholars working on ancient fiction, to which we shall return later in this chapter.[63]

In the aftermath of Bakhtin, the early modern period has provided hugely fruitful territory for the study of popular culture. Alongside the work of (inter alia) Natalie Zemon Davis discussed above, Peter Burke's now classic *Popular Culture in Early Modern Europe* (first edition 1978) has been of particular importance, as is clearly reflected in the work of those seeking to approach ancient popular culture.[64] Burke's cultural history, as discussed above, takes inspiration from cultural anthropology, in this case most importantly from the work of Robert Redfield's notions of the 'great' and 'little traditions'.[65] Burke's main thesis is that in early modern Europe there was a culture that was shared, albeit asymmetrically;[66] however, over time, this shared culture became

---

a revolutionary work of art.' There is a long-running dispute as to how far we should understand such 'rituals of rebellion' (see here Gluckman 1954) as acting as mere 'safety valves', ultimately preserving the status quo.

[59] 'It actually makes little sense to fight out the issue of whether or not carnivals are *intrinsically* radical or conservative, for to do so automatically involves the false essentialising of carnivalesque transgression.' Stallybrass and White 1986: 14.

[60] For instance, Bakhtin described Dostoyevsky's characters as free to speak in 'a plurality of independent and unmerged voices and consciousness, a genuine polyphony of fully valid voices', rather than being contained by the author: Bakhtin 1984: 6.

[61] Bakhtin 1981: 273. [62] Lears 1985: 591; LaCapra 1983.

[63] Though Peter Burke's call for historians to pay more attention Bakhtin's linguistic work is still relevant: Burke 1988: 90.

[64] This work is now in its third edition: Burke 2009.

[65] Redfield 1956: 67–104, though Burke 2009: 50 critiques Redfield's 'residual' definition of popular culture, and notes that it needs to be modified: 55.

[66] 'The elite participated in the little tradition, but the common people did not participate in the great tradition': Burke 2009: 552.

divided.[67] This is not to say that Burke at any point sees culture as univocal; rather he stresses 'unity and diversity' (to take the title of his Chapter 2) throughout.

Perhaps most importantly of all for scholarship in the field, Burke's book provided a clear and subtle methodology for the investigation of *premodern* popular culture. In search of such an 'elusive quarry' (Burke's Chapter 3), even an 'oblique' approach (i.e. using the largely elite records to approach non-elite culture) will not suffice. Firstly, therefore, the historian will need to use the 'regressive method', that is, read history *backwards* from later periods.[68] Secondly, the historian needs to use the comparative method, utilizing all available material and methodologies, particularly those of social anthropology. 'Since the popular culture of early modern Europe is so elusive, it has to be approached in a roundabout manner, recovered by indirect means, and interpreted by a series of analogies.'[69] This obviously applies, to an even greater extent, to the much earlier period covered by this book.[70] Burke set out his intention to deal with 'the code of popular culture rather than the individual messages';[71] nonetheless, his book is rich with material on the content of early modern popular culture, including popular heroes and villains and the importance of carnival.

While the limited 'evidence' available for the study of early modern popular culture was very cleverly used by Burke, the source materials available to scholars of earlier periods are even more challenging. This did not deter Aaron Gurevich from writing his *Medieval Popular Culture*, which covered the period from the sixth to the thirteenth centuries. As Gurevich stresses, this period is very different even from that of the later Middle Ages and the early modern period when, he argues, 'popular culture acquired a definition: it was the culture of the lower social strata in the process of secularization which also found its expression in written and printed form'.[72] For this early period, what is required, says Gurevich, is analysis 'perhaps closest to social anthropology',[73] although his metaphors are in fact more archaeological: an attempt to 'dig down' to the intellectual, ideational, affective and socio-psychological soil in which culture arose

---

[67] 'the clergy, the nobility, the merchants, the professional men – and their wives – had abandoned popular culture to the lower classes, from whom they were now separated, as never before, by profound differences in world view': Burke 2009: 366–7.
[68] Here Burke was indebted to the pioneering work of Marc Bloch, e.g. Bloch 1966.
[69] Burke 2009: 130.
[70] For discussion of Burke's methodology and its applicability to the ancient world, see Forsdyke 2012: *passim* and Kurke 2011: 7–8, 22–3.
[71] Burke 2009: xiv.   [72] Gurevich 1988: xv.   [73] Gurevich 1988: xviii.

and by which it was sustained' and as a 'mental substratum'.[74] The influence of Bakhtin is clear: Gurevich is interested in the meeting point between 'official' and popular culture, 'a complex and contradictory synthesis which I call a "dialogue-conflict" of the two forms of consciousness'.[75] It is Bakhtin's work on dialogism that is particularly important for Gurevich, who sees early medieval clerical texts, such as those of Caesarius of Arles, as what we might term 'multivocal'.[76] Ultimately, however, the 'popular culture' discussed by Gurevich is palpably more that of the lower clergy than their erstwhile congregations.

Having looked at a wide range of approaches to premodern popular culture it is now time to turn to our own ancient 'elusive quarry'.

Approaching Ancient Popular Culture

Accessing popular culture in the ancient world brings its own set of challenges, alongside those which are familiar from later periods. Not withstanding the flourishing, as we have seen, of the historical study of popular culture, ancient historians have been rather slow to turn to the subject. This in part reflects a general situation whereby ancient historians tend to be rather late adopters of disciplinary currents that have been vibrant in other areas of history. Part of the problem lies in the embeddedness of ancient history in the field of Classics, in that ancient historians have often been trained in philology rather than the historical method,[77] and can tend to approach their field in something of a historiographical vacuum. Nonetheless, as we shall see, the fundamentally interdisciplinary nature of Classics does offer great potential for the possibilities of studying ancient popular culture in the round, including literary, visual and material culture.

Social and economic historians have long sought to elucidate the lives of the non-elites of the Greek and Roman worlds. That this book does not need to discuss in particular freedmen and women, slaves and aliens of various types, rather than allowing them to intermix with non-elites, is down to the many admirable works of previous historians. Nonetheless,

---

[74] Gurevich 1988: xix. [75] Gurevich 1988: xx.
[76] Gurevich 1988: 5: 'The pages of popularizing medieval texts contain an ongoing hidden dialogue between official doctrine and folkloric consciousness, leading to their convergence but not to their fusion.'
[77] The institutional position of ancient historians does of course vary from country to country, and there is admittedly something of an Anglo-Saxon bias to this discussion.

the first dedicated study of ancient popular culture in English[78] actually came from a philologist, well-known as an expert on Virgil. Nicholas Horsfall's fascinating short book, *The Culture of the Roman Plebs* provides a fascinating window into a

> 'parallel' culture, in its own way rich, varied and robustly vigorous: it has little enough to do with those literary texts which have bequeathed to us such a magnificent set of cultural and social blinkers, but rests rather on theatre, games in various senses, music, songs, dance, memory and has amply demonstrated its ability to survive almost unaltered at least into late antiquity.[79]

As this suggests, Horsfall mined the literary corpus with a magpie eye, unearthing an array of tantalizing snippets of oral culture, embedded into the more familiar 'classical' culture we thought we knew. Song and memory are central planks of Horsfall's vision of ancient popular culture, which is very rich on the topic of the theatre and of performance, though it otherwise almost entirely neglects the world of the visual.

Roman popular culture has been approached from a more obvious perspective – that of the social historian – by Jerry Toner, a contributor to this volume. Toner's engagement with ancient popular culture began with his book *Leisure and Ancient Rome* (1995) but was fully developed in *Popular Culture in Ancient Rome* (2009). Toner defines popular culture, straightforwardly, as 'the culture of the non-elite',[80] and declares his intention to analyse this culture 'on its own terms, on a stand-alone basis'.[81] While Horsfall's ancient popular culture is rather close to the 'timeless' model, at the very least as something enjoying an extremely *longue durée*,[82] Toner's is changing and 'dynamic'.[83] In Toner's account there is a sense of culture as more than language, as something palpable: there is an attempt to write 'sensory history', including smell, touch and noise, although the visual is again absent.[84] Popular culture appears most often as a coping strategy (or rather a series of coping strategies) through which the non-elite faced the difficult world they lived in. This study is much more politically and theoretically attuned than that of Horsfall, for instance employing the work of Bakhtin, Scott and Thompson to look at the 'carnivalesque' and popular resistance.[85]

Ancient Greek popular culture, too, has recently come under sustained examination in two recent monographs. First is Leslie Kurke's *Aesopic*

---

[78] The work of Pedro Paulo Funari constitutes an important exception: see Funari 1989, with some of its key ideas recapitulated in English in Funari 1993.
[79] Horsfall 2003: 66–7.   [80] Toner 2009: 1.   [81] Toner 2009: 5.   [82] Horsfall 2003: 23–5.
[83] Toner 2009: 7.   [84] Toner 2009: esp. 123–61 (ch. 4: 'Common scents, common senses').
[85] Toner 2009: 92–122, 162–84 (ch. 3: 'The world turned bottom up' and ch. 5: 'Popular resistance').

Conversations (2011), even though Kurke herself states that the term is 'probably ... a misnomer' for the ancient world.[86] Kurke takes the *Life of Aesop* as her starting point.[87] Refreshingly for a work of classical scholarship, this author is upfront about 'a methodology that starts from cultural history, anthropology, and structuralist and poststructuralist literary and cultural theory'. The theoretical inventory is quite striking[88] and debts to this rich vein of theory are often explicit, as when Kurke states:

> Aesop, like other folkloric trickster figures in other cultural traditions, enabled or gave voice to power and inequitable power relations from below. In these terms, Aesop was a mobile figure within the common or 'little' cultural tradition in which nonelite and elite participated together, but a figure generally banned or excluded from elite high culture. As such, stories about Aesop should give us unique access to the rifts and tensions within Greek culture – divergent views, counterideologies, and resistances to all kinds of hegemonic positions, encoded in narrative form.[89]

Kurke argues that Aesop give us access to a dialogue between 'high' and 'low' and that we should see the *Life* as 'the layered bricolage of multiple acts and agents'.[90] However, in the end she chooses to pinpoint one particular origin for the text, back in the fifth century BCE.[91]

A search for origins is also carried out by Sara Forsdyke's *Slaves Tell Tales, and Other Episodes in the Politics of Popular Culture in Ancient Greece* (2012), though in this case the layers of elite texts are unpeeled in the search for a 'popular' core. Forsdyke, like Kurke, is keen to use theoretical, and particularly comparative, literature as a crucial tool. In fact, Forsdyke's method is explicitly to interpret ancient popular culture through the use of models taken from scholarship *outside* the classical world.[92] Hence Herodotus' account of the strange reforms of Cleisthenes of Sicyon is interpreted in a highly Bakhtinian fashion,[93] while Plutarch's account of rioting in sixth-century BCE Megara is interpreted with early modern carnival in mind.[94] Forsdyke's picture of ancient Greek popular culture is more obviously political than Kurke's,[95] with more than a nod to Subaltern Studies, concluding, 'To borrow a phrase from James Scott,

---

[86] Kurke 2011: 7.   [87] Discussed further below; see also Jennings, Chapter 9 in this volume.
[88] Kurke 2011: 23, including Althusser, Bourdieu, Certeau, Gramsci, Stallybrass and White and J. C. Scott, as well as Peter Burke and Robert Redfield.
[89] Kurke 2011: 53.   [90] Kurke 2011: 25.
[91] Whitmarsh 2011 aptly points out that in this way Kurke's study becomes much less radical, and more like a traditional study of literary history.
[92] Forsdyke 2012: 49.   [93] Forsdyke 2012: 90–113.   [94] Forsdyke 2012: 117–43, esp. 134–7.
[95] Forsdyke 2012 begins with a quote from Eric Hobsbawm (3) and invokes the relationship between popular culture and politics as a key theme of book: 11–14.

popular culture was, and continues to be, "a weapon of the weak".⁹⁶ What her study does reveal, however, is the difficulty of reconstructing 'the people' on the available evidence: the popular communities whose cultures are imagined by Forsdyke remain rather obscure in their social and economic position and identity. In this volume, Mirko Canevaro's chapter provides a critique of Forsdyke's book, arguing that the 'official' culture of democratic Athens was in fact 'popular'.

These works show that scholarly interest in ancient popular culture is burgeoning, but also reveal that there is still much work to be done. A truly interdisciplinary examination of ancient popular culture is required, one that applies diachronic, as well as synchronic analysis. A sceptical social historian, for instance, might wish to seek more clarity about who exactly *were* 'the people' at stake in a history of popular culture. Forsdyke's, as we saw, were decidedly obscure. Jerry Toner sensibly admits that:

> The non-elite were too great a hotchpotch of differing groups to be united by a single, monolithic culture. They inhabited a complex world of different geographies, wealth and status levels that meant that no uniform way of life could ever exist.⁹⁷

The various cleavages involved include such polarities as slave/free, citizen/non-citizen, male/female, adult/child, urban/rural. The differences between Greece and Rome also need flagging up clearly at this point. The picture of the culture of the Roman non-elite is clearer in scholarship not just due to the vast disparities in available evidence, but also arguably because of the strikingly different degrees of inequality between Greece and Rome, i.e. the different degrees of *subalternity*. With these caveats in mind, it is necessary to consider a brief picture of the social world in which our putative popular culture was embedded.

A still prevalent scholarly picture of classical Greece depicts a highly polarized society, in which a wealthy leisured elite (*hoi plousioi*) making up not even 5 per cent of the population⁹⁸ are to be contrasted with the non-elite mass, characterized as poor (*hoi penetes*). How far we can properly trace a middle class (Aristotle's *hoi mesoi*: *Pol.* 1295b) is a moot point: clearly Athenian society, like all societies, had gradations of wealth and social status, but they are hard to specify historically, though a clear hint comes from the existence of the three traditional military classes: *hippeis*, hoplites and *thetes*.

Current scholarship is slowly edging towards a more nuanced picture of Athenian society, stressing that Athenian citizens at least enjoyed levels of

---

⁹⁶ Forsdyke 2012: 178.   ⁹⁷ Toner 2009: 2.
⁹⁸ The figures are derived from the eligibility to pay liturgies in Athens: only *c.* 1,200 citizens, an estimated 4 per cent of the citizen population, paid them: see Canevaro's chapter below, p. 47.

inequality that were very low indeed in comparison to other premodern (and even modern) states.[99] Nonetheless, in the absence of clear economic and archaeological data on the one hand, and a hugely ideologically skewed literary tradition on the other, the situation is still cloudy. The citizen famers of Attica certainly do not fit the stereotype of the downtrodden, subaltern peasant;[100] most notably, in common with other 'poor' Athenians, they typically owned slaves, and they also participated in politics.[101] While the life of the farmer was respected in elite discourse,[102] manual labour of other kinds was despised as *banausic*, so degrading, although of course many, if not most, of the *banausoi* were citizens.[103] The urban non-elite (though crucially made up of foreigners, slaves and ex-slaves alongside citizens), traders and craftsmen of various kinds were consistently treated in pejorative terms as dishonest and low.[104]

Even in the vastly better-documented case of ancient Rome it remains tricky to produce a properly complex picture of Roman society. It is clear we need to avoid viewing Roman society in terms of a tiny 'elite' atop a huge, non-differentiated 'non-elite'.[105] The social stratification of the Roman non-elite,[106] comprising complex and overlapping social and economic statuses, is too broad a subject to deal with here in any but the most sweeping of terms,[107] although individual chapters of the book do take up the challenge.[108] That the *populus* of Rome, for example, cannot be shown as a coherent group is shown by Cyril Courrier's chapter, which takes an

---

[99] See, most strikingly, Ober 2015: esp. 71–100 as well as Kron 2011, using evidence for eligibility for liturgies.

[100] Bresson 2007: 150 stresses the inequality of land tenure, but the evidential basis for his estimated figures is far from secure. The use of the term 'peasant' for Athenian citizens has been debated, but is plausibly defended by Cartledge 1993: 132.

[101] The two are connected: that slave-owning gave peasant citizens time to participate in politics is now largely accepted. See Jameson 1977–8, though refuted by Wood 1988: esp. ch. 2. Literary evidence does depict the 'poor' owning slaves, e.g. the poor famer Chremylos in Aristophanes' *Ploutos* owns several slaves: 228, 1105.

[102] Dover 1974: 112–14.

[103] E.g. Arist. *Pol.* 1337 b7: 'We therefore call mechanical those skills which have a deleterious effect on the body's condition, and all work that is paid for'; see here Dover 1974: 40 on the contempt for economic dependency.

[104] Xenophon, albeit a clearly problematic witness, claimed that the Assembly was made up of 'fullers, cobblers, carpenters, blacksmiths, farmers, and traders': *Memorabilia* 3.7.6.

[105] Alföldy's famous schematic depiction of Roman society as a pyramid (Alföld 1988: fig. 1) avoids this caricature, though it is still understandably oversimplified. See, for an interesting attempt to provide a more nuanced picture of social stratification, Jones 2009.

[106] Again, it can only be very briefly pointed out that the Roman elite, too, was itself stratified: see, for a thoughtful discussion, Brown 2000b.

[107] Mayer 2012 takes up the challenge to identify an ancient middle class, though his arguments have not been met with universal acceptance.

[108] See here, too, Purcell 1994.

illuminating look at the *plebs urbana*. The question of social status in the Roman world as a whole became more and more complex over time.[109] We might think, for instance, of the ambiguity and contradictions involved in the status of the freedman or woman. The Empire-wide grant of citizenship made by Caracalla in 212 resulted in the devaluation of citizenship, and ultimately new levels of distinction or differentiation: legal evidence shows a deepening distinction between the treatment of *honestiores* and *humiliores* in Late Antiquity.[110] What is clear is that the Roman world, in especially marked contrast to the classical Greek period, combined striking levels of social mobility alongside equally striking levels of social and economic inequality.

While considering the complex social positioning of ancient popular culture we also need to consider its *location*. As ever, the nature of our source material will tend to bias urban over rural settings, despite the clear interdependence of town and countryside in the ancient world, not to mention the great numerical preponderance of peasants.[111] The city appears, in scholarship at least, to be the most natural locus for the development of a rich popular culture, due to the density of population, the prominence of horizontal as well as vertical associations, and the multiplicity of many key institutions and structures such as public entertainments, religious buildings and political bodies.[112] Courrier, Cristina Rosillo-López and Alexandre Vincent all deal with the fascinating *caput mundi* in their chapters. Vincent deals with the subjection of city-dwellers of all classes to hegemonic culture in the case of the 'sounds of power'. He reminds us that public and even private urban space was dominated by what we can only see as top-down delivery of decibels. High levels of urbanization in North Africa, meanwhile, allowed for popular channels of communication and protest, as discussed by Julio-Cesar Magalhães de Oliveira. Towns and cities also provide the locations for the sermons of the famous preachers of Late Antiquity, whose texts provide such crucial evidence for social and cultural history, as studied by Jaclyn Maxwell. However, the late antique source material for the Kalends of January, as discussed in my own chapter, makes it clear that it had both urban and rural components, reminding us that ancient cities were inextricably connected with their rural hinterlands.[113]

---

[109] For a helpful discussion, see Peachin 2011: 3–36.   [110] See here still Garnsey 1970.
[111] Grey 2011: 5 suggests that peasants made up 'something over eighty percent' of the population of the ancient Mediterranean.
[112] Horsfall's culture of the Roman plebs, for instance, appears almost entirely urban.
[113] See Klingshirn 1994: 208–9, citing Kroeber: 'the peasant society of sixth-century Arles was a "part-society" with a "part-culture"'.

Accessing the rural, peasant cultures[114] of ancient Greece and Rome requires particular methodological complexity, and detective work in order to shed light on a particularly recalcitrant evidential base.[115] Anthropological and comparative as well as archaeological studies are obviously crucial.[116] In the meantime rural popular culture in the guise of 'folk culture' has been the often-idealized focus of scholarship since Herder, who favoured a 'pure' peasantry, declaring 'The people are not the mob of the streets, who never sing or compose but shriek and mutilate.'[117] The timeless, traditional nature of peasant culture continues to feature in modern scholarship,[118] although peasant studies have also felt significant impact from subaltern and postcolonial studies.[119]

Just as urban popular culture is easier to access than its rural counterpart, so too popular culture is much more visible in the public than the private sphere. The household as locus for popular culture is considered in April Pudsey's chapter, which looks at children. The idea that children and young people have their own subordinate, alternative culture is one that clearly demands more historiographical attention.[120] In general, in this volume we are keen to encourage the study of new, less thronged avenues of study, pursuing both new types of source and new types of history. This includes, for instance, tackling the growing field of sensory history, such as Vincent's discussion of the history of sound.[121] It also involves taking the history of popular culture beyond the obvious, clichéd areas, such as the now well-known 'lower bodily stratum'. There is more to popular culture than fart jokes and rioting over food prices; in this sense, Toner's and Maxwell's serious studies of popular intellectual life represent clear advances in scholarship.

---

[114] Note the caveats discussed above in the case of Greece. A useful 'minimal' definition of a 'peasant' is suggested by Grey 2011: 29: 'settled cultivators, whose agricultural exploitation was essentially for subsistence, who performed agricultural tasks personally and controlled their own labour and land'.

[115] See Forsdyke 2012: *passim*.

[116] For a fascinating example of what can be done, here for the late antique period, see Dossey 2010 and Grey 2011. The Roman Peasant Project, directed by Kim Bowes represents an important step forward: see www.sas.upenn.edu/romanpeasants/index.html, including preliminary reports.

[117] Cited in Burke 2009: 47.

[118] E.g. Klingshirn 1994: 208–9, apropos of the countryside surrounding Arles: 'Where peasant culture diverged from urban culture was above all in its traditional way of life, which survived because of its proven value for success.'

[119] See Bernstein and Byres 2001, reflecting on the discipline of 'peasant studies': esp. 6–8 on 'peasantness'.

[120] Laes and Vuolanto forthcoming.

[121] See Vincent's chapter for bibliography. On sensory history and popular culture, particularly smell, see Toner 2009: 123–61, and note Toner 2014.

Having highlighted some of the aspects of popular culture to be dealt with here, the final section of this chapter will take a more sustained look at some of the most important areas of this field. While the volume makes no claim to comprehensiveness, this section will nonetheless round out the picture of ancient popular culture by highlighting several key areas that constitute popular culture: religion, literature, art and politics.

Key Themes in Ancient Popular Culture

The subject of 'popular religion', unlike other areas of 'popular culture' in the ancient world (and the Middle Ages) has long been on the scholarly agenda.[122] Indeed, in the case of the Middle Ages the study of medieval popular culture tends to blend into the study of medieval popular *religion*: here an influential 'two cultures' model has been suggested, configured out of various different binary opposites: clerical versus lay, learned versus 'folkloric', 'literate' versus 'oral'.[123] The very term 'popular religion' meanwhile remains highly vexed, having been used widely as part of a discourse which has sought to divide respectable, proper religion from its lesser 'popular' counterpart.[124] Robert Scribner provided a helpful starting point for definition and analysis in the case of Christianity:

popular religion is not a fixed category or set of practices, but something which has a continuing dynamic which occurs in two ways: both as developing practice and in relationship to the institutional church.[125]

Of course, in the case of the ancient world our investigation is made all the more challenging by the fact that 'popular religion' needs to be investigated across a particularly diverse religious landscape, encompassing polytheistic as well as monotheistic religions. The position of 'popular' or 'non-official' religion is clearly very different in a religious system that is highly centralized and defined by a standard set of doctrines and text,[126] as opposed to a system characterized by openness and diversity (albeit within limits).

---

[122] The bibliography is correspondingly large: a good starting point for Late Antiquity is Frankfurter 2005; Davis 1974 is still relevant; and see further Künzel 1992 and Schmitt 1976.

[123] Le Goff's idea of the 'two cultures' was laid out most fully in Le Goff 1977; his work has been much criticized, e.g. by Robert Markus, who notes that Le Goff has only really transposed traditional dichotomies 'from a religious into a cultural register': Markus 1990: 11–12. See p. 250 for further references.

[124] To 'separate the grain from the chaff' in the words of Davis 1974: 307.

[125] Scribner 1987: 44.

[126] The history of Christianity has suffered most obviously from an institutional bias: see here, for an interesting corrective, the recent *People's History of Christianity* series, seeking to offer

Indeed, the very concept of 'religion' is increasingly seen as problematic and anachronistic in the case of the ancient world.[127]

One attempt to locate 'popular' ancient religion might well be sociological, i.e. asking if certain religious practices and cults were more likely to appeal to non-elites than others. Generally, long-held notions here fall apart under closer scrutiny. For instance, scholars have often maintained that the cult of Isis was most closely identified with the socially marginalized, for slaves, freedmen, foreigners and women. Detailed epigraphic studies, however, have largely destroyed this notion. In Pompeii, for instance, where we have the most detailed evidence, the local elite played key roles in the cult.[128] Further afield, likewise, epigraphic data show that there were devotees across all social classes in the Roman world, with just as many *ingenui* as freedmen and slaves.[129] Notions about the 'popular' nature of this cult are thus shown to be based on outdated and condescending notions.[130]

One of the key concepts in discussions of popular religion both ancient and modern is that of 'superstition': *deisidaimonia* in Greek and *superstitio* in Latin. Neither term is of course an exact definition of the term: the Greek denotes a range of meanings, from (excessive) fear of the gods, to piety (with something like our 'superstition' in there too). Theophrastus' 'superstitious man', for instance, seems recognizable:

The superstitious man is the sort who < ....> washes his hands, sprinkles himself with water from a shrine, puts a sprig of laurel in his mouth and walks around that way all day. If a weasel crosses his path he goes no further until someone passes between them, or he throws three stones over the road. If he sees a snake in his house he invokes Sabazios if it is a reddish-brown one, but if it is a holy one he immediately founds a hero shrine on the spot.[131]

Plutarch's notion of superstition also involves excessive fear of the gods; his version of the superstitious man goes in for 'magic charms and spells, rushing about and beating of drums, impure purifications and unclean sanctifications, barbarous and outlandish penances and mortifications at

---

a history of the people, rather than 'the hierarchical-institutional-bureaucratic corporation': Burrus 2005: xiii.

[127] On the emergence of the concept of religion, see now Nongbri 2013.
[128] The temple of Isis at Pompeii was the first and only complete temple restoration in the aftermath of the earthquake of 63 CE, suggesting the local prominence and prestige of the cult and a high level of involvement of the decurion class; see still Tran Tam Tinh 1964.
[129] See here Malaise 1972 and Takács 1995.
[130] A similar characterization of the early adherents of Christianity, once common in scholarship, is now generally rejected.
[131] Theophrastus, *Char.* 16.1–4.

the shrines'.[132] Polybius however, in his discussion of the Roman constitution famously remarked that the Romans as a whole were distinguished by their *deisidaimonia* whereby fear of the gods meant that the Romans, unlike the Greeks, kept their faith.[133]

The relevant Latin term is rather less ambiguous, consistently denoting the wrong kind of religion: *superstitio* versus *religio*.[134] Like the Greek, the Latin term includes the idea of an excessive religiosity, but also denotes, more sharply, the idea of irregular (even dangerously so) religious practice. This division, between *religio* and *superstitio* can be seen as a starting point for the religious self-definition of the Roman elite, who set boundaries between the legitimate and illegitimate, 'us' and 'them', including the identification of a set of transgressive religious stereotypes against whom they set themselves.[135] *Superstitio* was most likely to be attributed to people the elite felt most superior to: the poor, women (especially elderly ones) and foreigners.[136] These people, excluded from the processes of state, posed structural problems, and were thus frequently seen as subversive, deviant, or as demons and witches. The classic case in point in ancient Rome is of course that of the suppression of Bacchic cult in the second century BCE, just as much later in Europe women were focused upon as witches. Meanwhile, with the expansion of empire, especially from the second century CE onwards, the beliefs of foreign people were increasingly described (and attacked) as *superstitio*, most strikingly those of Druids, Egyptians and Jews, as the Roman elite sought to define their superiority vis-à-vis provincial elites.[137] A growing focus on magic as the

---

[132] *Mor.* 171B.
[133] Polybius 6.56.7; it is striking that Polybius treats Roman religion as a device for manipulating the masses, although he actually attributes the same behaviour to Roman magistrates, i.e. the elite.
[134] For instance, *religio* honours the gods, *superstitio* wrongs them: Seneca, *De Clementia* 2.5.1 In Greek there is a polarity between *deisidaimonia* and *theosebeia* or *eusebeia*, but it is less striking and less common.
[135] Beard, North and Price 1998: 215.
[136] Christianity of course was regarded as a particularly pernicious *superstitio*. Though in fact a Christian caricature of anti-Christian polemic, this description is telling: 'They have collected from the absolute dregs of society the ill-educated and the women, who tend because of their sex to be more credulous and unstable, and have created a rabble of blasphemous conspirators, which is bound together by nocturnal gatherings, ritual fasts and unnatural feasts, not for any rite but for profanation. They form a secretive people that shuns the light, silent in public, talkative in corners, they despise temples as being only tombs, they spit on the gods, they mock our rites, these pitiful people pity (incredible though it is) our priests, they despise public offices and their purple robes, while they themselves go half-naked': Minucius Felix, *Octavius* 8.4.
[137] E.g. Tacitus on the *superstitio* of the Druids (*Hist.* 4.54.4) and the people of Alexandria (*Hist.* 4.81.2); see here Beard, North and Price 1998: 211–44, esp. 217, 221–2, 227, and Gordon 1990.

ultimate *superstitio* also developed, particularly in the fourth century CE and thereafter. In a striking ideological takeover, meanwhile, Christians inherited, and made their own, the distinction between *religio* and *superstitio* and this new Christian dichotomy would ultimately be even more powerful.[138]

While 'superstition' is clearly a term to be avoided, the utility of the concept of 'popular religion' is maintained by a number of scholars. In his *Athenian Popular Religion*, John Mikalson clearly states that he is not using the term in a social (i.e. lower class) or pejorative sense, but argues that it designates the religious views and attitudes and activities shared by 'the majority of Athenians' and 'the common cultural experience of the Athenians',[139] stressing consensus and homogeneity.[140] In the case of Late Antiquity, Ramsay MacMullen has recently sought to reclaim the notion of popular Christianity, with his book *The Second Church*. He argues, in a manner reminiscent of Le Goff, that there were 'two Christianities', the first representing 'the Establishment: ecclesiastical leadership, councils and theology, scriptural citations ..... clergy ... chanting ... a laity almost wholly recruited from the local aristocracy' and a second: 'the 95 per cent, worshiping in their own way'.[141] MacMullen is thus unrepentant about his famous claim that church congregations were made up of only of the social elite (estimated more precisely here at 5 per cent).[142] The 95 per cent meanwhile, according to MacMullen, worshipped in their own ways, 'outside the walls', particularly in funerary basilicas. Martyr cult, for MacMullen, provided just about the only opportunity for a rapprochement of the 'two Christianities'.[143] Scholars wishing to highlight the agency of the 'people' in ancient history will doubtless sympathize with MacMullen's determination not to occlude their religious practices from the record, but we might doubt the subtlety of his methodology.[144]

MacMullen is reacting against the influential work of Peter Brown, who powerfully attacked pejorative notions of 'popular religion' in his seminal

---

[138] Nicely put by Momigliano 1972: 11: 'The Christians ... set up their palisade between religion and superstition to coincide with the frontier between Christianity and Paganism.'

[139] Mikalson 1983: 5.

[140] Mikalson 1983: 107. Cf. Victoria Jennings' discussion of ancient popular religion in Chapter 9 below.

[141] MacMullen 2009: 110. [142] MacMullen 1989 versus Allen 1996.

[143] MacMullen 2009: 108.

[144] Counting the number of places available in churches, MacMullen estimates, based on 255 churches in 125 towns and cities, that attendance at church could have included only between 1 and 8 per cent of the population: 2009: 101. A comparison with the seating provided by the medieval church (or another period of history) would surely be crucial here; the estimates, in any case, provide a rather a blunt tool for analysis of this kind.

work *The Cult of the Saints*. Brown showed how a historiographical legacy, which he traced back as far as David Hume's essay *The Natural History of Religion*, has bedevilled analysis of Christian religion in particular.[145] Brown demonstrated that Hume's attack on the religious failures of 'the vulgar' had its heirs in an enduring 'two-tiered' model of religion, opposing the enlightened views of the elites to the limitations of the 'vulgar' masses.

Whether it is presented, bluntly, as "popular superstition" or categorized as "lower forms of belief", it is assumed that "popular religion" exhibits modes of thinking and worshiping that are best intelligible in terms of a failure to be something else.[146]

Moreover, and crucially, Brown lucidly pointed out how scholarship had consistently understood 'popular religion' 'from the view-point of the elite'.[147] The aim of this book, of course, is precisely to avoid taking a top-down view of ancient culture. In this context we can place Maxwell's chapter, which takes non-elite religion seriously, showing 'there was no clear distinction between theology and popular religion'.[148]

Most scholars working in the field of late antique religion today continue to critique the concept of popular religion from one angle or another. David Frankfurter, writing about Roman Egypt, argues that the concept of 'local religion'[149] is more fruitful:

Within (or at least in the context of) local religion one can accommodate and highlight the important continuities in religious practice between socioeconomic classes, a problem that previous constructions of 'popular religion' have been unable to negotiate.[150]

Frankfurter, like others, draws on the approach of Redfield, stressing the interaction between the 'great' tradition (Greco-Roman civic religion, temple religion), interacting with a 'little' tradition (local religions and cultures). He is determined that we take this local religion seriously, not as 'irrelevant veneers' on a general piety, but rather as 'idioms through which local religions and cultures can articulate their worlds'.[151] This idea of

---

[145] Brown 1981: 12–122.   [146] Brown 1981: 19.
[147] Brown 1981: 19. In a now classic article Momigliano argued forcefully that the notion of 'popular religion' is an invention of Christianity, though he himself retains something of the views criticized by Brown, e.g. writing of 'the Christian abolition of the internal frontiers between the learned and the vulgar': Momigliano 1972: 17.
[148] E.g., as David Frankfurter observes, 'the devotions of the poor and uneducated typically come off as a soup of magic, crisis rites, image worship, festival hilarity and superstition in contrast to the staid and rational religion ascribed to the upper classes': Frankfurter 2005: 255–6. See Maxwell in this volume, p. 297.
[149] As formulated by Christian 1981 for the case of early modern Spain.
[150] Frankfurter 1998: 34.   [151] Frankfurter 1998: 6.

religion as world-constructing is clearly crucial in any analysis of religion as part of popular culture.[152]

Looking at 'lived' or 'quotidian' religion, the approach taken by Nicola Denzey Lewis in her chapter[153] brings about similarly rich findings. It can be argued that 'lived religion' is a particularly appropriate approach for ancient religion, which is so demonstrably embedded in culture, as well as for the desire to investigate religion *as part of* popular culture.[154] It is in this sense that we can consider a huge range of activities, both public and private, to which we have access via a wonderful selection of source material, particularly from material culture. Do-it-yourself oracles are explored by Lewis, Jennings and Toner. The rubbish dumps of Oxyrhynchus have yielded a number of examples of papyrus slips which were used to ask questions of the gods: the individual would hand in two slips of papyrus, asking positive and negative versions of the same question. The god would 'choose' the answer, and the appropriate slip would be handed back. Surviving examples suggest that on occasions temple scribes were taking dictation, while on others the spelling and script suggest that individuals wrote their own. The gods addressed in this way included the falcon god Thonisis but also, later, the 'God of our protector St Philoxenos'.[155] As Lewis has shown, meanwhile, the catacombs of Rome have yielded many more interesting and varied objects of apotropaic and other significance than the official narratives of early Christian archaeology would suggest.

Lived, embedded religion also involves the very many festivals and celebrations both small, and large scale, that dotted and marked the year in the ancient world.[156] Chapter 11 looks at one such festival, the Kalends of January, that existed both on the official, 'top-down' level and on a much more local level, involving practices that were frequently targeted by the ecclesiastical authorities in Late Antiquity. The Kalends is just one of a number of festivals which could be considered to embrace particularly 'popular' themes, the most obvious being Saturnalia (the Greek Kronia)

---

[152] See here Davis 1974: 314, citing Geertz 1973: 87–125, a seminal discussion of religion as a cultural system. However, we should also note the critique of Asad 1983, reminding us that religion is created and defined by 'authorising discourses': 244; 'power create[s] religion': 252; see here too Arnold 2005: 6–19.

[153] See here Orsi 1997 and the discussion in Lewis' chapter.

[154] Frankfurter 2005: 268 reminds us of the need to *embed* our accounts of religious practices in their particular social contexts, which will enable us to see religious ritual acts as 'embedded in real social worlds and tensions', rather than labelling them as 'magic' or 'superstitious': 270.

[155] Parsons 2007: 175–6; *PGMP*8b. See pp. 186–7 for oracles discussed by Toner.

[156] Scullard 1981 remains the best guide to Roman festivals; see also Versnel 1994.

frequently compared to carnival, and interpreted along Bakhtinian lines.[157] In Greece festivals celebrating Dionysus and Demeter, for instance, were known for *aischrologia*, the shouting of obscene and abusive remarks, as well as for gender inversion.[158]

These festivals, of course, lie at the heart of one of the most important genres of ancient literature, that is, Greek comedy, the subject of James Robson's chapter. Aristophanes' plays, superficially at least, seem to offer the potential for accessing Greek popular culture: characters drawn from across a broad range of society, earthy language and humour, and often an apparently anti-establishment stance. Yet of course it is only with some difficulty that Aristophanes' plays can be truly identified as part of popular culture. His plays were early on claimed as part of the canon, and it is problematic to claim that they take a generally oppositional stance.[159] Nonetheless, ancient theatre, and comedy in particular, does constitute an obvious area for what we might see in Bakhtinian terms as the interpenetration of high and low culture. Nowhere is this more visible than in the case of the Roman mime. Mime was despised by the Roman elite as a definitely 'low' form and the very vitriol it attracted makes it a particularly good place to look for what we might call 'unauthorized culture', even for subaltern, oppositional voices.[160] Indeed, the Roman mime seems to have staged challenges to the dominant social order, hence its terrible reputation among elite critics.[161] The problem with reconstructing the ancient mime, however, lies in its improvised nature so that its textual traces are tantalizingly few.[162]

A quick glimpse at the history of scholarship on the ancient novel highlights the problems faced when examining the extant textual tradition. While earlier generations of scholars wished to see the ancient novels as 'low-brow' popular literature,[163] modern scholarship sees them very much as elite texts, often engaged in defining elite culture.[164] Once the Cinderella

[157] See Chapter 11 in this volume for bibliography. See also, on festive revelry, Forsdyke 2012: 124–43.
[158] For references and bibliography see Forsdyke 2012: 126, 130.
[159] Ste. Croix 1972 influentially argued for the conservative nature of Old Comedy; see esp. 355–71, although note the caveats expressed by Pritchard 2012. See Robson's chapter for further bibliography.
[160] Note briefly for introductions, Fantham 1989 and Panayotakis 2005.
[161] We might wish to contrast here the more 'authorized' Roman comedy of Plautus, which nonetheless liked to play at imagining challenges to the established order, particularly in the case of the master/slave relationship: see here McCarthy 2000.
[162] Herodas' 'literary' mime remains highly suggestive: see briefly Arnott 1971, Esposito 2010.
[163] E.g. Perry 1967: 98 as cited above; see Bowie 1994 for a useful survey of earlier views.
[164] E.g. Whitmarsh 2008c: esp. 72–4; there were nonetheless clear distinctions between the novels 'in terms of literary and stylistic elaboration', e.g. Hunter 2008: 265. Hofmann's definition is interesting: 'It certainly was a consumer literature but not a mass literature': Hofmann 1999: 6.

of classical literature, since the 1980s the Greek novel has undergone a startling renaissance in scholarship. Formerly popular ideas of these texts as 'proto-bourgeois', or as intended for female readers, have given way to much more theoretically informed and complex readings.[165] Does it make any sense to call them popular? A striking study counting surviving fragments of ancient literary papyri showed the ancient novel to be far less 'popular' (that is, in quantitative terms) than many more canonical works: we certainly need to move beyond approaches that try to assess the 'popular' status of a given text on the basis of wide distribution.[166] What else would make them popular? Attempting to define a distinctively popular literary aesthetic (for instance, positing the primacy of content over form) is problematic.[167] As so often in the study of popular culture, one possibility is to look to Bakhtin, who stressed the multivocality of the (ancient) novel.[168] This works better yet if we expand our view of ancient fiction.

The 'classic' Greek novels of course made up just part of a much broader genre of 'ancient prose fiction', which includes texts such as the *Alexander Romance*, the Apocryphal Acts of the Apostles and other Christian hagiographical works, Jewish narratives, and other works such as the *Life of Aesop*.[169] This last text is perhaps particularly rich for scholars working on popular culture, as is clearly demonstrated by Victoria Jennings' chapter. Related features that might most likely be associated with putatively popular texts are, as Jennings has it, '"openness" ... "non-canonicity", "textual fluidity"'; moreover 'it is likely that their non-textual distribution – their audience and their "consumption" – was considerably broader than text-*qua*-text transmission can suggest'. A purely text-based approach is in any case highly problematic in a culture with such a high degree of orality.

At this point it is necessary to pause and consider issues of orality and literacy in the ancient world. Pessimistic estimates of literacy were influentially, if controversially, laid out by William Harris, who has declared, forcefully:

[165] The bibliography is huge but see, for instance, the essays collected in Karla 2009a, Whitmarsh 2008a, Whitmarsh and Thomson 2013.
[166] In quantitative terms ancient novels clearly were not the most 'popular' form of literature: papyrus fragments from Oxyrhynchus put novels far below Homer, lyric and drama: 'The conclusion seems to me inescapable that the novels were not popular with the denizens of Greco-Roman Egypt – Christian or otherwise': Stephens 1994: esp. 414.
[167] Hansen 1998: xiv–xv cites Bourdieu 1984 on the issue of the 'popular aesthetic', while attempting to define ancient Greek 'popular literature'.
[168] Bakhtin 1981.
[169] See, for discussions of a wide range of texts, Whitmarsh and Thomson 2013, Hofmann 1999; for Christian fiction in particular, see Perkins 1995.

there was no mass literacy, and even the level which I have called craftsmen's literacy was achieved only in certain limited milieux. The classical world, even at its most advanced, was so lacking in the characteristics which produce extensive literacy that we must suppose that the majority of people were always illiterate.[170]

What levels of literacy are we talking about? Rates obviously varied greatly according to both chronology and geography; Harris estimated 'below 15 per cent' over all,[171] with higher rates from Rome and Italy, though still 'well below 20–30 per cent'.[172] Harris's pessimistic rejection of the very possibility of mass literacy has not, of course, gone unchallenged.[173] In any case, this is not an area where much generalization is helpful: rates of literacy seem to have been much higher in classical Greece than in ancient Rome.[174] High rates of literacy in Athens are suggested by a range of evidence, from the practice of ostracism to the large number of extant rupestral inscriptions in rural areas, including the fascinating example of a poem in Homeric metre inscribed on a rock by a shepherd.[175] The writing of metrical poetry clearly takes us far beyond a purely 'functional' literacy and suggests that previous estimates, at least for ancient Greece, have been too pessimistic. Meanwhile, however, it is no longer thought that Christianity involved any particular predilection for literacy,[176] and indeed a late antique decline in literacy is likely.[177]

This is not to say that we should imagine a great gulf between the literate and non-literate worlds. Recent scholarship, particularly on classical Greece, has stressed the interplay between written and oral communication, with the nature of the interaction being shaped by the specific conditions of a given culture. Rosalind Thomas in particular has stressed the importance of oral tradition and communal memory in classical Greece well into the fourth century BCE.[178] Meanwhile interest in the relationship between literacy and the development of Greek democracy continues, although more recent work rejects a simple causal relationship between the two.[179] For ancient Rome, meanwhile, the work of Peter Wiseman (the title of one book, *Unwritten Rome* is indicative) has stressed the importance of

---

[170] Harris 1989: 13.   [171] Harris 1989: 267.   [172] Harris 1989: 259.
[173] See Humphrey 1991 for an interesting range of responses and challenges to Harris's account, including Corbier 1991, discussing evidence for lower-class literacy.
[174] Nonetheless, debate continues regarding its extent: divergent views in recent scholarship can be found, for instance, in Missiou 2011 versus Thomas 2009. Harris argues for greater rates of literacy in Hellenistic compared to classical Greece: Harris 1989: 329.
[175] See Goette 1994: esp. 124–8.
[176] On the interface between orality and literacy in early Christianity, see Grig 2013a.
[177] See Harris 1989: 321–2.   [178] See, in particular, Thomas 1989 and 1992.
[179] See here Missiou 2011.

performance and story-telling in the transmission of Roman historiography, particularly in the Early and Mid Republic.[180] Meanwhile, as we have already seen, Nicholas Horsfall has shown just how important memory, performance and song were in communicating culture.[181]

It is clearly much more productive to think of literature that goes beyond literary *texts*. This involves taking in oral elements: story-telling, drama and performance of all kinds and tracing their presence in the surviving texts we do have (and of course, some types of texts are more likely to have these traces than others). Again, as Jennings suggests 'It seems likely that there was a performed element at work in [the popular] milieu'. Our discussion of 'popular literature' began with the religious festivals that gave birth to Greek comedy. A link between the *aischrologia* and surviving (largely iambic) poetry that includes scurrilous, obscene and often explicit elements is just one way to link the oral and literature cultures, and the blurred lines between these categories are demonstrated in Tom Hawkins' chapter. Hawkins' discussion of invective, which he sees as an important example of performative speech, shows how both 'elite' and popular shared the same demotic invective.[182]

A whole range of different types of texts, going beyond poetry, plays and fiction, can of course be mined for what they can tell us about popular culture, and the chapters in this volume provide many stimulating examples of this. Fables, as discussed by Toner, are one such case. The scholar's task is to identify, indeed excavate, popular elements in existing textual traditions. However, we can also certainly look for popular literature beyond texts. Graffiti, for instance, provides striking evidence again for the interpenetration of high and low, including fascinating examples of what have been seen as 'sub-literary' texts.[183] Take, for instance, this famous doubly punning take on the first line of the Aeneid, found on the facade of the fullery of Fabius Ululitremulus in Pompeii: *Fullones ululamque cano, non arma virumq(ue)* ('I sing of fullers and the owl, not arms and the man').[184] Graffiti from Pompeii shows locals combining lines and motifs from established poets (notably Virgil and Ovid) with their own creations. Sometimes the literary and philosophical canons were mocked in graffiti and artworks, such as the famous fresco from Pompeii depicting Aeneas as a dog-headed ape.[185] In this context too we can consider the

---

[180] Wiseman 2009; see also Wiseman 1995, discussed further below.   [181] Horsfall 2003.
[182] See here too Ruffell 2003.   [183] See now Baird and Taylor 2011.
[184] *CIL* 4.9131 (IX.Xiii.5). The owl is the symbol of fullers, while punning on the name of the fuller Ululitremulus.
[185] See Clarke (2007): 151–7.

famous paintings from the Caupona of the Seven Sages in Ostia, which appear to mock philosophical traditions, depicting the Sages defecating with captions like 'Thales advised those who shit hard to really work at it.'[186] Images such as this remind us of the complex interplay of visuality and textuality, high and low in the ancient world.

As this suggests, any properly rounded account of popular culture cannot ignore material culture. It should be stated at the outset that this book does not offer a sustained archaeological engagement with the issue of popular culture: that would require a wholly different book. Nonetheless, artefacts including dolls, amulets and plates are included in Chapters 10, 11 and 12. What we are dealing with here is not to be dealt with most properly under the heading 'art',[187] but rather 'visual culture' on the one hand and 'material production' on the other.[188] Classical artistic production clearly encompassed a tremendous range, from what we might call 'elite' and official art, such as marble statuary and paintings by famous artists, down to the production of cheap artefacts in clay and wood. An example of just one genre – the terracotta figurine – has many thousands of examples from classical Greece alone. These include, for example, depictions of dramatic and comic actors, people at work (the famous groups from Boeotia) and deities; they were used as decorative objects, toys and religious offerings in domestic, funerary and religious settings.[189] Such objects clearly played an important role in defining people's identities and constructing their culture. In her chapter Pudsey considers the role played by dolls and other toys in constructing children's culture. Lewis meanwhile considers the role of a variety of intriguing amulets (and related objects) in 'lived religion'; in particular she offers us an opportunity to put these artefacts back into the now thoroughly sanitized context of the Roman catacombs, and their authorized history. Chapter 11 shows again how neglected objects can bring new angles to (textual) histories, showing how a local corpus of ceramics might relate to the popularity of the Kalends in late antique Gaul.

Considering the above material under the rubric of 'art' is not, therefore, particularly helpful. There is nonetheless a lively scholarly tradition

---

[186] See Clarke 2006, citing Bakhtin, plus Clarke 2003: 170–80.
[187] 'Scholars point out that the Romans did not have a clear notion of art as an elevated creation, cut off from the mundane practicality of other objects; they did not have the modern concept of "art for art's sake"; they did not even have a word for art, since the Latin *ars*, like the Greek *tekhnē*, refers to all kinds of craft and skill. Roman "artists" are perhaps often best equated with modern craftsmen, skilled workmen.' Stewart 2008: 2. Though Stewart is here talking about Roman art, pretty much the same can of course be said of Greek 'art'.
[188] See here Kampen 1995.   [189] See Higgins 1967.

attempting to define Roman 'popular' art in particular, going back to Rodenwaldt's discussion of a *Volkskunst*,[190] reformulated with a Marxist flavour by Bianchi Bandinelli as *arte plebea*.[191] Recently John R. Clarke stridently concluded his monograph *Art in the Lives of Ordinary Romans*:

> This book should demonstrate how wrongheaded it is to try to understand non-elite art as an expression of a particular group or class. In the end, there is no such thing as folk, plebeian, or freedman art: there is only art at the service of ordinary people who might use standard images for their house, shop, or tomb – or might not.[192]

Not all will wish to accept such a depoliticized view of material culture (moreover, the composition of Clarke's 'non-elite', which takes in the owners many of the most famous houses in Pompeii, is, in any case, problematic). Nonetheless, issues of the relationship between centre and periphery, official and non-official, Hellenized and indigenous, persist. Clearly Roman visual culture, and indeed Roman artistic production, represent a world of artistic pluralism, where indigenous traditions coexisted alongside Hellenized ones, the former becoming more dominant in Late Antiquity.[193] While traditional art-historical approaches persist, postcolonial influence has reached the study of Roman archaeology, allowing for more pluralist and decentralized views of Roman material production.[194]

The central questions relating to popular culture are posed sharply by the case of visual culture, perhaps most obviously the question as to whether what we can identify is a clear case of 'trickle-down' or not. Both Paul Zanker[195] and Andrew Wallace-Hadrill[196] have powerfully and influentially argued for the trickle-down of elite visual culture to sub-elites (though not much further). Discussions of trickle-down have often taken place in the context of studies of 'Romanization', and have been open to critique as such.[197] Even when used in the contexts of Pompeii and Herculaneum analysis of 'trickle-down' tends towards condescension, such

---

[190] See, in particular, Rodenwaldt 1940.

[191] 'Plebeian' chosen in preference to 'popular' (explicitly rejected), and contrasted with an 'arte aulica' – court art, as well as an 'arte patrizia'; clearly showing a debt to Gramsci, this plebeian art was defined by Bianchi Bandinelli as 'subalterno': 1967, 1970: 51–105; see now Hölscher 2012.

[192] Clarke 2003: 273.   [193] See here Carrié 2002a: 34–5.

[194] See, for instance, the essays collected in D'Ambra and Métraux 2006; Kampen 1995.

[195] Across a range of publications, including Zanker 1975 on sarcophagi, Zanker 1988 on Augustan imagery and Zanker 1998 on Pompeian houses.

[196] See, most recently, Wallace-Hadrill 2008: 313–55; see too 356–440. Mayer 2012: 23 notes how this analysis is in line with Bourdieu's 1984 concept of 'social distinction': the construction of social status through 'conspicuous consumption', a concept which goes back to Veblen 1899.

[197] See here Woolf 1998: 169–205, esp. 170–2, and Mattingly 2010: esp. 203–45.

as when scholars criticize the 'banalization' of elite decorative schemes in the houses of the sub-elite.[198] The case of 'freedman art' represents perhaps the clearest case of scholarly condescension, as strongly criticized by Lauren Hackworth Petersen in her analysis of what she has called 'Trimalchio vision'.[199] Attempting to look at the 'art' of the non-elite in their own terms allows us to see a visual culture that goes beyond notions of trickle-down, as with the huge number of funerary monuments in which Roman men and women proudly commemorated their working lives, representing values very different from those of the elite.[200]

This begs a key question: can we in fact identify specifically popular values, or indeed ideologies?[201] Throughout this chapter questions of the *ideology* of popular culture have consistently emerged, whether explicitly and implicitly – for instance in the case of carnival, and the carnivalesque and Scott's 'infrapolitics' – and, in particular, the question of popular *resistance* intervenes. We would probably do well to heed Peter Burke, when he warns of the danger of anachronism, and of assuming 'rather too easily' that subordinate social groups are indeed conscious of belonging to a dominated class, over and above any other more specific local identities.[202] There is no doubt a danger of seeking to equate the 'popular' with the 'radical',[203] leaving aside much clear evidence of popular conservatism. Ancient fables, for instance – classic cases of a 'hidden transcript' – are clearly ideologically diverse, including both conservative and radical themes.[204] Nonetheless, 'reading against the grain' clearly can produce interesting new readings of ancient texts and ancient culture more generally.[205] The case of ancient slavery, where slave subjectivity would seem impossible to access, nonetheless represents fertile ground here. Some scholars would seek to 'read against the grain' here in order to seek possible critiques of slavery, or indeed narratives even from the slave's

---

[198] See, for critique, Petersen 2006: 196 and Mayer 2012: 273, n. 5, on Wallace-Hadrill 1994: 173–4 ('banalization').

[199] Petersen 2006.

[200] See here, for instance, Kampen 1981, examining the ways in which Roman women at Ostia celebrated their working careers.

[201] On popular values and morality, see Dover 1974 on ancient Greece, and Morgan 2007 on the Roman world.

[202] Burke 2009: xviii.

[203] For instance, on the lines of E. P. Thompson's 'moral economy', Thompson 1971.

[204] See here Morgan 2007: esp. 63–7; on social relations: 176–7.

[205] As in the case of Peter Wiseman's subtle attempts to highlight a popular, alternative version of the history of early Rome, such as his interpretation of Romulus and Remus, which argues that the story of Remus comes out of the ideological conflicts of the Early and Mid Republic: Wiseman 1995. See also the essays collected in Wiseman 2009, which seek to establish a 'people's narrative' of the Late Republic.

point of view, in places that are at first unlikely, including ancient fiction. One such place is the *Life of Aesop*, the closest thing we have, for all its problems, to a slave biography.[206] The use of comparativist approaches to ancient slavery, meanwhile, remains an important but problematic methodology in current scholarship.[207]

The subject of ancient popular politics *qua* politics 'proper' is, by comparison, rather more easily accessed, though it clearly requires treatment on a diachronic, rather than a synchronic, level. Chapters in this volume treat polities ranging from democratic Athens, through the Roman Republic on to imperial Rome and therefore deal with very different contexts. Democratic Athens obviously presents a unique case study for studying a putative popular politics in the ancient world. A well-known historical paradox lies in the fact that despite the persistence of democratic rule in classical Athens, the majority of extant literary sources are hostile to democracy. The surviving speeches of the Attic orators represent an exception in that regard and have been mined for evidence of the nature and extent of popular participation. Josiah Ober's claim that the Athenian *demos* ultimately held 'ideological hegemony',[208] with upper-class politicians acting as their spokesmen, has been much discussed and debated;[209] David Cohen, for instance, has argued that the *demos* gave validation to *elite* claims for honour and status.[210] The most recent scholarship looks rather to establish the influence of an arguably popular (that is, peasant) culture, that of archaic Greece, in the politics and institutions of classical Athens.[211] Mirko Canevaro's chapter here argues strongly for the dominance of the popular in even the 'official' culture of democratic Athens.

The extent of popular participation in Roman republican politics, meanwhile, remains controversial, particularly for the Late Republic. The democratic element in the Roman constitution[212] was theoretically assured by the clear fact of the sovereignty of the *populus Romanus*. Crucially, too, the Roman people elected magistrates in a secret ballot

---

[206] On this theme see Hopkins 1993. Meanwhile another ancient novel, the *Metamorphoses* of Apuleius, it has been argued, contains an extended metaphor for the experience of the slave in the narrative of Lucius' transformation into an ass: see Bradley 2000.

[207] On the historiography of ancient slavery, see McKeown 2007.

[208] Ober 1989: 332; cf. 'the word *demokratia* was the name for a political society and culture in which the most basic and elemental human power – the power to assign meanings to symbols – belonged to the people': 339.

[209] See Canevaro's chapter for full bibliography and discussion.   [210] Cohen 1995: 193.

[211] Schmitz 2004 represents a significant advance in scholarship, enlightening our view of archaic peasant society, and its influence on the laws and culture of democratic Athens.

[212] Famously described by Polybius: 6.11–18. Cf. Syme's famously damning comment: 'The Roman constitution was a screen and a sham': Syme 1939: 15.

from the end of the second century BCE.[213] How far ordinary Romans participated in politics has been much disputed, with estimates of voting numbers ranging widely.[214] The case of the *plebs urbana*, whose stake in the politics of Rome is well known, is discussed in Cyril Courrier's chapter. The participation of the agrarian and Italian populations meanwhile, was both sporadic and unpredictable.[215] Even allowing for an optimistic assessment of the participation of the *plebs urbana*, in the *contiones* and assemblies, the extent to which non-elites held any real political influence was clearly limited. Even if recent scholarship has long abandoned notions of a politics entirely dominated by clientage,[216] the extent to which non-elites possessed political influence should not be overstated. First of all we need to consider the built-in advantage of the elite in the voting assemblies; however, the ideological sway held by elite politicians in both the *contiones* and the assemblies is just as important.[217] Certainly key issues of 'popular' politics can be seen emerging consistently, particular those around issues of land and food supply. However, even supposedly *popularis* politicians remained part of an oligarchic system, radical reconceptions of which were never truly possible.[218] Nonetheless there were persistent concerns about agitation among the urban plebs, as evidenced by the periodic legislation against *collegia* as well as by the mob violence which marked the final years of the Republic, as politicians such as Clodius mobilized discontents, largely relating to food supply.[219]

The challenge, therefore, for the historian of popular culture is to view the Roman non-elite beyond the confines of the ancient mob, and instead to restore a degree of agency to this group, as both Courrier and Rosillo-López show in this volume. Rather than understanding the urban plebs as

---

[213] The secret ballot was a crucial anti-oligarchic measure and as such was disliked by conservative politicians, e.g. Cicero, *De legibus* 3.15–16.

[214] Contrast the pessimistic view of Mouritsen 2001: esp. 132–3, with the optimistic arguments for participation of Millar 1995 and 1998. See Jehne 2006 for the most recent (low) estimates of participation.

[215] For instance, they came to Rome for Tiberius Gracchus, and to vote for the recall of Cicero from exile in 57 BCE.

[216] See North 1990a: 6–7 on the so-called 'frozen waste theory' of Roman politics.

[217] As has been demonstrated by Morstein-Marx 2004: esp. 31–3 and 280–1: e.g. '[public oratory] produced and perpetuated an ideological structure for the citizenry that reinforced the cultural hegemony of the political élite' (33); however, note the slight modification of position in Morstein-Marx 2013.

[218] Characteristically well put: 'Genuine social concern or personal ambition led nobles like the Gracchi, Caesar and Clodius to come forward as "popular" leaders from time to time, but there was no consistent and continuous opposition, no organized and enduring popular party': Brunt 1966: 7.

[219] See further Courrier's chapter for bibliography and discussion.

'rent-a-mob', Rosillo-López clearly demonstrates the unreliability of elite sources for our understanding of late republican politics. Her chapter reassigns political agency to the urban plebs by uncovering a neglected aspect of popular political culture in the construction of political nicknames. This concern with popular agency, shared by the chapters in this book, is neatly described in this case by Nicholas Purcell:

> The politics of the *plebs urbana* were in part its own. It was not a slate on which the schemers of the Senate wrote whatever they wanted. The culture and social forms of the many were not the product of skilled formation by the aristocrats: they were agents too.[220]

Purcell has clearly shown that the benefits received by the urban plebs in the form of subsidized (eventually free) grain and entertainment should not be seen as handouts to a parasitic, indolent population, but rather as 'a bonus to denote their status', with this elite/non-elite relationship continuing and developing under the Principate.[221] In this way we avoid accepting the infamous satirical claims of Juvenal[222] and other inherited, snobbish notions of the 'mob', which go back to ancient elite authors,[223] but have been all too willingly accepted by classical scholars as part of the legacy of the classical tradition.

One of the main aims of this volume is of course to escape a 'bread and circuses' view of ancient popular culture.[224] Instead, the book celebrates the richness and diversity of ancient popular culture. This culture need not be coterminous with a particular group of the population (such as the *demos* or the Roman plebs). It need not necessarily originate (solely) from the 'bottom up'. It is a culture that can be shared by various sub-groups, and which can have diverse possible relationships to elite and official culture(s). Ultimately, we might prefer instead to talk of a network of ancient popular *cultures*. What is crucial is that these ancient popular cultures were fully *embedded* in the broader sphere of ancient culture and ideology. As this introductory chapter has shown, we can find evidence of this network of cultures in diverse and divergent places and ways across the ancient world. Ultimately, of course, 'popular culture' is a heuristic model, the point of which is to enable a properly 'thick' description of (ancient) culture in all its richness. The chapters that follow mark considerable progress towards this end.

---

[220] Purcell 1994: 678. [221] Purcell 1996: esp. 805. [222] Juvenal, *Sat.* 10.75–81.
[223] E.g. Tacitus, *Hist.* 1.4, contrasting the *pars populi integra* with the *plebs sordida*.
[224] See still Yavetz 1969, written to contradict the idea of the selfish, fickle mob; also Garnsey 1988, for a detailed discussion of the corn dole, demonstrating that the Roman plebs were neither pampered nor lazy.

PART I

Classical Greece

2 | The Popular Culture of the Athenian Institutions: 'Authorized' Popular Culture and 'Unauthorized' Elite Culture in Classical Athens

MIRKO CANEVARO

Introduction

In a recent article Holt Parker provides a lucid discussion of the issues and the pitfalls with the most common definitions of popular culture.[1] Following Bennett and Storey, Parker isolates and discusses six definitions of popular culture as (1) quantitatively superior, (2) qualitatively inferior, (3) mass culture, (4) a product of 'the people', (5) a battlefield for hegemony, or (6) a chimera to be deconstructed by postmodernism, and he concludes that they all 'have much to offer, but none is completely satisfying'.[2] He provides a new definition of 'popular culture as products that require little cultural capital and as unauthorized culture'.[3] This definition shifts the focus from the difficult issue of who 'the people' actually are, and moves it to the cultural products themselves. Parker identifies 'mass culture' as part of popular culture, 'the authorized utterance in search of as large an audience as possible', examples of which are the works of Aristophanes, and distinguishes both of them from 'elite culture', 'the elite speaking to the elite'. This definition is useful in many ways, but some of its assumptions need pointing out: the first is that, although we no longer need to identify 'the people', Parker still assumes a clearly demarcated elite, which is characterized by high cultural and economic capital; the second is that institutions that authorize cultural utterances of any kind are somehow entirely alien from popular culture

---

I am grateful to Lucy Grig for inviting me to contribute to this volume, and to Douglas Cairns, David Lewis and Nino Luraghi, who read the first draft of this chapter in full and provided me with invaluable feedback.

[1] See the Introduction pp. 3, 8–9.   [2] Parker 2011. Cf. also Bennett 1980: 20–2 and Storey 2006.
[3] Parker 2011: esp. 165, 169. See Introduction, pp. 8–9, for Parker's theoretical framework.
  The notion of 'cultural capital' is borrowed from Bourdieu, who stated that 'By this is meant the structure of the distribution of instruments for the appropriation of symbolic wealth socially designated as worthy of being sought and possessed': 1973: 73. See on the development and the uses of this concept, Lamont and Lareu 1988. Parker 2011: 165 introduces the term 'authorize' as 'that which turns someone into an *auctor* (author, creator) with *auctoritas* (author-ity)'. Parker's reference is the artworld that authorizes specific forms of art.

stricto sensu, if not from mass culture, which requires low cultural and economic capital for its consumption, but high cultural and economic capital for its production, and is authorized. Within this scheme, the institutional forms of authorization must necessarily be connected with elites (with high cultural and economic capital) that somehow control the relevant institutions. It follows necessarily that elite culture is authorized culture, and that all forms of authorized culture must somehow be connected to the elite, either because they are addressed to the elite, or because the elite provides authorization through the institutions it controls.

This is correct of many societies, and yet, as I shall argue in this chapter, it causes some problems with a society like Athens (and arguably with most Greek democracies)[4] in which the 'official culture' is geared towards the vast majority of the people:[5] apart from the adult male citizens, on the one hand, citizen women and children, for all their subordinate position, had a very clear role in the citizen community and in the state;[6] on the other hand, foreigner residents (metics) were both allowed to take part in certain civic institutions[7] and had their own festivals and religious life expressly authorized and regulated by the *polis*.[8] I shall argue that in Athens the whole institutional framework that 'authorized' various forms of culture was controlled by a vast number of people (and subordinately of families, *oikoi*) which in no way could be considered elite, i.e. characterized by high cultural and economic capital.[9] In such a context, only independent cultural utterances of slaves can technically be considered, according to Parker's definition, popular culture. And yet one is also faced with the paradox that while most institutionally sanctioned forms of cultural utterance are definitely non-elite, several elite cultural forms, and the contexts in which they take place (e.g. the banquet/*symposion*, or the *hetairiai*), are

---

[4] Cf. Robinson 1997 and 2011 on archaic and classical Greek democracies, and Carlsson 2010, Grieb 2009, Mann and Scholz 2011 on Hellenistic democracy.

[5] For a sensible guess, based on recent scholarship, regarding the number of male adult citizens, female adult citizens, citizen children, adult male metics, women and children, and slaves, see Ober 2010: 280, Appendix.

[6] Athenian women were effectively citizens, and recognized as such – after Pericles' citizenship law only sons of two citizens inherited citizenship (Arist. *Pol.* 1278a; cf. now Blok 2009). Their public citizen role was recognized, e.g. in specifically female public festivals such as the Thesmophoriai. On women's religious life, see Dillon 2001.

[7] E.g. metics had access to some lawcourts, in some cases directly, in others through a patron, and the court of the polemarch dealt specifically with cases concerning metics. Cf. MacDowell 1978: 75–8, 221–4, and Whitehead 1977: 89–97.

[8] On cults reserved to metics and their role in citizen festivals such as the Panathenaia, see Whitehead 1977: 86–8.

[9] For recent attempts at calculating the wealth and income distribution in Athens, see Ober 2010 and Kron 2011.

not institutionally 'authorized', and sometimes oppose or resist the institutional order (e.g. in the oligarchic revolutions of the late fifth century).

The most recent and the only comprehensive attempt to explore popular culture (and popular justice) in the Greek world is that of Sara Forsdyke. Forsdyke's working definition of popular culture is markedly different from Parker's: the object of her book is 'the ways that ordinary farmers, craftsmen, and slaves in ancient Greece made sense of their world and their place in it'. 'Popular' is defined as pertaining to 'ordinary farmers, craftsmen, and slaves'. Forsdyke contrasts these with the 'wealthy elites, who produced written texts illustrating their worldviews'. The ordinary farmers and craftsmen (let alone the slaves) did not, the extant texts having very little to say about their worldview, which was expressed instead 'in "living" forms such as festivals and storytelling'. Her definition seems therefore to be a mixture of Storey's number (2) (popular culture as what is left once we define high culture) and (4) (popular culture as the culture of 'the people'). Forsdyke undertakes therefore to excavate 'popular forms of culture that lie barely discernible beneath the surface of ancient Greek literature': festival revelry, oral story-telling and spontaneous collective punishment of social offenders are identified as examples of 'sites of vital political discourses and practices that ... operated alongside, within, and sometimes even in opposition to the formal institutions of the Greek city-state'.[10] Here we do find a point of contact with Parker's definition, inasmuch as Forsdyke follows the Bakhtinian understanding of popular culture as (also) 'unofficial culture', the same 'unauthorized' cultural utterances discussed by Parker.[11] The method used by Forsdyke is avowedly comparative: she draws on 'the approaches of historians of other premodern societies, as well as the interpretations of social scientists who study modern peasant cultures'.[12] Forsdyke does not spend much time drawing her own picture of the Greek societies she studies, yet the underlying assumptions are clear: there is an elite that is completely separate, politically, economically, socially and therefore culturally, from the rest of the population (slaves, of course, but also farmers and craftsmen), and our evidence reflects the worldview of this lucky minority (except for the 'traces' in it that can help us dig out something of the lost popular culture). This elite institutionally controlled all forms of 'official' culture of which our evidence is a sample. Once again, although these assumptions are fair enough for many societies, it is difficult to reconcile them with the reality of ancient Athens (and

---

[10] Forsdyke 2012: 3–4.
[11] Bakhtin 1968: 6–7, 11, 72, 90, 153–4. Cf. Parker 2011: 165–6, n. 82. See also Burke 2009: xiii.
[12] Her models are e.g. Bakhtin, Ginzburg, Zemon Davis, Burke.

probably most Greek democracies). I shall argue in this chapter that elite culture, as the cultural utterances produced by the elite for the elite, was not 'official' culture in Athens, and that ordinary farmers and craftsmen were very comfortable in the hegemonic institutions of the state, those that provided authorization, official sanction, for a wide range of cultural utterances. This has important implications for our understanding of ancient popular culture and highlights the importance of taking into account the nature and workings of the formal 'state' institutions of a society in order to understand correctly the place of popular culture and its relationship with elite culture.

In the first section of this chapter I attempt to show that the institutions of the Athenian state (the Council, the Assembly, the lawcourts) were not controlled by the Athenian elite, but by the vast majority of the Athenian population. Participation in the institutions of the democracy was very widespread, and therefore the average Athenian was perfectly comfortable in them, and the cultural forms that were authorized by them, although 'official', reflected the cultural conventions and ideologies of the masses rather than of the elite. The next section argues that elite culture found its fora outside the institutions of the state, and almost in opposition to them, to such an extent that political participation and elite lifestyle could be represented as antithetical. In Athens, it was elite culture that was in fact 'unofficial' and 'unauthorized', and therefore could become subversive.

'Popular' Institutions and 'Popular' Authorization

As in one of the most famous works for the study of popular culture, Carlo Ginzburg's *The Cheese and the Worms*,[13] my starting point will be the judicial process. Ginzburg's hero, Domenico Scandella, known as Menocchio, was a sixteenth-century peasant from Montereale, in Friuli, northern Italy. We know about him and his story from the records of two successive legal proceedings conducted against him by the Inquisition. He was eventually convicted as a heresiarch and burnt at the stake in 1599, at the age of sixty-seven. He made a living, in his words, as 'miller, carpenter, sawyer, mason, and other things', but he was mostly a miller. He described himself as 'very poor': 'I do not have anything but two rented mills and two fields in perpetual lease, and with these I have supported and continue to support my poor family.'[14] Despite his words, it is clear that Menocchio's

---

[13] Ginzburg 1980, first published in Italian in 1976.   [14] Ginzburg 1980: 1–2.

social standing in Montereale was not negligible: he was mayor of the village in 1581, and was at some point *camararo*, administrator of the local parish church, which suggests that he had probably attended an elementary school. He could certainly read and write. Nevertheless there can be no doubt that Menocchio was not a member of the elite. The records of the legal proceedings against him make abundantly clear how ill at ease he was in the official context of a lawcourt, despite the help of an advocate. His recorded statements often display naivety and incomprehension of the issues: Menocchio often incriminates himself with his own words. He speaks freely, too freely, because he feels he has done nothing wrong. The image we get is one of a peasant judged by his superiors in an institutional context that clearly puts him at a disadvantage. And Ginzburg has made a compelling case that his strange beliefs, although partially influenced by some readings, find their origin to a great extent in an undercurrent of popular culture.

When a historian of ancient Athens looks for a window into the social and economic reality of the daily life of the Athenians, the main sources are invariably the speeches of the Attic orators. And yet because the orators were either famous politicians speaking for themselves, or expensive logographers composing speeches for a fee, most of our extant speeches are meant to be pronounced by litigants who were by no means poor.[15] There is, however, one exception: Lysias' *For the Invalid* 24. We do not know much about the speaker, not even his name. We know that he had been at the time of the trial the recipient of an invalidity pension of 1 obol per day (Lys. 24.13, 26) for many years (Lys. 24.7, 22, 26). We learn from [Arist.] *Ath. Pol.* 49.4 that such pensions were given in the late fourth century by the Athenian state to citizens who had a wealth of less than three mnai and, because of disability, could not work.[16] The rules must, however, have changed at some point between the early and the late fourth century, because, first, the speaker admits openly that he has some kind of shop and makes some money for himself (Lys. 24.6) and, second, [Arist.] *Ath. Pol.* 49.4 speaks about 2 obols a day instead of 1.[17] The very figure of 1 obol a day suggests that this was intended as a small help for the disabled rather than their entire income.[18] Scheidel has studied the real wages of unskilled labourers in many ancient and medieval communities by converting them into wheat

---

[15] On logographers, see Lavency 1964 and Rubinstein 2000: 14–15, 125–6.
[16] Cf. Rhodes 1981: 570.   [17] On disability benefits in Athens, cf. Dillon 1995: 27–57.
[18] Wolpert and Kapparis 2011: 68, n. 8 and Dillon 1995: 38: the regulations changed. Carey 1990: 94: the regulations were not followed to the letter.

measures and has been able to check how close they were to bare subsistence. He found that the lower limit of income for a male adult head of family was in the region of 3.5 litres of wheat per day, which must have been close to the limit of subsistence.[19] In late fifth-century Athens the normal wage for unskilled labourers was 1 drachma per day.[20] The wheat price at the same time was 6 drachmas per medimnos, which means that the daily wage of an unskilled labourer could buy 9 litres of wheat (considerably more than bare subsistence).[21] One obol could therefore buy only 1.5 litres of wheat, well below the limit of subsistence. It is unthinkable that the condition for receiving such a minimal subsidy could be that the beneficiary (a male citizen, so hypothetically the head of a household) should not work at all. In that case an invalid would have starved. Conversely, in the later fourth century wheat prices were between 5 and 6 drachmas per medimnos, and therefore 2 obols could buy between 3.6 and 3 litres, close or just over subsistence levels, which could be supplemented through pay for Assembly (1.5 drachmas per *kyria ekklesia*; 1 drachma per ordinary *ekklesia*; cf. [Arist.] *Ath. Pol.* 62.2) and lawcourt attendance (3 obols per day; cf. Ar. *Eq.* 255; [Arist.] *Ath. Pol.* 62.2).

Beneficiaries of invalidity benefits had to undergo a *dokimasia* (scrutiny) before the Council annually. This was a formality, unless someone stood up and challenged the right of the beneficiary to the benefit on grounds of law. This is what happened in this case: the speaker's opponent questioned his right to the subsidy, and the speech is the response to these accusations, written by Lysias for the speaker, and pronounced before the Council (Lys. 24.1). Many scholars have doubted the speech's authenticity[22] on the grounds of the irreverent tone, the alleged lack of structure of the speech and the weakness of the case. Yet, as Carey has shown, the structure of the speech is quite clear, and depends closely on the order of the arguments of the opponent.[23] As for the tone and the irreverence, 'Lysias created a character, somewhat eccentric, sly, and witty, but also likeable and trustworthy, hoping that such a character would carry the jury'.[24] The *ethopoeia* in this speech is very typical of

---

[19] Scheidel and Friesen 2009; Scheidel 2010.
[20] Cf. the epigraphic and literary sources collected and discussed in Loomis 1998: 111–13; Markle 1985. Cf. Scheidel 2010: 441–2, 455–6.
[21] This is 2.6 times the lower level for subsistence, which puts Athenian wages above the 'middling' level of most other premodern societies, see Ober 2010: 262.
[22] Harpocration (*s.v. adynaton*) had already argued against its authenticity. See, among modern scholars, e.g. Darkow 1917: 73–7; Roussel 1966.
[23] Carey 1990.   [24] Wolpert and Kapparis 2011: 66.

Lysias, and should not make us doubt its authenticity.[25] Moreover, the details in the disability benefits are at odds with the account of the *Ath. Pol.*, a text very well-known in antiquity and from which one would expect the relevant information would come, were this a later rhetorical exercise.[26] The chief objection against authenticity is that if the speaker is really as poor as he claims to be, how could he possibly afford the services of Lysias? Todd suggests that the speaker may not be as poor as he wants the judges to believe,[27] but it is difficult to see what use a subsidy as low as one obol per day would be to anyone who is not really destitute. The very fact that the speaker fights to retain this benefit is evidence that his economic situation must have been dire indeed. On the other hand, the speaker admits, following his opponent's allegations, that his trade put him in contact with many rich people (Lys. 24.5) and it is not unthinkable that someone may have helped him to afford Lysias' fees, or that Lysias himself may have waived his fee on account of their acquaintance. In any case, the fact that Lysias wrote the speech cannot overturn the evidence of the speaker's poverty, which is proven both by the fact that he retained such a low subsidy for many years, and that he found it necessary to fight for it when challenged.

There is no doubt, therefore, that we have here a speech pronounced by a citizen at the very lowest end of the social and economic scale.[28] The speaker claims not to be able to afford even a saddled mule, let alone a horse (he borrowed horses from richer acquaintances; see Lys. 24.10–12), and although he could have used a slave to help with his *technē*, he has not so far been able to afford one (Lys. 24.6). This must be true, otherwise the opponent would have brought it up. And in Athens only the poorest of citizens could not afford a slave.[29] He claims not to have received any form of inheritance from his father, and to have just stopped supporting his late mother two years before. He has no children (Lys. 24.6) and is now an old man (Lys. 24.7). In many ways, he is worse off than Menocchio, with his 'two rented mills and two fields in perpetual lease' and his wife and the eleven children he is able to support. And yet his accuser can claim that he spent his time with wealthy people on account of his *technē* (Lys. 24.4–5),

---

[25] See in favour of authenticity, Jebb 1893: 251–2; Adams 1905: 234–5; Albini 1952: 28–38; Usher 1965; Dillon 1995: 38–9; Todd 1990: 166–7; 2000: 253–54; Wolpert and Kapparis 2011: 66.

[26] On rhetorical exercises in the Hellenistic period, see Canevaro 2013: 329–42 and forthcoming 1 with further bibliography.

[27] Todd 2000: 253.

[28] Even based on an income distribution, like that calculated in Ober 2010, that also included slaves and metics.

[29] See e.g. Ar. *Eccl.* 593; Xen. *Mem.* 2.3.3 and Arist. *Pol.* 1252b15.

and the speaker himself could claim that he borrowed horses from wealthy people, without it sounding absurd that such an individual could have wealthy acquaintances. This already points towards less marked social distinctions, however much we believe the speaker's or his accuser's statements. It gives a stark impression of a society in which a poor man could be mistaken for a rich man, and a rich man could pass for a poor one.

Of further interest is the relationship between the speaker and his audience, and his tone: the speaker seems completely comfortable, at ease in the institutional setting of the Athenian Council, and shows an obvious familiarity with the audience, so as to imply that he is one of them. Of course, the speech was written by Lysias, and not by the speaker, but the speaker pronounced it in person, so the persona of the speaker, his tone and approach, had to be both believable and strike a sympathetic cord with the *bouleutai*. It is unthinkable that a lowly citizen could speak to the *bouleutai* as our speaker did, showing such an easy familiarity with the institutional framework and discursive habits of *dokimasia* cases, and even a certain comfortable irreverence, if the audience were not made up of his actual peers and if the institutional framework which authorized his utterance were not designed to make him secure and comfortable. The speech in fact starts with a tongue-in-cheek mockery of a typical opening of *dokimasia* speeches pronounced by those who are selected for important magistracies. The speaker opens with the words: 'I am almost grateful to my accuser, members of the Council, for having devised these proceedings against me. In the past, I had no reason to give an account of my life, but now, because of him, I have one' (trans. Todd). This strikingly resembles the opening of Lys. 16 (*For Manthitheos*), yet that is a *dokimasia* speech by a confident young aristocrat who has been selected to be a *bouleutes*, whereas this is a speech by an old and destitute cripple who attempts to retain his pension. The impression of mockery is strengthened at Lys. 24.2, when the speaker wonders: 'Could he possibly be bringing charges against me for money as a sycophant?' (trans. Todd). Once again, alleging that the accuser has disreputable motives, is a sycophant and would drop the charge in exchange for money are stock motives in *dokimasia* and public speeches (e.g. Lys. 7.39–40, Ant. 6.48–49, Isoc. 15.5, Hyp. *Licophr.* 2), and the *bouleutai* must have heard such claims hundreds of times, yet it is absurd in the context of a speech pronounced by a poor man trying to retain a pension of 1 obol per day.[30] Along the same lines, the rhetorical question at Lys. 24.25 ('Or is it because I was in power

---

[30] Carey 1990: 46–7 for this interpretation of Lys. 26.1–2. Cf. also Adams 1905: 236–7.

under the Thirty and harmed many of the citizens? But I went into exile at Chalcis with your democracy, and although I could have shared in the *politeia* with them, I preferred to share in the danger with all of you', trans. Todd) is also a mockery of a stock motive of *dokimasia* (and judicial) speeches in the years following the democratic restoration of 403 BCE: accusers alleged that the defendants had been thriving under, and collaborating with, the Thirty, and defendants boasted their democratic credentials (cf. Lys. 16.3–5, 25.1–2, 26.5, 9–10, 16–18). Yet for the speaker, a very poor man, to claim that he could have shared in the *politeia* of the Thirty, aristocratic and elitist, is yet another joke.[31]

Likewise, the argument brought forward by the speaker against the allegations of the accuser that he is a rich man at Lys. 24.9 is also ironical: the speaker counters that if he was ever appointed *choregos* and challenged his opponent to an *antidosis*, his opponent would never accept. Only about 1,200 citizens in Athens were liable to be selected to perform liturgies,[32] around 4 per cent of the citizen population, and these all had wealth in excess of 3–4 talents,[33] which put them at the opposite end of the social and economic scale to our speaker. The very suggestion that he may be selected as a liturgist is both a mockery of the rhetorical strategies used by elite speakers, and a nod to the *bouleutai* that his opponent is indeed a member of that elite. And these covert allegations match the speaker's counter-arguments to the accusations against his moral character: at Lys. 24.15–18 the speaker counters the accuser's allegations that he is 'full of *hybris*, violent and dissolute', and argues that *hybris*, violence and dissolute behaviour are typical of the wealthy not of the poor, of the young not of the old. These are the same arguments used, for example, by Demosthenes (21.112, 158) against Meidias, and rely on the audience's dislike for the wealthy who behave as if they were above the rest of the citizens. Such arguments show that the speaker expected to receive a sympathetic hearing from the *bouleutai* precisely because he was poor, and expected them to be negatively disposed towards his accuser if he could single him out as a member of the elite.

It is likely that the speaker's reliance on the *bouleutai*'s sympathy, his implied familiarity with them, as if they belonged to the same class and milieu (and were not, at least predominantly, elite), was not unjustified.

---

[31] Cf. Carey 1990: 48.
[32] Cf. Rhodes 1982: 1–19; Gabrielsen 1994: 178–82; Van Wees 2011: 111–12, *pace* Davies 1981: 26–7; and recently Kron 2011: 129.
[33] See Davies 1971: xxiv and 1981: 28–37. Cf. also Rhodes 1982: 5 and 2006: 331–2; Gabrielsen 1994: 45–53, 176–82.

The Council reflected quite closely the demographics of the Athenian male citizen population, even though it might have slightly favoured the better-off.[34] Although the rules forbidding iteration were not applied to the *bouleutai*,[35] one could not be a councillor before thirty years of age, and no more than once every two years. Bouleutic quota inscriptions show, however, that citizens were rarely *bouleutai* more than once,[36] and therefore every year the Athenians had to find *c.* 375–400 new *bouleutai*.[37] Hansen has also found epigraphical evidence that the average age of first-time *bouleutai* was forty, and has calculated therefore that the vast majority of *bouleutai* had to be selected from a pool of about 600 persons in any given year, given the likely demographic structure of Attica. This means that the selection of the *bouleutai* put quite a strain on the citizen population of Athens, and, in Hansen's words, 'over a third of all citizens over eighteen, and about two thirds of all citizens over forty, became councillors, some of them twice'.[38] The councillors were selected from all demes, therefore from all parts of Attica, which means that citizens from the urban demes were no better represented than those from coastal and inland demes. The Council as an institution was not any more alien for those living in the countryside than for those living in Athens itself. Even though the evidence shows that the better-off were overrepresented in relation to their proportion in the Athenian citizen population, the Council could not have worked without the significant participation of all sections of the Athenian population, including the very worst-off. Therefore, when the speaker of Lys. 24, a poor and disabled man, came to be judged by one of the highest governmental organs of the Athenian state, it is likely that a significant part of the *bouleutai* may have identified to some extent with his economic and social position, and that the majority would not have belonged to the elite, and would have looked to them with some hostility. And moreover, because the speaker is an old man, there are two chances in three that he may have himself been a *bouleutes* before. In Athens the highest institutions of the state, those that authorized cultural utterances of various kinds, and made them official, were not controlled by the elite, they were not alien for a poor man, as the Inquisition tribunal was for Menocchio, and they did not express different (elite) cultural values. They were familiar and recognizable.[39]

[34] Rhodes 1972: 5–6 and Carey 1990: 46.   [35] [Arist.] *Ath. Pol.* 62.3, cf. Rhodes 1980; 1984.
[36] Cf. Hansen 1985: 51–5.   [37] Hansen 1991: 249.   [38] Hansen 1991: 249.
[39] Ober 1989 recognizes the high level of popular control over the institutions, but still assumes that they would be used for the most part by the elite. In this, his position still envisages e.g. the lawcourts as an arena for elite competition (see e.g. Osborne 1985 and Cohen 1995), albeit one

This is even truer for the lawcourts. Among the names of demes represented in the surviving heliastic plaques (from burials) coastal and inland demes are found more often than urban demes.[40] Immigration into the city can account for some of these plaques, but there is no denying that Athenians from all parts of Attica served as judges, and therefore the judicial institutions were equally familiar to (and found representation in) all Athenians, from all parts of Attica. This is confirmed by the literary sources: a character of Aristophanes' *Birds* remarks that the 'unheliastic' plant, although it can still occasionally be found in the country, is very rare (Ar. *Av.* 109–12).[41] The literary sources are also clear about the average composition of the lawcourts, and suggest that, unlike the Council, the lawcourts were preponderantly manned by the poor, for whom the 3 obols pay was often their only source of income.[42] Demosthenes (21.182) gives an example of this when he states: 'Yet when Pyrrhus, the Eteobutad, men of Athens, was denounced for serving as judge when he owed money to the treasury, some of you thought that he must be put to death, and after being convicted in your court, he was executed. And yet he tried to receive his payment because of poverty, not to commit abuse' (trans. Harris). And Isocrates (7.54) laments: 'These days what sensible individual would not be upset at what is happening when he sees many citizens drawing lots at the entrance of the courts to see whether they will have the necessities of life or not' (trans. Too). An extreme picture of the average Athenian judge as an elderly citizen, thoroughly destitute and dependent on the daily 3 obols for the survival of his family, is provided by Aristophanes' *Wasps*. The eponymous wasps are none other than the fellow judges of the main character, Philocleon, represented as a swarm of decrepit old men on their way to the courts (ll. 230–47). At ll. 291–315 we are witnesses to the dialogue between one of them and his young son, who asks the father for dried figs to eat. The father's answer is a harsh no, because, he laments, with the miserable heliastic pay he has to buy firewood, groats (partially crushed cereals to make a kind of cake)[43] and something to go with them for 3 obols. To this the son reacts with the desperate question: 'If the archon today does not summon the lawcourts, where will we find the money to eat?' The father has no solution. This picture is grotesque and exaggerated,

---

in which the *demos* was the ultimate arbiter. I argue here that these institutions were in fact a familiar context open to non-elite citizens, which expressed their worldview, their culture and their morality (see below pp. 50–7).

[40] Hansen 1989: 75, 87.   [41] Cf. Hansen 1991: 184 for other examples.
[42] Cf. [Xen.] *Ath. Pol.* 1.18; Dem. 24.123 with Markle 1985: 282–9; Hansen 1991: 184–6 and Rhodes 1981: 691.
[43] Cf. MacDowell 1971: 174–5.

but it must have resonated with the audience as believable in order to be funny, and there is no reason to doubt that the courts in Athens were manned for the most part by those at the lower end of the social and economic scale, and in particular by the older among them, because the pay of 3 obols was only half the daily wage of an unskilled labourer.[44] So the lawcourts, one of the highest political institutions in Athens, with powers over both the political and the private lives of the Athenians, were manned for the most part by lower-class Athenians.

Far from being alien to the cultural milieu of ordinary Athenians, as the Inquisition court was for Menocchio, the Athenian lawcourts were to a large extent controlled by them. Ordinary, poor Athenians over thirty years of age from all over Attica served in them to the number of 6,000 a year, out of a population of *c.* 30,000 male citizens over eighteen. In the context of the lawcourts, as in that of the Assembly and of the Council (and equally in that of the civic festivals) most 'official', 'authorized' cultural forms received their formal 'authorization', and this validation was provided not by the elite, but overwhelmingly by the lower classes. This should always be kept in mind when we dismiss the most prominent among Athenian cultural forms as elite culture. In a recent essay, Allan and Kelly rightly stress that in studying the meaning and the appeal of tragedy as an art form one should always keep in mind its audience, a multivocal, popular audience. They advance therefore an interpretation of tragedy as a form of popular art.[45] They understand it as mass entertainment, and this is consistent with Parker's definition of mass culture as authorized culture that requires high economic and cultural capital to be produced and low economic and cultural capital to consume. And yet what is even more

---

[44] Jones 1957: 36–7, 124 argued that in the fourth century the judges were mainly middle-class; contra Markle 1985, Rhodes 1981: 691, Hansen 1991: 185–6 and Todd 1990. Todd's discussion is the most detailed, but his conclusion that the courts represented a distinctive class of farmers with their own values that constituted the majority of the Athenian population is dependent on an outdated picture of the social and economic composition of the Athenian population (see Harris 2002 and Lewis, Harris and Woolmer 2015 for the prominence of market exchange and horizontal work specialization, and Hansen 2006: 67–84 for the high level of urbanization). MacDowell 1995: 156–8 believes that, despite some exaggeration, the picture of the judges provided in the *Wasps* is reliable.

[45] Allan and Kelly 2013. That it was a very wide audience with a strong popular element must be true even if we accept Goette's findings (1995, and his appendix to Csapo 2007) that the capacity of the theatre in the fifth century was between 5,500 and 7,000, much lower than usually assumed. (Dawson 1997: 7 estimates an even lower 3,700.) The sources speak of a space in the south slope of the Acropolis, beneath a poplar tree, from which many more watched the performances (Cratinus fr. 372 Kessel-Austin; Eust. ε 64; cf. Roselli 2011: 72–5), which suggests that demand for seats was higher than the capacity of the theatre allowed. Cf. Roselli 2011 and Akrigg and Tordoff 2013: 37–41, and Robson in this volume pp. 70–2.

remarkable within this scheme is that the authorizing institutions are in this case, unlike in the forms of mass culture to which Parker refers, controlled by those with low economic and cultural capital, and not by the elite. Tragedies and comedies were performed in the context of dramatic competitions, which a wide section of the population attended,[46] and which were judged by ten more or less randomly selected Athenians.[47] Deme performances widened even further the participation of the entire Athenian population.

Likewise, in the lawcourts, even in political speeches pronounced by famous politicians, the cultural references exploited, whether they are historical, poetic or artistic, are validated and authorized by an institution that is popular in its composition, and which lays a strong claim to the ownership and control of these cultural references. A case in point is the long series of poetic quotations introduced by Aeschines in his speech *Against Timarchus* (Aeschin. 1.141–54). Aeschines quotes four passages from Homer and two from Euripides (*Il.* 18.324–9; 333–5; 23.77–91; 18.95–9; Eur. fr. 672 Nauck; fr. 812 Nauck). It is easy to dismiss these as elite culture, and yet it is interesting how Aeschines introduces them:

But since you remember Achilles and Patroclus and Homer and other poets, as though the judges are men without education, and represent yourselves as impressive figures whose erudition allows you to look down on the people, to show you that we have already acquired a little knowledge and learning, we, too, shall say something on the subject.[48]

Some scholars interpret these lines as accusing Aeschines' opponents of posing as men whose superior knowledge and education sets them apart from the judges, which would exploit some measure of resentment of the judges towards an educated elite and their obscure culture.[49] Yet the rhetorical argument here works rather in the opposite direction: the orator is not relying on the judges' ignorance of poetry, nor is he relying on their mistrust of those that have a poetical education (in the way in which, for example, Menocchio mistrusts those who use Latin to confuse and trick peasants).[50] He rather portrays his opponents as questioning the

---

[46] See Robson in this volume pp. 69–74 for the social composition of the audience at the theatrical festivals.
[47] Cf. Pickard-Cambridge 1988: 95–9; Pope 1986: 322–6; Csapo and Slater 1995: 157–65; Wilson 2000: 98–102 and 346–47, nn. 222–37.
[48] Aeschin. 1.141 trans. Carey.
[49] Cf. Dover 1974: 25–8, Ostwald 1986: 256–7, Ober 1989: 170–7, Hesk 2000: 207–9.
[50] Cf. Ginzburg 1980: 9–10. Manzoni in *The Betrothed* has Renzo express all his resentment and suspicion for the 'latinorum' of priests and lawyers.

audience's culture, their knowledge of poetry, assuming that they will be offended by the insinuation that they do not know their Homer and their Euripides, and then he rescues the public from this imagined accusation of poetic ignorance by claiming that 'we, too, have already acquired a little knowledge and learning, we, too, shall say something on the subject'. It is a cunning strategy that relies on the popular audience having cultural pretensions and laying a strong claim to these cultural forms. Aeschines himself recognizes this when he states: 'the reason I think we learn by heart the poets' thoughts as children is to make use of them when we are men' (3.135).[51] In general, the orators always paint a picture of the popular judges as knowledgeable men who remember their laws, their poetry and their history and have a good ear for gossip.[52] Because these are the people the orators are trying to convince, this picture must have resonated with them. If not completely accurate, this is a picture that must have been pleasing to them, and must have reflected their own cultural world and pretensions. The cultural forms to which the orators allude cannot have been elite culture perceived as alien by the ordinary men that manned the lawcourts (and the Assembly and the Council).

The composition of the main institutions of the Athenian state has a remarkable consequence on the nature of the 'official', 'authorized' culture of ancient Athens: unlike in most premodern (and modern) societies, these cultural forms have a solid claim to be considered popular culture, not only because they require low (although not inconsiderable) economic and cultural capital in their audience to be enjoyed, but also because the institutions that authorize them are themselves controlled by their eventual audience, which acquires through political participation the capital necessary to directly secure their production. In this, they cannot be identified straightforwardly as forms of mass culture (on Parker's definition), because unlike normal forms of mass culture it is not an elite that authorizes them (although it is mostly, yet not exclusively, an elite that produces them). But it is not only in the composition of the chief Athenian institutions that we find a strong popular element. It is in the very values they reflect, in their very structure and substantive ideological content. Several Athenian statutes prescribe practices that in other societies scholars would not hesitate to define as forms of popular justice, and therefore popular culture. And yet these practices are embedded in the legal system, explicitly authorized and prescribed by the formal institutions of the city.

[51] Cf. Canevaro forthcoming 2 for a more extensive analysis of this passage, and a discussion of cultural references in the orators.
[52] Cf. Canevaro forthcoming 2.

As Forsdyke correctly recognizes, 'the "formal" institutions of the Athenian democracy incorporated various forms of popular justice within the "official" frame', and therefore 'the categories "formal" and "informal" or "official" and "popular" are highly misleading when applied to classical Athens'.[53] Forsdyke also argues that 'popular justice was frequently used alongside more "official" forms of punishment' and stresses the element of informality – institutions can incorporate forms of popular justice, but 'the masses, including ordinary farmers and craftsmen' must have had a distinctive cultural space with forms of justice as spontaneous collective punishment separate from the formal justice of the state. One wonders why the masses would have needed such a separate space and such separate forms of popular justice, when the 'formal' legal system of the *polis* was in fact controlled by them, and many of its laws reflected their beliefs and prescribed exactly those forms of justice that in other societies are separate from the formal institutions of the state.

The forms of punishment and public humiliation for seducers are particularly interesting from this point of view.[54] In Athens, if a *kyrios* caught a man in the act of having sexual intercourse with one of his free dependent women, he could kill him straightaway, and have the case heard by the Delphinion, arguing for acquittal on the grounds that that was a form of justifiable homicide among those explicitly listed in the relevant law.[55] But this was not the only possibility: he could maltreat the seducer, and the sources inform us of maltreatments such as pushing radishes up his anus or pulling out his pubic hair.[56] A further alternative was demanding a sum of money in compensation and keeping the seducer (or a surety) imprisoned until he paid. The seducer or anyone on his behalf could bring a public charge for wrongful imprisonment, and if he won, he was released without obligation to pay, but if he lost, the offended *kyrios* was authorized to do to him anything he wished, short of using a knife, in front of the

---

[53] Forsdyke 2012: 145–6.

[54] The relevant laws also applied to unmarried women, because the offence was committed against the *kyrios* of the *oikos*, not necessarily against the husband: cf. Paoli 1950: 123–82; Harrison 1968: 32–6; Dover 1974: 209; Cantarella 1991: 289–96; Foxhall 1991; Carey 1995: 407–8; Canevaro 2013: 190–6. *Pace* Cohen 1984; 1991: 98–132. Cohen 1985 has doubted the historicity of the forms of humiliation described in our sources, but see Roy 1991 and Carey 1993 against his arguments. See also Schmitz 2004: 338–47. Cf. for seduction and rape Harris 2006: 283–332.

[55] The law is preserved at Dem. 23.53 as a reliable document: cf. Canevaro 2013: 64–70. This is also the law on the basis of which Euphiletus asks for acquittal in Lys. 1 (the law is read out by the secretary at Lys. 1.30): see Harris 2006: 285; Carey 1995: 409–10; Todd 2007: 43–6, 126–8.

[56] Lys. 1.49; Ar. *Nub.* 1083; *Pl.* 168. Cf. Carey 1993.

court.⁵⁷ The *kyrios* could also bring a *graphe moicheias* (public charge for seduction), for which it is not clear whether the penalty was fixed or was assessed through *timesis*,⁵⁸ or a *graphe hybreos* (public charge for outrage).⁵⁹ There can be no doubt that these various remedies against a seducer were explicitly prescribed or authorized in the relevant laws: [Dem.] 59.85–6 is evidence that there were one or more specific *nomoi* regarding *moicheia*, and that they specified the punishments against the offenders;⁶⁰ we also know that the law discussed at Lys. 1.28 must have mentioned the possibility of killing the *moichos*, and likewise the possibility of imprisoning the *moichos* (seducer) and asking for a ransom, otherwise the *graphe* for wrongful imprisonment of a *moichos* mentioned at [Dem.] 59.65–6 could not have existed. And there is no reason to doubt that the laws must have also defined what sort of maltreatments of the seducer were allowed:⁶¹ the law discussed at [Dem.] 59.65–6 explicitly authorized that the *kyrios* who was attacked in a *graphe* for wrongful imprisonment of a *moichos* and won could do to the seducer anything he pleased short of using a knife. This is a form of extreme public humiliation which is specifically prescribed in the relevant laws, and is meant to happen in court. It seems perfectly reasonable to infer that the laws on *moicheia* also defined what kinds of humiliation were allowed against a *moichos* caught in the act, and in fact at Lys. 1.49, in an 'official' legal context, Euphiletus states that the laws instruct 'the man who catches an adulterer to treat him in any way he pleases'. They also prescribed forms of public humiliation for women who had been seduced. Aeschin. 1.183 (confirmed by [Dem.] 59.85–7) attributes the relevant law to Solon and states that:

the woman with whom a seducer is caught, he does not permit to adorn herself, nor to attend the public cult ceremonies, in order that she should not mix with the innocent women and corrupt them. But if she does attend, or adorn herself, he tells anyone who meets her to tear off her clothes, strip off her adornment and beat her – it is forbidden to kill or mutilate her.

---

[57] Lys. 1.25; [Dem.] 59.65–6; Callias fr. 1 and Cratinos fr. 81 Kassel and Austin. Harris 2006: 289 believes, against Cole 1984: 104 (cf. Kapparis 1995: 115; 1996: 65) that the ban on using a knife was meant to avoid bloodshed and therefore pollution in the court.

[58] [Arist.] *Ath. Pol.* 59.3. This is the law Euphiletus asks the secretary to read at Lys. 1.28: cf. Harris 2006: 291–3 and Carey 1995: 412, *pace* Paoli 1950: 153; Cohen 1991: 110–13; Todd 1993: 276–8 who believe this is the law on *apagoge*.

[59] See Harris 2006: 288.

[60] But the document at [Dem.] 59.87 is probably a forgery: cf. Canevaro 2013: 190–6.

[61] Cf. Carey 1995: 412.

Forms of collective, spontaneous humiliation, typical of popular justice, are here sanctioned and explicitly authorized by the laws of the city, and therefore made 'official'.[62]

Forsdyke, in discussing these statutes and these practices, claims that these were 'primarily extra-legal practices[s]' and stresses their 'informal' status. She dismisses the importance of their 'official' status by arguing that even when we find 'the overlap between institutional and popular justice', this is 'not evidence that formal law suppressed popular justice and that ritual humiliation could only take place through institutional channels'. She claims that 'the "formal" laws relating to adultery deal primarily with resolving disputes over whether the informal practices were properly followed, rather than with meting out punishment for the offense itself'.[63] This is problematic: first, the fact that the laws left to the private initiative of the victim the choice between precisely defined options (which allowed also for a certain measure of self-help) does not make the role of the laws any less key, because if the victim failed to follow the relevant instructions, he could himself be punished. The various options are explicitly sanctioned in the laws, and therefore they have the same legal status as punishments directly inflicted by the organs of the state. Second, when she argues that 'as long as the treatment of the adulterer fell within certain generally accepted practices ... cases of adultery probably rarely reached the courts' and denies that 'formal legal procedures were the primary route for dealing with such offenses', her view of the workings of the law is excessively narrow. In our modern world most drivers abide by the speed limits set by the laws without any concrete intervention by the authorities, and the authorities only intervene when someone breaks the law. Does this mean that the existence of the relevant laws, and of a legal system that can enforce them, has no or little role in determining the drivers' behaviour? Surely not. In the majority of cases, the chief sign that the laws are working is that no legal procedure is necessary. The laws authorize and prescribe a clearly defined behaviour and succeed when individuals conform to this behavioural rule without further intervention from the institutions.[64]

---

[62] Cf. Canevaro 2013: 191–5 on these provisions and the authenticity of the document at [Dem.] 59.87.

[63] Forsdyke 2012: 146–8.

[64] Forsdyke's views here are indebted to interpretations of Athenian law as purely procedural, that hold that Athenian laws only aimed to bring disputes to court, without concerning themselves with particular substantive behaviours (see e.g. Hansen 1980: 94; 1991: 165; Osborne 1985; and Todd 1993). Such a view, once popular, is contradicted by the evidence: see Harris 2013: 138–74.

The fact that Athenian law sanctions and prescribes practices that in other societies are typical of popular, 'unofficial' justice is evidence that because of the popular control over the formal institutions of the Athenian *polis*, Athens came to formalize popular forms of justice. This does not mean, however, that these laws cannot be used by historians as evidence of informal practices: as Schmitz has shown, the formal legal practices of classical Athens can be used to shed light on informal popular justice in the archaic period, which later on, with the development of democracy, came to be institutionalized.[65] They are important evidence for popular culture, but they need to be tackled through the 'regressive method' advocated by Burke.[66] But as for fifth- and fourth-century Athens, there is no need to find 'unauthorized' and unofficial venues of popular justice, because popular justice is embodied in the formal institutions of the *polis*.

The existence of these practices, sanctioned by the laws of the city, is further evidence that in classical Athens the formal institutions of the *polis* were the most genuine manifestation of the practices, the convictions, and the beliefs of the vast majority of the Athenians. They were 'popular' in the sense that the culture they fostered was controlled by, and reflected the worldview of, the 'people' of Athens. It is remarkable that in the provisions against seducers found in the Gortyn code (*IG* IV 72, ll. 16–45) the only penalties contemplated are financial, and the only case in which one can deal with a seducer as one pleases is if the seducer is not ransomed within five days.[67] No forms of public humiliation for the woman seem to be contemplated, and as long as the seducer pays what he owes in time, the law forbids any form of 'private' punishment against him, and any form of humiliation. Gortyn, like the other Cretan *poleis*, was an oligarchy controlled by the elite, in which only a minority of the inhabitants had any representation in the formal institutions of the state.[68] And, accordingly, the laws and legal institutions reflect the culture and practices of the elite, and show no trace of the forms of popular justice reflected instead in the Athenian legal system. In Athens the formal legal institutions can indeed be conceptualized as popular justice because they are controlled by the people, and reflect their beliefs, their practices, their cultural values and their worldview. In Gortyn the formal legal institutions were instead

---

[65] Cf. Schmitz 2004: 338–47, 401–9.
[66] Burke 2009: 120–30, borrowing the 'regressive' method from Marc Bloch, who used it most notably in Bloch 1966.
[67] For text and translation, see Willets 1967. For an introduction, see Davies 2005. For whether this is actually a 'code', and how it originated, see Davies 1998; Kristensen 2004.
[68] On the constitution of the Cretan *poleis* and on whether it is legitimate to speak of a Cretan constitution, see Perlman 1992 and Chaniotis 2005.

carriers of elite justice and lacked the popular elements common in Athens, because they reflected the practices and worldview of the elite. Identifying popular culture as 'unofficial', 'unauthorized' culture can be misleading. The institutional sanction of such a cultural form is not in itself a sign that such cultural forms cannot be truly popular, because 'the people' do not necessarily have to be passive subjects of institutions controlled by the elite. When the institutions are controlled by and represent the concerns and worldview of the majority, the culture they foster and 'authorize' can be truly popular. And, likewise, as we shall see in the next section, the lack of 'authorization' is in itself no guarantee that a cultural form is popular.

Unauthorized Elite Culture

The main character of Aristophanes' *Wasps*, Philocleon, is affected by a strange disease: he has an addiction to being a judge in the popular courts of Athens, to judging cases and making convictions (Ar. *Vesp.* 67–111). This 'disease' is, at a later point in the play, explained in detail and justified by Philocleon himself (Ar. *Vesp.* 548–727), who provides a remarkable (if parodic) account of the psychology of the Athenian judge: he claims that there is no one more blessed (Ar. *Vesp.* 550–1) or more powerful than a judge (Ar. *Vesp.* 619–30). The powerful prostrate themselves before him (Ar. *Vesp.* 55258); the trials in court provide him with entertainment, and the litigants flatter him (Ar. *Vesp.* 560–75, 578–82); he can make whatever decision he pleases (Ar. *Vesp.* 583–7) and is universally recognized as the highest authority in the city (Ar. *Vesp.* 590–600). And he is even paid 3 obols a day for all this (Ar. *Vesp.* 605–18).[69] Although Philocleon is not technically one of the wasps, the chorus of poor old judges whose condition we have discussed above (at least he is not dressed like one),[70] he is clearly pictured in the play as one of them: he is old, as they are, he has a very bad temper, as they do (Ar. *Vesp.* 223–4, 251–8), he is very fond of the time of his youth, with his dubious military exploits (set anachronistically in the Persian Wars), as they are (Ar. *Vesp.* 236–8), and he is fully devoted to the lawcourts, as they are (Ar. *Vesp.* 215–18, 240–5, 286–9). And indeed, when the chorus of wasps first appears (Ar. *Vesp.* 273), they have come to the

---

[69] Cf. Olson 1996: 132–8. *Pace* Konstan 1985: 31 and *passim* who argues that Philocleon is little more than the personification of an addiction, and dismisses these arguments as evidence of Philocleon's 'childish desire for flattery ... that transparently betrays the pathetic self-importance of the weak and powerless'.

[70] See MacDowell 1995: 155 and n. 7.

house, as they do every morning, to collect Philocleon, who would normally join them, becoming therefore himself a wasp. The only reason this does not happen is that Philocleon's son, Bdelycleon, with the help of two slaves, has shut him in the house, and is preventing him from joining his fellow judges. Konstan has argued that these similarities hide a remarkable difference: the chorus is composed of poor men who need court service not to starve, whereas Philocleon has the option of being supported by his wealthy son.[71] Yet the play consistently gives the impression that the fate of the chorus as a whole will be the same as that of Philocleon, even to the extent that when eventually Philocleon agrees to lead a life of apolitical leisure, the chorus speak as if his decision applies to them too, and they too will abandon the lawcourts for a life of leisure (Ar. *Vesp.* 872–3, 887–90).[72]

The initial situation of the play is therefore one in which Philocleon and the wasps, who represent here the *demos*, with a stress on their poverty and on their dependence on the dicastic *misthos*, are addicted to the courts and in general to the formal institutions of the state. That is their environment, where they are most comfortable and which they believe is their natural setting. They are the ordinary citizens of Athens, and the lawcourts, the institutions, are the political, social and cultural context they find most congenial. This is the situation that Philocleon finds desirable, and at Ar. *Vesp.* 548–727 he explains why. Bdelycleon's answer is a subtle political critique that does not so much challenge the existence of the lawcourts and of the democratic institutions of the state,[73] but rather highlights how the *demos* is deceived by clever politicians, how the power of the judges is not real, and how the real decisions are taken elsewhere, through bribery and the deception of the demagogues (Ar. *Vesp.* 665–711). To prove this, Bdelycleon argues that the revenues of the Empire, won by the people with their blood and labour, could guarantee everyone a life of leisure, but they are stolen by dishonest demagogues, and the *demos* receives only the crumbs. The politicians, on the other hand, get plenty of 'jars (of pickled fish), wine, carpets, cheese,

---

[71] Konstan 1985: 36–7.
[72] Konstan reads this as a serious problem, concealed by Aristophanes through a rather crude sleight of hand, but see Olson 1996: 132–8, who highlights the parallel between Philocleon's situation at home (the resources of the son can feed the dependent father) and that of the state (the resources are enough to allow citizens to live a life of leisure). The recognition of the politicians' deception is instrumental to Philocleon's enjoying his son's wealth, but also to the judges enjoying the resources of the Empire. Philocleon and the poor judges are in the same situation, vis-à-vis the *polis* (i.e. they are deceived by the politicians). MacDowell 1971: 8–10 and Rothwell 1995: 241 also agree that Philocleon is meant to be seen as a poor citizen.
[73] Cf. MacDowell 1995: 162–5.

honey, sesame seeds, pillows, libation-bowls, fine cloaks, garlands, necklaces, goblets, health-and-wealth' (Ar. *Vesp.* 676–7). These goods are representative of the high life, and in particular of luxurious banquets and *symposia*.[74] They are mentioned as typical of the kind of lifestyle that the judges, as representative of the *demos*, would find alien. The implication is that the demagogues, whatever their claims to be on the side of the people, are members of the elite, and live a life very different from that of the judges. While the *demos*, through its obsessive participation in the formal institutions of the state, believes itself to be in control and to reap the fruits of Athens' hegemony, it is the elite that gets the better share. Bdelycleon argues that if the people stopped following dishonest demagogues, that lifestyle of banquets, *symposia* and prelibacies could be shared by everyone (Ar. *Vesp.* 676–7).

Bdelycleon's speech convinces both Philocleon and the chorus (Ar. *Vesp.* 696–7, 713–14, 725–7), and the result is that eventually, in the final part of the play, Philocleon, as a representative of the wasps and of the *demos*, enjoys exactly the luxurious lifestyle that Bdelycleon had promised to him and to all Athenians. But first he has to abandon the formal institutions of the state. The domestic trial of the dog serves as a transition that eventually cures Philocleon of his addiction to judging, while parodying even more the working of the lawcourts.[75] What is interesting here is that Philocleon's move from the life of the masses to the life of the elite occurs through his abandonment of the formal institutions of the state in favour of more informal social and cultural contexts: first the domestic lawcourt, and finally the *symposion*. For Philocleon (and vicariously for the wasps, representing the *demos*), joining the elite equates to moving from 'authorized' institutional contexts, to use Parker's terminology, to 'unauthorized' ones. And it is clear that these different contexts come with very different cultural standards, which require the re-education of Philocleon to make him suitable for a *symposion*. In the final part of the play, much of the comedic effect is built upon the behaviour of a commoner, Philocleon, with his 'waspish' instincts, in the luxurious world of the elite.[76] That the culture involved is

---

[74] Cf. Olson 1996: 135.   [75] Cf. MacDowell 1995: 165–70; Olson 1996: 138–42.
[76] Cf. Cooper and Morris 1990: 77–8, Davidson 1997: 53, Donlan 1980: 159–62, Murray 1990: 150, Slater 1997: 38, Hobden 2013: 140 and Pritchard 2012: 22–4, who all identify in the class difference, and in Philocleon's ignorance of elite lifestyle and culture, the key comedic element of the scene. Various explanations have been offered for the puzzling class difference between father and son, which range from simple inconsistencies in the comic characterization (e.g. Pütz 2003: 125) to social changes that involved increased social mobility and generational conflict (Fisher 2000: 357).

very different indeed is made clear from the outset, when Philocleon has to change his clothes, because members of the elite dress differently from commoners (Ar. *Vesp.* 1122–73). Since the Persian Wars he has always worn a *tribon*, the cheapest kind of cloak, but is now given a thicker and warmer cloak, a *chlaina* of a type called *kaunakes*, which has been imported from Persia, and new shoes of the Laconian type.[77] Needless to say, Philocleon initially refuses to wear these fancy clothes, and shows how uncomfortable his re-education and rebranding make him. Bdelycleon then proceeds to instruct him in the etiquette of the *symposion* (1174–1264). First he asks him if he knows any good stories to tell in the company of learned men, and Philocleon offers first some vulgar myths, and then a fable about mice and ferrets.[78] Bdelycleon immediately reproaches him, calling him an 'ignorant knave' and making it clear that such stories are inappropriate among high-class people. This is not in fact the first or the last time that Philocleon makes use of Aesopic fables in the play, and later one of them actually has Aesop himself as the main character (cf. ll. 566–7, 1256–61, 1401–5, 1427–32, 1435–40, 1446–8). Among Aristophanes' characters Philocleon is the one that makes the most use of such stories.[79] Aesopic fables are prominent forms of popular culture, as has been persuasively argued in recent years by Forsdyke and Kurke,[80] and Philocleon's clumsy and inappropriate use of them in a sympotic context stresses just how out of place he is in an elite context.[81] It is interesting that at ll. 566–7 Philocleon mentions that litigants in court entertain the judges with these kind of stories, showing that they are perfectly appropriate in that context. This is confirmed by Arist. *Rhet.* 2.20 1393b12–1394a4.[82] It appears then that the forms of popular culture that Philocleon finds natural and congenial are perfectly appropriate in the official context of the lawcourts, but terribly vulgar in the 'unauthorized' elite context of the *symposion*.[83] Apart from telling inappropriate stories, Philocleon makes a fool of himself, mentioning as his most magnificent endeavour joining a delegation to Paros as a rower, as his bravest an episode of theft, and as a youthful athletic victory the time when he convicted a runner in a lawcourt.[84]

---

[77] See, on these clothes, Stone 1984: 162–3, 156 and 225–7; Geddes 1987: 311–15; Miller 2010: 317–21.
[78] Probably *Aesopica* 165; cf. Rothwell 1995: 248.   [79] See Rothwell 1995.
[80] Forsdyke 2012: 37–89 and Kurke 2011. Cf. the Introduction to this volume pp. 15–17.
[81] See Rothwell 1995.
[82] See Rothwell 1995: 245–7, with examples of orators using them from the Aesopic corpus.
[83] See Rothwell 1995: 348–52.   [84] See Hobden 2013: 141.

His behaviour is even more out of control when he joins a real *symposion*, as related by the slave Xanthias (Ar. *Vesp.* 1292–1325). Philocleon gets drunk and composes insulting *eikasmoi*, mocks his companions, makes vulgar jokes, recites ignorant stories and generally behaves in a manner completely inappropriate to the occasion. Philocleon's conversion and introduction into high society in the end shows just how ingrained popular habits are in him, and how alien they are from the sympotic context and from the culture of high society: in Hobden's words, 'Philocleon's revolutionary revelry demonstrates the hazards of abandoning the existing political system entirely, while also establishing the former juror's lack of aptitude ... for the replacement lifestyle of sumptuous feasting that Bdelycleon wishes for his father'.[85] Within this framework it is interesting to note that the cultural habits that the play connects with Philocleon and vicariously with the *demos*, the popular culture which is opposed to the cultural world of Bdelycleon and of the elite, finds its natural setting in the formal institutions of the state. This is consistent with the arguments made on pp. 42–57. Leaving this culture in favour of joining the elite is connected in the play with abandoning the formal institutions of the state, the 'authorized' spaces of *polis* life. And the setting of the elite's cultural life, exemplified in the play by the *symposion*, is explicitly a private space, an unofficial and 'unauthorized' one. In Athens the perception seemed to be that popular culture was official culture, while elite culture was unofficial culture.

Meanwhile a quick look at Athenian history shows that 'unofficial' in this case often means in opposition to the common folk and even sometimes to the formal institutions of the state. In Lysias' *Against Alcibiades* (Lys. 14.25 and *passim*), for instance, the speaker shows very well how accusations of taking part in *symposia*, and behaving inappropriately in those contexts, could be connected with hybristic and ultimately anti-democratic behaviour,[86] and the same connection is clear in Dem. 54.3, where hybristic behaviour is connected with revelling all day and night.

---

[85] Hobden 2013: 144. Pütz 2003: 111–33, on the one hand, recognizes that Philocleon's performance is that of a commoner ignorant of the conventions of high society, but on the other suggests that his ignorance may be a deception aimed at mocking his son and upper-class life in general. As noted by Pritchard 2012: 22–3, n. 51, there is no doubt that Philocleon's performance, in the context of the play, works also as a mockery of high-society lifestyle (and Pritchard uses this as a further argument to support Aristophanes' 'popular' credentials), but this does not mean that the character must be aware of the sympotic conventions and that his mockery is deliberate. In fact, various passages seem to stress exactly the opposite: his lack of understanding of the context (e.g. ll. 1299–1449).

[86] Cf. Hobden 2013: 144–8.

The *symposion* was traditionally an aristocratic pursuit.[87] It is interesting that in the late fifth century, at a time when sympotic activity was finally spreading as a pastime even for the moderately wealthy,[88] and even public dining spaces were progressively fashioned according to sympotic models,[89] the reality of the *symposion* was closely connected in popular imagination with anti-democratic tendencies, but this is fully justified by the events of the late fifth century. Aristocratic *symposia* were the key form of social gathering for *hetairiai*, informal groupings of upper-class males who engaged jointly in politics. Secrecy and devotion to the *hetairoi* before any other loyalty was paramount.[90] In Hobden's words, 'Hetaireiai focused their loyalties inwards and by default away from citizens outside their social group.'[91] A *symposion* of a *hetairia* was probably the most suitable occasion for expressing anti-democratic views.[92] Thucydides makes very clear that these realities were often involved with *stasis* and oligarchic revolutions (Thuc. 3.82.5–6). And in fact we find them prominently in connection with both the oligarchic revolution of 411 (Thuc. 8.54.4; 65.2; also mentioned as *xynomosiai*) and that of 404 in Athens ([Arist.] *Ath. Pol.* 34.3; Lys. 12.43), and moreover with the scandal of the mutilation of the Herms and of the mockery of the Eleusinian Mysteries in 415. They are often associated with mutual support in court and with manipulation of elections (Thuc. 8.54.4; Ar. *Lys.* 577–8). They were banned at some point in the late fifth century, and the law on *eisangelia* made their members liable to prosecution, and yet we still find them mentioned in the fourth century, and their members are typically associated with drunken violence, *hybris*, contempt for democracy and for their fellow citizens, and represented as willing to commit perjury for one another (Dem. 54.13–17, 20, 35–6 and 21.20, 139). Evidence of the continuity of the elite's opposition to the institutions of the state throughout the classical age is also Theophr. *Char.* 26, *Oligarchias*. Here, the oligarchic man complains about the official institutions of the state (Assembly, lawcourts, system of liturgies) and how they are either full of the unwashed rabble or oppress the rich. This shows that even a century after the oligarchic revolutions of the late fifth century the stereotypical elite snob was set against the structure of state institutions, not above them.

[87] On the origins of the *symposion* see Wecowski 2014. Cf. on the political significance of the symposion and *hetairia* in classical Greece, Connor 1971, esp. 25–30; Murray 1993: 201–20; 1983; Hobden 2013: 117–94.
[88] Cf. Fisher 2000.   [89] Cf. Steiner 2002.
[90] On the *hetairiai* in fifth-century Athens, see e.g. Sartori 1967; Murray 1990; McGlew 1999; Bearzot 2013: 53–62, 145–50.
[91] Hobden 2013: 151.   [92] Ober 1998: 45.

The evidence from classical Athens shows therefore that in a society in which the masses had considerable control over the formal institutions of the state, it was elite culture rather than popular culture that tended to articulate itself in unofficial, 'unauthorized' forms, even to the extent of fostering political subversion. Official culture was suspicious of such cultural forms, and of the associated social contexts, which were confined to a private and even occasionally to a clandestine dimension. Once again, comparison with the reality of oligarchic *poleis* is instructive: while in Athens *symposia* and *hetairiai* were strictly private realities, 'unauthorized' and autonomous from the formal political institutions, because they did not reflect the culture of those that controlled these institutions (the masses), in Crete and Sparta forms of banquet/*symposion* were embedded in the political institutions. Participation in the Spartan *syssitia*/*phiditia* (Arist. *Pol.* 1271a26–37, 1272a12–21; Xen. *Lac.* 5; Plut. *Lyc.* 12; Ath. 4.138b–43a) and in the Cretan *andreia* (Ephoros in *FGrH* 70 F 149; Arist. *Pol.* 1271a26–37, 1272a12–21; Ath. 4.143a–f) were an essential condition of citizenship, and in Crete and Cyrene the *hetairiai* were formal social sub-divisions of the *polis*. As Nafissi has argued, the Spartan *syssitia* are likely to have originated from informal sympotic reunions, which later became institutionalized.[93] In oligarchic states controlled by the elite, progressive institutionalization formalized social and cultural forms that were typical of the elite. In democratic Athens these forms remained unofficial and 'unauthorized', while it was the popular culture of the masses that was progressively institutionalized.

Conclusion

Athens is atypical among most premodern societies for the extent to which the formal institutions of the state involved a large number of its citizens, overwhelmingly non-elite citizens, and for the level of concrete participation that was required of them. In this chapter I have argued that this has significant consequences when we try to identify and study Athenian popular culture, which can make the use of comparative material, as well as of theoretical frameworks developed with other societies in mind, problematic when applied to the Athenian evidence. In particular, most discussions of popular culture tend to assume that the elite, however

---

[93] Nafissi 2009: 128–9, 132–3.

defined, has control of the formal institutions of the state, and therefore whatever form of culture these institutions may express cannot be genuinely popular, although it can be addressed to the people, or can make creative use of popular cultural forms. Another assumption usually follows: popular culture must be to some extent subversive, whether it is consciously and politically so, performing some sort of reversal of the social and political order, or is simply 'unauthorized' and unofficial.[94]

The Athenian case forces us to revise some of these assumptions about the relations between institutions, popular culture and elite culture. Institutions evolve and change, mostly in accordance with their own structure, in a path-dependent fashion.[95] Which concerns, which culture they represent and foster, is determined partially by the individuals that concretely control them at a given moment, but perhaps to a greater extent by the ideas that have originally shaped them (which could in earlier contexts have had an independent existence) and by their successive evolution, by the ideology and by the discursive practices that are embedded in their workings.[96] Athenian institutions, under close analysis, are revealed to be democratic not only because they provide the people with representation and give the masses an unparalleled level of institutional control, but also because they appear to have evolved to perform exactly this function, and reflect to a large extent the substantive concerns of non-elite citizens. The comparisons with Sparta and Crete show that while the institutions of oligarchies have formalized aristocratic cultural and social forms, the institutions of Athenian democracy have to a large extent formalized non-elite social and cultural forms, often leaving elite culture outside of the official space of the *polis* (and sometimes integrating it into the popular culture of the masses). In such a context, one cannot expect to find a popular culture that is as subversive, and popular cultural forms that are institutionally 'unauthorized', as in most premodern societies. In Athens popular culture seems to live rather inside the formal institutions of the state, fostered and validated by them, and the institutions are a comfortable place of cultural and social

---

[94] An influential statement of this view is James C. Scott's (1990) distinction between 'public transcripts', the public interactions between dominators and oppressed, and 'hidden transcripts', the undercurrent of critique of power that the elite cannot see. Scott generalizes this model to all societies, in which subordinate groups, he argues, resist similarly through 'hidden transcripts'.

[95] The foundational essay of new institutionalism is March and Olsen 1984. See March and Olsen 2006 for a survey of the field, and a synthesis of relevant research.

[96] See Schmidt 2008; 2010, 2011 for an account of 'discursive institutionalism' and Smith 2008 and Lieberman 2002 for 'ideational historical institutionalism'.

expression for the ordinary Athenian craftsmen and farmers. It is elite culture, rejected to a considerable extent by the institutional framework of the *polis*, that has to find different forms and venues of expression, which are unofficial and 'unauthorized', and that can therefore become subversive.[97]

[97] Of course, it is not only elite culture that is unauthorized in Athens, and the culture of other sections of the population, such as slaves and to a lesser extent metics, shared this status with that of the elite. Nevertheless the institutions of the *polis* do not reflect the concerns of the elite among the citizens, but rather those of the vast majority of Athenians. Therefore the elite had to find unofficial, and often subversive, forms of expression.

3 | Humouring the Masses: The Theatre Audience and the Highs and Lows of Aristophanic Comedy

JAMES ROBSON

If, as it has been suggested, popular culture is hard to define, 'but we know it when we see it',[1] then it is perhaps legitimate to claim that Old Comedy just instinctively feels 'popular'. Many of the vital ingredients are there: this is a genre that was performed for mass audiences, which is bursting with 'low' elements such as obscenity, slapstick and references to humdrum everyday life, and which was even categorized as 'low' by the likes of Plato and Aristotle (lower than tragedy and epic, that is, and appealing to less sophisticated spectators).[2] Yet despite this popular feel, there are nevertheless ways in which Old Comedy fits the categorization of 'popular culture' rather poorly. Old Comedy is hardly a product of the masses for the masses, after all: rather, its authors, as educated Athenian citizens, are by definition part of Athens' social elite, and its more recherché jokes and allusions would presumably have made most sense to educated Athenians, too.

Importantly, then, Aristophanic comedy is self-consciously designed to appeal to Athens' social and intellectual elite as well as the masses and clearly draws inspiration from both 'high' and 'low' genres and much in between. Indeed, the ways in which Aristophanes explores and exploits the tensions between high and low in his plays is striking. On a lexical level, we not only find sustained passages of either heightened or low expression, but also lexical 'clashes' where high- and low-register vocabulary are conspicuously juxtaposed in a single line or phrase.[3] In a similar vein, as a song-writer Aristophanes produces not just high-flown lyrics on the one hand and plain-speaking, comic verse on the other, but also an original blend of high and low – what Silk has called

---

[1] Parker 2011: 147, borrowing Justice Potter Stewart's much-quoted comments handed down in his 1964 Supreme Court judgement on whether the film *Les amants* qualified as 'hard-core pornography' (Jacobellis *v.* Ohio, 378 U.S. 184): 'I shall not today attempt further to define the kinds of material I understand to be embraced within that shorthand description; and perhaps I could never succeed in intelligibly doing so. But I know it when I see it, and the motion picture involved in this case is not that.' The translations from Aristophanes in this chapter are taken from (or based on) Sommerstein 1981, 1982, 1985, 1990, 1998a and 2001.

[2] Arist. *Po.* 1448b24–7; Pl. *Leg.* 658a–e (on which, see n. 66 below).   [3] Robson 2006: 176–82.

'low lyric *plus*'.[4] Nor is Aristophanes uninterested in talking about the particular place that his plays occupy on the high–low spectrum, regularly distancing his supposedly clever and original comedy from the work of his 'vulgar' rivals.[5] Rosen suggests that Aristophanes, by positioning his plays towards the 'high' end of the spectrum, 'had his own cultural élites in the audience with whom he wanted to align himself'; but Rosen is careful to emphasize, too, that these *claims* to seek a cultural elite may be no more than that: 'a *pretense* or *conceit* that his comedy was not "popular" in the sense of "popularizing"'.[6] Regardless of how we are to understand the numerous self-aggrandizing comments that Aristophanes makes about his own plays, however, the point remains that notions of high and low, and of what makes comedy superior or inferior in the eyes of the social and intellectual elite, are explicitly brought to the fore.[7]

This chapter seeks to explore these notions of elite/non-elite and high/low as far as they apply to one particular aspect of the plays: namely, Aristophanes' audience. The aim in particular is to plot how Aristophanes' comedies configure, relate to and engage with different social groups in the city – the rich and the poor, citizens and non-citizens, Athenians and non-Athenians, old and young – and to explore some of the means by which tensions and divisions are created in the audience. Notions of elite and non-elite and high and low surface in a variety of ways in the formation of sub-groups, with wealth, status, age and level of intellectual sophistication all playing key roles. As we shall see, the picture that emerges is one in which a whole variety of sub-groups in the audience are acknowledged and catered for, and where subaltern spectators are, for the most part, skilfully kept on side, but where the social, political and intellectual elite of Athens routinely enjoy the most attention.

At this point, it is worth briefly outlining the social make-up of Aristophanes' Athens and the way in which the terms 'elite' and 'non-elite'/'subaltern' are used in this chapter. Despite the various lines along

---

[4] Lyric which is 'not a mere mixture', but which combines 'the vigour ... of the low ... with the formal grace and discipline of the high', resulting in 'an enlarged tonal and expressive range all round' (Silk 2000: 129).
[5] Ar. *Nu.* 524.
[6] R. M. Rosen, 'Aesthetics, taste and the question of "popular" comedy in classical Athens', unpublished paper, delivered at the *Popular Comedy* conference, University of Glasgow, 28 August 2013.
[7] This interpenetration of high and low elements has inevitably led to Bakhtinian/carnivalesque readings of Aristophanes' plays: see e.g. Platter 2007 and the special edition of *Arethusa* 26 (1993) on 'Bakhtin and Ancient Studies' (ed. C. Platter and P. A. Miller).

which classical Athenians could potentially be divided (e.g. property class, occupation, tribe, place of residence), the marked tendency of contemporary authors, as Pritchard has noted, was to divide the population up into 'rich' citizens on the one hand, *hoi plousioi* or *kaloikagathoi*, and 'poor' on the other, *hoi penetes*.[8] Pritchard estimates that the social elite, characterized inter alia by their lives of leisure and relative luxury, their exclusive pastimes and, importantly, their education, comprised no more than 5 per cent of the citizen body.[9] But while the political movers and shakers in Athens were drawn disproportionately from the ranks of *hoi plousioi*, the 95 per cent of non-rich citizen men, many of whom would have earnt their living as traders and artisans or as farmers in Attica's countryside, nevertheless had a say in the running of the *polis* through the Assembly.[10] Non-elite citizens would have regularly assumed positions of power in the city, too, most notably by serving on Athens' Council: the sheer numbers required here (500 per year) and the rules surrounding membership (men had to be over thirty and could not serve more than twice) presumably guaranteed that large numbers of the social non-elite regularly held political office.[11] As for non-citizens, they might not have enjoyed the same legal and political rights as citizens, but certain metics (resident immigrants) nevertheless moved in the most elevated of circles (as the fourth-century examples of Lysias and Aristotle demonstrate; Athens' high-profile courtesans typically belonged to the metic class, too). That said, the vast bulk of metics can no doubt be comfortably categorized as non-elite: these were typically working men and their families based in or around the city of Athens itself. A further significant subaltern group in Athens were its slaves: these ranged from workers in Laurion's silver mines to sex workers, domestic slaves, *paidagogoi* and the occasional relatively independent man of means.

While the terms 'elite' and 'non-elite' map onto an important distinction made by classical Athenians themselves between 'rich' and 'poor', even this brief overview of the sociology of classical Athens begins to reveal something of the fuzziness of these categories and the diversity in individual

---

[8] Pritchard 2012: 20.
[9] Pritchard 2012: 20–1. Since less wealthy citizens might also occasionally move in elite circles (Socrates is a prime example here), it is perhaps wise to use the term 'social elite' with a certain amount of flexibility for fear of making too rigid a distinction based on wealth alone.
[10] Xenophon (*Mem.* 3.7.6) lists the professions practised by attendees of the citizen assembly as: 'fullers ... cobblers ... builders ... smiths ... farmers ... merchants ... traffickers in the market-place'. A useful catalogue of occupations in Athens (500–250 BCE) is offered by Harris 2002: 88–97.
[11] Citizens could also not serve on the Council for two years in a row: see Canevaro, this volume, p. 48.

circumstances that this binary distinction serves to disguise (see pp. 17–18). Some individuals cause us particular pause for thought, such as Socrates, someone who lacked personal wealth but who regularly rubbed shoulders with Athens' social elite. What is more, some rich Athenians were richer than others, and 'poor' Athenians might differ radically in terms of the wealth and political influence to which they could lay claim. A further dynamic to bear in mind is the relative permeability of social categories, especially during the turbulent years of the Peloponnesian War, where we find instances of citizen status being granted to non-Athenians (e.g. the Plataeans in 427 BCE) and even slaves (following the battle of Arginusae in 406 BCE), as well as citizens being disenfranchised: for example, through debt (*Lys.* 581) or involvement in the oligarchic coup of 411 BCE.[12]

This chapter is structured as follows. In the first section, I look at the size and make-up of the original audiences of Aristophanes' plays. Drawing on recent scholarship in this area, I aim to build up a picture of both who attended the theatre and the effects that social status might have had on the kind of theatrical experience that different categories of spectators enjoyed. In the second section, I go on to examine the ways in which the plays engage with key sub-groups (e.g. the city's officials, working Athenians, metics), exploring the ways in which Aristophanes uses factors such as wealth, education, social status and political influence in Athens temporarily to create in- and out-groups. In the third section, I look at Aristophanes' construct of high- and low-brow comedy, which exposes a further example of a division created in the Aristophanic audience – one made this time on the basis of intellectual sophistication. Fascinating here, as we shall see, is the way in which Aristophanes' conception of 'bad' comedy maps on to modern prejudices concerning 'popular' culture as something low-brow and crowd-pleasing: something fit for the masses, but not for the intellectual elite.

The Audience of Comedy

Who watched Old Comic plays at their first staging in Athens? The size and make-up of the audience is currently a subject of lively interest, prompted by a recent strand of scholarship which has overturned traditional views about the size of the fifth-century and early fourth-century

---

[12] The changes wrought to Athens' citizen body are famously discussed in the *parabasis* of *Frogs* (*Ra.* 674–737).

BCE auditorium. Significant here has been the recognition by scholars of the importance of the excavations carried out by Dörpfeld on the southern slope of the Acropolis in the nineteenth century.[13] These reveal the presence in the fifth century BCE of a road, housing and wells built into the rocky surface of the slope, which would have severely limited the space that any contemporary auditorium could have occupied.[14] Whereas the stone Lycurgan theatre of the later fourth century BCE expanded up the slope to accommodate around 14–17,000 spectators, the wooden seats of the fifth-century theatre may have been able to hold only one-third of this number. Estimates vary as to the theatre capacity in this earlier period: Dawson, for instance, suggests that the auditorium might have held just 3,700 spectators; Korres plumps for about 5,500; while Goette's estimate is slightly higher, his suggestion being that the classical theatre might have held 'just a little more than one-third of the *c.* 17,000 seats of the later rounded *theatron*'.[15]

A further prompt for this interest in the audiences of Athenian drama is David Roselli's provocative book, *Theater of the People*.[16] Roselli undertakes a wholesale examination of the sociology of Athenian theatre audiences, a major concern of his being to map the contours of the spectators in terms of their class and social status (as well as gender) and how this changed over time. Significantly for the question of the size of the audience at the time when Aristophanes' plays were first performed, he also revisits the scattered references to 'the view from the poplar' or 'view beside the poplar' found in ancient lexicographers.[17] Roselli's seductive thesis is that this phrase denotes a viewing space on the Acropolis slope, beyond the road and above the

---

[13] Published as Dörpfeld and Reisch 1896: see esp. 25–36. Csapo provides a summary of the process by which this re-evaluation has taken place in Csapo and Goette 2007: 98–9.

[14] The evidence is neatly laid out by Goette in Csapo and Goette 2007: 116–21.

[15] Dawson 1997: 7; Korres 2002: 540; Csapo and Goette 2007: 120. (In the same dual-authored article, Csapo hedges his bets with a figure of 4,000–7,000: Csapo and Goette 2007: 97.)

[16] Roselli 2011.

[17] Roselli 2011: 72–5. Photius α 505: '"View from the poplar" or "the view beside the poplar": At Athens there was a poplar tree, near which they assembled the bleachers [i.e. wooden seats of the auditorium] before there was a theater. So Cratinus [fr. 372].' Hesychius π 513: '"View beside the poplar": Eratosthenes [fr. 3 Strecker] says that the view near some poplar ... close to the bleachers. It was up to this plant they extended and constructed the bleachers, which are wooden uprights with planks attached like steps, in which they sat before the theater was built' (both passages, trans. Rusten 2011: 400). Eustathios ε 64: 'Behind the theatre at Athens there was indeed, they say, a poplar tree from which people watched who did not have a seat. Whence comes the expression "the view from the poplar". And the view beside the poplar is the view from the back. The view beside the poplar was also the cheapest, they say.' These passages are also discussed by Scullion (1994: 56–7), who reaches a similar conclusion to Roselli about their significance.

wooden seats of the auditorium, from which fifth- and early fourth-century spectators could have watched the spectacle either at low cost or for free.[18] He does not commit himself to a precise number of Athenians who might have experienced the plays in this way, but his best guess of 2,000, when added to the 3,700–6,000 invited and paying spectators in the auditorium itself, suggests an audience of up to 8,000 – not so far off the round figure of 10,000 audience members found at *Ra.* 676–7. The number of 'unofficial' spectators may possibly have been higher. If the figure of '13,000' mentioned at *Wealth* 1082 is (i) in fact a reference to the theatre audience and (ii) represents an accurate estimate of its size, then the 'view from the poplar' spectators may even have outnumbered those in the auditorium.[19]

The 'view from the poplar' is particularly important for Roselli's discussion of class and status since it represents a free or inexpensive vantage point. It is a place where those unable or unwilling to pay the 2 obol entrance fee for the theatre might choose to gather – in addition to those simply unable to obtain a seat once the places in the auditorium were filled.[20] For Roselli, then, this location above the theatre becomes home to what he calls a 'motley group' and is, significantly, the place where non-elite viewers were most likely to be found. This in turn allows him to talk in terms of audience stratification: Roselli envisages the 'view from the poplar' crowd as forming a third stratum in addition to two further strata present in the auditorium itself: on the one hand, those occupying the privileged seating closest to the acting space; on the other, the fee-paying spectators in the higher rows of the auditorium.[21]

While *prohedria* (privileged seating) might have been granted to a public benefactor or distinguished foreign visitor as a public honour,[22] in the late

---

[18] Roselli 2011: 72–5. 'Free' seems more likely than 'low cost', but owing to Eusthathios' description of this area as the 'cheapest' (see previous note), some kind of fee cannot be ruled out.

[19] At *Pl.* 1081–2 an Old Woman is said to have been 'shagged to pieces by 13,000 ... years (*etōn*)', instead of the expected 'men': for discussion, see Sommerstein 2001: ad loc. Cf. the hyperbolic figure of 'countless myriads/10,000s' of audience members given at *V.* 1010. In his unpublished paper, 'How "popular" was Athenian comedy?', delivered at the *Popular Comedy* conference, University of Glasgow 28 August 2013, Sommerstein chooses the figure of 12,000 audience members (presumably as an extreme upper limit) to explore the consequences of Roselli's thesis.

[20] There has been considerable debate as to whether there were theoric payments in the fifth century. The evidence is laid out in Wilson 2011: 38–43, who also problematizes the question of when entrance charges began (41).

[21] Lech criticizes some of Roselli's ideas about the different characteristics of these three strata and finds his assertions about their social make-up 'a bit incoherent' (Lech 2011).

[22] The evidence collected by Roselli (2011: 78–9) shows that this was an established practice by the mid fourth century, at least. On the composition of *prohedria* spectators, see Roselli 2011: 78–81.

fifth and early fourth centuries the vast majority of their occupants each year were city officials. These included the Priest of Dionysus Eleuthereus;[23] the ten elected generals;[24] Athens' archons; the judges whose votes would determine the outcome of the dramatic contest[25] – and also the 500 members of the Athens' Council, who had a designated section of their own (the *bouleutikon*).[26] As various scholars have noted, the kinds of civic roles that ensured these spectators their free and close-up view of the action, while nominally open to all citizens, were in all probability undertaken by those who were relatively wealthy more often than the poor.[27] But this is not the same as saying that the front rows were the exclusive home of *hoi plousioi*. Not only is 'relatively wealthy' a far broader category than 'rich', but front-row privileges were also generally short-lived and so incapable of being hogged by any group: while the Priest of Dionysus or a re-elected general might find himself in the same seat two years in a row, officials chosen by lot each year, such the members of the Council, the archons – and the ten judges of the dramatic competition, for that matter – generally did not. In short, the occupants of the front rows would have formed another kind of 'motley group' – a substantial body of (almost exclusively) citizen men drawn from across Athenian society whose make-up changed radically each year and whose members were, almost by definition given their civic roles, relatively well informed about the city's problems, politics and personalities.[28]

What of the middle section of the theatre audience – those spectators occupying the benches behind the privileged seats? The fact that seats in this area cost money, plus the fact that attendance at the theatre demanded leisure time, might once again imply that wealthier Athenians were more

---

[23] See *Ra.* 297 and the scholiast on this passage.

[24] On the evidence of Ar. *Eq.* 573–7 and 702–4, it would appear that, while *prohedria* were originally awarded to generals only in exceptional circumstances, this privilege was fast becoming an expectation towards the end of the fifth century.

[25] Commenting on *Ach.* 1224, Olson (2002: ad loc.) suggests that the judges probably sat in the front row along with the official responsible for the festival (the *archon basileus* in the case of the Lenaia; the eponymous archon in the case of the City Dionysia).

[26] *Av.* 794 (cf. *Pax* 882–908) and Pollux 4.122. The scholiast on *Pax* 878 locates the Council's seating as somewhere in the middle of the auditorium.

[27] Since these were time-consuming and poorly remunerated. See Canevaro, this volume, p. 48, for discussion of the make-up of the Council.

[28] Or, as Roselli (2011: 81) puts it: 'The front seating in the *theatron* was not exactly a space for "who's who" in Athens, but it did present a legible picture of the city's social and political hierarchy.' As an advocate of female attendance in the auditorium, Roselli also comments (81) that the *prohedria* would have been a 'prominent "men only" area', while also noting the possibility that the possible presence there during the classical era of the Priestess of Athena Polias (180).

likely to be found here than the poor. Indeed, as Sommerstein points out in 'How "popular" was Athenian comedy?', the 2 obol fee might prove expensive if this was indeed the fee per day, especially for a man taking other family members along.[29] But while the better-off in Athens may have been disproportionately represented in the paying seats, many scholars (Sommerstein and Roselli included) support the notion of a healthy subaltern presence, too.[30] Indeed, as we shall see, Aristophanes' plays themselves regularly make reference to these non-elite groups.

One important aspect of Roselli's work has been to draw attention to the large numbers of non-citizens among the spectators. In particular he singles out wealthier and 'monetized' metics, men who could plausibly afford to pay for seats and who often lived 'near the commercial centre in urban demes', their proximity to the Theatre of Dionysus further easing their attendance.[31] Slaves, too, were to be found in the theatre: some seated in the paying seats of the auditorium as *paidagogoi* supervising children or as attendants for the wealthy,[32] others working as stage-hands or charged with throwing nuts and dried fruit into the crowd.[33] At the City Dionysia in particular, there were also significant numbers of foreign visitors.[34] The question of whether women attended in any great numbers remains highly controversial:[35] Roselli argues for a limited female presence, especially in regard to working women who were accustomed to rubbing shoulders with men in public, but he avoids making any guesses as to numbers.[36]

---

[29] Sommerstein 1998b: 47.

[30] For discussion, see Sommerstein, unpublished paper. On mentions of, and attitudes towards, Athens' poor and working classes in comedy, see esp. Roselli 2011: 113–15. Sommerstein (1998b: 52–5) controversially argues for an increased admission charge to the theatre from around 440 BCE, serving to skew upwards the average wealth of theatre-goers.

[31] Roselli 2011: 121, following Sommerstein 1998b: 44.

[32] Fourth-century sources attest to the presence of *paidagogoi* (Thphr. *Char.* 9.5–6; Pl. *Grg.* 502d; but see Carter 2011: 52 for comment); other slave attendants are mentioned at Thphr. *Char.* 2.11. On slave spectators, see Roselli 2011: 148–54.

[33] *V.* 58–9; *Pl.* 797–9 (cf. *Pax* 962–5). Other wealthier, more independent slaves may even have attended in their own right: see Roselli 2011: 149. During the repartee with the audience at *V.* 78–9, one of the imaginary audience members who hazards a guess as to Philocleon's illness bears the slave name Sosias.

[34] Not only did allied states send delegates to the City Dionysia with tribute, possibly accompanied by phallus-bearers, but the City Dionysia, as a major international festival, plausibly attracted the kind of foreign visitors whom the shameless man at Thphr. *Char.* 9.5 takes with him to the theatre. Foreigners are also to be found in the audience at Ael. *VH* 2.13. At Ar. *Pax* 43–5, 'some Ionian' supposedly speaks from the front rows (although Rosen 1984 argues that this ethnicity may primarily have been selected by Aristophanes for its association with iambic abuse). See further Roselli 2011: 119–25.

[35] Roselli 2011: 158–94; see also Carter 2011: 50–3 for recent discussion and bibliography.

[36] Sommerstein 1997: 65 makes the point that 'whether or not their audience actually was male or even nearly so, dramatists seem to regard it as such ... dramatists, tragic and comic alike, wrote

Roselli has been criticized for a lack of clarity surrounding the ways in which he envisages the three strata of theatre audience to be characterized. As Lech points out in his review of *Theater of the People*, Roselli at times seems to be suggesting that the three tiers can be broadly seen as 'elite – working class – poor', while simultaneously arguing for better recognition of the presence in the middle tier of groups such as monetized metics, wealthy foreigners, slave attendants and elite women.[37] In Roselli's defence, characterizing the differences between the different strata in economic terms is far from straightforward; indeed, perhaps the only safe conclusion is that *on average* the 'view from the poplar' viewers were likely to be somewhat poorer than those in the auditorium. Sommerstein's vision of audience composition avoids such questions by looking beyond the different strata: he argues for a socially mixed spectatorship which nevertheless contained a 'skewed sample' of Athenians 'in which the better-off and better-educated were disproportionately represented'.[38] The view that both these and other scholars share, however, is one of a diverse crowd of spectators – a crowd which it fell to Aristophanes and the other poets of Old Comedy each year to entertain.

Audience Interaction and the Sociology of Aristophanic Comedy

So far we have been considering the audience of Aristophanic comedy: the bums on the seats of the auditorium and the spectators perched on the slopes of the Acropolis. But to what extent was the social make-up of this audience reflected in the plays themselves? A brief glance at the *dramatis personae* reveals a broad range of personnel: citizens ranging from the elite to the poor, foreigners (both Greek and non-Greek), women and slaves are all there. Male metics are perhaps less easy to locate, but since many of these would have worked in similar professions to Athenian citizens, it is perhaps unnecessary to see this as a missing group. Metic women – or at least a particular sub-section of metic women – are certainly in evidence, however. Since prostitute-entertainers were characteristically metic, many of the nude, mute figures in Aristophanes' plays, such as the dancing girls in *Acharnians* and Theoria (Showtime) in *Peace*, are probably to be thought of as belonging to this social group.[39]

---

as male Athenian citizens for male Athenian citizens'. The tension between actual and notional audience is explored by Henderson 1991: 134 and Carter 2011: 49.

[37] Lech 2011.   [38] Sommerstein (unpublished paper).

[39] For discussion of these figures, see Zweig 1992 and Robson 2015.

The people of Aristophanes' plays may span the breadth of Athenian society and beyond, but the social groups to which his protagonists belong are relatively limited. In the extant plays, when a single character carries the action, this is either a woman (*Lysistrata* and *Assemblywomen*) or, more often, an older citizen country-dweller: Dicaeopolis in *Acharnians*; Trygaeus in *Peace*; Strepsiades in *Clouds*. In other plays, we find double acts: either two citizen men (Bdelycleon and Philocleon in *Wasps*; Euripides and his in-law in *Thesmophoriazusae*; Paphlagon/Cleon and Sausage-Seller in *Knights*; cf. *Clouds* where Strepsiades' son, Pheidippides, also plays a significant supporting role) or a master and his slave (Chremylus and Carion in *Wealth*). In *Frogs*, the master/slave pairing of the god Dionysus and Xanthias at the beginning of the play gives way to the threesome of Dionysus, Euripides and Aeschylus in the second half, whereas in *Birds*, Euelpides fades from the double act of ageing Athenian citizens to leave Peisetaerus as ring-master in the second half of the play. In broad terms, then, we might say that when there is a single character with a 'Great Idea' for change, the audience is invited to view events from the point of view of someone on the fringes of the citizen world (a citizen wife or a more rather than less marginalized man): this is hardly the view from the *prohedria*, but nor is it the perspective of the most downtrodden in Athenian society either. Where double acts feature, the situation is more complex: characteristically there is a difference in age, social status and/or social standing between the two figures,[40] with perspectives ranging from that of a god (Dionysus), to citizen men of influence in Athens (tragic poets and politicians), relatively powerless older citizens (Philocleon and the in-law) and a long-suffering slave (Xanthias).[41] Of course, some of these characters are represented more sympathetically than others by Aristophanes: Cleon notoriously gets the worst press of all, whereas older men and slaves, for example, tend to be more sympathetically portrayed.[42]

The mention of figures such as Cleon and Euripides brings us onto the broader subject of *komoidoumenoi*. Leaving the thorny issue of Aristophanic politics and the 'seriousness' of personal attacks to one side, however, I want here simply to consider the real-life Athenians named in the plays in terms of their potential location in the theatre audience. In his

---

[40] *Birds* is an exception here.
[41] Interestingly, the world of the double act is one from which metics (and women) are excluded in these surviving plays.
[42] Various studies have highlighted patterns in the portrayal of various social groups: young men tend to be portrayed negatively as a group (Sommerstein 1996), whereas the portrayal of Spartans is largely positive (Harvey 1994). On the figure of the Aristophanic slave, see Walin 2009.

1996 article, 'How to avoid being a *komoidoumenos*',[43] Sommerstein concludes that the largest single category of *komoidoumenoi* comprises people who are active in the institutions of the *polis*. In addition to 'politicians' like Cleon, he lists office-holders, military men and priests: in short, figures who might typically be found in the theatre's front rows. The next largest category is that of men active in the theatre, such as rival comic poets, tragedians, actors, dancers and *choregoi*: people whose interest in theatre would, one supposes, all but guarantee their presence at the dramatic festivals and who would plausibly be more rather than less prepared to pay for seats in the auditorium. Other significant categories include men active in given trades or professions and Athens' conspicuous consumers: in other words, monetized, high-profile individuals, who might reasonably be expected to afford the entrance fee with ease. There is no guarantee that any given individual would be present to hear himself (or herself) abused, of course, and there are also further categories of *komoidoumenoi* whose likely presence at, let alone position in, the theatre is less easy to predict (those held in high regard either for their 'good looks' or 'witty conversation', for example).[44] But it seems reasonable to suppose that the targets of comic abuse would often be present in the auditorium: either seated in the *prohedria* by dint of their civic role, or as paying customers in the upper rows.

When it came to performance, the bunching together of public officials in the *prohedria* must have been a godsend for actors: this would regularly have allowed them to locate a given individual in the auditorium and thus help them to make the most of a choice piece of comic mockery. A neat example of this comes in *Peace*, where an extended sequence is built around Trygaeus' handling of the prostitute figure Theoria (Showtime) to the city's Prytaneis (who would have sat in the *bouleutikon*, along with the other members of the Council).[45] Trygaeus first asks for someone in the audience to 'take care' of Theoria – probably played by a man in body padding – and he and his slave pick out a supposedly enthusiastic spectator, one Ariphrades, who is supposedly 'begging' for her to be taken to him (*Pax* 881-4).[46] The handover of Theoria is delayed, however, while

---

[43] Sommerstein 1996.
[44] Sommerstein 1996: 331. Indeed, while elite Athenians were no doubt more likely to fall victim to comic abuse than the poor, as Sommerstein comments (1996: 331), 'virtually anyone in the public eye could expect to become a target of comic satire'.
[45] Further references to the Prytaneis in Aristophanes include: *Ach.* 23 and 40, *Eq.* 167 and 300 and *Th.* 854, 929–46 (where a Prytanis features as a mute character).
[46] Ariphrades is further mocked by the slave, who claims that 'he'll fall upon her and lap up her broth' (*Pax* 885); cf. *Eq.* 1280-7 and *V.* 1280-3. As Olson comments (1998: ad loc.), 'The implication of this passage is that [Ariphrades] was a member of the Boule in 422/1.'

Trygaeus lingers in front of the Councillors, teasing them with descriptions of Theoria's sexual availability (*Pax* 887–90).

TRYGAEUS: Councillors, Prytaneis, behold Showtime. Look what a bundle of blessings I'm bringing to hand over to you – you can raise up her legs in the air straight away, and then have a feast of a time! ...

When Theoria is finally handed over, this padded figure presumably lands in an individual's lap (*Pax* 905–6):[47]

TRYGAEUS: Now, Prytaneis, take possession of Showtime! [*He gives Showtime to the chairman of the Prytaneis.*] Look how eagerly the chairman took her from me!

The interplay between actors and the front rows was not confined to the mockery, abuse and embarrassment of individuals. Other forms of audience interaction were also disproportionately directed at these 'privileged' spectators: references to public officials in the audience such as the Priest of Dionysus (*Ra.* 297), for example, or the various addresses to the judges (e.g. *Av.* 445 and 1102–17; *Nu.* 1115–30; *Ec.* 1154–62). Repartee, too, such as in the prologue of *Wasps* (*V.* 73–82), where audience members are invited to guess the nature of Philocleon's illness, would also presumably have engaged those sitting in the front rows of the theatre rather than the back.[48] And in the prologue of *Peace*, we also find the males in the audience segmented first in terms of age and then in terms of civic position, with two sections of the *prohedria* – the Council and the front-row magistrates and priests, perhaps – singled out for special mention (*Pax* 50–3).[49]

SECOND SLAVE: I'm going to explain the plot to the children (*toisi paidiois*) and the striplings (*tois andrioisi*) and the men (*tois andrasin*) and the men of high position (*tois hypertatoisin andrasin*) and yes, even to those proud supermen (*hyperēnoreousin*) there.

---

[47] Thus Slater 1999: 356–7; Olson (1998: ad loc.) suggests that Aristophanes may have had a 'confederate' among the Prytaneis whom he had 'coached in advance' as to how to receive Theoria. Sommerstein chooses to translate *prytanis* here as 'chairman' (following its use with this meaning at Thuc. 6.14.1), but the word could equally denote any member of this body.

[48] In performance, this passage may have involved fielding genuine suggestions and heckles, *pace* Slater (1999: 356), who asserts that these comments were 'all scripted in advance' while at the same time suggesting that 'this comic sequence indicates audience familiarity with a kind of improvisational insult comedy in which performers did react to comments shouted out from the audience'.

[49] Thus Sommerstein (1985: ad loc.). If Olson is right (1998: ad loc.) that *andrioisi* denotes 'half-men, creatures resembling men but inferior to them', there is always the possibility that a particular group is being targeted here, too. See also Roselli 2011: 154–5 on this passage.

In short, those seated in the *prohedria* were routinely mentioned, interacted with and drawn into the play that much more than the other spectators of the play.

The front rows may have received more than their fair share of attention from the actors, but there are still plenty of instances in Aristophanes of the theatre audience as a whole being drawn into the action. Famously, the presence of spectators is often explicitly acknowledged in the plays, with the entire audience directly addressed, abused, flattered or asked to show their support for the play.[50] Alternatively, Aristophanes picks out subgroups, not only highlighting social differences between his audience members, but potentially generating divergent reactions from these groups in the process. In the notoriously political *parabasis* of *Frogs*, for instance, a contrast is drawn between members of Athens' aristocratic families who were disenfranchised owing to their involvement in the oligarchic coup of 411 BCE and its new citizens – the slaves who fought at Arginusae the previous year (406 BCE) and who were subsequently granted citizen rights (*Ra.* 686–737). Conflicts on stage may likewise have played on social fault lines to create divisions among the spectators depending on their allegiances or political and cultural leanings – the pro-Spartan Dicaeopolis pitched against the anti-Spartan chorus in the early part of *Acharnians*, for instance, or the contest between the older, more traditional Aeschylus and the iconoclastic, 'democratic' Euripides in *Frogs* [51] – with factors such as social status, occupation and wealth often playing key roles in determining which side (if either) a given audience member favoured. Furthermore, those who found themselves aligned with one of the sides in an on-stage debate will often have made their feelings clear: Revermann talks of 'constant feedback on [the] part of the onlookers', with laughter, clapping and heckling being just three ways in which audiences could make their feelings known.[52] Feedback could even be actively solicited from the stage, such as the enthusiastic response, 'a splash with eleven oars', solicited at *Knights* 544–50 – with possibly a nod to Athens' (socially non-elite) rowers.[53] Not

---

[50] Addressed: esp. in prologues and *parabases*, but also at, e.g., *Ach.* 497; *Nu.* 1437; *Pax* 82 1; *Av.* 479–80; *Ec.* 336–40, 1002–4. Abused: e.g. *Nu.* 1089–1100; *Pax* 819–23; *Ra.* 274–6 and 783; *Ec.* 434–40. Flattered: e.g. *V.* 65, 1014; *Ra.* 676–7, 700, 1109–18. Asked to show support: e.g. *Eq.* 37–9; *Pax* 768.

[51] *Ra.* 952; see Roselli 2011: 114 for a useful overview of the elite/non-elite tensions inherent in the characterization of these tragic poets in *Frogs*.

[52] Revermann 2006a: 34. See Slater 1999: 353–4, Revermann 2006a: 33–6 and 161 and Roselli 2011: 45–51 on feedback from the audiences of comedy, which may also have included hissing, walking out of the theatre, clucking and heel-banging.

[53] This is much debated. The reference may be an allusion to Athens' rowers, citizen poor par excellence (Roselli 2011: 29), but may alternatively signify ten fingers and the tongue (i.e.

that members of the audience were always encouraged to make a rowdy response. One section of Athenian society that gains a series of affectionate yet subdued mentions in Aristophanes' plays is its metics. In the *parabasis* of *Acharnians*, for instance, their closeness to the citizenry of Athens is underlined by a metaphor which describes them as the civic bran (508), in contrast to other foreigners who are the husks (507). A similar image of metic integration is to be found in *Lysistrata*. In her wool-working speech where she compares solving the city's problems to handling a skein of wool, Lysistrata recommends 'carding the wool into the work-basket of union and concord, mixing everyone in', including the metics (579–80). She goes on to say that the resulting ball of wool should be woven into a 'warm cloak for the people to wear' (586).

Particularly interesting from the perspective of subaltern sub-groups is an indirect address to the audience from *Peace*. To aid his efforts to recover the goddess Peace from the deep cavern in which she is buried, Trygaeus calls on others to help in a theatrical moment in which the identities of the stage audience (i.e. the chorus) and the actual audience are momentarily merged (*Pax* 296–9).

You farmers and merchants and carpenters and craftsmen and immigrants and foreigners and islanders, come hither, all ye people, as quickly as you can, bringing shovels and crowbars and ropes . . . !

Insofar as this address is directed at the spectators, it specifically takes in large swathes of Athens' (citizen) working classes, while also recognizing the presence of non-Athenians in the audience, both metics and visitors to the city.[54] Instructively, free working-class citizens are categorized into four major groups according to their occupation with the importance of their ability to perform physical labour underscored by the implements they are asked to bring. Non-Athenians, on the other hand, are split into three groups, differentiated by the nature of their attachment to Athens: residents (metics), non-residents (*xenoi*) and allied subjects (islanders). What links the people in this list is that they are all ostensibly opposed to

---

applause and cheers: see Sommerstein 1981: ad loc.). Athens' 'upper-oar' rowers are specifically called the 'saviours of the city' at *Ach.* 161–2.

[54] Adapting Dover's comments on this passage (1972: 138), Sommerstein (1985: ad loc.) remarks that these lines comprise 'a complete list of the categories of adult males one would expect to find in the theatre at the City Dionysia (except for "privileged" groups such as politicians, priests and generals)' ('free adult males' may be more accurate, since slaves are absent from this list). Olson (1998: ad loc.) distinguishes between 'traders' (*emporoi*) who *are* mentioned and 'local retail merchants' (*kapeloi*) who are *not* and for whom, he claims, 'Ar. normally displays little sympathy'. He also notes that here and in other such lists farmers 'who made up the great majority of the free population of Attika' are given 'pride of place' (cf. *Pl.* 903–5; Xen. *Lac.* 8.1).

the war – but it is a list from which Athens' elite and its slaves are notably absent. Indeed, this division between supposed war-lovers and peace-lovers reappears throughout the play, but with subtle shifts in the constituency of the supposed pro- and anti-war factions. At *Peace* 543–50, for example, Hermes and Trygaeus note the various reactions in the audience to the advent of peace: good news for the farmers who can now return to their fields and also the mattock- and the sickle-maker; but bad news for other craftsmen whose businesses profit from war, namely the crest-maker and swordsmith.

One last point I shall address in relation to sub-groups is the role that humour and laughter may have played in creating audible and visible in- and out-groups among the spectators. The principle here is that some audience members would inevitably have been better equipped to understand some jokes than others: humour that relies on knowledge of public figures in the city (from Socrates and Cleon to Ariphrades or the chairman of the Prytaneis), or on familiarity with previous dramatic performances (from paratragedy to jokes at the expense of comic rivals). Factors such as education and civic status are once again relevant here, as is up-to-date knowledge of the city's affairs (potentially less well developed in the case of categories such as country-dwellers, children, foreign visitors and citizens who had been absent from Athens: for example, as soldiers, sailors or envoys). Civic status is also a factor: the pastiche-cum-parody of the proceedings of the Athens' Assembly in *Thesmophoriazusae* and *Assemblywomen*, for example, would presumably be best appreciated by citizen men. Not that divided laughter will always have split the audience in straightforward ways: a spectator who was in the know might fail to find the joke funny or choose to supress their laughter, most notably, perhaps, in the case of a personal attack. And in addition to those in the audience who 'got' the joke and found it amusing, laughter might also be elicited from audience members who pretended to get the joke, or who were simply swept up into laughing.[55]

While humour has the potential to be divisive at times, Aristophanes is also careful to create comic scenes that are comprehensible on some level to the full breadth of his audience members: something akin to what Revermann alternatively calls 'layered inclusion' and 'stratification'.[56] Even a personal attack can be turned into a joke with mass appeal through

---

[55] See Goldhill 2006: 96–9, who explores the effects of a 'fissured audience response' among the tragic audience, i.e. where some spectators laugh at a line, but others do not.
[56] Revermann 2006b: 101 and 103.

the simple device employed in the following extract from *Clouds*, where the basis of a series of jibes is 'explained' to his audience each time in anticipation of the punch line. Here Socrates is telling Strepsiades why the chorus members of *Clouds* who have just appeared 'look just like mortal women' (*Nu.* 341; 346–55):

SOCRATES: Have you ever looked up and seen a cloud that looked like a centaur, or a leopard, or a wolf, or a bull?
STREPSIADES: Yes I have, by Zeus! What of it?
SOCRATES: They can assume any shape they like. So, if they see some hairy, wild looking guy – one of those shaggy fellows like the son of Xenophantus – they make fun of his passions by taking the form of centaurs.
STREPSIADES: So what do they do if they catch sight of an embezzler of public funds like Simon?
SOCRATES: They immediately show him up for what he is by turning into wolves.
STREPSIADES: Right! So that's why, when they saw Cleonymus the shield-thrower yesterday and recognized what a great coward he is, they turned into deer.
SOCRATES: And now, because they have seen Cleisthenes – do you see? Because of this they've turned into women!

In these lines, then, the audience is informed that Hieronymus (the son of Xenophantus) is 'shaggy' (hence the Clouds turning into centaurs); that Simon is an 'embezzler' (hence wolves) and that Cleonymus is a 'shield-thrower' (hence deer). In short, for every character mentioned – with the exception of the stock *komoidoumenos*, Cleisthenes – Aristophanes is careful to tell his audience the basis of each joke before he makes it, thus ensuring that the audience are able to engage in collective laughter.

To sum up, differences in wealth, occupation and social status among his spectators were regularly exploited by Aristophanes to create divisions and tensions – an important dynamic in the creation of lively drama, no doubt. But these divisions were also balanced by addresses, flattery, abuse and humour aimed at the audience as a whole. The sub-groups in society to which individuals belonged clearly affected the theatrical experience that they enjoyed, just as their physical position in the theatre affected the degree of interaction they enjoyed with the performers. But the audience is also drawn together at times – both in the ways already outlined and also in some of the subtler ways that Slater outlines in 'Making the Aristophanic audience', such as the capturing of the audience's collective good will, settling spectators down at the beginning of the play or the shaping of their responses to the play's humour and aesthetics.[57] And it is to Old Comedy's aesthetics to which we now turn in the final part of this chapter.

High-Brow and Low-Brow Comedy

The final area that I shall explore in this chapter is the distinction that Aristophanes makes between his intellectually sophisticated and non-sophisticated spectators. This is a division we find articulated in *Assemblywomen*, for instance, where the chorus leader proposes that the judges of the comic competition largely fall into two types: those who appreciate the 'intellectual bits' of comedy, and those who appreciate 'laughs' (*Ec.* 1154–7):

But I want to give a little piece of advice to the judges: to those who are intellectual (*tois sophois*), to remember the intellectual bits (*tōn sophōn*) and vote for me; to those who enjoy a laugh (*tois gelōsi*), to think of the laughs (*ton gelōn*) they've had and vote for me.

This striking contrast between 'intellectual' spectators on the one hand and 'those who enjoy a laugh' on the other deserves some scrutiny. After all, this opposition might at first glance seem counter-intuitive: spectators who are smarter might arguably be said to be in a better position to appreciate a broader range of jokes and therefore to laugh more, not less, than other audience members. So, what does this division signify?

To understand these comments better, we need to position them in the broader context of the rhetoric we find in Aristophanes about what constitutes 'good' and 'bad' comedy. In the prologues and *parabases* of his plays, as well as in addresses to the judges, we find no shortage of remarks as to what makes Aristophanes' comedies superior to those of his rivals, with similar virtues and shortcomings articulated with remarkable consistency over the course of his career. How we are meant to understand these comments is unclear, however: some of the assertions that are made about Aristophanes' plays are simply untrue (e.g. that he avoids certain types of well-worn, comic routine: see below); and as Wright has recently shown, Aristophanes' claims to cleverness and originality seem to be somewhat

---

[57] Slater (1999: 361) may overstate his case when he suggests that 'the comic viewing experience was meant to evoke a shared and unified response', but he is no doubt right that the audience as a whole is, as a rule, exhorted to look favourably on Aristophanes' play and its fictive world. Certainly the whole audience is not infrequently invited to come together for the purposes of celebration at the end of the plays (e.g. *Ec.* 1140–6).

typical of the genre, too, echoed as they are in the fragments of other Old Comic poets.[58] But regardless of whether such comments are intended as playful, posturing or sincere, the consistent message is that what sets Aristophanes' plays apart is their intelligence, originality and their avoidance of 'vulgarity'. Aristophanes' plays are *dexios*, 'skilful, clever' (*Nu.* 548; *V.* 65), *sophos*, 'clever, ingenious, wise' (*Nu.* 522; *V.* 66), and full of 'new ideas' (*kainas ideas*: *Nu.* 547). The kind of slapstick routines they avoid, we are told, include Heracles being cheated of his dinner (*V.* 60; *Pax* 741) and slaves running away, getting beaten or burnt (*Pax* 742–3; *Lys.* 1217–8). Importantly, too, his plays are not *phortikos*, 'vulgar': rather, they are distinct from 'vulgar comedy' (*komōidias . . . phortikēs*: *V.* 66), they avoid 'vulgarity' (*ho phortos*: *Pl.* 796) and vulgar routines (*phortikon to chorion*: *Lys.* 1218), and are therefore vastly superior to the efforts of his rivals who are characterized as 'vulgar men' (*andrōn phortikōn*: *Nu.* 524). Indeed, as Rosen has argued, in *ho phortos* and its cognate adjective *phortikos*, we have a concept which bears strong similarities to the modern term 'popular', with its negative connotations of low entertainment and appeal to the masses rather than the intellectual elite: '*Phortikon* implied something that appealed to people who didn't know any better, those without education, and so without refinement and taste, slaves to their bodily cravings and passions, and always seeking easy gratification – in other words the vast majority of people, the "populace".'[59]

So, *phortikos* comedy is 'vulgar', unintelligent, unoriginal, low-brow and readily employs stock routines and well-worn jokes.[60] And insofar as it embraces the low and hackneyed, it characteristically makes use of crowd-pleasing gestures, too, such as the distribution of treats to the spectators (something which caters to the body rather than the mind, we might note). In Aristophanes' *Wealth*, Ploutos himself states that crowd-pleasing 'vulgarity' is something the play's *didaskalos* avoids. Instructively, too, he also claims that the scattering of food can be used a bribe to elicit laughter (*Pl.* 796–9).[61]

---

[58] Wright 2012: 25–30 and 70–8.
[59] Rosen (unpublished paper), whose key passages outside Aristophanes are Arist. *Po.* 1461b26–9, *Pol.* 1342a18–21 and Plut. *Solon* 3.1.2.
[60] The opening lines of *Frogs* (*Ra.* 1–32) has it both ways in articulating a number of the 'usual' jokes that Xanthias is instructed by Dionysus to avoid. Interestingly, while these are jokes made in connection with the 'burden' that the slave is carrying for his master, the word *ho phortos*, which also means 'burden', is avoided.
[61] The scattering of nuts by slaves is also mentioned in close proximity to 'laughter stolen from Megara' at *V.* 57–9. At *Pax* 962–7 'barley seed' is thrown into the audience: presumably this consisted of figs and/or nuts but called *krithē* (also a slang word for 'penis') for the sake of the pun.

That way [i.e. by showering Ploutos with nuts and sweetmeats inside the house rather than outside] we can also avoid vulgarity (*ton phorton*); it doesn't befit our producer to throw dried figs and nibbles to his audience (*tois theōmenois*) and then make them feel obliged to laugh on account of that.

In this rhetoric of 'good' and 'bad' comedy, then, the unoriginal and unintellectual sit alongside physical routines, crowd-pleasing gestures, and also *laughter*, at the 'low' end of the spectrum.[62] Laughter is similarly associated with 'low' comedy in the following much-discussed passage from *Clouds*, where the chorus details some of the techniques supposedly used by other comic playwrights to amuse their audiences. The chorus personifies the play as a young girl, saying (*Nu.* 537–44):[63]

Look at how modest her nature is. For a start, she has not come with a bit of stitched, dangling leather, red at the end and thick so as to give the boys (*paidiois*) a laugh (*gelōs*). Nor has she made fun of bald men, nor danced a cordax. Nor is there an old man (one with a speaking part) hitting whoever's around with a stick in an attempt to disguise bad jokes (*ponēra skōmmata*). Nor does she rush on with torches, nor shout 'help, help!' Rather, she has come trusting in herself and her script (*tois epesin*).

In this passage we find a list of physical routines that *Clouds* supposedly eschews, with the use of *phalloi*, in particular, specifically connected both with laughter and with the entertainment of one particular group of less sophisticated spectators: namely, boys. Notable, too, is the contrast between these physical routines on the one hand and words (*tois epesi*) on the other. The fact that Aristophanes uses most of the physical routines he names here either in *Clouds* itself or elsewhere in his comedies has naturally given scholars pause for thought: to what extent is Aristophanes being conventional, provocative or simply tongue-in-cheek here? But whatever the answer may be, the position that Aristophanes claims to adopt about what 'good' and 'bad' comedy comprises is nevertheless clear and consistent enough. And so to summarize, 'good' comedy relies on words; it is characterized by originality and cleverness; and it appeals to the intelligent and more discerning members of the audience: *dexios* and *sophos* spectators.[64] 'Bad' comedy, on the other hand, uses physical objects

---

[62] As Rosen points out (unpublished paper), there is a certain inevitability about laughter's 'low' status: as 'a *universally* human *physiological* response … its associations have always tended to be "populist"'.

[63] The gender of the play matches that of 'comedy' (*hē kōmōidia*) and also the analogy that Aristophanes makes between Electra and his play which – instead of a long-lost Orestes – is hoping to find intelligent spectators (*Nu.* 534–5).

[64] *Nu.* 521, 526, 527, 535; cf. *Eq.* 228 and 233; *Ra.* 1109–18. At times, the whole audience is characterized as intelligent, e.g. *Nu.* 521, *Ra.* 1109–18. Elsewhere, intelligent spectators are

and physical routines and is designed to make the unsophisticated members of his audience (such as boys) laugh.[65] Or to phrase it another way: 'good' comedy is high-brow, appeals to intellectual spectators and is perceived with the ears; 'bad' comedy is low-brow, crowd-pleasing and is perceived with the eyes.[66]

An interesting question to ask in relation to this rhetorical division is what sections of society Aristophanes' intellectual spectators might be thought to come from. Importantly, there is a sense in which this category floats free of social class: after all, anyone in the audience was entitled to think of themselves as 'intellectual' and to consider their tastes superior to those of supposedly unsophisticated spectators (see Canevaro, this volume, on the cultural pretensions of ordinary Athenians). An alternative tack is broadly to align the 'cultural elite' being appealed to by Aristophanes with the city's social elite, *hoi plousioi*, since this section of society was the best educated – or, to turn things around, it certainly seems plausible that wealthy Athenians, by dint of their superior education, would be inclined to think of themselves as discerning. But another specific group suggests itself for categorization as *dexios* and *sophos*, too. In 'The competence of theatre audiences in fifth- and fourth-century Athens', Revermann builds a compelling case for what he calls the greater 'theatrical competence' of spectators who have participated first-hand in dramatic (and dithyrambic) performances as chorus members. Through 'expertise by exposure', he argues, these *choreutai* learnt about the dynamics of theatre performance, interaction

---

spoken of more as a sub-section, e.g. *Eq.* 228, *Nu.* 525–6, *Pax* 43–5. When it comes to questions of familiarity and innovation the (metatheatrical) comments on audiences at *Ec.* 583–7 make for interesting reading: Praxagora expresses the fear that audiences will cling on to the old and not accept the new.

[65] An exception to this rule is to be found at *Pax* 736–50. During a series of conventional boasts about Aristophanes' innovations and avoidance of *ho phortos*, the chorus differentiate between the ignoble buffoonery (*bōmolocheumat' agenē*) he has removed from comedy and the 'mighty words and ideas and jokes that are not unrefined (*skōmmasin ouk agoraiois*)' that he has supposedly introduced. In the prologue of *Frogs*, too, the initial exchange between Dionysus and Xanthias revolves around questions of refined and unrefined humour (thus Rosen, unpublished paper). Interestingly, at *Rh.* 2.12.16 (1389b), Aristotle calls the young 'fond of laughter' (*philogelōs*), a quality that he connects with *hybris*: as Goldhill suggests, laughter and *hybris* might both be said to involve a certain lack of rationality and self-control (Goldhill 2006: 83–5).

[66] These prejudices against visual elements surface elsewhere in Greek culture. For Aristotle spectacle (*opsis*) is the least artistic part of poetry (*Poet.* 1450b16–20; as Revermann 2006b: 106–7 plausibly argues, because the visuals are there for all to see and take in since they supposedly require the least decoding). At Pl. *Leg.* 658a–e, small children are said to like (visual) puppet shows, while old men prefer (aural) epic recitation; comedy's relatively lowly status is underlined by the fact that it is preferred by older boys (*hoi meizous paides*), while tragedy is favoured by young men (*nea meirakia*), educated women and, interestingly, the masses (*to plēthos*).

with an audience and the effective delivery of verse, enabling them to view dramatic performance with a connoisseur's eye.[67] Importantly for the present discussion, Revermann suggests that *choreutai*, who had traditionally come from Athens' wealthier classes, were increasingly drawn from non-elite sections of the citizen body towards the end of the fifth century.[68] Here, then, we have another group who might plausibly identify themselves as 'sophisticated' spectators whose membership is plausibly split between Athens' 'rich' and 'poor'.

We might not buy into Aristophanes' rhetoric about 'good' and 'bad' comedy and his crude division of spectators into laughers and thinkers – can't spectators be both? – but we cannot avoid the fact that throughout his career Aristophanes challenges his audience to consider the issue of what it means to be a sophisticated spectator. Revermann's work suggests that the practical learning gained by an increasingly non-elite group of *choreutai* is an important factor in 'theatrical competence', but the cultural pretensions of the masses can hardly be ignored – nor can the formal education of the elite (it is, after all, 'free and educated' spectators that Aristotle contrasts with vulgar ones, who are said to be drawn from the lowest class of citizen: *Pol.* 8.1342a18–21; cf. Arist. *Po.* 1461b26–9).[69] In short, Aristophanes' discussions of 'good' and 'bad' comedy subtly raise a whole series of questions for his audience about the relationship between class and cultural sophistication.

Conclusions

Aristophanes' plays, it turns out, reveal a deep preoccupation with the notions of high and low, and elite and non-elite, that lie at the heart of discussions of popular culture. In many ways, his plays are self-consciously aimed at the masses and are inclusive in the ways in which they conceive of Athenian society. His comedies are rich not only in 'low' cultural

---

[67] Revermann 2006b: 112–15.
[68] Revermann 2006b: 109–10, drawing on the work of Wilson 2000: 75–80 and 123–30, who provides a useful overview of 'the vexed question of the socioeconomic status of *khoreutai* . . . in Athens' (2000: 124); on the 'rise of often lower-class professionals and virtuosi' after the middle of the fifth century, see Wilson 2011: 28. Choral performance extended far beyond dramatic festivals, of course: see Swift 2010: 36–9.
[69] Wright sees Aristophanes and his fellow comic poets adopting an 'elitist' outlook, foreshadowing later 'literary' approaches to literature and its criticism (2012: 3). More controversially, he argues that comedians were, in part, producing works ultimately to be read by a select book-reading public (141–71).

elements (e.g. slapstick, obscenity and that other low feature, laughter) but also in socially 'low' personnel (e.g. the slaves and farmers who feature as characters in the plays and the various working-class occupations that are specifically mentioned on stage). The discussions of what makes for 'good' and 'bad' comedy also reveal a self-consciousness about catering to the masses – albeit by means of 'low' humour (especially appreciated, we are told, by unsophisticated spectators, such as boys).

In his statements as to what makes for 'good' comedy, however, it is the more exclusive elements of his comedies of which Aristophanes claims to be proudest: new ideas that are *dexios* and *sophos* and which require intelligence to appreciate (notwithstanding the fact that these rhetorical claims may be disingenuous or playful, of course). In addition, there is also a tendency to exclusiveness in the way in which the actors interact with spectators, as revealed in the earlier discussion of theatre audiences. It is the viewers in the front rows with whom the actors most often interact, for example, and in broad terms it is the social elite and those with recent experience of public office for whom personal and political jokes would arguably make the most sense.

In summary, Old Comedy might reasonably be said to display both popular and elite – inclusive and exclusive – tendencies: this is, perhaps, hardly controversial. But what this chapter has allowed us to map are some of the different ways in which Aristophanes' comedy constructs its 'elite' in-groups. The wealthy in Athens; audience members who are granted *prohedria* seats in any given year; those who consider themselves 'intellectual' spectators: all these groups are given special treatment in the plays – as the 'social elite', 'auditorium elite' and 'cultural elite', one might say. As we have seen, these groups are not coterminous (indeed, how could they be when the make-up of the 'auditorium elite' would have changed significantly year on year?) and significantly, too, the 'special treatment' that elite groups received included a certain amount of scrutiny and ridicule.[70] There is a sense, then, in which what it meant to be elite was a live question for Aristophanes' audiences – wealthy and poor, citizen and non-citizen alike. For all its popular elements, then, Old Comedy is certainly no straightforward example of popular culture. But perhaps that is only to be expected from a self-consciously subversive genre operating in a radical democracy where questions of what it means to be elite or non-elite are as persistent as they are complex.

---

[70] See Pritchard 2012: 22–4 for a brief overview of the humour directed at the wealthy and the ways in which tensions and misunderstandings between rich and poor are exploited on the comic stage.

PART II

Rome

4 | Popular Public Opinion in a Nutshell: Nicknames and Non-Elite Political Culture in the Late Republic

CRISTINA ROSILLO-LÓPEZ

The existence of a plebeian or popular collective memory is connected to the debate over the existence of a similarly independent popular political culture. Did the popular classes have an alternative memory of the past and an autonomous interpretation of the political present? Or were they completely dependent on elite political discourse? This chapter proposes that a political culture of the Roman people existed, especially in informal settings, influenced by the elite, but with independent aspects. This political culture was not conducted in secret, but is nonetheless absent from our sources because the elite did not usually pay it any real attention, although they did not entirely ignore it. Instead of directly opposing the elite, popular political culture adapted elite forms and modes of expression and enriched them with new meanings.[1] In order to test this premise, we shall turn to the study of popular nicknames in the first century BCE, examining them as a means of expressing a political discourse independent of that of the elite.

During the Republic, several elite sources tell us that nicknames were attributed to important political figures by the people. In fact, as we shall see, these nicknames reflected the appropriation and reinterpretation by non-elite citizens of the political history and the shared memory of past politicians. They offer an alternative interpretation to the more familiar elite point of view, putting into perspective the claims of an elite-dominated political discourse and memory. First, it is necessary to survey the places and locations in the city of Rome in which popular political opinions and ideas circulated.

This research has been financed by the project 'Opinión pública y comunicación política en la República Romana (siglos II–I a de C.)' (2013–43496-P) through the Ministerio de Economía y Competitividad, Spain. On the definition of non-elite and popular strata of the Roman citizens, see Courrier in this volume. All dates are BCE.

[1] See a similar point in Magalhães de Oliveira in this volume for the Late Empire. See Scott 1990 on his theory of 'hidden transcripts': the ways in which popular opinion was expressed in a political context dominated by an elite discourse.

Our understanding of popular political activity and political culture should not be restricted to the performance of formal political acts, such as voting or attending an assembly. Informal participation in politics was not controlled by the state and, therefore, provided more flexibility for those engaged in it, who were not subject to rules and controls. In Rome, freedom of speech existed, but not freedom of public speaking, since magistrates controlled public discourse in the *contiones*: only they or those whom they invited could address the people.[2] Facing such restrictions, informal participation in politics eschewed these rules and bypassed them. Rumours, gossip, shouts in the theatre or the games and other expressions of public opinion, for instance, allowed non-elite citizens to engage in political debate in an informal but equally effective way. How far the elite paid attention to such activities is a matter of debate, but, especially in troubled circumstances or when they catered to the desires of certain politicians, they could not be ignored.[3]

Popular public opinion could be located all around the city: people gossiped, talked and exchanged comments, not only in the Forum, but also in the adjacent streets, on street corners and even at fountains located in other parts of the city.[4] Walking was the most effective way of moving information.[5] Both busy streets and pedestrian spaces had advantages and disadvantages for the circulation of information. Bumping into an acquaintance was more likely to happen in busy streets, thus being conducive to small talk and therefore to cementing networks.[6] Nevertheless, in the case of very busy streets, noises, cries and shops that covered the whole pavement and carts travelling around the city could have made conducting a calm conversation arduous, burdensome and irritating.[7] On the other hand, pedestrian spaces (or even promenading spaces, such as porticos) offered calmer surroundings, where conversations could be conducted

---

[2] *Contiones* were one of the sources from which non-elite citizens could gain information, not only about current political events, but also about the past. See Pina Polo 1996 (political information) and forthcoming (on historical information as discussed in *contiones*).

[3] For such debate, see Rosillo-López forthcoming. See Magalhães de Oliveira in this volume on plebeian sociability in the Late Empire.

[4] On gossip in Rome, see Laurence 1994b; Rosillo-López 2007; Pina Polo 2010; Rosillo-López forthcoming. On popular invective, see Hawkins in this volume.

[5] O'Sullivan 2011.

[6] Gehl 1987. On the importance of informal networks and sociability, see Courrier and Magalhães de Oliveira in this volume.

[7] Pavements in Rome were not as developed as those of Pompeii: most were narrow or non-existent. Only four appear in the *Forma Urbis Romae*, although arcades and colonnades also functioned as such (see Holleran 2011: 248–9).

without raising one's voice too much. However, in those places the number of people crossing each other's paths would be correspondingly lower.

The Forum, access to which was not restricted during the republican period, was evidently one of the main places for sociability. It was not a place of exclusively political character, as it was also one of the main economic and financial centres of the city, thus ensuring a constant turnout of people who came into contact with each other.[8] Distinctions of class did not always preclude such contacts: non-elite citizens could directly address senators or even magistrates. For instance, an auctioneer mocked a consul about his taking bribes from foreign envoys.[9] Similar anecdotes feature during election times, when members of the elite had to behave more considerately to their fellow citizens in order to gain their votes.[10] Thus, even though authors like Cicero wanted to paint a picture of an aloof political elite who did not share sociability with the common people, the reality looks rather different. Cries in the theatre were heard regardless of the socio-economic status of the shouter. This fact allowed public opinion, information and gossip of any kind to flow freely and to move easily from one level or group of public opinion to another. There was no question of a closely guarded elite, detached and uninterested in what people were saying.

The streets near the Forum were places for making comments and for trying to get information in return.[11] Well-connected people could stop politicians and converse with them here.[12] These places also hosted groups of people who commented on political news or were interested in it: from informal *circuli* to the *columnarii*, *susurratores* and *subrostrani*.[13] A probably similar concept was that of *subbasilicani*, mentioned by Plautus.[14] Shackleton Bailey has translated them as 'pavement-gossips'.[15] All these groups fulfilled the same objectives: the collection and spreading of information and opinions.

Street corners and crossroads (*compita*) guaranteed a high turnover of people, as the high concentration of graffiti in these places attests.[16] Gossip and assorted comments featured in the graffiti of the *trivium*, where three streets crossed each other.[17] The presence of fountains at crossroads also

---

[8] Newsome 2010: 121–4 has highlighted how the Forum was surrounded by commercial areas, such as the Vicus Tuscus, the Velabrum and the Forum Boarium. On food markets, see De Ruyt 1983: 236–50; Papi 2002: 48–54; Carandini 2010: 49–51. Mansouri 2002 has studied the informal space of politics in the agora of Athens, especially in the marketplace, and how it played a role in forming public opinion.
[9] Cic. *Planc.* 33.   [10] See Yakobson 1999.   [11] Macrob. *Sat.* 2.7.11.   [12] Hor. *Sat.* 2.6.51–6.
[13] Cic. *Fam.* 8.9.5, 8.1.4, 8.1.5. On the *circuli*, see O'Neill 2001; 2003.   [14] Plaut. *Capt.* 815.
[15] Shackleton Bailey 1977: 383.   [16] Franklin 1986: 319–20.
[17] E.g. Cic. *Agr.* 1.3.7; Cic. *Mur.* 13.

made them a place for the exchange of information, since they provided a place for sociability. Laurence, for instance, has located fountains in Pompeii as always being located near street junctions; in that town, most people lived within 80 metres of a fountain.[18] The *compita* too were closely related to politics. Horace, for instance, described a rumour which travelled from the *rostra* to the *compita*.[19] After his popular monetary reform of 85, statues were spontaneously erected to the praetor Marius Gratidianus in the *compita*.[20] This represented an innovation, as the cult of a living person: most probably his *genius* would be worshipped, that is, the divine part of a man.[21] Furthermore, *compita* had become places of *popularis* connotations. After the quartering of Gratidianus by Sulla's partisans, the dictator ordered the destruction of all the former praetor's statues, recognizing their meanings and importance.[22] Not only that, they contributed to the consolidation of plebeian opinion.[23] Tiberius and Caius Gracchus' statues, erected after their death, were probably also located in the *compita*.[24] The Roman people used to make sacrifices before them. Statues maintain a special meaning even after a very long period of time; the groups that feel attached to them may react and respond to them daily or on specific occasions.[25] The politician Murena was abused by the people in a *trivium* and called a *saltator* – a dancer.[26]

The theatre and the games also constituted prime locations for sociability and for the circulation of public opinion and information.[27] Expressions of public opinion were not restricted merely to clapping or to the well-known repetition of verses that supported or denigrated certain politicians.[28] In fact, rumours and information circulated freely, as in 168, when the news of the victory in Pydna in the Third Macedonian War arrived in the city before the messengers did, a fact that was interpreted as an omen, although the account clearly shows the circulation of the rumour within the games.[29]

---

[18] Laurence 1994a: 42–50 (map establishing a relation between fountains and neighbourhoods: 49).

[19] Hor. *Sat.* 2.6.50.

[20] Plin. *HN.* 33.132; Cic. *Off.* 3.80; Sen. *De ira* 3.18.1. On Gratidianus' reform see Crawford 1970: 42; Barlow 1980: 217–19.

[21] Marco Simón and Pina Polo 2000: 163–9 suggest that Augustus, ordering that his *genius* should be worshipped, would have appropriated this custom of the plebs.

[22] Luc. 2.173–87; Sen. *De ira* 3.18.1–2; Asc. 75, 78C. On Sullan propaganda during the 80s, see Frier 1971.

[23] Marco Simón and Pina Polo 2000: 155–61.   [24] Plut. *Cai. Grac.* 18.3.

[25] Gregory 1994: 81.   [26] Cic. *Mur.* 13.

[27] Cf. Abbott 1907; Clavel-Lévêque 1984; Morgan 1990; Beacham 1991: 122–40; Flaig 1994; Flower 1995; Laser 1997: 92–102.

[28] On this practice, see Cic. *Sest.* 118, 120–2 (in favour of Cicero).   [29] Liv. 45.1.2–3.

Aside from public spaces, private places were also important locations for sociability, and hence potential exchange of information, gossip and public opinion. In the Plautus play *Epidicus*, the homonymous slave looks for the father of his master all around the city of Rome, mentioning shops: in particular doctors, perfumers, bankers, markets, butchers and barbers.[30] People did not only socialize in the Forum, but in the adjacent streets, and even outside the centre of the city, where such businesses could be found. *Tonsores* (barbers) have been considered a vehicle for circulating opinions in many civilizations, such as Athens, the Roman world or sixteenth-century Venice.[31] Roman men only shaved at home when in mourning, so they had to go to the barber or *tonsor* to keep their faces smooth.[32] Barbers' reputations as sources for rumours and gossip were well known.[33] Even popular wisdom linked barbers and public opinion: *res nota lippis et tonsoribus*, to speak of something well known by everybody.[34] Taverns were also popular spaces for lower-class socializing, which Juvenal associated with gossip.[35] Hermasen has noted that 20 per cent of identified taverns in Ostia were located on street corners. In Pompeii, Laurence has located the *cauponae* or inns just by the gates of the city, whereas *popinae* or taverns spread all around the city, but notably away from the houses of the elite.[36]

All these places, whether public or private, allowed for contact between members of the popular classes, and even between them and the elite. They ensured the circulation of opinions, information, gossip and rumours, which developed into a way of participating in politics for non-elite citizens, outside the elite's sphere of control. They also set the framework for the existence of an independent political culture. And, through sociability, they allowed the inclusion of people who were not Roman citizens, such as women or foreigners, since public opinion, as an informal institution, did not differentiate between these categories.

Nicknames represent a useful method of testing this premise of an independent popular political culture. These names constituted a snippet of public opinion, which could circulate quickly due to their oral nature, the concise message conveyed, and at times their comical effect. Establishing a comparison with contemporary information theory,

---

[30] Plaut. *Epid.* 196–200; similar places covered in Plaut. *Amphitr.* 1011–14.
[31] Venice: De Vivo 2007.   [32] E.g. Plut. *Ant.* 1.2; Artemid. 1.22.
[33] Plaut. *Asin.* 343ff.; Polyb. 3.20.5; Plut. *De garrul.* 7, 13.
[34] Hor. *Sat.* 1.7.3, and the scholiast Pomponius Porfirius on these verses.
[35] Juv. 9.102; on sociability in taverns: Laurence 1994a: 86; Purcell 1994: 659–73 (on the Roman plebs and the world of the tavern).
[36] Laurence 1994a: 81–7 with maps of their location.

Roman political nicknames would be similar to a bit, the smallest unit of information, as it would condense many meanings into a single word. If the nickname was going to be successful and circulate around the city, it needed to be appealing, accurate, well-aimed, even slightly daring, so people would be encouraged to pass it on. Only the most successful nicknames would survive in this Darwinian competition. As we shall see, nicknames were the result of the exchange of political information among the non-elite: in sum, a popular political culture, independent of elite influence.

Nicknames or *cognomina*, the frequency of use of which increased during the first century, were a constituent part of the Roman onomastic system.[37] *Cognomina* mainly described physical or mental peculiarities.[38] The negative connotations of a nickname, including those from sharing it with other, infamous, persons, could be damaging.[39] *Cognomina* could be inherited or earned during a politician's lifetime, usually relating to a deed or fact that had marked his career. For instance, they could relate to military victories and glorious deeds (*cognomina ex victa gente*), such as *Africanus, Macedonicus* or *Creticus*.[40] They might even have an expiry date: Cicero once commented that Pompey's *Magnus* had started to seem old.[41] The name of a politician, of any man, gave access to the moral kernel of his character, which could be used against him in political confrontations and in the courts of justice.[42] Favonius was nicknamed 'Cato's ape', alluding to his imitation of Cato the Younger.[43] Lucius Calpurnius Piso's honest administration earned him the *cognomen Frugi* (honest), so that his political enemy Caius Gracchus recognized it as attributed to him, even though he refused to employ it.[44] Cicero claimed that just as *Frugi* had lived his name, so Verres, the brute uncastrated boar, had lived his.[45]

---

[37] See Nicolet 1977: 55–6 for statistical data comparing their usage during the second and first centuries. On the Roman onomastic system, see Salway 1994. On *cognomina* see RE s.v. cognomen (Mau); Axtell 1915: 391–2; Matthews 1973; Kajanto 1965; Salomies 2008; Montanari 2009: ch. 7. Weaver 1972: 90–2 on the importance of *agnomina* for the onomastics of freedmen.

[38] Kajanto 1965: 131 (44 per cent of all *cognomina* recorded, especially physical traits); 13.6 per cent were related to geographical meanings.

[39] E.g. Cic. *Caec.* 27. McCartney 1919 on puns and *cognomina*. Corbeill 1996: 74–97 on abuse and *cognomina*.

[40] Linderski 1990 has argued that these nicknames, related to military victories, were assumed unofficially. Some of them were officially confirmed if a triumph was granted. Linderski 2007: 117–18: the triumphal *agnomina* were entered in the *Fasti Triumphales Capitolini*.

[41] Cic. *Att.* 2.13.2.5.   [42] Cic. *Font.* 39; Cic. *Inv.* 2.28; Corbeill 1996: 74–8.

[43] On Favonius' imitation of Cato, see Plut. *Cat. Mi.* 46.1; Cass. Dio 38.7.

[44] Cic. *Font.* 39. He was consul in 133.

[45] Cic. *2Verr.* 4.57. On the pun on Verres' name see Corbeill 1996: 91–5.

Could we equate a nickname and *cognomen*? Many *cognomina* started as personal nicknames, but turned later into a hereditary name that progeny would adopt. In fact, a *cognomen* could be defined as a nickname that, with the passing of time, lost its original purpose of pointing to a specific characteristic. Probably not all members of the family with the *cognomen* Rufus were red-haired or all the Caesars were bald.

Modern scholarship has offered a variety of interpretations of the origin and use of nicknames. Mommsen considered *cognomina* in a utilitarian fashion, as a way of distinguishing members of the same family; in his view, they also established a boundary between the upper class and the rest of the population.[46] Alföldi regarded *cognomina* of the elite as having been created and bestowed upon them by the crowd of the Forum or by soldiers, as a way of mocking their superiors and also as a way of distinguishing them by their salient traits.[47] However, his hypothesis regarding the popular origin of *all* nicknames is not corroborated by the sources in the majority of the cases, since these names were frequently bestowed by the elite upon their peers. Meanwhile Corbeill has proposed that pejorative nicknames were a tool for political stability, since they acted as a check on the elite by the elite in a context of fierce aristocratic competition.[48]

Non-elite citizens did express political messages and opinions through *cognomina*. Popular nicknames feature more abundantly in sources from the imperial period because historians focused exclusively on the emperor and his successor and thus were more likely to collect them.[49] Like many instances of non-elite public opinion, our sources are rather tight-lipped about popular nicknames. When mentioned, they are either scorned or even subverted, as we shall see. In this way they were discredited and their role as a representation of non-elite public opinion undermined.

Popular *cognomina* circulated and were exchanged in places where non-elite citizens socialized, especially street corners throughout the city. Horace the poet conversed with his friend Damasippus, who was ruined due to his financial speculations as well as his excessive expenditure on works of art.[50] At one point, Damasippus' renown as an art collector was so well known throughout Rome that he himself remarked: 'hence the crowded *compita* gave me the nickname of Mercury's pet (*Mercurialis*)', meaning that he was the favourite of the god of commerce and good business.[51] During the prosecution of Lucius Murena for electoral

---

[46] Mommsen 1864: 49, 59–60.   [47] Alföldi 1966: 710, 718–19.   [48] Corbeill 1996: 63–8.
[49] On imperial nicknames see Bruun 2003: 80–8.
[50] Hor. *Sat.* 2.3.17; 2.3.35. Damasippus later adhered to Stoicism.
[51] Hor. *Sat.* 2.3.25–6, 2.3.68; see commentary in Villeneuve 2001.

corruption (*ambitus*), Cicero tried to defend the reputation of the accused, dismissing the charges uttered by Cato the Younger, one of the prosecutors.[52] The latter had reported in court that he had heard Murena being called a *saltator* (dancer) on a street corner.[53] This insult was not uncommon: it was used by Cicero himself as a term of abuse against Gabinius, drawing on the *infamia* and effeminacy which were ascribed to dancers in Rome.[54] In both cases, people on street corners had attributed such names to them, thus linking the propagation of nicknames with the popular circulation of information.

Plebeian pejorative nicknames stemmed directly from popular political vocabulary and attest to the use of such political slang by non-elite citizens. Scipio Nasica Serapio, consul in 138 and *pontifex maximus*, led the senatorial lynch mob that murdered Tiberius Gracchus and his followers. In the aftermath, he was harassed in the streets, with people calling him 'tyrant' and an accursed man.[55] The Roman people, as is well known, greatly cherished the memory of the Gracchi (see below). These catcalls, which we could see as a kind of popular justice, proved too much for Nasica Serapio, who left Italy and died in Pergamum.[56]

Analysis of the rare instances when elite sources attribute a popular origin to a specific nickname provides three interesting cases of *positive* popular nicknames, which expressed both a positive non-elite opinion and an independent political culture. Interestingly, they are related to the memory of popular defenders of the people, that is, to three popular tribunes of the plebs: the Gracchi brothers and Appuleius Saturninus.

Such nicknames are especially concentrated during the turbulent years of 58–6, when we are dependent on the highly tendentious, and occasionally unreliable, testimony of Cicero. In his *Pro Sestio*, in 56, he surveyed the previous tumultuous years and attempted to provide a narrative of his exile and return, which he crafted carefully in order to present it in the most positive light possible and to improve his public image after his return. This

---

[52] On Cato's accusations against Murena see Nelson 1950: 66.
[53] Cic. *Mur.* 13. Moreau 1980 on the rewriting of the *Pro Murena* to suit the later political context.
[54] Cic. *Red. Sen.* 13 (*huius calamistrati saltatoris*); *Pis.* 22; *Dom.* 60; *Planc.* 87. Gabinius was praised indeed for his skills as a dancer (Macrob. *Sat.* 3.14,15). Catiline's supporters used to dance naked, according to Cicero (Cic. *Cat.* 2.23). See Gonfroy 1978 on the term *saltator* being linked to passive homosexuality and slavery; Corbeill 1997: 104–7 on *saltator* as a term of abuse.
[55] Plut. *TG* 21. 3. See Briscoe 1974: 133–4 on Nasica Serapio's opposition to Gracchus.
[56] Plut. *TG* 21. He left Rome even though his religious position precluded him from abandoning the city. He was also trying to avoid a trial (Pina Polo 2006: 93–4). On the figure of Nasica and his political role see Binot 2001.

narrative, which Kaster has dubbed 'the standard version', is in fact full of silences, misrepresentations, half-truths and, at times, falsehoods.[57]

In this speech, Cicero mentioned one of the tribunes of the plebs, Q. Numerius Rufus, who opposed his return, in a derogatory manner:

> The tribunes of the plebs entered office, having unanimously affirmed that they would publish a measure concerning my recall. For starters, my enemies bought one of these – the one whom people, in mockery and grief, called 'Gracchus', because it was the community's fate that that little Weld mouse, when plucked from the thorn-bushes, would try to nibble away at the commonwealth.[58]

Therefore, according to Cicero, people (*homines*) named Numerius *Gracchus* as a joke, with the pun also implying that he was not a match for those great homonymous tribunes.[59] The joke on the name is accompanied by a further allusion to a reddish mouse (*nitedula*). Later on in the text, Numerius is mentioned only by his nickname, when Cicero describes how he hid away when Sestius was attacked and, allegedly, the attackers turned on him.[60] The reason behind the nickname *Gracchus* and Cicero's explanation have long puzzled readers of the text. The scholiast, unconvinced by Cicero's convoluted explanation, tried to offer an alternative viewpoint: 'he called him *nitedula* because he was not only short in stature, but red in color'.[61] Other scholars have opted for linking the colour of the mouse to that of Numerius' cognomen, *Rufus* (red-haired);[62] the mouse would also refer to Numerius' rural origins, similarly mentioned in the speech.[63] Scholars have tried to propose alternative conjectures to fit Cicero's explanation: thus, Skutsch opted for *Brocchus*, referring to projecting front teeth, which would explain the allusions to rodents, although he later defended *Gracchus*.[64] The reading *Brocchus* could explain this joke, but does not fit with a second mention of Numerius Rufus, where it was a question of 'killing their own Gracchus'.[65] Furthermore, the word *Gracchus* is clearly transmitted by the manuscript.

All these interpretations assume that the nickname *Gracchus* was of humorous origin, blindly following Cicero's lead. However, an alternative

---

[57] Kaster 2006: 12.   [58] Cic. *Sest.* 72. Translation Kaster 2006.
[59] Kaster 2006: 278–9: 'he was what a Roman might call Gracchus dimidiatus, a half-pint Gracchus'.
[60] Cic. *Sest.* 82.
[61] *Schol. Bob.* 134 Stangl: 'quod esset non tantum statura depressus, verum etiam colore rubidus, nitedulam nominavit', trans. Corbeill 1996: 86.
[62] Corbeill 1996: 86–7; Kaster 2006: 278–9.
[63] Cic. *Sest.* 82. Numerius Rufus would probably have come from Picenum (Taylor 1960: 63).
[64] On *Brocchus*, see Varro *Rust.* 2.7.3, 2.9.4; Plin. *HN* 11.169.
[65] Cic. *Sest.* 82; Kaster 2006: 278–9.

hypothesis could be suggested: that the nickname was popular in origin and serious in tone, that is, it was a nickname, bestowed upon Numerius in all earnest by the plebs. As we shall see, the implications of this interpretation conflict directly with Cicero's 'standard version', which he was trying to present during his public appearances. A review of the political situation of late 58 and 57 provides an answer to this puzzle, and explains why people chose to call Numerius *Gracchus*.[66]

The attacks of Clodius against Cicero had crystallized since the beginning of the former's term as tribune of the plebs. He had promulgated laws *de capite civis*, which were actually aimed at punishing the murder of Roman citizens without trial during the conspiracy of Catiline.[67] The orator and his friends tried to counter these attacks during the weeks that followed. The attitude of Pompey was crucial: he abandoned Cicero, even though the latter threw himself at his feet as a suppliant.[68] Desperate, though reassured that his absence would be only be a matter of weeks, Cicero left Rome on 18/19 March 58.[69] Over the next few days, Clodius promulgated a law which named him explicitly as an exile.[70] The elections for the tribunate of the plebs traditionally took place in July.[71] Eight tribunes of the plebs, among them Sestius, declared themselves favourable to working for Cicero's return. The discordant two were Sextus Atilius Serranus Gavianus and Quintus Numerius Rufus. Cicero demonized these two hostile voices, arguing that they had been bribed by his enemies.[72] Furthermore, he heavily criticized Numerius during the *Pro Sestio*: he depicted him as a coward who hid under a shameful disguise (that of a muleteer); he mentioned his rural origins, almost omitted mentioning his name, and distorted his popular nickname *Gracchus*.

---

[66] A very helpful chronology is available in Kaster 2006: 395–408.
[67] Cic. *Sest.* 56–7. Kaster 2006: 395, n. 3 points out that Cicero's narrative suggests that they were passed after his exile, but this corresponds to a strategy in the speech.
[68] Cass. Dio 38.17.6; Cic. *QF* 1.4.4. On Pompey's attitude during 58, see Kaster 2006: 13–14. He had broken with Clodius, but had been tolerant towards him in the previous months, even acting as augur during his *transitio ad plebem*.
[69] Cic. *Sest.* 53–4.   [70] Cic. *Sest.* 65; Cic. *Att.* 3.1.   [71] Cic. *Att.* 1.1.1, 14.15.7–8; *Fam.* 8.4.
[72] Cic. *Pis.* 35; *Sest.* 94. Scholars who consider Numerius Rufus a 'Clodian tribune': Shackleton Bailey 1979: 271; Rawson 1977; Welch 1998: 102; Vanderbroeck 1985: 205, Ap-33; Benner 1987: 174–5; Flambard 1977: 154–5. Tatum speculates that, due to his Picenian origins, he may have sided with Pompey (Tatum 1999: 177, n. 8). Other politicians, though, who also came from that region, such as Marcus Caelius Rufus, did not number among the Pompeian supporters. Gruen has proposed that he was perhaps attached to Caesar, taking into account an inscription attesting that he served on Caesar's staff in Gaul in 56 (*CIL* I^2 2.759; Gruen 1974: 187). However, Caesar's legates came from various political backgrounds: e.g. Quintus Cicero, who is not considered a pro-Caesar politician. Numerius Rufus may not have been so dependent on Clodius after all.

The question remains: why would non-elite citizens have bestowed this nickname upon Numerius Rufus? In this case we can see that the plebs were not dependent on the elite for the transmission of historical knowledge about the Gracchi, since they had their own independent tradition.[73] For the plebs, the Gracchi were highly respected popular heroes. Shortly after Gaius' death, the people erected unofficial statues to honour the two brothers, even sacrificing to them, and consecrated the places where they had been murdered.[74] It is striking that when Cicero pronounced speeches before the people, his treatment of the two tribunes was positive, describing them as true friends of the Roman citizens.[75] In 102, an unknown man called Equitius claimed to be the son of Tiberius Gracchus, and won the favour of the plebs solely by the power of such a name.[76]

The plebs could have conferred the nickname *Gracchus* on Numerius Rufus in earnest for at least two reasons, which are not mutually exclusive, but rather complementary. First of all, the turbulent period of Numerius Rufus' tribunate allowed him plenty of time to address the citizens. If the people considered that he was defending their interests against the 'aristocrats', it is likely that the nickname *Gracchus* was granted to him in this light. In his second *De lege agraria*, pronounced before the people, Cicero mentioned the idea that the brothers had always struggled for the welfare of the plebs.[77] The second, complementary, reason would involve his intervention in probably the most problematic issue of 57, despite Cicero's self-centred narrative: the increase of grain prices, popular riots and the fear of famine.[78] The situation was somewhat problematic in 58, and worsened still more in the following year. In January 58, Clodius' law abolished the charge for state distributions of grain and lengthened the list of recipients;[79] by March grain was expensive. In fact, Virlouvet has suggested that the start of the crisis should be placed beforehand and that the *lex Clodia* was in fact attempting to alleviate a worsening situation.[80] Garnsey

---

[73] On the different traditions related to the Gracchi, see Flower 2006: 76–81; Wiseman 2009: 177–89 on the political divisions as a consequence of their murder; Van der Blom 2010: 103–7 on the views of the elite on the Gracchi; Pina Polo forthcoming on the use of the memoir of the Gracchi in speeches before the people.

[74] Plut. *CG* 18.3. See Marco Simón and Pina Polo 2000: esp. 158, n. 23; Morstein-Marx 2004: 119–59.

[75] Van der Blom 2010: 103–6, e.g. Cic. *Leg. Agr.* 2.10.31. By contrast, the speech *De lege agraria* delivered before the Senate contained a negative view of the Gracchi (Cic. *Leg. Agr.* 1.21).

[76] See Benness and Hillard 1990; Pina Polo 2014.   [77] Cic. *Leg. Agr.* 2.81.

[78] On this issue, see esp. Virlouvet 1985: 15–16; Garnsey 1988: 200–11.

[79] Cass. Dio 38.13.1–2.

[80] Virlouvet 1985: 45, especially if, through that law, Sextus Clodius (or Cloelius), a close collaborator of the tribune, received special powers to oversee and control the grain supply

has attributed the crisis in the grain supply of 57 to several reasons.[81] Harvest failure was mentioned by Cicero;[82] speculation is another likely possibility, linked to this previous factor.[83] Furthermore, Clodius augmented the number of grain recipients, which further strained the distributions. This deteriorating situation exploded during the *ludi Apollinares* (6–13 July 57), which saw a serious riot related to the high price of grain.[84] The plays performed at the *ludi* were pro-Ciceronian (as was the organizer), but the plebs had other concerns.[85] A large group of lower-class people (*infima multitudo*) invaded the theatre and compelled the spectators to evacuate the premises in a hurry.[86] At the same time, Clodius' gangs assaulted the house of Lucius Caecilius Rufus, the organizer of the games and the highest authority in Rome in charge of the grain supply, who had a background of opposition to agrarian problems.[87]

The Senate could not ignore these circumstances and felt compelled to react. In fact, the severity of the problem and of the popular reaction made the government regulate the shipping of grain for the first time.[88] Prices fell in July 57, coinciding with the news of the recall of Cicero.[89] Virlouvet speculates that the decrease in the prices was temporary, since we know they were falling again on 7 September.[90] Cicero delivered a speech that day and proposed granting extraordinary powers to Pompey as a commissioner for the corn supply (*cura annonae*).[91] Cicero's proposal was backed unanimously by the people.[92] Just beforehand, the plebs made their complaints heard during the sitting of the Senate in another riot, in which they confronted the senators:

---

similar to those that Pompey would receive the following year (Virlouvet 1985: 44–5; 96–102; Benner 1987: 119–21). On Sextus Clodius/Cloelius, the *scriba* and *operarum dux* of Clodius, see Shackleton Bailey 1960 (on the establishment of his name as Cloelius); Flambard 1977: 126–8; Vanderbroeck 1987: 55; Damon 1992.

[81] Garnsey 1988: 203. Further explanations in Virlouvet 1985: 42–8.   [82] Cic. *Dom.* 11.
[83] Garnsey 1988: 205–8 (esp. 206–8 on popular reactions to speculation).
[84] Asc. 48.20–2C; Courrier 2014. Bernstein 1998: 171–86 for the *ludi Apollinares*. Marshall 1985: 200 suggests that Asconius had confused the *ludi Apollinares* with the *ludi Romani*.
[85] Flower 1995: 175. The *fabula praetexta Brutus*, by the playwriter Accius, was programmed for the games by the organizer, L. Caecilius Rufus, urban praetor. The lines regarding King Servius Tullius served to express support for Cicero (Cic. *Sest.* 123).
[86] Asc. 48C; Cic. *Dom.* 14; *Mil.* 38.   [87] Cic. *Sull.* 65; Tatum 1999: 183.
[88] On grain supply to the city, see Rickman 1980: 122–55; Erdkamp 2005: 258–316.
[89] Cic. *Dom.* 14.   [90] Cic. *Quir.* 14; Virlouvet 1985: 15–16.
[91] The plebs requested him to be in charge: Cic. *Att.* 4.1.6–7; *Fam.* 5.17.2.
[92] Cic. *Att.* 4.1.6; *Dom.* 16. The crowd applauded wildly when the decree was read. Cicero addressed them in a *contio*, the *Post reditum ad Quirites*; even though the date of its delivery has also been suggested as two days earlier, after his address to the Senate, *Post reditum in Senatu*, see Kaster 2006: 401–2, n. 27.

'threatening at first to slay them with their own hands, and later to burn them alive, temples and all'.[93] The risk or at least the likelihood of famine seems to have spurred the plebs into action; Virlouvet is therefore probably right to suggest that these riots should not only be linked to the actions of Clodius and his gangs.[94] After discussion of the powers bestowed upon Pompey, an extraordinary command of five years was decided.[95] Nevertheless, the shortage did not disappear quickly enough and the problem remained.[96] In February 56 Clodius and his partisans tried to rouse the plebs under the banner of the grain supply;[97] in April, the Senate voted the allocation of 40 million sesterces as additional funds for the provision of the grain supply.[98]

This context of a grain crisis establishes a suitable background against which a tribune could earn the surname *Gracchus*.[99] The main objective of the *lex Sempronia frumentaria* was to introduce regularity into the grain supply;[100] these subsidized allowances had been abolished by Sulla, although they were reinstated in 73.[101] Cato the Younger, during his term as tribune of the plebs, extended the right of distribution.[102] In the historical memory of the plebs, Caius Gracchus' grain law had established the distribution of grain at reduced and fixed prices. Agrarian laws were generally, of course, very popular among the people.[103] Numerius Rufus may have been highly active in dealing with the grain problem and thus have earned his nickname *Gracchus*, earnestly bestowed on him by the plebs. It is thus understandable that Cicero tried to subvert the name: he could not deny or hide its existence, as it was clearly widely known. He could, however, offer another interpretation of its origin. The acceptance of the nickname *Gracchus* granted by the plebs could suggest that Cicero's 'standard version', which posited a universal consensus of elite and plebs regarding his return, would crumble. Non-elite citizens seem to have been at least equally concerned (if not more so) with the problem of the high prices of grain than with Cicero's return from exile. We can see that Cicero himself, meanwhile, was clearly aware of this fact, since his

---

[93] Cass. Dio 39.9.2–3. Cic. *Att.* 4.1.6–7; *Fam.* 5.17.2.   [94] Virlouvet 1985: 41.
[95] Pompey's command: Cic. *Att.* 4.1.7; *QF* 2.5; *Dom.* 11; Plut. *Pomp.* 49.5; Cass. Dio 39.9. The tribune of the plebs Messius proposed granting Pompey even further powers (Cic. *Att.* 4.1.7).
[96] Cic. *QF* 2.3.2–4; *Dom.* 25–6; Plut. *Pomp.* 50.1–2.   [97] Cic. *QF* 2.3.2.14.
[98] Cic. *QF* 2.6.1, 2.5.1.
[99] Garnsey and Rathbone 1985 on the context of the grain law of Caius Gracchus; Boren 1958 on the consequences of the grain crisis in the city.
[100] Garnsey and Rathbone 1985: 24; Nicolet 1976: 259–80.
[101] Sulla: Sall. *Hist.* 1.55.11. Restoration in 73: Sall. *Hist.* 3.48.19; Cic. *2Verr.* 3.163.
[102] Plut. *Cat. Mi.* 26.1.   [103] Cic. *Leg. Agr.* 2.63.

political interventions upon his return were linked to solving the problem of grain supply.

Was the bestowal by the plebs of the positive nickname *Gracchus* upon Numerius Rufus something exceptional or even unique? In fact, taking into account the fondness of the Romans for nicknames, together with the latter's effectiveness in conveying both a political message and a political opinion, it was probably a not infrequent usage. The identification of such popular nicknames is difficult, because they were not likely to have been recorded by elite sources. Numerius Rufus' nickname, which has been shown here to have been of popular origin, was certainly not an isolated case, since other popular politicians had them, most famously the most popular politician of the 50s, Publius Clodius Pulcher.

In a letter to Atticus dated in May 55, Cicero sneeringly referred to his hated rival as 'the people's Appuleia' (*illa populi Appuleia*), equating Clodius with the tribune L. Appuleius Saturninus. Like the Gracchi, Saturninus had been a popular tribune, who was likewise murdered during a confrontation with the conservative part of the Senate.[104] After his death, repression ensued: a tribune of the plebs was even condemned because he was found to have possessed an *imago* of Saturninus.[105] However, Saturninus and his memory were cherished by the people; Cicero once abused him in a speech in a court of justice, and the reaction of the crowd surrounding the trial was fierce: shouts and boos could be clearly heard. Much as he tried to downplay such expressions of public opinion, attributing them to a minority, Cicero could not deny their existence.[106] Decades after his murder, Saturninus was still a part of the historical memory and political culture of at least a part of the plebs. For the elite, meanwhile, he was the model of the radical and destructive tribune.[107] The difference between popular interpretation of this political culture and that of the elite attests to the divergence between non-elite and elite political culture.

---

[104] Cavaggioni 1998: 137ff. on the events which led to his demise. *Pace* Beness 1991 who has questioned the popularity of Saturninus among the plebs during his life. After his death, however, she states that he became a 'popularis martyr' (Beness 1991: 56).

[105] Cic. *Rab. Perd.* 9.24; see Cic. *Off.* 2.48; 265; Val. Max. 8.1.3. On the importance of the veneration of *imagines* see Gregory 1994; Marco Simón and Pina Polo 2000.

[106] Cic. *Rab. Post.* 18. This reaction may hint that the crowd that surrounded the court of justice was composed mainly of non-elite citizens, since it is extremely unlikely that the Roman elite would had been offended by Cicero's comments about Saturninus (see Pina Polo forthcoming).

[107] Van der Blom 2010: 107.

Conscious of their popularity, Saturninus had indeed modelled himself according to the example of the Gracchi;[108] he associated with L. Equitius, who claimed to be Tiberius Gracchus' son.[109] This positive image of Saturninus might have produced in turn a highly positive popular nickname for Clodius. As in the case of Numerius Rufus *Gracchus*, Cicero could here have subverted a popular *cognomen*, part of non-elite political culture, and turned it into an effeminate insult.[110]

A third possible popular nickname is more controversial. In his *Pro domo sua*, Cicero asserted that his followers called Clodius *felix Catilina*.[111] In the orator's mind-set, of course, this represented a powerful insult, which equated his loathed rival with the greatest danger to the Roman Republic in recent years.[112] Nevertheless, Clodius' role during the conspiracy had been unambiguous. He had helped to suppress it, and in 65 he had brought Catiline to trial for extortion, though some accused him of collusion with the accused.[113] The deeply loaded title therefore raises doubts about its attribution to Clodius' followers. The popularity of Catiline among non-elite citizens has been the subject of debate,[114] along with his status as *popularis* martyr.[115] Throughout the writings of Cicero, in any case, both in private letters and public speeches, Clodius was assimilated to Catiline and considered as his successor.[116] The orator even alleged that Clodius' followers contained former associates and supporters of Catiline.[117] However, these affirmations are firmly rooted in Cicero's rhetorical strategy of the 50s, which consisted of demonizing his rival by linking him to the man whom he presented as the greatest danger to Rome in decades, Catiline. By attributing the nickname to the plebs, Cicero was shifting it away from himself, thus giving it more weight as an

---

[108] Cavaggioni 1998; Flower 2006: 81–5. *Rhet Her.* 4.67 mentioned Appuleius Saturninus in comparison with the Gracchi.

[109] See Beness and Hillard 1990; Pina Polo 2014.

[110] Richlin 1983; Corbeill 1997 in general on the effeminate male, esp. 111–12 on other politicians described as women (such as Julius Caesar as the queen of Bithynia), although more as a mixture of passive effeminacy and aggressive masculine lust; for other instances of insults to Clodius related to effeminacy, see Pina Polo 1991: 145–6.

[111] Cic. *Dom.* 72.

[112] Pina Polo 1991: 135, n. 18 on other enemies of Cicero named also *Catilina*.

[113] Cic. *Att.* 1.2.1 (in fact Cicero considered defending Catiline in the trial). Lintott 1967: 158–9; Pina Polo 1991: 135–6; Tatum 1999; Harrison 2008: 115.

[114] See Harrison 2008: esp. 97, n. 14 for full bibliographical details on the debate.

[115] Harrison 2008: 99–100. Cic. *Flacc.* 95: flowers on the tomb of Catiline when C. Antonius, one of his enemies, was condemned for provincial extortion.

[116] Cic. *Attt.* 1.14.5; 1.16.9; 4.33; *Red. Sen.* 33; *Dom.* 13, 58, 61, 72, 75; *Sest.* 42; *Pis.* 15–16, 23; *Mil.* 37, 63; *Asc.* 9C. On Clodius as Catiline's successor, see Tatum 1999: 142–5.

[117] Cic. *Red. Quir.* 13; *Pis.* 11, 16, 23; *Dom.* 61; *Planc.* 35. Harrison 2008: 115–16.

expression of public opinion. Nevertheless, taking into account the numerous instances in which he deployed the pairing Clodius = Catiline, it is probable that in this case the origin of the nickname was not in fact to be related to Roman non-elite citizens. The use of *Gracchus* and *Appuleius* by Cicero is different. He did not subvert the nickname *(felix) Catilina*. In the two previous cases, however, he tried to undermine the connotations behind the popular names, either by providing a different and unsatisfactory explanation or by turning it into an insult. In these cases we can see that Cicero was appropriating a powerful expression of popular political culture and reinterpreting it according to his own interests.

In conclusion, these popular, highly favourable nicknames were the expression of a collective popular memory and culture, based on the reverence for certain politicians, who were felt to have fought for the interest of the plebs, such as the Gracchi brothers, Saturninus and Gratidianus. This memory was not only expressed through visual and material means: that is, with statues erected in Rome by the people and the offering of sacrifices, as attested for both the Gracchi and Gratidianus.[118] Indeed Cicero himself mentioned the popularity of anyone who could relate in some way to the Gracchi or Saturninus, since the mere name and memory of these politicians could rally wide support from the plebs.[119]

The analysis of popular *cognomina* for Roman politicians suggests that popular public opinion was more dynamic and independent than has previously been thought. Non-elite citizens used political slang when they stated and circulated their opinions in the Forum and throughout the city. The bestowal by the plebs of a flattering nickname, based on previous popular figures, on a contemporary politician offered an alternative view of history to that of the elite. To name someone as *Gracchus* or *Appuleius* ranged him in a long line of defenders of non-elite interests and placed a heavy burden of hopes and expectations upon his shoulders. Tracing the various mentions of positive popular nicknames has allowed us to discern the popularity with the plebs of several political figures, presenting at the same time an alternative and independent political memory to that of the elite. Popular *cognomina*, therefore, represent the most condensed or concise expression of non-elite public opinion and reflect nothing less than an independent, cohesive and indeed genuinely challenging popular political culture.

[118] Plut. *CG* 18.3 (statues of the Gracchi); Cic. *Off.* 3.80 (statues of Gratidianus); Marco Simón and Pina Polo 2000.
[119] Cic. *2Verr.* 1.151. E.g. the already mentioned Equitius as the supposed son of Tiberius Gracchus.

5 | Plebeian Culture in the City of Rome, from the Late Republic to the Early Empire

CYRIL COURRIER

> Est animus tibi, sunt mores, est lingua fidesque, / sed quadringentis sex septem milia desunt: / plebs eris. (Hor. *Ep.* 1.1.56–8)[1]

Horace here observes that, during the Late Republic and Early Empire, the *plebs urbana* was composed of citizens of Rome whose property qualifications in the census were inferior to that required of the equestrian order (400,000 sesterces).[2] The literature of the time commonly delineates three categories according to which plebeians differed from *equites* and senators.[3] The plebs, however, cannot be regarded as a homogeneous group; on the contrary, this category itself comprised multiple internal hierarchies:[4] being born free or enslaved was a primary distinction; belonging to the *ordines*, for some privileged plebeians, was another. There was, more generally, a sharp contrast between what Andreau has influentially termed '*affairistes*'[5] ('entrepreneurs'), and the 'average workers' who owned or rented their *taberna*,[6] and even more so with the labourers who made their living on a day-to-day basis. Therefore, it is far from likely that one single congruent 'culture' can represent such diverse legal and socio-economic strata. Indeed, sociologists and anthropologists understand the notion of culture as representing 'symbolic coherence in the set

---

The following pages draw on ideas developed in my book devoted to the Roman plebs: Courrier 2014. I am much indebted to Sabine Lauret for the translation into English, and to Yves Roman and Jean-Pierre Guilhembet for their reading. My warmest thanks go to Lucy Grig for her reading and suggestions.

[1] 'You have sense, you have morals, eloquence and honour, but you are six or seven thousands short of the four hundred; you'll be one of the plebs.'
[2] Purcell 1994: 644; Courrier 2014: 1–25.
[3] Cic. *Pis.* 64; *Planc.* 21; *Sest.* 24; Liv. 26.36.4–8 and 12; Ov. *Fast.* 2.127; 4.291; *Tr.* 4.15; Mart. 5.27.
[4] Nicolet 1985.   [5] Andreau 2001: 101–6.
[6] That is, people living above the poverty line. See Virlouvet 2009: 1: 'ceux qui, dans les cités du monde romain, vivaient hors de la précarité, possédaient un toit, un métier, une famille, entretenaient des liens sociaux avec leurs semblables, sans pour autant être de riches propriétaires de l'élite'. See also Veyne 2005: 117–61 on the locution *plebs media* and the reassessment in Courrier 2014: 299–365 (the expression probably does not designate a 'middling' plebs in the modern sense of the term but rather the most well-off categories of the population who did not belong to the equestrian or senatorial elites). There was without doubt no ancient equivalent of the contemporary expression ' middle classes'.

of practices (social, economic, political, religious, etc.) of a community or of a group of individuals'.[7] This raises the following question: in spite of their differences and heterogeneity, is it possible to identify – as with the elite – a combination of symptomatic behaviours that defined the plebs as a group? In particular, how did the plebeians construct their role in the daily, extraordinary and ritual relationships that structured the Roman social order?[8]

This leads to another question. While many sociologists and anthropologists conceive of culture as largely ruled by subconscious mechanisms, others, like Richard Hoggart, have pointed out the strongly felt (if also at times conflicted) sense shared by members of a given culture, of belonging to the same group, subject to the same limitations and constraints.[9] In other words – and without necessarily going as far as adopting such clearly formulated claims as those implied by the concept of 'identity'[10] – 'culture' implies a bipartition of the world ('us' versus 'them') according to the shared values of a given group. Adapting this concept, I will ask, could the *plebs urbana* have possessed a group consciousness, and if so how was this signified? Was there a common sentiment that drove plebeians to group themselves around collective values that they considered representative? In which case, what were these values, and did they form a system that we can analyse as a coherent whole? This volume is, however, dedicated to popular culture: is it possible to juxtapose plebeian culture and popular culture? This question must, therefore, deal also with the social and economic dimensions of cultural forms, together with the very meaning (and applicability) of the adjective 'popular'.

These questions, even in the context of ancient Rome, inevitably echo the theoretical debates of the early 1970s, initiated by the ground-breaking works of Robert Mandrou (1964) and Mikhail Bakhtin (first published in 1965, in English in 1968) which prepared the foundations for the study of the 'popular culture' of the French *Ancien Régime*. To return to the terms of the definition formulated (not uncritically) by Roger Chartier, the 'popular' was defined negatively, in terms of what it was *not*: it was not erudite

---

[7] Cuche 1996: 5. For a recent overview of the notion of 'culture', see Blandenet, Chillet and Courrier 2010: 5–17 and Grig's Introduction.

[8] This analysis is grounded in Agier's research: see Agier 2010: 55–64, 99–104.

[9] Hoggart 1957: 19: 'I admitted earlier that working-class people probably do not feel themselves to be members of a "lower" group as strongly as they did a generation or two ago. Yet those I have in mind still to a considerable extent retain a sense of being in a group of their own, and this without there being necessarily implied any feeling of inferiority or pride; they feel rather that they are "working-class" in the things they admire and dislike, in "belonging".'

[10] Cuche 1996: 83–4. See further below.

literature or the normative religion of the Catholic church.[11] But this new historical method – which primarily consisted of studying cheap, widely distributed pamphlets in order to produce an inventory of what were seen as autonomous cultural forms and practices – was severely criticized and scholarly focus quickly shifted to consider the role of cultural intermediaries and the process of cultural transformation and hybridization.[12] However, in recent publications dealing with the ancient world, we find a definition of popular culture that is reminiscent of these earlier theories:[13] defined in opposition to the 'elite', the 'non-elite' are a group of individuals 'united by broadly similar interests, facing the same day-to-day problems of making a living, and equipped with the same tried-and-tested ways of trying to get things done in a tough, hierarchical world run by the elite for the elite ... Popular culture was how people survived'.[14] In other words, steering clear of the pitfalls of cultural relativism, this contention is based on the understanding that a popular culture is first and foremost the culture of dominated groups. On the one hand, when it comes to the plebs of the capital, in a position of social, economic and political inferiority vis-à-vis the equestrian and senatorial classes, this definition indeed seems to provide both an operational method and a richly heuristic perspective. I will thus explore how far 'plebeian culture' was shaped by its need to acknowledge the culture of a dominant group.[15] On the other hand, the quasi-systematic assimilation of 'popular' and 'poor' in recent scholarship clearly raises issues;[16] this assimilation has coloured the debate, and has palpably modified our interpretation of 'the culture of the plebs'.

In this chapter it will not be possible to deal with all these issues, nor to survey every aspect of plebeian culture. My focus will be on the sociological and cultural implications of the recent analyses of the plebs in terms of

---

[11] Chartier 1986: 174–9.
[12] See, in particular, Ginzburg 1980 on the miller Menocchio; Roche 1981 on the people of Paris and the question of material culture; Chartier 1982 on the texts dubbed 'popular' and on the impossibility of considering them as such. See also Certeau 1974, 1984 and, most recently, Kalifa 2010: 994–9.
[13] Even if they are not explicitly referenced.
[14] Toner 2009: 2. See also Knapp 2011. For a strictly cultural approach, see Horsfall 2003.
[15] I rely here on the definition of popular culture given by Hoggart 1957 and Grignon and Passeron 1989.
[16] See, for example, Toner 2009: 2; also Knapp 2011 (who, interestingly, excludes the Roman plebs from poverty due to their economic situation and political importance). The analysis of ancient popular cultures in terms of poverty largely rests on Scheidel's economic theories and Scobie's description of living conditions (Scheidel 2003, 2010, 2014; Scobie 1986). *Contra* (for Late Antiquity): Magalhães de Oliveira 2012: 38–84.

poverty. I will then offer a fresh approach, proposing some new points, which, while partial in conclusion, will nonetheless nuance our image of the plebs.

A Culture of Poverty? Living Conditions and Subsistence Culture

This question echoes a much wider debate on the living conditions in a megalopolis such as Rome and on the demographic model known as the 'urban graveyard effect'. Recent scholarship – essentially by comparison with much later development in cities like London and Paris – lays emphasis on how urban sprawl resulted in squalor and promiscuity.[17] In the wake of Alex Scobie's now-classic article,[18] many have written about the top floors of the buildings where lower-status Romans lived. These constructions were basically unsteady hovels, homes that grew smaller the higher one went, as the population increased. Rent was very high, leaving people with barely enough to maintain a miserable subsistence. Unable to afford a decent diet, eating mostly bread and pulses, the urban poor suffered from chronic malnutrition. Their water may have been contaminated, because of the lead in the pipes and stagnancy in *lacus*. Water pollution would in this analysis constitute one of the main vectors of disease, the spread of which was facilitated by the rudimentary sanitary conditions of a city overwhelmed by rubbish.

I shall not go into detail regarding the conclusions drawn in such studies, except to underline how they influenced many demographic historians to construct their models of Rome as a demographic black hole, where immigrants came to die. In this picture, Rome falls into the universal pattern of the pre-industrial megalopolis, as described by Henri W. Pleket:

the iron law that the population of large pre-industrial megalopolises was incapable of reproducing itself sufficiently. In this respect Rome fully obeys the demographic law according to which big cities largely depended on immigration for keeping the population up to the mark. Life in such cities was far from healthy and as a result mortality rates vastly exceeded birth rates.[19]

The implications of such studies are important, considering that they posit that temporary residents of Rome, or those who lived a hand-to-mouth

---

[17] For example, Whittaker 1992: 347–50 or Pleket 1993: 17. For full references see Courrier 2014: 28–43.
[18] Scobie 1986.   [19] Pleket 1993: 17.

existence, represented a much larger proportion of the population than a hypothetical community of permanent city-dwellers.[20] As a result, the culture of the plebs could ever only be a culture of uprooted people – people who could not afford to have children, with all the cultural ties this implied. They could not develop roots in the city itself; they had no capacity to develop a collective memory, for want of successors to pass it on to. In other words, their culture was a culture of poverty. As Walter Scheidel has put it, 'if correct, these findings are of considerable relevance to appraisals of family formation, social structure, political activity and the preservation of civic memory in the capital'.[21] Even though it will not be possible to scrutinize in detail all aspects of this thesis,[22] this chapter will note some important objections, because the consequences in terms of culture are significant.

First, let us consider the handling of source material by historians writing in the wake of Alex Scobie's work: every single text, anecdotal as it might have been, that gave a negative impression of Rome as a deeply insalubrious city, was considered to have the validity of a general principle, and pieced together to shed negative light on the city. In this way, Juvenal was considered almost an ethnographer! Ray Laurence was justly able to use the word 'dystopian' to describe these studies.[23] In fact, as Elio Lo Cascio recently suggested, it is very likely that there has been too much insistence on the negative aspects of living in Rome (noise, squalor, smell, lack of privacy, insecurity and disease), while the advantages the city provided to large groups of its inhabitants have been overlooked.[24]

The distribution of grain is clearly the first of these positive factors. Starting in 123 BCE – when the state implemented *frumentationes* – a growing sector of the plebs of the *Urbs* was entitled to a significant monthly allowance (5 *modii*, approximately 35 kg) of reduced-price grain (6 $^{1/3}$ *as* for 1 modius) and, after 58 BCE, of free grain.[25] Given the market price of the modius in the Late Republic and Early Empire (6–8 HS per modius, according to Richard Duncan-Jones)[26] on the one hand and, on the other, what we know about the plebeians' wages and incomes, such

---

[20] As suggested, for example, by Purcell 1994: 650. [21] Scheidel 2003: 158; Scheidel 2014.
[22] See Courrier 2014: 27–125. [23] See Laurence 1997 and Courrier 2014.
[24] Lo Cascio 2001. [25] Virlouvet 1995: 9.
[26] See Duncan-Jones 1982: 345–7; Garnsey 1998: 237, who used Plin. *HN* 18.90. Considering that the prices given by Pliny mostly refer to the period after Nero had devalued the Roman currency (Corbier 1985), it would be wise to leave a margin for slight inflation. On the other hand, Cic. *Verr.* 3.148 does not give any indication about the free market price, only mentioning the fixed price paid by the Senate for wheat from Sicily (i.e. 3–4 HS per modius) as part of the second tithe Rome levied on the island. See Rickman 1980: 170–1 and Virlouvet 1994: 22.

assistance was far from negligible. It represented something between 30 to 60 per cent of a person's income at the time: that is, if we stick with the 'canonical' salary mentioned by Cicero,[27] and consider the increasing numbers of holidays that affected the number of working days.[28] Yet, while the *plebs frumentaria* and *plebs urbana* were never strictly equivalent, it must not be forgotten that the list of beneficiaries included up to 320,000 adult male[29] Roman citizens and permanent residents registered as such. According to Lo Cascio's estimates for the Augustan era, this amounted to a population of about 600,000 registered residents (women and children included),[30] at least from 46 BCE, when *frumentationes* were granted on the basis of domicile.[31] Furthermore, in 2 BCE, when a system of *subsortitio* (which may have been tried out under Caesar's rule)[32] was adopted, the number of beneficiaries was capped. This suggests that the plebs entitled to the distribution of grain represented a stable demographic group[33] whose standard of living was above subsistence levels.

This conclusion helps shed new light on the huge quantity of food products that were transported each day to the capital – products that those who were eligible for free grain could afford. Taking into account the available information in order to establish the consumption of four staple products (oil, bread, wine and meat), I have estimated elsewhere – at least according to hypothetical levels of consumption – that daily nutritional intake oscillated between 1,900 and 3,500 calories – enough to meet the needs of a sedentary woman as well as an active man. Similarly, the quality and amount of water – 61 to 142 litres per head per day from the 30s onwards,[34] provided by *lacus* alone, regardless of the resources of rainwater and, of course, the *balnea*[35] – reveal a pattern in which the people of the *Urbs* were doing far better than merely eking out a precarious existence. Their living conditions could, indeed, be considered somewhat exceptional for the pre-industrial era, as numerous recent studies on sanitation issues in the megalopolis illustrate.[36] In this regard, we can see the plebs as a sovereign people in an imperial capital, beneficiaries of free grain as

---

[27] Cic. *Q. Rosc.* 28.　[28] For more detail, see Courrier 2014: 50–4.　[29] Suet. *Jul.* 41.5.
[30] Lo Cascio 2001: 195.
[31] Although it might be argued that this criterion had been used since 123 BCE – Virlouvet 1995: 19–21.
[32] Suet. *Jul.* 41.5. On Augustus, see Cass. Dio 55.10.
[33] Lo Cascio 1990: 292–304; 1997: 8–14; 1998: 370–2.
[34] Courrier 2014: 97. See also De Kleijn 2001: 58–60 and Bruun 1997.
[35] This point is highlighted by Purcell 1994: 650.
[36] See notably Dupré Raventós and Anton Remolà 2000 and Ballet, Cordier and Dieudonné-Glad 2003.

well as the largesse of the emperor (the *congiarum* was probably far from negligible). There is thus an inherent paradox attached to the culture of this social group, as viewed by the plebs themselves: that of a dominated group, united by a civic privilege, that conceived itself as master of the world.[37]

From this standpoint, the culture of the plebs (or at least those benefiting from the grain dole) appears no longer to be a culture of poverty shared by a deracinated population. On the contrary, this sub-section of the plebs was chiefly composed of people living above the poverty threshold, who had an occupation, and who rented or owned their accommodation. Both natural reproduction and the transmission of shared memory could take place,[38] at the same time as a number of activities which contributed to a pattern of an '*être-en-ville*'[39] shared not by a group of uprooted individuals, but by a stable population whose life was anchored around a few well-known streets and marked by patterns of sociability, solidarity and hierarchy that had been established over several generations.

Urban Culture and Social Practices of the Plebs

Looking at everyday life (I will come to the political aspect later on), plebeians seemed to have gathered in a few well-known streets, busy with people, and particularly around the focal points of a plebeian life, ordered by localized activities.[40] Each neighbourhood[41] was organized in a way that

---

[37] Virlouvet 2009.

[38] That is to say, a common knowledge and a common *imaginaire*, born out of experiences and memories, which played a foundational role in the construction of a collective memory belonging to different strata of the plebs, and not only to the citizen members of this ensemble. This *imaginaire* allowed the plebs to assume a consciousness of themselves and their identity through time. *Contra*, see Flower 2006: 53: 'Roman memory was political memory: Roman republican history was synonymous with the gentilitial traditions and pretentions of office-holding families.' For an in-depth discussion of the memory mechanisms of the plebs, see Courrier 2012, 2014: 547–99 and Rosillo-López in this volume.

[39] Agier 2010: 77 forged this expression in reference to that of Heidegger's 'Dasein', to describe the modes of appropriation of the city, the styles of living in a city, that are specific to an individual or a group, especially the *familiar* city (as opposed to the city of others, of the unknown) in which each creates his or her own sense, his or her own history, his or her own itinerary.

[40] Courrier 2014: 127–91.

[41] Neighbourhood is understood here not as a modern equivalent of the Latin term *vicus* – which referred above all to an administrative and official division of urban space (see Lott 2004: esp. 4–5 and 23; Lo Cascio 2007: 149–50 and 156–7; Tarpin 2008; Courrier 2014: 128–41) – but from a sociological perspective, as a contained urban space, the limits of which primarily make sense to its residents. See Choay and Merlin 1987 who define neighbourhood as 'fraction[s] du territoire d'une ville, dotée[s] d'une physionomie propre et caractérisée[s] par des traits distinctifs [leur] conférant une certaine unité et une individualité'. This is taken up and

enabled people to live their lives centred around their micro-communities, except when interacting with the authorities was necessary. One finds traces of this illustrated in the probable intersections of domestic and professional life at the *taberna*. As clearly shown by Nicholas Purcell, this diffusion was so common in the Late Republic that it was almost taken as the very definition of the plebs;[42] and recent studies have suggested that *tabernae* buildings may in fact have been the most common type of housing.[43] When people did not live in the shops themselves (in the mezzanine or an adjacent room), *tabernarii* inhabited rooms on the upper floors of the same buildings in which *tabernae* occupied the ground floor. This is clearly demonstrated by both epigraphic[44] and archaeological evidence: the vast majority of buildings excavated (primarily in Ostia, but also in Rome)[45] share this pattern, with shops on the ground floor, connected by stairs on the side and topped by apartments. Indeed, the *Forma Urbis Marmorea* offers a specific sign – V – to indicate the multiple floors, and sometimes even depicts the stairs.[46]

From a sociological standpoint, such a layout implies a very limited range of daily movement and a highly localized use of urban space.[47] This space was then further mapped by strong neighbourhood dynamics, and given rhythm by rites and collective celebrations such as Compitalia,[48] as well as being delineated by places where people socialized, such as *collegia*[49] and corner shops. To illustrate these urban habits, let us consider Plutarch's story of a poor plebeian (*penēs kai demotikos*) who offered shelter to the orator Mark Antony, of whom he was a follower, during the civil war between Sulla and Marius when Rome was controlled by the

---

critiqued by Lussault 2003: 758–60, who counters with the case of contemporary cities in developed countries, where geographical proximity of residence is less important in the construction of social groups than proximity of taste or common practices. In our case, it is lived space that is of interest above all: that is, in the overlap between the physical setting and the sense of belonging to a collectivity (see Staszak 2003: 341–2; Agier 2010: 67). In his work on the Augustan *vici*, Lott also proposes useful theoretical considerations, based on sociological and geographical schemas and the concept of neighbourhood, defined more broadly as 'a social structure operating in a physical container, a continuous and stable population in a pattern of physical structures and spaces' (D. Greer, cited by Lott 2004: 12).

[42] Purcell 1994: 659–73. See also Magalhães de Oliveira in this volume.
[43] Reynolds 1996: 150–8; Guilhembet 2011.
[44] *CIL* 4.138, 1136; *CIL* 5.4488, and *CIL* 6.1682 and 29791, discussed in Courrier 2014: 146–8, 153–4.
[45] See, for example, the buildings of the 'vicus Capitis Africae' (Cavallo, Coppola and Pavolini 1998), the Ara Coeli (Packer 1968–9 and Priester 2002), the Piazza del Cinquecento (Pettinau 1996) or the ancient Via Lata/Flaminia (Gros 2001: 115).
[46] Pedroni 1992; Reynolds 1996; Madeleine 2008. [47] See Courrier 2014: 154–7.
[48] Among many others, see most recently Tarpin 2008.
[49] Note most recently Tran 2006 and Dondin-Payre and Tran 2012 (with up-to-date references).

latter. To show respect to his distinguished guest, he sent a slave to the local tavern for wine – the same place he would usually buy the cheap wine that was all he could afford. This time, however, the slave took his time to taste the wine more carefully and chose some of better quality. He must have been a very regular customer, for the tavern owner immediately noticed the change in his habits. He thus questioned the slave, who – thinking he could trust this man he had been interacting with every day for years, and whom he considered to be an old acquaintance – told the innkeeper that his master was hosting Mark Antony himself. Unfortunately for the orator, as soon as the slave left, the innkeeper went straight to Marius.[50] While one is aware of the double stereotype at play here (naïve slave/crooked innkeeper eager to gossip), the religious undertones used by Plutarch should not go unnoticed. He calls the innkeeper impious (*asebēs kai miaros*), to indicate that the betrayal of a resident of his own neighbourhood was an act of sacrilege, even if the innkeeper was one of Marius' followers. This *exemplum* reveals that, for daily errands, people would just 'go downstairs' or 'go round the corner': it is notable in this respect that the fragments of the *Forma Urbis Marmorea*, including those most recently discovered, indicate that there were shops on almost every street.[51] Above all, it illustrates that, within a given neighbourhood, everyone knew everyone else,[52] and formed a clearly delimited group.[53]

In the same way, the communal quality of apartment buildings, structured around courtyards with shops opening on to the courtyards rather than on to the street (common on the *FVM* and in Ostia) is highly suggestive. Even though the courtyard was not designed to exclude 'non-residents' as such, it nevertheless functioned as a kind of private *macellum*, while collective services clearly went beyond money matters. Indeed, the sense of belonging to a community, to a geographically specific place, was

---

[50] Plu. *Mar.* 44.1–3. This anecdote is found in very similar terms in Appian (App. *B.C.* 1.72. 333–5), with the exception of one – major – element: Mark Antony takes refuge not in Rome but 'in the countryside'. This difference is inexplicable.

[51] See Reynolds 1996; Meneghini and Santangeli Valenziani 2006; Madeleine 2008.

[52] Sources and analyses are gathered in Courrier 2014: 142–85. The dossier of modes of orientation and of rumour as tools of communication are particularly revealing of this state of affairs, as is the genealogical stability of the quarter, which can also be reconstructed epigraphically.

[53] Lott 2004 comes to similar conclusions (a specific identity proper to each quarter of Rome) with regard to the *vici* of the *Urbs*. In Courrier 2014: 135–41, I show that the scale of these sentiments of belonging was, in fact, without doubt lesser in this case. In effect, the *vicus*, which housed between 2,500 and 4,500 inhabitants (according to the sources) in areas of more than 5 hectares on average, was most probably too large to foster what we could see as a true 'daily sociability' of the quarter.

heightened by elements such as *lacus, balnea, collegia* and even *sacella*. At Ostia (our principal source of information on this point), the House of the Lararium was furnished with a basin in the interior courtyard and a *lararium* (which gave the building its name). This domestic furniture gave the inhabitants a sense of belonging to the same community or collective.[54] The House of Diana was divided into apartments which shared common services: a latrine and a fountain. The Building of Serapis and the Building of the Charioteers formed a single complex with the Baths of the Seven Sages, the ensemble having been conceived from the start as a single building project. Although the baths were not private, or even reserved for the inhabitants or users of these two *insulae* alone, the porticoed courtyard of the Building of Serapis functioned as a sort of vestibule for the baths, just as the layout of the Building of the Charioteers was clearly designed to facilitate access for the inhabitants to the bath establishment: two north–south corridors traversed the complex and gave on to a third east–west *ambulacra*, directly opening on to the baths. At Rome, *insula* E (dating from the beginning of the second century CE, uncovered at the time of the construction of Termini railway station), was provided with a bath complex that was private property (it was linked to a *domus*) but for public use (between the *domus* and the baths an independent entrance gave on to a staircase which led to the apartments on the upper floors). The scale of the baths suggests that it served the needs of the whole quarter (five adjacent buildings have been discovered here).[55]

Epitaphs which list both a place and an occupation provide further evidence of a meaningful connection between people and neighbourhood. For example, that of Lucius Statius Onesimus reads 'viae Appiae multorum annorum negotia(n)s' (trader on the Via Appia for many years).[56] Moreover, this sense of belonging so deeply shaped neighbourhood culture that it determined the residents' collective behaviour: that is, the interests of the community prevailed over those of individuals. We see this in 121 BCE, when M. Fulvius Flaccus, on the run from the consul L. Opimius and his followers, took refuge with a shopkeeper whom he knew. Not knowing in which house he was hiding, his pursuers threatened to burn down the whole neighbourhood. The shopkeeper did not want to betray Flaccus (perhaps for reasons of clientage) and did not want to put the neighbourhood in danger: rather than turn Flaccus in

---

[54] For a detailed account of these building complexes, see Packer 1971; Gros 2001: 125–6.
[55] Wallace-Hadrill 2000: 206–8.
[56] *CIL* 6.9663. See the documentation gathered in Virlouvet 2006: 52–4; Monteix 2012: 341; Courrier 2014: 185–9.

himself, he asked another resident to hand him over.[57] As Lott has suggested, this threat in itself implies the existence of a neighbourhood community – a community whose interests and activities were bound to a particular space. The concerns of this community were not limited to the celebration of Compitalia. This was a community of people who knew exactly who lived where, and who were capable of pressurizing their fellow residents to act for the sake of the community as a whole.

The daily life of the plebs, then, took place on a local scale, sustained by the hustle and bustle of the neighbourhood, within which each plebeian found his own community of belonging, organized around family, work and neighbours. The megalopolis was structured by individual neighbourhoods, creating spaces where people could interact, establish collective memory and define their identity.[58] These neighbourhoods bore witness to the existence of a stable demographic group, entirely alien to the model presented by the 'urban graveyard effect'. It is clear that a large proportion of the plebs were attached to their neighbourhoods and maintained a rapport with this urban space which would have been impossible for a deracinated population. This stability is further illustrated in the activities men and women developed in the *Urbs* and to which they formed substantial attachments. The first of these was professional activity. The plebs was not, of course, a group of idlers. On the contrary, professional occupation constituted an essential characteristic of the plebeian *habitus*.

Professional Culture and Plebeian Identity

Following the work of Francesco M. de Robertis,[59] the aristocratic disdain for work has generally been contrasted with plebeian professional pride. It is true that Cicero's[60] disdain for small businesses is clear, and this sharply contrasts with the positive image of work illustrated by the numerous funerary monuments erected by plebeians.[61] Even here, however, social stratification is made visible in details such as the size of the funerary plot, the material used and the scale: from simple epitaphs to carefully engraved altars. Admittedly, these details reveal a striking social

---

[57] App. *B.C.* 1.26.118. On this passage, see Lott 2004: 47–8. [58] Agier 2010: 74.
[59] De Robertis 1963: 49–83.
[60] For example, Cic. *Off.* 1.150–1. However, this general feeling of disdain is not universal in Roman literature, not even in Cicero's work; at times, a sense of aristocratic recognition of work well done can be found: see here Tran 2011: 126–32; Courrier 2014: 286–92; and D'Ercole 2014.
[61] Joshel 1992 counted 1,262 men and 208 women in Rome who mentioned their work in their epitaph.

heterogeneity. But they also point to the fact that professional pride did not always equate with success in business.[62] In fact, pride might also come from *savoir-faire*, from technical expertise, from an honest reputation and even from sensitivity to *labor* as a moral value.[63] In this sense, we may identify a single[64] shared vision of professional activity, which brought plebeians together around shared values. These values can be briefly summarized: first, a job well done provided a way for individuals to gain honour and excellence within a group that is often depicted in the literary sources as an unformed mass without hierarchy or distinctions. Second, it furnished a justification for making money (providing it was done honestly) and improving one's standard of living, in spite of the scorn this aroused in the Roman aristocratic mentality. An exceptional document, found in Rome and dating to the end of the Republic or the very beginning of the Empire, epitomizes this concept of work well and honestly done. Composed by the deceased himself, M. Valerius Celer, the epitaph presents an honest and parsimonious tradesman, but also a tireless worker: 'M. Valerius Celer | bublarius qui plura maluit emereri | quam consumere. Hic | fide et amicitia sanctissimus | sibi et suis fec(it)'.[65] The dead man presents two different ways of life: the dogged pursuit of economic success through hard work and a comfortable lifestyle of careless expenditure. He himself prefers the first path – the regular increase of earnings through consistent effort. This is reflected in the term *emereri* – the concept of deserved and honestly gained success, founded on bonds of trust with friends and clients (*fide et amicitia*).

Finally, work could provide a basis for social ascent for the professional plebs in their own circles[66] and, sometimes, though more rarely, even among the social elite of Roman society.[67] The prevalence of such a discourse – regardless of the quite diverse social realities it implied – is significant. In terms of social psychology, we can understand such pride as

---

[62] Courrier 2014: 232–52: cases of workers proud of their professions, even though the evidence clearly shows that these did not make them rich; *contra* Veyne 2005: 137.

[63] See Tran 2013 for a recent analysis of these plebeian professional values.

[64] Of course, there were many nuances to take into account. Cf., for instance, the way the *plebs media* – which did not represent the 'average' plebs, but rather an infra-equestrian elite – conceived of professional activities. See here Courrier 2014: 368–400.

[65] AE 1991.122: 'Marcus Valerius Celer, beef trader, who preferred to earn rather than squander; a man for whom keeping his word and friendship were the most sacred things. He made [this tomb] for himself and his family.'

[66] On the monuments of the *plebs media*, such as the tomb of M. Vergilius Eurysaces, see Courrier 2014: 368–400. Eurysaces could not omit the very thing that enabled him to 'arrive', his *métier* as *pistor*. On this monument see most recently Petersen 2003 and 2006.

[67] Examples are very rare (*CLE* 1868; *CIL* 8.11824; *AE* 1960.116) and all from North Africa.

a 'coping mechanism', as plebeians sought personal fulfilment where it was available: in this case, in the field of professional activity. Even if this did not quite take the form of a *collective* apologia for work (professional merits were nearly always individually praised), the very repetitiveness of the values conveyed by these professional epitaphs is revealing of a culture that ruled the workers' behaviours among themselves and, beyond, within the Roman social order as a whole.[68]

Macrobius gives a telling example of this in a book dedicated to *bons mots* from the past. He recounts a misfortune experienced in court by L. Munatius Plancus.[69] While pleading for a friend, he set out to ruin the reputation of the prosecution witness whom he knew to be a cobbler (*sutor*). He asked the witness how he made a living. The cobbler replied: *gallam subigo* ('I grind the gall-nut': the pun does not work in English). He wittily played on the name of one of his tools (oak gall)[70] in order to allude to the rumour of adultery that targeted Plancus and a certain Maevia Galla. In other words, the consul-to-be in 42 BCE intended to undermine the credibility of a witness by employing classic aristocratic stereotypes that looked down on the world of work, such as the servitude induced by *labor*, dishonesty of material gain, and the stigma of dependency. He was instead outwitted as the cobbler turned the object of his scorn against him. The cobbler's sense of humour epitomizes the self-awareness and dignity of a man who took pride in his profession, using the tools of his trade to make a political point. It also highlights, in its own way, the conflict between the two systems of representation of work. Professional pride therefore was not only expressed among the plebs. It also provided a way of affirming the place of workers in Roman society in the public sphere (for this tale concerns the credibility of a witness who was challenged precisely about his professional occupation) and to counter-balance aristocratic disdain.

The assertion of professional pride in a context of politicized humour and criticism is akin to another specific characteristic shared by subaltern groups who turn the very grounds of their social exclusion back against the groups who exclude them. That is, the culture of the *plebs urbana* shares some characteristics of a culture of resistance, something often seen as typical of popular cultures, at least as defined by many sociologists. Claude Grignon, Jean-Claude Passeron, Richard Hoggart and Stuart Hall have

---

[68] Agier 2010: 40–4.
[69] Macr. 2.2.6. I am grateful to Pascal Montlahuc (Université Paris 7) who shared this anecdote. For an in-depth study of the pride shoemakers took in their expertise, see D'Ercole 2014.
[70] For the technical aspects of *sutores*' work, see D'Ercole 2014: 237–8.

shown that popular cultures are often constructed in the context of the domination of an official/accepted 'model' culture, to which they oppose their own standards.[71] As we saw in Macrobius' anecdote, these standards owe much to the plebs' attempt at resistance to cultural domination. The dominated section of a population usually reacts to the cultural model that is imposed on them with (variously) derision, provocation or a deliberate display of bad taste. These are traditional, or indeed typical, devices of ironic subversion or manipulation of cultural inculcation.[72] In this sense, popular cultures are counter-cultures/cultures of contestation – and that of the *plebs urbana* was no exception.

Political Culture and Collective Action

A crucial point here is the fact that a large part of the *plebs urbana* in Rome – *c.* 150,000 to 200,000 inhabitants and their families (at least from the time of Julius Caesar onwards) – benefited from *frumentationes* and enjoyed privileged living conditions such as owning or renting property of some kind,[73] as well as belonging to a social network and having a professional activity, all of which inculcated a strong sense of belonging in the city. This is precisely what we saw in the case of Macrobius' *sutor*. Of course, Macrobius' text does not reveal whether or not the shoemaker benefited from the *frumentationes*. It does, however, show us a craftsman who is able to testify in court and to rebut aristocratic contempt[74] (which is in itself the sign of a certain degree of culture). Above all, the use the *sutor* made of the *rumor* proves him to be clearly embedded in social relationships between people of the same background and fully integrated into the political life of the city.

This example can be connected to a large number of ancient texts which show that plebeians in literary sources do not represent the dregs of Roman society.[75] Admittedly, it is impossible to determine strict rules according to which one can associate a specific social category with a specific Latin or Greek word, and we must concede that the vague terms describing Rome's

---

[71] Among others, see Hoggart 1957; Hall 1973 (and, more broadly, the works of the Centre for Contemporary Cultural Studies); Grignon and Passeron 1989 and Scott 1990. For antiquity, Purcell 1994: 678 (see the passage by Purcell in Grig's Introduction (p. 36) as well as the chapters by Toner and Rosillo-López in this volume).
[72] Toner 2009: 92–122.   [73] Virlouvet 2009: 1.
[74] On the theory of cultural legitimacy, see Grignon and Passeron 1989: 18–60.
[75] Virlouvet 1985: 54–63.

citizen population (*plebs* and *populus* in Latin; *dēmos* and its derivatives *to dēmotikon, dēmotikoi, hoi Rōmaioi* in Greek) or mere crowds (*multitudo, vulgus, turba; homilos, okhlos, polloi, plēthos*) are ones that are used synonymously,[76] although they actually encompass diverse social categories. By contrast, it is worth mentioning how difficult it is to find any term explicitly stigmatizing the poverty of those who took part in elections and riots (*inopes; penētes*). One may find in the vagueness of this lexical field an echo of the fact that those texts generally contain no description at all of the rioters as *poor*: even when texts do give more details, the social categories that appear in the sources still say nothing about poor outcasts.

In 58 BCE, according to Cicero, Clodius repeatedly ordered the closing of shops so as to recruit his 'troops', which Cicero himself confirms when he admits that he owed his comeback to the Italian *municipia* rather than to the *tabernarii*.[77] We know that in 53 BCE the same Clodius, pursued by Antonius, also had to take shelter, this time in a bookshop (*taberna libraria*).[78] In April 52 BCE, T. Munatius Plancus invited the *populus* to take part in a *contio*, requesting the greatest number possible to be present in the Forum the next day in order to support Clodius and prevent Milo's acquittal; he was obeyed so completely that all the shops in the city were closed.[79] The shops were also the first to be closed when the news of Caesar's murder spread.[80] And when, in 37 BCE, M. Oppius contemplated resigning from his post as an aedile because he lacked the necessary funds to continue (he had been among the 'proscribed' and all his properties had been confiscated), he was such a favourite among the people (*dēmos*) that the craftsmen of the city (*kheirotekhnai*) performed the work required by Oppius' aedileship without being paid for it, in order to allow him to manage the expense. Appian also mentions that some spectators, a certain number of whom must have been the craftsmen he had just described, threw money into the pit of a theatre during the games Oppius had organized – enough to make him rich.[81] Even allowing for exaggeration, this is significant insofar as it shows that craftsmen were able, in Appian's eyes, to support a magistrate collectively. This suggests that their economic situation was not exactly one of poverty. Indeed, these plebeians were not outcasts in the politicians' pay: they were rather part of the world of small shops and craftsmen, owners of some kind of property, professionally

---

[76] See Yavetz 1969: 141–55 and Courrier 2014: 489–97.
[77] Cic. *Sen.* 32–3; *Red. pop.* 13; *Dom.* 54, 89, 129; *Sest.* 34; *Pis.* 23.
[78] Cic. *Mil.* 40; *Phil.* 2.21 and 49.
[79] Cic. *Mil.* 3; Asc. 40–2C; Plu. *Cic.* 35.1–5; App. *B.C.* 2.24.90; Cass. Dio 40.54.1–3.
[80] Plu. *Caes.* 67.1–6; Cass. Dio 44.20.   [81] App. *B.C.* 4.41.172–4.

active and financially independent. They could therefore act entirely in their own interests.[82] The (political) culture of the plebs did not entirely depend on the aristocratic system of senators[83] or on networks of clientage.[84]

Other examples of collective activities likewise demonstrate that the plebs had the means to act in their own interest. Despite the scorn expressed in literary sources for the urban population – always depicted as a volatile, incoherent and easily manipulated crowd[85] – a focus on the collective behaviour of the plebs proves otherwise. These instances of collective behaviour – that is, of people gathering together in order to promote or to protect their interests[86] – in fact suggest that Roman city-dwellers knew how to make themselves heard by those who governed them. Examples I have collected elsewhere (organized and freely accessible in an online database[87]) clearly demonstrate the existence of a political culture, centred around themes and values that went far beyond the cliché of bread and circuses. Even if problems with the food supply certainly constituted an important cause of popular mobilization under both the Republic and the Empire, this was not the only motivation for action by the plebeians, nor should such movements be seen as hunger riots, pure and simple.[88] Under the Republic, the people made themselves heard regarding

---

[82] See on this point Virlouvet 1985: 54–63 and Yavetz's classic study (1969). The bibliography is vast; for full citation see Courrier 2014, noting here only Nicolet 1976; Vanderbroeck 1987; Flaig 1994; Purcell 1994; Millar 1998; Yakobson 1999; Mouritsen 2001; and Hölkeskamp 2010.

[83] On the politicization of the plebs during the republican period: Courrier 2014: 427–603. *Contra* see, for example, Flaig 1994 and Hölkeskamp 2010. For an assessment of the historiographical debate engendered by the work of Fergus Millar, see most recently Hurlet 2012.

[84] On the insufficiency of interpretations purely in terms of patronage, see Le Gall 1971; Rouland 1979: 401–91; Nippel 1995: 70–84; and Flaig 1994: 19–20.

[85] On the manifold sources, see Courrier 2014: 1–3. During the republican period 'the crowd' of the *Urbs* was considered *imperitus* (ignorant), *inconditus* (disordered), *tumultuosus* (turbulent) and *ventosus* (changeable like the wind: that is, fickle and susceptible to sudden changes of attitude). The crowd was equally *perditus* (desperate, lost) and *infimus* (of the lowest level). No form of collective deliberation could be attributed to a group presented as a mass as numerous as it was uninformed – always treated collectively as a monolithic bloc, dependent on handouts, and politically menacing.

[86] Vanderbroeck 1987: 15 and 218 (with bibliographical references). Among the many works dealing with 'collective actions' or popular pressure, those of Charles Tilly and his theory of 'repertoires of contention' have been particularly influential.

[87] http://actoz.db.huma-num.fr/fmi/webd#. The following references to collective behaviour refer to the database, also published in Courrier 2014, where they are fully documented; here, the sources concerned are briefly indicated in brackets.

[88] As recently noted by Magalhães de Oliveira 2012: 18 – 'Les débats récents sur les conflits et les violences de la période [Late Antiquity] continuent en grande mesure à véhiculer ce que Edward P. Thompson a appelé "une vision spasmodique de l'histoire populaire", selon laquelle

matters of political morals – the behaviour of magistrates, for instance[89] – as well as the division of power within the *res publica*, particularly the area of responsibility of the Senate.[90] The plebs also voiced concerns about the extension of citizenship (before the Social War) and the division of the new citizens into tribes after the same war.[91] They addressed questions regarding what we could categorize as 'foreign policy',[92] but also economics: remission of debts and rent, as well as protests against taxes that were too high.[93]

While it is difficult to identify the precise composition of such a group, the political actions of the plebs as an entity in itself surface in both group consciousness and motivation. We can trace a widely shared sense among a large proportion of the plebs – that of being driven by the same feeling of belonging to one stratum, subject to the same constraints. In other words, the plebs shared a cultural identity which permitted them to coordinate their efforts on the basis of shared interests. They were aware that they shared a single culture, through which they could affirm points of social and cultural particularity.[94] The repetitiveness of the methods used in collective action – from votes to violence, from acclamation to riots – is also illustrative of this collective capacity to take a political stand. In this regard, the election for consulship of 107 BCE is enlightening. The plebeians' decision to vote for Marius was presented by Sallust as having been politically motivated by the contents of letters from Roman citizens stationed in Africa, sent to their contacts in Rome, relating the disastrous command of Metellus during the Jugurthine War.[95] Clearly politics, and foreign policy in particular, played a key role in this election, leading the electorate to take a position on military matters, the consequences of which, principally as regarded the food supply, could not be overlooked. The letters from the Romans on the ground were not about personal matters, but dealt with issues of public interest: the way in which the war was being conducted

les interventions du peuple dans la scène historique sont interprétées comme des réactions occasionnelles et compulsives à des stimulations extérieures.' See Thompson 1971.

[89] See in the database nos. 17 (Sall. *Iug.* 33–34), 37 (Cic. *Clu.* 4–5, 77, 79, 90, 93–5, 103–5, 108–13) and 120 (a magistrate's behaviour: Cic. *Fam.* 8.2.1); 19 (Cic. *de Orat.* 2.197; *Off.* 2.49), 102 (Plu. *Crass.* 16.4-7), 109–10 (Cic. *Q. fr.* 3.1.24; 3.5.7; Cass. Dio 39.59.1–63.5) and 148 (breaking a religious norm: Suet. *Aug.* 70.1–2) and 165 (Suet. *Cl.* 1.1; Cass. Dio 44.5); 166–7 (observance of the family rules: App. *B.C.* 4.41.172–174; Cass, Dio 48.53.4–6).

[90] E.g., no. 46: Asc. 58–9 and 74–6C; Cass. Dio 36.38.4–5, 39.1–4, 40.1.

[91] Nos. 27 (Cic. *Phil.* 8.7; Plu. *Sull.* 8.1–8; App. *B.C.* 1.55–56.240–9), 29 (App. *B.C.* 1.64.286–92; see also Cic. *Phil.* 8.7; Vell. 2.20.2 and Plu. *Mar.* 41.1). See Courrier 2014: 479.

[92] Nos. 1 (Plu. *TG* 5–7), 18 (Sall. *Iug.* 73.6), 42–4, 160. See Courrier 2014: 480–9.

[93] Nos. 56, 123 (Cass. Dio 41.38.1–3), 124, 125.   [94] Cuche 1996: 83–4.   [95] Sall. *Iug.* 73.3–6.

and the hope of quickly reaching peace, which would be better for business.[96] From a more general standpoint, the desire for peace and stability was a significant cause of the mobilization of the plebs.[97] Contrary to the stereotypes conveyed by writers such as Sallust, plebeians were not eager for major changes. The reason is simple: they did not constitute a *Lumpenproletariat*, always on the lookout for reasons to start a riot, but rather a stable, even conservative component of Roman society, who were attached to its activities and identified themselves with the city's institutions.

It was not easy to manipulate the plebs. Plebeians knew how to defend their own interests, even when these differed from the struggles that were steered by popular leaders, whom they did not always obey. Thus, in Cicero's account of the trouble caused by Clodius' factions, the plebeians became involved and followed the latter until early September 57 BCE.[98] But once the plebs was satisfied, which was clear when Pompey obtained *cura annonae*, the crowd deserted Clodius and calm returned to the *Urbs*.[99] The unrest was then not entirely down to the gangs of Clodius, and his leadership was not absolute. We can draw similar conclusions for 63–2 BCE, when the Senate, at the initiative of Cato, acted to dissipate the threat of sedition posed by Caesar by taking measures regarding the grain dole.[100] Likewise, in 48 BCE, if we accept the idea that Caesar's *remissio* was a response to the unrest caused by M. Caelius Rufus, the plebs stopped supporting the praetor[101] as soon as an acceptable financial settlement (in the case of rent) was assured. In these cases we see that the discontent of some of the people regarding food provision could converge with the political ambitions of one man;[102] it was, however, impossible entirely to channel and coordinate the collective actions of the plebeians.

Naturally, these political modes changed with the advent of the Principate. Once linked to the life of the Forum, to *contiones* and *comitia*, they were progressively integrated to the ludic scene.[103] The plebeians were

---

[96] Yakobson 1999: 158–9.
[97] Nos. 1 (Plu. *TG* 5–7), 121 (Plu. *Caes.* 30.2; *Pomp.* 58, 4–5; App. *B.C.* 2.27.106), 151 (Cic. *Ad Brut.* 1.3.1–3.2; *Phil.* 14.10 and 14–15), 160–2 (for the republican period).
[98] Nos. 86–7: Cic. *Att.* 4.1.6–7; *Fam.* 5.17.2; *Dom.* 6–7, 10–18; Cass. Dio 39.9.2–3.
[99] For more details on how the situation abated, see Virlouvet 1985: 41.
[100] No. 57: Plu. *Caes.* 8.5–7; *Cat. Mi.* 26.1; *Mor.* 818D.
[101] No. 124: The riots are only mentioned at Caes. *Civ.* 3.20–1 and Cass. Dio 42.22; the debt moratorium: Caes. *Civ.* 3.20–1; the remission of rents: Caes. *Civ.* 3.20–1; Cass. Dio 42.22; the *tabulae novae*: Caes. *Civ.* 3.20–1; Liv. 111; Vell. 2.68.1–3 and Cass. Dio 42.22. See Courrier 2014: 818–19.
[102] Virlouvet 1985: 41.
[103] Fraschetti 1990; Benoist 1999; Roman and Roman 2007; Courrier 2014: 650–82.

not, however, the depoliticized people depicted by Juvenal.[104] On the contrary, little by little, they formed a new privileged group that had direct contact with the most powerful *patronus* of all.[105] Every time they cheered for the emperor, they expressed both their privilege and its implications.[106] They had to take advantage of these moments when they met with the *princeps* – instances which did not just serve to legitimate the power of the ruler, but also as occasions to express their own political opinions. They seized opportunities given by entertainments at the circus, theatre and amphitheatre, privileged (even though not exclusive) sites for interaction between plebs and *princeps*, to express opinions on subjects that were not always to do with the spectacle they were attending. Needless to say, in a monarchical regime relying on the delegation of powers and the tacit acceptance of the right to rule of one individual, the stakes were high and the reaction of the ultimate authority was particularly important.[107]

Looking at entertainment venues alone, we can designate roughly three kinds of collective demands:[108]

- Demands as to the nature of the entertainment itself: people pleaded for comedians to be freed,[109] demanded to see certain actors or gladiators,[110] and protested against the choice of a victor in some theatre contest.[111] They also asked for gladiators to be executed,[112] for favours to be granted to certain factions[113] and for the *princeps* to organize certain types of games.[114]
- Socio-economic demands: plebeians protested against the high cost of wheat,[115] against tax increases or newly created taxes.[116] Certain other demands may also have taken place during the games: demands to reduce the price of wine (in 19 BCE)[117] and wheat (in 19 CE)[118] in

---

[104] Juv. 10.72–81. [105] See Flaig 1992: 38–92. [106] Aldrete 1999; Ménard 2004: 59.
[107] See also Tom Hawkins' paper in this volume.
[108] It is not possible to provide here an exhaustive analysis of the plebs' political interventions in imperial Rome. However, entertainment venues are an ideal lens through which one can scrutinize the collective actions and the political culture they claimed under the Empire.
[109] Nos. 197 (Sen. *Ben.* 2.19.1; Gel. 5.14; Ael. *De nat. anim.* 7.48; see also Plin. *Nat.* 8.56), 202 (Suet. *Tib.* 47).
[110] Nos. 199 (Cass. Dio 56.47.2; see also Tac. *Ann.* 1.54.2 and 77.1), 228 (Suet. *Cal.* 30), 240 (Cass. Dio 60.28.3), 252 (Tac. *Ann.* 16.21.7).
[111] Nos. 204 (Tac. *Ann.* 1.77.1), 212? (Tac. *Ann.* 4.14.3; Suet. *Tib.* 37; Cass. Dio 57.21.3), 246 (Tac. *Ann.* 13.25.4, 14.21.4). See Courrier 2014: 669–70.
[112] No. 229 (Suet. *Cal.* 30). [113] No. 282 (Suet. *Vit.* 14).
[114] Nos. 290 (Suet. *Vit.* 8), 291 (Suet. *Dom.* 4). [115] No. 221 (Tac. *Ann.* 6.13).
[116] No. 234 (Jos. *AJ* 19.4.24–7; Cass. Dio 59.28.11).
[117] No. 178 (Suet. *Aug.* 42.1; Cass. Dio 54.11.7).
[118] No. 208 (Tac. *Ann.* 87.1; see also Jos. *Ap.* 2.63; Tac. *Ann.* 2.59.1 and Suet. *Tib.* 52).

a pressurized economic situation. Protests against *centesima rerum venalium* in 15 CE,[119] against the tax *pro edulibus* in 40 CE[120] and the excesses of publicans in 58 CE,[121] unfolded the same way, with the crowd directly addressing the *princeps*.

– Political protests: this broadly references complaints driven by moral motivations – in other words, demands in response to the (bad) behaviour of the *princeps*. There are many examples. In the theatre, the plebeians requested that Tiberius gave back Lysippus' *Apoxyomenos*, a statue Agrippa had placed in front of his thermal baths and that Tiberius had transported to the *cubiculum* of the palace:[122] this complaint, made several times, was linked to the proprietorial sense felt by the Roman people – the sense that such ornaments should remain accessible to all in the city; it also speaks to the role of the artefact as a memory device, connected with Agrippa's policy of returning art to the public sphere, as well as the monitoring of water policy for which the *Apoxyomenos* functioned as a 'memory catalyst'.[123] Again, it was in the theatre that the plebs, feeling abandoned, protested against Tiberius' retreat to Capri.[124] At the theatre, the circus and the amphitheatre, there were demonstrations against Caligula's despotism, because not only did Caligula act against senators, but he also started victimizing the plebs in late 38.[125] In the theatre, the plebs also demonstrated against Galba's acquisitiveness.[126] In this category of protests, I would also add a few more instances which, although political in nature, were not directly linked to the behaviour of the *princeps*: most likely at the theatre, harsh taunts against a *consularis*;[127] at the theatre and circus, multiple demands for the execution of Tigellinus;[128] and, at the stadium, a special request to Domitian to have Palfurius Sura, an informer, reinstated as senator.[129]

This brief overview (for reasons of space, I deal only with sites associated with the *ludi*) highlights a few constants. The first is also the most evident: while the attention and reactions of plebeians sometimes did depend on

---

[119] No. 205 (Tac. *Ann.* 1.78.2). [120] No. 233 (Plin. *Nat.* 19.56; Suet. *Cal.* 40; Cass. Dio 59.28.8).
[121] No. 247 (Tac. *Ann.* 13.50–1; Suet. *Nero* 10). [122] No. 201 (Plin. *Nat.* 34.62).
[123] On Agrippa's project to put on public display works of art previously only visible in the private homes of the wealthy, see Plin. *Nat.* 35.26; for a full-scale analysis, see Courrier forthcoming.
[124] No. 215 (Suet. *Tib.* 43 and 45; see also Tac. *Ann.* 4.57–9; 67).
[125] Nos. 227 (Suet. *Cal.* 30; Cass. Dio 59.13.1–9; see also Sen. *Ir.* 3.19.2), 230 (Cass. Dio 59.13.6), 231 (Cass. Dio 59.13.7), 232 (Suet. *Cl.* 7).
[126] No. 266 (Suet. *Gal.* 12–13). [127] No. 242 (Tac. *Ann.* 11.13).
[128] Nos. 267 (Plu. *Gal.* 17.2–6), 272 (Tac. *Hist.* 1.72.1–4).
[129] No. 292 (Suet. *Dom.* 13; *Schol. ad Juv.* 4.53).

the *ludi*, issues were also raised that had nothing to do with the spectacles themselves. Nonetheless, the range of themes brought up was not particularly diverse. In fact, it focused more or less entirely on the behaviour of the *princeps*, whereby the plebs shared certain normative expectations and would protest if these were not respected. In such circumstances, as shown by Zvi Yavetz,[130] the emperor had to be in Rome (his absence gave significant grounds for the protests of the Roman people);[131] he had to abide by the conventions of public places (some places and objects were to remain at everyone's disposal). He also had to pay attention to the plebs' desires, well-being and dignity by ensuring the food supply and reasonable taxes. He had, in other words, to position himself as a generous benefactor, for avarice was not tolerated. Since the 10s BCE, the ceremonial context of the games had helped construct the *princeps* as the *only* spokesperson for the people of the *Urbs*, with a monopoly on communications with the masses. For their part, the people quickly latched onto the political implications of this change of regime, and they profited from the many occasions now at their disposal to address themselves directly to the source of power and to present their requests.

Conclusion: The Plebs and the City, a Politically and Professionally Integrated Urban Culture

It is clear that the image of famished masses living in conditions of the most basic sanitation is an out-dated stereotype. The 'average' plebeian in the *Urbs* had things to lose: a family, possessions, a job, a social life and sometimes even access to *frumentationes*. The grain supply was a civic privilege, and those who benefited from it understood the distinction it represented. This distinction meant that the plebs was part of the city and its institutions, and connected to its leaders. The culture of the plebs, then, was a culture of stability, an urban culture (that is, defined by a specific pattern of '*être-en-ville*'), professionally and politically integrated. The plebs was neither shapeless nor fickle, and in terms of politics, plebeians pursued matters beyond its stomach and its pleasures. From this standpoint, while power in Rome did not rely on public opinion, it was

---

[130] Yavetz 1969.
[131] See nos. 175–6 (Cass. Dio 54.6.1–3), 177 (Vell. 2.91.3–9 and 92.1–5; Cass. Dio 53.24.4–6 and 54.10.1–2; see also Sen. *Cl.* 3.7.6; Tac. *Ann.* 1.10.4), 215 (Suet. *Tib.* 43 and 45; see also Tac. *Ann.* 4. 57–9; 67), 216 (Tac. *Ann.* 4.62–3; Plin. *Ep.* 6.20; Suet. *Tib.* 40), 225 (Suet. *Cal.* 14), 237 (Suet. *Cl.* 12), 259 (Tac. *Ann.* 15.36), 275 (Tac. *Hist.* 1.90).

nonetheless a place where the governed could make themselves heard by those who ruled them. As a result of this socio-economic stability, the plebs was a group profoundly integrated into community life and therefore perfectly able both to reason and to justify its choices, based on a background of common interests, built on possessions and rights it had held for a long time. A number of elements combined to consolidate the place of the plebs in urban space. They were rooted in the city in *vici*, in daily proximity to the aristocracy, due to the general lack of urban zoning. By means of multiple ritual ceremonies (the *census*, the vote, games, festivals and even links of clientage) and, later, under the Empire, through the attention paid by the emperor to his people, the plebs came to represent a group of Roman citizens with firmly established rights. They were involved in all the activities that reinforced the civic pact of the *Urbs* and that sanctioned its existence as a political community, without ever erasing their autonomous existence as a specifically plebeian culture.

6 | Pollio's Paradox: Popular Invective and the Transition to Empire

TOM HAWKINS

> Quid enim gladiatoribus clamores innumerabilium civium? quid *populi* versus? (*Cic.* Phil. *1.36*)

'I'll keep quiet. For it's not easy to play the scribe against one who can *pro*scribe.' This was Asinius Pollio's retort to the Fescennine verses that Octavian had written about him some time during the triumvirate. Pollio's wit exemplifies the transformation of invective strategies at the end of the Republic that highlighted the political dimension of popular abuse directed at leading figures.[1] This exchange, in which an ex-consul calls attention to a triumvir's tyrannical abuses, continues a long Roman tradition of intra-elite status negotiation via invective sound-bites, but Octavian's increasing consolidation of political and military power had begun to change the parameters of such discourse. Yet popular political invective suffered no such attenuation. I will, thus, be using the term 'popular' in two interrelated ways: first, as the unmarked social opposite of the marked category of 'elite', and, second, as a sign of invective's rhetorical directionality, which (however facetiously) attempts to erode the social status of the target.[2] The first sense will apply largely to the anonymous chants, verses and shouts of mass audiences, which in any given instance may or may not have been fomented by elite agents, but which emerge in our sources as an anonymous, broadly non-elite voice; and the second usage will support my argument that, while the *princeps* constrained the freedom of elite speakers, non-elite invective, because of its diffuse nature, could engage the emperor more freely. In Hall's terms of the dialectic between popular and hegemonic culture, therefore, I see popular invective as a bottom-up admonitory rhetoric that became increasingly important as aristocrats' freedom to chastise Roman leadership decreased.[3]

---

[1] Macrobius preserves this anecdote without social contextualization in a list of quips attributed to Octavian/Augustus (*Sat.* 2.4.21): 'Temporibus triumviralibus Pollio, cum Fescenninos in eum Augustus scripsisset, ait: at ego taceo. Non est enim facile in eum scribere qui potest proscribere.'
[2] This definition of 'popular' follows that of Toner 2009: 1.
[3] See Hall 1981 and the Introduction to this volume.

In the coming pages I will first discuss invective in terms of its social register and the difference between literary analysis and interpersonal communication. I will then outline some prominent popular and elite republican patterns of politicized invective before focusing on the imperial situation. I will argue that the presence of the emperor changed the rules of the Roman invective game such that popular invective took on a greater role in Roman life. The two primary reasons for this change were the constraints on elite behaviour and the close relationship between the imperial regime and massive, monumentalized spectacle architecture.

Popular Invective

Invective is a verbal assault upon a target.[4] We can attempt to sub-divide this definition between elite and popular forms – though these categories prove messier than they might first appear, particularly in terms of the question (thoroughly presented in the Introduction) of what groups should be considered 'popular'. In this case, 'elite' and 'popular' function better as poles that define a spectrum than as exclusive categories. Content and context tend to be the best markers of invective register. Ovid's *Ibis*, for example, displays a poetic economy and an allusive erudition in its curse catalogue that derives from the privileged educational elite. By contrast, Xenophon's account of the abusive banter in Cyrus' military camp (e.g. *Cyr.* 2.2.28–31) does not demand such erudition, but it is located within an exclusive banquet held for the top brass and Xenophon targets an audience within the upper echelon of Greek society. In these cases, the verbal aggression centres on the sensibilities, education, or exclusive habits of the social elite in a manner that would tend to exclude non-elite audiences from access to or full appreciation of the invective. From this notion of invective involving elite content or deriving from elite contexts, I suggest that we can approach popular invective as invective that does not satisfy these constraints. Yet content and context can only get us so far. Pollio's response to Octavian, for example, derives from the highest social stratum and treats the forced appropriation of wealth from rich citizens, yet the lilt of his words and the rustic connotations of Fescennine abuse may have popularized his comment among a more diverse audience.[5] One

---

[4] See, for example, Dundes *et al.* 1970, Irvine 1992, Pagliai 2009, Neu 2009 and Smith 2013.
[5] For Fescennine *opprobria rustica*, see Hor. *Ep.* 2.1.145–6 and Graf 2005a: 201–3. Such a popularization of Pollio's words suggests a rare example of the little tradition participating in the great (cf. Toner 2009: 5).

aspect of 'Pollio's paradox', therefore, is the manner in which invective often blurs hierarchical categorizations even as it seeks to negotiate statuses.

These examples seek to differentiate elite from popular invective, but at least three major issues thwart this process. First, 'the elite' were not always a unified group.[6] In a *polis* of average size from the classical era, an aristocratic oligarchy could probably be identified without much difficulty as the group with a virtual monopoly on Aristotle's three pillars of elite status: birth, wealth and *paideia* (*Pol.* 1317b39–41).[7] Already in Sarpedon's speech to his cousin Glaucus in *Iliad* 12 we can see how a family's continued claim to birth status is fundamentally connected to its wealth, which, in turn, fosters the cultural skill-sets (such as speech-making, courtly manners and athletic-military training) that distinguished elites from non-elites.[8] Yet, in other circumstances, these three elements could split. Thus, Demosthenes railed against Aeschines' humble origins despite his elite rhetorical training and social prominence. A similar rift typifies the Roman aristocratic disdain for upstarts, who could, through their ingenuity, luck or industriousness, amass phenomenal wealth but who lacked the nobility of birth and/or cultured education. Cicero, a *novus homo*, offers a real-world example of this, and Petronius' Trimalchio presents a more salacious extreme: for all his opulence he remains, in terms of birth and culture, a sub-elite boor.

The second main impediment to neatly demarcating elite from popular invective is that even in exclusively elite circles, a great deal of invective boils down to a handful of abusive typologies decrying the target's body, mental capabilities, family, public and private behaviour and so forth. In this sense, even elite invective often reveals a deeply demotic slant, since it regularly emerges from an inversion of the traits that typify elite pretension. Thus, when Semonides categorizes all wives as corresponding to various animals (*fr.* 7), he distinguishes between the squalorous pig-wife and the regal mare, but both types are slandered according to a calculus of likening humans to animals that can be heard in playgrounds around the world. Centuries later, this same de-humanizing logic informs Dio's claim that the people of Agae and Adana mocked their regional rivals in Tarsus by calling them a bunch of Cercopes (33.8). Or again, Demosthenes' sexual

---

[6] Nor, of course, were 'the people'. For a parsing of rhetoric invoking the *populus Romanus*, see Morstein-Marx 2004: 119–59.
[7] Ober 1989 discusses 'mass' and 'elite' status in classical Athens; for Rome, see Mayer 2012 and Arena 2012.
[8] Tandy 1997: 107–9 explores the economic implications of this scene.

allegations against Timarchus closely resemble those enumerated by Lucian in his attack on an unnamed rival in his *Pseudologista*. And Pollio's pun on the lexical similarities and power discrepancies of the words *scribere* and *proscribere* speaks most directly to property-owners, who stood to lose their land in proscriptions, but the propertyless would have easily understood the pun and may well have circulated it because of its wit or anti-Octavian sentiment. Thus, even this bit of elitist invective can gain popular traction.[9] From this primarily formalist perspective, then, elite invective seems easier to delimit than popular invective, since the former represents the marked and more constrained sub-category, whereas the latter encompasses any invective that does not satisfy the conditions of elite content and/or context.

A final challenge to evaluating invective involves its relationship to insult. The former is a formal category of verbal aggression, whereas the latter represents a hostile communicative exchange. In narrow literary terms invective can be recognized by its 'outrageous speech' or its grammar of attack, but without an understanding of the social context, we cannot hope to understand its impact. Rituals such as the Eleusinian *gephurismos*, Horace's Atellan-Aristophanic exchange in *Satire* 1.5 and the later imperial festival of the Kalends of January all featured licensed invective notionally devoid of insult.[10] Similarly, examples abound of invective that serves to build and strengthen social bonds, like Nagy's claim that archaic *iambos* affirmed *philotês* within a community, or the banter of the Spartan mess-hall.[11] Cross-cultural anthropological studies confirm that thoroughly aggressive and transgressive invective often serves to promote friendships within certain socially designated contexts.[12] These examples demonstrate that the literary record of invective speech does not, in itself, help us access the social experience of invective.

All this points to the importance of social contextualization in evaluating invective. Whether we look to examples of public mockery, such as the abuse Aristophanes heaped upon the likes of Cleon, Socrates and Euripides, or more intimate banter, such as Catullus' savage threats of

---

[9] Graf 2015: 168–75 presents a parallel case involving the late antique Lupercalia: Pope Gelasius (492–6) condemned the revived festival because aristocrats were composing invectives about the clergy, which were then sung in the streets by a motley assortment of non-elite figures. Thus, the invective is elite in terms of composition and popular in terms of performance.
[10] For Horace's invective exchange, see Gowers 2012: 199–200.
[11] Nagy 1979: 251. For the Spartan practice: Plut. *Lyc.* 12.4.
[12] E.g. Dundes *et al.* 1970 on Turkish boys; Wald 2012 on the African American game most often called 'The Dozens'; Askew 2002: 123–56 analyses both the bonding and segregating/chastising power of Tanzanian Taarab music. Smith 2013: 130–2 summarizes several similar examples.

sexual violence in Carmen 16 against Aurelius and Furius, who are elsewhere described as the poet's friends (11.1), we constantly bump up against our inability to differentiate angry exchanges from friendly banter that is made more enjoyable by adopting a posture of mock hostility. All such cases attempt to generate interest by luring us into the 'persistent tension between fiction and reality' that emerges from directing verbal abuse at recognizably historical figures in ancient poetry.[13] Whether such invective was intended or received as an insult is usually impossible to determine.

We are fortunate to have one ancient text that discusses invective in general terms, and it corroborates this need for fine-grained social contextualization. Among other topics, Plutarch's *Table-talk* evaluates how to tease (*skōmmata*) without sliding into insult (*loidoria*). Plutarch begins with a warning that holds as true today as it did in antiquity: 'Anyone who can't deliver a joke at just the right moment and with just the right tone should avoid it altogether' (*Mor.* 631 c = *Table-talk* 2.1.4). And later in the same section he admits that our response to rough banter changes depending on our company: 'People laugh at things among friends and colleagues that they would find disgusting (*dyskherainousin*) if spoken in the presence of their spouse or parent or teacher, unless, of course, such banter is pleasing to them as well' (634a = 2.1.11). Plutarch confirms that the difference between humour and offence rests on a razor's edge. Yet even if we hope to use his text as an insider's guide, we often encounter frustration, as when we try to apply its teachings to Horace's *Epode* 3. At one point Plutarch says that 'joking blame' (*skōmma kai mempsis*) delivered with appropriate flair expresses gratitude more elegantly than does straightforward thanks, and he even gives the specific example of a dinner guest who pleasantly sasses a generous host to good effect (632e–33a = 2.1.7). This scenario seems to map precisely onto Horace's poem, which expresses mock outrage at Maecenas for serving so much garlic at a meal. Yet Plutarch goes on to note that people easily accept being teased for baldness but take offence at jokes about their bad breath (633 c = 2.1.9). So when Horace complains about his garlicky dinner and hopes that Maecenas will reek so badly that his girlfriend will turn away, which bit of Plutarchan advice wins out? Is this friendly teasing that positively disrupts the dynamics of patronage or does the hyperbolic comparison of garlic to Medea's poisons provide rhetorical cover for real anger? Does Maecenas take offence at or enjoy this banter? Or does he laugh to counter Horace's dissembled aggression? To none of these questions can we

---

[13] Rosen 2007: 27 and, more generally, 3–32.

provide a convincing answer, because we cannot access the subtlest social cues within this exchange and have only the lexical skeleton of communication. As we will see in the next section, during the Late Republic a rich and diverse invective culture flourished, but triumviral and (far more so) imperial politics constrained this repartee in such a way that only popular invective, by which I mean invective attributable only to mass gatherings, spectacle audiences and the perception of a *vox populi*, continued to provide a safe means of commenting upon and resisting the top-down exercise of power.

Republican Roman Patterns of Political Invective

Throughout the Republic, Roman elites and non-elites engaged in invective exchanges that helped shape civic life. At times this discourse brought the two strata (overlooking, for the moment, the shortcomings of a two-tiered model) into close communication. After the murder of Caesar, for example, Cicero asked Atticus to gauge the people's sentiment by noting the crowd's positive and negative reactions to leading figures at the mime shows (*Att.* 14.3.3). Such demonstrations allowed audiences to voice their opinions in a space where elites could hear. Elites also frequently butted heads with each other through invective verse in what seems to have been an expected aspect of a prominent political career.[14] At the end of the Republic, however, this free-flowing game of one-upmanship changed, and popular invective played a key part in the emergence of the new social role that would eventually be called the *princeps*. Although this process was more complex than can be dealt with here, we can see key examples in the careers of Caesar, Octavian and Pompey (whom I postpone for reasons that will become clear).

First, Caesar may have manipulated habits of sexualized invective to create a new role for himself in Roman society. Suetonius records that while Caesar was celebrating his Gallic commission in 58 he boasted that he would 'mount the heads' of his enemies (*insultaturum omnium*

---

[14] Lucilius famously attacked the leading men of Rome in his satires; Cato the Younger wrote Archilochean poetry against Metellus Scipio for stealing his bride (Plut. *Cat. Mi.* 7.2); Calvus took aim at Pompey (fr. 18) and Catullus did the same with various figures, including Caesar (e.g. 54 and 93; cf. Suet. *Caes.* 73). Furius Bibaculus wrote iambic poetry (Quint. 10.1.96) and lampoons on Octavian (and perhaps also Caesar) that, according to Tacitus, brooked no response (*Ann.* 4.34.8). C. Trebonius, the henchman-turned-assassin of Caesar, composed an invective poem (*versiculi*) against Antony that he sent to Cicero and which he justified via an appeal to Lucilius' *libertas* (*Ad fam.* 12.16.3).

capitibus); someone quipped that this would be difficult for a woman, and Caesar responded by likening himself to Semiramis and the Amazons (*Caes*. 22.2). This insult connects rumours about Caesar's effeminacy to a standard and simple logic that equates masculinity with power and, in this case, the threat of silencing speech via forced fellatio. Caesar's riposte, however, wins out because he embraced what most would expect to be the disempowered role.[15] With this exchange in mind, we can reconsider the stories about similar taunts directed at Caesar by his troops.[16] Ruffell, stressing the Bakhtinian idea of carnivalesque transgression over the more commonly discussed inversion, suggests that this discourse about Caesar's gender and sexual identity may have proclaimed how anomalous he had become in terms of traditional categories. He proposes that such characterization 'diffuses the Foucauldian equation of penetrated' with passivity, femininity and powerlessness.[17] On this analysis, Caesar emerges as a radically individual figure, much like Derrida's notions, developed throughout *The Beast and the Sovereign*, that autocrat and animal exist outside normative rules; Caesar's troops claim that he is categorically different from earlier charismatic generals and now inhabits a role that would remain underdefined until the aftermath of Actium. Thus, in addition to releasing tensions, inverting hierarchies or enacting apotropaic ritual, this triumphal abuse may also have participated in an ongoing social dialogue about how Caesar had moved outside familiar social hierarchies altogether.[18] Zanker has led the way in showing that Augustan propaganda was not a unidirectional, top-down dissemination of a clearly articulated message but was, rather, a process of negotiation and cultural dialogue.[19] In the invective of Caesar's troops, scurrilous speech may have served as a bottom-up overture in a similar process.[20]

---

[15] Similarly, Archilochus and Hipponax may have presented themselves in ways that chafed against normative sexual politics, though the evidence is fragmentary. Cratinus' empowering self-presentation as a drunk and adulterer in *Pytine* and Catullus' endorsement of *otium* over *negotium* parallel Caesar's move, though without such pointedly political implications. Nero's enthusiasm for public performance, Commodus' self-presentation as a hunter and gladiator, and Julian's preference for philosophical austerity over imperial pomp perhaps offer better parallels in terms of leading political figures seeking innovative ways to vaunt their masculinity. Modern examples are easier to adduce; e.g. Lil' Kim's song 'Suck my dick' hinges on a similar gender dynamic, but her words, which repeat the phrase 'if I was a dude ... ', highlight rather than transcend the gendered implications of insults about oral sex.

[16] Extant examples include *versus triumphales* 1–4 (Courtney 1993) upon which Calvus fr. 17 is modelled.

[17] Ruffell 2003: 48.   [18] For the ritual aspects of satirical speech, see Graf 2005a.

[19] Zanker 1988.

[20] Caesar's assassination on the festival of Anna Perenna, a carnivalesque celebration that could have distracted the plebs and thereby facilitated the murderous plot, may also associate Caesar

My second example shows that while Caesar was shaping a new role for himself, intra-elite political invective was declining. Indeed such discourse can rarely exist in any autocratic regime outside carefully delimited parameters of ritual or joking, since the hegemon's authority is by implicit definition inviolate and since unmitigated invective aims to negotiate statuses.[21] We can see how this decline in elite political invective happened in Pollio's response to Octavian. *Fescennini* were ritualized blame poetry, but Pollio does not reply with *Fescennini* of his own. He claims that tyrannical power has made any such response impossible and his quip suggests that Octavian's verses were composed outside a ritual context or that the old rustic licence no longer existed. This retort continues the elite trend of exchanging barbed comments, but Pollio highlights the power differential that split the senatorial elite from the triumvirs, who had authority to proscribe citizens (including Pollio's father-in-law). Pollio shows that inveighing against a triumvir is difficult but not quite impossible, since his words box Octavian into an awkward position. Had he responded violently to Pollio's insolence, Octavian would have confirmed the truth of Pollio's description of him as presiding over a reign of terror.

Similar examples of cornering an autocrat are nearly impossible to adduce from antiquity, and our evidence for republican-style political invective all but disappears with Octavian's consolidation of power.[22] Cicero's *Philippics*, delivered during 44–3, represent the last extant outburst of robust Roman oratorical invective, and Antony's assassination of Cicero underlines the danger of using republican strategies to influence triumviral politics. Less formally, we hear of Octavian being pilloried (in uncertain performance contexts) for effeminacy and sexual improprieties by Sextus Pompeius, Antony and Antony's brother Lucius, but their actual words do not survive; Suetonius pairs this account of slander among elites with a story about a theatre crowd cheering maliciously at a line about a eunuch that they understood as a reference to Octavian's unmanliness (*Aug.* 68).[23]

---

with bottom-up movements. The best historical sources do not connect the festival and the killing, though it seems that Ovid has done so at *Fasti* 3.523–696, as argued by Herbert-Brown 2009:131–2. Parenti 2003: *passim* takes such a view of Caesar to an extreme.

[21] Analyses of the annual Swazi Ncwala ritual, in which carefully scripted invective against the king provides apotropaic security and promotes fertility, bear out this basic point. Most fundamental is Kuper 1944; most relevant to my discussion is Dirks 1988. Smith 2013: 129 offers a similar analysis of the connection between invective and egalitarianism.

[22] The exchange between Diogenes and Alexander at Dio Chrys. 4.59 offers perhaps the closest parallel.

[23] Suet. *Aug.* 53 preserves a different sort of interaction between actor, crowd and an elite target. Sometime after Actium a comic actor spoke the line *O dominum aequum et bonum*, 'O great and gracious master', which the crowd (perhaps sycophantically) took to be a reference to

Suetonius thus connects elite and non-elite attacks as part of the overall discourse of anti-Octavian sentiment.[24] Yet these seem to be among the last examples of elite political invective in the republican mould, and not surprisingly the final extant example of such compositions comes from none other than Octavian himself (fr. 1 = Martial 11.20, against Antony).[25] As Octavian's control of Rome increased and solidified into the early Principate, popular political invective continued, however, since it could be voiced through the anonymity and traditional *licentia* of the crowd.[26] Yet although this anonymity existed in terms of the officials' logistical challenge of identifying individual speakers, Fagan has shown that the subjective experience of members of a crowd rarely leads to a loss of identity. Instead Fagan argues that the 'crowd might ... be one of the few places where people can freely express who they really feel themselves to be, where an "imagined community" can share an expression of how they see the world'.[27] Part of Fagan's thesis is that audiences in the arena (as opposed to the rowdier theatre audiences) so rarely rioted because they primarily saw the arena as divided between stands and sands, with the in-group of Romans (from *editor* to plebs) above and out-group performers (animals, criminals, gladiators) below. Yet at moments when that sense of in-group solidarity became untenable, what Fagan calls the 'spasms of divisiveness', sub-groups may well have perceived the organization of performance spaces differently, with representatives of the imperial regime looking more like an out-group than the head of the in-group. Such moments, amid the heightened sense of sub-group identity that Fagan describes, could lead to outbursts of invective against the imperial leadership.

My third and final example of the shift in the politics of invective deals with the trend towards monumentalized spectacle venues. As is well known, throughout most of the republican period, spectacle venues in Rome, such as theatres and the Circus Maximus, lacked permanent monumental structures.[28] Particularly successful generals could, with senatorial

---

Augustus himself. The *princeps* quickly quieted the unwanted flattery and issued an edict chastising such obsequiousness.

[24] Suet. *Aug.* 70 offers a similar pairing of elite and popular censure in its description of Octavian's mock *theoxenia*, which is corroborated by reference to a bitter letter from Antony and the full quotation of a popular lampoon.

[25] Dated by Courtney 1993: 282 to the end of 41. Later examples of invectives delivered against living emperors by named individuals are few and problematic, with Philo's speech against Caligula being the best example (for a reaction to which, see Eusebius *HE* 2.5.1–2).

[26] The standard discussion of *theatralis licentia* is Bollinger 1969.   [27] Fagan 2011: 279.

[28] This may, though with no certainty, be connected to Valerius Maximus' story of a senatorial ban on spectacle seating in Rome, supposedly intended to display Roman manliness by forcing audiences to stand (2.4.2).

permission, build temples or other monuments to commemorate their achievements, but these building projects did not include spectacle venues. Extraordinary spectacles, such as funerary commemorations or the fulfilment of a battlefield vow, could be staged in dual-use venues, such as the Forum or, later, the Saepta, or held in temporary structures. The annual cycle of fixed shows, the responsibility of the aediles, took place in just such temporary venues. This costly habit of constructing and dismantling buildings each year probably reflects the Senate's desire to avoid connecting any individual's name and reputation to a permanent structure designed to entertain the people, and sponsors of shows clearly sought to surpass their peers with the extravagance of their displays.[29]

Yet in 55 BCE, not long after Caesar's riposte about Semiramis, the ground rules of spectacle architecture fundamentally changed when Pompey dedicated his monumental theatre complex, an innovation that set him above his rivals. His phenomenal military successes allowed him to transcend senatorial conservatism regarding entertainment venues, and he ushered in a new architectural era by attaching his name to a permanent stone structure where the public could connect their enjoyment directly and enduringly to him. Once the Empire had become a reality, the *princeps* alone had the authority to sponsor such public works, a privilege modelled on Pompey's precedent. Caesar, too, had planned to build a theatre, which Octavian eventually completed. This project, the Theatre of Marcellus (dedicated in 12 BCE), and the transfer of Caesar's dream to Octavian's sponsorship in the name of Marcellus, demonstrates the dynastic implications of this venue.[30] Yet it was Pompey who first broke through in this arena, and the consequences, in terms of popular invective, were immediate and in some cases quite probably unanticipated.[31]

Surely Pompey expected his architectural triumph to earn him great popularity, since his lack of popular support had been painfully revealed at shows.[32] In a letter from 59 BCE, Cicero demonstrates some of the

---

[29] See, for example, Tate 2008: 85–7; Beacham 2007: 217 presents a different view. Pliny describes the mind-boggling opulence of the temporary structures built by Aemilius Scaurus in 58 and Curio the younger in 52 (*HN* 36.114–20).

[30] During Octavian-Augustus' reign Pompey's theatre complex received other neighbours: in 29 BCE the relatively small amphitheatre of Statilius Taurus and in 13 BCE the Theatre of Balbus.

[31] For discussions of Pompey's theatre complex within the history of Roman spectacle architecture, see Tate 2008: 80–98 and Kuttner 1999. For broader assessments of spectacle architecture at this time, see Welch 2007: 38–71, 108–26, Bomgardner 2000: 32–120, and Coleman 2003 on the surprising absence of a large monumentalized amphitheatre in Augustan Rome.

[32] Cic. *Q. fr.* 2.3.4 reveals Pompey's anxiety in 56 that his popularity was bottoming out.

complexity of theatre politics when he claims that Pompey was booed, Caesar's entrance was met with prickly silence and, to the irritation of the triumvirs, cheers of approval greeted Curio's arrival.[33] Cicero adds a parallel incident in which the crowd erupted into applause when they interpreted an actor's line as a reference to Pompey: *miseria nostra Magnus es*, 'through our misfortune you are Great'. So in 55 BCE, Pompey aimed to overawe his audience with a spectacle like no other. He even sought to forestall objections to his architectural innovation by claiming that it was primarily a temple to Venus Victrix to which the theatre was a comparatively minor accessory.[34] Yet both Cicero and Pliny record how the crowd disliked the extravagant elephant hunt in the Circus, and Cicero adds that his theatrical shows were generally a flop.[35] Although such negative reviews may not reflect the general response to Pompey's shows, they do reveal one of the dangers associated with his innovative theatre complex, namely that crowds could attach negative, as well as positive, sentiments to their architectural patron.

To be sure, Roman crowds had often expressed themselves at spectacles, but Pompey's theatre reconfigured crowd response in several ways.[36] First, it provided a more focused visual arena than did many dual-use venues, such as the Forum or the Saepta. Theatre and circus designs offered clearer lines of sight and better acoustics to more people than was possible at these other locations. This, in turn, must have fostered a more cohesive sense of Fagan's 'imagined community'.[37] And so it must have been easier for the audience to work together at cheering, jeering, chanting and generally expressing themselves than at, say, a gladiatorial show in the Forum. Second, compared to temporary structures, Pompey's building complex overcame the Senate's conservatism and therefore made a more impressive statement than did the structures built within, rather than in transgression of, senatorial tradition. And finally, Pompey's theatre was simply much

---

[33] Cic. *Att.* 2.19; cf. Val. Max. 6.2.9.
[34] Tac. *Ann.* 14.20.4–6, Plin. *HN* 8.7.20, Tert. *De spect.* 10.
[35] Cic. *Ad fam.* 7.1; Plin. *HN* 8.20–1.
[36] Cicero (*Sest.* 106–24) pairs spectacles with elections and assemblies as the three typical occasions for expressing popular sentiments, but he notes that elections and assemblies had already become a sham and that spectacle crowds offered the best indication of popular opinion. Tacitus provides an imperial-era parallel in describing the theatres and circuses as the places *ubi plurima vulga licentia*, 'where most of all the crowds have licence' (*Hist.* 1.72; cf. Tert. *De spect.* 16).
[37] Pliny the Younger (*Pan.* 51) emphasizes that the Circus layout fostered visual communication between Trajan and the audience. Yavetz 1969 discusses the idea of group identity in spectacle venues. Gunderson 1996: 115 compares the Roman arena (generally) to 'a social organ of sight on the order of Foucault's Panopticon'.

bigger. His was the largest theatre in Rome, and that scale meant that crowd responses of any sort involved more people and created a larger stir than had been possible previously.[38]

As we leave the triumviral era and move into the Empire, we can see that popular invective participated in the transition from Republic to Empire in at least three significant ways. First, it seems to have had a role in the dialogical articulation of new social roles, as in the triumphal chants of Caesar's troops. Second, the move towards the Principate curtailed the elite game of vying for status via invective poetry. Once the figure of the emperor had fully emerged, pre-eminent status was no longer a matter of debate, and intra-elite invective became a dangerous game with fewer tangible benefits. This, in turn, meant that anonymous popular invective was the only form of verbal critique and aggression that the emperor would hear. And third, the rise of massive, monumental, permanent spectacle venues that were associated with specific individuals (first Pompey, soon the imperial family) meant that mass audiences had larger and better venues in which to express themselves. And because the emperor became the only visible civic benefactor, he was all but obligated to attend the spectacles and thereby acknowledge and respond to the crowds. With this changed apparatus in place, we can now move into the imperial era to survey this new invective landscape in which elites were significantly constrained from inveighing against leading figures and the emperor heard both praise and blame at the shows that afforded the autocrat and the masses a direct, if blunt, line of communication.

Popular Invective and the Emperor

For roughly the last half-century, historians have been developing new strategies for understanding the Roman *plebs*. Rostovtzeff took a traditional line in noting that with the rise of the Empire, the urban population of Rome 'readily acquiesced' to losing official political influence but 'insisted on their right ... to be fed and amused by the government'.[39] Ste. Croix saw the emergence of the Empire as the curtailment of 'all

---

[38] Pliny claims that Scaurus' theatre seated about 80,000 spectators whereas Pompey's only held about 40,000. Both figures are suspicious, but we can at least surmise that Pompey's permanent theatre soon welcomed cumulatively far more spectators than Scaurus' temporary venue could boast.

[39] Rostovtzeff 1957: 80. On the Roman plebs see, in this volume in particular, Courrier and Rosillo-López.

protection against exploitation and oppression by the powerful, and indeed of all effective opportunity of even voicing [popular] grievances by constitutional means'.[40] Yet a different perspective had already arisen with Yavetz's *Plebs and Princeps*, the title of which announces a new attention to the role of the people that goes beyond condemning (Rostovtzeff) or lamenting (Ste. Croix) their plight and begins to see them as an important player in imperial history.[41] In a similar vein, Alan Cameron's inaugural lecture at Kings College gave a preview of his soon-to-be-published *Circus Factions* by asserting that 'the man to whom [the urban population] now turned for help in their troubles and redress of their grievances was the emperor – a more accessible and a more responsive patron than ever the consul or praetor had proved'.[42] Two decades later Millar claimed that the collapse of the Republic must be understood in terms of the 'two-way relationship between *plebs* and *princeps*'.[43] This shift in attitudes bespeaks a fundamental transformation in conceptualizing Roman history, and my goal here is to bring the role of popular invective into that discourse.

Millar has promoted the study of republican expansion in terms of how it satisfied 'the interests of the voters, the *populus Romanus*'.[44] Yet the evidence for invective permits the extension of this exercise into the imperial era, when the *populus Romanus* were no longer voters. In the last section I showed how the tradition of intra-elite invective disappeared with the rise of the emperor, as a natural reaction to the new monopoly on violence. Tacitus, showing how careful elites now had to be, describes Agricola spending his tribunician year 'unobtrusively in private pursuits', because he knew that under Nero *inertia pro sapientia fuit*, 'inactivity was a sign of wisdom' (*Ag.* 6).[45] Yet politicized popular invective continued largely unchanged, even as the venues became larger and the marketplace of targets shrank from the republican oligarchy of political powerhouses to a single monarch. Thus, even as Agricola was ducking his way through the *cursus honorum*, Nero showed himself remarkably lenient towards popular abuse. As Suetonius notes: 'it was particularly amazing that amid [political setbacks] he bore nothing so patiently as the curses and abuses of the people and he endured nothing more mildly than those who attacked him in conversation and verse' (*Ner.* 39.1). Although it is certainly true that

---

[40] Ste. Croix 1981: 317.   [41] Yavetz 1969.   [42] Cameron 1973: 4.
[43] Millar 1995/2002: 107/176.   [44] Millar 1995/2002: 97/168.
[45] Under particularly volatile emperors, even seemingly insignificant acts could become grounds for punishment, as when Commodus executed someone whom he caught reading Suetonius' biography of Caligula (*HA Comm.* 10.2–3). The problems of relying upon the *Historia Augusta* are well known, and I use such anecdotes in this piece because at the very least they reflect the attitudes that connect certain types of emperors with scenarios involving popular invective.

mass spectacle venues provided crowds with the cover of anonymity, in this case the Senate identified the individuals accused of composing or propagating these invectives and yet Nero forbade their punishment (*Ner.* 39.2).

It is also true that even if the people could exert some influence via invective, the *princeps* maintained his monopoly on violence. We have the clearest evidence in the case of Caligula for how an emperor could try to restrain popular dissent by use of force: Josephus, Dio Cassius and Suetonius offer parallel accounts highlighting his efforts to curtail popular criticism.[46] But Caligula was far from alone. Domitian happened to overhear a barbed comment from a spectator and had the unfortunate man thrown to the beasts (Suet. *Dom.* 10). The fanciful author of the *Historia Augusta* depicts Commodus as so paranoid that he mistook the crowd's cheers for taunts and in response had soldiers carry out wholesale slaughter in the Colosseum (*HA Comm.* 15.6). And, most horrifically, Justinian had thousands butchered in the Hippodrome at Constantinople during the Nika Riots (Procop. *Pers.* 1.24).[47] Even this handful of examples serves to underline that that it was the emperor who always maintained the upper hand in terms of the use of force.

With violent repression representing one extreme limit to the effectiveness of popular invective, we can now examine how popular rhetoric could work in less extreme situations. In several cases, verbal abuse seems to emerge from deeply held popular opinion and generate effective responses. For example, when a crowd believed that Claudius had been assassinated, they shouted curse-laden accusations at the army and Senate until official representatives convinced them that their favoured emperor was safe (Suet. *Claud.* 12). Domitian changed his plan for agricultural reform because of anonymous verses that threatened his death (Suet. *Dom.* 14). And when Didius Julianus, who ruled for only nine weeks in 193, came to power, urban crowds demonstrated in various locations including the Circus Maximus, where they pilloried him despite his offers of largesse (Cass. Dio 74.13.2–5 and *HA Did. Iul.* 4.2–7). Surely such staunch popular opposition contributed to Julianus' failure to ensconce his regime more securely. Much later, Valens (ruled 364–78) was ridiculed in the hippodrome of Constantinople for failing to provide sufficiently energetic

---

[46] J. *AJ* 19.24; Cass. Dio 59.28.11; Suet. *Calig.* 27.

[47] Amid the complexities of the Nika Riots, we should note that at one point crowds were abusing (*hybrizon*, 1.24.17) two officials while running amok in the streets, and Justinian promptly fired the two men. Although this is not a simple case, invective was part of the popular tactics and the emperor tried to avert escalation by responding to popular demands.

leadership in defence of the city, which was then being threatened by an army of Goths; the emperor responded with abuse of his own, promising to level the city altogether, but he did march against the Goths, only to die in the battle of Adrianople (Soc. *HE* 4.38). From these examples, we can see that popular invective could be used as a direct and effective tool for influencing imperial politics. Such cases are rare, to be sure, but they show that the extra-constitutional power of popular invective could be used to the people's benefit.

Even in cases when we do not hear of such dramatic outcomes as Valens' deciding to lead out his army after being heckled by the people, popular invective may well have been a tool with real, if limited, power to influence an emperor's behaviour. For example, Suetonius claims that during Tiberius' reign some people turned to invective verse (*nonnulli versiculis ... exprobrarent*) such as the following (59.1–2):

> Asper et immitis, breviter vis omnia dicam?
> Dispeream, si te mater amare potest.
> Non es eques; quare? non sunt tibi milia centum;
> Omnia si quaeras, et Rhodus exilium est.
> Aurea mutasti Saturni saecula, Caesar:
> Incolumi nam te ferrea semper erunt.
> Fastidit vinum, quia iam sitit iste cruorem:
> Tam bibit hunc avide, quam bibit ante merum.
> Aspice felicem sibi, non tibi, Romule, Sullam
> et Marium, si vis, aspice sed reducem,
> nec non Antoni civilia bella mouentis
> non semel infectas aspice caede manus,
> et dic: Roma perit! regnavit sanguine multo,
> ad regnum quisquis venit ab exilio.

> O you harsh and hard one, should I briefly say all I can?
> Let me die, if even your mother can love you.
> You're no knight. Why? You don't have the hundred thousand.
> If you want the whole tale, it's your exile on Rhodes.
> You've degraded the Golden Ages of Saturn, Caesar.
> For while you're alive, they'll always be iron.
> He turns from wine, since he now thirsts for gore.
> He drinks it as greedily as before he drank straight wine.
> Behold, Romulus, Sulla is happy – for himself, not for you –
> And, if you'd like, behold Marius, though in his re-conquest,
> And the hands of Antony rousing up civil wars,
> Behold, hands stained with slaughter more than once,

> And then say: Rome is dead! Whoever has come to the throne from exile,
> has ruled by blood.

Suetonius claims the source of such poetry is the indefinite *nonnulli*, which means that whatever its actual provenance he presents it as non-elite commentary. What is more, Suetonius' description of the emperor trying to explain away these lines as the result of impatience over his pace of reform indicates that they were known to the *princeps* and that he sought to respond in a manner indicative of an ongoing dialogue.[48]

Similar anecdotes can be adduced from across the Empire (both in time and space). Suetonius claims that Vitellius harboured lasting irritation towards astrologers and satirists because, in response to an edict banishing all astrologers from Italy, a mock counter-edict circulated predicting the day of his death (*Vit.* 14). In Alexandria, where citizens expecting a gift became angry at an imperial tax hike, Vespasian endured anapestic mockery at some mass gathering, quite possibly in the city's theatre (Cass. Dio 65.8).[49] Dio provides many details, including Titus' efforts to moderate Vespasian's position, which shows that the emperor's heir, although ultimately unsuccessful, interceded on behalf of the Alexandrians in response to their combination of complaints and insults. Opellius Macrinus (ruled 217–18), the first emperor from the equestrian class, was derided for his stern and stuffy demeanour in a particularly creative way: in the Forum someone posted both a satirical epigram on the emperor by a certain (*quisdam*) Greek poet and an accompanying Latin translation; as with Suetonius' anonymous poem on Tiberius, the anonymous (*nescio qui*) but public presentation of the Latin version means that it emerged as part of a popular, rather than an elite, discourse. Macrinus responded with a Latin epigram of his own, and the author of the *Historia Augusta* claims that both the emperor and the unknown Latin translator were derided for the quality of their verse (*HA Op. Mac.* 11). Macrinus was also so harsh in his disciplining of the army (at whose hands he eventually met his death) that he supposedly coined the term 'centimate' as a lenient respite from his frequent decimations; and his brutal and degrading treatment of the army, no doubt a matter of popular concern, earned him derogatory taunts from the crowd in the Circus Maximus (*HA*

---

[48] Tac. *Ann.* 6.13 describes the breakdown of communication between Tiberius and spectacle audiences.

[49] The anapestic rhythm suggests a procession, so it could be that a group marched through the streets voicing their complaints in this metre. Fritz Graf has suggested to me that such anapestic abuse could be equivalent to the *versus quadratus* used by soldiers to abuse their general during Roman triumphs. On the popular uses of the *versus quadratus*, see Gerick 1996: 37–42.

Op. Mac. 12).[50] In a similar expression of popular discontent, the people of Antioch lampooned Julian in anapestic verses during the festival of the Kalends of January in 363. With this example, we can recall Plutarch's warning about the need for careful social contextualization of invective. It can easily be argued that the Antiochenes' ridicule of the emperor was merely meant as a permissible part of a carnivalesque festival that featured such raillery. Yet either this abuse went too far (whatever that means) or Julian was too sensitive or some combination of both. In any case, these chants (and Julian's strange, self-mocking response in his *Beard-Hater*) participate in a well-documented exchange that went from bad to worse between a civic population and an emperor.[51]

It is no surprise that in most cases our sources for popular invective directed at Roman emperors provide some explanatory motivation for the verbal assaults (e.g. high taxes), but in a few instances we can wonder if something else was at work. Thus, before he seems to have lost general support, Nero butted heads with Otho (the future emperor) over the affection of Poppaea Sabina; Suetonius tells us that although Nero was more embarrassed than angry and tried to deal with the incident quietly, a lampoon circulated that made fun of the whole situation (*Oth.* 3 = *vers. pop.* fr. 16). Or again, Marcus Aurelius was supposedly ridiculed because his wife conducted her adulterous affairs so openly (*HA Marc.* 29.2). In such cases, the people may have felt that the emperor's personal relationships were a matter of direct concern to them. Yet whether or not such scrupulous concern for *Romanitas* is at issue here, I would like to suggest another model, namely that the people bruited about these gossipy titbits as part of ongoing political negotiations between *plebs* and *princeps* in which imperial peccadillos could be used to popular advantage.

'Political Language *Is* Political Reality'

If we keep in mind Certeau's description of 'the ingenious ways in which the weak make use of the strong', we can see that the emperor and the plebs (and, of course, other groups, such as the army and the Senate) constantly

---

[50] Although the important division within the army between citizens and non-citizens had effectively disappeared after Caracalla's massive expansion of Roman citizenship in 212, the general demographic make-up of the military must have remained largely the same: most soldiers came from humble backgrounds and therefore policies that impacted the rank and file must have been matters of some popular concern.

[51] Gleason 1986 analyses Julian's text in terms of its carnivalesque festival context. Hawkins 2012 and 2014: 262–99 provide updated discussions.

jockeyed with one another to achieve their respective goals.[52] The emperor wanted praise, continued wealth, a minimum of domestic headaches and immunity from 'regime-change'; the people wanted low taxes, cheap and plentiful grain, economic stability and personal safety. Yet in this scenario, the optimization of all these desiderata comes not from exclusionary competition (as, for example, between sports teams involved in a contest that only one can win) but from some amount of compromise and cooperation (as with two people who get over a high wall quickly by taking the time to help each other). Roman spectacles were a primary means of negotiating and experiencing cooperative compromise (often called 'symmetric compromise').[53] In some (perhaps most) cases, these spectacles may have worked their magic largely on their own. The emperor sponsors a show, the crowd cheers; the imperial ego is stroked, the masses forget the daily grind; the event keeps the urban population satisfied and everyone is reassured by the pageantry of power. Yet our sources make it patently clear that in many cases one side or the other needed to work a little harder to grease the skids of cooperative compromise and thereby optimize the situation for everyone. In these circumstances each party had certain tools available. The emperor, for example, could put on particularly impressive shows and offer particularly generous donatives, as Pompey did at the dedication of his theatre complex in 55 BCE and Titus at the Colosseum in 80 CE, and as many an emperor did at the beginning of his reign. But he could also make choices about how to display himself at shows (at the circus, Augustus watched from the *pulvinar*, whereas Caligula sat in the front row and Trajan sat among the audience);[54] he could opt to present himself as an impartial sponsor (Marcus Aurelius) or as a devoted fan (many emperors supported the Greens, a few the Blues; Anastasius favoured the Reds), and he could adopt popular behaviours connecting him to his subjects (Claudius distributed gifts to the people with his left hand exposed 'in the plebeian style'; Titus argued with the crowd about the superiority of Thracian gladiators).[55] By carefully adjusting his approach to spectacles (particularly in relation to that of his imperial predecessor), an emperor could earn for himself more cheers than jeers, but to achieve such an end, he had to participate according to

---

[52] Certeau 1984: 25. [53] E.g. Weinberger and Rosenschein 2004.
[54] Augustus: Suet. *Aug.* 45; Caligula: Cass. Dio 59.7.4; Trajan: Plin. Min. *Pan.* 51.
[55] Marcus: *Med.* 1.5; for emperors as fans, see Cameron 1976: 45–73; the case of Anastasius is particularly interesting, since Malalas (p. 393, Bonn) suggests that he favoured the Reds as a strategy for political negotiations with the Greens and Blues; Claudius: Suet. *Claud.* 21; Titus: *Tit.* 8.

the basic rules of engagement. Emperors who withdrew from the spectacles, disdained them (such as by doing work while in attendance), or used violence to obliterate discourse would lose popular support and thereby make things harder for themselves.

For crowds, the options were fewer: essentially they could use their voice as a carrot or a stick. They could cheer, which would gratify the emperor, and this would be a safe strategy for expressing thanks or coaxing benefits from their patron, though it might convey a sense that they were satisfied and thereby weaken their leverage. Or they could use invective.[56] This option could rouse imperial ire, though *licentia theatralis* provided some protection; more optimistically their heckling could prompt the emperor to act, as when Valens decided to march towards Adrianople. On countless other occasions, the crowd must have won smaller benefits by teasing an emperor and putting him in the position of being able to buy a thunderous ovation. Such a dynamic may lie behind the examples of emperors proactively courting favour with the people, such as when Claudius called them *domini* or Titus promised to refuse no request made to him during a gladiatorial show.[57] But an emperor who did not seek popular favour might have to contend with popular abuse. This is all to say that if we take the crowd's invective directed at the *princeps* as an example of 'working with force' rather than seeing it as mere carnivalesque inversion or as a release of pent-up social tensions, then we can recognize such slanders and calumniations as a fundamental part of Roman politics. As Edelman puts it 'political language *is* political reality'.[58]

To claim that the chants of the crowd are political language necessitates expanding traditional delimitations of this concept. The responses of republican crowds to the words and actions of the elite figures in the Forum (studied incisively by Millar and Morstein-Marx) are more directly and obviously political, but the voice of the people at other venues could 'do things' in Austin's sense of performance and they gain power through

---

[56] In the most extreme cases, they could riot, though this was likely to prompt brutal reprisals.

[57] Suet. *Claud.* 21 and *Tit.* 8. Claudius' use of *domini* pairs with Juvenal's description of the authority of crowds in the amphitheatre (3.36–7): '[sponsors] put on shows and, when the crowd gives the order with a turn of the thumb (*verso pollice vulgus cum iubet*), they kill populistly (*populariter*)'.

[58] 'Working with force': Fowler 1911: 264. This concept is closely related to 'skilled crafting' as discussed by Helms 1993: 91–170 and brought into classical scholarship by Kurke 2011: 98–101. Edelman 1988: 104. The emphasis is original, but Edelman probably did not expect that the shouts and chants of a crowd would be understood as falling under his rubric of 'political language'. Besnier 2009, however, has already broadened Edelman's phrase in an extreme way by applying it to his study of gossip.

repetition, as Butler has shown.[59] In the case of Pollio, with which I began, his elegance in drawing attention to Octavian's role in the proscriptions protected him from any violent response, and his clever turn may have become widely known. In the case of mass audiences, their numbers and tradition provided similar cover, allowing them to engage in crowd-sourced political discourse on the model of social insects, who exhibit 'swarm intelligence': not mindless group-think but a heightened sense of purpose deriving from group or sub-group identification.[60] That is to say that an individual member of a Roman crowd could do little either to engage the emperor personally or to shape the reaction of the entire crowd, yet as Cicero knew when he sought to judge the political landscape immediately after Caesar's death, crowds conveyed simple, clear and important information expressed through a collective voice. It would be wrong to extend this argument so far as to suggest that this voice of Roman crowds amounted to a form of direct democracy in any strong sense. But we may have gone too far in assuming that popular discourse at massive gatherings had virtually no influence on Roman imperial politics.

---

[59] Austin 1962; Butler 1997. Morstein-Marx 2013 builds upon his earlier work in interesting ways and suggests that 'plebian "insubordination" did not represent a breakdown in the [republican] system but was integral to the functioning of the system itself' (46).

[60] An approach explored in terms of modern business practices by Miller 2010.

7 | The Music of Power and the Power of Music: Studying Popular Auditory Culture in Ancient Rome

ALEXANDRE VINCENT

Music is one of the topics that has been the least explored by historians of ancient Rome. Largely ignored by musicologists (for whom 'ancient music' is pre-Renaissance, but still no earlier than the fourteenth-century invention of *Ars Nova*) and treated as a minor subject by ancient historians, Roman music has only recently started to garner scholarly attention.[1] The lack of ancient sources is of course principally responsible for this indifference: fragmentary survivals of ancient material culture continue to be discovered, but testimonia about musical life in ancient Rome are few and far between. Few ancient instruments have been preserved, and attempts to reconstruct ancient melodies amount to mere guesswork: no Roman score has survived from antiquity. We can, of course, make some broad comparisons with ancient Greek music, which has received greater scholarly attention than its poorer Roman sibling.[2] It is certain, however, that since the publication of Gunther Wille's monumental *Musica Romana* (1967), historians now commonly – and rightly – assert the importance of Roman music as an integral feature of everyday life in the capital and the major Western cities.[3] The abundant literary, epigraphic, iconographic and numismatic evidence gathered by Wille makes this clear, even if the full potential of these sources remains to be exploited. The exact nature of Roman melodies may be unrecoverable, but the concept of 'Roman music' is nevertheless accessible if we forego reconstructing music and focus instead on constructing a musical praxis. A social history of Roman

---

[1] Dufour and Fauquet 1987 deal with similar themes to those treated here, and are particularly revealing on this chronological partition. The general book on ancient Rome edited by Umberto Eco features a section on music (Eco 2012: 996–1031). Though this section is much more modest than the hundred or so pages devoted to visual arts in the same book, its very presence does signal a notable change, as does the chapter dedicated to music in Rüpke's recent Roman religion textbook (Fless and Moede 2007) and, more recently, the creation of a journal entirely devoted to the subject, *Greek and Roman Musical Studies*.

[2] The most relevant sources are Greek and concern the Orient; see the collection of sources in Pöhlmann and West 2001.

[3] Wille 1967; among the first studies to follow Wille, Baudot 1973 remains one of the few to deal exclusively with Roman musicians.

musical culture must embrace the conclusion that the sound itself matters less than the social identity of those who produced and listened to it, and the context in which it was emitted. Roman music was a means of communication and can be analysed accordingly: it was not a sensory ornament with minimal connection to an extraneous event, but was integral to the social fabric of each and every event. At stake in studying music in such a framework is an understanding of the meaning of an act of communication that connects the source with the target of the sound.

This approach to auditory perception taps into a particularly vibrant field in contemporary historiography: sensory history, or the exploration of the historicity of the senses.[4] Interest in an anthropology of the senses developed in the early 1980s, predominantly in the work of the Canadian scholars David Howes and Constance Classen, and it has since been enthusiastically embraced by the Anglo-American academy. In a nutshell, sensory data are cultural phenomena which are historically and spatially constructed.[5] We do not feel, nor do we hear, in the same manner as a Roman from the first century BCE. The sounds that the Romans heard should not, therefore, be interpreted according to our own sensory and cultural standards, but as far as possible according to theirs. This concept – a cornerstone of the historian's craft – nonetheless needs emphasizing in the preamble to any study on ancient music. An objective of this chapter is to apply this approach to one particular category of sounds, which I call the *music of power*.

In their studies of Roman popular culture, both Nicholas Horsfall and Jerry Toner have signalled the importance of music for the plebeians.[6] However, both have focused on music that was played or sung in moments of leisure (the theatre or popular celebrations like the festival of Anna Perenna) or for the sake of *paideia*. In order to complement these studies, this chapter focuses on 'music employed by the Romans in their public ceremonies', a phrase by Strabo that I employ as a preliminary definition of the music of power.[7] For Strabo, the word *dēmosia* ('in public') references the city. But the term should also be understood more concretely as 'played

---

[4] Scholarly production in recent years is huge; for an assessment of Anglo-American historiography and a methodological introduction, see Smith 2007 and Schwartz 2011. Useful recent syntheses, incorporating French research, can be found in Palazzo 2012 and Krampl and Beck 2013.

[5] See Classen 1993, 1997; Howes 2003, 2005. In France, this approach has been communicated more widely by D. Le Breton. Le Breton 2007 presents a clear overview of his work.

[6] Horsfall 2003: see in particular ch. 1 on songs, and ch. 3, 'Music returns to Rome'.

[7] Strab. *Geog.* 5.2.2: *mousikē, hosa dēmosia chrōntai Rōmaioi*. Unless otherwise indicated, all translations come from the Loeb editions.

in public', in front of – at least in theory – an audience of citizens without distinction of rank or class.[8] The double meaning of the term 'public' is significant because it denotes a tension between the collective and the particular; between the city as a whole and the population as an ensemble of singular individuals. The population whose cultural capital this chapter will examine was noticeably affected by the music of power, which they heard repeatedly throughout the course of their lives.[9] We shall explore to what extent the sounds to which the masses were exposed would become a significant part of their culture (taking as a given the proposition that the plebeians *had* a culture). Finally, building on the work of Egyptologist Jan Assmann on rituals, culture and the notion of cultural memory, the role of music in Roman popular culture will be assessed.[10] I use 'Roman' advisedly: while I make occasional forays into other large cities of the Western Empire, this chapter focuses on the inhabitants of the city of Rome, since, for the most part, our historical sources are concentrated on this population.

Listening to the Music of Power: Soundmakers

A simple method for better understanding the communicative impact of a musical performance is to separate the different agents involved. Concentrating on basic analytical structures enables us to distinguish between those making sounds and those receiving the auditory information. For example, musicians performing in public ceremonies did so for reasons beyond their own personal pleasure; they cannot be considered the target of their own performance, in that they were not performing on their own initiative – rather, they were fulfilling a demand. In the final analysis, then, musicians would be considered rather as 'vectors' of sounds neither aimed at them nor initiated by them. This demonstrates that, in order better to understand the involvement of the different agents present at a

---

[8] On the double meaning of 'public' when associated with religion, see Scheid 2013: 122.
[9] A definition of what constitutes 'the people' is not the main object of this chapter. I will use it here as a synonym for the plebs in its negative definition: that is, the population as a whole to the exclusion of the families of knights and senators. I am aware of the great sociological, financial and cultural diversity that such a loose definition implies. See Courrier in this volume (esp. pp. 107–8). The notion of cultural capital derives of course from the classic work of Pierre Bourdieu, *La distinction* (first published in French 1979: Bourdieu 1984). It refers to the amount of cultural resources an individual has at his disposal, whether transmitted by family, school or living in society in general.
[10] Assmann 2010.

musical performance, it is necessary to analyse the specific context of the musical performance with care.

Thanks to the brilliant, muscular soundtracks beloved by directors of epic films, what immediately comes to mind today when thinking about Roman music is the music played during the Roman games.[11] There is some basis for this in our historical narratives: as famously depicted by Dionysius of Halicarnassus, musicians played during the procession bringing the participants of the games to the space where these took place.[12] Ostensibly describing the specific *pompa circensis* of the *ludi votivi* promised by the dictator Aulus Postumius after the battle of Lake Regillus in 499 BCE, Dionysius of Halicarnassus details a typical procession, with elements he had himself witnessed, as well as others borrowed from the annalist Fabius Pictor.[13] *Auloi*, lyre and lute players marched in these processions, a fact confirmed by other narrative and iconographic sources.[14] Yet, starting from the end of the Republic, a third category of instruments, brass instruments, came to be preferred. Juvenal satirizes a games organizer who is surrounded by *cornicines* (musicians playing large bronze instruments turned in on themselves), and these musicians are often featured in Roman relief sculptures along with *tubicines* (musicians playing long, straight bronze instruments).[15] Later, Tertullian mentions the *tibia* and the *tuba* as the two instruments dominating the music of processions for the games.[16]

The organization of games – be they theatrical, musical or gymnastic, circus races or gladiatorial combats – was the prerogative of curule magistrates. More specifically, the aediles were in charge of staging the annual games.[17] Starting with the reign of Augustus, the organization of ritual festivals changed. Even if some republican habits remained unaltered, the emperor progressively gained greater control.[18] No matter who held the

---

[11] See, for instance, the numerous images from films featuring musicians playing bronze instruments reproduced in Martin 2003 and Dumont 2009.

[12] Dion. Hal. *Ant. Rom.* 7.72.   [13] Piganiol 1923: 15–32.

[14] On *auloi/tibia*, see notably Cic. *Har.* 11.23 and Ov. *Am.* 3.13.11–12. For a visual representation, see the relief of Castel San Elia, cf. Ronke 1987: figs. 15–19. The *tibia* is pictured with chord instruments on the Pesaro relief (Fless 1995: pl. 10, fig. 1).

[15] Juv. 10.43–6. See the relief from the Stabian Gate necropolis in Pompeii that depicts the procession preceding the games on the first of the three levels of sculpture (Junkelmann 2000: 131, figs. 205 and 209). See also the funeral monument of a *sevir Augustalis* at Amiternum (Ronke 1987: figs. 10–14 and Guidetti 2006).

[16] Tert. *De spect.*10.2.

[17] Bernstein 1998: 51–78. An exception: the gladiatorial games were theoretically private events, organized for religious ends, until the end of the Republic.

[18] Benoist 1999: 73–82.

upper hand, organizing the games was an important task for whoever was in charge of the city. As the games were part of the religious rituals of public life, they were the responsibility of those who interceded between the gods and the citizens – that is, priests and politicians, who both hailed from the same social group. These priests and politicians hired the participants of the games: the actors, charioteers and gladiators, and also the musicians who played in the *pompa*. A Roman inscription written in memory of a *cornicen* called Titus Avienus suggests that, by the latest at the end of the first or start of the second century CE, musicians were attached to the imperial *ludus* permanently, or at least for lengthy periods.[19]

The same process of imperial appropriation of ceremonies with a musical component can be seen in the case of the triumph.[20] In both republican and imperial times, the decision to celebrate a victorious general was considered a public matter and thus had to be ratified by a vote in the Senate. The musicians taking part in triumphs – mostly players of large bronze aerophones and *tubicines* – were therefore acting on the order of the public. These musicians were, as described by Plutarch and Appian, at the head of the parade for the triumph of Aemilius Paulus in 167 BCE.[21] Likewise, the frieze of the triumphal relief on the Temple of Apollo Sosianus features a *tubicen* blowing his horn while bearers are about to lift a *ferculum* holding a trophy, which suggests that the scene is at the beginning of the procession.[22] The presence of these musicians became so emblematic of the ceremony as a whole that on the well-known panel of Marcus Aurelius' triumphal arch the emperor has only one *tubicen* by his side, who thus serves metonymically for the entire *pompa*.[23]

Both the games and the triumph were manifestations of Roman public religion. Yet there was another rite, perhaps the most important of all, which necessitated the presence of musicians: the sacrifice. Here, too, the available iconography testifies to the importance of music. Altars from the Augustan period systematically feature a *tibicen* by the side of the

---

[19] AE 1988, 23 = EAOR 1, pp. 42–3, n. 36, pl. 11, 2 = EDR 080574: D(is) [M(anibus)] | T(iti) Avieni [- - -] | cornic[inis - - -] | lud[i - - -].

[20] The privatization of the triumph by emperors, starting with Augustus, is a well-known phenomenon: see Bastien 2007.

[21] Plut. *Aem.* 33.1; App. *Pun.* 66.

[22] This relief is currently in the Montemartini Museum (inv. no. MC 2776). *Tubicines* are also found in the same position at the start of a procession on the Medinaceli relief depicting the triumph of Augustus in 29 BCE (after his victory in Actium). This exceptional monument can be seen in full in the catalogue of the 2013–14 Augustus exhibition: La Rocca *et al.* 2013: 321–3.

[23] Currently in the Capitoline Museums, Palazzo dei Conservatori (inv. no. MC 0808). For an analysis of the role of musicians in triumphal processions, see Podini 2004.

sacrificant.[24] Pliny the Elder suggests that the *tibicen* was there because he added to the ritual's completeness. The *tibicen*'s role was to insulate, as it were, the sacrificant with a wall of sound, shielding him from any extraneous sounds that might distract him from performing the sacrifice as tradition dictated.[25] The episode known as the '*Tibicines* protest' of 311 BCE highlights the fact that the presence of musicians was absolutely necessary in order for sacrifices to be carried out.[26] Because ritual communication with the gods could no longer be properly effected, the musicians' voluntary exile to Tibur endangered the functioning of the city. In order for them to return, magistrates were forced into a course of action that mingled deception with compromise.[27] During sacrifices, therefore, the *tibicines* were directly in the service of the priests and magistrates of the Roman religion. Unsurprisingly, the law regulating the colony of Urso, in Baetica, stipulated that magistrates had one of these musicians at their disposition.[28] Article 62 specifies that the city's *duumviri* and aediles had a right to have on their staff a herald, a *haruspex* and a *tibicen*.[29] The *tibicen*, in sum, allowed magistrates to carry out properly the public religious rites that their office required.

Another example – perhaps less obvious in this context but nonetheless precisely documented – must be added to these instances of the music of power: that of public assemblies of the Roman populace. Dionysius of Halicarnassus describes how, in the early days of Rome, animal horns were used to make the call to assemblies.[30] In later periods, sources stipulate the type of instrument used for the call – making it possible to distinguish between the different types of *comitia*. According to Aulus Gellius, centuriate assemblies were called by a *cornu*, while curiate

---

[24] For illustrations, see Fless 1995 and Ryberg 1955. For a preliminary analysis of the systematization of their representation, see Vincent 2013. For an analysis of the ritual, see Scheid 2005 and Prescendi 2007.

[25] Plin. *HN* 28.3.11.

[26] The story is told by Ov. *Fast* 6. 650–711; Plut. *Quaest. Rom.* 55; Liv. 9.30.5; Val. Max. 2.5.4. The same episode is told by Julius Paris, who epitomized the works of Valerius Maximus, and is briefly mentioned by Quint. *Inst.* 5.11.9.

[27] There are many interpretations of the causes of their departure from the city and the circumstances of their return: see Basanoff 1949, Palmer 1965, Dumézil 1973, Girard 1973, Storchi Marino 1979, Massa-Pairault 1985: 92–6, Pailler 2001, Humm 2005: 469–73, Buchet 2010, Vincent 2016. The ancient sources nonetheless agree that the exile was voluntary and the return advantageous to the musicians.

[28] This document was engraved on bronze tablets dating from the Flavian epoch, although the text itself is older, from the pre-Augustan period.

[29] Crawford 1996: 400. In this case, this refers to three types of priests shared by the magistrates.

[30] Dion. Hal. *Ant. Rom.* 2.8.4, see below.

assemblies were sounded by the voice of a herald.[31] Such a differentiation is not surprising if one considers the nature of the centuriate assembly, which brought together Roman citizens according to their military rank: the *cornu* was one of the three instruments present in Roman camps, along with the *tuba* and the *bucina*. Calling together citizens with the *cornu* was therefore a way to reassert the military contours of Roman citizenship. Before 218 BCE centuriate assemblies were called in order to vote on laws, to ratify declarations of war and to confirm the capital sentences pronounced by judges in trials *de perduellione*. In his text on the Latin language, Varro illuminates this latter function by pointing to an edict prior to 242 BCE, which details the procedure for the unfolding of centuriate assemblies in high treason trials:

In the same *Commentary on the Indictment*, this is the summing up of the edict written at the end: 'Likewise in what pertains to those who have received from the censors the contract for the trumpeter who gives the summons to the centuriate assembly, they shall see to it that on that day, on which the assembly shall take place, the trumpeter shall sound the trumpet (*classicus canat*) on the Citadel and around the walls, and shall sound it before the house-entrance of this accursed Titus Quintius Trogus, and that he be present in the Campus Martius at daybreak.'[32]

This excerpt from the edict forcefully brings out the construction of the music of power. Musicians who were in charge of bringing together the centuriate assemblies clearly acted on behalf of the civic authorities. They held their mandate thanks to a system of deputization which made them temporarily servants of the city.[33] But the interest of this passage also lies in the fact that it sheds light on the other pole of communication dynamics, that of the receivers of sound.

Receivers

One of the most constructive ways to explore the audience of the music of power is to retrace, from the perspective of spatial semiotics, the steps of

---

[31] Gell. 15.27.2: 'Eorum autem alia esse "curiata", alia "centuriata"; "curiata" per lictorem curiatum "calari", id est "convocari", "centuriata" per cornicinem.'

[32] Var. *Ling.* 6.92: 'In eodem commentario anquisitionis ad extremum scriptum caput edicti hoc est: 'Item quod attingat qui de censoribus redemptum habent, uti curent eo die quo die comitia erunt, in arce classicus canat tum circumque moeros et ante privati huiusce T. Quincti Trogi scelerosi ostium canat et ut in Campo cum primo luci adsiet.'

[33] On this juridical condition and the social consequences that it had for the musicians concerned, see Vincent 2016. On adjudications by Roman authorities in general, see Trisciuoglio 1998 and Aubert 1994: esp. 112–14 (a legal description of *locatio-conductio*).

the musician in charge of calling these public assemblies. The first sound of the horn was blown on the Arx, the oldest citadel of Rome and its most impregnable fortress.[34] During the mid-republican period the Arx was still the military heart of the city.[35] The fact that the *cornicen* was located on the Arx indicated the seriousness of the capital charge, which was carried out by the military authorities in the guise of the praetor, temporarily acting *cum imperio*, who assumed the function of public prosecutor. More practically speaking, the Arx was the highest point in the city, so no other building could block the resonance of the *cornicen*'s sounds. The repeated calls of the *cornicen* along the city walls (*tum circumque moeros canat*, as Varro stressed) designated the target audience, which was the city as a whole. Every citizen, regardless of social class, wealth or reputation, was affected by a capital trial. This encircling of the *Urbs* by the musicians is thus akin to a rite of inclusion, whereby the community of citizens is created acoustically. By contrast, the musician's last call, played at the door of the condemned, worked to differentiate and exclude, by drawing attention to the convict, who stood apart from the rest of the civic population. The sound of the *cornu* resonated within the city walls, breaking the monotony and silence of the Roman night.[36] Absent from Varro's text, the audience is nevertheless omnipresent in the musical journey: an entire citizenry targeted in an acoustic dramatization of justice.

Other scenes related to the carrying out of capital punishment demonstrate how music solemnized such moments for the whole of the civic body – represented, again, as the target audience. Seneca the Elder gives a brief account of the moments preceding an execution in the Forum:

> The praetor takes his place on the tribunal, under the gaze of the province. The guilty man's hands are tied behind his back; he stands, facing everyone's intense and reproving stare; the herald asks for silence, the ritual sentence is pronounced, the *classicum* is blown from the other side.[37]

The *classicum* in question was a melody – the only one whose name has been preserved. It was primarily played in a military setting in the case of

---

[34] On the Capitol as the last refuge for Romans, see the story of the taking of Rome by the Gauls led by Brennus found in, among others, Liv. 5.39–43, 47. On the etymology of Arx, stemming from *arcere* (to push away), see Var. *Ling.* 5.151.

[35] Gianelli 1993.

[36] As the musician had to be at the Campus Martius at the first light of dawn, this implies that he crossed the city at night.

[37] Sen. *Controv.* 9.2.10: 'deinde descripsit, quanto aliter in foro decolletur: ascendit praetor tribunal inspectante provincia. Noxio post terga deligantur manus; stat intento ac tristi omnium vultu. Fit a praecone silentium; adhibentur deinde legitima verba, canitur ex altera parte classicum.'

an emergency (the attack of a camp at night, for example) or to render official honours to magistrates *cum imperio* when they were in the camp. During the Republic, when conscripts manned the army, citizen-soldiers were habituated to the sound of the horn. In the same text, Seneca the Elder contrasts the *classicum* with the *symphonia*, which was generally played in a private setting.[38] While the *symphonia* was totally inappropriate for public ceremonies, the *gravitas* of the *classicum* reinforced the majesty of the Roman people. The *classicum* was thus a familiar tune, at least for the citizen-soldiers, played in order to highlight the dramatic qualities of the event unfolding before the eyes of the Roman population. Capito's words – *omnium vultu*, literally 'in front of the faces of everyone' – emphasize the public space. It was not so much that the entire population of Rome could be found in the Forum – that would be to confuse rhetoric and statistics – but the point is that this ceremony was meant for all citizens, who were all free to come and listen – *in silence* – to the final notes for the condemned man.

Medium

The responsibility for summoning people's assemblies and dramatizing justice in republican and imperial times fell upon the horns. Present in the processions for games and during triumphs, they were the instruments of choice for the music of power. This can, of course, be explained in practical terms: Julius Pollux, the Greek lexicographer whose *Onomasticon* was composed in the second half of the second century CE, notes that the sound of the *tuba* could be heard at a distance of 50 stades, or about 10 kilometres.[39] The most suitable instruments for communicating to the masses and over a large distance, the *tubae* guaranteed that all citizens heard these soundings of the music of power. It was no longer the case that there were distinct calls according to social rank, as Dionysius of Halicarnassus relates in relation to the regal period: 'whenever the kings thought proper to assemble the patricians, the heralds called them both by their names and by the names of their fathers, whereas public servants

---

[38] Sen. *Con.* 9.2.14: 'Dic enim mihi, si, cum animadvertere debeat non legitimo cultu ac more solemni usus, interdiu tribunal conscenderit convivali veste, si, cum classicum canere debeat, symphoniam canere iusserit, non laedet maiestatem?'

[39] Poll. *Onom.* 4.88. The Greek term is *salpinx*, which is the equivalent of the Latin *tuba*. On the organologic and acoustic qualities of the *tuba*, see Vendries 2007, the most complete study to date. The size of the inner rim diameter and of the bore of the tuba of Neuvy-en-Sullias seems to confirm Pollux's statement.

summoned the plebeians *en masse* to the assemblies by the sound of ox horns'.[40] By contrast, the music of power in later times made no distinction between social classes, with both plebeians and senators hearing the same call.

The acoustic strength of large aerophones partly explains why they were used to transmit information to a very large number of people. This can be deduced from an Augustan document, the epigraphic report of the Secular Games organized in 17 BCE.[41] This long text leads one to believe that more citizens than originally planned participated in the rites of these games, which were designed to inaugurate a new century and a new era for Rome. Initially meant to take place on a single day, the distribution of *suffimenta* (torches, sulphur and asphalt) purifying the participants in the rite was extended to three days.[42] This was done in an edict of the *quindecemviri* dating from 24 May, only four days before the scheduled date.[43] Such overwhelming enthusiasm for a ritual event which one was supposed to attend only once in a lifetime suggests that a very large number of residents of Rome took part, and probably a large number of citizens from outside the capital.[44] The city might then have looked rather like Suetonius' description of the games given by Caesar: taken over by visiting spectators, who took up positions wherever they could during the celebrations.[45] It is this enormous crowd, made up of several hundreds of thousands of individuals, that the trumpet players (*aenatores*) addressed through song on 30 May, calling the citizens to take part in the religious rites (*sacri*) relating to the theatrical games, which were also organized as part of these exceptional celebrations.[46]

A few days later, on 3 June, the mass of citizens again heard these musicians, but this time accompanied by another category of instrumentalists: lyre and *tibia* players. They all accompanied the procession from the Palatine Hill to the Capitol. A narrative of this event is found in the epigraphic account of the Secular Games of Septimius Severus (204 CE).

---

[40] Dion. Hal. *Ant. Rom.* 2.8.4.
[41] For the edition of this text, see most recently Schnegg-Köhler 2002.
[42] Zos. 2. 5.1; Schnegg-Köhler 2002: 30, l. 48.   [43] Schnegg-Köhler 2002: 32, l. 62–7.
[44] This is the meaning of the Roman *saeculum*, cf. Zos. 2.1.1. On the fact that only citizens were authorized to participate in these rituals of the civic religion, see Scheid 2013: 121–43, esp. 130–43, based on Zos. 2.5.1.
[45] Suet. *Iul.* 39.7: 'Such a throng flocked to all these shows from every quarter that many strangers had to lodge in tents in the streets or along the roads and the press was often such that many were crushed to death, including two senators.'
[46] Schnegg-Köhler 2002: 34, l. 86–8 (with commentary, p. 114): 'Item cum ad caerimonias sacro [rum - - -] | certiores esse volumnus omnes m[- - -] | aenatores in funere canere [- - - (vacat ?)].'

This inscription describes the procession between the two hills where the *Carmen saeculare* was sung, with the musicians accompanying chariots, dancers and even horseback acrobats.[47] On this occasion the musicians paraded on the *sacra via* and crossed the Forum. This is where, according to the inscription, they met the *populus* (*adstante et intercedente populo*) who had not been able to attend the performance given by twenty-seven each of young noble men and women in front of the temples of Apollo Palatinus and Jupiter Capitolinus.

Remarkable for their rich documentary remains, these musical events during the secular games are paradigmatic examples of the music of power. Played by command of the civil authorities, in the name of the entire populace, and on instruments suitable for mass communication, this music was meant to be heard by the entire citizen body of the city, plebeians included. Does this mean that this particular music of power – music that was heard by all – penetrated into popular culture?

The Music of Power and Popular Culture

Ancient popular culture is difficult to access and assess today because so few truly popular testimonies have reached us. For example, Martial's vituperations regarding his alleged poverty and the hardships of being a *cliens* begging for patronage do not fool anyone: his voice was not a *vox populi*.[48] Epigraphy – which we might consider one of the most useful alternative sources for accessing non-elite history – is of little assistance when it comes to the music of power. Inscriptions supply the names of some musicians, thus allowing us to analyse their social class, but this does not actually enlighten historians as to how musical performances were actually received.[49] The best one can say is that some musicians were indeed in the service of the city and were thus the official emissaries of the music of power.

---

[47] Pighi 1965: '[- - - Inde XVuiri duxerunt] et tibi[cinum fidicinum cornic]inum aeneatorum et tubicin[u]m translatum, et togarum [- - -| a]sinariorum [- - -]m et tiron[u]mque ludionum quadr[igarum binarum et bi]garum binarum item desultorum cu[rsor]umque factionu[m singularum pompam] publicis et c[alatoribus ordinantibus, adstante et i]ntercede[nte popull]o, per [Via]m Sacram forumque Romanu[m] arcum Seue[ri et Antoni]ni Aug[[g. et Getae Caes.]].'

[48] See, for instance, Balland 2010.

[49] For a sociological study of professional musicians, see Vincent 2016. The study of the inscriptions highlights the difference between private musicians and musicians playing for the city, the latter enjoying better conditions, especially post-Augustus.

Other methodological tools are necessary to fill in these gaps. Among them, the concept of 'cultural memory' elaborated by the Egyptologist Jan Assmann proves particularly useful, not least because it was developed by a specialist in ancient history.[50] The concept of cultural memory offers a series of criteria for analysis that are especially adapted to the study of ancient societies. It deals with collective culture, including popular culture, through the prism of a category of events that are among the most richly documented. For Assmann, cultural memory corresponds to a mode of transmission and commemoration of cultural content within a population, regardless of its social components. Cultural memory is at the crossroads of identity, continuity and a certain relationship to the past – all of which make up the very foundations of a community.[51] It is distinguished from 'communicational memory', which corresponds to the memories of a recent past that individuals share with their contemporaries. Cultural memory is developed over a longer period and its content serves as a structural framework for human societies. In order to exist and endure, cultural memory needs to be manifested in concrete moments, such as rituals, defined here as mimetic routines which have acquired meaning beyond their immediate utility.[52] These rituals are repeated in order to anchor memory in a lengthier temporal continuity.[53] Addressed to each and every member of the community, the iteration of these rituals allows for a sharing of cultural givens by the whole community. In this respect festivals and celebrations are of prime importance because they gather together a substantial part of the population, which then collectively integrates or reinvigorates its cultural memory.

The testimonia regarding the music of power that I present here offer elements that would seem to be part of the cultural memory of the inhabitants of Rome. These relate to ritual moments, often of celebration, in collective life. The term 'ritual' should not be understood here in exclusively religious terms, as in the cases discussed above (the triumph, *pompa ludi* and sacrificial rites). Since rituals are defined first and foremost by their normative and repetitive organization, they can be religious or they can relate to an ensemble of purely political actions and traditions.

---

[50] Assmann 1995 provides a short summary of the idea; the most comprehensive account is Assmann 2010.

[51] The foundation of Assmann's ideas lies in the work of Halbwachs, who developed the notion of 'collective memory', which presupposes that all memory experience becomes lodged in a group and that an individual, by him- or herself, does not have any memory. See the summary in Assmann 2010: 32–43.

[52] Assmann 2010: 19.

[53] Rudhardt 1988: 2–14 on the value of ritual for insertion in an historical chain.

Ceremonies such as assemblies of the people or the execution of a convict were framed by a raft of traditional, inherited procedures, which is why they are fully congruent with what Christer Bruun has called, with reference to Ostia, 'civic rituals'.[54]

Of all the rituals mentioned in this chapter, the sounds of religious sacrifices were probably the most familiar to the inhabitants of Rome. The rigorous organization of the Roman religious calendar, as evidenced by the records of numerous *fasti* in many cities of the Empire, allowed for sacrificial music to be performed frequently. In addition to fixed, calendrical dates, further sacrifices were added due to events that necessitated communication with the gods (military victories, natural catastrophes, births, weddings, etc.). Sacrificial music was anchored in the city's acoustic culture because these permanent rituals were, by their very nature, repeated regularly through the years. Every iteration was an opportunity to reinvigorate this culture and make it part of the population's collective knowledge. The concrete circumstances of these musical performances also played an important role in the diffusion of such knowledge. According to iconographic and numismatic sources, these rituals took place mostly outdoors, in front of temples.[55] This likely facilitated the dispersion of sound in the city space, so that it could be heard by large numbers of people. Moreover, sacrifices were not held in one single space in the city: the vicinity of the temple of Jupiter Capitolinus was used as often as the sanctuaries of the Campus Martius. Thus, throughout the year, the entire urban space would be filled with the sounds of sacrifices, thereby reacquainting the inhabitants' ears with the acoustic culture of ritual.

Processions were clearly one of the preferred modes of diffusion of the music of power. Playing on the order of political authorities, musicians marched through the city streets in order to lead participants to the site of games (usually the temple of the divinity being honoured), to accompany a triumphant general or the participants in a religious ritual, or to inform citizens of an imminent conviction. In so doing, they increased the potential for sound diffusion and enabled their performances to enter the acoustic range of the whole city.

The capillary diffusion of ritual music in urban space and across social classes expanded further during the reign of Augustus when, in 7 BCE, the

---

[54] Bruun 2009 notes in a similar manner, concerning the inhabitants of the Ostian colony during the imperial period, that the function of these 'civic rituals' was to reinforce the historical and memorial conscience of the community. Bruun does not refer to Assmann's work on cultural memory.

[55] See, on the iconographic representation of musicians, Fless 1995.

city was reorganized into fourteen *regiones* and *c*. 265 *vici*.[56] This reform of urban planning prompted the first *princeps* to re-establish abandoned neighbourhood cults honouring the gods of crossroads (*Lares compitales*). To these ancient gods, Augustus added the worship of his own genius (*genius Augusti*), which laid the foundations for imperial worship during popular assemblies.[57] The importance of this initiative is well known. In relation to this present study, it embedded the sounds of power even deeper within the fabric of the city. Surviving altar reliefs illustrate the quotidian presence of *tibicines* during sacrifices by neighbourhood officials (*vicomagistri*) in honour of the emperor's genius.[58] Likewise, the large historical relief discovered under the Palazzo della Cancelleria, and today conserved in the Vatican Museums, allows one to associate *tubicines* with *tibicines* in the sacrifices organized during these crossroad rituals. A procession scene shows *vicomagistri* holding statuettes representing the *Lares compitales* and *genius Augusti*, while in the background three *tubicines* blow into their instruments.[59] Each year, then, each urban cell of the *Urbs* – all at the same time – was filled with the sounds of the music of power, imposing upon the citizens of Rome a layer of communal acoustic culture.[60]

The choice of the word 'imposing' to describe this process does not seem excessive given the nature of the instruments concerned. Imagine three *tubae* playing at the same time – three of those instruments that Julius Pollux said could be heard at a distance of 10 kilometres.[61] Could one possibly escape their sounds? The coercive qualities of these sounds, especially those emitted by large aerophones in bronze, should not be underestimated. In his *Apocolocyntosis* Seneca parodies these instruments as being able literally to wake the dead: 'It was certainly a most gorgeous spectacle, got up regardless of expense, clear it was that a god was being borne to the grave: tootling of trumpets, roaring of horns, an immense

---

[56] The figure of 265 *vici* is given by Pliny the Elder (for his time; the figure does not seem unreasonable for a few decades earlier, cf. Lott 2004: 84–98).

[57] There is a vast literature on the Augustan reorganization of the city and on the cult of the crossroads. See, in particular, Fraschetti 1990 and Lott 2004.

[58] See Hano 1986 for the iconography of these altars, as well as Vincent 2013 for a preliminary analysis of this exact point.

[59] For images, see Ryberg 1955: pl. 23; Fless 1995: 51–4, pl. 13, fig. 2 and pl. 17, fig. 1–2.

[60] One can postulate that not all of the *vici* took part in a procession as important as the one represented on the frieze of the Palazzo della Cancelleria, as the city did not have enough *tubicines*. The frieze is more likely a depiction of an ideal *pompa* or one that took place for a particularly important *vicus*.

[61] Wille 1967: 71. This suggests that attending the parade of a *pompa* amounted to exposing oneself to the maximum acoustic volume that one could have in the pre-industrial era.

brass band of all sorts, such a din that even Claudius could hear it.'[62] The sounds emitted by these instruments spread throughout the urban space and into the ears of those who, *volens nolens*, had no other choice but to accept them and to integrate them into a known repertoire. The music of power did not need to be present at the heart of the event since it could be heard far beyond the limits of the visible – a fact that probably did not escape officials seeking to diffuse communications about the political regime. In this respect, one must underline the significant difference between diffusing information visually and aurally. Art historians of ancient Rome rightly attempt to interpret the details of figures featured on coins and on painted or sculpted iconographic programmes, assigning precise meaning to the representation of a god, an animal or a vegetal element.[63] Reflecting upon the power of images, they try to understand whether the iconographical programmes of monuments were seen and understood, and if so by which section(s) of the population.[64] However, the primacy of sight over the other senses in contemporary Western culture is mirrored, we find, in its historiography,[65] and this purely visual approach rarely takes into account the role of music and the sound environment in general. If one accepts, as I have shown here, that there is indeed a soundscape of political power, then one must also take into consideration that these sounds were, by their very nature, an efficient, familiar and indeed effective tool of communication for the Roman population. The music of power spread through the city and touched its audience in a way that figural representations could not.

The means at the disposal of the city for acoustic communication were great, and their efficiency was reinforced by the material contexts of musical performances. However, it is not possible to differentiate between hearers: the city's sounds were imposed without distinction. In this sense,

---

[62] Sen. *Apocol.* 12: 'Et erat omnium formosissimum et impensa cura, plane ut scires deum efferri: tubicinum, cornicinum, omnis generis aenatorum tanta turba, tantus concentus, ut etiam Claudius audire posset.'

[63] Here I am thinking specifically of Sauron's interpretations of vegetal friezes decorating the lower level of the Ara Pacis and the diverse reactions that they have elicited (enumerated in Sauron 2000: 50–64).

[64] The very fact that monuments and their ornaments existed is enough to ensure their communicative efficacy, even if no one could comprehend or differentiate the precise details. Cf. Veyne 2002, who takes up the question of the efficacy of Trajan's Column with breathtaking intellectual power.

[65] See Smith 2007 on the hierarchy of the senses and the history of the pre-eminence of vision. For a similar critique, see Howes 2003: xi–xx and Howes 2005. Smith underlines the importance of Foucault's thought for contemporary historiography, and its impact on the dominant position of sight.

the cultural memory of the music of power was universal, and the plebs were part of it but not its sole holder. The mastery of this common acoustic environment defined the contours of what, in discussing contemporary contexts, Barry Truax has called the 'acoustic community'.[66] In our case, we can say that this acoustic community had borders that were geographical (residing in an urban setting where musical performances were held) or political (for instance, knowing the *classicum* by having served in the legions during the period of the Republic), rather than social.

Conclusions

The results of this study might appear slight, especially for those who, following Jerry Toner, believe that Roman popular culture was more than a few 'half-remembered songs from the theatre'.[67] In fact, in the case of the music of power – defined as music played in public at the behest of political authorities – it is not possible to investigate further into the exact nature of what city-dwellers heard. With the exception of the *classicum*, the historical sources do not allow us to go beyond the study of the specific settings of musical performances. The content of these cultural forms escapes us almost entirely. Furthermore, the music of power was not a form of culture that was exclusively tied to the urban plebeian class. Produced in a public space by mass communication tools – the large bronze instruments such as the *tuba* and *cornu* – these sonorities imposed themselves above and beyond any social divisions. More than a popular culture, properly speaking, these sonorities are closer to constituting a Roman culture – or, indeed, a culture specific to the city of Rome, as the frequency and lavishness of celebrations in the capital exceeded all those of other cities. The music of power might thus be considered a unifying element of urban identity in which the plebeian took part, as did members of other social classes. As an integral part of a number of rites, this music was played frequently in civic space, imprinting itself in the Roman cultural memory as an identity-creating refrain. Such a conclusion, however modest, highlights a rarely studied aspect of our historical sources: even though we cannot access it in full, the soundscape of the past can certainly enlighten us about the culture and organization of ancient cities.

---

[66] Truax 1984 58–83, cf. p. 61: 'Sound signals, and the information they convey, bind the community together and contribute to its character.'
[67] Toner 2009: 2.

PART III

The Roman Empire: Greece, Rome and Beyond

8 | The Intellectual Life of the Roman Non-Elite

JERRY TONER

When Elizabeth Rawson wrote her book *Intellectual Life in the Late Roman Republic*, published in 1985, she felt it sufficient to concentrate on the philosophical and literary pursuits of the Roman elite. Almost no mention was made of Romans of other classes. On the other hand, academics of other periods who have looked at the culture of the lower classes, have often been influenced by Bakhtin's theory of carnival, which sought to locate popular culture primarily in the exuberance and inversions found during certain festivals. In such an approach, 'the popular' is often to be found in down-to-earth love of what Bakhtin rather delicately termed the 'lower bodily stratum' – the antithesis of anything intellectual. In this piece I seek to redress the balance, firstly by establishing that ordinary Romans can be seen as having had a serious side to their lives. I then set out to examine what characteristics we can discover about this intellectual life of the Roman non-elite, primarily in the imperial period. This will mean redefining what the term 'intellectual life' means. I argue for a far broader definition than that of Rawson: one that comprises those activities that involve creative or considered thought at all levels of society. Popular intellectual life did not centre on high cultural practices such as literature or formal philosophy. Instead, it revolved around finding solutions to more everyday problems and providing intellectual stimulation in an environment of limited resources.

The usual challenges stand in the way of such a project. Most of the surviving texts in the canon of classical literature pay little more than passing attention to the non-elite. When they do notice them, they are often sneering. Apuleius, for example, was keen that the uneducated should not try to imitate philosophy: 'I wish ... that the rude, vulgar, unskilled people who are only philosophers because they wear cloaks should not imitate them, nor should they debase the royal discipline [i.e. philosophy] ... by speaking badly and living in the same way'.[1] *Sordidi*, people of lower rank, had no place in an activity that was reserved for the

---

[1] Apul. *Fl.* 7.9–10: 'Quod utinam ... neu rudes, sordidi, imperiti pallio tenus philosophos imitarentur et disciplinam regalem ... male dicendo et similiter vivendo contaminarent.' Quoted in Hahn 2011: 135.

educated elite. But there is nevertheless a considerable amount of material that may offer us glimpses of the intellectual world of the ordinary Roman. This includes fables, proverbs, gaming-boards, jokebooks and theatrical events such as the pantomimes. Of course, there are serious methodological issues at stake here. These popular texts are no more transparent than any others; and some of them may not be as popular as they seem. But despite these difficulties, I hope to show that the traditional, closed view of intellectual life cannot be sustained in the face of evidence that strongly suggests that the non-elite enjoyed a wide range of intellectual inputs into their lives.

What Is Intellectual Life?

Rawson accepted that intellectual life is not altogether easy to define.[2] But most of her study is an investigation into scholars, writers and libraries. High-level literacy, in other words, sits at its core. Her focus was on questions relating to access to this book culture: 'I had a number of definite questions in mind as I worked ... what were the basic opportunities and constraints in intellectual activity? ... where were the books and other documents, and who could use them? How far could one do without written materials?' This understanding of intellectual life as a culture of book learning also informed Jonathan Rose's important study, *The Intellectual Life of the British Working Classes*.[3] Rose aimed to highlight the strong desire among the British working class to consume the written culture which had hitherto been the preserve of the highly educated elite. In doing so, his aim was to change the perception of popular culture from that of a group of uncritical consumers of low-brow entertainments into one that saw them as hungry for learning and self-improvement. The mass production of books made possible by the development of the printing press and industrialization meant that Rose's concentration on book culture was both sufficient and fruitful. The problem in the pre-literate, manuscript world of the Roman Empire is, of course, that such a narrow approach automatically condemns the non-elite to a life almost bereft of intellectual activity.

That is not to say that there was no non-elite literary life. As Rawson pointed out, many other 'more or less literate people' probably never read a 'real book', but did have access to the 'lowest forms' of text, which were

[2] Rawson 1985: vii. [3] Rose 2001.

jokebooks, anthologies of sayings or passages of verse, as well as astrological and magical texts.[4] The problem with this is that the numbers who were more or less literate enough to read one of these texts were probably small. Leaving aside the details of the literacy debate, it is clear that the overwhelming majority of the non-elite, especially when this includes the rural population, would not have been in a position to enjoy such texts. In the urban context of Pompeii, there does seem to have been some more widespread enjoyment of literary texts, with Virgil being cited in graffiti on at least sixty-five occasions.[5] Of these, sixteen are the first line of the epic, fourteen the first line of Book 2, with another twenty-two quotes from sixteen different passages, as well as thirteen from the Eclogues. The first line was sufficiently well known for it to be parodied in one example.[6] Tacitus also notes that Virgil's verses could be heard in the theatre, while Suetonius refers to repeated theatrical performances of the Eclogues.[7] But not all access to high culture depended on the book. This was an oral culture where there were public readings of Virgil's writings, and pantomimes were sometimes held with Virgilian themes.[8] As Horsfall has pointed out, the fact that literature was largely an elite product did not mean that the vast majority was 'bullied, exploited, poor and therefore naturally condemned by economic circumstances, aristocratic bullying and political manipulation to – if not illiteracy proper – then at least to a profound degree of intellectual impoverishment'.[9] Or as Rawson somewhat pejoratively put it, 'it is clear that even illiteracy would be no bar to some sort of quasi-intellectual activity'.[10]

What I want to suggest is that we should try to broaden out the concept of intellectual life beyond this kind of literary or quasi-literary activity. The risk with such text-based definitions is that the cultural practices of the non-elite come to be seen as being valuable only to the extent that they ape or participate in those of the elite. I hope to show that it is clear that there were many other non-elite practices which contained an intellectual element. How then are we to understand what the intellectual life entailed?

It would seem to be uncontroversial to start by requiring intellectual life to consist of activities that involve active intelligent thought, as opposed to simply an emotional or instinctual response. Some element of learning, not necessarily academic erudition, can be seen as part of this. Such learning informs the participants' approach to the activity and allows

---

[4] Rawson 1985: 50–1.   [5] See Milnor 2009. See also Introduction (p. 30).
[6] *CIL* 4.9131: 'fullones ululamqua cano, non arma virumque'.
[7] Tac. *Dial.* 13; Suet. *De Poetis* 103–4; see Panayotakis 2008.
[8] Horsfall 2003: 56. See also Adams 1999.   [9] Horsfall 2003: 66.   [10] Rawson 1985: 52.

them to engage in it critically, in the sense that they are able actively to appreciate the qualities of what is being done. Involving this kind of active, intelligent engagement, we can see that intellectual life is concerned with the production, dissemination and appreciation of ideas. To some extent, then, it is about philosophy and theology or what might be seen as thinking about the deeper problems of life and beyond.[11] Yet there is also a more creative element to intellectual life, representing the ability to understand and appreciate more artistic forms of expression. Putting the two elements together, we can also see intellectual life as encompassing the act of participating in the meta-commentaries that a culture produces. As in Geertz's classic analysis of the Balinese cockfight, these are the kind of important social activities that can be seen as representing abstract expressions of the principal themes that characterize that culture's normal life.[12] They are stories people tell themselves about themselves. When individual Romans uttered a proverb, went to the theatre or took part in a dice game, for example, they were not unthinking cultural automata, carrying out the cultural practices they had learned from birth. Rather, we should see them as actively and continuously reinterpreting the values that mattered in their lives.

If this kind of broad definition of intellectual life is to be applied outside the elite, four structural constraints must be removed. The first is not to limit artistic creations to those of a literary type. As we have already noted, in a largely illiterate society, such a restriction automatically disqualifies the majority from any participation in almost all forms of intellectual activity. Second, we need not see intellectual life as requiring long periods of reflection. The very ability to devote substantial temporal resources to thinking about the problems of life is something which only those of the leisured class could comfortably afford. Of course, there were probably periods of underemployment when many non-elite also had the free time to devote to greater reflection, but this was primarily not of their own choice and should not be seen as representing their only opportunity for engaging in intellectual activity. Third, no similar resource limitations should be applied to the concept of intellectual life. Neither books nor libraries nor theatres were necessary for an individual to partake in intellectual activity. All they needed was a brain and some means of exercising it. Finally, we should not limit abstraction and creativity to the serious.

---

[11] On the question of popular theology, see Maxwell in this volume. On characteristics of popular religion, see Toner 2009: 38–53.

[12] Geertz 1973: 412–53 ('Deep Play: Notes on the Balinese Cockfight'). For an attempt to apply this to the Roman games, see Toner 1995: 34–52.

As with the Balinese cockfight, so we should expect to find much popular intellectual activity being displayed in their entertainments.

When these constraints are removed, it becomes clear that the opportunities for non-elite intellectual life were considerable: we might see, for example, story-telling as giving voice to the relationship between the masses and their history; folk medicine as giving a way to theorize about the body and its relationship to the natural world; popular art as reflecting the decorative features that appealed to a less restrained aesthetic than elite art; and magic and divination as offering a set of rituals through which to explore theological issues such as the nature of the divine.[13] What I shall do in this chapter is to focus on three particular aspects of popular culture to try to establish the principle that a non-elite intellectual life existed. First, I shall look at popular philosophy as expressed in fables, proverbs and jokes; second, at non-elite participation in the creative life of pantomime; and finally at the abstractions that can be seen as being expressed in gambling and gaming. Space constraints mean that I am not going to try to pinpoint accurately which part of the non-elite we are looking at. Nor shall I discuss source issues.[14] None of these acts were uniformly expressed among the huge numbers of the non-elite in the Roman Empire; status, gender, geography, wealth and time all had an influence. But, taken together, I will argue that it is possible to discern a popular intellectual life, which was very different from the 'high cultural' practices of the elite, even if the boundary between the two was usually permeable and allowed for some level of elite participation.

Popular Philosophy

The elite view of the non-elite can be seen in Strabo's account of how, like children, they had no interest in abstract thought, preferring the simple attractions of myth and story:

Now every illiterate and uneducated man is, in a sense, a child, and, like a child, he is fond of stories; and for that matter, so is the half-educated man, for his reasoning faculty has not been fully developed, and, besides, the mental habits of his childhood persist in him. Now since the portentous is not only pleasing, but

---

[13] On popular medicine, see King and Toner 2014; on popular medicine in relation to mental disorders, see Toner 2009: 79–91; on popular art see Clarke 2003; on popular theology see Maxwell in this volume.

[14] On source issues, see Horsfall 2003: 20–30; Beard 2010; Toner 2015; Parker 2011.

fear-inspiring as well, we can employ both kinds of myth for children, and for grown-up people too.[15]

The philosopher cannot hope to influence by reason a crowd of women or a promiscuous mob. Philosophy, Strabo claims, is for the few. Yet if we look at popular fables, proverbs and jokes, we find considerable evidence for what we might call a popular philosophy. By this, I do not mean evidence of the familiarity with or the quotation of elite philosophical texts, even though, as with high literature, some such evidence does exist.[16] This would be to interpret popular philosophy purely in terms of the degree to which it had contact with elite philosophical thought. I mean the ability of popular forms to engage with discussions about abstract notions, albeit in an often practical context, which related closely to problems that ordinary people faced in their everyday lives.

The substantial body of fables and proverbs provided a treasure-trove of practical advice and moral guidance. Their popularity can be gauged from the fact that pithy and memorable phrases could generate applause in the theatres.[17] Their lack of context meant that they could be applied to a wide range of situations. Quintilian, in his guide to oratory, explains how fables appealed to the rough and uneducated.[18] They were the kind of morality tale that pleased simple folk, who were persuaded of the story's arguments because it gave them pleasure. As an example, Quintilian cites that of Menenius Agrippa, who was said to have reconciled the plebs to the patricians by his fable of the limbs' quarrel with the belly. He brackets proverbs alongside fables, which he argues should be seen as abridged fables that can be allegorically understood.

Clearly, in Quintilian's eyes, such simple tales and sayings did not constitute much by way of a philosophical system. Yet if we look more sympathetically at their subject matter, we can see popular wisdom literature as discussing a considerable variety of abstract notions by means of practical example. For example, the fact that truth is often a casualty of

---

[15] Strabo 1.2.8.
[16] See Horsfall 2003: 55, who notes that mime 'at a modest intellectual level seems to have been full of allusions to philosophical ideas, at least in simple formulation, with a definite vein of curiosity about Pythagoreanism'; and also that 'there is a good deal of philosophy, simplified but recognisable, in the graffiti of Pompeii, on metrical epitaphs, inscriptions for *xii scripta*, in proverbs, on the inscription of a Boscoreale cup and in the tipsy meditations of Trimalchio's guests'. It would, however, be wrong to assume that the characters portrayed in the *Satyricon* can be seen as authentic representations of the popular.
[17] See, for example, Cic. *Off.* 1.97; *Tusc.* 1.37; Sen. *Ep. Mor.* 108.8. On fable and proverbs, see Morgan 2007 and Forsdyke 2012: 59–73. On the theory of proverbs, see Obelkevich 1987.
[18] Quint. *Inst.* 5.11.19: 'ducere animos solent praecipue rusticorum et imperitorum'.

poverty is made clear in the saying, 'Want makes a needy man a liar.'[19] People had to be alert to the fact that not all was what it seemed: as one of the Sayings of Cato put it, 'Do not accept men who talk with smooth tongues, the pipe sings sweetly, when the fowler deceives the bird.'[20] Even when dealing with a spouse, the man had to be on his guard: 'Do not fear the words of an angry wife; for when a woman weeps, she fills the tears with ambushes.'[21] Above all, people had to be sceptical about those who claimed to provide them with intangible services. As the Aesop fable warns of the prophet who used to sit in the marketplace, how was it that he did not foretell that he himself was about to be burgled when he was charging people for professing to foresee their troubles?[22]

Abstract concepts such as friendship and justice are often debated within these texts. The fable of the eagle and fox who formed an intimate friendship tells how these two unlikely soul-mates decided to live near each other. Soon, when the eagle needed food for her young, she swooped down and grabbed one of the fox's cubs and fed it to her brood. The power of the feeling of injustice is noted in the fact that the fox felt less aggrieved for the death of her cub than for her inability to avenge them. That there is a natural and even divine justness in the world is made clear in the eagle's fate. While hovering near a sacrifice, she suddenly seized a piece of the flesh, and carried it, along with a burning cinder, to her nest. A strong breeze soon fanned the spark into a flame, and the eaglets, as yet unfledged and helpless, were roasted in their nest and dropped down dead at the bottom of the tree. There, in the sight of the eagle, the fox gobbled them up.[23]

The nature of power is a common theme. The fact that laws often apply differently to the most powerful is reflected in the proverb, 'Success makes some crimes honourable.' The danger for ordinary people in having contact with power is brought out by the saying 'It is not safe to joke with kings.'[24] Likewise, the fable of the lion captured by the farmer warns of the trouble that the weak can bring on their own heads by dealing with those more powerful than themselves. As the farmer's wife says to her husband after he has seen the lion kill his sheep and cattle, 'You got just what you deserved. Why did you want to shut in an animal you ought to have feared even at a distance?'[25] Some proverbs speak optimistically of the ability of the weak to harm the powerful: 'There is anger even in the ant.' Or, as the

---

[19] Pub. Syr. 534.   [20] *Sayings of Cato* 1.27.
[21] *Sayings of Cato* 3.20: 'Coniugis iratae noli tu verba timere; nam lacrimis struit insidias, cum femina plorat.'
[22] *Aesopica* 161 as numbered in Daly 1961.   [23] *Aesopica* 1. See Forsdyke 2012: 63–6.
[24] Pub. Syr. 326, 601.   [25] *Aesopica* 144.

fable of the mouse who ran over a sleeping lion asserts, 'Even mice can show their gratitude.'[26] But for the most part, popular wisdom literature advises that an attitude of resigned acceptance is the best way to cope with the abuse of the powerful. As one of the Sayings of Cato puts it, 'Just as you bear blows in school now and again from the teacher, accept your father's overlordship when he breaks out in anger in words.'[27]

The practical problems of poverty are often discussed: 'We live how we can, not how we want.'[28] A poor man who tries to raise himself up above his station is what one of Petronius' freedmen would call 'a dunghill cock'.[29] Like the ass who pretended he was a lion, he will end up being beaten by everyone with sticks when he is exposed as a fraud. As the moral to this fable states, 'A poor common man should not imitate the wealthy for fear of being laughed at and getting into trouble.'[30] Many stories also focus on the problems of slavery. Its state of powerlessness is encapsulated in the pithy phrase, 'The request of a master is a command.'[31] The desire of many to flee its rigours is brought out in the fable of the pet jackdaw, who could not endure his captive life but in trying to escape got himself killed.[32] The pitiable fate of slaves who bore children into servitude is lamented in the warning given to the dove by the crow: 'The more children you have, the more you will have to lament their servitude.'[33] And however unhappy a slave might be, 'An unwilling slave is wretched but he is still a slave.'[34] Issues of slavery are also presented from the owner's point of view. In the fable of the timorous old man who tries to persuade his donkey to flee an unexpected enemy attack, he is told in no uncertain terms how misguided it would be to rely on the loyalty of a slave: 'What does it matter to me whose slave I am', says the donkey, 'so long as I carry only one pack at a time?'[35] Indeed, masters should be alert to being conned by any clever slaves they own, for 'the clever slave has a share in power'.[36]

Perhaps the most important of the ideas is wisdom, *sapientia*. As Morgan has shown, intelligence was not valued for its own sake in the popular context.[37] There was no benefit to be gained from the intellectual pyrotechnics of elite sophists. Rather, fables and proverbs tells us that intelligence had to be applied for it to be popularly valued. In the context of looking for a non-elite intellectual life, we can see wisdom, therefore, as representing the accumulated practical intelligence of the non-elite. It resulted when intelligence was allied with experience. Such wisdom

[26] *Aesopica* 150. [27] *Sayings of Cato* 4.6. [28] Pub. Syr. 71. [29] Pet. *Sat.* 45.
[30] *Aesopica* 358. [31] Pub. Syr. 142. [32] *Aesopica* 131. [33] *Aesopica* 202.
[34] Pub. Syr. 757. [35] Phaedrus 1.15. [36] Pub. Syr. 596.
[37] On wisdom, see Morgan 2007: 43–8 on proverbs, 70–3 on fables, and 102–5 on *gnomai*.

was the opposite of foolishness. Cautious and conservative, it was a quality that fables and proverbs taught should be used to keep out of harm's way and to hang on to what little you had. It was a quality that was acquired by learning from the mistakes of the past and proceeded at a measured pace: 'The wise take their time', as one proverb held.[38] As Morgan also notes, such wisdom was not necessarily a social quality.[39] It was used by individuals in the pursuit of their own self-interest, not in the service of a more general cause. We can see this in the way that wisdom was often linked with cunning. It was a small step from applying intelligence to practical problems to using it to manipulate the social context in which such actions took place.[40] Not that such cunning was condemned. The wisdom attained in an environment of poverty could not afford such social niceties. But it was clear that this meant that individual intelligence often sat in conflict with the wider community.

Proverbs and fables, therefore, provided a vehicle for thinking about the various characteristics of what constituted a range of abstract ideas. They showed these qualities in action, with a moral commentary on what was considered socially necessary, acceptable or merely desirable. By doing so, this body of popular literature effectively analysed the nature of these notions, at least insofar as they applied to the context of non-elite daily life. Obviously this was not the kind of in-depth, logical analysis that we find in the philosophical texts of the highly educated. We often find that proverbs and fables provide somewhat contradictory messages and are inconsistent in the advice that they offer. Rather than seeing this as evidence for how bad such popular philosophy was, we should recognize that the practical contexts that gave rise to such general advice could not always be expected to produce a set of hard-and-fast rules. The non-elite individuals who found themselves in a tricky situation needed to interpret and apply these nuggets of wisdom to whatever difficulty they faced. In this respect, non-elite intellectual life consisted of actively thinking through the possibilities offered by the collected wisdom of the past. Through imagination and the creative interpretation of ancient stories and well-known sayings it was possible for the individual to add to meanings that had collectively been created and stored.

Fables were supposedly invented to enable slaves to express their sentiments couched in a form that would not cause offence to their owners.[41]

---

[38] Pub. Syr. 311. [39] Morgan 2007: 168. [40] Morgan 2007: 147.
[41] According, at least, to Phaedrus 3 pr. On the meanings of fables, see Morgan 2007: 19–22, 57–63; Toner 2009: 28–9, 36–7; on the hidden political meanings of fables, see Toner 2009: 165–7; Forsdyke 2012: 62–8.

This obfuscatory element to their structure meant that they necessarily required creative interpretation by those employing them. It also means it is impossible for us to ascertain all the various meanings that such sayings would have had for their non-elite users. They represented what Scott has called a 'hidden transcript', by which he means a subordinate discourse, which is cut off from that of a society's dominant groups. It is a discourse that operates beneath the public transcript of what was considered acceptable, and indeed safe, to say.[42] But such creative interpretation means that these subordinate texts allowed members of the non-elite to theorize about important issues that affected their lives. Many of the texts also saw the world through the eyes of the weak, allowing them to critique power without its even realizing it. The seemingly simple and harmless fable and proverb therefore served as a platform for all manner of popular philosophy concerning the nature of their social world.

One striking element of popular philosophy is its use of humour as a means of theorizing. Perhaps this stemmed from the same need to adopt a cloak of informality to conceal its more serious purpose from those above them in society. Or it may have resulted from the inversions that often characterized popular festivals such as Saturnalia and the Kalends (on which see Grig in this volume), which made it seem natural to express important matters in a non-serious way. Or did the use of humour reflect the fact that the non-elite did not share the same stake in society as the powerful and so refused to take it seriously? Whatever the reason, we find a variety of comic forms serving to analyse aspects of non-elite life.

The decoration of the Tavern of the Seven Sages in Ostia explicitly mocked the philosophy of the elite.[43] Phrases such as 'Thales advises those who shit hard to push hard' and 'Cunning Chilon taught how to fart silently' subverted the cerebral output of the educated by transforming it into a collection of scatological advice. In part, we can see this as a Bakhtinian refocusing on the lower stratum for comic effect.[44] We can also see in such texts a refusal to accept the usefulness of intellectual theorizing for its own sake. Empty theorizing by a philosopher becomes almost literally a load of vacuous crap. What matters is the down-to-earth, the everyday and the practical. Learning how 'to shit well' was in some ways

---

[42] See Scott 1990 on hidden and public transcripts, discussed by Forsdyke 2012: 40–9. Also see Scott 1985 for various forms of subordinate resistance. For an attempt to apply Scott's theories to the Roman context, see Toner 2009: 117–22; 162–84, 188–9.
[43] See Clarke 2003: 171–5.
[44] On carnival, see Bakhtin 1968. In the Roman context, see Toner 2009: 92–122; and Branham 2002.

a reduction of the practicality that epitomized popular life and represented an anti-intellectual intellectualization of non-elite life.

We also find jokes providing an anthropological meta-commentary on non-elite life.[45] If we take some examples from the surviving ancient jokebook, the Philogelos, we find humour acting as a vehicle to convey discussions of many of the anxieties of everyday life. Approximately 15 per cent of the jokes concern death and dying. The humour of some of these is pretty dark: when an intellectual was haggling over the price of a coffin for his dead wife, he asks the undertaker to 'throw in for free a small casket, in case I need it for my son'.[46] However inappropriate such jokes might seem to us, and may well have done to many Romans in the wrong context, they drew on generally accepted notions of the proximity of death and high rates of child mortality for their effect. It was because people knew they could die at any time that they found them funny.

Other jokes reveal a range of popular thought about other issues. Many exhibit concerns about status or identity. In one, a man, just back from a trip abroad, went to an incompetent fortune-teller to ask about the health of his family: 'Everyone is fine, especially your father.' When the man objected that his father had been dead for ten years, the fortune-teller replied, 'You have no clue who your real father is.'[47] In a world without paternity tests, such semi-paranoid patriarchal anxieties seem to have been commonplace. When a friend said to an intellectual, 'I want to congratulate you on the birth of your new son!' the intellectual said, 'It is because of friends like you that I have a new son!'[48] A man could never really know what his wife was up to while he was out working. But, more generally, identity jokes such as this underscore how fragile was an individual's position in society. It was birth that dictated status and established one's position in society. That even such a fundamental social bedrock could itself be uncertain emphasized just how insecure all types of status could be.

Many jokes relate to the nature of intelligence. Indeed, the 'intellectual', the *scholastikos*, is a frequent butt of the humour. What characterizes the intellectual, however, is of course that he is entirely lacking in common sense: 'That slave you sold me died', a man complained to an intellectual. 'Well, I swear by all the gods, he never did anything like that when I had him', comes the reply.[49] The non-elite take on intelligence is clear: that book learning is not enough or even of any use in the real world. We find

---

[45] On the theory of humour, see Critchley 2002; Beard 2014; and Toner 1995: 83–8.
[46] *Philogelos* 97.   [47] *Philogelos* 201.   [48] *Philogelos* 98.   [49] *Philogelos* 18.

something similar in the ancient equivalent of the Irish or Polish joke, which was aimed at the inhabitants of Abdera or Kyme. Seeing a eunuch chatting with a woman, an Abderite asked him if it was his wife. The eunuch replied that people like him could not have wives. 'Ah then she must be your daughter', he replies.[50] These are individuals who stand at the other end of the intelligence spectrum from the *scholastikos* but, like them, cannot even understand the most basic truths. The truly intelligent are those who are implicitly able to see through the charlatans they encounter in their everyday existence: the fake fortune-tellers and incompetent doctors and barbers. Intelligence in the jokebook is theorized as a practical commodity, a kind of streetwise *nous* which prevented the individual from being taken for a ride.

Popular Artistic Appreciation

I want now to look at the more creative side to non-elite intellectual life. In particular, whether ordinary people had not just passive exposure to art in the broad sense, but also the skill-set to act as critical consumers and connoisseurs of such creations. Again, I want to broaden out the discussion to think of such exposure to art in a non-literary sense. There is clear evidence for the popular appeal of poetry readings, with Strabo going on to describe how philosophy might be for the few but poetry is 'more useful to the people at large and can draw full houses, especially the poetry of Homer'.[51] But I want to argue that other artistic forms provided the means for the non-elite to engage fully with the more creative aspects of intellectual life, regardless of issues concerning their degree of literacy and education. The form I want to focus on is the pantomime.[52]

Pantomime was extremely popular. It played a central role in the entertainment of the Empire and, in Lada-Richards' words, possessed a 'formidable hold on public imagination'.[53] Seneca refers to the clamour and applause of the common people for the pantomime.[54] Its popularity was such that it persisted for centuries and resisted frequent attempts by later Christian emperors to ban it. But it also suffered from a long tradition

---

[50] *Philogelos* 115; cf. 112–27 for other Abderite jokes and 154–82 for those told at the expense of the inhabitants of Kyme.
[51] Strabo 1.2.8.
[52] On pantomime, see Slater 1996; Molloy 1996; Lada-Richards 2003 and 2007; Hall and Wyles 2008; and Webb 2008a: 168–96, 265–70.
[53] Lada-Richards 2008: 310.   [54] Sen. *Ep.* 29.12.

of elite censure, which liked to portray it as ignorant and uncritical. As Lada-Richards warns, to see it as such is to fall into an elite trap.[55]

The first thing to emphasize is that the pantomime, unlike the more down-to-earth mime, was an artistic form that clearly had aesthetic aspirations towards beauty. It was serious and visual, but also appealed to the ear through the use of a musical accompaniment, such as metronomic clacking which beat out the time, a range of instrumentalists, choirs and even water organs. Consisting of a graceful act in the style of modern ballet, the principal dancer relied on his or her vigorous physical training to be able to express a wide range of actions and emotions. Often the pantomimes used well-known myths for their storylines. Apuleius describes an act which dealt with the beauty contest between the gods that Paris adjudicated and led ultimately to the Trojan war.[56] His description of the scene makes it clear that the performance relied on some aesthetic subtlety:

Then Venus appeared displaying to all her perfect beauty, naked except for a sheer silk scarf which covered, or rather shaded, her quite remarkable hips ... Then two groups of attractive young maidens danced onto the stage, the Graces and the Seasons, who honoured the goddess by scattering flowers around her. They danced with great skill an intricate ballet movement. The flutes played sweet Lydian melodies, which soothed and delighted the spectators. But far more delightful was Venus, who began to move forward gracefully, rhythmically, slowly, swaying softly from side to side, gently inclining her head.

The use of such myth may in part have been the result of playing to a crowd who were multi-ethnic and possessed little by way of shared culture or language. Myth acted as a collective store of wisdom in the same way as fables and proverbs. And for those in the crowd that did not know the myths, then the pantomime also provided an education in them. Either way, the hoped-for result, as Strabo also argued, was that the people who lived in the cities would be 'incited to emulation by the myths that are pleasing'.[57] Hearing of the heroic deeds of mythology, they would be inspired to improve their own behaviour, but also learn of the divine punishments that awaited them if they acted shamefully. Myth, in other words, was an accessible way to reify abstract qualities in a manner that made them recognizably human and understandable to a broad audience.

It is also clear that pantomime was fundamentally physical.[58] The pantomime artist sought to create character by means of the

[55] Lada-Richards 2008: 292. [56] Apul. *Met.* 10.29. [57] Strabo 1.2.8.
[58] Huskinson 2008: 88.

movements of the body and the use of masks and costume. As Hall says, 'Much of the pleasure in pantomime seems to have been generated by the transformation of the dancer into different roles within the individual story.' But, as Hall also argues, this physicality did not mean that the pantomime had no intellectual qualities. Indeed, it 'trained its spectators in a sophisticated cognitive mode'.[59] It was a way of 'understanding with one's body'.[60] No doubt there were also some unintellectual elements to the enjoyment, such as male voyeurism. But by exploring the contrast between outward appearances and qualities within, the pantomime represented in a dramatic form some of the polarities that underpinned normal life in Rome.[61] The boundaries between male and female, passion and restraint, order and chaos were all questioned though the liminal personality of the pantomime artist. On the pantomime stage, identity was not fixed but a mutable, plastic concept. As Lucian argues in his stout appreciation of the art, *On Dance*, given through the words of the character Lycinus, pantomime at its best held up a mirror to the audience and allowed them to see and know themselves. It was nothing less than an instrument for moral self-reflection.[62]

Pantomime did not only consist of great feats of physical agility. The still poses which the pantomime dancer adopted may also have resonated with meaning and required active and intelligent popular participation. Lada-Richards has suggested that some of these poses may have imitated famous statues, thereby adding a layer of intertextuality to the performance. Of course, we can safely assume that not everyone in the audience will have got every reference, but when well-known, easily recognizable pieces of public statuary were being copied, it is reasonable to think that many, perhaps most, in the crowd will have picked up on them.[63] The audience also had to be alert to the various meanings that the artist was generating through the use of costume. Fronto describes how a pantomime might use a scarf to represent such diverse things as a swan's tail, Venus's hair or a Fury's scourge.[64]

The level of skill that the pantomime dancer had to attain in order to express such a range of concepts and emotions was considerable. The dancer needed to have a body like that of a professional gymnast, whose legs, Galen tells us, could assume positions that ordinary men could not hope to imitate, even if they tried to force them with their hands.[65]

---

[59] Hall and Wyles 2008: 22.   [60] Lada-Richards 2007: 131 quoting Bourdieu.
[61] See Lada-Richards 2007: 66–8.   [62] Luc. *Salt* 81; see Lada-Richards 2007: 88–9.
[63] See Lada-Richards 2004.   [64] Fronto *Orations* 5, quoted by Wyles: Wyles 2008: 76.
[65] Galen K4: 451, quoted by Webb 2008b: 53.

The pantomimes, Lycinus says in Lucian's work, have to know everything: 'all that is, that was, that shall be'. Nothing must escape their memory. Their job is an unenviable one: to faithfully represent their subject, to adequately express their own ideas, and to make everything clear and comprehensible.[66] The leading pantomime actor in Nero's reign was unsurpassed in the breadth of his range and the grace of his execution. When a cynic, Demetrius, who was unfamiliar with the form, asked to see him perform in order to make up his own mind, the pantomime represented the loves of Ares and Aphrodite, the whole story from the craft of Hephaestus, his capture of the two lovers in the net, the blushes of Aphrodite, and the embarrassment of Ares, all without the aid of the time-beaters, the flutes or even the chorus. Demetrius was amazed by the performance and cried, 'This is not seeing, but hearing and seeing at the same time. It is as if your hands were tongues!'[67] Again we should not concentrate only on the physical qualities. Lucian emphasizes that pantomime 'quickens the mental faculties at every turn'.[68] His description of the qualities that the artist needs also dwells on the broad range of high-cultural skills required: music, rhythm and metre, philosophy, both natural and moral, rhetoric, painting and even sculpture. All of these are needed to enable the artist to reveal human character and passions.[69]

The high technical ability of the performer does not of course mean that the non-elite members of the audience understood or appreciated it.[70] A passage from Cicero suggests that the theatre crowd in the Late Republic was well able to recognize the quality of the performance on offer: 'If an actor makes a movement that is a little out of time with the music or recites a verse that is one syllable too short or too long he is hissed and hooted off the stage.'[71] Lucian also describes how the collective tears at moments of pathos showed that the whole audience understood what was going on and could recognize what was being performed.[72] That did not mean that no degrees of connoisseurship existed in the crowd. Libanius says that the joy of watching pantomime lay in the ability to exercise one's gradually acquired knowledge. But he also describes how audiences relished the chance to test their knowledge, and so scrutinize 'the position of the feet, the directions of the hands, the harmony of the gestures . . . and, in general, the comeliness of the entire spectacle'.[73] And, as Lucian says of the audiences in Antioch, both highly intelligent and devoted to

---

[66] Luc. *Salt.* 36.   [67] Luc. *Salt.* 63.   [68] Luc. *Salt.* 85.   [69] Luc. *Salt.* 35.
[70] See Robson in this volume on different levels of audience.   [71] Cic. *Paradoxa* 25.
[72] Luc. *Salt.* 79; see Lada-Richards 2007: 88–9.
[73] Libanius *Oration* 64.57; see also Plotinus *Enneads* 4.4.33; and Lada-Richards 2007: 50–1, 134.

pantomime, 'each individual is all eyes and ears for the performance; not a word, not a gesture escapes them'. One overweight dancer was met with earnest entreaties to 'spare the platform'; a thin performer was recommended to 'take care of his health'. The fact that some of the audience criticism was humorous should not, as Lucian emphasizes, detract from the considerable interest that the city had in the show or from its ability to 'discern its merits and demerits'.[74]

The tradition of elite censure of the pantomime can conceal this popular discernment. Cicero elsewhere mocks the audience at a performance of a mime act, which represented a symposium of poets and philosophers, including, anachronistically, Euripides, Socrates, Menander and Epicurus, because the crowd loudly applauded 'in their ignorance'.[75] And we can find some of the same elements of elite disdain for the lesser quality of popular appreciation in Lucian's text on the pantomime. Criticizing an over-the-top performance of the madness of Ajax, he describes how the pantomime artist 'so lost control of himself, that one might have been excused for thinking his madness was something more than feigned'. The actor tore the clothes from the back of one of the time-beaters, snatched a flute from a player's hands, and used to it attack the nearby actor who was playing the part of Odysseus. Lucian condemns the 'illiterate riff-raff, who did not know good from bad, and had no idea of decency', because they regarded it as a 'supreme piece of acting'. But the more intelligent part of the audience, according to Lucian, concealed their disgust, and 'instead of reproaching the actor's folly by silence, smothered it under their plaudits'.[76]

Divisions clearly existed within the crowd, which may to some extent have reflected the often competitive nature of the performances. But that there was a section who preferred their performances more understated and low-key should not blind us to the fact that the majority were also judging and appreciating the performance according their own view of its aesthetic qualities. In this case, they were looking for acting skill and a faithful representation of the extreme emotions of madness. Lucian's censure can obscure the normal situation that he implicitly describes: that both sections of the audience would usually be watching and appreciating the same performance in the same way, without any disagreement as to its value. It was only an extreme, abnormal performance of this kind that generated any notable dissension among the crowd as to its merits. We should see in the pantomimes, therefore, evidence for a non-elite exposure to, and appreciation of, an artistic form that deliberately aimed

[74] Luc. *Salt.* 76. [75] Cic. *Pro Gall.* frag. 2. [76] Luc. *Salt.* 82–3.

to bring to life widely disseminated stories and myths in a sophisticated and nuanced way. Indeed, a performance of this quality relied on an audience's discerning faculties for its effect.

Popular Abstraction

The final aspect of popular intellectual life I shall look at is that of the formulation of abstractions. The ability for art to express in a concentrated form the culture that informs it is one of its most powerful features. That is, of course, not all that art does, but in performing this important task, artistic creations can allow us to glimpse a culture's main themes, issues and flashpoints. Nor is it only art that can do this. Play and leisure, for example, often copy elements of the serious world in which they occur, as Geertz showed in his analysis of the Balinese cockfight. I would argue that some of the 'non-serious' cultural activities of the Roman non-elite can be seen as carrying out a similar role. I finish, then, by examining how popular gambling and gaming can be seen as providing an abstract expression of many of the principles of non-elite culture. As such, we can see these activities as an example of the kind of practical intellectualization that characterized non-elite intellectual life. As Kurke has suggested, 'it is precisely their lowly, unexamined status that endows games with extraordinary power to inculcate values within culture'.[77]

Perhaps the first intellectual value that gambling expressed was the importance of having niche knowledge. Gambling and board games required the learning of a significant body of detailed knowledge. As Purcell has noted, they involved 'numerical sophistication', and in doing so argue for us to see numeracy as being a valued part of non-elite life.[78] Being quick with numbers and fractions acted as a kind of ancient technological advantage.[79] As with literacy, though, it is probably right to see a range of numeracies having existed.[80] Some will have been learnt in areas of commerce and bookkeeping, others in the army or the business of crop management. But whatever its source and form, such niche expertise also reflected the kind of specialization that was fundamental for members of the non-elite to improve their economic situation.[81] It was having the detailed knowledge that an artisanal skill or trade gave that could boost

---

[77] Kurke 1999: 247.   [78] Purcell 1995: 4.
[79] See Horsfall's excellent appendix on interest rate calculations to see how difficult this could be: Horsfall 2003: 17–19.
[80] Woolf 2009.   [81] See Toner 2009: 18–22.

incomes significantly above those of the manual day-labourer. Gambling was seen as a technical skill, as, for example, in Claudius' treatise on gambling.[82] It is striking that one of the brags inscribed on a surviving gaming board is that, 'You don't know how to play (*ludere nescis*).' Knowledge was what marked out the good gambler from the bad. It was having sufficient learning that allowed the participant to understand and appreciate what constituted good play.

Gambling also expressed the important social elements of non-elite life in an abstract form. In particular, it highlighted the importance of status. The whole point of gambling was that it enabled the good player to get more money and prestige and so improve his position in society. As Purcell notes of Suetonius' description of Caligula, it caricatures him as an 'extravagant, pushy, hopeful plebeian, who can get away with obvious cheating'.[83] The widespread censure we find in elite literature for popular gambling stemmed from concerns at what such social mobility meant for society and for its being achieved without work or birth.[84] But for the non-elite, gambling served as an expression, in a very practical form, of this popular appetite for social mobility. It is no surprise that when Claudius is punished in Seneca's *Apocolocyntosis* it is by being condemned to play *alea* endlessly and pointlessly. It was not the taking part that mattered, it was winning.

Status in the non-elite world was won in the local sphere. It was the ability to do well within the community context, often in a crowded and competitive urban environment, that singled out the successful non-elite male. Standing up for oneself was an important part of winning and maintaining status and local reputation. These are all qualities that we find the gambler expressing and learning at the table. Whether it was the abusive counters or the frequent fights that gambling seemed habitually to generate, it was all reflective of the kind of verbal and physical sparring such a competitive social environment produced.[85] People were prepared to go to considerable personal lengths to maintain their status within the gambling group, in what we can imagine was a similar way to how they went about their everyday lives. They would take advantage of another's weaknesses and ignorance or, if necessary, fight to protect their interests. Cheating, through such means as magic, was all part of what was normal behaviour.[86] It was not always possible simply to rely on niche expertise.

[82] Purcell 1995: 30. [83] Purcell 1995: 11 on Suet. *Cal.* 41.2. [84] See Toner 1995: 95–101.
[85] See *Digest* 11.5 for various laws concerning gambling-related violence. Wall paintings from the Caupona of Salvius in Pompeii also depict men fighting about the outcome of gaming.
[86] *PGM* 7.423–8.

But it is also striking that the form of gambling reflected a strong social side to this competitiveness. The camaraderie of the local group provided communal bonds and networks. As Ammianus describes, in Rome, 'where all friendships are rather cool', it was only those friendships created between gamblers that were sociable and intimate.[87] They had been forged through shared struggle and granted the individual a respected place within that gaming community. Any imputed slight to that reputation, based as it no doubt was on his knowing 'all the secrets of the dice', resulted in a grave and solemn response.

The counters, bearing such charming taunts as 'drunkard', 'tart' and 'adulterer', did not only reflect simple abuse, they also acted as symbols of the competitive banter that served to glue together these local male communities. This was not just abuse, it was jocular macho sparring. Men were expected to be able to invent and respond to witticisms as quickly as they could work out the odds on the gaming table.[88] Banter of this kind was itself an expression of street-smart nous. This was the kind of quick-witted thinking that enabled the non-elite to hold their own in such a competitive close-knit world. It was not purely designed to wound the recipient. The collective humour it generated supported group morale and established a hierarchy of wit. Reducing individuals to the vices expressed on the counters emphasized that the group came first. However competitive their world, the non-elite needed each other to survive. There was no room for the individual to be overly sensitive to such personal attacks. The non-elite male was expected to be tough enough to laugh off such abuse and share in the collective laughter. It was, however, a model of social relations that was patently aggressive and argumentative.

Gambling also expressed the popular valorization of risk-assessment. In a world where poverty was never far away, and incomes were always vulnerable to the knock-on effects of poor harvests or the arbitrary patronage of the elite, the average Roman needed to learn the skills to control the risks he and his family faced in life. Gambling taught people the necessary skills to be able to take life-affecting decisions under pressure within a communal context. It told them when to be cautious and risk-averse and when to risk more. As in the moves of ancient board games, it was necessary to display tactical nous.[89] Pliny the Elder notes that monkeys could be 'amazingly cunning' and could even play board games of this type.[90] Those people who did it well gained prestige: Piso was 'so good and

---

[87] Amm. Marc. 28.4.21. [88] For popular wit, see Hawkins in this volume.
[89] See, for example, Polyb. 1.84.7–8; Ovid, Ars 3.355–60. [90] Plin. HN 8.215.

clever in the game of little soldiers that people would gather round him as he played'.[91]

However much the non-elite might hope to improve their prospects by means of their local expertise, the popularity of gambling also reflected the major part that chance played in their life. As the moral of a fable said, 'So it is that chance often bestows what skill cannot provide.'[92] I suggest that we can see gambling, in this context, as expressing in an idealized form the kind of personality traits that the non-elite male needed to possess in order to deal with this kind of risky, volatile environment: competitive, communal, quick-witted, firm when necessary, yielding when not. I want now to end by showing how aleatory practices in a different, religious context can show us how these kinds of personal characteristics functioned to generate risk-assessments in practice. In dice oracles, with their use of dice or knuckle-bones to elicit the will of the gods, we can find a confluence of the chance of play and that of real life.

By way of example, let us look at the pillar of dice oracles, which stood in the forum at Kremna, in central Pisidia. This four-sided advice column was inscribed with replies to the fifty-six possible throws of five knuckle-bones.[93] Other almost identical pillars have been discovered elsewhere in the region. In the answers, choosing the right time to act becomes all-important. It was crucial not to act intemperately. As throw 10, called the throw of Tyche the Helmsman, states, this was no time for frivolous enthusiasm, which would do 'great harm'. The advice is to wait because it is the right time for waiting. If the consulter can manage to do that, then he will 'accomplish everything'. Or as throw 22 puts it, 'Stay calm for the time is not yet ripe. If you make frivolous haste in vain, you will pursue a goal that is out of reach. I do not yet see the right moment, but if you relax a little, you will achieve success.'

Success also required experience and intelligence: the practical wisdom we encountered before. It meant having a plan. It meant accepting the weak and lowly place of humanity in the universe: 'You are struggling against waves that oppose you. You are looking for a fish in the ocean, don't hurry into the matter. It is not profitable for you to force the gods inopportunely' (throw 14). But for all their acceptance of human frailty, these were texts written for those looking to fight their fate actively. They might obey the gods but they were always looking for the right moment to burst into

---

[91] [Probus] *Note on Juvenal's Satire* 5.109. On this source, probably fourth-century, which survives in Lorenzo Valla's 1486 edition of Juvenal, see Peirano 2012: 152–3.
[92] *Aesopica* 21.
[93] The dice oracle can be found in Horsley and Mitchell 2000: 22–38; see also Graf 2005b.

action. This desire for things to happen was itself a reflection of the desire for personal improvement that characterized the aspirational non-elite small businessmen.

Inaction was sometimes the best move: 'Scorpions stand in your way. Don't hurry to do the business which you intend. Stay and what you want will happen later. This is better, neither to buy or sell' (throw 23). But if you bided your time and struck at the right moment, victory would be yours. As throw 7, Of Victory, states: 'You will win, you will take what you wish, and everything will be yours.' Not only that, but the gods themselves will respect you: 'The Daimon treats you as worthy of honour and you will overcome your enemies.' Success in such a world meant not only financial improvement, but a concomitant rise up the status and respect ladder.

A proverb put it this way: 'We must master our good fortune or it will master us.'[94] What we see in both gambling and dice oracles is a belief that chance was not overwhelming but was something that could be managed and influenced. To see the world in this way was to leave room for hope and individual agency. Rather than see their life as simply being dominated by chance, gambling and dice oracles reflected a conception of the world in which non-elite individuals, however modest their station, had an opportunity to improve their lot. To be sure, this required knowledge, skill, experience, nous and guts, but the opportunity did still exist. It enabled the average Roman, who had to survive in an environment where risks abounded, to cope with this high level of uncertainty. Life was not simply a matter of destiny, rather the vagaries of chance could be directed to the individual's benefit and, conversely, to the detriment of enemies. It was not simply humanity's lot to accept its fate with resignation.

We can see in gambling and aleatory divination practices how randomness was imbued with meaning, how the chance that played so large a part in non-elite life was conceptualized, but how that concept was itself constructed in such a way that it gave the non-elite an opportunity for agency and purpose. Chance became a malleable force, which, if managed successfully, could help the non-elite fulfil their social aspirations. Risk may have been an inherent part of ordinary life, but a culture developed in response that used beliefs and practices to soften its impact. Of course, the centrality of chance to non-elite thought also reflected the fact that they were fundamentally powerless to avoid the risks that they were structurally exposed to throughout their life. What we find, therefore, in the forms of gambling and the oracles are translations of chance into practice. They are

---

[94] Pub. Syr. 109.

an abstract expression of the ideal set of life skills and characteristics that the non-elite needed to possess to thrive in such a world.

This part of non-elite culture was, like most others, largely accessible to those at the top of society. There was nothing secret about the activities of gambling. But the significance of what was learned there resonated far more greatly with those who were themselves structurally exposed to greater risk. We must be careful not to see this subculture as a degraded form of elite culture. As Woolf says, commentating on Purcell's idea of popular gambling knowledge as a form of calque or parody of high culture, the danger is that in such a view 'popular knowledge is in some respects secondary to that mastered by the social elite'.[95] The idea of a non-elite take-off of elite culture does at least emphasize the agency of the adopters. But, however less complex or sophisticated or erudite such non-elite thinking was in comparison with that of the elite, popular aleatory practices can be seen as representing an abstract intellectualization of their own way of life – a meta-commentary that told them what they needed to know to do well. Taken alongside popular philosophy and evidence for widespread appreciation of artistic activity, it was just another facet of what we can reasonably describe as a non-elite intellectual life.

[95] Woolf 2009: 50–1 discussing Purcell 1995: 31.

9 | Divination and Popular Culture

VICTORIA JENNINGS

Popular Literature: A Question of Words

> Master, if it is a question of words, I have comebacks at the ready; but about this ... I am no *mantis* (*oute gar eimi mantis*).
>
> (*Life of Aesop* G84)[1]

This chapter is concerned with popular or non-elite literary texts, in particular the *Life of Aesop*. I suggest that thinking about divination is a good starting point for thinking more broadly about how the representation of popular religion in popular literature offers us a way 'in' to popular culture. There is a real sense in which 'popular literature' is a hopefully but vainly grasped-at will-o'-the-wisp. The evidence is entirely against a literature of or for the people. A critical mass of 'lower' readers is never likely to have existed to shape literary tastes.[2] The dominance of Homeric texts in the papyrological record presents us with something of a demographic dead-end in gauging popular (rather, 'populous') in the sense of the 'entertainment' value of a text.[3] Another way to look at 'popular' is offered by the *Alexander Romance*, translated into twenty-four languages and second only in popularity to the Bible. 'Popular' here equates with 'best-seller': 'How can it be that works of such questionable literary merit achieved such outstanding popularity?'[4] Yet wide distribution tells us almost nothing about *who* is reading or listening or engaging with a text. And 'questionable literary merit' raises another series of questions altogether. In this chapter, popular texts will include novelistic texts, fictional biographies, fables, proverbs, jokes, mimes and oracle books. What characterizes many of

---

[1] Greek text: Perry 1952; translations are my own. G(rottaferrata) is the oldest (tenth/eleventh century) manuscript and closest in form to a first-/second-century archetype of the *Life of Aesop*. I am grateful to audiences in Edinburgh and Sydney for discussion of earlier versions of this chapter.
[2] Stephens 1994: 407–8.   [3] Stephens 1994: 410–16; Morgan 2007: 4   [4] Dowden 2009: 156.

these is their 'openness': non-canonicity, 'textual fluidity'[5] and existence in multiple versions, 'authored by no one and so authored by each one who writes it down'.[6] It seems likely that there was a performed element at work in this milieu (the episodic, comedic,[7] bodily obsessed *Life of Aesop* seems ideally suited for performance), and it is likely that their non-textual distribution – their audience and their 'consumption' – was considerably broader than text *qua* text transmission can suggest.[8] Not every consumer of a popular text will consume it at the same level of understanding, and this understanding cannot be simply quantified by level of education: some slaves, for instance, possess a level of literacy enabling them to read aloud to their masters. Do they also read aloud to their fellow slaves? (And what would they make of the *Life of Aesop*?[9]) The element of 'updating', seen in the multiple versions of the *Life of Aesop* (replacement of divine characters; expurgation/addition of scenes) or the oracle books makes us consider factors such as constant (rather than consistent) use and re-use, and even an ordinariness (and a meaningfulness) in non-canonicity, rather than a 'deviance'.[10] Jokes well illustrate another constituent of 'popular' (and the link with performativity), namely an interplay of the 'popular oral tradition and elite written text in ongoing dialogue'.[11] A compendium like *Philogelos* is essentially a toolkit for adaptive re-use, whether that be written or oral. There is also the question of the relationship between fictional texts and the performed mime.[12] An element of timelessness is noteworthy, whether this lies in the timelessness of 'adventure time' in the novels

---

[5] Hansen 1998: xxii; Thomas 1998: 280 ('Although these characteristics of "fluidity" are not sufficient to define a genre, precisely this lack of an original text is significant in assessing the type of writing these works were considered to be by their ancient audience').

[6] Kurke 2011: 10; Thomas 1998: 288; Whitmarsh 2008c: 82.

[7] Goins 1989–90. Kurke 2011: 356 suggests the loss of a number of comic Aesops restricts our understanding of the reception of the *Life*.

[8] Karla 2009b: 22–3.

[9] A particularly significant question if one subscribes to the 'participatory' and 'interrogative relationship to the text' postulated by Konstan 2009.

[10] Thomas 1998: 280 (meaningful); Jouannou 2009: 34 (deviance). Fixed categories of genre are not resistant to the unique, but are not necessarily helpful; thus Whitmarsh 2008c: 81 on Lucian's *True History* as 'not a Greek novel as the term is conventionally understood, but certainly a Congregationalist in the broad church of imperial Greek fiction'. Cf. Morgan's suggestion (2007: 283) regarding the *Lives* of Aesop and Secundus as members of a 'fusion genre', 'between high philosophy and popular wisdom ... drawing on elements from both to create something not quite like either'.

[11] Kurke 2011: 46.

[12] Lightfoot 2000: 230 on Herodas' 'mimesis of urban low life' in 'language ... incompatible with the idea that they were intended for an unlettered public'. Cf. Morgan 2007: 4 – mimes and farces 'occupy an ambivalent position between the vulgar and the sophisticated: the examples

(with their anachronistic facades of historicity and a near complete disregard for periodization: Isis, Croesus *and* Ahiqar[13] in a 'biography' of Aesop) or the absolute timelessness of the proverb and generic fable. The urban setting of many texts is also a factor in thinking about popular in terms of access and – as Avlamis has sensitively nuanced with regard to the *Life of Aesop* – 'relatability' and conventionality of themes.[14]

Tastes change, and tastes are driven by a variety of external forces (for instance, emperors[15]). I have already noted the element of constant change with these texts – their 'dynamic resistance to fixity'.[16] Popular culture in any time or place should not be viewed as a homogeneous phenomenon, although there are pressures regarding our evidence that make this a tempting supposition.[17] Yet there is also a sense in which the popular texts of the Greek imperial world – looking back with a certain deliberately traditional view of classical and Hellenistic Greece – provide a good case study for what appeals to a segment of the population who have access through text and, likely, performance (listening to texts; viewing actual performances).[18]

Popular Literature, Religion, Reality and Risk

> 'Samian men! ... take counsel in defence of your own freedom; this is a portent (*sēmeion*) of besiegement and a sure sign (*tekmērion*) of enslavement'.
>
> (G91)

'Popular religion was embedded in every area of non-elite life.'[19] All of the texts I have located under the umbrella of 'popular' bear out this close

---

that survive may have been written by the relatively highly cultured, but they derive from popular entertainment and continued to draw on it'.

[13] Ahiqar and Aesop: Konstantakos 2013.   [14] Avlamis 2011. Conventionality: Hägg 1997.
[15] Horsfall 2003: 70.   [16] Karla 2009b: 26.
[17] So, Horsfall 2003: 55 on a spike in 'popular culture' 50–100 CE. Some suppositions may be consequent on modern scholarship's 'taste' for the Greek imperial world.
[18] Stephens 2008: 56–7 on this acquired 'new Hellenism' of the novel world which 'expressed itself as an accumulated set of predispositions and practices held in common by the dominant social orders in the cities that encircled the Mediterranean'.
[19] Toner 2009: 38. 'Popular religion' readily attracts the pejorative shading laid on other 'populars'. My reading of 'popular religion' is broadly based on Mikalson 1983: 5 – 'religious views and attitudes that were acceptable to the majority'. This definition should permit the coexistence of individualized everyday practice (as in the *Life* G77 when an individual seeks a bird omen for personal guidance) alongside participation in mass consumption (as when an assembly of citizens seeks an interpretation for the collective benefit of the city: G81). As Fowler

involvement of the religious and the everyday: dreams, omens, oracles, sign-reading, prayer, offerings and sacrifices fill these works in more or less 'realistic', reflexive and rational ways.[20] A text like the *Life* perfectly illustrates by its representation of the everyday life of master and slave how a narrative can make use of the ordinary to extraordinary effect.[21] I do not suggest that popular literature is a precise mirror of everyday life.[22] There is an obvious sense in which supernatural phenomena are used in, for instance, the ancient novels as part and parcel of the narrative structure: they foreshadow, indicate and misdirect narrative expectations.[23] So, in Achilles Tatius 4.1, 'I told Leucippe about this dream, and ceased forcing myself on her.'[24] The sophisticated game that popular religion can be made to play – wrong interpretations, multiple interpretations – can be seen in episodes in which 'incorrect exegesis is crucial to the fulfilment of true prefigurement'[25] and to the narrative needs. These games are clever, and they help the narrative along or defer narrative inevitability, but can they – amid plentiful other evidence of how the everyday functions in the narrative – also offer insight into how popular religion plays an equally reflexive role in the parallel social world – the real world – where signs are taken seriously?[26]

Bakhtin has put forward an interesting explanation for the predominance of dreams and oracles in Greek prose romances, and for characters' reliance on them as guides to action: because the events of the novels' 'adventure time' are controlled by chance alone, experience and analysis are useless aids; the

---

2000: 322–3 notes regarding the distinction between public ritual/private magic or oracles/oracle-mongers, 'Context and social approval make all the difference.' Concepts such as the respectability of popular religion and the limits of 'non-official' religious practice are well addressed by Lucy Grig in the Introduction.

[20] Whitmarsh 2008b: 12 on novels 'composed by and for people whose daily lives were saturated with religiosity'.

[21] The methodological legitimacy of eliding slaves among lower consumers ('subordinate groups') of popular culture is discussed by Forsdyke 2012: 18–89.

[22] Hopkins 1993 remains fundamental for exploring the 'contention that the social history which can be squeezed from "real histories" and from fiction may be broadly similar, and that, for the interpretation of culture, there is little justification for privileging one above the other'.

[23] Bartsch 1989: 81 on the 'inferential walk'.

[24] Achilles Tatius 5.4: Leucippe collides with a swallow being chased by a hawk and Clitophon sees a painting of the rape of Philomena, leading to their plans changing – these events are recognized as signs.

[25] Bartsch 1989: 85. Examples of differing interpretations, wrong and misleading dreams: Heliodorus 2.16, 4.15, 10.3; Xenophon of Ephesus 1.12.

[26] One can take this practically (Shiner 1998: 167: 'It seems likely that reliance on divine causation in ancient narrative is not merely a literary device but reflects a shared understanding of the nature of causation in the world') or theoretically (Struck 2005: 147–8, 'divinatory thinking' encodes narratives as a mode of thought).

kaleidoscope of events is 'better understood through fortune-telling, omens, legends, oracular predictions, prophetic dreams and premonitions'.[27]

Can this narrative reliance on the supernatural by powerless protagonists be expanded to the everyday world? The concept of risk management – 'the theory that risks are socially constructed'[28] – is particularly interesting in terms of how religious use operates in relationships between powerless and powerful, such as (but not restricted to) slave and master.[29] We likely go too far[30] if we compare overtly the construction of fiction and the construction of social realities (in the sense that elements of religious improvisation[31] evoke an echo of 'adventure time' and that both groups share a 'common cultural experience'[32]). However, as Guinan has so well explored, an omen itself triggers 'generic expectations ... they operate in the mind to organize the observation into a signifying structure that makes attribution of divinatory meaning possible'.[33] In her study of oracles and risk, Eidinow sees curse tablets – 'unselfconscious emotional responses of ancient Greek men and women, from all levels of society, in fervent, sometimes ferocious, appeals to the gods' – as vivid records of ordinary life which can be read agonistically ('weapons in situations of rivalry and competition between individuals') and as 'a way for people to regain the initiative in a situation of essential powerlessness'.[34] Let us think more closely about how divination functions as a tool for managing the possibilities presented by the everyday life experience.

Why Divination?

> The Samians were anxious, unable to regard this omen (*sēmeion*) as anything but misfortune (*symphoran*). At once they summoned seers and priests (*manteis kai hiereis*) to settle the omen.
>
> (G81)

Divination is but one manifestation of the consumption of popular religion, but for considering popular culture it is a significant one. Divination is ubiquitous in the ancient world, at all levels of society, and over

---

[27] Bartsch 1989: 81, n. 1.   [28] Eidinow 2007: 5.   [29] 'Patron-management': Toner 2009: 32.
[30] Fusillo 2008: 330 on the *Life* as a 'text on slavery and story-telling'.
[31] Gould 1985: 7; Parker 2011: 4: 'the religion of crisis situations'.
[32] Mikalson 1983: 5 ('spoken of and acted upon daily'). Cf. Burkert 2005: 30 on the role of divination in 'modeling reality' in life and literature.
[33] Guinan 2002: 22.   [34] Eidinow 2007: 7, 154.

a remarkably broad period of time. It is a conservative phenomenon: this longevity and relative ritual stasis offer a stable platform for thinking about how people thought about and used divination. These factors emphasize a crucial point about divination, namely that it must be taken seriously, and that the predominately negative value ascribed to divination-as-superstition in our society obscures how tremendously important it was in daily life in the Greco-Roman world.[35] Divination is not something odd;[36] rather, we must consider divination – as its ubiquity suggests – as a normative response,[37] a 'rationality ... coherently included in the entire body of social thought'.[38] It is an everyday event, the 'white background noise to the city',[39] 'solidly rooted in the ordinary':[40] 'It's likely that in antiquity most people practiced or witnessed some form of divination at least once every few days.'[41] In this sense, divination is a useful phenomenon through which to approach popular life.

Material evidence (notably dice and lot oracles) suggests that divination was an accessible form of social participation for the non-elite.[42] Seeking divine guidance through divination can be a big ticket, high-status enterprise, requiring travel, time and money: things which demarcate the enquirer as elite. The 'ordinary' man was never likely to go one-on-one with the Pythia.[43] Certain forms of divination did require outlay on the means of divining (divination from entrails requires beast sacrifice[44]) or a professional to interpret the signs (as with dreams) or the ability to consult an interpretive text (dice oracles; dreams). The requirement of literacy closes down certain divinatory avenues. However, one route

[35] Modern opinions of 'superstition' as a non-rational phenomenon (and one linked, sometimes frivolously but primarily pejoratively, with notions of primitiveness, foreignness, lower levels of education and low social class) have coloured perspectives not only on ancient (and modern) divination, but also ancient superstition. Ancient superstition as a rational pious response taken to excess or perverted to caricature is well demonstrated by the Superstitious Man of Theophrastus *Characters* 16, whose exaggerated personal agency in the name of piety takes 'superstition' well beyond a rational, functional level of ordinary daily living.

[36] Divination *can* influence a wide mainstream audience in the modern world: thus 'Paul the Octopus' at the World Cup in 2010, 'the world's most famous octopus, the underwater Nostradamus, the eight-armed cephalopod prophet of the football pitch' (Roger Boyes, *Times Online* 27 October 2010, available at: www.theaustralian.com.au/sport/football/paul-the-octopus-didnt-see-his-death-coming/story-fn63e0vj-1225944119474.

[37] Flower 2008a: 246. [38] Vernant 1991: 304. [39] Ripat 2006: 156. [40] Miller 1994: 8.
[41] Johnston 2008: 3.
[42] Slaves at oracles: Eidinow 2012. The questions of the transparency of any divinatory system (elements of external, non-neutral control) and whether signs hold similar weight for elite v. non-elite consumers is beyond the scope of this chapter, but studies of dream interpretation note different interpretations given to different social classes: Pomeroy 1991; Hall 2011.
[43] Potter 1994: 23.
[44] Herodas *Mimiamb* 4: a cock substitutes for an ox on the alleged grounds of financial strain.

remains open: although receiving the optimum divinatory solution required a professional *mantis*,[45] do-it-yourself divination has a long literary pedigree. Away from the organized oracular centres, divination's entrenchment in the ordinary gains, for the seeker of popular culture, further cachet by the ordinariness of its instruments. Divination is rooted physically in the common, shared world of everyday chance and happenstance. This is particularly true of divination from birds.

Bird Divination and Popular Space

> Xanthus said to Aesop, 'Since I am a bird-interpreter (*oiōnistēs*), go and check if there's any troublesome bird at the entrance (*oiōnos . . . dyskolos*).
> (G77)

Bird divination is the earliest and most important form of Greek *manteia*, culturally entrenched by its significant role in Hesiod, Homer and the tragedians. Even when divination from entrails becomes the predominant form of divination from the classical period onwards, bird divination maintains a constant presence, a position reinforced by linguistic embedding: the Greek for 'bird' (*oiōnos*) means 'omen'.[46] The 'value', we might say, of a bird sign hardly diminishes. Unlike 'natural' divination by prophetic or inspired means, divination from birds is a technical or artificial *technē*. In terms of popular use, this is significant: bird divination can be *learned*. This do-it-yourself divination has a long history in elite texts, and while these instances are generally framed in elite contexts, there is little suggestion of a 'closed shop': Greek bird divination requires little technical know-how and it is not the protected baby of a specialist group. Xenophon offers a good example of the trained layperson at work: on campaign he travels with a professional *mantis*, but reveals that he has learned to read bird signs (and entrails) by observation.[47] The idea that one can learn without formal training is significant, as is the medium: Xenophon has to obtain a beast for entrail-reading, with all of the associated costs and paraphernalia. As well as representing an authoritative direct line from the heavens because of their ability to travel between the mortal/immortal

---

[45] Dillon 1996: 117 (an amateur's superstitions could influence interpretation).
[46] Dillon 1996: 102.
[47] Mikalson 1983: 40, 42, 127, n. 18; Johnston 2008: 115; Flower 2008a: 54. The history of this do-it-yourself is not without ambiguity: see Flower 2008b: 215–18 and Trampedach 2008 on Polydamas' amateur interpreting at *Iliad* 12.195–258.

realms, birds are also free and readily available. Bird divination is 'useful in that the worshipper can ask the gods for an answer to a specific enquiry and receive an immediate response without the necessity of consulting an oracle or a professional *mantis*, or even moving position'.[48] Bird divination is readily 'adaptable to home use'.[49] To summarize: bird divination is good to think about in popular terms because it is authoritative, free, easy to use, instant; its relative cultural stability is rarely debased or rendered déclassé;[50] and its arena of performance renders public/private boundaries immaterial. Bird divination is ideal for the 'everyman' seeking immediate quality divine guidance. Xenophon's proficiency as a *mantis* offers one further consideration: the self-trained interpreter can interpret for his own personal guidance, and he can interpret for the guidance of others, whether they be neighbours, masters or an army.

The Ideal Seer: Social Realities and Divinatory Conservatism

> ... it's not easy to figure out an omen (*sēmeion*). If someone's not effectively educated (*empraktos paideias*), he can't fully interpret an omen.
>
> (G81)

One turns to divination as a 'method of ending dissent and confusion and of deciding what is to be done'.[51] Divination legitimizes decisions; facilitates action; brings in objectivity; reassures.[52] It is a 'guide to action', 'and not ... a means of stripping the veil from the future to satisfy simple curiosity'.[53] Flower notes the 'high value that society placed on divination and an attendant anxiety about its proper performance'.[54] Divination, as we will see, can be 'a high-stakes performance' in which the interpreter gains access to riches and social mobility if things turn out well.[55] Interpreting signs, within and outside popular texts, is very much about

---

[48] Dillon 1996: 108.   [49] Johnston 2008: 132.
[50] Cicero describes dice/lot oracles as 'vulgar' (part of his negative case: *Div.* 2.41.86–8). Intellectuals despising lot oracles: Grottanelli 2005: 138–44. As Potter 1994: 26–7 notes on a civic dice oracle of Asia Minor, 'it was not a "lower-class" oracle, even though members of the lower classes could certainly use it. These texts were civic monuments erected with the full knowledge and quite probably the active encouragement of the town councils'; cf. Lane Fox 1986: 209.
[51] Burkert 2005: 29.   [52] Flower 2008a: 74–5, 243–4; Johnston 2005: 300–1.
[53] Parker 2000: 77.   [54] Flower 2008b: 204; Collins 2002: 41: it is a 'performed truth'.
[55] Flower 2008a: 189.

recognizing the 'concerns of the moment'.[56] In the *Alexander Romance*, Alexander is concerned when birds swoop down and eat the grain being used to lay out Alexandria's foundations. But his interpreters accentuate the positive: 'The city that you, King, have ordered to be built will nourish the whole world, and men born in it will be found everywhere: birds fly round the whole world.'[57] This is a 'spin' of great appeal to Alexander, that most generous rewarder of interpreters.[58] It is no surprise that doubts regarding the value of interpretation focus on the interpreters' self-interests rather than divination itself,[59] as at Phaedrus 3.3 where a worried farmer calls in the soothsayers after his ewes give birth to lambs with human heads. The *harioli* suggest some costly sacrifices; along comes Aesop who counters with the suggestion that the farmer give his shepherds wives: thus, 'The one experienced through practice is generally held as more truthful than the soothsayer' (*usu peritus hariolo veracior / vulgo perhibetur*).[60] Alexander's establishment of a city and a farmer's mongrel sheep seem far removed in terms of social status. What unites the interpretations is a good understanding of social realities. The ideal seer is a good reader of the social context of the problem as well as the sign.[61] An element of practicality – of a realistic solution – is at work in the divinatory performance, so it is not particularly surprising given that, removed from an extravagant prestige-driven divinatory space such as the *Alexander Romance*, much divination deals with the everyday: 'Am I going to marry my girlfriend?' – 'Will I be harmed in the business affair?' – 'Will the traveller return?' (*Sortes Astrampsychi* 70, 31, 27). These seem 'banal' – yet, unquestionably, banality must be important for us as a means of accessing the ordinary or popular life in which the lot oracles 'were a marriage bureau and a career service, a medical surgery and a farmers' bulletin'.[62] And the

---

[56] Flower 2008a: 73.
[57] *Alexander Romance* 1.32 (trans. Dowden 1998); further sign 'massaging': *Alexander Romance* 1.8, 1.11. Cf. Heliodorus 1.19.1 where Thyamis' 'desire' motivates an explanation that suits his purpose.
[58] Morgan 2007: 133; cf. *Alexander Romance* 1.42.
[59] Flower 2008a: 13. Humour at the expense of 'experts' is a good indicator of societal anxieties about status figures: prophets who cannot foretell their own fates (*Aesopica* 161, 236); fake doctors (Phaedrus 1.14); dubious fortune-tellers (*Greek Anthology* 11.159–64; *Philogelos* 201–4).
[60] Cicero *Div.* 1.18.34 similarly links observation and guesswork from experience.
[61] Social context: Flower 2008a: 154–5, 191; Trampedach 2008: 212, 233. For anthropologists, 'divination ... reveals the actors' understanding of their social structure': Zeitlin 1995: 196. Artemidorus would have dream interpreters first investigate the dreamers, especially their social class: Miller 1994: 83–5.
[62] Lane Fox 1986: 210, 214.

answers they give are essentially conservative: avoiding confrontation and reflecting social realities.[63] Xenophon makes the point in *Memorabilia* 1.1.9 – and given his prominent public use of divination it is important for thinking about the realities of divination – that Socrates objects to asking the gods about things that common sense would best answer: 'Is it better to get an experienced coachman to drive my carriage or a man without experience? Is it better to get an experienced seaman to steer my ship or a man without experience? ... To put such questions to the gods seemed to his mind profane.'[64] From high literature to lower genres, in Babrius 20, an ox-driver who regards Heracles as his one true divine patron loses his wagon in a gully. He prays to Heracles for help, and the god appears, saying, 'Grasp the wheels and goad the oxen! Pray to the gods when you're doing something yourself – rather than pray idly.' Fables are perceived as 'socially low in origin',[65] and Babrius' fable is just one of many instances of a culture of conservatism in the literature of advice. The reader of fable is struck by how limited are the opportunities to improve one's lot or gain tacit approval of a grasp at social mobility.[66]

Whose *Life of Aesop*?

> A limitation and an irony of popular sayings and stories is that the more popular we take them to be, the less we know about most of the people who used them.[67]

The *Life of Aesop* can be read as a journey of social and cultural progression: from slave to culture hero, and from low culture to high. Simultaneously it can be read as a constant agonistic engagement between low and high culture, whether that be the victory of Aesop's earthy wisdom over his philosopher-master's educated learning, or the antagonism between lower and higher religious cultures played out between Isis, patroness of the lowly slave fieldworker, against Apollo, vindictive

---

[63] Toner 2009: 44–8 (thus long-lived and popular). [64] Trans. Marchant 1923.
[65] Morgan 2007: 6. On 'low' as 'popular' see Kurke 2011: 2–6, 157–8.
[66] Toner 2009: 36–7; Forsdyke 2012: 70–3 Proverbs reinforce a 'strong sense of appropriate social hierarchy' (Morgan 2007: 42) and 'express popular wisdom's attitude that life is very difficult and that much is done in vain' (Knapp 2011: 105). See Whitmarsh 2008c: 84–7 on class and conservatism in the novel.
[67] Morgan 2007: 22.

protector of the realm of the Muses.[68] Who formed the audience[69] of a story about a hideously ugly, clever slave in open warfare with all the perfections and values of the elite world? To whose 'tastes' did this appeal? Is it a unique instance of the literature of social protest?[70] The bleak end to the hero's cultural progress makes this reading problematic. Is it part of an odd literature of leisure, a sort of *nostalgie de la boue* like a *Satyricon*?[71] Labels such as 'Saturnalian'[72] and 'Menippean' are not out of place. The first half of the *Life* has been likened to a satiric piece aimed by students at a *pepaideumenos* like Aesop's master Xanthus.[73] Fable illustrates how difficult it is to place an audience and how varied an audience may be: who consumed Phaedrus' tricky little fables? – child? slave? freeman? emperor?[74] The obvious divisions in the *Life* have occasioned considerable scholarly gymnastics to assert an underlying structural and narrative unity.[75] They suggest to this reader, in the context of 'popular' texts, that we should consider both the 'popularity' of this particular version of the *Life* and the extent to which this version's popularity is indebted to a structure of multiple agonistically themed episodes, in which the small man continually bests the grander opponent.[76] What can this, in turn, suggest about its audience? The audience would appear to enjoy episodic narratives:[77] that is, short pieces, on the domestic and social

---

[68] Isis accepts all worshippers, hence her popularity among slaves: Witt 1971: 23–84; Snowden 1983: 97–9. In the *Life* it is Isis, not Apollo, who asks the Muses to confer their gifts on Aesop – a curious instance of syncretism, and a signal of trouble to come. See Finkelpearl 2003: 39–43 on the association of Isis with verbal and literary 'lowness' and Hunter 2007 on Aesop, Isis and 'the linked rise of linguistic sophistication and socio-legal status' (2007: 57) in the *Life*.

[69] Bowie 1994: 438 notes that 'ability to read is not in itself a condition of "readership" in a broader sense'. On reading and the novels: Konstan 2009.

[70] Cf. Forsdyke 2012: 40–9 on slave stories as 'lower-level resistance to power'.

[71] Whitmarsh and Bartsch 2008: 255 on Encolpius as 'surely the first buggered man to voice a personal narrative in a text for the elite'.

[72] Pervo 1998: 101 suggests 'read aloud in a household of masters and slaves during Saturnalia'.

[73] Kurke 2011: 38, 52; Shiner 1998: 162; Morgan 2007: 283.

[74] Henderson 1977: 25 on Phaedrus' fables as 'a rare glimpse ... into the mental furniture of the man in the ancient (Hellenistic) street'. While considered a low genre, fable is open to manipulation at the highest levels and in multiple genres, low and high. It easily adapts from oral performance to written work, and its stories are open to ready expansion and compression. Fable entertains and instructs; masked by humour and apparent lowness of content, it acts as a form of critical speech directed at higher powers: Jennings 2009.

[75] Holzberg 1992.

[76] For instance, G contains only thirteen fables, although it perhaps circulated with a collection. The manuscript containing G offers a glimpse of how texts become associated by type: as well as the *Life* and 226 Augustana fables, we find the *Physiologus*, *Kalilah and Dimnah*, thirty-one Babrian fables and the *Philogelos*: Avery 1941.

[77] Did episodes form a narrative, or was the narrative composed as a series of episodes? Episodic style is a feature of much prose, but it also draws on a story-telling tradition: see Shiner 1998 on

conventions[78] of the lives of famous men. This might suggest a context for the *Life* in oral performance. As I noted, judgements on 'literary merit' are problematic: does bad writing make something 'popular'? Elements of the *Life* betray familiarity with educated conceits, as we will see, but the Greek can be appalling.[79] The theme of display of competitive wisdom is prominent,[80] as is the theme of the little trickster besting the big man with his native wit. However, things do not work out for the little man in the *Life* the way that they do for the displaced elite hero of the Greek novel.[81] Is that, too, part of what popular texts are about – reinforcing social stasis?

Can thinking about the function of popular religion, specifically divination, help approach these problems? That is, can thinking about the common cultural experience of popular religion – the religion of the ordinary – help us approach the popular audience of popular literature? Let us examine two episodes of divination from the *Life of Aesop*.

Divining in Private: Aesop and the Two Crows (G77)

G77 is one of a series of self-contained episodes in which the clever slave Aesop betters his educated philosopher-master by turning his own beliefs – particularly his belief in a *degré zéro* of language – against him. This passage also neatly demonstrates how sophisticated language can exist simultaneously with low themes in a 'sub-elite' text.

---

episodic style and plotting in the *Life*. Thomas 1998 notes 'textless' works and works subject to a 'performance' attitude. Can we link the *Life* to mime tradition? On novels and mimes: Webb 2013; Whitmarsh 2008b: 11; Stephens 1994: 408. *P. Oxy.* 413 may represent (an) Aesop in second-century CE mime: Andreassi 2001.

[78] Hägg 1997; Hunter 2009: 51–7.
[79] How elite a product is a *Life of Aesop*? On how much engagement with high culture is necessary to appreciate an ancient novel, see Whitmarsh 2008c: 82–3. See Hunter 2008 on social interconnections between characters and audience in the novels. One can be educated but not elite in origin: Johnson 2010: 204–5. As Lightfoot 2000: 233 asks, 'might a broadly common value-system allow quite large sections of the public to appreciate fairly demanding material – not to understand it in every single details and nuance, but to be familiar enough with its background and conventions to be able to enjoy it?'
[80] This fits generally with an agonistic culture interested in wisdom competition – a 'dialogical spirit', as Konstan 2009: 7 would suggest novel audiences possessed. Futre Pinheiro 2009: 18 notes that the 'dialogic nature ... encompasses multiple resonances of social voices and their several relations and correlations, of their incessant mutual relationships'.
[81] Jouannou 2009: 42–5. On Aesop as trickster, see Shiner 1998: 162 ('Tricksters are often populist figures in the sense that they unmask the foibles of the elite'); Toner 2009: 29 (does the *Life* 'capture the personal characteristics that the non-elite told themselves were good traits for their hero to have and, presumably, good to emulate'?); and Forsdyke 2012: 37–49.

Xanthus said to Aesop, 'Since I am a bird-interpreter, go and see if there's any troublesome bird at the entrance. If you see a pair of crows (*dikorōnon*) at the entrance, call me; for this is clearly a sign of good things (*euphrosynē*) for the one seeing it.

Going out, Aesop saw, by chance (*kata tykhēn*), a pair of crows at the entrance and coming in he said to Xanthus, 'Master! The time is right (*kairos*) for you to go out – a pair of crows stands there.'

His master said, 'Let's go.'

While this was happening, one crow flew off, and coming out, his master saw only one crow and said, 'Curse you! Did I not say, "Call me if you see a pair of crows"? But you call me seeing but one crow (*monokorōnon*).'

Aesop replied, 'One flew off, master.'

His master said, 'Now you've really done wrong. Strip him! Fetch the straps!'

Aesop was thoroughly flayed. While he was still being whipped, a slave of one of Xanthus' friends arrived, inviting Xanthus to dinner. Aesop said, 'Master, you whip me unjustly (*adikōs*).'

Xanthus asked, 'Why unjustly?'

Aesop: 'You yourself said that a pair of crows was good *(kalon)* and lucky (*euphrosynon*). I saw the pair of crows and while coming to let you know, one flew off. You, who went out and saw only the single crow – you were asked to dinner. But I, the one who saw the pair of crows, received a beating. So, aren't omen-interpretation and signs (*oiōnismoi kai sēmeia*) senseless (*eis matēn*)?'

Divining in Public: Aesop and the Eagle (G81)

The Samian assembly is meeting to elect a new Guardian of the Laws when an eagle swoops down and snatches the public seal. This is regarded as a 'great portent', and seers and priests are called, who fail to offer an interpretation. As they deliberate, an old man addresses the worried assembly:

'Samian men, we were about to attend to those sorts who fill their stomachs from the sacrificial offerings and dice away their living as though gentlemen. It's not easy to solve an omen *(sēmeion)*. If someone's not effectively educated, he can't fully interpret an omen. But Xanthus the philosopher is among us – that man known to all Greece. Let's ask him to interpret the omen.'

...

The assembly was about to break up when the eagle, flying down again, dropped the seal-ring onto the lap of a public slave. They requested that Xanthus find a solution to this second omen. (G81–2)

Xanthus must beg his clever slave Aesop for help, but their relationship is at an all-time low, with Aesop locked up after Xanthus refused his freedom as a reward for finding a fabulous treasure. Aesop plays hard to get, claiming that he is no seer: 'if it is a question of words, I have comebacks at the ready; but about this ... I am no *mantis (oute gar eimi mantis)*' (G84). Xanthus decides the best option is suicide, but Aesop intervenes: Xanthus is to make up an excuse 'about the decorum of philosophy' to avoid interpreting, and Aesop the grotesque slave is given the floor at the democratic assembly of the free citizen population of Samos.

The assembly's reaction riffs on a recurring theme in the *Life*, that of external appearance versus internal quality, with the freak interpreter of the portent described in the language of a freaky portent:

> The Samians began laughing on seeing Aesop and said, 'Bring another interpreter (*sēmeiolytēs*), to figure out this omen *(sēmeion)*! Look what a monster *(teras)* he is! ... He could be a frog, a hedgehog, or a humped jar, or a captain of apes, or some sort of shaped flagon, or a cook's store, or a dog in a basket. (G87)

Of course, Aesop sways them, masterminds his freedom from slavery as the price of interpretation,[82] then interprets the eagle portent as bringing enslavement to the free citizens who have just freed him:

> Samian men! ... take council in defence of your own freedom; this is a portent *(sēmeion)* of besiegement and a sure sign *(tekmērion)* of enslavement. First, there will be war. I want you to understand this, because the eagle is king of the birds and most mighty of all. Flying down, he snatched the seal-ring – representing command – from the laws and threw it down on to the lap of a public slave. He dragged the security of free men into the fickle yoke of slavery. The interpretation of your omen *(tou sēmeiou lysis)* is this then. (G91)

In one of fiction's convenient coincidences, Samos falls immediately into enemy hands, and Aesop waltzes off to become adviser to the enslaver.

Cooking, Gardening, Divining

> Any culture which admits the use of oracles and divination is committed to a distinction between appearances and reality. The oracle offers a way of reaching behind appearance to another source of knowledge.[83]

How do we approach divination in the *Life*? Does an episode of divination function like any number of other episodes in the text that subvert the

---

[82] The repetition of forms of *luō* (solving and dissolving) in these episodes is in keeping with other instances of playful double-speak in the *Life*.
[83] Douglas 1999: 119.

master's orders and values in order to extract a perverted didactic moral in an orgy of Bakhtinian foci such as cooking, gardening, defecating and copulating?[84] The inclusion of divination amid the everyday is important for understanding the normality – the ordinariness, the reflex response – of religious experience for slave and master. In this reading, the episode of the two crows allows the slave to manipulate quotidian realia to score a point over his master. For instance, when Aesop exasperates his philosopher-master with his literal realization of the instruction 'go cook lentil' (and the supper pan contains but one lentil), the philosopher-master is taught a lesson about linguistic precision. The lesson the philosopher-seer learns from his I-am-not-a-seer-slave is the uselessness of another facet of his learning:[85] I am *oiōnistēs*, bird-interpreter, he had boasted. Kurke has asked why Xanthus presents himself as an bird-interpreter, when, as a philosopher, he (also) espouses rational means of enquiry.[86] Two factors, one explicit in the text, the other implicit in the divinatory experience, suggest another reading: first, Xanthus-the-philosopher is Samos's great all-rounder, a *pepaideumenos*, a man of learning 'known to all Greece'. Second, as I have discussed, divination is not irrational: it represents another legitimate form of rationality,[87] a form of expertise that *leaders* must demonstrate. It is how Themistocles manipulates the oracle of the wooden walls,[88] and it is what Xenophon represents himself as doing all the time. The educated man divines from birds: that is the message presented in elite literature (and in G81), and that is what Xanthus-the-professor should demonstrate: it is 'the weaponry of the elite, enabling them to exert and maintain social control through privileged religious knowledge and practice'.[89] However, in the topsy-turvy world of the sub-elite text, control of meaning – and thus mastery per se – is up for grabs.

I have noted that some of the novels use religious devices (dreams and oracles) to manipulate the reader's generic expectations. In this sense, the episode of the two crows may draw on the protective vague temporality of sign-reading, and symbolically prefigure events to come. In this reading, the endgame is not a dinner invitation but another lesson in reading wrongly: now there are two crows – master and slave; soon there will be

---

[84] As Kurke 2011: 203–4 notes, these episodes 'undermine the high tradition from below'.
[85] Whitmarsh 2008c: 74: the *pepaideumenos* is also judged, and this 'cultural capital' is 'a dangerous, unstable investment', based as it is on public perception and ideals. Kurke 2011: 204: 'the Aesopic parody often works by exposing how such claims to high wisdom endorse and enable inequitable power relations and the oppression of the weak by the strong'.
[86] Kurke 2011: 168–72.   [87] Vernant 1991: 303–4.   [88] Kurke 2011: 172–3.
[89] Kurke 2011: 205 (Hesiod *Works and Days* 826–8 is programmatic).

but one, when the ex-slave takes off to the East.[90] But does the appearance of supernatural phenomena in fictional narrative also serve to demarcate a space that legitimizes the transformative power of popular religious experience for the everyman without options?[91] Not every space is as overtly delimited as the *locus amoenus* of G6–7 in which the mute Aesop's voice is restored by Isis in epiphany, but one notes that the divinatory episodes of G77 and G81 both occur in liminal zones: at the gate with the crows, and as a slave in the free man's assembly on the cusp of becoming free himself.

A Troublesome Bird

> So, aren't omen-interpretation and signs senseless (*eis matēn*)?
>
> (G77)

And what of those crows? Their importance is signposted by the two hapaxlegomena for 'one crow' and 'two crows'.[92] Crows are proverbially long-lived, faithful to their partners (which is why one crow is a bad thing) and truth-tellers.[93] Aesop too is a survivor, touched by divinity, superficially assiduous (but *dyskolos*?) in aiding his master and even blackish in colouring (G1). Bird signs are Apollo's speciality and the crow is Apollo's mantic bird.[94] As I have noted, the *Life of Aesop* weaves a thread through the narrative of Apolline antagonism to Aesop and Aesopic disrespect to Apollo. It would seem that mantic privilege is also up for grabs. For instance, early in the *Life*, Aesop tells the story that, tired of Apollo's boastfulness, Zeus decided to humble him by sending out true dreams that would thus downgrade the prestige of Apollo's oracle. When Apollo apologized, Zeus sent false dreams to drive men back to the oracle (G33). This is not a story in which Apollo or divination come out well. And Aesop

---

[90] This sort of symbolic prefiguration can also be seen, as Pervo 1998: 104, n. 120 suggests, in G69–70, where Xanthus stakes his seal ring in a bet that seems impossible to win (without Aesop's aid).

[91] Forsdyke (2012): 63–70 suggests that this 'hopeful', transformative role may also be at work in fable.

[92] Perry 1939: 32.

[93] Crows: McCartney 1921: 90; Dillon 1996: 113–14; Schmidt 2002; Foufopoulos and Litinas 2005; Arnott 2007: 113–15; Patera 2011. As faithful (*Physiologus* 41; Aelian *De natura animalium* 3.9), long-lived (Babrius 46; *Philogelos* 255) and trainable, but also malicious (feeding on the soft, accessible parts), vociferous (ill-omened), aggressive tormenters of more powerful birds.

[94] Aristophanes *Birds* 716–22: birds are mantic Apollos for humans. See Dillon 1996: 102; Collins 2002: 33.

will die, after a long career in wisdom-merchandizing, at Delphi, the centre of Apolline divinatory wisdom. In G77 Aesop criticizes the assurance that his master, representative of high culture, places in divination – a criticism that can also be considered a further slight to Apollo. Divination, like *paideia*, is a confrontational and contested business in this text.

It is apt that a motif among mythic bird diviners is 'their opposition to the authority of kings'.[95] The epic diviner, too, is an outsider (despite his often aristocratic status), and is often itinerant.[96] These diviners attract stories of generational conflict and contests of authority between each other and between *mantis* and audience.[97] While these features are part of the general picture of being a culture hero in a society that values the contest, the parallel is not without interest.[98] Bird divination gives rise to 'oppositional forces'.[99] Divinatory space offers potential for interaction between the separated zones of divine and human. The eagle who snatches the seal and throws it down to a public slave represents far more in narrative terms than Aesop offers in his interpretation. It also, very obviously, signifies his coming freedom: that the moment is right – kairotic[100] – for his movement between slavery and freedom. In this space, meanings can reverse (as with the two crows) and meanings can multiply (as with the slave and the seal).[101] This is a zone of contestation – and how appropriate that it is an assembly-place – where the best performance is just as significant as the best interpretation.[102] In the *Life*, the role of the narrative is similar to a divinatory hermeneusis: 'The unconscious process that formulates an omen externalizes it and attributes it to an outside force. The process, however, conceals as much as it reveals. Its

---

[95] Dillery 2005: 172–5, 192, 223 on Teiresias and Calchas.

[96] Bremmer 1996; Muir 2011: 30–2. The higher social class of the epic diviner might suggest that the slave-diviner is doomed from the onset, his fate akin to the jackdaw in borrowed finery of Babrius 72.

[97] Burkert 2005: 40 notes the risk of 'singularity'.

[98] Manetti 1993: 29–30 discusses Apollo, divination, riddles and contestation, and interpretation 'as a dialectic confrontation between two opposing opinions'.

[99] Perceived self-interest is a great problem, as Dillery 2005: 173 notes regarding Teiresias, accused of self-promotion and loving money (Soph. *OT* 556; *Ant.* 1055). Cf. Johnston 2001: 109: 'although interpretation is viewed by those who listen to it as a *de*randomizing device because it seems to organize and clarify the chaotic raw material of the divination, in reality, interpretation is often a *secondary randomizer* insofar as it allows the interpreter, consciously or unconsciously, to shift meaning in any of several directions'.

[100] Kurke 2011: 143–5, 197–8 discusses *kairos* in the *Life*.

[101] Guinan 2002: 20. Horoscopes illustrate the 'semantic gaps' that offer multiple valid readings: Graf 2005b: 70. The multi-purpose oracular text of the fraudulent priests in Apul. *Met.* 9.8 functions similarly: Grottanelli 2005: 133–4.

[102] Eur. fr. 973 Nauck (cf. Cic. *Div.* 2.4.12): 'the best seer is the one who guesses well'.

very success depends on suppressing the fact the receiver played a part in the sending, the reader had a hand in the writing.'[103] What is being suppressed by this text?

'Will I Be Freed from Servitude?'

> ... 'stories' provide the decorative container of a *narrativity* for everyday practice.[104]

Why send someone outside to look for a good omen when you need to see it for yourself?[105] Aesop saw two crows; he ought to have the good luck. Can a slave not even be allowed to be lucky?[106] Consider how questions of status figure in lot and dice oracles: 'Will I be freed from servitude?' 'Will I come to terms with my masters?' 'Am I going to be sold?'[107] Should I run away from my master?[108] Does the lot *ever* return a resounding Yes?[109] This is the passive, powerless face of divination – the user helpless against social stasis. The dynamic face, in the *Life*, is the diviner in active pursuit of his own status change.[110]

Who has the power to say what a bird omen properly means – the slave who reads it or the master who wields the whip? The slave may read the signs, but the master has the power to constitute the slave's future as he will ... Those with power ... constitute meaning.[111]

Divination is about power: the Roman Empire provides a fine example of the importance of this when divination is banned if it concerns the emperor.[112] Aesop's victories may seem hollow while he remains enslaved,

---

[103] Guinan 2002: 21 (on Mesopotamian divination). Parker 2000: 76 suggests that 'The important distinction between "besought" and "self-offering" signs is that the authority of the former was increased by the decision to seek them.'

[104] Certeau 1984: 70.   [105] As the repeated 'seeing' words in G77 suggest.

[106] In the Roman world the lowly recipient of an omen should escalate the omen to a higher authority: Ripat 2006: 160–2. (A slave could, however, be called 'Lucky': Toner 2009: 97.)

[107] *Sortes Astrampsychi* 32, 46, 74.   [108] Eidinow 2007: 100–1, 131.

[109] Gell. *NA* 3.3.7–8 offers a Plautinesque oracle choice: death if you do not and flogging if you do.

[110] See Potter 1994: 5 on oracles as 'the essential vehicles of "active" religious experience'. At G80 the imprisoned Aesop tells Xanthus, 'Watch out, master: you'll end up freeing me by your own choice and forced against your will.'

[111] Kurke 2011: 210; cf. North 1990b: 58–60. Note *Apollonius of Tyre* 32 on the risks in obeying a dubious order (murder) with the expectation of freedom.

[112] Cf. the slave punished for enquiring about the health of the master: Paulus *Sent.* 5.21. Potter 1994: 15: 'The gods were manifestly not under human control, and it was this simple fact that made prophecy a vehicle for social disturbance and social commentary as well as one for social order.'

but in the *Life* fiction plays out the divinatory power gamble on the big screen, the miserable reality of which is the powerless man at the dice oracle using divination to appropriate what small power he has over his destiny.[113] In fiction, divinatory space offers a rare opportunity for the lowly to perform in a high-stakes[114] game of authority with or against the elite, with social mobility the ultimate prize. In fiction, your fate *can* change and you can do it yourself.[115] We see too how masterly is the choice of a common, everyday signifier – the bird – in the narrative: what other character can move so smoothly from the private and domestic to the public and political spheres?[116] But, then, it can still go horribly wrong: who tells this story, and who grasps the moral? Popular texts are not necessarily simple texts, and it is wholly frustrating to know almost nothing about the audience and the audience's reception of these preserved divinatory performances in the *Life* of a slave who becomes one of Western civilization's most durable and popular cultural icons.

---

[113] See Toner 2009: 37; Johnston 2005: 301; Forsdyke 2012: 84. Karla 2009b: 20–1 suggests that the *Life* 'has a wider social appeal' because of this element of control.

[114] As Collins 2002: 18 notes regarding epic divination. Vernant 1991: 307: 'What then is the attitude of the social body towards the keepers of a knowledge that, at its extreme, lays claim to omniscience?'

[115] Fortune is not immutable: Potter 1994: 22. Omens foretell but do not cause events: Cic. *Div.* 1.17.29.

[116] Dillon 1996: 115, 121.

10 | Children's Cultures in Roman Egypt

APRIL PUDSEY

Introduction: The Child's World

Can we view ancient children and their cultural history through a lens of popular culture? In demographically young populations, such as those found across the Roman world, children and young people under the age of twenty-five outnumbered those of any other age group; their lives, concerns, outlook and cultures played out in a vast range of 'official' and 'everyday' spheres of life which are the focus of discussion on the nature of what precisely popular culture is, and its relationship to 'official' culture. We can envisage children's lives and growing up processes as, in part, a process of socialization into adulthood in which children's agency in shaping this process is the crux of the relationship between 'children' and 'adults' as social groups. Since all adults were once children, how can we examine a child culture in terms of leading, responding to, or embedded within adult culture, as one morphed into the other? Theories of popular culture, and how best to understand it, provide a springboard for studying ancient children from as close to their own perspective as we have thus far been able to approach.

 The answer to these questions lies in the nature of relationships between adult expectations of children on the one hand and, on the other, children's environments and their interaction with them, taking into account their own agency and concerns in shaping and negotiating these relationships. Are we to read children's cultures as entirely separate from those of adults, and children themselves as a group subordinate to the dominant group (of adults) with an autonomous – or subaltern – popular culture of their own? If we view adult/child relationships in these dominant/subordinate terms, then can we observe children's cultures as in any way subverting the expected norms and values of adult behaviour and activity? Children, of course, do not remain children indefinitely and so cannot be thought of as a social and cultural group entirely distinct from their surrounding adults, but in antiquity there were various spheres of life in which only children

I would like to thank Micaela Langellotti and Ville Vuolanto for their comments and suggestions on earlier versions of this work.

participated in a very distinct set of activities, rituals and behaviours, in particular ways. Taking a cue from Stuart Hall's approach to popular culture, we are able in principle to examine the extent to which children as a group produced and consumed culture; further, it is also possible to explore the degree to which children's activities and experiences in various spheres overlapped with, responded to, or even subverted those of adults, and children's own roles in shaping their cultures and their transitions to adulthood.[1]

Children's cultures in the Roman world, then, may be studied from these perspectives. Since Beryl Rawson's pioneering research into Roman families reinvigorated scholarly interest in the study of Greek and Roman children and childhood, albeit largely from adult perspectives, subsequent research has flourished, though it has tended to focus on the media through which children in Athens and Rome learned and adopted the dominant cultural principles of their social groups, through the *ephebeia*, *gymnasium* and Roman magistracies.[2] This is perhaps no surprise given the political and philosophical preoccupations of the key authors and texts at our disposal: elite notions of a socially appropriate childhood through education, preparation for civic duty and marriage occupy the classical authors,[3] and anxieties surrounding child mortality were often framed in similar terms in commemorations and funerary reliefs.[4] Yet children's spheres of interaction were – and still are – often less formal, and broader-ranging, than those of adults: work, religion, family and household, other children, and local community provided the common means through which many children understood and engaged with their immediate physical and social environment and community, and viewed the world and their place within it. Children's outlook on life, and their immediate concerns and activities played out in a range of less officially designated spaces and spheres: their household, shared courtyards, streets, neighbourhoods, workshops, fields and other areas they lived, played, worked and learned in and moved around.

To paint a more textured picture of children's cultures in the ancient world we must explore their experience and relationships within both

---

[1] As discussed in detail in Grig's introductory chapter in this volume.
[2] Most notably Rawson 2003. See, most recently, Dasen and Späth 2010; Evans Grubbs and Parkin 2013; Horn and Phoenix 2009; Laes 2011; Mustakallio *et al.* 2005. For a comprehensive review of scholarship see Vuolanto 2014.
[3] E.g. Aristot. *Pol.* 3.1275a 14–33; Pol. 4.20.8–10, 6.8.4; Pliny, *Ep.* 5.16. 2–4; Sen, *Ira* 2.21.1–6; Sen. *De Constantia Sapientis* 12.
[4] E.g. *SEG* 29 (1979) 1003, the epitaph of four-year-old L. Minicius Anthimianus, third century CE Asia Minor; Cohen and Rutter 2007.

formal and informal spheres, their own agency in shaping their experience, and the ways in which these interacted with symbolic notions of childhood within those contexts – in essence, the ancient child's world. Egypt in the Roman period presents us with an ideal setting for such an exploration: the wealth of papyrological material documenting and detailing aspects of everyday life combine with an array of archaeological material to provide a window through which we may glimpse the worlds of children within their homes, workshops, streets and places of religious activity. In this material we see children's involvement in work, learning and play in the contexts of their families, peer groups and local communities.

Our approach to this material within the framework of a study of the dynamics of children's and adults' cultures also benefits from sociological approaches to the study of children's experience. Recent historical and archaeological work on ancient childhood has begun to explore the ways in which children's roles as cultural and social actors can be observed through their socialization: that is, the manner in which they were taught and raised by family members, community and educators in the customs, norms and values of their social, religious and kin groups.[5] This approach runs the risk of treating children almost as passive recipients of adult-taught culture and focusing on adults as teachers rather than children as learners, whose particular imaginative abilities and interpretations played a huge part in sculpting their own experiences and drove their production, consumption and transmission of cultures.[6] Archaeologists have developed the notion of socialization for studying past children's cultures and experience in a more focused way, taking into account children's own agency and cognitive abilities in shaping their learning, play, working, use of space and relationships within and beyond their families.[7] These studies and others have begun to approach the study of children in the past from the perspective of looking for their agency: children were active participants in producing and consuming their cultures, not simply recipients of predetermined (adult?) cultures.[8]

---

[5] Socialization: Harlow and Laurence 2002; Harders 2010; Horn 2005. For more nuanced approaches, see Katajala-Peltomaa and Vuolanto 2011; Prescendi 2010; Pudsey, 2015; Pudsey and Vuolanto forthcoming.

[6] See Hirschfeld 2002 on anthropological work on children as learners. An example of ancient children as creative producers and innovators of culture in this sense from material culture of early Greece: Langdon 2013.

[7] Children's material culture and agency: Baxter 2005; Sofaer Derevenski 1997, 2000; Lillehammer 1989, 2000; Moore and Scott 1997. In a case study of graffiti in Roman Campania, the cognitive development of children can be clearly identified: Huntley 2010.

[8] Baxter 2005: 2.

Further, a 'decentralized' study of children's cultures allows the study of identities, activities and relationships within a textured world of particular socio-political structures, familial obligations, religion, environmental space and peer relationships from children's perspectives.[9] Decentralizing the worlds of ancient children is useful in exploring relationships between children's cultures and wider experience. Classic studies of Roman children have typically broken these down into themes such as 'education and schooling', 'labour', 'religion', 'family' and 'slaves', but these categories are born of a number of presuppositions about the fixed nature of these spheres of life.[10] In Roman Egypt at least, children's education was not limited to schooling but incorporated aspects of learning a craft or trade, or learning through religious activity. Similarly, 'labour' is a problematic category because of its connotations of harsh conditions and financially exploitative objectives, which were not the most prominent features of working life for children throughout Roman Egypt. Familial continuity, tradition and connections beyond the home rendered children's experience of family one which overlapped significantly with their experience of religion, work and learning in various other spheres.

A comprehensive study of ancient children's experiences, activities, emotions and concerns is near impossible given the elite focus of most of our Greek and Roman sources, whose references to children are aimed at promoting particular behaviours in, and treatment of, them.[11] But the wealth of documentary papyri and material culture from Roman Egypt at least reflects a wide range of elements of both elite and non-elite children's cultures through their experience within family life, peers, local community, work, learning, play and cultic activity. This constitutes some of the most detailed source material on children's lives we have from the ancient world. In this chapter, in order to explore the 'world of the child' and children's cultures in Roman Egypt, I adopt an approach to understanding children's cultures as a form of popular culture in dialogue with adult cultures. The adoption of Lillehammer's division of children's agency and

---

[9] Decentralized approaches: Hengst 2005; James and Prout 1997a; James, Jenks and Prout 2005; Qvortup 1994.
[10] For example, Bradley 1991; Dixon 2001.
[11] E.g. Xenophon on what boys ought to learn to become men (Xen. *Cyr.* 4.3); Aristotle's often-cited division of ages at which children should or should not be exposed to particular aspects of life (Arist. *Pol.* 1336b19–20) and youths' responsibilities in taking the ephebic oath (Arist. *Pol.* 42.2–5); Polybius' presentation of childhood as an essential character-building phase of life (Pol. 4.20.8–10, 6.8.4); and late Roman sources on the childhoods of holy men (see Papaconstantinou and Talbot 2009: 1–14; and Pudsey 2015 for childhood in hagiography specific to Egypt).

cultures into three components will complement this approach: culture that is created through day-to-day experience and interactions between children and their environment; culture that is shared between children; and culture that is transmitted down from parents to their children.[12] In what follows, I examine the source material in relation to these three components and theories of popular culture, asking what it reveals of the nature of children's cultures in Roman Egypt.

How did children engage with their immediate environment, their peer groups and relationships with adults? How were children's cultures and experiences related to preparations for particular aspects of adult social life? And in what ways can we observe children actively shaping their own cultural processes? In terms of the key aspects of life that constitute popular culture, this chapter will engage with material related to children's experience and agency within a number of spheres of life, and within children's homes and local environments where they were frequently engaged in 'situated learning' through apprenticeships.[13] This chapter aims at least to raise some questions about the level to which popular culture approaches can be used, in conjunction with a decentralized study of children's cultures and agency, to examine the relationships between children's cultures and wider society – or, where possible, children's experience of it.

Shaping Culture: Day-to-Day Experience and Agency

Children's immediate environment, their homes and neighbourhoods were the setting for most of their interactions, both with adults and with one another. It is therefore a reasonable place to start when examining children's cultures through their experience and agency in day-to-day life. In the villages and towns of Roman Egypt a rather flexible and communal attitude towards familial living arrangements and housing structures resulted in the creation of space for familial and communal use in the form of courtyards and areas both within and around houses. Children living in typically large families were afforded both space and opportunity to form peer groups in very localized communities:[14] their use of this space was a key feature of children's everyday experience, shaping their activities

---

[12] Lillehammer 1989: 90.
[13] 'Situated learning' is a term coined by Coy 1989 to reflect the learning of a trade or craft in a work context, under specific types of guidance.
[14] Pudsey under review. See also Pudsey 2011.

of playing, eating and learning and their relationships with family, local community and peers.[15] In the Fayum village of Karanis housing was such that the family home provided communal space for use in daily household activities, production and play of adults and children from the extended family, and from more than one family.[16] For instance, the well-known Taesion/Taesis archive details a widow sharing one of the multi-roomed houses with her sons and their children, and other houses indicated shared use of courtyards or passageways. In houses in the nearby villages of Tebtynis and Soknopaiou Nesos we find similar patterns in the use and adaptation of communal space in and between houses.[17] The primary entrance to each house was through a vestibule and a further space, usually on the north side of the house, and a separately entered courtyard lay at the south of each house. In most houses such an open courtyard was designed to be shared with neighbouring households, and in Tebtynis this trend stretches over time to the gradual building of houses in the spaces between houses and further building on the communal courtyards and outdoor space.[18] This particular type of sharing of space is not unknown elsewhere in the housing of the Roman world, but its connection with the patterns of kinship and connected family groups is particular to the Fayum villages of Egypt.[19]

This sharing of space across families is supported by evidence from the Romano-Egyptian household census registers, which gives information on the living arrangements of the inhabitants of the villages of the Fayum region and of some of the towns and metropoleis within and surrounding the Arsinoite nome.[20] If we look at these recorded households from the vantage point of children it becomes clear that their domestic world was one filled with other children – siblings, half-siblings, cousins and the children of lodgers and slaves.[21] It was a common experience for households to contain female adult slaves and their multiple children alongside multiple freeborn children of similar ages, most likely a consequence of the

---

[15] Revell 2010: 61; See also Holloway and Valentine 2000. See Bourdieu 1977: 89–90 on how children learn their position within family and society, and the accepted rules of gender and age performance, through their interactions with space in (and in the case of Roman Egypt, around) the house.

[16] Pudsey 2013: 490–1.

[17] Bagnall and Davoli 2011; Gallazzi and Hadji-Minaglou 2000; Hadji-Minaglou, 2007, 2008: esp. 124–6. Also Pudsey under review.

[18] See also: Alston 1997, 29–31; Hadji-Minaglou 2007 and 2008, 124–5; 127–8.

[19] See Baird 2014 for housing and social structures in Dura Europos, and Baird and Pudsey under review for recent studies of housing across the Graeco-Roman world.

[20] Bagnall and Frier 2006; Pudsey 2011.

[21] Pudsey 2013: 490–503 esp. tables 24.1, 24.2, 24.3, 24.4, 24.5.

practice of obtaining and retaining wet-nurses.[22] The day-to-day interaction between children of slave and free status in the same household would not necessarily have been limited, given the predominant physical environment discussed above, and the common age ranges between free and slave children in the same households being cared for by the same adult women (usually slaves).

Beyond the census material there is evidence of the affectionate bonds shared between freeborn and slave children growing up in the same house. An *epikrisis* registration document from the Hellenized metropolis of Oxyrhynchus hints at such a bond between slave and non-slave children who had been raised from birth together. Thirteen-year-old Apollonius and his sister Helena – both Greek – jointly owned through inheritance a house-born Egyptian slave, Sarapion, who was the same age as Apollonius; in the *epikrisis* application put forward by Apollonius himself, he registered Sarapion in the same proud terms as he registered himself, leaving us to speculate on the degree of friendship and affection between children in such household circumstances; we are also left to ponder on the space for children who were slaves to develop friendships with other children, given that Sarapion appears to have lived and grown up with Apollonius and Helena for quite some time before turning thirteen.[23] In another example, Aurelius Aphynchis petitioned a high-ranking official (the local *strategos*). Aurelius was here seeking redress from a pastry-cook who had allegedly assaulted the young slave girl, Sarapias (again, an Egyptian), who belonged to his son (both are referred to as minors); the claim is that the assailant caused injury to Sarapias' lip and went on to assault Aurelius himself on being confronted about the incident. The family 'hand[s] in the petition and request[s] you to order him to be brought before you and to proceed against his outrages so that the girl can receive redress and treatment'.[24] The tone of the petition, from a particularly well-connected family, is suggestive of a good deal of affection for the slave girl on the part of that family, and is presented in personal terms rather than the more typical type of petition for injury to slaves as a purely financial concern.

Children of slave status were also contracted as apprentices and worked and learned trades alongside their freeborn peers in the workshop.[25] For instance, in a third-century contract from the village of Karanis, Aurelius

---

[22] Wet-nurse contracts: Masciadri and Montevecchi 1984.
[23] W. Chr. 217 (172–3 CE); see also discussion of this text in Johnson 1936: 254.
[24] P. Oxy. XXXIII 2672 (218 CE).
[25] E.g. P. Oxy. XLI 2977 (239 CE), 2988 (second century CE). See discussion below on apprentices.

Ision arranged with a (female) weaver, Aurelia Libouke (who had a number of apprentices) to teach the craft of weaving to his young (female) slave over a period of a year with the clear intention of learning the trade: 'when the slave child has completed the agreed time without fault, the teacher shall return her after she has learned the craft with skill equal to those of her own age'.[26] Similarly, a contract from the nearby town of Tebtynis details an agreement between Herakleon and the prominent weaver Orsenouphis to teach Herakleon's slave girl, Helene, the art of weaving during an apprenticeship of two and a half years.[27] It is clear that children in Roman Egypt shared their day-to-day lives at home with many other children, and these would very often have included children of slave status and of similar ages, all being cared for by the same adults.

The social environment of children stretched beyond the immediate physical confines of the household. Freeborn children in the Roman world are recorded as engaged in paid work from the age of ten years upwards, often in agricultural contexts and usually in groups of their peers.[28] In two documents detailing the tasks and wages paid on Epimachus' estate and the wages paid for farm work on Gemellus' land nearby, we read that children were paid for work. Listed either as *paides* (all under the age of fourteen) or *aphelikes* (under the age of twenty-five, but still dependent) they were paid much lower wages than adult workers for the same tasks.[29] It is on the basis of documents such as these that we tend to think of child work in the ancient world as universally exploitative, harsh and in relation only to economic concerns. But the unique documentation on apprenticeships in Roman Egypt suggests a widespread practice in which apprenticed children in villages and metropoleis were expected to learn the technical skills of a trade or craft, and the values associated with it, rather than simply have their labour exploited for financial gain (though the one, of course, did not always preclude the other).[30] We find in the papyri apprentices of both slave and free status, and evidence of both girls and boys working and learning as apprentices. A common feature of apprenticeship arrangements was a loan made to the parents or guardian in return for the child's work for a specified number of years, guaranteeing the repayment of the

---

[26] *P. Mich. inv.* 5191 (271 CE).   [27] *P. Mich.* V 241 (16 CE).

[28] Laes 2011: 189–97, 207–16. Varro *Rust.* 210.1 suggests children work as shepherds. Mirković 2005: 145–6; Rathbone 1991: 155–66 (tables 5 and 12); Laes 2011: 206–10.

[29] *P. Lond.* 131 (78–9 CE) and *P. Fay.* 102 (105 CE). See discussion in Mirković 2005: 43–147.

[30] Collation of published contracts: Bergamasco 1995; Bradley 1991. For discussion of some apprenticeship contracts as thinly disguised means of pledging children in return for a loan: Vuolanto 2015.

loan for the master in addition to the work of the child.[31] But these contracts indicate that apprenticeships were more than simple pledging of a child's work as loan security, and the language and focus of the contracted arrangements are squarely on outlining an agreement for the responsibilities of teaching and learning the relevant skills, and the daily conditions of work for the child apprentice.

Children's experience of apprenticeship depended in part on their agency in shaping how they worked, understood and interpreted the skills and values they were meant simply to pick up. In terms of children's cultures, can we observe in the practice of apprenticeship in Roman Egypt any evidence that children were able to respond to intended socialization with their own negotiation of relationships, activities and interactions with their wider (adult) community? The most prominent trade requiring apprenticed workers in Egypt was weaving.[32] Freeborn and slave children were frequently apprenticed to weavers in the Fayum village of Karanis, such as in the case where Satornilos apprenticed his nephew to the weaver Theabennis, with whom the boy was to reside day and night and whose orders he was to obey in order to learn the craft.[33] A similar arrangement was made in a contract from Tebtynis in which Tephersais apprenticed her son, Kronion, to the weaver Heron for two years to learn the trade: 'at the end of the period Heron shall deliver up the boy knowing the trade in its entirety'.[34] Two brothers in Tebtynis apprenticed their younger brother for one year in return for a loan, as is typical of many of these contracts.[35] Arrangements for such apprenticeships were typically made by family members, and on occasion we see apprentice boys working with their own fathers in the villages of the Fayum.[36] It is a feature of the village apprenticeship contracts in particular that this type of situated learning appears to have taken place within the context of the wider kin or community, but beyond the immediate family, with the apprentice remaining in residence at the family home and working with the apprentice master in the stipulated hours from sunrise to sunset. If the purpose was to learn and continue the family trade in a serious way, then it could be argued that the discipline of a master and routine outside familiar

---

[31] Mirković 2005: 140. See also *P. Mich.* II 121 recto II, viii (42 CE), a register of contracts from Tebtynis. For discussion of the use of the *paramone* clause, see Vuolanto 2015. For example, see *P. Oxy.* XVI 1895 (554 CE) (=Rowlandson 1998: 234) in which a widowed mother claimed she was unable to support her nine-year-old daughter after the death of the girl's father.

[32] See Kelly 2011: 131–3; Rowlandson 1998: 112–17.   [33] *P. Oslo* III 141 (50 CE).

[34] *P. Tebt.* II 385 (117 CE).   [35] *P. Tebt.* II 384 (10 CE).

[36] For example: *P. Mich.* III 170 (49 CE), 171 (58 CE), 172 (62 CE).

surroundings might have been more conducive to focused learning (there was also less risk to a household economy if the child apprentice learned her or his craft elsewhere).[37]

The emergence of apprenticeship as a social institution is tied in many ways to local modes of production in villages and metropoleis in Egypt, but it also provided children with the social and psychological process of learning through craft, trade, work and travel in new surroundings and among new people. This was a key issue for apprenticeship in the larger towns and the metropoleis of Roman Egypt, and in Oxyrhynchus there survive no examples of apprentices working with their fathers as we saw above in the villages of the Fayum.[38] Typically, apprenticeship appears to have taken place outside the home on the basis that the child would work from sunrise to sunset in return for a specified wage and a clothing and food allowance.[39]

The obligation on the part of the master was to teach the craft, and on the part of the apprentice to learn. In one example from the metropolis of Oxyrhynchus, a contract gives further insight into such an arrangement:

Taseus, daughter of Heraclas, with her full brother ... as guardian, and Seuthes son of Diogenes, son of Dionysius, weaver, acknowledge to one another, Taseus that she has handed over to Seuthes her son Heraclas, son of Apollo ... who is not yet of age, to learn the craft of weaving for a period of two years and six months from the present day, (the boy) carrying out all the instructions given to him by Seuthes pertaining to the craft of weaving. Seuthes for his part will teach him in accordance with his own knowledge, the boy being maintained and clothed by the teacher Seuthes, and Seuthes too is to pay the trade-tax due on the boy, together with the fine, for the two and a half years; and if during that time the boy shall be required to pay poll-tax or dike-tax or pig-tax, these too shall be incumbent on the said Seuthes. If the boy does not wish to be maintained by the teacher, Seuthes is to pay Taseus for his maintenance each month 5 silver drachmas, and after the period he is to give the boy on his departure a tunic worth 12 drachmas, or the 12 drachmas themselves. The boy will have holidays ... at the Amesysia ... but for as many days as the boy is idle besides these, Taseus shall deliver him for an equal number of days after the period, or pay a penalty of a drachma for each day; but for withdrawing him before the period is up she shall pay a fine of 100 silver drachmas and the same sum to the state. Should Seuthes for his part not teach the boy, he shall be liable to the same fine.

---

[37] See Goody 1989.
[38] Though there is the occasional uncle who is apprentice master to his nephew, as in *P. Oxy. Hels.* 29 (54 CE), in which the boy lived with his grandmother who had arranged this apprenticeship. See discussion in Pudsey and Vuolanto forthcoming.
[39] Further examples: *P. Oxy.* II 322 (36 CE); *P. Oxy. Hels.* 29 (54 CE); *P. Oxy.* II 275 (66 CE); *P. Oxy.* IV 725 (183 CE); *P. Oxy* XLI 2977 (239 CE).

This contract of apprenticeship is valid. The twelfth year of Nero Claudius Caesar Augustus Germanicus Imperator, Phamenoth 15.

(Second hand) I, Seuthes, son of Diogenes, shall teach the boy and shall do as aforesaid. The twelfth year of Nero Claudius Caesar Augustus Germanicus Imperator, Pharmenoth 15.[40]

Taseus, acting with her brother as official guardian, here arranged for her twelve-year-old, fatherless son Heraclas to learn the craft of weaving for two years and six months, with holiday allowance, from the weaver Seuthes. The contract specified that Heraclas was to follow all instructions in learning weaving from Seuthes and that Seuthes himself was contractually obliged to ensure that Heracles learned the craft sufficiently well, under threat of a fine should he fail in this. A number of interesting features arise from this contract: first, that Heraclas would be entitled to holidays for religious festivals, here the Amesysia; second, that should Heraclas for some reason dislike being maintained by the teacher he would be entitled to choose for himself whether to stay with him or continue living at home with his mother and travel to Seuthes' workshop on a daily basis.

In this case, young Heraclas (most likely aged twelve to fourteen years, given his eligibility for various taxes) was permitted a degree of freedom in determining the nature of his apprenticeship under Seuthes; his mother and maternal uncle arranged his contract in such a manner as to allow him some flexibility. It is unfortunate that we have no further documentation of how Heraclas chose to act upon his freedom here; nonetheless, it is clear that the expectation was for Heraclas to make his own decisions regarding his learning and working arrangements, and there is no suggestion in the contract that this might have been an unusual or atypical arrangement.

Children would not typically have been apprenticed to work alone: in a number of cases we see that they worked and learned alongside other children. In this rather proud letter from a young man to his former apprentice master, Agathangelus boasts of his achievements and sends greetings to his former peers:

Agathangelus, to Panares the barber, very many greetings. I salute Heliodora too. I make obeisance before the gods here and I make your obeisance each day. By the gods' will I am already barber to the master and I am barber to everyone in the

---

[40] *P. Oxy.* XLI 2971 (66 CE). All papyrological translations quoted in this chapter are by multiple editors and translators of the print volumes of each collection. Standard papyrological referencing conventions are in accordance with the *Checklist of Editions of Greek, Latin, Demotic, and Coptic Papyri, Ostraca and Tablets,* where publisher, editor and translator details are given in full: http://papyri.info/docs/checklist.

house. Whichever day I have barber's work to do it is my custom to make the obeisance. Salute to all my fellow apprentices!

I pray for your health![41]

In other contracts we see evidence of multiple apprentices working together:

Thonis, a minor, to be taught the art of weaving for a period of five years starting from the first of next month, Phaophi, and will produce him to attend the teacher for the stipulated period every day from sunrise to sunset, performing all the orders that may be given to him by the said teacher on the same terms as the other apprentices.[42]

The widespread nature of apprenticeship of the kind outlined above would have provided children from the age of twelve the means to engage with adults and with their peers, both free and slave, in an environment beyond their home; their obligations were clear, in that they were to learn to become proficient in their craft over a specified number of years, from sunrise to sunset and in some cases would live with the master. It was possible for freeborn children to be given a degree of choice about his or her living arrangements; a ubiquitous clause stating that any days lost through absence or illness need to be made up at the end of the term of contract, suggests that in practice child apprentices could, and did, exercise some agency in their relationships with the work and the master. It is difficult to argue on the basis of the surviving evidence that child apprentices, on the whole, subverted the intended working process by frequently absenting themselves and choosing when, where and how to do their work, but it seems they did at least exercise some flexibility. They were often entitled to holidays in full expectation that they would participate in local religious festivals.

Girls made up a large proportion of apprentices in the villages, and in most cases these were slaves.[43] Freeborn girls featured less as apprentices in urban contexts, except in relation to (potentially as security on) a loan.[44]

---

[41] *P. Oxy.* XLV 3809 (second/third century CE).

[42] *P. Oxy.* IV 725 (183 CE). See also *P. Fouad.* 37 (48 CE).

[43] *CPGr* I 17 r 4 vii: a house-born slave girl of unspecified age. *O. Trim.* 1 289 (350–70 CE) is an ostraka receipt for a slave girl from Trimithis (Oasis Magna). In *P. Col.* VIII 213 (84–105 CE) Kronion registered properties inherited from his mother and father, including land, part of a house and a slave girl. *P. Mich.* V 346a (13 CE), 346b (16 CE), Tebtynis. *SPP* XII 40 (150 CE), Soknopaiou Nesos. *P. Oxy.* 1674 (second century CE), Oxyrhynchus. *PSI* 241 (second to third century CE), Antinopolis. *P. Mich. inv.* 5191a (271 CE), Karanis.

[44] E.g. *P. Oxy.* LXVII 4596 (264 CE): Aurelius Polydeuces arranged for his underage daughter Aurelia Aphrodite to learn the craft of weaving for four years, living with the weaver until the loan was repaid. See discussion in Vuolanto 2015.

Girls who were contracted as apprentices, whether slave or free, appear in the record only in connection with the weaving trade, though they were still subject to the same clauses in the contracts regarding their obligations and those of the master in terms of work, learning and distribution of the costs of feeding and clothing them. In the relatively small number of apprentice contracts for girls there was a tendency for them to reside with the master, though this was perhaps in connection with the loan arrangements attached to these contracts rather than an indication that it was preferred for girls to live away from home, for example: 'for this period of time her father will see that his daughter abides with Thonis, not spending a night or a day away, being fed and clothed for the whole period by Thonis instead of receiving wages'.[45]

In fact, it may have been financially preferable in most cases for boys to have lived with their apprentice master, since this arrangement was connected in the contracts with the master's obligation to pay various taxes due only on apprentice boys. For boys, the experience of apprenticeships in weaving, carpentry and stone-cutting was undoubtedly focused on their learning the craft, rather than on exploiting their labour, and they exercised some limited choice in their negotiation of this experience, often alongside their freeborn and slave peers. Girls who were apprenticed were mostly slaves, and mostly worked and learned under the same types of contracts. The experience for freeborn girls would most likely have differed, in that many examples related to their being apprenticed to live and work with the apprentice master away from their families, and one is left to speculate on whether these sorts of contracts were in fact a convenient means of pledging freeborn girls in return for a loan.

Children in Roman Egypt related to their physical and social environment in particular ways. At home day-to-day life was filled with other children in the form of siblings, cousins, slaves, lodgers and, in the villages in particular, neighbours; they grew up together and we see them refer to one another in affectionate and thoughtful terms. They engaged in work, learning, play and daily living alongside their peers in closely connected spaces, and were often cared for and under the day-to-day supervision of the same adults in the home, workshop or school, irrespective of whether they were slaves or freeborn, related or unrelated. These children may have exercised a degree of agency in cultivating their own relationships in local communities, particularly in urban contexts where their learning took place beyond the branches of their own family

---

[45] *P. Oxy.* LXVII 4596 (264 CE).

group.[46] In terms of forming and shaping their own cultures, children in these circumstances and contexts were able in many cases to engage on their own terms with those children and adults around them, and with the skills and crafts they may have been learning. This poses the question of the extent to which children were therefore able to produce and consume their day-to-day experience and activity not just as individuals, but with one another.

Shared Children's Cultures

The second of Lillehammer's aspects of children's culture mentioned at the start of this chapter is in their shared experience, activity and concerns. Children across Roman Egypt shared their day-to-day lives with many other children both at home and away from home. Can we explore children's cultures in these contexts as shared cultures, differing from, or in flux with, adult (dominant) cultures? Evidence of children's own expressions of their shared lives with other children is rare for the ancient world, but we do see elements of this in the documents from Oxyrhynchus in particular. For instance, in one letter to a deputy *epistrategos* a father pleaded for his fourteen-year-old son to be allowed to join his friends in enjoying the shared activities of the gymnasium with them, as his name had been omitted from the official list – a reflection of the nature of the gymnasium on a day-to-day basis for teenage boys.[47] Another boy approaching adulthood through gymnasial circles cordially invited his friends to join him at his home for a feast in celebration of his successful *epikrisis* application.[48] And a mother wrote to her son who was away at school, mentioning that his cousins at home were missing him.[49]

There is very little in the documentary record from Roman Egypt containing the words of children themselves, but we do have one clear example. In a letter a homesick schoolboy wrote home in frustration at the lack of visits from his father, and clearly missed even his pet pigeons.[50] But childhood experience was of course also constructed through material

---

[46] On children's roles in forming varied relationships: James and Prout 1997a; Qvortup et al. 1994.
[47] *P. Oxy.* IX 1202 (217 CE). [48] *P. Oxy.* VI 926 (third century CE).
[49] *P. Oxy.* VI 930 (late second or early third century CE).
[50] *SB* III 6262 (third century CE) discussed in Cribiore 2001: 112. Cf. Pudsey 2013: 504–6 and *P. Oxy.* I 119 (second/third century CE) in which a young boy sulkily expressed dissatisfaction at his father's refusal to bring him along on a visit to Alexandria.

culture, of which much survives from Roman Egypt.[51] In archaeological studies of children's material culture in the past, items which were child-specific such as toys, dolls and clothes often reflect parental attempts to pass on particular aspects of behaviour, which were usually defined along age and gender lines as well as socio-economic groups and ideals.[52] We could read much of the material of this sort in terms of socialization processes, children having very little say in the way that dominant adult cultures were introduced to them for them to learn. But while children are directed and guided in their play by adults, more significantly they mark out and develop their own rules, structures and boundaries; their participation in various aspects of play can range from the simple to the imaginative, creative and even subversive – as such, play is one aspect of children's culture that can be considered in terms of a 'subaltern' culture in relation to adults' expected behaviours and norms.

One item pertaining to children's material culture we find widely across the Roman world is the small doll, made from cloth, ivory or bone; dolls like these survive in their as a consequence largely of burial with girls. Dolls have been interpreted as simple playthings for girls and/or to have held some ritual meaning and function.[53] Almost all of the surviving dolls from the Roman world are representations of girls and women and, as such, were at least intended as specifically gendered toys, which children would have been expected to have understood as such.[54] Dolls found across the Roman world were arguably modelled on imperial women as well as on ideals of femininity, and were clearly designed as luxury items aimed at passing on particular messages to girls in the upper echelons of Roman society.[55]

But we can view dolls as more than simple tools for the socialization of girls into an idealized femininity in accordance with their social group; they can be examined as objects through which girls actively played and responded to such messages of gendered norms and values with their own interpretations of their world.[56] In particular, dolls that had the capacity to

[51] On children's material culture, see Sofaer Derevenski 2000: esp. 5–12.
[52] Wilkie 2000: 107–8.
[53] Especially Manson 1987, 1991, 1992. See also Horn 2005: 102–5; Rawson 2003.
[54] E.g. Janssen 1996: 239; but see Dolansky 2012: 258–9.
[55] See Dolansky 2012: 284–5 on imperial ideologies intended in doll manufacture.
[56] The best-known example of this sort of children's subversion of adult expectations was in the treatment of the doll collection of one Irene Cordes in early twentieth-century America. Irene had deliberately smashed, beheaded and broken her dolls in a direct and antagonistic response to her parents' giving them to her as representations of expected female values within her social class: motherhood, childcare and household concerns. 'Children can also destroy or lose those objects that contradict their image of themselves or the expectations of their peer group.

be moved and dressed up enabled children to understand and play with them in different and imaginative ways, and to share this play with whomever they chose, and however they chose. One is left to wonder how many upper-class Roman girls would have deliberately injured or disfigured their 'Lady Faustina' ivory dolls; however, it is worth exploring the capacity that the toys and dolls found in Roman Egypt had for imaginative play.

A number of cloth dolls from Egypt have been discussed as playthings, and as tools for gendered socialization, with their adult female forms and pronounced breasts and pubic regions.[57] One first-century CE linen doll stuffed with papyrus and rags, with moulded breasts, painted nipples and painted jewellery and with movable attached arms comes from Hawara, and two dolls from the fourth century CE have very similar features.[58] These dolls, like others found across the Mediterranean world, appear to have embodied both gender and status ideals: adult women's reproductive and mothering capacity was emphasized by their shape, along with implied status through hairstyles, jewellery and facial cosmetic paint. As such, these dolls were most likely symbolic of adult attempts to encourage their young girls into accepting the values associated with womanhood in their particular social group, and to learn the important roles played by aspects of female appearance and adornment in displaying social status and culture, especially in conjunction with small toilette items recovered alongside them.[59]

But what of young girls' own experience of playing with such dolls? These dolls were more than objects on which girls could practise their dressing and cosmetics. As cloth dolls they were particularly malleable, all with movable limbs which allowed their owners to move, position and engage them in a pretence of some sort of activity. Janssen's original study of items in Oxyrhynchus reveals what appears to be a ball for a doll, with which a doll could be made to play.[60] The capacity of these Egyptian cloth

---

Archaeologically, it is the act of discard, loss and destruction of child-specific artefacts that we are most likely to encounter.' Wilkie 2000: 103. Further examples of this kind of subversion in contemporary girls' play with Barbie dolls are discussed by Dolansky 2012: 280–2.

[57] Janssen 1996 figs. 1–6. See also Dolansky 2012: 265–7.

[58] Manchester University Museum 2094, Janssen, 1996: 234; Petrie Museum of Egyptian Archaeology, University College London, UC 28024, Janssen, 1996: 231–2; and Ashmolean Museum 1888.818, Jansen, 1996: 232–3. See discussion and images in Dolansky 2012: 266 and figs. 4, 5 and 6.

[59] See Dolansky 2012: 275.

[60] A wool ball, stuffed with papyrus, found in Behnasa, Oxyrhynchus, features in Janssen 1996: 238 and fig. 8 (Victoria and Albert Museum, inv. no. 1937-1897) as cited in Dolansky 2012: 276, n. 77.

dolls to be dressed with additional clothing,[61] posed, moved and brought to imaginative life in various ways allows us to read into them as objects with the potential for imaginative play of the sort that drew not only on the intended messages of femininity and motherhood of dolls, but also on the range of experiences of those playing together (or alone) with them. Children of both freeborn and slave status would undoubtedly have played together with dolls and toys in their homes, and facets of their play with these objects would have focused more on their shared experience of being children, rather than on their different social statuses and genders.

The urban inhabitants of Oxyrhynchus have left us with a number of further examples of such dolls. While the children of Oxyrhynchus were not elite in the same sense as Roman aristocrats were, those belonging to the hereditary gymnasial and metropolitan groups were invested with particular administrative, judicial and other expectations, and as such their children would have been expected to conform to particular social and gendered behaviours and values inherent in the typical design of dolls.[62] However, the dolls found in Egypt appear to have differed from those imperial dolls found elsewhere in the Empire. A well-preserved linen rag doll, stuffed with papyrus, dated to between the first and the fifth century CE, had the capacity for a great deal of activity in the hands of a small child.[63] The doll has arms attached in a similar fashion to others from Egypt: that is, in the form of a long roll of linen attached to the back to the doll's torso, rendering them movable and hugely poseable. Another, dated from between the fifth and the tenth century and made of bone, shows careful detailing of the eyes, navel and breasts, in line with the feminine ideals aimed at girls within the urban elite, but also has movable arms which have been attached to the torso as a separate unit, thus rendering the dolls of metropolite girls active and malleable playthings which could, and seem to have been, used imaginary activities beyond those expected of metropolite girls – for instance, sporting activity in the example of the doll with the ball.[64]

Other toys from Oxyrhynchus are indicative of a degree of children's agency, imagination and shared play on the part of the child(ren) playing with them. For instance, a terracotta model of a Nile boat dated to the first

---

[61] Such as the dolls' clothing from Hawara in the Petrie Museum of Egyptian Archaeology, University College London, UC28030.
[62] On the gymnasia and gymnasial groups in the metropoleis of Roman Egypt see Bowman and Rathbone 1992: 107–27; Montevecchi 1975, 1993; Nelson 2002; Ruffini 2006; Sijpesteijn 1976; Yiftach-Firanko 2010.
[63] British Museum, GR 1905, 1021.13.   [64] British Museum, GR 1979, 1017.209.

or second century CE features details of the pointed stern and rounded bows, along with various other decorative elements and pierced holes in the bow and cabin for fitting with thread which could be used to pull it along.[65] There are also some wooden figurines of horses dated to the Roman period with a hole in the head for attaching string or thread so that they can be used as pull-along toys.[66] These toys also had holes in both forelegs and hind legs in which some had wheels attached to them with a peg.[67] This type of pull-along wooden horse was very popular in the village of Karanis where many have been found, and their popularity hints at an intention to display and encourage the activities and values associated with military status and pursuits.[68] Karanis was closely associated with auxiliary and cavalry soldiers and veterans in the Roman period, many of whom settled and formed families and communities within the village,[69] and it is quite reasonable to expect that veterans' children would have been given plenty of toy horses to play with in and around their houses and the courtyards they shared with children of other families. While the intention of such toys was to give Karanis' children the opportunity to play at being cavalry, the potential of these toys to be dragged and wheeled around by the children of non-military families, and often children of slave status, would have lessened their 'socializing' impact and heightened their use in imaginative and creative, possibly even subversive, play shared between children across social groups (given that riders were painted on some of these horses, using different colours, actively racing these horses in emulation of sporting activity is one obvious possibility).

From the village of Karanis a large proportion of all the items we classify as toys had similar potential for active play: from the pull-along animals and objects and movable dolls discussed above to a series of noisy clappers[70] and marbles and game pieces for more structured games.[71]

---

[65] British Museum, GR 1922, 1021.3.

[66] Petrie Museum of Egyptian Archaeology, University College London, UC59352, UC59353, UC59354.

[67] Petrie Museum of Egyptian Archaeology, University College London, UC45015.

[68] Kelsey Museum of Archaeology, no. 7692 is a particularly well-preserved example, but see also the twelve other wooden pull-along horses from Karanis, Kelsey Museum, nos. 7487–91, 7652, 7692, 01.0034, 01.0035, 02.6399, 02.6401, 02.6402 and numerous other pull-along objects and animals.

[69] Alston 1995: esp. 117–42.

[70] Kelsey Museum of Archaeology, nos. 3530–4, 3843, 3852, 7620, 01.0767, 01.0768, 01.0769, 02.3933, 02.6356–9, 02.6362, 02.6372.

[71] For example the gaming pieces in Kelsey Museum of Archaeology, nos. 4748, 4750–2, 10041, 02.2786–7. See also the intriguing item in the Kelsey Museum of Archaeology, no. 7571, a miniature version of a weaver's comb and wooden hammer. Was this intended as a toy, or to be used in working and/or learning?

These toys are far from socializing tools: many of them are perfect for games of pretence within groups (and potentially establishing hierarchies/inviting competition between children) regardless of their intended purpose. Movement was a function of all the dolls, pull-along animals, clappers and gaming pieces, which were all conducive to shared activity and play often requiring multiple players and allowing flexibility in respect of game 'rules' and objectives. In a world where children of different ages, sexes and social status were living, working, learning and playing together it is hard not to imagine that such shared imaginative play formed a large part of uniquely child-centric and child-produced cultures distinct from, and yet in dialogue with, those dominant cultures of adults and their expectations of how their children should be.

The 'Symbolic Child': Passing Down Culture through Children

Children were an essential focus for the transmission of social ideals, values and memory through families, and ultimately social groups.[72] It is this role that makes children and their progression to adulthood an important focus for the study of varied cultural interactions across and between quite diverse social, ethnic and cultural groups. Throughout this chapter I have explored how we may be able to consider children's activities and concerns as a form of culture distinct from that of the adults around them, and the extent to which they shared more in common with other children in their day-to-day lives, than the expectations of their social position would have suggested. In playing with this theme it has become apparent that the children of Roman Egypt both produced and consumed cultures of play, identity, space and learning in a range of different ways, often in response to the expectations of the more dominant adult-produced cultures. But the process of growing up and becoming an adult must have lent a further dynamic to this relationship.

Cultural values, practices and attitudes were passed down the generations and through children in many ways. Children were very much the focus of localized political and religious values within their social group, a focus which is evidenced by parental expression of their children's association with social status, gendered behaviours and local and national

---

[72] See Prescendi 2010: esp. 74–5, 90–2, for children's roles in the transition of cultural memory in religious terms within the framework of 'deliberate' and 'mechanical' memory.

cults and deities. These symbolic aspects of children and their lives, and the hopes their parents, other family members and associated adults placed in them, were expressed through the activities of political and religious institutions. In the remainder of this chapter I consider what sort of hopes and values adults expressed through children symbolically, particularly at the point of their growing up into adults. Did the dialogues between adult expectations and children's experience within these spheres change as children grew older? How might this have impacted on the position of children as a kind of 'subaltern' group?

In the metropoleis of Roman Egypt, entrance into the gymnasial and metropolitan groups of those liable for only 12 drachma tax status was the means through which boys would continue their parents' lineage and status traditions in their admission into adult society. The privileges and responsibilities associated with these groups were tied to the ways in which local and regional economic and administrative power was distributed.[73] From the mid first century onwards all of the metropoleis in Egypt were divided into districts, and boys approaching age fourteen were entered into the *ephebate* for examination (through an application of *epikrisis*), the records for which reveal the nature of children's status and their lineage. Those entered were to demonstrate that both of their parents were of the same status, and the applications were fairly standard and typical:

From Sarapion, son of Harpocration, grandson of Sarapion, [whose] mother [is] Demetria alias Asclatarion, daughter of Heracleides, from the city of the Oxyrhynchi. In accordance with the orders concerning scrutiny of those entering the class of thirteen-year-olds to discover if they are born of parents both of the category of the gymnasial class I was registered in the Tenth District as having entered the class of thirteen-year-olds in the twelfth year of the deified Hadrian. Therefore I have presented myself for my own scrutiny and declare that my grandfather Sarapion son of Harpocration was scrutinized in the scrutiny which took place in the fifth year of the deified Vespasian under Sutorius Sosibus then strategos and Nicander then royal scribe.[74]

Here a father wrote that his son was eligible for the 12 drachma tax rate group, and provided details of his lineage and proof of when and where he himself had registered. Some interesting issues emanate from these documents regarding children's family lives, the expectations placed upon them and the important role played by the gymnasial groups in preserving

---

[73] See Bowman and Rathbone 1992. On the importance of the maternal line within the gymnasial group, see Depaw 2009. See Pudsey and Vuolanto forthcoming for Oxyrhynchus' gymnasium and family members' involvement in putting forward boys for application.

[74] *P. Oxy.* XLVI 3282 (148/9 CE).

privileged social status, ideals and values through their teenage children. In the majority of these documents it was the father who put forward the child for examination, though we do see cases where this role was played by the boy's mother in the absence of a living or resident father,[75] or even in instances where there was a resident father.[76] In one case the boy's mother made great efforts to point out her son's literacy, which was neither a necessity nor common practice, but clearly a factor in her mind as something which might have proved a significant bolster to her son's successful application, leaving us to wonder whether she thought this necessary because his father was not making the application.[77]

The desires of family or guardians to present their children for entrance into this privileged urban elite group, along with its associated political privileges, is clearly strong: so much so that many did not fit the strict criteria and looked for ways around the rules in order to have their children remain connected with their traditions and to continue them. In fact we have evidence that some boys were presented long before they turned thirteen or fourteen. An eleven-year-old boy was presented by his father in the cavalry camp district of Oxyrhynchus:

I wish to have registered for the first time in the district in which I am myself registered, the cavalry camp district, the son born to me from my wife who lives with me, Aurelia Nice or Taias, from the same city, Aurelius Eudaemon, who is liable to the 12 drachma poll-tax and of the gymnasial class and is in the present year eleven years old.[78]

In one case the parents and maternal uncle of a four-year-old boy submitted a registration of their son for the third share of a house, and mentioned him as having been registered as a payer of the 12 drachma tax.[79] Children of slave status were occasionally put forward in application by their owners, as a means of attempting to keep the family associated with the traditions of the privileged group:

To Philonicus also called Hermodorus, basilica-grammateus, and Dionysius and a second Dionysius, keepers of the archives and officers in charge of the selection, and to Apollonius, ex-exegetes and scribe of the city, from Apollonius ... of the city of Oxyrhynchus, living in the West Quay quarter. My slave ... born in the house to my female slave ... has reached the age of thirteen years in the past fifth year of Hadrianus Caesar the lord. I therefore declare that I am rated at 12

---

[75] E.g. *P. Oxy.* III 478 (132 CE) cited below, p. 229. [76] *P. Oxy.* XLVI 3295 (285 CE).
[77] *P. Oxy.* XXII 2345 (224 CE). [78] *P. Oxy.* XLVI 3295 (285 CE).
[79] *P. Oxy.* XXXVIII 2858 (171 CE).

drachmae by a poll-tax list of the second year of Hadrianus Caesar the lord at the said quarter.[80]

In a case discussed earlier, two siblings registered a slave boy aged thirteen.[81] And in another case, a freedwoman applied for her son to be registered, citing the connections of his father as legitimate qualification.[82] Non-kin such as freedmen or guardians were sometimes responsible for the applications in cases where there appear to have been no living family members.[83] In some cases applications for girls were also submitted, as in this example of the application for an eleven-year-old girl:

> a copy is appended, with declarations of three witnesses to the effect that Trunnia Marcella is the sister of Trunnius Lucillianus, and of the examination of my slaves Euphrosynus, [...]olytus and Plutarchus; and I swear the usual oath made by the Romans that they are my children and I have made no false return.[84]

The document goes on to reveal that the girl was illegitimate and also lists a slave boy of the age of five. We also know of cases where parents felt the need to provide as much proof as possible, sometimes providing copies of records of previous registrations in the family line which they retrieved from an archive: one such case from Oxyrhynchus demonstrates this practice.[85]

Similar formal processes passing traditional values down through children were common in priesthoods and the priestly class, in both villages and towns.[86] In the villages of the Arsinoite region we see the importance attached to connecting one's children with the local priesthood for both religious and social purposes. Circumcision of boys was a prerequisite for entrance into the priesthood, and parents made formal applications and petitions to priests for permission to have their sons circumcised.[87] Examples range from large villages and towns like

---

[80] *P. Oxy.* IV 714 (122 CE) in which the boy's mother was also a slave in the house.
[81] *W. Chr.* 217 (172–3 CE).   [82] *P. Oxy.* III 478 (132 CE). See also *BGU* I 324 (166–7 CE).
[83] *P. Oxy.* LXVII 4585 (189 CE) in which a freedman appeared to have be responsible for this boy, and *P. Mich.* XIV 676 (272 CE) for the guardian.
[84] *P. Oxy.* XII 1451 (175 CE) regarding the gymnasial group at Alexandria, though the document was kept in Oxyrhynchus. This eleven-year-old girl's father was a veteran and she was being submitted for consideration on the same terms as her older brother, and at the same time. See also *BGU* I 113 (60–61 CE) for an example of the daughter of a veteran.
[85] *P. Mich. inv.* 261 (238–44) discussed by Leon 2012: 95–108. As noted by Leon, the mother's name in this case suggests she may have been from a different district altogether and was using this process of registering her child as a means of cementing her family's relations with the local metropolitan group.
[86] Hickey 2009: esp. 506.
[87] For instance, *BGU* I 347 (171 CE) Arsinoites region, giving of permission for the circumcision.

Tebtynis[88] and Soknopaiou Nesos[89] to the metropoleis such as Oxyrhynchus.[90] In Tebtynis a mother, Isidora, wrote a formal application to the *strategos* for permission to have both her seven-year-old son and her eleven-year-old cousin circumcised. Isidora specifically highlighted the boys' ancestry and pointed out that the family requests this: 'that in accordance with custom a letter should be written by you to his highness the high-priest in order that, his permission being given, the boys may be able to be circumcised and to perform the sacred offices assigned to them'.[91]

In a private letter Chaireas, father of Kronion, informed the addressee about some problems regarding the circumcision of a boy,[92] and a report of proceedings before a priest in Soknopaiou Nesos listed many children in relation to permission to circumcise.[93] Priests formally accepted applications for circumcision on these terms,[94] and a number of these applications related to the regionally important Apis cult, association with which was a means of expression of social (and often gendered) identity. Parents in particular locales were keen to ensure their sons were formally recognized and entered into the priestly class associated with these local cults.

These instances show parents, uncles, guardians and masters apparently going to great lengths to ensure their children's place within important social and political groups at the turning point of their children's lives. They demonstrate on the part of these adults – who of course had once been children experiencing the same processes – an attachment to specific symbolic notions of the bridge between what it meant to be a child and what it meant to be an adult. The adults in the cases discussed above made every effort to shape and determine the environment for their children very much in terms of the dominant cultures surrounding them (cults and gymnasial groups). But in shaping these environments for their children, many would bend the already flexible rules of social status and gender to ensure continued tradition.

This sort of complex relationship between parental expectations and hopes for their children, and idealized images of them through expressions of their children's religious and social identity, are further expressed in

---

[88] *BGU* 15 2470 (192–3 CE) Arsinoite nome, request for permission to circumcise.
[89] *SPP* 22 51 (153 CE).
[90] *P. Oxy.* 50 3567 (252 CE); *PSI* 5 454 (320 CE); *SB* 18 13129 (207–8 CE).
[91] *P. Tebt.* 2 292 (189–90 CE).   [92] *P. Tebt.* 2 314 (second century CE).
[93] *BGU* 13 2216 (156 CE). See also *BGU* 1 347 (171 CE) Memphis; *P. Tebt.* 2 291 (161–2 CE) Tebtynis report of judicial examinations for priests, include references to circumcision.
[94] *P.Tebt.* 2 293 (187 CE) Tebtynis report on application for circumcision; *SB* VI 9027 (148 CE) Soknopaiou Nesos.

funerary art relating to children in Roman Egypt. Funerary representations of adults and children varied between regions,[95] but many factors were common. Children's symbolic presence was gendered and they were closely associated with local cults, particularly child-god cults dating from Pharaonic times and experiencing a surge in popularity under Roman rule, particularly cults associated with Horus, Harpokrates, Isis and Apis.[96] Funerary art in Roman Egypt ranges from the mummy cases from Akhmim in Upper Egypt[97] to painted shrouds from the Fayum region (Hawara in particular)[98] and painted mummy portraits from across Egypt.[99]

Children's coffins had strikingly gendered features, reflecting a symbolic set of their parents' ideals. For instance, the Akhmin coffins featured delineated breasts, nipples, wide hips and indented navels, in a similar manner as we observe in many dolls.[100] Throughout most funerary art representing children, boys are closely associated with Osiris and girls with Hathor. The boy's coffin now known as the 'shrine sarcophagus' presents an image of a boy wearing his hair with Horus locks, the very symbol of youth, and wearing his mantle in an arm sling style: at once he is associated both with the child-protector god and also with the identity of his particular social group through his dress.[101] Two girls were buried with this same group and their shrouds emphasize particular aspects of their girlhood, such as a Roman hairstyle, a floral wreath, a tunic with a *clavus* and representations of Anubis.[102] Boys' association with the Serapis cult was indicated by a particular diagonal folding of the mantle in a number of shrouds.[103] The boy's shaved head, with four patches remaining on his forehead, associated him closely with the protection of the god Horus. This was also common at Karanis in the Fayum, along with images of the child-god Harpokrates.[104]

---

[95] Riggs 2002: 86.
[96] Many symbolic figurines (intended for children as toys?) from the Fayum village of Karanis feature Harpokrates: Kelsey Museum of Archaeology, no. 6456, Harpokrates the child-god, son of Isis, riding a horse; or no. 3452, a female figurine doll.
[97] Schweitzer 1998.   [98] Parlasca 1966.
[99] Borg 1996: 183–90; Also Bierbrier 1997; Walker and Bierbrier 1997.
[100] See Riggs 2005: figs. 24–8.
[101] Berlin, Ägyptische Museum und Papyrussammlung 17126, 17127; see Riggs 2005: 149, 151, fig. 70. In third-century Deir el-Medina (in Thebes) the painted shroud of an adolescent boy also expresses his symbolic position within his social group. Deir el-Medina Tomb 1447, see Riggs 2005: 225, fig. 112.
[102] Turin, Museo Egizio 2265 and Paris, Louvre, 3398, discussed in Riggs 2005: 228–9, figs. 113, 114.
[103] For example London, British Museum EA6715, cited in Riggs 2005: 231 fig. 116.
[104] Boak and Peterson 1931: 34, plate 25, fig. 49; Rowlandson 1998: 51, fig. ii.

The Fayum mummy portraits featured children, and we see images again of boys with the 'Horus locks' on a shaved head, along with hair tufts, the result of a hair-cutting *mallokouria* ceremony in relation to the Isis cult.[105] This type of hair-cutting was also associated with the protection of Horus across pre-Roman Egyptian history.[106] The identification of children with these child-focused protector deities and local cults clearly indicates parental desire to ensure their sons and daughters identified with the local community, especially in villages. Further, the mummy portraits appear to identify boys with the age-focused values of the urban gymnasial groups discussed above, to which many of the boys represented had likely belonged. While portraits of younger boys featured typically youthful symbols, those approaching adulthood were regularly pictured with moustaches, and often with garlands and other symbols of ephebic dress.[107]

These boys and the girls would be pictured in mummy portraits wearing amulets containing papyri with spells for protection against disease and the evil eye. This protection of children was common across both urban and rural sites in Egypt in the Roman period; indeed, the plea for protection for the children of family members, friends and associates appears across the salutations of private letters in the documents from Oxyrhynchus, in the format 'whom the evil eye shall not touch', a salutation that we never see in reference to adults.[108] In a population for whom mortality was an ever-looming threat, especially for the very young, it is not surprising to see so much evidence of anxiety regarding the protection of children against ill health.[109] The child-focused protection of particular deities, together with hairstyles and visual representations, were key to the expression of local and cultural identity, but these images also represent the symbolic child's role within social and political groups and the importance of the expression of shared cultural values and practices.

---

[105] Mummy portrait of a boy, 150–200 CE, J. Paul Getty Museum 78.AP.262, from Oxyrhynchus; cf. British Museum EA 6715. See also Monsterrat 1991, 1993; Riggs 2002.

[106] Ikram 2003 esp. 247–50.

[107] See discussion in Ikram 2003; Monsterrat 1993: esp. 218–22; and, for example, London, Petrie Museum UC 19613.

[108] E.g. *P. Oxy.* IX 1218 (third century CE) family letter; *P. Oxy.* XLI 2981 (second century CE) business letter; *P. Oxy.* XLVI 3312 (second century CE) family letter; *P. Oxy.* XLVI 3313 (second century CE) family letter; *P. Oxy. Hels.* 50 (third century CE) business letter. See Pudsey and Vuolanto forthcoming.

[109] Parkin 2013; Pudsey 2013: 486–90.

Conclusions

In spite of the relative lack of historical and archaeological evidence produced by children themselves in the ancient world, it has been possible to observe aspects of children's culture in Roman Egypt through the material that survives. In this chapter I hope to have shown that a picture of children's culture in Roman Egypt can be drawn with the help of some of the theories and concepts of modern sociological studies of children's cultures in the present day, and archaeological approaches to children's cultures across a range of periods and places. The notion of children's culture as a 'subaltern' culture is a very useful one, which enables us to think of the ways in which children themselves produced and consumed culture, and how their experience of this related to what adults expected of them.

Parents, family and guardians vividly expressed their hopes and expectations for future generations in largely gendered and socially stratified terms, but the reality of life for children was not as straightforward. Children shared their activities and experiences largely with other children, whether in their homes, their immediate neighbourhood, the gymnasium, through local cults or as apprentices. Their work and learning relied on the successful negotiation of relationships with other children and adults, and they clearly had a great deal of agency in shaping their own lives. Shared play and active engagement with surroundings and other children at younger ages were an important part of life, and were also more complex than simple socialization along gender lines. The documentary and archaeological sources relating to children's lived experience in Roman Egypt are not without problems: it is still largely through words and objects produced by adults that we hear and see children, but we can observe aspects of children's culture if we approach that material through the lens of sociological and archaeological approaches to understanding the child's world.

The child's world in Roman Egypt was one in which day-to-day lived experiences, values and concerns played out through their interaction with their physical and social environment, their shared cultures and the relationship between the 'symbolic child' and children's experience. It is clear that children, individually, had some degree of agency in shaping their environment and relationships, particularly in cases where their work or learning took them outside their family home and into engagement with adults and children beyond the family group. Moreover, children as a group understood and responded to adult expectations of them and adult cultures of religion, work and life in the household. Shared culture between children was an important aspect of their experience of work, home life, play, learning and religious activity, and such shared activity allowed for greater depth of experience as a child growing up in Roman Egypt. The distinction between children's cultures and adults' cultures, if we can discern one, and the dynamics of engagement between the two, can be viewed in terms of popular culture theories and approaches and helps us to understand what it meant to be a child in the world of Roman Egypt.

PART IV

Late Antiquity

11 | Interpreting the Kalends of January: A Case Study for Late Antique Popular Culture?

LUCY GRIG

The festival of the Kalends represents a veritable bounty for the scholar of popular culture in Late Antiquity. This festival was, most unusually, celebrated Empire-wide, in town and countryside alike, and was conspicuous and noisy enough to attract the attention of a large number of commentators, generally disapproving. It contains several elements traditionally seen as characteristic of popular culture: masquerade, satire and role reversal, as well as the usual eating, drinking, dancing and carousing generally involved in festivals. Moreover, the Kalends is particularly suitable as a case study for *late antique* popular culture in that it seems to be a distinctively *late antique* phenomenon, first rising to prominence in our sources during the fourth century, and retaining visibility in the ecclesiastical record until remarkably late on, as we shall see. This chapter will examine the key elements of the celebration of the Kalends and their representation in the historical record, with a particular eye to the issue of popular culture. In this way it will consider some important methodological issues for the study of the 'popular' and its representation in the largely ecclesiastical literary sources.

In my reading of the late antique texts, I shall flag up the key strategies of clerical discourse regarding popular culture, which need to be deconstructed and analysed carefully in order to improve our understanding of both ecclesiastical responses to popular culture, and this popular culture itself. This study will thus take on the challenge of reading against the grain in order to attempt to understand the history of the late antique Kalends in its own right. With limited space, my discussion will largely focus on the late antique West, with particular focus on Gaul, where the evidence is especially rich. Even the Gallic evidence, as we shall see, is highly problematic. The dominant figure of Caesarius of Arles plays a central role in the story;[1] as *the* most influential critic of the Kalends, his attacks on the festival would be repeated and rephrased throughout a lengthy early

---

This chapter has benefited from the insights of audiences in Budapest, Edinburgh and Tvärminne.
[1] The key texts are Caesarius' two sermons on the Kalends: *Serm.* 192–3; see also *Serm.* 13.5.

medieval literary tradition in the West, encompassing largely France and Spain, but stretching as far north as Germany, and even some way into the second millennium. Getting *beyond* Caesarius and his colleagues is the challenge at hand. Earlier scholars would of course have thought this an entirely fruitless endeavour: for instance, Samuel Dill who wrote that 'The most penetrating imagination, with the fullest learning, could never wake to life that dim, sunken mass who dragged out their lives in indigence, with no hope, and probably no desire, of any change.'[2] However, in this chapter I shall attempt to restore agency to the individuals who made up the congregations of Caesarius and his ilk, in part by examining, alongside the usual ecclesiastical texts, some source material hitherto untapped in this context: late antique ceramics.

To begin with a brief history of the festival: the Kalends of January was a date of long-standing importance in the official Roman calendar.[3] It was the date when the consuls for the year were sworn in and, during the imperial period, the date when the army, and also the Senate, swore an oath of allegiance to the emperor.[4] The public rites, which went on for three days, included the *vota publica*, the distribution of donatives (to the army) and gifts of various kinds (including tokens, trinkets and silver coins) to the people, as well as *ludi* and related processions.[5] While the feast was very likely traditionally one of the *dies fasti*, its status as a public holiday is first officially attested only in 389.[6] Traditionally closely associated with Rome and Roman traditions, it is most likely during the fourth century that celebration of the Kalends began to spread Empire-wide, with activities encompassing the public and private, formal and informal, official and unofficial.[7] This growth is shown by the wide geographical spread of our sources from the fourth and fifth centuries, originating from locations as far flung as Amasea (in Pontus),[8] Antioch,[9]

---

[2] Dill 1926: 235.
[3] For a full account of the history of the Kalends, see Meslin 1970, to which all recent scholarship is indebted; more recently, see too Graf 2015 (which appeared late in the production of this volume) and 1998; Harris 2011: 11–21; Hawkins 2012; Kaldellis 2012.
[4] The other date being on the anniversary of his accession.
[5] See Meslin 1970: 53–70 on the civic activities celebrating the Kalends in Late Antiquity.
[6] *CTh* 2.8.19 (Rome, 389). Graf argues that Theodosius' endorsement of the festival is the impetus behind the cluster of anti-Kalends sermons in the years that follow: Graf 2015:138–9.
[7] It had seemingly spread to North Africa considerably earlier, judging by the references in Tertullian: *Apol.* 42 and *De idol.* 14. Its growth in popularity during the fourth century is shown by Meslin 1970: 50–2. That it was unusual for a festival to be celebrated Empire-wide is noted by Libanius: *Or.* 9.4 and *Descr.* 5.2 (for texts see n. 9 below).
[8] Asterius of Amasea, *Hom.* 4, in Datema 1970: 38–52; see further Driver 2005.
[9] John Chrysostom, *Hom. in Kalendas* (*PG* 48: 954); Libanius, *Or.* 9; *Descr.* 5 (see Gibson 2008: 437–41). See further Gleason 1986; Graf 2012; Hawkins 2012. A further Syriac text, Isaac of

Barcelona,[10] Carthage,[11] Milan,[12] Ravenna[13] and Turin.[14] Ecclesiastical sources from the sixth and seventh centuries and beyond seemingly show that Kalends celebrations continued to be widespread, with testimony from Andalusia,[15] Constantinople,[16] Galicia,[17] Lydia[18] and Rome.[19] The largest body of evidence for this later period, however, comes from Gaul, which will form much of focus of this chapter.

Alongside the official public events put on in the large cities by the secular authorities, and more particularly the focus of the ecclesiastical naysayers, were the unofficial Kalends activities enjoyed across a broad swathe of society, across the Empire. Some seem familiar from other festivals, especially Saturnalia and its Greek counterpart Kronia. The temptation for the historian of popular culture to wish to compare, and in some sense elide, the festival of the Kalends with that of Saturnalia is obvious. Calendrically, they are very close together: Saturnalia ran from 17 to 23 December during the imperial period.[20] Midwinter was a period traditionally marked by extended feasting and celebration. In the Roman calendar Saturnalia was followed not long after by Compitalia (3–5 January), another festival with a distinctly 'popular' flavour, at least in its urban form.[21] Unlike Saturnalia, but like the later Kalends celebrations, Compitalia had its own associated *ludi* in Rome. In general, Compitalia shared key features with Saturnalia: it involved feasting and household celebrations, and was particularly associated with slaves.[22] It is Saturnalia,

---

Antioch's 'Homily on the Night Vigils at Antioch' has also been discussed as a description of the Kalends: see Gleason 1986: 112.

[10] Pacianus, *Paranesis* 1 (*PL* 13: 108) 1; cf. Jerome, *De vir. inl.* 106.
[11] Augustine, *Serm.* Mainz 62/Dolbeau 198: Dolbeau 1992.
[12] Ambrose, *De interpellatione Iob et David* 4[2].1.4 (*CSEL* 32.2.271).
[13] Peter Chrysologus, *Serm* 155 (*PL* 52: 609–11).   [14] Max. Tur. *Serm.* 63 and 98 (*CCL* 43).
[15] Isidore of Seville, *De Off. Ecc.* 1.41 (*PL* 83: 774–5).
[16] Council of Constantinople 680; Council of Trullo 692 can. 62 in Hefele 1829–1912 (V) 232; see further Kaldellis 2012.
[17] Martin of Braga, *De corr. rust.* 10,16; see too Second Council of Braga (572), canon 73: Barlow 1950: 123–44.
[18] John Lydus, *De mensibus* 4.2.
[19] Boniface, *Ep.* 50 (*MGH Epp. sel.* 3.1.301); *Conc. romanum* 743 c. 9 (*MGH Conc.* 2.1: 15–16).
[20] On Saturnalia, see in particular Versnel 1994: 136–227 and Dolansky 2011.
[21] The urban version, at least, was known for its popular dimension during the Late Republic, when it was considered potentially dangerous. The *collegia compitalicia* were abolished in 64 BCE, only to be re-established by Clodius six years later (Cic. *Pis.* 81), then seemingly abolished again by Caesar, though he gave the *ludi*; Augustus revived the institution with a new focus. Compitalia was also a rural festival, marking the end of the agricultural year. See Scullard 1981: 58–69; Lott 2004: 33, 35–7, 45–60, 114–15.
[22] Cicero chose not to visit Pompey at his villa on Compitalia so as not to disturb his slaves' festivities: Cic. *Att.* 2.3.4.

however, that looms large in the minds of scholars of popular culture working in many different periods,[23] who like to associate it with carnival, and to assert that it held a comparable symbolic importance in ancient popular culture.[24] Similarly, in Toner's account of Roman popular culture its symbolic centrality is assured: 'The Saturnalia were more than a mere holiday; they were an alternative world sanctioned by the authorities. Everything that was culturally dominant was overturned ... A new world order was established in direct opposition to the serious high culture.'[25] It is perhaps surprising, therefore, that so few *ancient* sources link the Kalends with Saturnalia.[26] While it is clear that Compitalia was moribund by Late Antiquity, it also seems likely that the festival of the Kalends overtook Saturnalia in popularity during this period.[27] An examination of the reasons for the success, and longevity, of the Kalends forms the heart of this chapter.

So what did celebrating the Kalends involve? In Carthage in 404, for instance, Augustine suggests several characteristic activities:

Are you going to join in today in the celebration of good luck presents with a pagan, going to play at dice with a pagan, going to get drunk with a pagan?[28]

The *strenae* are a ubiquitous feature in accounts of the Kalends, from our earliest evidence onwards.[29] Christian preachers considered them an example of the wrong kind of giving and contrasted them with the alms

---

[23] Note, for instance, the title of the final chapter of Scott 1990: 202–29, 'A Saturnalia of Power: The First Public Declaration of the Hidden Transcript'.

[24] References here are legion, but see, most influentially, Bakhtin 1968 and Stallybrass and White 1986.

[25] Toner 2009: 93; he also asserts that 'Saturnalia was not ... a festival given for the people but one they gave themselves': 95. However, that this was not always the case is made clear by the Kalends shows put on by Domitian: see *Silvae* 1.6 and, further, Newlands 2002: 227–59.

[26] For rare exceptions see Tert. *Apol.* 42 and *De idol.* 14 and Max. Tur. *Serm.* 98.1, referring scornfully to 'ebrietatem ... Saturnaliam ... lasciviam kalendarum'. At times there is clear confusion between the two in Christian texts, as in the *Acts of Dasius*, discussed below.

[27] An interesting alternative late antique comparator for the Kalends would be the Jewish festival of Purim, the subject of prohibitive imperial legislation in 408: *CTh* 16.8.18. This festival, like the Kalends and Saturnalia, involved jests and mockery, but it was the specific mockery of the Christian faith and its rituals that seemed to concern the authorities, as well as its potential to stir intercommunal tensions: see here Sivan 2008: 144–68.

[28] Augustine, *Serm.* Mainz 62.2/Dolbeau 198.2: 'Acturus es hodie celebrationem strenarum cum pagano, lusurus alea cum pagano, inebriaturus es te cum pagano?' Gambling is also at mentioned at 198.8.

[29] Glossed by Festus as follows: 'Strenam vocamus, quae datur die religioso ominis boni gratia' (410, 21ff.). Suetonius tells us that Tiberius forbade their exchange (*Tib.* 34.2) during a discussion of his various frugality measures, designed to characterize him as stingy and joyless; see further Baudy 1987 and Meslin 1970: 39–46.

given by good Christians.[30] *Strenae* can obviously be compared with the *sigillaria* given at Saturnalia, particularly on Sigillaria itself (23 December 23); *strenae*, like *sigillaria*, were given both horizontally and vertically, encompassing tips from employers and patrons, as well as gifts among friends.[31] As well as giving presents, the exchange of New Year greetings, including kissing, is mentioned several times with disapproval.[32] Dice-playing, a key feature of Saturnalia,[33] is less prominent in accounts of the Kalends,[34] though gaming and gambling are attacked by preachers in general.[35] Drinking, it scarcely needs to be said, was a universal feature of festivities of all kinds, and it is unsurprising that it is criticized in attacks on the Kalends.[36] For moralizing preachers drinking is invariably associated with general dissipation, with lust, with 'bawdy' singing and immodest dancing.[37] Opportunities for licence, and role-reversal for slaves in particular, so characteristic of Saturnalia, are less prominent in accounts of the Kalends.[38] However, laughter, jesting and

---

[30] E.g. Augustine, *Serm.* Dolbeau 198.2: 'Dant ergo illi strenas, vos date eleemosynas'. Asterius concentrates much of his ire on the exchange of *strenae*, which he sees as corrupting rather than sustaining civic relations: *Hom.* 4 esp. 3–4. The pleasure brought by the gifts is lauded, however, by Lib. *Or.* 9.8–9 and 16–17 and *Descr.* 5.5. For Caesarius of Arles the gifts are 'diabolicas ... strenas': *Serm.* 192.3 and criticized again at 193.3.

[31] See here Versnel 1994: 148–9.

[32] These greetings were, like the official ones, known as *vota*; the Kalends kiss is disparaged by Asterius as venal and lacking in charity: *Hom.* 4.3.

[33] Saturnalia was famous for gambling with both dice and knucklebones, being the one time of the year when it was not officially illegal. Dice are depicted in the image for December in the Calendar of 354: see here Salzman 1990: 74–6. See further on dice in the Kronia/Saturnalia, Versnel 1994: 211. Versnel sees dice as thematically central to Saturnalia, due to the element of dangerous unpredictability, whereby chance can reverse roles.

[34] Gaming in taverns is mentioned by Chrysostom: *In Kalend.* 2; Libanius says that slaves were allowed to play dice: Lib. *Descr.* 5. 11; *Or.* 9.11.

[35] E.g. Caes. *Serm.* 61.3; 207.3.

[36] E.g. John Chrys. *In Kalend.* 2, complaining about the consumption of unmixed wine all day and night; like Augustine, Caesarius criticizes excessive drinking and wishes his congregation would fast instead: *Serm.* 193.3. Filotas 2005: 162–4 notes that early medieval texts pay less attention to drinking and suggests it might have become more acceptable: the sermon embedded in the *Vita Eligii* 2.16 is a rare exception: *MGH SRM* 4: 705. For Libanius, excessive eating and drinking are part and parcel of the festival: Libanius, *Or.* 9.7; *Descr.* 5.9, 12.

[37] E.g. Maximus of Turin, *Serm.* 63.1; Augustine, *Serm.* Dolbeau 198.8. Caes. *Serm.* 193.1. On attacks on singing and dancing as attacks on popular culture, see further Grig 2013b.

[38] Accounts of Saturnalia frequently recount that at this time masters waited on their slaves (or at least dined *with* them): Macrob. *Sat.* 1.22–3; Auson. *Eclog.* 23. 15–16; and that the household enjoyed a period of licence and relaxation, e.g. Plin. *Ep.* 2.17 and Cato, *Agr.* 57; see here especially Dolanksy 2011. However, only Libanius specifically mentions licence for slaves during the Kalends: *Or.* 9.11; *Descr.* 5.12, including slaves and masters playing dice together: *Descr.* 5.11. It might indeed be objected that here, as at various other points, Libanius' account has a rather artificial flavour.

licence in general seem to have been characteristic of the Kalends, like Saturnalia.[39]

Who took part in the festival? It is clear that involvement was spread across society, from the bottom right to the very top, where generous provision of Kalends gifts and entertainment was expected of the political elite, who provided the civic side of the festivities. Libanius' account in *Or.* 9 (which we should probably read as part of an ongoing debate with Christian rival orators) stresses the universality of the celebration.[40] According to Libanius, it was celebrated by both rich and poor (*Or.* 9.6), including slaves (9.11) and prisoners (9.12), with gifts being given from the emperor downwards (9.15), including the consuls (9.18). He emphasizes the festival's ability to bring unity to society (9.14) and its stress on equality (*Descr.* 5.12).[41] As with so many festivals in antiquity, the Kalends would, of course, have brought country-dwellers into the town for both the official and unofficial aspects of the celebration.[42]

That the festival was celebrated by the military as well as the civilian population is well known, but two tantalizing, if problematic, passages suggest a particularly interesting aspect of military Kalends customs. An association of the Kalends with satire and ridicule, as suggested by a number of sources,[43] has an intriguing military dimension. A scandalous military 'carnival' is depicted in the *Acts of Dasius*, there ascribed to Saturnalia/Kronia, but more generally taken as the Kalends.[44] While the narrative, the tale of a human sacrifice thwarted by the brave Christian soldier Dasius, is clearly fictional, the text as a whole is clearly designed, like Kalends sermons, to dissuade Christians from taking part in 'pagan' New Year festivities. Asterius of Amasea attacks what he sees as obscene skits performed by soldiers at New Year, including, most offensively of all to the bishop, men imitating women in dress and behaviour (*Hom.* 4.7). Caesarius also claims that it is soldiers in particular who are engaging in cross-dressing festivities;[45] it is unclear whether this is just an exaggeration,

---

[39] As particularly focused on by Gleason 1986 and Hawkins 2012.
[40] Graf 2012 argues that Libanius is responding to sermons such as John Chrysostom's.
[41] As already seen, Christian orators disputed this interpretation of the festival and its gift-giving.
[42] As explicitly discussed by both Asterius (*Hom.* 4.6) and Libanius (*Or.* 9.8).
[43] See here Gleason 1986.
[44] *Acts of Dasius* in Musurillo 1972: 272–9; see further Cumont 1897, Weinstock 1964 and Pillinger 1988. Cf. a similar fictional martyr story which explicitly links human sacrifice with the Kalends, preserved in four extant versions, probably from the sixth century: *Acta S. Caesarii* in *AASS* I: 106–26.
[45] *Caes. Serm.* 192.2: 'non erubescentes tunicis muliebribus inserere militares lacertos ... Et merito virilem iam fortitudinem non habent, qui in muliebres transierunt; iusto enim iudicio

to heighten the perversion of gender-switching, or whether Caesarius is referring to the same kind of military carnival described by Asterius.[46]

To a certain extent, the description of the festival as 'popular' is a familiar aspect of hostile polemic. Asterius refers to Kalends celebrants as the 'rabble without' (*Hom.* 4.1). As we shall see, Caesarius makes an association of the festival with the lower orders, with *inperiti homines et rustici*;[47] however, he also described Kalends customs as being practised by *plures in populo christiano* and speaks of his desire to drive the custom of dressing as stags (to be discussed below) *de hac civitate* (*Serm.* 192.3), suggesting its practice in urban as well as rural settings.[48] Writing on the Kalends in Byzantium, Antony Kaldellis argues for the continuing celebration of the festival across the whole of society up to 1200, and that attacks on the festival as 'popular' are polemical, and designed to discredit it: this is highly persuasive.[49]

But what was unique to the Kalends? Where did the secret of its longevity lie, in the teeth of consistent ecclesiastical prohibition? Indeed, what was the reason for the persistent vehemence of clerical disapproval?[50] Let us return to Augustine: this is the longest extant sermon Augustine ever delivered – coming in at a whopping two and a half hours. A deliberate filibuster, as Augustine's translator Edmund Hill puts it, this sermon was designed to keep his Carthage congregation from the Kalends celebrations for as long as possible.[51] Augustine begins by complaining about the noise being made outside the church by the revellers, including 'silly and

---

dei evenisse credendum est, ut militarem virtutem amitterent, qui feminarum se specie deformassent.'

[46] Scholars remain generally unsure regarding the reliability of Caesarius' claims, e.g. Arbesmann 1979: 115; Twycross and Carpenter 2002: 34.

[47] Caes. *Serm.* 192.1; this has left its legacy in the account of the festival in the Golden Legend from 1260, which is largely based on Caesarius (although Augustine gets the credit!), and talks about the persistence of the customs: *The Golden Legend, Feast of the Circumcision*, in Graesse 1846: 86. The practice of laying out tables is specifically ascribed to *rustici* by Caes. *Serm.* 192.3. See further n. 57 below.

[48] Caesarius' orbit took in both the city of Arles and the *vici* and *pagi* of the outlying districts: generally it is impossible to know which audiences he is addressing, even assuming the published sermons give us access to particular historical audiences.

[49] Kaldellis 2012: 200–3.

[50] As Filotas comments: 'The New Year was the main focus of the church's efforts to Christianise seasonal celebrations. Here she failed utterly.' Filotas 2005: 155.

[51] Hill 1997: 229, n. 1; see Chadwick 1996: 71, noting that Augustine himself commented on how he liked to prolong his sermons on days of big pagan festivals, to try to deter his flock from getting involved: *Tract. in ev. Joh.* 7.24. The very length of the Kalends day sermon is seemingly what put off generations of later copyists, as the sermon was generally only known in shortened versions. Bede tried to read it, but, 'his eyes soon glazed over': Brown 2000a: 444; see too Dolbeau 1996b.

disgraceful songs'.[52] He presents the day as one of frivolity, where people indulge their love of the world, their passion for destructive pleasures (*Serm.* Dolbeau 198.8). He constructs a binary rhetoric of separation, demarcating the church, the saved, from the nations (as in his biblical text for the day: Ps. 106.47). This binary distinction would turn out to be hugely influential on ecclesiastical attacks on the Kalends, as well as those on popular culture more generally. The features of the festival attacked by Augustine – gift exchange, dice-playing, New Year's greetings and visits to the homes of friends and neighbours, drinking and singing – are crucially associated with 'paganism'.[53] None of these features, of course, would actually seem to have much to do with 'paganism' – and yet this is the association Augustine is determined to make, and indeed the association is consistently made by many preachers, as we shall see.

The claim that celebrating the Kalends was 'pagan' was most simply demonstrated by preachers pointing out that the origins of the festival lay in the worship of the two-faced god Janus. For instance, Caesarius employs the usual Christian polemic against the pagan gods, asserting simultaneously both their monstrous, demonic nature and their human origin.[54] The focus on Janus, it should be stressed, is purely polemical: despite the distant original association, it is abundantly clear that actual worship of Janus was not a feature of the late antique festival.[55] There was more mileage for preachers in attacking as 'superstitious' a series of practices that were distinctively attached to the Kalends as the festival of the New Year. Kalends rituals involved a number of rites that were both apotropaic and prognostic. Martin of Braga has the longest list of these (including such seemingly bizarre omens as putting cloth and bread in a box for mice and moths), but they turn up in other texts as well.[56]

---

[52] 'strepitu vanissimarum turpissimarumque cantionum': *Serm.* Dolbeau 198.1.

[53] As we saw above: *Serm.* Dolbeau 198.2.

[54] Briefly Maximus of Turin, *Serm.* 63.2; at greater length, Caes. *Serm.* 192.1: Janus was really 'dux quondam et princeps hominum paganorum', worshipped 'like a god' by the foolish, though in reality a demon. His two-faced appearance rendered him particularly monstrous: 'monstrum esse fecerunt'. Cf. the prohibition against the Kalends in the Council of Tours of 567: c. 23 (see Chambers 1903 (II): 300): 'Enimvero quoniam cognovimus nonnullos inveniri sequipedes erroris antiqui, qui Kalendas Ianuarii colunt, cum Ianus homo gentilis fuerit, rex quidam, sed esse Deus non potuit.'

[55] Libanius does not name Janus (it is, of course, unlikely that he would name a Roman deity), but refers to the festival as being in honour of a 'mighty daimon': *Or.* 9.1. Graf suggests, persuasively, that this is most likely the emperor (2012: 178). It is notable that Libanius laments the fact that sacrifices no longer form part of the festival's rituals: *Or.* 9.18. (These original consular sacrifices would of course have been not to Janus but to Jupiter Optimus Maximus, and later to the imperial cult.)

[56] *De corr. rust.* 11. For detailed discussion see Filotas 2005: 165–72.

Practices include laying out samples of food and drink on tables in order to ensure bounty throughout the year,[57] and a variety of rites related to fire.[58]

However, despite the recurrent list of 'pagan' and 'superstitious' practices that recur again and again in ecclesiastical attacks on the Kalends, it is clear that the problem with the Kalends was not really 'paganism'. Ordinary churchgoers knew this, as recounted by Peter Chrysologus in his sermon on the day:

> But one of you says: This isn't the deliberate pursuit of sacrilege, these good luck visits are just for fun; this is a celebration of the new, not an error from the past; this is just New Year, not the offence of paganism.[59]

That the Kalends was not really 'pagan' is not a new assertion. Robert Markus made this clear, stressing in his analysis that the late antique church would brook no rival and, specifically, that the Kalends represented a rival to Christian ideas of time and renewal, as represented liturgically by Christmas and its related calendar.[60] William Klingshirn has similarly argued that the Kalends should really be understood more as a secular festival that offended the church with its worldly emphases than as a religious opponent, with Caesarius' objections to the festival being in fact largely moral.[61] Indeed, these 'moral' objections focus more particularly on the Kalends as an example of popular culture, against which, I am arguing, the church waged a particularly forceful, if unsuccessful, war in Late Antiquity.

This becomes particularly clear when we turn to what is the most distinctive aspect of the Kalends celebrations: the masquerade. This would constitute a crucial target of Western criticism in particular: it has fascinated generations of scholars and represents a tantalizing glimpse of a particularly suggestive aspect of popular culture. The Kalends

---

[57] E.g. Caes. *Serm.* 192.3; Martin Brag. *De corr. rust.* 11, 16, 742–3. This was practised in Rome as late as the eighth century to the horror of Boniface: *Ep.* 50 (*MGH Epp. sel.* 1: 84) and then proscribed: *Conc. romanum* 743 c.9 (*MGH Conc.* 2.1: 15–16).

[58] Libation of food and wine on the fire: Martin Brag. *De corr. rust.* 16; refusal to share fire: Caes. *Serm.* 192.3, 193.3; lighting fires in the forum: John Chrys. *In Kalend.* 2.

[59] *Serm.* 155: 'Sed dicit aliquis, Non sunt haec sacrilegiorum studia, vota sunt haec iocorum; et hoc esse novitatis laetitiam, non vetustatis errorem; esse hoc anni principium, non gentilitatis offensam.' The preacher gave this imagined reply pretty short shrift, continuing: 'Erras, homo! Non sunt, non sunt haec ludicra, sunt crimina.'

[60] Markus 1990: 103–6; see also, on the church's desire to privilege a Christian concept of time, Meslin 1970: 109–12.

[61] Klingshirn 1994: 216–18. MacMullen 1997: 36–8 is unusual among modern scholars in seeing the Kalends as representing 'paganism'.

masquerade involved dressing up in costume, including masks, and travelling about either in public procession (in major urban settings) or going door to door (in both urban and rural settings), particularly at night. In Ravenna, Peter Chrysologus seems to describe both sorts of masquerade. His most developed description of the first type is worth quoting at length:

> The days are now coming, the days that mark the new year are coming, and the demons arrive with all their pomp (*tota daemonum pompa procedit*), a fully-fledged workshop of idols (*idolorum ... officina*) is set up. And the new year is consecrated with age-old sacrilege. They fashion Saturn, they make Jupiter, they form Hercules, they exhibit Diana with her young servants, they lead Vulcan around roaring out tales of his obscenities, and there are even more, whose names must be left unmentioned, since they are hideous monsters (*portenta*).[62]

Meanwhile John Chrysostom speaks of *daimones* processing (*pompeusantōn*) in the *agora* in Antioch but it is unclear whether this is directly comparable to the procession in Ravenna.[63]

Peter Chrysologus also has unofficial, door-to-door visits in mind.[64] These boisterous affairs, whether costumed or not, are obviously an important feature of the Kalends, involving songs, jests and the exchange (or extortion!) of gifts.[65] The dressing up here might well be of the improvised kind, possibly involving the use of charcoal (for face blackening), straw, rags, even dung, according to Peter Chrysologus.[66] For several commentators, most notably Caesarius, it is the dressing up that constitutes the most reprehensible aspect of the Kalends.

> For in these days miserable men and, what is worse, even some who are baptized, assume false forms and unnatural appearances, and certain features in them are especially worthy of laughter or rather of sorrow.[67]

---

[62] Pet. Chrys. *Serm.* 155 *bis* (*CCL* 24B), trans. Palardy 2005. Cf. the very similar *Serm.* 155: 'Hinc est, fratres, hinc est quod hodie gentiles deos suos, foeditatibus exquisitis, excogitato dedecore, et ipsa turpitudine turpiores – deos suos videndos trahunt, distrahunt, pertrahunt, quos faciunt non videndos.'

[63] John Chrys. *In Kalend.* 1.

[64] *Serm.* 155 *bis* : 'Et hoc christiani vident, christiani expectant, admittunt in domus suas, in domibus suis recipiunt christiani.'

[65] See too Lib. *Descr.* 5.6; Asterius, *Hom.* 4.6.

[66] *Serm.* 155b: 'Namque talium deorum facies ut pernigrari possint, carbo deficit; et ut eorum habitus pleno cumuletur horrore, paleae, pelles, panni, stercora toto saeculo perquiruntur, et quicquid est confusionis humanae in eorum facie collocatur.'

[67] Caes. *Serm.* 192.2: 'In istis enim diebus miseri homines et, quod peius et, etiam aliqui baptizati sumunt formas adulteras, species monstruosas, in quibus quidem quae primum ridenda aut potius dolenda sint nescio.'

This stress on the unnatural and the monstrous is consistent, even when we are far from clear as to what exactly is being described.

The first kind of dressing up attacked by Caesarius involved animal costume:

For what wise man can believe that men are found to be of sound mind, if they are willing to make themselves a small stag (*cervulum facientes*) or to be changed into the condition of wild beasts? Some are clothed in the skins of sheep, and others take the heads of wild beasts, rejoicing and exulting if they have transformed themselves into the appearance of animals in such a way that they do not seem to be men.[68]

The practice of dressing up as animals appears in Kalends texts from France, Germany, Italy and Spain.[69] The first disguise mentioned, the *cervulus*, appears in our sources as early as the 380s, in the writings of Ambrose of Milan;[70] shortly afterwards Pacianus, bishop of Barcelona, wrote a work entitled *Cervulus* criticizing the practice.[71] As Caesarius noted, the *cervulus* is generally joined by a supporting cast of other animals, both wild and agricultural. One lively account comes in the *vita* of Hilary of Mende (in Languedoc, 100 miles from Arles), a monk bishop contemporary of Caesarius (the *vita* itself is probably seventh century). It tells how Hilary went out to meet a group of villagers whom he found ready to go out masquerading, all decked out with antlers on their heads into order to look like wild beasts (*praefixo ... cervi capite ad imitandum ferae formam*) but he successfully persuaded them to abandon the practice.[72]

The popularity of the stag is striking in the literary ecclesiastical sources, but it can also be traced in a very different type of evidence. A number of depictions of the *cervulus* can in fact be found in the indigenous pottery of

---

[68] *Serm.* 192.2: 'Quis enim sapiens credere poterit, inveniri aliquos sanae mentis, qui cervulum facientes in ferarum se velint habitus commutare? Alii vestiuntur pellibus pecudum; alii adsumunt capita bestiarum, gaudentes et exultantes, si taliter se in ferinas species transformaverint, ut homines non esse videantur.'

[69] Cf. Pet. Chrys.: 'vestiuntur homines in pecudes', *Serm.* 155 bis. There are almost thirty references to animal costumes counted by Filotas 2005: 161, all from the Latin West.

[70] Ambrose, *De interpellatione Iob et David* 4(2)1.

[71] Pacianus later worried that he had, in fact taught people how to do it: 'Puto nescierant cervulum facere nisi illis reprehendendo monstrassem' (*PL* 13: 1081). Jerome (*De vir. inl.* 106) thought the title of the work was *Cervus*, but this is clearly a mistake.

[72] 'Cum more solito mense, quem gentiles a Jano rege januarium vocitavere, vulgus ignobile ludis, cantibus exerceretur vel epulis, antiquus ille serpens per speciem laetitiae mortis venena diffudit; ludum simulat ut sacrilegio corda subvertat. Praefixo quidem cervi capite, ad imitandum ferae formam conditionem humanam persuasionis diabolicae scelus inclinat. Mala haec geri haud procul a monasterio suo pater agnovit: et duobus adscitis fratribus, infelicem plebem sanctaque correcturus exortatione progressus est.' *Vita B. Hilari episcopi* in *AASS* Oct. 11: 638–9 at 638.

248 LUCY GRIG

Figure 11.1. Drawing of DSP plate featuring a stag. Drawn by Belinda Washington, after Rigoir, Rigoir and Meffre 1973: 207–63 at 255, no. 901.

south and western Gaul in Late Antiquity, the so-called 'dérivées des sigillés paléochrétiennes' (DSP).[73] The deer is a very popular motif on this pottery, especially as a central motif on the centre of plates, where it appears in combination with diverse symbols: trees, humans and other animals, including dogs, as well as crosses (see Figs. 11.1 and 11.2). While earlier scholars, when looking for symbolic meaning in the presence of the deer, wanted to see a spiritual significance relating to the deer of the psalms panting for water, this seems tenuous in the case of these particular ceramics.[74] (There is no water, for one thing, and a general lack of Christian iconography in the corpus suggests such readings are not plausible.) Could not the popularity of the stag on late antique Gallic ceramics instead have more to do with the popularity of the stag as an emblem of the Kalends celebrations?

[73] This term describes the stamped fineware (largely grey, though there are also some orange-coloured examples) that was the local version of the dominant African red slipware (ARS) of Late Antiquity, produced in a number of locations across southern and south-western Gaul, primarily between the middle and the end of the fifth century, through to the seventh century. It was produced in a number of regional locations, including Languedoc, Aquitaine and Provence, with a notable concentration of production in Marseilles. See Bonifay, Raynaud *et al.* 2007, Rigoir 1960 and Rigoir, Rigoir and Meffre 1973.

[74] E.g. Béraud-Sudreau 1938–40: 536, 540–1; see too Girault 1876.

Interpreting the Kalends of January 249

Figure 11.2. Drawing of DSP plate featuring stags and a human figure. Drawn by Belinda Washington, after Rigoir, Rigoir and Meffre 1973: 207–63, at 254, no. 898.

The stag is certainly not the only animal costume worn by Kalends revellers: different versions of clerical prohibitions against beast mumming feature a bewildering number of terminological variants referring to what is most probably the *vitulus* or *vitula*: a young cow.[75] These prohibitions extend some way into the medieval period and are stupefying in their volume and monotony. As E. K. Chambers put it: 'Homily followed homily, canon followed canon, capitulary followed capitulary, penitential followed penitential, for half a thousand years. But the Kalends died hard.'[76] The canons of Gallic councils and Frankish penitentials are a fertile source up to the tenth century, but references go as late and as far north as Burchard of Worms in the eleventh century (his *Decretorum* is a famously ragbag text).[77] The most immediately tempting conclusion to draw from this textual morass is that made over thirty years ago by Rudolph Arbesmann: that the later tradition of the Kalends animal dressing up is 'purely literary': that is, it represents a clear case of 'cutting and pasting' in the textual tradition, and refers to a moribund practice.[78] This brings us back to the huge methodological problem posed

---

[75] Including *cervula, annicula, vecola, vetola, vecola, vaecola, vitula*; see here Arbesmann 1979.
[76] Chambers 1903 (I): 246.
[77] Burchard, *Decretorum* 10.39 (*PL* 140: 538–1058, col. 839). See here Filotas 2005: 61, 181.
[78] Arbesmann 1979: esp. 104. Sometimes the confusion in the early medieval texts is palpable, e.g. 'Si quis, quod kalendas ianuarii vel alias kalendas colunt ... et cerenus, quod dicitur circerlus, aut in vecula vadunt' ('If anyone honours the Kalends of January or any other Kalends, and goes

250 LUCY GRIG

Figure 11.3. Man dressed as a stag from the *Roman d'Alexandre*. MS Bodley 264, fol. 70r. Bodleian Libraries, University of Oxford.

by the repetitive nature of early medieval ecclesiastical accounts of 'popular religion' and indeed popular culture: how far can we take the constant iteration of stereotypes to represent anything other than lazy plagiarism?[79] How far can we imagine real people actually dressing up like this?

There are in fact tantalizing suggestions that animal mumming did enjoy real continuity well beyond the early medieval period.[80] Two late medieval manuscripts clearly depict this activity. In a French manuscript of the *Histoire du Graal* preserved in the Bibliothèque Nationale in Paris there is what looks like a hollow tree trunk with a stag's head on top, but we can see human feet beneath the bottom of the costume and a human face emerging from a hole about halfway up; this costumed man is dancing to a musician playing the bagpipes.[81] In the famous illuminated manuscript of the *Roman d'Alexandre* from Tournai, now in the Bodleian Library in Oxford, we have two separate illustrations (Figs. 11.3 and 11.4).[82] Fig. 11.3 depicts a man in a highly impressive stag costume dancing to a musician; his costume is so

about as a *cerenus*, as the *circulus* is called or in/as? a *vecula*'): *Poen. Oxoniense* 29 (*CCL* 156: 91) (first half of the eighth century) = Filotas 2005: 161. It is obvious that the scribe here had no idea what exactly he was prohibiting!

[79] See, for a range of approaches, Filotas 2005, Gurevich 1988, Harmening 1979, Hen 1995 and 2012, and Künzel 1992. A cautionary tale is provided by the example of the fictive festival of the 'Spurcalia', a medieval clerical construction further reified by eighteenth- and nineteenth-century scholarship: see Ristuccia 2013.

[80] See Twycross and Carpenter 2002: 14–100 and Camille 1998: 232–75.

[81] Robert de Boron, *Histoire de Graal*, BNF, MS fonds français 95, fol. 273r. For a reproduction see Twycross and Carpenter 2002: 32.

[82] *Roman d'Alexandre*, illustrated by Jehan de Grise, produced in Tournai in 1344. Oxford, Bodleian Library, MS Bodley 264.

Figure 11.4. Animal mummers and dancers from the *Roman d'Alexandre*. MS Bodley 264, fol. 21v. Bodleian Libraries, University of Oxford.

striking it seems he has frightened away a woman and two children. In the second illustration (Fig. 11.4) we see three men dressed as animals: a stag, a hare, an ass/boar, accompanied by female dancers (or men dressed as women?); towering over this group is a tonsured cleric with a threatening club; in an added twist, under his tunic he has animal legs.

Is this a serious case of continuity of 'animal' mumming in medieval Gaul? The case for pagan 'continuity' across the *longue durée* has been strongly argued for not just by medieval churchmen, but also by a rather different type of writer: folklorists and other scholars from the late nineteenth and twentieth centuries, who employed the very same 'cut and paste' methodology to argue their case, albeit to serve rather different agendas. Herein of course lies another layer in the complex history and historiography of the late antique Kalends: it has played a key role in scholarship on medieval theatre, been wrapped up with the prehistory of the Feast of Fools, as well as being touched upon by those interested in Celtic religion. The fundamentally antique and 'pagan' nature of popular culture, though deplored by ecclesiastical writers over an exceedingly long time, has instead been celebrated by several generations of scholars interested in anthropology, folklore and the ancient origins of the theatre; these same scholars, however, have tended to employ their sources with rather less attention to context than we might wish. Here we should point to E. K. Chambers, the great and influential historian of the English stage, whose work was impressively wide-ranging and inclusive, including folk drama, religion and 'minstrelsy'. Chambers, influenced by the theories of J. G. Frazer and other contemporary anthropologists,[83] took a keen interest in ritual, and was eager to seek significance in and connections between apparently scattered, long-neglected cultural phenomena. Despite the huge importance of his work, there remains an important side effect: 'his tendency to draw scattered fragments of evidence into a single, a-historic, overarching pattern of residual pre-Christian worship can seriously distort the local and immediate meanings and functions of particular masking customs'.[84]

For some scholars, the ubiquity of the mention of the *cervulus* has its origins in the Celtic deity of Cernunnos.[85] This horned god, generally associated in scholarship with the renewal of nature, sexual power, abundance and riches, has been identified in over forty iconographical depictions.[86] His most common attributes are deer's antlers, torc(s), a container of coins/grains held in the lap, and crossed legs. His depictions hail mostly from eastern Gaul, from the first century CE onwards (though covering a strikingly wide chronological and geographical reach). However, the case of 'Cernunnos' is rather more problematic than many scholars would have us believe. The sole labelled image of the deity is from the 'Pillar of the Boatman', a stone bas-relief depicting a mixture of Roman and Gallic deities (happily dated by its dedication to Tiberius), from a temple in Lutetia.[87] It is tempting, and perhaps not going too far, to be rather more sceptical, and see Cernunnos as a purely scholarly creation, constructed from various types of Celtic horned god, by scholars overly keen to construct a homogeneous, even timeless pan-Celtic religious tradition.[88] There are certainly those keen to believe that the stags of

---

[83] E.g. Chambers 1903 (I): 102–3, 134–50.

[84] Twycross and Carpenter 2002: 3; note too, regarding ostensibly similar customs: 'that does not mean that a fifth-century Spanish Kalends masker and a fifteenth-century English mummer were necessarily doing and meaning the same thing' (2); see, for further critique of Chambers and the decontextualized use of sources, Harris 2011: 3–5.

[85] E.g. Arbesmann 1979: 117–19; Meslin 1970: 88–9, but going back to Arnold 1894: 174 and Nilsson 1969-19. See too the connection made between the deer as Christ and the deer as Cernunnos in the late antique ceramics: Béraud-Sudreau 1938–40: 540–1.

[86] For a brief summary: Maier 1997: 69–70. A comprehensive survey with catalogue (also arguing unusually that Cernunnos should in fact be associated with the underworld): Bober 1951. Fickett-Wilbar 2003 argues that Cernunnos' iconography is deliberately ambiguous, as he was an intentionally ambiguous deity. See, with caution, Green 1989: *passim*, 'Cernunnos'.

[87] Musée Cluny National du Moyen Age in Paris; *CIL* 13.3026a; Espérandieu 1911 nos. 3132–5 (3133).

[88] See, for an important critique, Fitzpatrick 1991.

Kalends represent a continuation of pre-Christian Celtic religion,[89] but the evidence is not really there for such an assertion, and the reason behind the popularity of the stag remains mysterious.

In any case, although the popularity of the stag seems to show a remarkable continuity, this is in fact overshadowed by another type of Kalends dressing up abhorred by the church: cross-dressing. Caesarius of Arles considered cross-dressing to be perhaps the most disturbing Kalends practice of all.

Moreover how shameful and how disgraceful it is when those who were born as men are clothed in the tunics of women. By a most unseemly change they make their manly strength womanish by means of girlish fashions, not blushing to put the arms of a soldier into the tunics of women. They show bearded faces, but want to appear like women.[90]

Caesarius returns to this theme again in another sermon:

For what is so absurd as by shameful dress to change the sex of a man into the form of a woman? What is so foolish as to disfigure one's face, to assume an appearance, which even the demons themselves greatly fear?[91]

Asterius was equally appalled:

But their other doings, how can one mention them? Does not the champion, the lion-hearted man, the man who when armed is the admiration of his friends and the terror of his foes, loose his tunic to his ankles, twine a girdle about his breast, use a woman's sandal, put a roll of hair on his head in feminine fashion, and ply the distaff full of wool, and with that right hand which once bore the trophy, draw out the thread, and changing the tone of his voice utter his words in the sharper feminine treble?[92]

As we saw earlier, both Caesarius and Asterius depict this shameful drag show as forming a particular part of *military* revels in particular.[93] References to cross-dressing during Kalends celebrations are not nearly as numerous as references to animal costuming, but they do recur in

---

[89] 'Like the other forms of pagan worship, his cult could be destroyed, but not the customs and jollifications which had been connected with it since time immemorial. Though their initial significance had long been forgotten, they lived on: in the countryside, where the peasants practiced them in the form of simple, old-fashioned fertility magic, and in the cities and towns, where the masquerade had to all appearances taken on the features of pure carnival-sport': Arbesmann 1979: 119.

[90] Caes. *Serm.* 192.2.

[91] *Serm.* 193.1: 'Quid enim est tam demens, quam virilem sexum in formam mulieris turpi habitu commutare? Quid tam demens, quam deformare faciem, et vultus induere, quos ipsi etiam daemones expavescunt?'

[92] Asterius, *Hom.* 4.   [93] See pp. 242–3.

a number of sources, from both East and West.[94] Although the sources normally specify men dressing up as women, others suggest that the cross-dressing could also be practised by women.[95]

These practices of dressing up, as we have seen, are attacked by late antique churchmen as unnatural, as monstrous, as a perversion of God's creation, as apostasy, as the opposite of what is Christian, indeed as *pagan*. Returning to the *longue durée*, familiar denunciations continue to appear in the thunderings of ecclesiasts from far more recent eras. One lively example attacks monstrous dressing up and cross-dressing as part of carnival celebrations in sixteenth-century Zurich:

Men are often in women's clothes, and also women in men's clothes, as if to belie their fair and virtuous sex. Some, besides, are so deformed that you would say they had put off all human appearance, for with horns, beaks, boar's teeth, flaming eyes, breathing smoke and sparks, curved talons, tails, shaggy hair, they aim to seem, and to terrify, like monstrous and terrible demons.[96]

Another early modern example, this time from Scotland, is a confession from a penitent brought before the kirk session in Elgin, for 'dansyng and guysing'. He admits that:

he haid his sisters coat upon him and the rest that were with him haid claythis dammaskit about thame and thair faces blaikit ... Archie Hayes haid a faise [face = mask] about his loynes and ane kerche [woman's kerchief] about his face.[97]

---

[94] While Isidore of Seville is an apparent source for cross-dressing (or at least female pantomiming) in the West, his dependence on Caesarius is all too clear: 'etiam fideles, sumentes species monstruosas, in ferarum habitu transformantur: alii femineo gestu demutati, virile vultum effeminant' *De ecclesiasticis officiis* 1.41(47)2. Peter Chrysologus is a more reliably independent source for cross-dressing: 'in feminas viros vertunt', *Serm.* 155 *bis*.

[95] E.g. in the West (though highly dependent on earlier sources), *Dicta Abbatis Primini* c. 22: 'Viri vestes femineas, femine vestes virilis in ipsis Kalandas [sic] vel in alia lusa quam plurima nolite vestire.' In the East: in 680 the Council of Constantinople ruled against *both* sexes cross-dressing, invoking Deuteronomy 22:5, although the context is not clear: Twycross and Carpenter 2002: 35–6. See too the Council in Trullo in 692 against cross-dressing and mask-wearing: versio Latina c. 62 in Chambers 1903 (II): 302: 'ut nullus vir deinceps muliebri veste induatur vel mulier veste viro conveniente'.

[96] 'viri frequenter veste foeminea, interdum etiam foeminae veste virili, tanquam si pulchrum aut honestum foret sexum mentiri. Nonnunquam insuper quidam sic deformati, ut figuram omnem humanam prorsus exuisse diceres: nam cornuti, rostrati, dentibus aprinis, flammantibus oculis, fumum et scintillas ex ore exhalantes, curvis unguibus, caudati hirsute, denique & monstrosi terribilesque cacodaemonas videri atque timeri affectant.' Rodolphus Hospinianus, *Festa christianorum: hoc est de origine, progressu, ceremoniis et ritibus festorum dierum christianorum* (Zurich, 1593), 37–8, trans. Twycross and Carpenter 2002: 72.

[97] 1598 Elgin Rec. II. 69, cited in Twycross and Carpenter 2002: 81.

Clearly people have always dressed up in whatever they had to hand – blacking their faces[98] and borrowing clothes from a household member of the opposite sex providing particularly popular, cheap and convenient practices. Dressing up in 'monstrous' forms, as well as in the clothes of the opposite sex, continued to form an important part of popular festivities, and therefore, indeed, of popular culture.

Kalends practices do seem to provide us with a tantalizing snapshot of a continuing 'Kulturkampf'. Occasionally even our dominant ecclesiastical literary sources let us get a glimpse of the 'other side' of the struggle. As we have already seen, in Ravenna, Peter Chrysologus did give us something, at least, of his congregation's side of the story:

> But one of you says: This isn't the deliberate pursuit of sacrilege, these good luck visits are just for fun; this is a celebration of a new beginning, not a superstition from the past; this is just New Year, not the threat of paganism.[99]

Meanwhile, a text from early medieval Gaul, the *Vita Eligii*, provides a spirited defence of traditional culture in the form of a fictionalized speech from the pagan opponents of its titular hero. While we saw earlier in this chapter that St Hilary of Mende was able to persuade a band of Kalends revellers to hang up their antler horns, Eligius met a group of peasants, from a *vicus* outside Noyon, that were made of stronger stuff:

> No matter how often you talk, Roman, you will never be able to uproot our customs, but we will continue always and forever to carry on our feasts as we have hitherto. No man will ever be able to forbid us the ancient entertainments that are so dear to us.[100]

(Admittedly, in this particular instance, the customs in questions are not specifically those of the Kalends; however, Kalends practices are criticized elsewhere in this text.)[101] Ramsay MacMullen has very aptly compared this speech to 'the passionate speeches invented by Tacitus for oppressed barbarians'.[102] It certainly provides a neat example of one particular

---

[98] As we saw, Peter Chrysologus thundered disapproval at Kalends revellers blacking their faces with charcoal: *Serm.* 155 *bis*.

[99] Pet. Chrys. *Serm.* 155.

[100] 'Numquam tu, Romane, quamvis haec frequenter taxes, consuetudines nostras evellere poteris, sed sollemnia nostra sicut hactenus fecimus, perpetuo semperque frequentabimus, nec ullus hominum erit, qui priscos atque gratissimos possit nobis umquam prohibere ludos.' *Vita Eligii* 2.20, *MGH SRM* 4: 634–763, at 712); see Banniard 1992.

[101] The sermon gives a very standard denunciation: *MGH SRM* 4: 705 (2.16): 'nullus in Kalendas Ianuarii nefanda et ridiculosa, vetulas aut cervulos vel iotticos faciat neque mensas super noctem conponat neque strenas aut bibitiones superfluas exerceat.'

[102] MacMullen 1997: 18.

model of the relationship between popular and dominant cultures, as one of conflict, and indeed resistance.

Pulling together the diverse threads of the late antique Kalends material, a definitive analysis of the 'meaning' of the festival remains elusive. Attempts to find an origin for beast mumming in Celtic religion can only remain speculative at best. Cross-dressing, meanwhile, is a popular element in carnivalistic celebrations, with its connotations of the 'world turned upside-down'. Its combination of elements clearly made it a truly popular festival with considerable resilience. Quite how resilient the festival really was remains something of a moot point, however. While late antique and medieval churchmen cut and pasted from earlier works to construct a genealogy of 'paganism' that threatened the cultural hegemony of the church, twentieth-century scholars indulged in a 'snippetology' of their own in order to construct a perhaps equally fictitious genealogy of popular paganism which lay at the heart of a continuing folkloric tradition. Nevertheless, I hope to have shown through my own readings of clerical texts on the one hand, and an examination of the much less well-known visual material on the other, that the late antique Kalends is not entirely unreachable.

Ultimately therefore I would like to suggest that studying the Kalends of January provides an encouraging case study for the pursuit of late antique popular culture, It reminds us, of course, of the many methodological pitfalls of attempting to study 'ordinary people' from clerical sources. It does, however, encourage us to see these people as far more than Dill's 'dim, sunken, mass'. It encourages us to see the cultural history of Late Antiquity as one of dynamic cultural interchange rather than as submission to the inevitable triumph of hegemonic culture. And even if we do not want to go this far, we can perhaps take heart from the persistence of a festival persistently characterized as *iocorum ... laetitiam.*[103]

---

[103] Pet. Chrys. *Serm.* 155.

12 | Popular Christianity and Lived Religion in Late Antique Rome: Seeing Magic in the Catacombs

NICOLA DENZEY LEWIS

> Since the dead are very much involved in luck, if you are on good terms with them, you have an excellent chance of success in everything from love to the lottery. The dead are a vital part of that chaotic network that connects past and present in Naples, and they are ubiquitous and hyperactive, as befits a place that was once a Greek necropolis. For a short period after death, it is believed, the spirit hovers close to the living world and may be able to intercede with the Divine to get favors or even miracles for those left behind.[1]

In his article 'Death in Naples', journalist Michael Ledeen writes gracefully about Naples' Fontanelle Cemetery caves, a massive charnel complex on the outskirts of the city which holds the bodies of tens of thousands of Neapolitans. Spasms of plague through the centuries saw corpses abandoned in grotesque piles, until in 1872 a priest by the name of Gaetano Barbati began to sort the bones into discrete bundles, artfully arranging them in the style of Europe's great ossuaries.[2] But then something rather curious happened. Volunteers (reputedly, elderly women) began to name the anonymous dead, often developing a close bond with the skulls that they claimed spoke to them. The women would return to stuff rolled-up requests for boons, small or large, into gaping eye sockets. Skulls that delivered reliable oracles were rewarded by being placed in special 'houses' and were visited for years, even for generations. The skulls specialized in providing winning lottery numbers, but they might also help heal the sick or bring other minor favours. One 'public' skull was worn smooth by women coming to touch it to request help for infertility.

The Fontanelle caves became, at the close of the nineteenth century and again at the close of World War II, a potent site for receiving oracles or even, some people feared, dabbling in the dark arts. To annul demonic powers and set Catholic believers on the right path, a small chapel, Maria Santissima del Carmine, was erected near the cave's mouth. No one visited it much. The Vatican eventually tired of such dangerous, 'wildcat, highly

---

[1] Ledeen 2009.   [2] For more on Fontanelle, see Koudounaris 2011: 133–41.

entrepreneurial' behaviours around Fontanelle.[3] The cardinal of Naples, Corrado Ursi, ordered the caves to be closed in 1969 following a highly charged ecclesiastical tribunal. But using vivid dreams as their medium, the skulls raised a sorrowful lament from the darkness: 'Why have you abandoned us?' Gradually, the women of Fontanelle returned, reunited with their adopted kin.

The case of the Fontanelle Cemetery caves offers us a fascinating glimpse into the interplay between 'popular culture' – that is, unsanctioned, informal religious activity and performance – and the catalyst for these performances, in this case, the priest who in seeking to give the bones a respectful permanent rest inadvertently created an oracular shrine. The women with their oracular skulls work the margins of religious behaviour; likely they fully understood themselves to be faithful Catholics, and yet their unsanctioned acts pressed them into the shadows of a tradition. Not quite 'heretical', not quite 'unorthodox', these women offer us a new way of seeing the unseen in antiquity, by becoming attuned to ordinary actors and their sometimes extraordinary actions in an unusually marginal setting.

In an extraordinary essay on what he and others have termed 'lived religion', the American religious historian Robert Orsi writes about the ordinary places and moments where what he calls 'everyday miracles' occur:

> Workplaces, homes, and streets – as well as churches, temples, shrines, class meetings, and other more immediately recognizable sites of religious activity – are the places where humans make something of the worlds they have found themselves thrown into, and in turn, it is through these subtle, intimate, quotidian actions on the world that meanings are made, known, and verified.[4]

In this chapter, my chosen setting for uncovering 'everyday miracles' consists of the cemeteries and catacombs of late antique Rome. Here, I have been looking for instances not of 'popular culture' precisely, but 'lived religion'. 'Lived religion', for Orsi, is the experience of ordinary people taking matters into their own hands: 'All religious ideas and impulses', he writes, 'are of the moment, invented, taken, borrowed, and improvised at the intersections of life.'[5] In these moments, these intersections, people become religious actors; they create actions that come from, and bear with them, deep meaning.

Orsi's description of 'lived religion' comes very close to what I call 'ordinary Christianity' in antiquity: it too is quotidian, often mundane, performed by non-specialists, often improvised, and virtually never

---

[3] The assessment is that of Leeden 2009.   [4] Orsi 1997: 7.   [5] Orsi 1997: 8.

sanctioned by Christian authorities. My research on 'lived religion' or 'ordinary Christianity' in the fourth century concerns that set of behaviours that were often dismissed by the authorizing voices of early Christianity as 'mere' superstition. My hope is to highlight the practices and sensibilities of non-elites, some of whom were performing Christianity in the private – that is to say, domestic – sphere and some of whom were doing so publicly. Their Christianity was 'ordinary' in the sense that it often ran counter to what Roman Christian elites or the clergy (which, as we know, often amounted in the late antique world to the same thing) were performing. It was also 'ordinary' in the sense of being 'quotidian', or performed outside the logic of the sacred/profane *limes* that the church attempted, with greater or lesser degrees of success, to impose on the varied expressions of piety.

Magic as 'Lived Religion' in Late Antique Christianity

For the purposes of this chapter, I will consider here only one class of 'quotidian' or 'ordinary' Christianity that was both widespread and unsanctioned: small acts of ritual power – what we can call with the oversimplifying and unfortunately denigrating term, 'magic'.[6] Magic was not a 'popular' practice in an unreconstructed Humean sense; it transcended divisions of social class. Magic also transgressed the slowly coalescing margin between licit and illicit Christian behaviour. The degree to which it was censured may in fact have been less than we might think. There are relatively few condemnations of Christian magic in patristic literature. Augustine, for example, condemns 'superstitious' practices, as does John Chrysostom, but their influence was no doubt limited.[7] What we might consider 'garden variety' magical practices – the casting of spells and curses, the deposition of magical items in baths, springs or cemeteries, for example – are mentioned only very rarely. The Council of Laodicea (363–4 CE) includes a canon that censures amulet use:

They who are of the priesthood, or of the clergy, shall not be magicians, enchanters, mathematicians, or astrologers; nor shall they make what are called amulets, which

---

[6] There is no space here to discuss substantial bibliography on terminology, but for a very modest beginning see Bremmer 1999; Graf 1997.
[7] Augustine, *In Io. Evang. Tr.* VII, 6 = CCL 36: 69–71; John Chrysostom, *Discourses Against Judaizing Christians*, see Harkins 1979.

are chains for their own souls. And those who wear such, we command to be cast out of the church.[8]

It is directed, notably, at the clergy, not at laypeople.[9] The practice of ordinary magic by ordinary people, in short, continued presumably undiminished as the Empire gradually 'Christianized', its practitioners drawn from a variety of social classes and operating in pursuit of a variety of ends.

Most studies of magic in Christian antiquity draw on the copious papyri and amulets from late antique Egypt. I, however, will consider the case of ancient Christian magic using an unusual data set: the Roman catacombs. The catacombs, presented nowadays by the Catholic church as holy sites that preserve inviolate evidence for early and authentic Catholic life, hardly spring to mind as profitable sites for uncovering practices of magic. Yet, behind a carefully controlled facade, the catacombs reveal an unexpected world. That late antique Christians practised magic complicates simplistic ideas about the supposed doctrinal rigidity of early Christianity, but my hope in this chapter is to let that discomfort simmer. My intention is not merely to emphasize that late antique Roman Christians practised magic, but to focus on the ordinary ritual practices of ordinary people while suppressing the need to label them as 'Christian' or 'not Christian'. Similarly, my aim here is not to argue that magic was 'popular', while 'proper religion' – whatever that may be – was what necessarily ruled in the business of death and burial in Christian Rome. The catacombs provide a peculiar site for comprehensive reconstructions, largely because they represent only one specific lens on the past. As Brent Shaw has observed, most of the graves are not elite; neither do they generally contain the graves of the indigent.[10] They contain the graves of poor to moderately wealthy urban late antique individuals. The greatest problem, however, is that with the exception of very recently excavated catacombs, they were improperly and haphazardly excavated since the Renaissance, then tidied up to be transformed into showcases of paleo-Catholic piety. Magical materials – from graffiti to amulets to objects secondarily deposited in graves – have therefore largely been expurgated, moved to private collections, or have disappeared from view altogether. Fortunately, a new class of Christian archaeologists work to correct the sins of their predecessors, and I draw crucially upon their work here.

---

[8] Canon 36, in 'The Canons of the Councils of Ancyra, Gangra, Neocaesarea, Antioch and Laodicea, which Canons were Accepted and Received by the Ecumenical Synods', see Schaff and Wace 1988.
[9] The famous 'magic trials' of the fourth century recorded by Ammianus Marcellinus are really about something other than 'ordinary religion'. On these, see Barb 1963; Aune 1980.
[10] Shaw 1996: 102.

Death, Fear and the Dead: Rethinking the Late Antique Cemetery

We must begin earlier than Late Antiquity if we wish to consider the catacombs and magical activity around them anew. In imperial Rome the burial ground was liminal space: dangerous and supercharged with malevolent beings. This information comes not from funerary inscriptions, but from Latin literature, which was replete with stories of ghosts, the undead and werewolves thought to haunt cemeteries.[11] Lucan features, in Book 6 of his *Pharsalia*, the witch Erictho, who lives among tombs and violates human corpses. Erictho's horrifying activities include necromancy, both for the purpose of gaining information about the outcome of a distant war and for sending information to the shades trapped in the underworld below. Horace, in a more satirical vein, gives an account of two crones on Rome's Esquiline Hill who dig up corpses for necromantic purposes (*Sat.* 1.8). Among second-century Roman writers, Apuleius includes in *The Golden Ass* the character Pamphile, a witch who draws upon a stable of conventional objects drawn from corpses and cemeteries, including crucifixion nails and body parts (*Met.* 3.15–18).[12]

If the burial ground was a fearsome place in the High Empire, there is absolutely nothing to indicate that late antique Christians thought of cemeteries in different new ways. The introduction of the new name *koimetērion* – although indicating a new eschatological hope for the dead – should not be conceived as signalling a radical conceptual shift.[13] Even those Christians in deep sleep could have their bones violated or their souls threatened.[14] And although, ideally, Christians believed that those who died 'in Christ' had found eternal refreshment, those who were refreshed were surely not the ones to be feared – for the cemetery brought all types.[15] Even the promise of a blessed afterlife might not cancel out the wariness brought on by proximity to those who had died violent deaths, or to those who had not been fortunate enough to have been ritually 'hedged in' by baptism *in extremis*.

Besides the fear of the restless dead, there was another concern: demons, who waged continual, silent war against individuals. Demons were known

---

[11] E.g. Hor. *Epod.* 5, *Sat.* 1.8; Tib. 1.5.53; Petron. *Sat.* 61–2. The bibliography on Roman magic is similarly extensive; most germane to this chapter are Ogden 2001; Janowitz 2001.
[12] Stratton 2014.   [13] Rebillard 2009: 1–12.
[14] On the fear of tomb violation, see Rebillard 2009: 57–88.
[15] On the Christian catacombs as not really Christian, see Bodel 2008; Rebillard 2009: 1–36; Johnson 1997.

to lurk in hollows, and the vast darkness of the catacombs must have been absolutely terrifying. We have few such testimonials, but one often cited from Jerome (recalling his youthful days exploring the catacombs on Sundays) stands out:

> While it is pitch dark, the words of the prophet seem to come true: 'may they go down alive into Sheol' [Psalm 55:15]; only occasionally light enters from above that helps to diminish the horrors of darkness; and when one returns step by step and the darkness of night surrounds you entirely, the following verse of Virgil comes to mind: 'Everywhere dread fills my heart; the very silence too dismays' [*Aen.* 2.755].[16]

This passage nicely highlights the sense of fear and dread accompanying a tour of a vast subterranean necropolis, and properly balances out modern-day assessments of the catacombs as 'sacred space' where late antique Christians gathered. This 'sacred space' is, ironically, a largely Protestant picture: it ignores entirely the vast, imaginative, unseen universe of late antique Roman conceptualization.

Both inscriptions and material culture from Rome's catacombs indicate that the saints did not dwell alone in the afterlife, but jostled for space with the souls of the ordinary dead and a panoply of others for whom cognitive scientists have coined the useful term 'non-obvious beings'.[17] These non-obvious beings were ancestral spirits, other minor divinities such as nymphs or river gods and, by the fourth century, malevolent entities that late antique Roman Christians would not have hesitated to term *daimones*. Rome, as a city of immigrants and a broadly inclusive and assimilating religious culture, found itself home not only to major foreign cults like that of Isis and Atargatis, but to unwanted and feared threats which tagged along with transient populations, such as Abzou, the killer of infants. Other demons, like Baccus (a corruption of Bacchus), had been demoted from powerful gods in this new pantheon of saints, angels and demons. Some, like Hecate, lingered as ever on the periphery of the city and the Roman imagination.

But the climate of nervous caution that these non-obvious beings evoked is almost invisible from the Christian catacombs today, scoured clean of any indications of magic. We only see mere glimpses of it. Rodolfo Lanciani, writing in the hot July of 1886, tells us of the discovery of the mausoleum of the Lucilii family off the Via Triumphalis north of the city.[18]

---

[16] Jerome, *Comment. In Ezech.* XX.40.
[17] See, for example, Stowers 2008 for the use of the term applied to early Christianity and Roman religions.
[18] Lanciani 1892: 285–6.

In the fourth century, Christians had reused it for burial space, sinking *loculi* into the side walls of the central corridor and scattering the ashes of the Lucilii on the floor. Two of these *loculi*, Lanciani reports, contained the skeletons of children with 'magic circlets' around their necks. He was clearly impressed:

They [the circlets] are most extraordinary objects in both material and variety of shape. The pendants are cut in bone, ivory, rock crystal, onyx, jasper, amethyst, amber, touch-stone, metal, glass, and enamel; and they represent elephants, bells, doves, pastoral flutes, hares, knives, rabbits, poniards, rats, Fortuna, jellyfish, human arms, hammers, symbols of fecundity, helms, marbles, boar's tusks, loaves of bread, and so on.[19]

Unfortunately, these necklaces have disappeared. But a range of amulets have been recovered from the catacombs.[20] It is impossible to determine how many were once in there, since these small finds were often pocketed by catacomb tourists from the sixteenth century onwards. A number show up in the Kircherian and Lateran collections, now incorporated into the Vatican Museums and the Museo Nazionale delle Terme.[21] Currently on display at the Vatican are a number of iron finger rings and magical gems, often inscribed with christograms, names, adjurations ('*Nika!*'), or the names of angels or other celestial beings.[22] From the catacombs are derived a small number of rock-crystal objects including figurines, small plaques and amulets. Of those objects currently on display at the Vatican Museum, perhaps one of the most striking pieces of this genre is a cut rock-crystal sculpture, diminutive but very fine, of a young male deity standing on a globe (inv. 60443). In his hand he appears to have once held a long staff. Another amuletic object, less ambiguously Christian, is a diminutive ivory ship, exquisitely carved, of Jonah pitched overboard, with the inscription in Greek *Eusebii zeseis!*

---

[19] Lanciani 1892: 285–6. For attestations of iron nails and gems in the catacombs, see Février 1978: 262–3; for animal teeth, see Engemann 1990: 529.

[20] Even De Rossi 1888: 262 admits to discovering a late fourth-century gold *capsella* containing four tiny nails in the grave of Maximus, *praepositus de via Flaminia*, in the *sub divo* catacomb of Valentinus to the north of the city.

[21] Objects from the catacombs are also included in the collections of the Cabinet des Médailles and the British Museum. For the British Museum collections, see Dalton 1901: 1 (no. 3, inscribed gem with name 'ΙΗΣΟΥΣ', dove, and fish); 11 (no. 73, bronze signet ring with christogram, found at Rome).

[22] According to Testini 1966: 218, there are relatively few iron rings from the catacombs because they do not survive the conditions of the tomb well; more resilient are objects of bone or ivory. Note the six bone rings with fluted sides and traces of mortar remaining from the catacombs in Dalton 1901: 175 no. 988, also cited in De Rossi, 1864–7 (III): 583.

('Eusebius, may you live') (inv. 62588).[23] More frequently found at the catacombs are gorgon heads, often embedded into tomb closures.[24] The non-Christian nature of many apotropaic objects do not seem to have deterred Christians.

Egyptian or pseudo-Egyptian amulets seem to have been particularly favoured by late antique Roman Christians. A bone token from the catacombs features a curious image of the Sphinx, with a bald masculine human head, leonine torso and a long lizard-like tail (inv. 62608) (Fig. 12.1). A lapis lazuli plate is inscribed with an image of Bes Pantheos bearing a pole with two snakes and pseudo-hieroglyphic script. Found embedded in mortar around a tomb at the catacombs of Hippolytus, it had apparently been worn as a pendant.[25] Catacomb archaeologist Donatella Nuzzo also notes the case of an Egyptian terracotta relief featuring Isis, Horus and Serapis. The relief dates stylistically to the first century, but it had been reused to cover a grave in the catacombs of Praetextatus in perhaps the third century. Nuzzo argues, convincingly, that the apotropaic power of the relief was still known, in that whoever had closed the tomb with the terracotta slab chose to position the carved images facing outwards.[26] Another small porphyritic slab from the catacombs of Novatian, still in situ, features a border of Egyptian-style 'hieroglyphs' around a snake-headed mummy, most likely a demon or decan figure.[27]

If Egyptian-looking artefacts were magically powerful, so were other objects from even farther east. The Vatican collection of catacomb small finds includes two curious chalcedony *phalerae* in low relief, with flat backs and holes for stringing. Six other very similar chalcedony *phalerae* appear embedded in an elaborate gold piece crafted by Luigi Valadier in 1741, a mount designed to showcase an oversized onyx cameo of the Emperor Augustus.[28] The *phalerae*, along with other curious objects of

---

[23] The Vatican collection preserves a number of ivory objects from the catacombs, most more clearly part of daily use (hair pins, combs, bracelets (inv. 62630, 62637)), but some are possibly apotropaic, including small figurines (inv. 62528; 62524 (broken arm of a youth); inv. 62520 (head of a young girl), inv. 60518 (*eros* still embedded in mortar)). Parts of diptychs (e.g. Dalton 1901: 48, no. 290) in the mortar may also have been amuletic. Ferrua 1957: 12 mentions the discovery of a small ivory plate with Egyptian figures on it in the catacombs of Domitilla, now lost.

[24] Nuzzo 2000:253, fig. 26.5.   [25] Nuzzo 2000: 251, fig. 26.1.8.

[26] Nuzzo 2000:251; the slab is detailed in Dolzani 1975.

[27] Nuzzo 2000:251, fig. 26.2; see also Testini 1966, fig. 99 (unpaginated); this was erroneously identified as gnostic by Lietzmann 1934. Nuzzo notes Athanasius' condemnation of Alexandrian Christians who still venerate animal-headed deities (*Contra Gentes* 9 = *PG* 25: 18–22).

[28] Accession number: Louvre Bj 1839. Formerly in the collection of Cardinal Gaspare Carpegna, this object was purchased by the Vatican in 1741; it was seized by Napoleon (by the Treaty of Tolentino) in 1797 and transferred to the Louvre four years later, where it remains today.

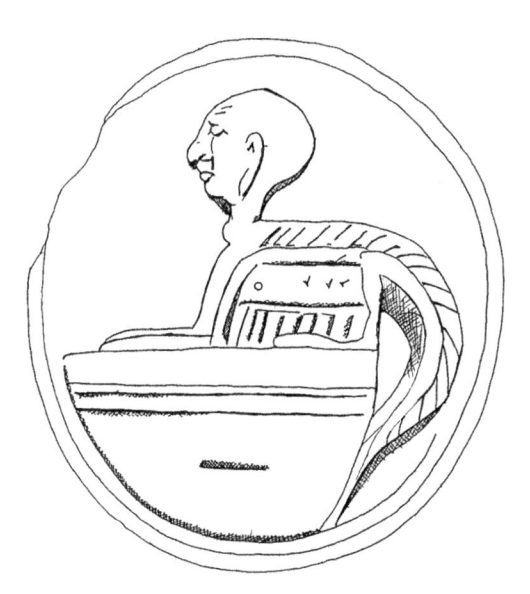

Figure 12.1. Drawing of bone token from the catacombs featuring a bald sphinx: Vat. Mus. inv. 60628. Drawn by Belinda Washington.

rock crystal and glass used in the piece, came from the catacombs of Priscilla by way of the papal collections. The distinctive style and material of these objects suggest that they derived originally from the Kushan Empire, with which Rome engaged in a lively trade.[29] Their precise placement in the catacombs of Priscilla is lost, but their amuletic function is self-evident.

Other objects inserted into the mortar around tombs are more difficult to identify as clearly apotropaic. Some of these include lamps, miniature sundials, glass bowls and phials, dice, a terracotta piglet, small spoons and rattles.[30] Glass bowls may have been prestige goods used merely for decoration or to hold perfumes or oil, but they also evoke Aramaic curse bowls, placed around graves facing downwards to trap and 'bind' demons.[31] One *cubiculum* on the lower level of the catacomb of Pamphilus contained an *arcosolium* grave with more than a dozen glass bowls of different sizes – some quite large – affixed sideways to the wall with mortar.[32]

---

[29] Parker 2008.

[30] Besides those objects on display at the Vatican, there is a collection of photographs in Testini 1966: fig. 99; see 211–20 for brief descriptions, with the (rare) concession that late antique Christians practised magic (219).

[31] On glass vessels in catacombs, see De Santis 2000; more generally in late antique Italian graves: Stiaffini 1993. On Aramaic demon bowls, see Shaked, Ford and Bhayro 2013.

[32] De Santis 2000: 239.

Dolls are a common find (see Chapter 10); whether or not these should be interpreted as magical objects – that is, as apotropaic or dedications to the gods – or as grave goods intended merely to mark and identify a particular child by burying her with her toy(s) remains hotly disputed.[33] The evidence for ivory dolls marking graves (or included in burials) is certainly earlier than Late Antiquity and by no means confined to Christian practice. As Stefanie Martin-Kilcher has noted, the practice of depositing a doll in or near the grave of a nubile girl was primarily a dedication to the gods which perdured through Late Antiquity, at which point it likely acquired a 'magical meaning', like other miniature representations of real things.[34]

There is some indication that children's graves in the catacombs were considered particularly vulnerable. It should be noted that young children's graves are extraordinarily rare in the catacombs, comprising only a minuscule percentage of the total. Since this in no way represents the total number of infant deaths, one wonders where late antique infants were buried, and how their corpses were valued.[35] The children buried in the catacombs are never neonates, but generally those who had lived for at least a year or more. The *loculi* of children are sometimes marked by small bronze or even copper bells, a curious practice concerning which Donatella Nuzzo invokes one of John Chrysostom's homilies where he condemns those who entrust the safety of their children in their cribs to small bells placed nearby to ward off demons.[36] Last century, a small gold bell with the inscription *tois hommasi hypotētagmai* was discovered in the vicinity of the ancient funerary grounds of the Esquiline, indicating that the very sound of

---

[33] See the discussion and bibliography in Martin-Kilcher 2000.

[34] Martin-Kilcher 2000: 67. Ogden 2001: 184–7 includes dolls in his section on technologies and materials used in necromantic rites, although these seem primarily to be wax effigies (akin to modern 'voodoo dolls') rather than the ivory and bone ones not uncommon in the catacombs. All the dolls from Christian catacombs were found embedded in the mortar of the tomb closure rather than in the graves themselves, suggesting they were not so much 'grave goods' as deliberately positioned to be visible and fixed into place, like a phylactery.

[35] Children's burials in general (but not specifically in Christian Rome): Dasen 2012; 2010. On a late Roman infant burial ground and the apotropaic items found within, see Crummy 2010.

[36] Nuzzo 2000: 247, 252, fig. 26.3. John Chrysostom (*Hom. in 1. Cor.* 7 = *PG* 61: 105–8). Nuzzo notes two bronze bells in the mortar of children's graves in Gallery Four of the Coemeterium Maius and two more, also from children's graves, at the catacomb of Pamphilius (Nuzzo 2000: 247). As Nuzzo points out, a number of prominent catacomb archaeologists from Boldetti to Enrico Iosi have discovered bells around children's graves; some are on display at the Vatican, while others are still visible in situ or in the collections of small objects pooled in the catacombs and viewable during public catacomb tours.

a bell could ward off the evil eye.[37] Even children who had died were apparently in need of protection from demons who might come to find their souls lurking around the grave.

The act of writing itself could wield magical power.[38] The engraving of a tomb closure was as much an act of power and ritual protection as a tattooed symbol on a body or a word of power inscribed on a curse tablet. The occasional acts of mirror-writing or backward-writing in the catacombs also underscore the apotropaic, as opposed to purely documentary, function of funerary inscriptions. At the catacomb of Sant'Agnese, a tomb inscription commemorating one Laurentius is written from right to left; the letters are also flipped over.[39] Words can also be hedged in by magical *charaktēres*.[40] A *loculus* from the catacombs of Marcus and Marcellinus bears the magical name IAΩ, a celestial being able to drive away demons.[41]

A symbol or emblem upon a grave need not conform to the canon of magical iconography. The epigrapher Carlo Carletti notes that around 350 CE, the letters E, F, L and P, corresponding to different teams competing in local chariot races, appear often as monograms on the mortar of *loculus* closures.[42] We must also think differently about common emblems on graves; the *chi rho*, I argue, was not a 'label' identifying a Christian grave and conveniently dating it to the Constantinian or post-Constantinian era, but a powerfully apotropaic sign.[43] The IXΘΥΣ symbol, less frequently found in the catacombs, may well have functioned similarly, just like *alpha/omega* pairings, anchors and doves. The late antique Jewish catacombs of Beth She'arim, which contain graffiti of provisioned ships and bound gladiators, provides a useful comparandum.[44] In both the Jewish and the Christian catacombs, the dead are protected from demonic intervention by the act of inscribing prophylactic images and words upon or around the

---

[37] Bruzza 1875: 50–68.   [38] Frankfurter 1994: 189–211; Beard 1991; Bowman and Woolf 1994.

[39] ICUR 8.21140. With gratitude to Rebekah Junkermeier for her unpublished work on this inscription. Junkermeier finds other inscriptions written backwards: ICUR 2.4351; ICUR 3, tab. XV, b. 10; ICUR 4.12551.

[40] ICUR 7.19893b (catacombs of Cyriaca); ICUR 3.8713b (catacombs of Commodilla); ICUR 7.20332b (catacombs of Hippolytus). The images are reproduced in Nuzzo 2000: 250, figs. 26.1.3, 26.1.4 and 26.1.5.

[41] ICUR 4.12990. See Bonner 1950: 134–5 on the power of the name IAΩ to drive away demons. Nuzzo 2000: 249 notes the instance of another engraved amulet with the name IAΩ from a grave in the catacombs of San Gennaro, Naples; see Miranda 1991.

[42] Carletti 1998: 127–42.

[43] Also noting the *chi rho* as apotropaic: Ferrua 1940: 79–80; Nuzzo 2000: 254; Russell 1995: 50. For the cross as the most powerful apotropaic sign in later and Byzantine antiquity, see Caseau 2012 on stamps. Used in many households, the cross was combined with words of prayer to exorcise demons. See John Chrysostom, *Hom. in 1 Cor.* 7 = PG 61: 106.

[44] Stern 2013.

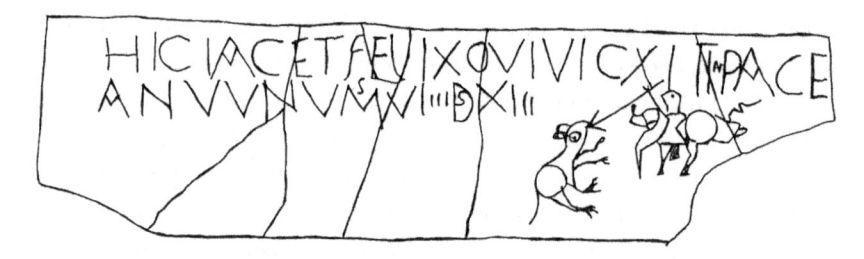

Figure 12.2. Drawing of *loculus* closing depicting a rider-god spearing a demon. Drawn by Belinda Washington, after Nuzzo 2000: 249–56 at 250, Fig. 26.1.7.

loculus closing of graves.[45] These images or signs may be conventionally 'magical', symbolic or *nomina sacra*.

In an important article on magical objects in the catacombs, Donatella Nuzzo mentions a *loculus* closure from the catacombs dating from 398 CE, invoking God to protect the dead from the evil spirit Bacus (sic): 'hic con<s>iste deus, nic ... / ne Bacus inqus temptet T{}/ epositus Sabin [_]/ XVIII kal(endas d[ecembres] / d(omino) n(ostro) Honor [io IIII] et Fl(avio) Eutych{iano cons(ulibus)s.'[46] She also reproduces a line-drawing of a *loculus* closure featuring a crude image of a rider-god spearing a demon, which in this case looks rather like a mouse (Fig. 12.2).[47] The rider god was, as Gary Vikan notes, 'one of late antiquity's most popular amuletic motifs'.[48] It remains a question whether this rider-god was intended to be Solomon – known widely in antiquity to overpower demons – or St Sissinios, whose particular skill was vanquishing the demon(s) of infant mortality.[49] It is suggestive, however, that the grave in question holds the body of a one-year-old boy.

Frescoes of biblical scenes in catacomb paintings around and covering burials may also have functioned apotropaically. Gary Vikan identifies the following scenes as 'substantially amuletic': the Adoration of the Magi; the Nativity; the women at the tomb; and indeed any image featuring Christ.[50] Vikan reminds us to think of catacomb paintings as polyvalent, rather than as merely 'paupers' Bibles' to illustrate typological lessons to an unschooled audience. The painting-as-amulet theory may help us make better sense of

---

[45] Stern 2013: 144–7. [46] Nuzzo 2000: 249; Ferrua 1940: 19–20.
[47] *ICUR* 2.6190, with the reproduction in Nuzzo 2000: 250, fig. 26.1.7. Nuzzo also notes Solomon amulets found at late antique sites in Sicily and Palestine.
[48] Vikan 1984: 79.
[49] On Sissinios generally: Frankfurter 1998: 3; on the connection with infant mortality, see Greenfield 1989: 83–142. Solomon the rider: see Calza 1917 for a Solomon amulet discovered in a grave in Ostia; Nuzzo 2000: 251.
[50] Vikan 1984: 79. See, too, the helpful work of Grig 2013a.

the number of catacomb *loculi* burials that apparently were dug literally into an image *after* it had been painted; what appears to us a lack of respect for the image may in fact be the opposite: a desire to fully embrace and even exploit the painting's apotropaic power by situating the dead literally within a scriptural scene.

A final category of phylactery to consider are spells or requests for victory or good luck. One victory amulet from the catacombs is on display at the Vatican. A thin piece of green jasper, each one of its four long sides reads 'Νίκα/ Σεβαστίαν/ Μαρια/Ιη(σοὺς)', along with inscribed crosses. At the top and bottom of the amulet are the letters A and Ω.[51] A special category of phylactery, the victory charm, is rendered moot after the death of its owner. Nevertheless, this category of amulet is often found in graves, perhaps because they had held special significance for the bearer. It is difficult to ascertain, though, why such goods were placed in the tomb. One might bring up the example of a small gold *lamella* first reported in 1852 as having been discovered rolled up and placed within the mouth of a skull contained within a terracotta cinerary urn at the Vigna Codini just south of the Porta San Sebastiano.[52] The *lamella* soon went missing, and various scholars took a crack at interpreting its inscription as recorded. The similar circumstances between the *lamella*'s emplacement and that of some of the so-called Orphic *lamellae* led some to suspect that it was put in the skull's mouth intentionally as instructions for the afterlife; however, the item was identified as having been moved to the Cabinet des Médailles in Paris, and examined anew.[53] In a brief article, D. R. Jordan re-examined the inscription and determined that it was a victory charm invoking Serapis rather than directions for the afterlife.[54] Uncovering the ritual act behind the object's deposition would be the key to determining whether the *lamella* was necromantic or whether it was a mere grave good, a 'good luck charm' secondarily deposited with the burial because it had been valued by its owners and seemed appropriate to be buried along with them. Of course, these options are not necessarily mutually exclusive.

Curses and Aggressive Magic

So far, my investigations have highlighted one particular category of magic evident in the Roman catacombs: the use of phylacteries in a variety of

---

[51] Inv. 64294 (fourth–fifth century CE). [52] Jordan 1985; Bonner 1944.
[53] On the Orphic *lamellae* (one also known from Rome): Johnston and Graf 2013.
[54] Jordan 1985: 162–7.

media to ward off malevolent forces. This may be classified as 'passive' or 'protective' magic. It is relatively easy to see examples of protective magic in catacombs, since they are attached directly to grave closures, and many still remain in situ. Less easy to see, however, are acts of 'aggressive' magic, involving the deposit of curse tablets (*defixiones*) or objects secondarily into graves. The successful deployment of these curse materials required access to the catacombs as well as a stable environment for such materials to remain in place long enough to be efficacious. Christopher Faraone and Joseph Rife's examination of a curse tablet discovered at a cemetery excavation in Cenchreae provides a great deal of insight into the placement of a *defixio* in a stable archaeological and social context.[55] In this case, neither the grave nor the curse was Christian, but most remarkable is Faraone's claim that the *defixio* was in place in the grave from the time that the corpse was deposited; no one sought to remove it as inappropriate or a mark of disrespect to the dead or his family.[56]

It is impossible to assess how many objects may have been added secondarily to catacomb tombs for necromantic purposes. Given the Catholic church's insistence that the catacombs were subjected to centralized oversight from the third century, those Christian archaeologists who have excavated the catacombs were not likely to have advertised the presence of any traces of aggressive magic. However, at least one Roman catacomb excavated at the turn of the last century yielded, according to excavation reports, a curse tablet on papyrus in a small capsule, set into a child's grave.[57] Likely the report only mentioned it because the catacombs were then (and still are today) identified as Jewish, although the excavation reports clearly state that there were Christian graves there as well.

Lead tablets or other magical objects need not have been deposited in the Christian catacombs for them to have been commissioned by Christians, even if deposited elsewhere. In his book on aggressive magic in antiquity, John Gager cites a number of *defixiones* from fourth-century Rome.[58] All were written primarily in Greek, all were deposited in tombs, and all draw on language more Christian than not. One, a restraining spell, invokes the 'lord angels' and 'lord gods' to prevent one woman's slave owner from assigning her to a workhouse: 'Lord Gods, restrain the matron of the workhouse, Clodia Valeria Sophrone and do not let her drag Poletoria to suffer (?) the fate of lifelessness there.'[59] Another necromantic *lamella*,

---

[55] Faraone and Rife 2007.   [56] Faraone and Rife 2007: 154.
[57] Müller 1915: 250, excavating the now destroyed 'Jewish' catacombs of Monteverde.
[58] Gager 1992: 67–74, 169–71.   [59] Gager 1992: 169–71.

found on the Via Appia near the Porta San Sebastiano, is inscribed on both sides, with every other line written upside-down and backwards. It was a part of a cache of fifty-six *defixiones*, rolled up and pierced through with nails, found within a terracotta sarcophagus inside a mausoleum, all dating to the reigns of Theodosius I or Honorius. All the *defixiones* in this cache invoke archangels and angels as well as more traditional Roman deities and other powerful figures such as Osiris. The best preserved *defixio* displays images as well as *charaktēres*, and clearly was intended to throw the results of a chariot race in the Hippodrome.[60] Part of Side A reads:

EULAMON restrain. OUSIRI OUSIRI APHI OUSIRI MNE PHRI. I invoke you, holy angels and archangels by the (one in the) underworld in order that just as I hand over to you that impious, lawless and accursed Kardelos, to whom his mother Pholgentia gave birth, so put him on a bed of torment and make him suffer the penalty of an evil death and expire within five days. Quickly, quickly![61]

As John Gager nicely articulates, this *lamella* 'symbolized the invisible world of Rome – a world of gods, spirits, and *daimones* on the one side, of aspirations, tensions, and implicit power on the other – in short, a world where emperors, senators, and bishops were not in command.'[62]

While necromantic curses are hard to come by in catacombs in the form of *lamellae*, we do find curses inscribed on funerary inscriptions. One, from the catacombs of Sant'Agnese, reads 'male pereat insepultus iaceat non resurgat cum Iuda partem habeat si quis sepulcrum hunc violarit' ('May whoever violates this tomb die a terrible death, lie unburied, never rise again, and share the fate of Judas').[63] Eric Rebillard rightly notes that such curses were inscribed for their own 'performative value'.[64] This curse against tomb violators is not an act of aggressive magic; what it expresses, however, is not necessarily anxiety about tomb 'squatters' looking to bury someone else in an already claimed spot, but perhaps a more visceral fear of necromancers coming to make use of bones, or to nestle a curse tablet by the body.

Necromancy and Oracular Magic

The phenomenon of aggressive magic and traces of it at the catacombs brings us to a final category: necromancy and oracular magic. Although the

---

[60] Gager 1992: 67–74.
[61] Gager 1992: 70. Some of the *lamellae*, with reproductions of the line drawings, are on display at the Museo Nazionale delle Terme.
[62] Gager 1992: 46.   [63] *ILCV* 3845 = *ICUR* 8.21396.   [64] Rebillard 2009: 22.

term 'necromancy' evokes fearsome images of sorcerers or witches like Erictho performing the darkest arts, Roman necromancy was likely more prosaic. A large percentage of curse tablets and victory spells derive from graves; Faraone's claim that the *defixio* excavated at Cenchreae lay within sight of visitors to the tomb (and was not subsequently removed) indicated that while the dead were still puissant, the desire to draw upon these powers was neither particularly unusual nor particularly censured. As Daniel Ogden notes, there were few condemnations of necromantic practices in Roman literature and law; even within Christian practice, the Witch of Endor presented a model for necromancy that was positive rather than negative.[65]

Were catacomb bones ever used for cephalomancy, the type of fortune-telling by oracular skulls that the Fontanelle women performed? Unfortunately, this type of ritual performance cannot be discerned from the material culture of the catacombs alone. The practice was not uncommon in Greek and Roman antiquity, and there are indications that elsewhere in the late Roman Empire cults emerged in Late Antiquity that venerated *martyria* as oracular sites.[66] Around the year 370 in Egypt, Athanasius complained that people sought out saints' shrines for healing and exorcisms. There, around the relics, people claimed to be possessed by the spirits of the dead. 'These people', Athanasius railed, 'give glory to them and ask them about what will happen ... they dare to question the unclean spirits!' Noting that people assumed naively that the spirits of the dead were 'the prophets of the martyrs', Athanasius argues that the martyrs themselves nowhere professed that they would speak through the medium of 'demons'.[67] In Egypt, then, the saint's shrine was an oracular space where the spirits of the dead communicated with the living. This practice evidently continued; David Frankfurter observes that in the mid fifth century, Shenoute claims that Christians 'sleep in the tombs to gain visions and ... question the dead about the living'.[68] Relic veneration in martyr shrines was linked to dream incubation and oracular spirit possession. The 'problem' of the improper use of bones for oracular purposes brings to mind the ruling at the Council of Elvira that forbade women to hold overnight vigils in tombs.[69] It remains an open question, however, to what degree this practice extended to Rome.

---

[65] Ogden 2001: 159; Smelik 1979: 160–79; Greer and Mitchell 2007.
[66] For Greek and Roman cephalomancy, see Ogden 2001: 208–16.
[67] Athanasius, *Festal Letter* 42, fr. 15 cited in Frankfurter 2010: 31.
[68] Shenoute of Atripe, *Those Who Work Evil*, cited in Frankfurter 2010: 32.
[69] Canon 35: 'Placuit prohiberi ne foeminae in coemeterio pervigilent, eo quod saepe sub obtentu orationis latentur scelera committunt.' See Hefele 1829–1912 (I): 150–1.

In his illuminating article on spirit possession in Late Antiquity, David Frankfurter remarks on the essentially locative nature of demons and the demonic in Late Antiquity as a 'threat revealed and distributed in landscape features', where a visit to something as innocuous in the urban landscape as the theatre or the baths could instigate a full-on episode of demonic possession.[70] To this dangerous 'urban landscape' must be added liminal suburban spaces such as cemeteries and *hypogaea*, where the margins between the world of the living and the world of the dead overlapped uncomfortably. In this particular space, humans encountered a range of spirits and beings, in what Frankfurter terms evocatively 'conflict and collusion'.[71] Frankfurter is also properly sensitive to the element of spectacle at martyrs' shrines, for, as he states, 'people went *out to* the shrines in order to experience the new pantheon and its powers through dramatic possessions; and naturally they expected some consequences of the demons' appearance, whether exorcisms, oracles, or simply drama'.[72]

Frankfurter's comments hold some utility for us when we conceptualize the complex pattern of magic in the catacombs, from apotropaic signs to patterns of practice and ritual that surely occurred but are harder to tease out from what remains. At the heart of magic, ancient or otherwise, lies a series of performative acts in which the individual gains some form of agency. Some of these acts took place in the vicinity of the catacomb – whether in their earlier phase as communal cemeteries, or their later phase as *martyria*. In either case, the power of the catacomb lay in the pantheon of beings who populated the site, from demons, the 'ordinary' spirits of the dead, to those saints whose power drew from their mastery of the non-obvious beings who lurked there.

Conclusions

Why did late antique Christians practise magic? Because they, like others, believed that magic worked.[73] Evans-Pritchard's work on witchcraft among the Azande highlighted significant social work that magic did: it could explain personal misfortune or a plague of 'bad luck' and exonerate individuals from public failure.[74] At the risk of drawing too reductively on theories of deprivation and compensation, magic helped people to get something they wanted. These wants were not served by what the

---

[70] Frankfurter 2010: 39. [71] Frankfurter 2010: 40. [72] Frankfurter 2010: 40.
[73] See Gager 1992: 22–7 for the question 'Did magic work?'
[74] Evans-Pritchard 1976; 18–55. See also Graf 1997: magic helps us cope with a difficult life.

authorized rites of the church – or its dogma – provided. The promise of a blessed afterlife offered some relief from anxiety perhaps. But what could Christianity do to help bring or restore good fortune? Magic also helped to keep away what was unwanted – bad luck, the evil eye of envy, the brittle infertility of female demons that made them want to steal away the life force of a human infant – all the personified forces of greed, fear and hostility that raged even against the unfortunate. In the dizzying world of seen and unseen threats and insecurities, the controlled and the frankly uncontrolled, it is hardly surprising that the sanctioned, measured interventions of a clergy that had not yet hit its stride would not have won the full reassurance of the populace. What succour could bishops offer against the tyranny of subterranean darkness? As Rangar Cline sagely noted in his study of late antique protective magic at Miletus, 'when it comes to protective magic, efficacy is more important than orthodoxy'.[75] Harnessing the powers of a 'truly democratic pantheon', in the words of Gary Vikan, was not to exclude the light-bringing blessedness of Jesus and the saints, but to stand them alongside other powers at least as worthy of consideration.[76]

The undercurrent of magical praxis and a preference for 'efficacy over orthodoxy' may have put ordinary Christians who used or 'believed in' magic at odds with a nascent ecclesiastical hierarchy. Kim Bowes articulates this beautifully: 'lying even deeper beneath most magical accusations', she writes, 'lay the volatile, tectonic boundary created when power invested in public institutions collided with that based on personal or charismatic abilities'. She continues, 'behind the relatively infrequent accusations of *superstitio* and *magia* there lay a certain tension between public, that is, civic, religiosity, and various kinds of "the private"'.[77]

Although I do not dispute that those performing (private) magic may have come into tension with ecclesiastical displays of might and control, this is not the only interpretive model that may be useful to us. Here, the old women of Fontanelle may help us to think differently. As private practitioners in unsanctioned rites, it is unlikely that they saw themselves as being across a boundary from licit, public Catholicism. All religious practices that are spontaneous, of the moment, unauthorized, private and 'popular' need not be counter-performances to the sacramental system of a developed church. Rather, they likely acted as necessary 'gap-fillers', filling in where a specific need was perceived: the need for good fortune, or protection or vindication. Similarly, in Late Antiquity, those who affixed

---

[75] Cline 2011: 69.   [76] Vikan 1984: 85.   [77] Bowes 2008: 46.

rings or bells to the mortar of tomb closures likely had little sense of their behaviour as 'un-Christian', just as they had little sense of participating in 'popular culture' by so doing. Seeing a problem, they responded appropriately and spontaneously.

Perhaps the Fontanelle women teach us more than this, the power of gap-filling rituals. In Ledeen's thoughtful article on the living and the dead in Naples, he records an offhand comment from a local curator of the site: that the oracular women of Fontanelle tended to be those who had, in the wake of World War II, lost family members. In essence, these women sought out the dead to build for themselves new kinship networks and models; although they were not related to their oracular skulls by ties of blood, they forged new spiritual ties. As Peter Brown has already so beautifully expressed, the rise of the cult of the saints – and with it, a new sense of who constituted 'patron' or 'ancestor' – helped ease widespread deracination as Rome shuddered its way through massive population shifts and social change in the fifth century.[78] Perhaps the traces of magical practice in the catacombs allow us to 'see', for a brief moment, the plight of the city's many deracinated, socially marginalized individuals building new connections for themselves.

Along with the need to create a fictive but potently 'real' network of kin, magical practices also, in a real sense, held together the world of the living and the world of the dead. For contemporary Neapolitans, their ongoing relationship with their dead accomplished much work. Ledeen writes:

I think the vagueness of the boundary between the living and the dead has a lot to do with the ongoing creativity of the city. It eases anxiety about death in the contemporary world, an enormous and largely unspoken fear that stifles the range of thought and art. The Neapolitan ease with the dead reminds the living that they are part of a continuum, and it gives them the faith to believe that their own identity and their own endeavors will continue after they have passed on.[79]

The parallels between contemporary Naples (and, specifically, the women of Fontanelle) and the late ancient world are, of course, imperfect. Yet it strikes me as useful to keep in the foreground the practitioners of magic, and not just to consider what materials they left behind. To say that ordinary Christians practised magic because they believed it worked is not an explanation; it is perhaps more fruitful to use the phenomenon to think with – to consider, rather, what sort of work these practices accomplished, and for whom. None of this, then, has much to do with Christianization, or with power disputes between Christian laypeople

[78] Brown 1981.   [79] Ledeen 2009.

and the clergy. Roman bishops and clergy may have become, in the fourth and fifth centuries, the new civic arbiters, but ordinary people controlled and patrolled those hollow black spaces in which the living and the dead could meet, shoring up those vulnerable, liminal areas of potential demonic or malevolent interest, seeking to ensure small daily victories in a harsh world – a healed limb, a bad end to the wrong charioteer, a relief from a short miserable life of toil in the workhouse, the assurance that a dead child is no longer vulnerable to the evil eye. Hence we return to Orsi's world of quotidian religion, in which ordinary people take matters into their own hands, 'making do' with bewildering circumstances, at the intersections of life and death.

13 | Popular Theology in Late Antiquity

JACLYN MAXWELL

When approaching the study of popular culture in the ancient world, we might not expect intellectual pursuits such as theology to be included, especially given the relatively low levels of literacy in antiquity. Discussions of ideas, however, do not actually require literary training. In the context of theology, becoming an expert requires years of training, but having an interest in these matters does not. If theological ideas are presented to a broad audience, then, I would argue, we can view them as part of popular culture, or, more specifically, 'popular religion'.[1] When considering whether any given aspect of culture is 'popular', we should focus on its social context and its accessibility rather than rely on our perception of how complex or 'highbrow' it is.[2] As Lucy Grig points out in the Introduction to this volume (p. 21), the concept of 'popular religion' has been used 'to divide respectable, proper religion from its lesser "popular" counterpart'. Instead of slipping back into these (elitist) value judgements, we should consider 'popular religion' to include the religious beliefs, practices and experiences of the general population. From this perspective, ideas associated with 'proper' religion, such as theological speculation, can be seen as belonging to 'popular religion' as well.

In most cases, studies of popular religion aim, justifiably, to turn our attention away from the concerns of intellectuals and towards the experiences of ordinary people. Theological speculation seems to belong exclusively to the learned, elite culture at the other end of the social spectrum from popular practices. Complex arguments about abstract ideas *appear* to be quite different from other popular interests such as pantomime and

---

[1] Holt Parker defines popular culture as including the 'unauthorized' aspects of culture that is produced by the non-elites as well as any culture that is accessible and appealing to the general population, regardless of their training or 'cultural capital': Parker 2011: 161–7. In this case, theology is 'authorized', but accessible to a general audience.

[2] See Lawrence Levine's study of how high culture of the twentieth century, from Shakespeare to the opera, was previously the popular culture – or, more precisely, shared culture – in the nineteenth century: Levine 1988. Parker points out that in pre-industrial Europe, culture was mass-consumed in cities: Parker 2011: 153. I thank Kevin Mattson for suggesting Levine's book as a comparison.

gambling.[3] To some extent, theologians as early as Tertullian and Origen made this distinction when they considered their understanding of religious questions to be quite different from the majority of Christians' views.[4] Modern scholars have tended to follow this line of thinking, pursuing theology and popular religion as separate fields of study. Even some scientists (as we shall see) approach religion in these discrete terms. But the separation of theology from popular religion implies that, outside intellectual circles, most people were *only* interested in 'popular' practices, such as exorcism, and *never* concerned about questions about the nature of God, the existence of a soul, or the fate of the soul after death (unless the soul is envisioned as a ghost or featured in a folk-tale). Likewise, this distinction implies that theologians were *never* concerned about demons or healing, because they *only* focused on abstract debates about the nature of divinity. Assumptions like these underestimate everyone's capabilities for wide-ranging questions and experiences. As David Frankfurter observes, 'the devotions of the poor and uneducated typically come off as a soup of magic, crisis rites, image worship, festival hilarity and superstition in contrast to the staid and rational religion ascribed to the upper classes'.[5] These categories, with magic and 'superstition' at one end of the spectrum and careful, rational thought about religion at the other, associate particular aspects of religion with different social contexts, even though the experience and understanding of religion at all levels of society were linked in many ways.

Recent studies of popular culture and popular religion in antiquity support this notion of fluidity and shared culture, demonstrating that 'popular' culture was not necessarily different from what we would consider mainstream or elite culture.[6] Most famously, Peter Brown's *The Cult of the Saints* challenged the idea that there were two tiers of Christian worship and belief: a superior version based on theological understanding and an inferior version based on popular practices such as the veneration of martyrs. Brown demonstrates that these seemingly 'popular' practices were actually shared by all levels of society.[7] Likewise, the discussions of morality among the elites and masses were not so different: Teresa Morgan

---

[3] In this volume Jerry Toner argues to the contrary, pointing out the intellectual dimensions of these forms of entertainment.

[4] Carpenter 1963: 308–9.   [5] Frankfurter 2005: 255–6.

[6] Many studies examine aspects of ancient culture shared by elites and masses: Horsfall 1996; Morgan 2007; Toner 2009. For more references, see Peachin 2011: 22–4, as well as further chapters in the same volume.

[7] Brown 1981. For another example breaking down the divide between elite and popular, see Frankfurter 2005: 262 on the widespread belief in the powers of holy oil. For a recent

has demonstrated that popular morality consisted of 'ethical ideas that were widely shared up and down the social spectrum'.[8] In a similar vein, Jerry Toner proposes that opportunities for intellectual pursuits did not necessarily require literacy: popular jokes, fables and entertainment reflect philosophical concerns.[9] Theology can also be thought of in these terms, as a part of the religious 'common sense' of Late Antiquity shared by people with varying levels of social status, wealth and education. If we look more closely at the descriptions of theological debates and the social contexts of many sermons, we can find a great deal of evidence that non-elite Christians were engaged with religious concepts even though they did not strive to be theologians themselves.

In Late Antiquity in particular, theology was no ivory tower pursuit: in ordinary church gatherings and during conflicts among rival theologians, Christian leaders had to reach out to broad audiences and address the questions and concerns of ordinary laypeople. While official doctrines were formulated by educated men, these ideas were part of a religious culture shared by people across the social and economic spectrum. This chapter will draw on ideas about the fluidity between 'elite' and 'popular' culture in order to understand better the relationship between theology and the religious concerns of ordinary people in Late Antiquity. The active, at times aggressive, participation of ordinary people in theological controversies of the fourth and fifth centuries CE indicates that Christian theology was, to some extent, a popular field of enquiry in this period. The widespread interest in theological teachings can also be seen in the festivals that attracted crowds to martyr shrines, where priests or bishops spoke publicly to honour the martyrs.[10] The sermons presented during celebrations of the martyrs in certain Greek-speaking cities (the focus here will be on cities in Asia Minor and Syria) reveal some of the religious concepts that were accessible to ordinary people. These sermons indicate that some theological concepts were common knowledge, while others were subject to ongoing debates. There was no distinction between 'popular' martyr cult and 'elite' intellectual enquiry: in these cases, ordinary

---

intervention in favour of the two-tiered view, see Ramsey MacMullen's argument that popular martyr veneration existed separate from the elite official church: MacMullen 2009.

[8] Morgan 2007: 1–2. Morgan argues that a great deal of culture took the form of public performances, 3–4. On the connections between philosophers' discussions and common sense, see 298.

[9] Toner in this volume.

[10] Limberis emphasizes the resources that the Cappadocians put into cultivating the martyrs, including the shrines themselves: Limberis 2011: 66–96.

Christians engaged with theological ideas during the celebrations at the martyrs' shrines.

Cognitive Science, Theology and Popular Religion

Before examining popular engagement in theology during Late Antiquity, we should consider another argument, one based in cognitive science, that there *is* a fundamental, neurological divide between theology and popular religion. The perceived gulf between theology and popular religion plays an important role in current work on cognitive theories of religion. Robert McCauley, in *Why Religion is Natural and Science is Not*, argues that some ways of thinking are intuitive and 'natural', while others are more difficult to attain and therefore less 'natural'. In this framework, he considers popular religion to be cognitively natural and easy, and theology, like science, to be unnatural and difficult.[11] In his view, popular religion includes devotion to icons, sacred spaces and rituals, and falls into the same category as interest in fairytales and fantasy literature. These tendencies stand in sharp contrast to both theological and scientific thinking. Popular religion, he argues, is rooted in the 'theory of mind' that evolved in such a way as to make us perceive aspects of the natural world as resulting from some sort of intelligent being with a mind like ours.[12]

An important part of McCauley's argument hinges on a distinction between popular religion (intuitive and easy to grasp) and theology (counter-intuitive and as difficult as science). In his view, the core of religious belief is not intellectual. Certain conditions – such as the competition between belief systems – can lead religious experts to formulate doctrine based on reasoning, and then to enforce their doctrines. This theological approach to religious beliefs, based on the use of inference and abstractions, 'departs from our natural cognitive systems'.[13] One of his most interesting (and problematic) conclusions is the 'inevitability of theological incorrectness' – people will tend to drift away from orthodoxy back to the types of beliefs to which our brains are more predisposed.[14]

---

[11] McCauley categorizes popular religion with technology as basic human endeavours rooted in prehistoric times, possibly predating language. McCauley 2012: 148–50.

[12] McCauley 2012: 235–6.

[13] McCauley 2012: 153–4. By contrast, popular religion 'employs ideas and forms of thought that are *naturally appealing* to the human mind', because they draw on 'natural cognitive dispositions'.

[14] McCauley illustrates the development of theology and the 'inevitable' theological incorrectness with examples from an Afro-Brazilian religious group: McCauley 2012: 238–43.

This approach to studying religion has been subject to criticism, not least because the assumptions and conclusions boil down to religion being a mere side effect of evolutionary adaptation.[15] But McCauley's view that popular religion and theology are separate, one natural and universal and the other the unnatural realm of experts, can also be called into question. Some scholars of early Christianity have shared his view, assuming that a deep divide existed between the theologians' carefully formulated understanding and the religious practices of the masses.[16]

From the evidence from Late Antiquity, however, we can see that theology was not always isolated from popular religion – unless popular discussions are automatically excluded from what counts as theology. One problem with McCauley's (and others') use of the term 'theology' is that it is *by definition* separate from popular religion. If theology is defined as religious thought that is too complicated for non-experts to engage in, then it must always be an impenetrable subject.[17] However, if theology includes discussions of a religion's basic premises and explanations of beliefs about the divine, then theology consists of a spectrum of thought reaching from the most basic ideas to the esoteric. This broader understanding of the term allows us to see a great deal of overlap between the religious beliefs and experiences of theologians and those of everyone else.

From Primitive Christianity to Speculative Theology

According to one narrative of early Christian theology and institutional structure, the unified 'primitive' Christianity of the second and third centuries gave way to speculative theology that would be dominated by educated experts, just as the clergy would become the domain of local elites. Before the fourth century, debates within Christian communities centred on moral behaviour and how the church should be run, while disagreements over beliefs did not result in complex theological explanations. More technical and complicated theology began to emerge in the late second and early third centuries, due to the growing importance of Paul's

---

[15] Scholars have also criticized the evolutionary theorists' narrow conception of religion and their lack of interest in the historical and cultural contexts of the beliefs. For these critiques and suggestions for new directions for cognitive theories of religion, see Barrett 2010.

[16] MacMullen 1990 and 2009; Harnack 1957. Adolf von Harnack saw a stark divide between primitive Christianity and speculative theology, which he refers to as 'scientific' religion.

[17] Likewise, McCauley's definition of 'science' only includes post-Enlightenment Western science, as seeking knowledge and testing hypotheses outside this context does not count as 'science': McCauley 2012.

letters and the Gospel of John.[18] The increased involvement of highly educated men as bishops and apologists led to more learned theological debates, first against pagan critics and then among Christians, which culminated in the Trinitarian and Christological controversies of the fourth and fifth centuries CE. These changes are sometimes seen as problematic because they left behind the ordinary Christians, the non-theologians. For instance, the influential church historian and Lutheran theologian Adolf von Harnack viewed the development of complex theological discussions as an unfortunate movement away from the universally accessible 'primitive Christianity'. For Harnack, the use of methods drawn from classical education in philosophy shifted Christianity onto a path 'toward a scientific religion and toward a theological science', which would be intelligible only to experts and 'a mystery to the great majority of Christians'.[19]

For some Christian thinkers, there was a division among Christians based on one's ability to learn the 'theological science'. According to both Origen and Clement of Alexandria, God had given basic doctrines to the simple people and advanced theology only to a few.[20] Simple people would have to be persuaded with rhetoric or won over by miracles because they could not grasp philosophical argumentation. Irrational faith was less than ideal, but it was a fact of life and better than no faith at all.[21] Origen's opponents within the Christian community in Alexandria (who likely outnumbered his supporters) claimed simplicity to be a virtue and tarred his intellectual approach to scripture as 'wordiness'.[22] Origen's community thus provides an example of a rift between theology and popular religion.

Yet, the assumption that theology was *always* inaccessible to ordinary Christians is based on a vision of educated theologians always isolated in ivory towers, engaged in discussion only with each other. In Late Antiquity, in contrast with Origen's community, most theologians did not envision the divide between themselves and the majority of Christians in such stark terms. Rather, many of the most influential theologians of Late Antiquity were engaged with their lay congregations as bishops and pastors. Furthermore, the laity do not seem to have been passive listeners to sermons and unthinking reciters of creeds – there is a great deal of evidence

---

[18] Carpenter 1963.
[19] Harnack 1957: 149–50; 193–4. For a more positive assessment of the Hellenization of Christian thought, see Pelikan 1993.
[20] Hällström 1984: 7–8.
[21] Origen recognized that not everyone had time for philosophizing. Hällström 1984: 28; Carpenter 1963: 309.
[22] Hällström 1984: 25, 30.

that they provided feedback to their preachers in the form of questions, disbelief or applause.[23] Also, historians describe the disruptions caused in major cities due to theological controversies, which sometimes led urban populations to demonstrate or even riot.[24]

Popular Religion and Theological Controversies in Late Antiquity

In the fourth century, the controversy over the nature of the Trinity occupied much of the preaching and writing of leading Christians, with bishops in many cities competing for followers and support from the emperors. Although the theological vocabulary and methods of argumentation originated in the milieu of men educated in classical philosophy, rhetoric and Christian texts, these debates became part of a broader discourse. Religious authorities from different sects tried to convince the laity that their theological arguments were correct. Although it is clear that the Christian public were involved in these rivalries, scholars have disagreed about the extent to which ordinary people engaged in these debates, as opposed to merely learning 'slogans' or chants and following their bishop/patron. Ramsay MacMullen has argued that the participation of the laity in these conflicts was important – bishops needed their followers' support just as the traditional elites needed the plebs. Yet, MacMullen maintains that the laity did not engage in or understand the theological issues; the only messages that were available and appealing to the masses were 'labels and slogans ... set to music'.[25] In his view, ordinary people were concerned about having powerful religious patrons and, as a result, God's protection from harm.

These practical concerns were undoubtedly important, but they do not rule out interest in actual theological differences. Popular engagement in these conflicts indicates that there were popular discussions of theology. Most recently, Carlos Galvão-Sobrinho's work on the social setting of theological controversies has emphasized the efforts made by church leaders to win over ordinary Christians: their appeals to the laypeople clearly included explanations of their theological positions.[26] Indeed, some church authorities grumbled that there was too much public

---

[23] On laypeople as the audience of sermons and as participants in theological discussions, see Lim 1995; Mayer 1998, 2000; Maxwell 2006.
[24] Gregory 1979; Gaddis 2005; Shaw 2011; see too Magalhães de Oliveira in this volume.
[25] MacMullen 1990: 271–2, n. 49.   [26] Galvão-Sobrinho 2013: 47–65.

discussion of theology. Gregory of Nyssa, the Cappadocian theologian and bishop, complains in a very famous passage that unqualified people insisted on discussing the Trinity:

> The whole city is full of [theological controversy], the squares, the marketplaces, the cross-roads, the alleyways; money changers, food sellers: they are all busy arguing. If you ask someone to give you change, he philosophises about the Begotten [Son] and the Unbegotten [Father]; if you inquire about the price of a loaf, you are told by way of reply that the Father is greater and the Son inferior; if you ask 'Is my bath ready?' the attendant answers that the Son was made out of nothing.[27]

Clearly, Gregory disapproved of popular participation in theological controversies. He and some of his contemporaries worried about people being won over by theological errors, but they also seem to scoff at the idea that people in the marketplaces and dinner parties were *able* to take these matters seriously. Another Cappadocian theologian and bishop, Gregory of Nazianzus, also referred to the ubiquity of theological discussions and asked people to leave these matters to experts like himself:

> Discussion of theology is not for everyone, I tell you, not for everyone – it is no such inexpensive or effortless pursuit. Nor, I would add, is it for every occasion, or every audience; neither are all its aspects open to inquiry. It must be reserved for certain occasions, for certain audiences, and certain limits must be observed. It is not for all men, but only for those who have been tested and have found a sound footing in study, and, more importantly, have undergone, or at the very least are undergoing, purification of body and soul.[28]

The problem these bishops encountered was not a lack of interest in theology, but a lack of complete control over the discussions. Richard Lim has described how the Cappadocian Fathers, John Chrysostom and others aimed to discourage popular debates and speculation by emphasizing that divine truths are 'unknowable'. Discussions that they had previously tolerated or even encouraged were no longer welcome by the late fourth century. By that time, definitions of orthodox beliefs had been refined to such a degree that theological positions had to be expressed precisely, or else they would be considered heretical. Leading theologians attempted to avoid complicated discussions through 'mystification', attempting to persuade the laity that they could not fully understand divinity and so they should stop grappling with these questions.[29] Lim also illustrates that the Church Fathers' concerns were not limited to heresy

---

[27] Gr. Nys. *De deitate filii et spiritus oratio* (*PG* 46: 557B). Cf. Gr. Naz. *Or.* 27.2 (*SC* 250: 75).
[28] Gr. Naz. *Or.* 27.3 (*SC* 250: 76); quoted in Lim 1995: 159–60.   [29] Lim 1995: 152–7, 168.

and orthodoxy: they also viewed public theological disputation as a threat to their claims on religious authority.[30]

However, the public engagement in these debates continued into the fifth century, when public demonstrations erupted in major cities such as Ephesus and Alexandria in favour of particular Christological positions. William Frend observes that popular interest in Christology was not surprising because of the matter's implications for personal salvation through Christ – questions about the nature of Christ could be quite relevant to any believer.[31] Frend provides an example illustrating this concern from Severus of Antioch, who warned his congregation that if they did not get the sacrament from an orthodox priest, a demon would capture their soul.[32] The public demonstrations, which sometimes resulted in violence, clearly show the public's engagement in these issues. Our interpretation of their engagement in theology depends on our definition of theology. For instance, Severus' comment about demons might lead us to take the Christological concerns less seriously. Likewise, MacMullen sees the following case as a demonstration of ordinary Christians' lack of interest in the content of theological discussions: when a bishop suffered a stroke during a theological debate, the townspeople took this to mean he had lost the debate.[33] For MacMullen, this anecdote indicates that the townspeople were not interested in ideas, but only in supernatural intervention. In this case, however, it is likely that most people, educated or not, would have come to the same conclusion about the meaning of the bishop's ailment. If anything, the dramatic end of the debate might have reinforced the public's concerns about these issues. In general, it seems unlikely that the same laypeople who were overly enthused about theological controversies had no real interest in or aptitude for theology. A much simpler explanation would be to consider theology to have been an aspect of the popular culture of this period.

Martyr Sermons and their Audiences

The Church Fathers that Lim describes as discouraging public theological discourse regularly preached to the laity. They might have avoided certain

---

[30] Lim 1995: 168–75.
[31] Frend 1971: 19–20. For descriptions of these demonstrations: 22–4. Frend interprets the public interest as stemming from the widespread belief that Christ must unambiguously be God for the redemption of humans to work and for the fight against demons to succeed, 25–7. On popular demonstrations and riots, see Gregory 1979.
[32] Frend 1971: 28.   [33] MacMullen 1990: 271–2, n. 48.

questions that divided Christians into rival sects, but they did not steer clear of all theological issues. Theological concepts inevitably came up during their sermons. The most well-attended sermons were the ones presented at the martyr festivals, many of which were established commemorations in Eastern cities and towns in Late Antiquity. The martyrs' shrines were sites of private worship and prayers for people seeking healing or various other kinds of aid. Each year, there would be a *panegyris*, lasting one or two days, which featured one or more homilies in the martyr's honour, often at shrines built at the martyrs' tombs outside the city. In the sermons from these events, the preachers remark on the size and diversity of the crowds, the presence of men and women, old and young, rich and poor, urban and rural.[34] Not surprisingly, we also hear about the noise-level that resulted from the crowds.[35]

The homilies presented on these occasions usually concentrated on basic elements of the martyr narrative: for instance, the devil inspired the persecution of Christians, and God had allowed the devil to do so, in order to provide an opportunity for martyrs to show the strength of their beliefs.[36] The martyrs defied the government's laws and professed their faith without fear of punishments. Usually, the Roman officials resorted to both bribes and torture, to no avail. Sometimes, the violence – the blood and guts – is described in graphic detail. The sermons usually refer to the martyrs' relics as an inspiration for the congregation and also as a source of practical miracles. The sermons also sometimes include descriptions of the paintings of the martyrs' deeds that decorate the shrine, as well as references to unofficial aspects of the festivals: the drinking, dancing and joking around.[37]

The sermons at martyrs' festivals also presented a great deal of theological content, if one thinks of theology in the broad sense of the beliefs about cosmic order, the nature of God, human salvation and related topics. These matters overlap with aspects of 'popular' religion, such as concerns

---

[34] For an argument that the preacher's audience consisted mostly of wealthy people and their dependants, see MacMullen 1989 and 2009: 14–15. For the view that sermons in Late Antiquity were presented to more diverse audiences, see Cunningham 1986; Mayer 1998: 109–14; Mayer 2000; Maxwell 2006: 65–87; Rylaarsdam 2014: 214–18.

[35] Limberis 2011: 20–3; Leemans 2004: 264–5.

[36] On martyr narratives as performing miracles while providing religious instruction, see Grig 2004: 3–4.

[37] On the decoration of the shrine, see Gregory of Nyssa, *Hom. de S. Theodoro* (*GNO* 62). On the physical context of martyr festivals, see Limberis 2011: 53–95; on drinking and dancing: 24–5. For a calendar of martyrs' festivals in Cappadocia, see Limberis 2011: 52. On the distractions at festivals, see John Chrys. *Hom. in S. Julianum* 4 (*PG* 50: 672–3); *Hom. in S. Pelagiam* 3 (*PG* 50: 582).

about demons and angels and the power of the relics.[38] In the context of public preaching, these bishops do not appear to have approached theological concepts as separate from popular beliefs. They taught ethical instructions in conjunction with theological concepts: sinful or upright behaviour had consequences for each individual's salvation. The presentation of theology to broad audiences as well as the overlap between theology and popular religion allows us to see more clearly how popular culture worked in late antique society. In the case of theology, cultural authorities interacted with ordinary people. The interaction was not merely a top-down transmission (or 'trickle-down') of ideas. Instead, the questions and concerns from the general population shaped the content of sermons. Also, the allegiances of the masses were key to their leaders' claim to authority.[39]

Basic Theological Knowledge

Numerous aspects of Christian cosmology can be found dispersed throughout the homilies. Many of these points appear to have been common knowledge, because they did not require in-depth explanation or clarification: angels, demons and the devil existed and participated in the events on earth and in the hereafter; rewards and punishments (even the rewards for the martyrs) will be meted out in the future, at the time of the resurrection and judgement. The homilies give no indication that people needed to be convinced of these beliefs, and the mechanics of these processes do not appear to have been up for debate.[40] Most of the listeners would have had some experience with Christian teachings – they were not complete beginners. John Chrysostom describes how the first encounter with Christian teachings was the most difficult: 'What is now being heard for the first time confuses the mind of the audience and throws up many issues for those doing the teaching.' But, according to Chrysostom, once people had experience of these teachings, they understood more easily.[41] It is also clearly taken for granted that the martyrs could act as intercessors, effecting cures and miracles in this world, and also improving one's standing in the next world. The martyrs were praised for helping the

---

[38] On the theological content in Basil and Gregory of Nyssa's homilies on the Forty Martyrs and on Stephen, see Mühlenberg 2012: 128–32.
[39] Galvão-Sobrinho 2013: 47–65; Van Dam 2003: 9–13.
[40] An exception can be found in Gregory of Nyssa's *Hom. de S. Theodoro* (*GNO* 64). Gregory remarks that some people do not believe in life after death.
[41] *Hom. in S. Ignatium*, 9 (*PG* 50: 591).

needy, the sick, the hungry and the wandering poor. They were called on for communal help. For instance, Gregory of Nyssa invokes the martyr Theodore to protect the Christian community from a war with the Scythians, and also to protect them from heresies.[42] The shrines, the relics themselves and other reminders of the martyrs, such as images and the use of the saint's name, are described as simultaneously reminding people to be virtuous and protecting them from harm.[43] These preachers were the highly educated Church Fathers: seeking protection and well-being from the martyrs was not exclusively the preserve of 'popular' Christianity – it was everyone's Christianity.

The accounts of the martyrs' trials and torture taught Christians that the more they suffered on earth while adhering to their religious beliefs, the greater their rewards would be at the final judgement. On several occasions, the priest or bishop clarifies that wealth and high standing in this life are not to be taken as foreshadowing one's ultimate destiny. Wealth and poverty were both meaningless, and both were only temporary.[44] Homilies on the martyrs frequently come back to the point of the inferiority of this world and the implications for how to live one's life. In this case, the preachers are insistent, not because the concept was complex or contested, but rather, it seems, because of the difficulty in living consistently with this belief.

More Advanced Theology

Aside from future judgement in a separate and superior divine realm, to what degree was Christian doctrine a part of general knowledge? Numerous references to biblical narratives indicate that people were already familiar with them: the Book of Daniel, in particular, was a favourite point of reference in martyr homilies.[45] Some of the martyr

---

[42] Gr. Nys. *Hom. de S. Theodoro* 70.29 (*GNO* 69–70). For people seeking general safety and health, see Basil, *Hom. in XL martyres* 8 (*PG* 31: 524); Asterius, *Hom.* 9 (Datema 9.9.2–3, trans. B. Dehandschutter 2003: 171).

[43] Asterius, *Hom.* 9 (Datema 9.1.1–9.2.2, trans. B. Dehanschutter 2003: 168–9); John Chrys. *Hom. in S. Meletium* 2–3 (*PG* 50: 515–16); John Chrys. *Hom. in S. Lucianum* 2–4 (*PG* 50: 521–2).

[44] Wealth and poverty are both meaningless after 'you come and see the martyr's wealth and scorn the money out in the world'. John Chrys. *Hom. in Sanctum Julianum* 4 (*PG* 50: 673); *Hom. in S. Pelagiam* 3 (*PG* 50: 582); *Hom. in S. Eustathium* 2 (*PG* 50: 599–600); Basil, *Hom. in XL martyres* 4 and 6 (*PG* 31: 512–13, 517). On the complex attitudes towards wealth, see Brown 2012.

[45] In Basil's version of the forty martyrs, the martyrs quote from Ephesians, Genesis, Psalms, Matthew, Daniel, Romans: *Hom. in XL martyres* 6 (*PG* 31: 517). Gregory of Nyssa's *Encomium in XL martyres* 1b refers to Job as well as various other scriptures, and assumes the audience

sermons also include references to and/or detailed explanations of more complex issues that relied on some prior knowledge of the scriptures.

In connection with the martyrs and their rewards, the Cappadocian brothers and bishops Basil of Caesarea and Gregory of Nyssa hark back to Adam and Eve and the fall from grace. Gregory of Nyssa's *Homily on the Forty Martyrs of Sebaste* (a group of soldiers martyred together) describes the angels watching the wrestling match between the devil and the martyrs. In the first round of this fight, the serpent had floored Adam, but in this round, the men laughed at the devil's ploys. Gregory then elaborates: Adam and Eve had degraded human nature and brought on death, while the martyrs restored human nature and overcame death.[46] Basil's *Homily on the Forty Martyrs* also refers to this parallel in the context of the martyrs being ordered to freeze to death in the winter cold without clothes. Basil describes one of the martyrs making the best of a difficult situation: 'Since we [humans] put on clothes because of the snake, let us take them off [to freeze] because of Christ.'[47] In this last allusion, Basil appears to have made his point without having to explain the details. This part of the cosmic narrative, the fall from grace and later redemption through Christ, appears to have been familiar to the Christian community and uncontested.

One particularly striking reference to theological questions in the martyr homilies is an aside about free will by John Chrysostom. In his *Homily on Babylas*, Chrysostom describes how this martyr's relics were removed from their original resting place on the orders of the pagan emperor Julian. Julian aimed to ridicule the Christian veneration of relics. In the context of discussing relics and how pagans considered the dead bodies to be pollution, Chrysostom remarks, 'the bodies of the living are more full of wickedness than those of the dead are impure. My point is that the former [living bodies] serve the soul's commands, while the latter [dead bodies] lie motionless.' He takes the position that the depravity of living people comes from their decisions, not from physical existence. He clarifies his position: 'I personally wouldn't say that the bodies of the living are by nature impure, but rather that in every case the wicked and distorted will is accountable for

---

know the story of the three boys in the furnace (*GNO* 10 1/2: 147). John Chrysostom's *Hom. in Sanctum Julianum* 3–4 (*PG* 50: 670–2) refers to Lot, Noah and Daniel; *Hom. in S. Meletium* 7 (*PG* 50: 518) and *Hom. in S. Lucianum* 7 (*PG* 50: 524) refers to the Book of Daniel and the three boys. Asterius' *Hom.* 12 on Stephen (Datema 12.2.2, trans. B. Dehanschutter 2003: 178) refers to Cain and Abel, as well as, of course, Stephen from Acts.

[46] Gr. Nys. *Encomium in XL martyres* 1b (*GNO* 10 1/2: 149). For a discussion of Basil and Gregory's sermons on the forty martyrs, see Van Dam 2003: 132–50.

[47] Basil, *Hom. in XL martyres* 6 (*PG* 31: 517).

the charges brought by all.'[48] In this case, at a local martyr's festival, John Chrysostom briefly addresses the issues of theodicy and free will. He wanted to clarify that he did not consider evil to be inherent in physical bodies themselves. It appears to have been an extempore comment, because it is a digression from his main point in that section. He expressed this view in the course of his discussion of the pagans' disdain for the relics of the martyr. This is one example indicating that even if church authorities such as Chrysostom attempted to curb debates over Trinitarian and Christological questions, this does not mean that *all* theological discussions were discouraged.

God's Intervention and Why Bad Things Happen to Good People

Two theological topics received extensive attention in several martyr sermons: why God allowed certain events to happen and the nature of the Trinity. In these cases the preachers attempted to convince their listeners to believe something, perhaps because they did not understand or perhaps because they were susceptible to competing (heretical) explanations. In these cases, far from shutting down the discussion, the preachers prepared their listeners to engage in these arguments on their own.

God's direct intervention in human events is referred to on many occasions in sermons honouring the martyrs. During their trials and tortures, the bravery of the martyrs was due to God's help, not to human nature.[49] God also intervened to provide the martyrs with a more glorious and honourable death: for instance, he protected virgin martyrs from rape and oglers. These actions made sense: God was helping his own cause. But in the cases of exiled bishops (whom John Chrysostom considered as martyrs), why would God allow heretics to gain the upper hand? This required explanation. In his homily about the former bishop of Antioch, Meletius, Chrysostom explained that God allowed Meletius to be expelled in order to benefit the Nicene Christians.

---

[48] John Chrys. *Hom. de S. Babyla* 5 (SC 362: 304).

[49] John Chrys. *Hom. de S. Pelagia* 1 (*PG* 50: 579–80); Asterius, *Hom.* 9 on Phocas (Datema 9.13.3, trans. B. Dehandschutter 2003: 173); Asterius, *Hom.* 12 on Stephen (Datema 12.5.1, trans. B. Dehanschutter 2003: 179); John Chrys. *Hom. de Sanctis Bernice, Prosdoce et Domnina* 11–14 (*PG* 50: 634–6). In another case of God's intervention, lightning struck the temple of Apollo when the pagan Emperor Julian moved the relics of Babylas away from Daphne: John Chrys. *Hom. de S. Babyla* 8–9 (SC 362: 308–10).

Meletius' exile led his congregation to show their virtue and unity, while the bishop was able to interact with more communities during his exile.[50] Chrysostom made a more extensive argument in his homily on Bishop Eustathius, Meletius' predecessor, who was also sent into exile and considered to have been a martyr. The question, again, was why did God allow this to happen?

For what reason, then, was he expelled, and did God agree to their leading him away? For what reason? Whatever you do, don't think that what I say is the solution to just this question. Rather, whether you happen to argue about such matters with Greeks or other heretics, what I am about to say is enough to solve every question. Whereas God agrees to his true and apostolic faith being warred against in many ways, he allows the heresies and Greco-Roman religions to enjoy indemnity. What on earth for? So that, on the one hand, you might learn the latter's feebleness, since without being harassed they fold of their own accord; while, on the other, you may recognize the faith's strength, in that despite being embattled it grows even by means of the people blocking it.[51]

He repeats this idea a few times within a short passage:

God *allowed* his servants to be whipped, driven away, to suffer countless tortures, so that he might show his own power ... Do you see that it's for this reason that God *allowed* Satan's angels to keep up their assault on his servants and to provide countless opportunities so that his power might be obvious? For truly, whether we dispute with Greeks or with the miserable Jews, this suffices for us as a proof of the divine power.[52]

Chrysostom explains that the ones who were tortured prevailed, and the same would be the case with the suffering of Nicene leaders at the hands of the heretics. In this particular sermon, it seems that he needed to emphasize God's approval of the bishop's exile, while God's approval of martyrs (and that he allowed the persecutions) did not raise questions. Also, it is significant that Chrysostom envisioned discussions led by the laypeople: 'whether you happen to argue about such matters with Greeks or other heretics' and 'whether we dispute with Greeks or with the miserable Jews'. These statements indicate that the fate of the bishop Eustathius and its meaning was up for discussion in the broader community. These passages (and others) also indicate that Chrysostom encouraged some theological discussions to take place outside of church.[53]

---

[50] John Chrys. *Hom. in S. Meletium* 4, 7 (*PG* 50: 516, 18).
[51] John Chrys. *Hom. in S. Eustathium* 8 (*PG* 50: 602–3).
[52] John Chrys. *Hom. in S. Eustathium* 8–9 (*PG* 50: 603).
[53] Rylaarsdam 2014: 218–26; Maxwell 2006: 113–16.

The Trinity

The most important theological controversy of the fourth century was the relationship between God the Father and Christ the Son. An extensive discussion of this issue appears in the homily on Stephen the proto-martyr by Bishop Asterius (~330–420) of Amasea in north-eastern Asia Minor. This sermon starts off with theological topics and vocabulary by referring to the previous day's festival, Christmas, which celebrated the 'begetting of the One who yesterday was born according to the flesh, existing eternally according to the godhead'.[54] Asterius continues: 'the One without flesh put on the flesh, and so then also accepted the suffering for our sake, for nothing else than for his concern about us'. Asterius also refers to Cain, who first spilled blood, as the counterpart to Stephen who first sanctified the earth with blood.[55]

Asterius delves into a detailed discussion of the Trinity in the context of Stephen's vision of God, described in the Acts of the Apostles. In direct speech from God's perspective, Asterius observes that 'it scandalised many that God embraced a body on earth. But now consider Him [the son] on high together with Me as celestial and even supracelestial, to confirm in His human shape the economy of salvation.'[56] Asterius then describes God encouraging Stephen to leave his body and to 'despise it as an earthly bond, a house of decay, a perishable vessel of the potter' and aim for heaven. Stephen's body will be food for dogs, but his soul will join the angels.[57]

In his description of Stephen's vision, Asterius emphasizes that God appeared to Stephen as a form, not just as a voice. Asterius claims that the vision provided a refutation of future heresies:

[The heretic Sabellius] introduced the evil doctrine of the mixture of the persons of the Trinity, therefore, as an anticipation of the future and a confirmation of the souls beforehand, God shows himself to Stephen in His very own glory; and moreover he shows the Son as a person on His own, standing at His right side, so that by a clear distinction of the Persons, the hypostases are manifest.[58]

Asterius then turns to the next possible problem: 'But probably someone would say: "The question about the Father and the Son has been treated

---

[54] Asterius, *Hom.* 12 on Stephen (Datema 12.1.1, trans. B. Dehandschutter 2003: 177). See Matthews 2010: 123, 129–30.
[55] Asterius, *Hom.* 12 on Stephen (Datema 12.2.2, trans. B. Dehandschutter 2003: 178).
[56] Asterius, *Hom.* 12 on Stephen (Datema 12.7.3, trans. B. Dehandschutter 2003: 181).
[57] Asterius, *Hom.* 12 on Stephen (Datema 12.7.4, trans. B. Dehandschutter 2003: 181).
[58] Asterius *Hom.* 12 on Stephen (Datema 12.12.1, trans. B. Dehandschutter 2003: 183); here, Sabellianism refers to modalism.

sufficiently by you but what about the Holy Spirit?"[59] Asterius informs his listeners that just before the vision in Acts, the scripture refers to 'the Spirit through whom he spoke'.[60] He reassures his listeners that the scriptures mention the different persons of the Trinity separately, but they are always all three present. Although the Holy Spirit's role in the Trinity had been agreed upon at the Council of Constantinople in 381, and the Nicene position on the Son and the Father much earlier, it was still useful for Asterius in the early fifth century to clarify these issues and provide arguments against objections.

In his sermon on the martyr Phocas presented in 400 CE in Constantinople, John Chrysostom veered away from the martyr's narrative and focused on the Trinity. He complains that heretics 'twist scripture' to find backing for their claim that 'the Son of God is not Son, but a created being'.[61] He also takes care to explain that these heresies do not harm God – they only harm the people who fall for them. This clarification indicates that this question had been raised. Also on the topic of damage caused by heresies, Chrysostom explains that people fall into error because of a lack of judgement. Judas is his example of someone with bad judgement, while Job is someone who had good judgement. But, Chrysostom warned his listeners, the ability to use scriptural passages in one's support should not be impressive or persuasive: even the devil used references from scripture.[62]

In his homily on Phocas, Chrysostom also argues against a very specific claim by the Arians: they argued that the term 'Father' is the same as God, while the term 'Son' is the same as Lord, and that this implies a distinction of greater and lesser between them.[63] Chrysostom argues that both terms are equal, quoting Isaiah 45:18, 'Lord made heaven, God made earth', to prove his point.[64] He tells his listeners that if they understand this, they will be ready for battle with the heretics. At the end of the homily (which contained almost no references to the martyr Phocas), he provides a summary, telling his listeners that they should be able to reiterate his points when talking with others: 'If [the person you converse with is] a heretic, you set them straight, if it's a friend who's lazy, you drag them along, if it's an incorrigible wife, you make her more modest.'[65]

---

[59] Asterius *Hom.* 12 on Stephen (Datema 12.13.1, trans. B. Dehandschutter 2003: 183).
[60] Asterius *Hom.* 12 on Stephen (Datema 12.13.2, trans. B. Dehandschutter 2003: 184); Acts 6:10.
[61] John Chrys. *Hom. de S. Phoca* 8 (*PG* 50: 703).
[62] John Chrys. *Hom. de S. Phoca* 8 (*PG* 50: 703).
[63] John Chrys. *Hom. de S. Phoca* 8–9 (*PG* 50: 703–4).
[64] John Chrys. *Hom. de S. Phoca* 9 (*PG* 50: 704).
[65] John Chrys. *Hom. de S. Phoca* 12 (*PG* 50: 706). Earlier in *Hom. de S. Phoca*, 4, Chrysostom encourages people to take up their battle array against heretics, and to pursue heretics verbally

A Brief Dispute with a Pagan

One of the homilies by Gregory of Nyssa depicts a brief discussion between the soon-to-be-martyr Theodore and a soldier who mocked him. This discussion might reflect the tenor of theological discussions among ordinary people. In Gregory's account, after Theodore had been arrested, another soldier asked him, contemptuously, 'Theodore, has your God a Son? Does he beget, just like man, with passion?' Theodore replied that this was not the case, and added, 'You, however, O pitiable man with the intellect of a child, don't you blush or hide due to your confession in a female god and your veneration for her, a mother of twelve children, a kind of very fertile goddess who just like a hare or a sow effortlessly conceives and gives birth!'[66] This brief exchange does not quite reach the level of an eloquent, reasoned theological disputation, but it was considered heroic. The retort offered the congregation at the martyr's festival a model for expressing and defending their religious beliefs. Other references in these martyr homilies hint at disputations among ordinary people outside church. When Chrysostom remarks that the Greeks would laugh about the idea of people performing miracles after they had been buried, he implies that Christians discussed these matters with others. Chrysostom goes on to explain that God gave the relics power in order to teach people that a better life awaits us after death.[67] Again, it is clear that there was no clear distinction between theological discussions and popular religion.

Conclusions

Sermons presented to crowds at martyr festivals include a range of concepts, including some that would typically be considered 'theology' and others 'popular religion'. It could be argued that these events were so crowded and noisy that few people would have heard the sermons. The preachers complained about the noise and about how people were easily distracted from the religious content of the events. But, they also

---

(*PG* 50: 700–1). In *Hom. in S. Lucianum* 9 (*PG* 50: 526), Chrysostom encourages people 'let us confess the faith with boldness. Let us mock their error.'

[66] Gr. Nys. *Hom. in S. Theodoro* (*GNO* 64). In the following passage, Gregory tells us that when Theodore was briefly freed from jail, he took the opportunity to burn down a temple of the mother goddess.

[67] *Hom. de S. Babyla* 2 (*SC* 362: 296).

expressed confidence that some people were listening and hoped that the listeners would encourage other Christians. It is reasonable to assume that these well-known religious leaders, famous for their oratory, would have attracted the attention of many of the people who gathered to listen to them. The content of their homilies, especially when studied within the social context of the martyr festivals, demonstrate that there was no distinction between theology and popular religion. Based on the concepts presented in these martyr sermons, it does not seem that popular engagement in theological controversies must have relied on the memorization of slogans. Rather, many ordinary people had some background on various theological issues, either from sermons or from discussions of these topics outside official church gatherings. There is no indication that devotion to the martyrs was separate from other aspects of Christian teachings. Theological and scriptural explanations did not operate independent of popular beliefs about relics, healing and divine protection; instead, all of these beliefs were part of the common culture. The educated theologians were not isolated from the laypeople. Although these church authorities did not approve of popular discussions of the most controversial topics, they continued to present theological concepts to the public and even encouraged independent discussions.

These sermons and martyr festivals do not indicate that there was a clear separation between natural, popular religion versus unintuitive theology. Whether this sort of distinction is made in terms of cognitive science, or in reference to elite versus popular culture, it does not square with these accounts of martyr festivals. In order to conceive of theology as separate from the rest of religious life, theology must exclude concepts that were understood and accepted by many. But, in many of these cases, discussions of the Trinity by some of the most highly regarded Church Fathers were presented to the crowds gathered at martyrs' shrines. Distinctions between elite and popular culture, between theology and popular religion, or between cognitively natural and unnatural aspects of religion do not hold up when they are tested by these historically contextualized examples of popular theological discussions in Late Antiquity.

14 | Communication and Plebeian Sociability in Late Antiquity: The View from North Africa in the Age of Augustine

JULIO CESAR MAGALHÃES DE OLIVEIRA

Introduction

The question of 'popular culture' is one of power relations. Even defined in the seemingly most neutral terms as 'the culture of the non-elite' or 'the forms of thinking and acting of the politically or economically subordinate groups',[1] the concept should still not be dissociated from more general considerations regarding the relations of power and cultural domination in society at large. In practice, however, historians of popular culture have not always escaped the double temptation, well summarized by Roger Chartier, of seeing the cultures of the common people either as totally independent from or as totally determined by dominant cultures.[2]

The first problem with these diametrically opposed conceptions is that both fail to recognize the deeply contradictory condition of any subordinate group, and even of each of its members. As Antonio Gramsci once observed, the 'man-in-the-mass' has not one but

> two theoretical consciousnesses (or one contradictory consciousness): one which is implicit in his activity and which in reality unites him with all his fellow-workers in the practical transformation of the real world; and one, superficially explicit or verbal, which he has inherited from the past and uncritically absorbed.[3]

What this notion of 'contradictory consciousness' stresses is that any subordinate group, according to its social and material experiences, can effectively create its own conception of the world and translate it into

---

I am grateful to Lucy Grig for the invitation to publish in this book the communication presented at the conference 'Locating Popular Culture in the Ancient World'. Much gratitude goes to her, as well as to Pedro Paulo Funari, Carlos Galvão-Sobrinho, Silvia Heshiki, Claude Lepelley, Carlos Machado, Monica Selvatici, Kostas Vlassopoulos and an anonymous reader from Cambridge University Press for their generous comments on the text, and for references and corrections.
I would also like to express my thanks for the comments and suggestions of the audience at the conference, particularly those of Cristina Rosillo-López and Jerry Toner. However, I am solely responsible for the errors and idiosyncrasies that still persist.

[1] The quoted definitions are respectively that of Burke 2009: xiii; and Beik 1993: 213.
[2] Chartier 1993.   [3] Gramsci 1971: 333.

traditions and practices. But the concept also reminds us that, at the same time and precisely because they are not hegemonic, the cultures of the subaltern classes are never self-defined, and neither are they immune from external influences.[4]

Another still more fundamental problem behind the duality of the complete 'autonomy' or the complete 'encapsulation' of popular culture is a tacit conception of cultural forms as whole and coherent. For most anthropologists and historians, culture has been defined as 'a system of shared meanings, attitudes and values, and the symbolic forms (performances, artefacts) in which they are embodied'.[5] But, as E. P. Thompson wrote:

a culture is also a pool of diverse resources, in which traffic passes between the literate and the oral, the superordinate and the subordinate, the village and the metropolis; it is an arena of conflictual elements, which requires some compelling pressure – as, for example, nationalism, or prevalent religious orthodoxy or class consciousness – to take form as a 'system'.[6]

In this light, we should rather see culture as an 'ambience' or, in Pierre Bourdieu's term, as a *habitus*, a set of cultivated dispositions that could be adapted and employed by different actors, for different performances and in different times and places.[7]

Conscious of these problems, some historians and social theorists have promoted an important shift of emphasis, a shift that can be described, in the words of Peter Burke, as 'the most important contribution to the popular culture debate since the 1970s'.[8] Instead of classifying the objects of culture along previously established lines, these scholars have been more concerned about its uses, appropriations and adaptations by different groups and for different purposes. According to Michel de Certeau, 'popular culture' would be conceived not as a corpus, but as the 'arts of making' this or that and, in particular, as the 'popular' ways of using an imposed system.[9] In a similar way, Stuart Hall has insisted that, because the meaning of a cultural symbol is given in part by the social field in which it is incorporated, what matters in the study of popular culture are '*not* the intrinsic or historically fixed objects of culture, but the state of play in cultural relations: to put it bluntly and in an oversimplified form – what counts is the class struggle in and over culture'.[10]

---

[4] On the Gramscian concepts of 'cultural hegemony' and 'contradictory consciousness', see Lears 1985.
[5] Burke 2009: xiii. On anthropological definitions of culture, see Kuper 1999.
[6] Thompson 1991: 6.   [7] Bourdieu 1977: 72 (*habitus*); Thompson 1993: 102 ('ambience').
[8] Burke 2009: 14.   [9] Certeau 1984: xi–xxiii, 15–41.   [10] Hall 1981: 235.

The objective of this chapter is to explore the implications of this approach for the study of plebeian forms of communication and everyday sociability in late Roman cities, as expressed in our sources, and more specifically in the works of St Augustine. As we shall see, the realm of plebeian sociability (understood here in the sociological sense of the French word *sociabilité*, as the networks of interpersonal relations and the forms taken by these relations)[11] was neither a world of its own, nor the simple by-product of the culture of the elite. On the contrary, phenomena like rumour and gossip, popular songs and chants, the public readings of books and pamphlets, and the brief or enduring forms of popular association (for friendship and conviviality, as well as for social protest) were all shaped in an arena of conflicting interests. Yet even when mobilized and exploited by the social, political or religious elites of the time, such channels of popular communication, association and protest could never be entirely controlled from above. This is because the everyday practices of plebeian sociability not only allowed the common people to express their own concerns; they also enabled them to adapt, transform and even subvert any cultural product that the members of the elite wished to diffuse in a popular milieu.

The Roots of Plebeian Sociability

Let us start by defining the wider context in which these everyday practices of communication and social interaction among plebeians had developed, beginning with the formative experiences of plebeian life.

The ancient Mediterranean town was always linked to its agricultural base. Small wonder, then, that its primary economic activities consisted, at all times, in the processing and redistribution of the products of agriculture and pastoralism, and in the intensification of production in various ways.[12] However, until the Hellenistic period, much urban productive activity had been limited in scale and contained within the framework of the patriarchal household.[13] The integration of these relatively autonomous, 'face-to-face' societies into the wider structures of the Hellenistic kingdoms and ultimately of the Roman Empire was therefore not without consequences. To begin with, these wider horizons progressively replaced the traditional embedded exchange networks with the more market-oriented, large-scale

---

[11] Rivière 2004.   [12] Purcell 1994: 658–9; Horden and Purcell 2000: 108; 263–9, 354–9.
[13] On archaic Rome, see Cornell 1995: 284–8.

economy of the Empire.[14] The influx of wealth to Rome and Italy promoted by Roman expansion and, later, the reversal of this tendency with the rise of provincial economies, resulted in a growing specialization of labour and in the spreading of high-quality goods widely in society.[15] As a consequence of this, urban production was progressively emancipated from its former patriarchal household framework, when even activities that had been treated as a domestic service became a trade and many others were created to supply the expanding middle and lower markets.[16] This is what we can see from the archaeological record in the development of the continuous rows of *tabernae* as a hallmark of Roman urbanism[17] or in the expansion in many towns, notably harbour cities, of entire districts of workshops and commercial activity interspersed with densely packed low-status housing.[18] The growth of urbanization and the increase in population, with its related problems of sanitation, mortality and disease, and the intensified monetization of the urban economy, with its imperative to earn cash and the risks derived from debt, also implied that the majority of the urban population came to be united by the shared experience of insecurity and instability, given greater opportunities for personal advancement, but living under the constant threat of impoverishment.[19]

The impact of these developments on the behaviour and values of the urban populace was twofold. On the one hand, the growth of urban production and retail activity in specialized establishments and the plebeian emancipation from the households of the elite implied that the forms of paternalistic control over the subaltern classes no longer extended to the entire life of the working population. In fact, however pervasive the economic domination of aristocratic patrons might have remained, the majority of ordinary inhabitants of cities came to work and live outside any direct control by social superiors.[20] The model of the 'big house' offered by Ariès and employed by Wallace-Hadrill to characterize the Pompeian houses as the crucial focal points in urban life 'where friends, clients, relatives and protégés could meet and talk',[21] is not at all appropriate for

---

[14] On the 'disembedding' of the economy after the Roman conquest, see Fentress 2006. On the market-oriented economy of the Empire, see Temin 2006.
[15] Ward-Perkins 2005: 87–137.
[16] A transformation recognized by the Romans themselves: Pliny, *HN* 13.107; 7.211 (the appearance of bakers and barbers in Rome after the third century BCE).
[17] Purcell 1994: 659–73; MacMahon 2003, 2006. [18] Wilson 2002.
[19] Purcell 1994: 678; Brown 2002: 15.
[20] See Alston and Alston 1997 (for the example of cities in Roman Egypt); and Flohr 2007 (for the case of Pompeii).
[21] Wallace-Hadrill 1994: 91, quoting Ariès 1962: 391–2.

the understanding of a Roman world in which all forms of plebeian sociability came to be located *outside* the household, in the streets, taverns, shops and places of entertainment.[22]

On the other hand, the insecurity that pervaded plebeian life also infused in various ways the cultural horizons of the mass of the populace. The popularity of gaming and gambling, for instance, epitomized the hopes of the urban poor for survival and advancement, as well as their insouciance in taking risk.[23] Gladiators and charioteers became popular heroes in large measure because they could reflect attributes of strength, skill and endurance that the common people needed to survive in cities.[24] The very pursuit of pleasure in public places might be viewed as a way found by the ordinary inhabitants of cities to counterweight the precariousness of their existence.[25] While we may assume that many of these aspirations stemmed from pressures favouring competition in city life, it is this same context that encouraged cooperation by neighbourhood groups and fellow-workers among plebeians.[26] This is what we can see, above all, in the proliferation in Rome and across the Empire of the various kinds of voluntary associations of employees, craftsmen and tradesmen, all of whom provided a measure of mutual support and a sense of belonging for these otherwise unstable groups.[27]

Aristocratic Hegemony, Plebeian Culture

There is little doubt, therefore, that these structural factors contributed to fostering a popular culture of discussion and sociability throughout the imperial period. We must not forget, however, that plebeian cultural practices only took shape defensively and in a continuing tension, at the same time accommodating and resisting the limits imposed by aristocratic domination. Let us consider the nature of these constraints.

Already by the second century BCE, the forms of power and authority promoted by the aristocracy in Rome and the local elites in other Roman cities came to be founded on their proper use of money and time to the

---

[22] See Courrier in this volume.   [23] Purcell 1995; Toner 1995: 89–10; 2009: 30–1 and 110–11.
[24] Toner 2009: 115–16. For the different images of gladiators construed in elite and popular milieux, see Funari 1989: 40–2, 63–6; Garraffoni and Funari 2008.
[25] Funari 1989: 18–19; Purcell 1994: 678–87. On popular coping strategies, see Toner 2009: 11–53.
[26] On cooperation in the work process, see Marichal 1986.
[27] On this 'associative phenomenon', see De Robertis 1955. For Rome, see Flambard 1981; Purcell 1994: 673–80; and Lott 2004. On Italy and Gaul, see Tran 2006 and the texts assembled in Dondin-Payre and Tran 2012. For the eastern part of the Empire, see Van Nijf 1997.

benefit of the body politic and on their exclusive rights to speak authoritatively in public. From this time forth, popular leisure became constantly criticized as time-wasting in the moralizing discourses of the elite, while the informal meetings of the populace were despised by those in power and seen as unworthy of serious attention.[28] To be sure, by the end of the Roman Republic, within a high level of public debate, some politicians did not hesitate to mobilize popular traditions of speech, association and riot, while the populace themselves grew in self-confidence to assert their demands.[29] However, with the coming of the Principate, political leaders no longer dared to seek power by championing the discontented masses, and new measures to reduce the political power of the urban populace were actively supported by the emperor in the capital, and by local notables elsewhere.[30] Under these new conditions, a highly formalized style of politics in which urban aristocracies exercised a monopoly over public speech was reinforced.[31] Local notables, while selectively accommodating the desires of the populace, insistently attempted to restrict the 'licence of the crowd' to entertainment venues, rendering whole areas of popular activity illegitimate.[32]

Three consequences follow from this dynamic of public speech, which came to characterize city life up to the fourth century. One was the serious limitations imposed on popular speech made in public. In authorized meetings such as the assembly, the court and the shows, popular feeling could be expressed by the crowd's reactions, but communication was always vertical, hierarchical and governed by specific rituals. In theatres and amphitheatres, for example, a visible hierarchy was enforced by law and architecture, and everything was prepared to ensure that the elite entered an audience to be acclaimed.[33] Certainly, as Tacitus wrote, 'in the circus and theatres there was the greatest licence to the crowds'.[34] But this was a licence confined to limits of time and space defined by authorities. It is significant, for example, that the notorious riot led by the

---

[28] Purcell 1995; Toner 1995: 65–88.
[29] Flambard 1977; Nippel 1995: 47–84; Millar 1998: 124–96.
[30] These measures included suppression of pamphleteering: Cass Dio, 55.27.1–3; crackdown on subversion: Suet. *Aug.* 19; Cass. Dio, 55.27.1–3; ban on private societies (and their later, stricter regulation): Suet. *Aug.* 42, Gaius, *Inst.* 3.4.1, with De Robertis 1955; and the co-optation of the Roman neighbourhoods into a new system of civic administration (suppressing their former spontaneous political activity): Lott 2004: 118–20. On the impact of these measures on the life of the urban populace (and especially of slaves and freedpersons), see Galvão-Sobrinho 2012: 141–8.
[31] Brown 1992: 35–58 and 78–89.
[32] O'Neill 2003: 157–62. See Courrier and Hawkins in this volume.
[33] Kolendo 1981; Rawson 1987; Parker 1999.   [34] Tac. *Hist.* 1.72.

silversmiths of Ephesus against Paul could be dispersed by a magistrate under the allegation that those involved in an unauthorized meeting at the theatre would be charged with subversion and attract the retaliation of the Roman power.[35] Under these conditions, a more horizontal, egalitarian popular speech was restricted to the convivial activities of the *collegia*, to the sequestered space of the tavern or to the informal meetings of the *circuli*, the small groups of plebeians which elite sources often describe with scorn and fear precisely because they were not conducted by a member of the elite.[36]

The second consequence of this state of affairs was the restriction of much of the daily expression of popular opinions and criticism to situations that James Scott defined as 'a politics of disguise and anonymity': the forms of communication and expression that take place in public view but that are designed to have a double meaning or to shield the identity of the authors.[37] This is the case with caricatures and jokes, folktales and songs and with rumour and gossip, all of which may be seen as opportunities for the expression of criticisms otherwise hardly ever set forth openly, as well as for the enforcement of social bonds.[38] To take a crucial example: the graffiti found at Pompeii were perhaps no more a vehicle for the expression of class-war sentiments from below than had been Roman graffiti at the time of the Gracchi.[39] They remained, however, a safe medium for the disempowered to laugh at the high and the mighty, to criticize local authorities and even to spread rumours about the workings of the imperial court.[40]

Finally, it is within these same political constraints that the paramilitary politics of the Late Republic gave way, under the Empire, to swift, evanescent direct action as the only real mode of popular protest outside the licensed venues of theatres and arenas. By means of such forms of action, the urban populace continued to express what we might consider a reasoned discontent and a proper sense of outrage when it came to such crucial matters such as the urban food supply.[41] But these kinds of

---

[35] Acts 19: 25–7.
[36] On plebeian *circuli*, see O'Neill 2003. On the *collegia* as a forum for the lower classes, see Scheid 2003.
[37] Scott 1990: 18.
[38] Graphic caricature: Funari 1993, 1999. Songs: Horsfall 2003: 31–47. Rumour and gossip: Rosillo-López 2007 and Pina Polo 2010 (both, however, discussing the role of rumours in the rather different politics of the Late Republic). On the propagation of nicknames, see Rosillo-López in this volume.
[39] See Hillard 2013, and Plut. *TG* 8 (graffiti campaigns for land reform).
[40] See Funari 1993, 1999, and *CIL* 4.4533; 8075; 9226; and 9099.   [41] Erdkamp 2002.

action did not depend on any formal organization to be triggered. They might be seen, therefore, as yet another example of the popular uses of political disguise and anonymity, as discussed by Scott.[42]

The Transformations of Late Antiquity

How much did this situation change in the Later Empire? By the fourth and early fifth centuries, levels of prosperity and population varied across the Empire, but the overall economic circumstances of urban life continued to frame plebeian experiences in the way we described above.[43] In fact, the novelty in Late Antiquity may be found not in any supposedly generalized decline of the Roman economy, but rather in the more troubled political situation of the cities.

The drastic centralization of imperial power, which resulted from the crisis of the third century, did not put an end to self-government by the cities, but aggravated fractures that already existed among the urban upper classes as a result of the unequal distribution of taxes, charges and access to imperial dignities.[44] The outcome, as Peter Brown has observed, was increased infighting among members of the local elites, when competing groups began to derive their status and power from different sources.[45] Some were still attached to the city councils; others were empowered by the exercise of posts on the imperial career ladder.[46] The rise of Christian bishops as figures of authority added yet another new protagonist with whom civic notables had to reckon.[47] With the mounting of the Christian challenge, urban elites also fractured along religious, and then sectarian, lines. When the claims to authority multiplied and different groups and leaders became anxious to put their mark on the cities, the ability to mobilize and assemble the largest possible number of people became increasingly a source of legitimacy.[48] But precisely because urban elites had splintered, urban leaders were also

---

[42] Scott 1990: 151: 'Spontaneity, anonymity, and a lack of formal organization then became enabling modes of protest rather than a reflection on the slender political talents of popular classes.'

[43] Ward-Perkins 1998: 403–9. Regional overviews: Lepelley 1979: 15–36, 1989 (North Africa); Whittow 1990 (eastern Mediterranean); Février 1980 (southern Gaul). For the city of Rome, see Purcell 1999. For the later changes in Mediterranean urban economies, see Wickham 2005: 609–74.

[44] Lepelley 2001. [45] Brown 1992: 19. [46] Millar 1983.

[47] Brown 1992: 71–158; Liebeschuetz 2001: 137–68. [48] Harries 1999; Lim 1999.

forced to compete more than ever before for the allegiance and obedience of the populace.[49]

It is in this context that the aristocratic monopoly of political speech was contested and that new forms of popular power were brought into being. This was especially the case in Christian circles, where these changes were promoted by a new and more assertive type of church leader.[50] The Trinitarian and Christological controversies in the East and the Donatist schism in North Africa provided the inhabitants of cities with many occasions for argument and for confrontation.[51] This, in turn, forced church leaders to work hard to engineer support, expanding preaching and conceiving new forms of mass communication to make the people a partner in these disputes.[52] Unlike traditional aristocracies, therefore, the churchmen of Late Antiquity could no longer attempt only to contain and dismiss the traditional popular culture of discussion and sociability. They were also required to actively engage and transform it. But, precisely because the common people were given greater cultural space in this relationship, the plebeian forms of communication and expression were also continuously threatening to break out of their subaltern role.

The Evidence from Augustine

To illustrate how the traditional culture of plebeian sociability came to be mobilized, energized and exploited under these new conditions, not only by church leaders but also by the plebeians themselves, we may now turn from these more general arguments to the specific example of Augustine, the bishop of the coastal city of Hippo and one of the most combative leaders in the religious struggles that divided Roman Africa in his day.

Augustine exemplifies, above all, how church leaders in Late Antiquity were prepared to acknowledge and understand plebeian habits and attitudes, if only to transform them. Preaching at Hippo, Carthage and other cities, Augustine was often compelled to recognize how spectacles and games remained a distinctive feature of urban life and immensely dear to the people. For instance, when speaking to an urban audience, he was well aware that the very word 'allegory' would be understood as a reference to the pantomime.[53] In his own congregation, he knew that everyone had

---

[49] Brown 1992: 19–20; Purcell 1999: 146–9. [50] Galvão-Sobrinho 2013. Cf. Shaw 2011: 141–5.
[51] Brown 1992: 89. See also Maxwell in this volume. [52] Galvão-Sobrinho 2013: 47–65.
[53] Aug. *En. in Ps.* 103.1.3 (*CCL* 40: 1486).

learnt the story of Aeneas' journey to the Underworld told by Virgil, 'a few from the books, but many from the theatres'.[54] And at least in Carthage, if not in every other city, he did not overlook the fact that the songs of the theatre still set the pace for the work of journeymen in each workshop: 'Do we not know how all workmen give their hearts and tongues to the vanities and even to the filth of theatre-plays when their hands are set to work?'[55]

One must note how such perceptive observations, dictated by the pastoral concern to be understood by all, differed from the more distant, dismissive tropes of traditional elites.[56] To be sure, as a bishop, and one with an ascetic background, Augustine frequently thundered against the vainglory of the rich who sponsored the spectacles and against the spectators who wasted their time in the shows.[57] Time and again, reproducing a well-known *topos*, the bishop condemned the alienating and corrupting effects the spectacles had on the audiences,[58] while presenting the martyrs' stories as a better spectacle.[59] Yet in the carrying out of his routine pastoral duties, attempting to persuade a candidate for baptism to prefer attending church to the shows, Augustine was still capable of recognizing that the emotions evoked by the spectacles had important societal functions for their participants:

For if in public spectacles you wished to be in friendly company and to attach yourself closely to men who are united with you in a love for some charioteer, or some hunter, or some player, how much more ought you to find pleasure in associating with those who are at one with you in loving God.[60]

Not only does this passage show how mass spectacles encouraged social interaction, but it also allows one to infer a measure of continuity between those festive moments and everyday practices of sociability. As Augustine observed, the crowds of spectators in the shows were composed not of atomized individuals but of groups, whose members, even if not familiar with one another, were at any rate guided by a common sense of belonging and by the pleasure of being together.

---

[54] Aug. *Serm.* 241.5 (*PL* 38: 1135–6).
[55] Aug. *De op. monach.* 17. 20 (*PL* 40: 565), trans. Horsfall 2003: 16: 'An ignoramus, omnes opifices in quibus vanitatibus et plerumque etiam turpitudinibus theatricarum fabularum donent corda et linguas suas, cum manus ab opere non recedant?'
[56] MacCormack 2001.   [57] Hugoniot 1992: 11–21; Lugaresi 2007.   [58] Lim 1996.
[59] Grig 2004: 34–53.
[60] Aug. *De cat. Rud.* 25. 49 (*CCL* 46: 172–3): 'Nam si in spectaculis cum illis esse cupiebas et eis inhaerere, qui tecum vel aurigam, vel venatorem, vel aliquem histrionem simul amabant: quanto magis te delectare debet eorum coniunctio qui tecum amant Deum.'

In this, Augustine was not alone among his peers. The bishops assembled in council at Carthage in 401, for example, recognized these same continuities between the shows and the everyday forms of popular association. In a petition addressed to the emperors to avoid the coincidence of public entertainments with the holidays of the church, they justified their demand: 'above all because we must consider the pressures of *corporati* who, against the precepts of God, force each other with great fear to come together to the spectacles'.[61] These *corporati* might be 'partners' in the wide sense, but it is also possible to think of the members of the *corpora*. The *corpora* (or *collegia*) were the carefully organized associations of craftsmen and tradesmen, which remained important focuses for conviviality in Late Antiquity.[62] In many cities, these associations had seats reserved in theatres and amphitheatres where their members could present themselves as a recognizable group.[63]

Augustine did not overlook the significance of these professional associations.[64] But, when discussing the everyday forms of popular association, he seems to have been more concerned about what anthropologists define as 'non-corporate groups': the informal networks of friends or acquaintances and the more intimate but often temporary coalitions formed out of them.[65] This is what we can see in his observations about the connections established by the urban poor in various places of sociability. In his manual for the instruction of the uneducated, for example, he observed that there were poor persons that 'just want to have fun and lie in bars, whorehouses, theatres and to enjoy common shows that they can have for free in big cities':

In this way, they either consume their own slender resources in this luxurious living and then, because of their poverty and need, they advance to robberies, breaking and entering, and even to brazen banditry. Suddenly they are filled with many great fears: those who only recently sang songs in the bars are now sleeping in the noisy din of the prison.[66]

---

[61] *Reg. Eccl. Carth. Excerpt.* 61 (*CCL* 149: 197): 'Corporatorum enim maxime periculum considerandum est qui contra praecepta Dei magno terrore coguntur ad spectacula convenire.'
[62] Carrié 2002b. [63] Roueché 1993: 120–8. [64] Note Aug. *Ep.* 22*.2 (*CSEL* 88: 114).
[65] Boissevain 2013: 115–27.
[66] Aug. *De cat. Rud.* 16.25.7–8 (*CCL* 46: 149–50), trans. Shaw 2011: 457: 'Sunt autem homines, qui nec divites quaerunt esse nec ad vanas honorum pompas ambiunt pervenire, sed gaudere et requiescere volunt in popinis et in fornicationibus et in theatris atque spectaculis nugacitatis, quae in magnis civitatibus gratis habent. Sed sic etiam ipsi aut consumunt per luxuriam paupertatem suam, aut ab egestate postea in furta et effracturas et aliquando etiam in latrocinia prosiliunt, et subito multis et magnis timoribus implentur; et qui in popina paulo ante cantabant, iam planctus carceris somniant.'

As Shaw pointed out, through the heavy moralizing of this passage, 'it is possible to see the association between the raucous bonding of young males and paths that led to various kinds of collective violence'.[67] On other occasions, the bishop still recognized that one of the major attractions of the tavern was precisely this sort of camaraderie: just as the fans of a performer loved each other at the shows, so too did those who drank together in bars.[68]

The criticisms of Augustine against the world of the tavern were focused mainly on the disorderly behaviour of tavern customers and on the songs and excessive drinking that strengthened their ties to one another. But the tavern was also a place for free-speaking and irreverent chatter, a fact that was often seen with anxiety by political authorities. We are told, for example, by Ammianus Marcellinus that the Caesar Gallus himself once roamed in disguise around the taverns of Antioch to enquire what people actually thought about him.[69] For Augustine, however, the *platea* (the square or the colonnaded street) was the main focus for conversations among male friends, just as the *domus* (the house) was the locus of exchanges between husband and wife.[70] Making this comment to an audience, he did not fail to notice that it was in these settings that his own teachings would be discussed and contested.[71] On another instance, Augustine warned his parishioners not to take part in the banquets and festivities of the New Year. But he knew that on leaving the church they were going to meet their friends *in plateis*, that is, in the streets or squares of the town. The problem was that, in the conversations they would have, they would find many 'shameless and bad advisers'.[72]

The centrality of these open-air gatherings is characteristic of a Mediterranean society where people spent a large part of their lives in outdoor activities.[73] In fourth-century Rome, for example, Ammianus made a similar observation, noting 'the many circles gathered together in the fora, at the crossroads, in the streets and other meeting-places in which

---

[67] Shaw 2011: 457.
[68] Aug. *Serm.* 332.1 (*PL* 38: 1461): 'Diligunt invicem qui histriones simul spectant, diligunt invicem qui simul se in popinis inebriant.'
[69] Amm. Marc. 14.1.9.
[70] A gendered division of space that was recurrent in North African history: Brett and Fentress 1996: 231–70.
[71] Aug. *En. in Ps.* 93.20 (*CCL* 39: 1322): 'Et hoc forte non in platea tibi dicit amicus, sed in domo uxor, aut forte maritus uxori fideli bonae et sanctae, deceptor ipsius.'
[72] Aug. *Serm.* Dolbeau 26.7 (Dolbeau 1996a: 372): 'Atque utinam in solis plateis patiamini improbos dissuasores, et non forte in domibus vestris!'
[73] Boissevain 2013: 122.

people were engaged with one another in quarrelsome strife'.[74] Augustine, however, was making a more crucial point. For him, the unsupervised conversations in outdoor 'circles' were important (and potentially dangerous) because they could attract his parishioners away from their discipline to participate in various kinds of collective action, from the festivities he could not control to the open riot. Already as a priest, when he abolished the songs and drinking associated with the festivities of St Leontius, he noted to a friend that it was in these conversations that the opposition to his measures was first formed.[75] Later, as a bishop, he would comment in a more positive manner on the discussions that were held in these circles:

Brethren, see how it is when a feast of the martyrs or some holy place is mentioned, to which crowds might flow to hold high festival. See how they stir each other up, and say: 'Let us go, let us go.' And each one asks the other: 'Where to?' They say: 'To that place, that holy place.' They speak to each other, and as if each one of them were set alight, they form together one single blaze.[76]

What Augustine underscores in this passage is a lesson that modern scholars have realized only with great difficulty: that communication, especially by word of mouth, is never a 'pure' exchange of signs.[77] When interlocutors share information, they are simultaneously sharing values, identity, memory and everything that makes the social bond.[78] Even the spread of rumours and gossip, which earlier scholars tended to associate with a pathological state of mind, cannot be understood outside this social framework. After all, the bearer of a rumour does not just say anything, to anyone and at any time, but only in the context of a social relationship which is suitable for the exchange of confidences.[79] It is this sentiment of being together and among partners that Augustine noted in the extract cited above. In this specific case, the exchange of news in a circle of friends was clearly motivated by their desire to feast together and be together. But these same practices of communication could equally be employed in a much more tense situation to give voice to a common fear, anger or hatred.[80]

---

[74] Amm. Marc. 28.4.29: 'et videre licet per fora et compita et plateas et conventicula, circulos multos collectos in se controversis iurgiis ferri.'

[75] Aug. *Ep.* 29.8 (*CSEL* 34: 119), to Alypius of Thagaste. See Brown 1981: 26 and 34–5.

[76] Aug. *En. in Ps.* 121.2 (*CCL* 40: 1802), trans. Brown 2000a: 452–3: 'Fratres, veniat in mentem Caritati vestrae, si qua forte festivitas martyrum et locus aliquis sanctus nominatur, quo certo die turbae confluant ad celebrandam solemnitatem; illae turbae quomodo se exsuscitant, quomodo se hortantur et dicunt: Eamus, eamus. Et quaerunt: Quo eamus? Et dicitur: Ad illum locum, ad sanctum locum. Invicem sibi loquuntur, et tamquam incensi singillatim faciunt unam flammam.'

[77] Bourdieu 1982. [78] Aldrin 2005: 51. [79] Aldrin 2005: 54, 83–4; Kapferer 2013: 11.

[80] Aldrin 2005: 78.

The popular gatherings in the squares and streets of a town were also important because, as Adam Fox and Robert Darnton have observed for later contexts, they often enabled the overlapping of various kinds of media.[81] It is not a coincidence that Augustine contrasted the discussions of the uneducated in popular gatherings (*in circulis*) with the debates of the educated in the libraries: in both cases, texts of various kinds could be read aloud and commented upon.[82] Take the following example. Augustine once wrote how an anonymous collection of heretical works had been offered for sale by a book dealer and read aloud before 'a crowd of attentive hearers' on the *platea maritima* at Carthage (that is, at the heart of the most important artisanal and commercial districts of the city).[83] The main item of this collection was the work of a Marcionite or other heretic who thought that the God of the Old Testament was not the true God, but a very wicked demon. According to Augustine, the 'brothers' who purchased the book and informed him about it were at the place 'at the same moment that the book on sale was brought to the attention of a crowd gathered by dangerous curiosity and by the pleasure of hearing it read'.[84]

The 'dangerous curiosity' and the 'pleasure of hearing' that Augustine highlights in this passage show well how such popular gatherings were politically significant. Because they were never controlled by the authorities, they allowed plebeians to deliberate freely on any subject. Yet when faced with this challenge, Augustine's reaction was not to deny legitimacy to these popular assemblies, as traditional elites had done, but to write a response intended to be debated in the same popular circles. The result, in this case, was a booklet entitled 'Against an Adversary of the Law and the Prophets', which was explicitly designed to be read aloud and without a break before an audience, at least until the end of the first part, when the reader was invited to rest 'as an exhausted traveller in a hostel', before continuing its reading.[85]

---

[81] Fox 1997; Darnton 2003.

[82] Aug. *De duabus animabus*, 11.15 (*CSEL* 25.1): 'Nonne ista cantant ... et indocti in circulis, et docti in bibliothecis?' On the meaning of *circulus*, see O'Neill 2003: 137.

[83] Aug. *Retract.* 2.58.85 (*CCL* 57: 136). For the location of the *platea maritima*, see Magalhães de Oliveira 2012: 133.

[84] Aug. *Contra adv. legis et prophet.* 1.1.1 (*PL* 42: 603): 'cum venalis codex ipse ferretur et concurrentibus turbis periculosa curiositate et delectatione legeretur, ut quanto possem compendio responderem, prius quaesivi, cuiusnam esset erroris'.

[85] Aug. *Contra adv. legis et prophet.* 1.24.53 (*PL* 42: 636): 'reficitur lectoris intentio, sicut labor viatoris hospitio'.

Mobilizing Popular Culture

Augustine would certainly have preferred to stop such unrestrained popular discussions. As he wrote about the public disputation he once engaged in with Fortunius, the dissident bishop of Thubursicu Numidarum, he wished to keep the debate on religious matters away from the attention of the 'tumultuous mob'.[86] But he knew that this was impossible. It is for this reason that Augustine, like other church leaders in dispute in Africa, decided to resort to the most unconventional methods of diffusion of ideas to manage and control this popular power.[87]

As early as 393, as a recently ordained priest of the minority Catholic church of Hippo, Augustine's first act in combating his most formidable adversaries, the 'Donatist' dissidents, was to compose a popular song, the *Psalmus contra Partem Donati*.[88] The piece was a didactic, polemical sung sermon structured along the pattern of forensic oratory, but composed in rhythmical rather than quantitative verses. It suited the model of the popular ABC-song, with each stanza beginning with a letter of the alphabet and each verse ending in a rhyme. Using a popular idiom, it was intended, in the words of Augustine, 'to reach the knowledge of the very humblest folk and of the inexpert and uninstructed and, as far as I could, make it stick in their memory'.[89] Like the *Thalia* of Arius, more than half a century earlier, what made the *Psalmus* of Augustine attractive to ordinary Christians was not only its rhythm, based on a trochaic pattern reminiscent of the theatrical and popular songs, but its accusatory and argumentative tone that, as Galvão-Sobrinho puts it with respect to the *Thalia*, 'invested the ordinary faithful with authority to teach doctrine'.[90] Indeed, as we can see in the chorus, it was the faithful who were invited to judge the reasons of the dispute and to convert their fellows: 'All of you who take your joy in peace, now is the time to judge what is true.'[91]

---

[86] Aug. *Ep.* 44.1.1 (*CSEL* 34/2: 109–10): 'Cum autem apud eum consedissemus, rumore disperso non parua praeterea turba confluxit. Sed in tota illa multitudine perpauci apparebant, qui utiliter ac salubriter agi causam illam et tantam reique tantae quaestionem prudenter et pie discuti cuperent.'

[87] Brown 2000a: 134, 224; Shaw 2011: 442.

[88] See Nodes 2009; Hunink 2011; and, for the text, Lambot 1935.

[89] Aug. *Retract.* 1.20.19 (*CCL* 57: 61): 'Volens etiam causam Donatistarum ad ipsius humillimi vulgi et omnino imperitorum atque idiotarum notitiam pervenire, et eorum quantum fieri per nos posset inhaerere memoriae, Psalmum qui eis cantaretur per Latinas litteras feci, sed usque ad V litteram.'

[90] Galvão-Sobrinho 2013: 55.

[91] Aug. *Psalmus contra partem Donati*, 1, 7, 20, 33, etc.: 'Omnes qui gaudetis de pace, modo verum iudicate.'

The psalm may have been devised, at first sight, to be sung in church, with the stanzas being psalmodized by one or two singers and the refrain being sung in response by the congregation.[92] But the central preoccupation of Augustine with memorization reflects his awareness that Christian songs, once popularized, could be sung in a wider range of contexts: in private houses and workshops, in the streets and marketplaces, on the road and even in bathhouses.[93] Memorization also ensured that the song could be used in plebeian circles of discussion, where arguments were sometimes chanted in unison, rather than simply verbalized.[94] Finally, we must not forget that psalms and militant songs were also a regular accompaniment to violence in confrontations between Christian factions, as a way to unite and energize the fighters.[95]

Augustine, however, was not the only, nor even the first, African church leader to have composed such songs to instruct and mobilize the simple and uneducated.[96] We know from a later catalogue of heresies that Parmenian, the dissident bishop of Carthage, was already renowned for travelling around Africa in the 380s or early 390s spreading the new psalms he was composing against the Catholics.[97] Augustine himself would later comment to his parishioners that several of his own co-religionists were also composing new ABC-psalms in both Latin and Punic.[98] In fact, as Shaw points out, the composition of these popular songs is the clearest testimony of the crucial adjustments that church leaders would necessarily have to make in order to be able to communicate in a popular style in the context of a sectarian war.[99]

This preoccupation with the instruction of ordinary Christians and the need for them to memorize the Catholic arguments later led Augustine, now bishop, to write a series of pamphlets and pastoral tracts for wide distribution. Again, Augustine was far from the first to have resorted to this

---

[92] Hunink 2011: 400.

[93] Shaw 2011: 445. For the singing of psalms in the lavatory, see Aug. *De ord.* 1.8.22–3 (*CCL* 29: 99–100) (Licentius in the outhouse at Cassiciacum).

[94] See, for example, the disputations by rhythmic chanting between Christians and non-Christians in front of the closed temple of the goddess Caelestis in Carthage described by Quodvultdeus, *Liber de promissionis*, 3.38.44 (*SC* 102: 574–6).

[95] Aug. *Ep.* 185.27 (*CSEL* 57: 26): 'Deinde cum ab eis tandem relictum nostri cum psalmis auferre temptarent, illi ira ardentiore succensi eum de portantium manibus abstulerunt male mulcatis fugatisque Catholicis.' Cf. Shaw 2011: 442–3.

[96] Monceaux 1905: 451–97; Shaw 2011: 475–89.

[97] 'Praedestinatus', *Liber de haeresibus*, 1.44 (Oehler 1856: 247): 'Parmenianos a Parmeniano, qui per totam Africam libros contra nos conficiens et novos psalmos faciens circumibat, contra quem noster scripsit Optatus.'

[98] Aug. *En. 32 in Ps.* 118.8 (*CCL* 40: 1775–6).   [99] Shaw 2011: 477.

stratagem to mobilize the mass of ordinary Christians.[100] Since the very beginning of the schism, the imperial government had been forced to take repeated measures to control the spread of polemical written pamphlets by African Christians. These measures included the search and seizure of anonymous 'defamatory pamphlets' and their destruction by fire.[101] Augustine himself was often provoked to write in response to initiatives taken by his enemies. On one occasion, a dissident layman named Centurius came to the Catholic basilica at Hippo and put one of these chapbooks in his hands. The anonymous pamphlet, 'recorded under dictation or directly composed by its author', contained a brief and sharp defence of the dissident cause against the Catholics. It received from Augustine, an equally brief and sharp reply, in the same genre.[102]

As this example clearly shows, the crucial importance of these kinds of texts is that they could be quickly produced and widely distributed with the aid of the laymen themselves. This was a lesson that Augustine explicitly considered on another occasion, as he recounts in his *Retractationes*:

> Seeing that difficulty in reading prevented many people from learning how the party of Donatus lacked all logic and truth, I wrote a really short booklet in which I thought to instruct them only about the Maximianists. The ease of copying this booklet could send it into the hands of more people and, through its brevity, it could more easily be committed to memory.[103]

Here we can see how the dissemination of certain types of texts could be achieved even by relatively uneducated people, who not only learnt them by heart, but even recopied them for friends and neighbours. The extent to which people of Roman times could read and write has long been debated in scholarship.[104] But there is little doubt that, at least in towns and cities,

---

[100] Shaw 2011: 433–5.

[101] Measures against *libelli*: *CTh* 9.34.2 (Constantine to Aelianus, Proconsul of Africa, posted in Carthage on 25 February 315); *CTh* 9.34.1 (Constantine to Verinus, vicar of Africa, 29 March 319); *CTh* 9.34.3 (Constantine to Januarius, vicar, 4 December 320); *CTh* 9.34.5 (Constantius to the Africans, 18 June 338); *CTh* 9.34.6 (Constantius to the people, 21 October 355). On the first pamphlet wars between Donatists and Catholics, see Aug. *Ep.* 43.5.15; 88.2; and 93.4.13 (pamphlets against Caecilian at Carthage).

[102] Aug. *Retract.* 2.19.46 (*CCL* 57: 105): 'Cum adversus partem Donati multa crebris disputationibus ageremus, attulit ad ecclesiam quidam laicus tunc eorum nonnulla contra nos dictata vel scripta in paucis velut testimoniis, quae sua causa suffragari putant; his brevissime respondi. Huius libelli titulus est: Contra quod attulit Centurius a Donatistis.'

[103] Aug. *Retract.* 2.29.56 (*CCL* 57: 114): 'Cum viderem multos legendi labore impediri a discendo, quam nihil rationis atque veritatis habeat pars Donati, libellum brevissimum feci, quo eos de solis Maximianistis admonendos putavi, ut posset facilitate describendi in manus plurium pervenire, et ipsa sui brevitate facilius commendari memoriae.'

[104] Harris 1989; Humphrey 1991; Woolf 2000; Ward-Perkins 2005: 151–67. See also the Introduction to this volume.

people of various backgrounds participated in elementary education and that even the illiterate had recourse to a network of literates: the ubiquitous scribe, a relative, a friend, or a slave in a nearby household.[105] Indeed, the effectiveness of pamphlets could only be understood in relation to these informal networks of acquaintances.

The central preoccupation of Augustine with the memorization of his arguments is also a clue to the most common context in which these texts were used by ordinary Christians: in public readings and informal discussions among the faithful of different confessions who, as we have already seen, gathered in the squares and streets of North African cities. That pamphlets were mainly read and discussed in such open-air gatherings is also confirmed by the decision of Augustine in 405 to respond to an anonymous pamphlet that attacked the Catholics for having recently benefited from the confiscations of Donatist properties. In reply, Augustine not only composed his own pamphlet to justify the moral grounds of these seizures, but also ordered the text to be posted on the walls of the Donatist basilica recently seized by the Catholics, where the laypeople could meet to read it or hear it being read.[106]

It is with an eye to these open-air meetings of ordinary Christians that Augustine resorted to what Peter Brown has described as a 'journalistic style' in his preaching against the Donatists: that is, the constant recourse in his sermons to caricaturing his rivals and the diffusion of theological arguments in the form of a commentary on contemporary events.[107] This can be seen in the way he exploited the events of 393–4, which marked the Donatist leaders' suppression of Maximian's schism inside their camp.[108] Augustine made the most of official documents and stories of violence to prove that the Donatists, too, persecuted their own dissidents, but in the end reabsorbed most of the Maximianist bishops without rebaptism.[109] He even went on to detail the public humiliation of one of these bishops, who (it was said) had been forced to dance with a necklace of dead dogs around his neck.[110] The same can be said of the manner in which he publicized the brutality of the 'Circumcellions', the organized men of violence who sometimes cooperated with the Donatist church to enforce its aims. By narrating their 'atrocities' in the most sordid

---

[105] Botha 2012: 65–6. On the learning of letters in public and outside school, see Garraffoni and Laurence 2013.
[106] Aug. *Retract.* 2.27.53 (*CCL* 57: 112–13): 'Illa vero documenta quae promiseram, eidem libello quod eadem promiseram iunxi, et ex utroque unum esse volui; eumque edidi, ut in parietibus basilicae quae Donatistarum fuerat, prius propositus legeretur.'
[107] Brown 2000a: 224.   [108] De Veer 1965.   [109] Aug. *En. 2 in Ps.* 36 (*CCL* 38).
[110] Aug. *Contra ep. Parm.* 3.6.29 (*CSEL* 51: 139). See Shaw 2011: 131–9.

detail, Augustine amplified what were at best specific and isolated incidents.[111]

These were all rhetorical strategies deliberately intended to ensure the spread of rumours. The recourse to this weapon had a long history in African sectarian wars. Right from the beginning of the schism, the leaders of the parties in dispute had not hesitated to resort to a rumour campaign in order to undermine the credibility of their opponents. On one occasion, a merchant acting on behalf of the party of Donatus had been responsible for spreading rumours against Caecilian and those who consecrated him in markets and fairs in every locality of Numidia and Mauretania through which he passed for trade.[112] Preachers like Augustine were well aware that news communicated by sermons could be spread in a similar manner by the informal channels of exchange among the populace, who spread and discussed what they had heard.[113] Therefore, by presenting shocking revelations about his sectarian enemies, a bishop could activate, with an example drawn from immediate reality, a common, but often dormant, imaginary of hatred for 'the other' among the faithful. But, once again, the strategies of church leaders only worked because they could mobilize existing popular practices of social interaction.

Of course, these were all risky strategies, and not only because they could be employed by one's own rivals, as can we see in the accusations made against Augustine of being a covert Manichee.[114] These strategies were also dangerous because no Christian leader could ever be sure what the people would do with the messages broadcast in popular gatherings. This was implicitly recognized by Augustine himself in a sermon recently discovered by François Dolbeau and dated to 416, at the turning point of another controversy: the debate on grace between the bishop of Hippo and the British monk Pelagius.[115]

---

[111] Brown 2000a: 224–5. On the Augustinian rhetoric against the 'Circumcellions', see also Shaw 2011: 630–74.

[112] *Acta purgationis Felicis*, 28b (*CSEL* 26: 203): 'Apronianus dixit: dignare de eo quaerere, qua auctoritate, quo dolo, qua insania circuierit Mauritanias omnes, Numidias etiam, qua ratione seditionem commoverit catholicae ecclesiae. Aelianus proconsul dixit: ad Numidias fuisti? Respondit: non, domine, sit, qui probet. Aelianus proconsul dixit: nec in Mauritania? Respondit: negotiari ille fui.'

[113] Shaw 2011: 411, quoting Aug. *Ep. ad Cath. contra Donatist.* 18.47 (*CSEL* 52: 293): 'non in sermonibus et rumoribus Afrorum, non in conciliis episcoporum suorum, non in litteris quorumlibet disputatorum'.

[114] BeDuhn 2009.

[115] Dolbeau 1995, 1999. On the Pelagian controversy, see now Salamito 2005. On Augustine's preaching during this controversy, see Dupont 2012.

It was the first time Augustine had attacked Pelagius by name in a liturgical assembly. Hitherto he had denounced the 'new heresy' without naming the author, out of respect for him. But, as Augustine explained to his hearers, this time, in view of the serious news he had received from Palestine after the acquittal of Pelagius by the Synod of Diospolis, this reserve was no longer appropriate:

Why do I want to deliver this information to your faith? Because major problems seem to have occurred in Jerusalem and from there we have received very distressing news: two monasteries in Bethlehem seem even to have been burned in a popular uprising. I would not have told you that, if I had not known that the news had already reached some of you. It was better for you to hear all the facts from me, rather than being wounded by secret rumours.[116]

Rumours are always a sort of 'improvised news', developed in situations in which the demand for news is unsatisfied.[117] As a product of collective deliberation, they passed on news that official channels did not offer or were supposed to conceal. Rumours, indeed, reveal secrets.[118] But the extent of their spread depends on the ability of the habitual 'truth-holders' to authenticate, or conversely to disqualify, the veracity of this news.[119] The public response of Augustine in 416 was precisely an attempt to satisfy, through the authority of the pulpit, the demand for news of his parishioners, who had previously only been informed via *informal* channels of the news that circulated from the port of Hippo. The danger for Augustine was that the news about the acquittal of Pelagius would be viewed by the people as giving legitimacy to the arguments of Pelagius' followers. In response to this threat, the best the bishop could offer to the faithful was to alert them to how the Pelagian teachings threatened their most cherished traditions of piety, such as the benedictions and prayers, by rendering them useless.[120]

However, if the news of the Palestinian riots so distressed Augustine, it was also because they made him realize how unsupervised discussions in plebeian circles could potentially lead to autonomous popular action: the riots of Palestine could be repeated at Hippo. In this particular case, the concerns of Augustine seem to have been premature, but he knew well

---

[116] Aug. *Serm.* Dolbeau 30.7: 'Quare autem hoc insinuare volui fidei vestrae? Quia nescio qua magna perturbatio Hierosolymis facta est nobisque nuntiata plena tristitia, ut etiam tumultu populari duo monasteria in Bethlehem incensa esse dicantur. Quae vobis non opus erat dicere, nisi iam et ad aliquos vestrum pervenisse cognoscerem. Melius ergo a me totum audistis, quam occultis rumoribus vulneramini.'
[117] Shibutani 1966. [118] Kapferer 2013: 14–15. [119] Aldrin 2005: 84.
[120] Aug. *Serm.* Dolbeau 30.11–5.

how, on other occasions, overseas news had triggered uprisings. In June 401, with a council of African Catholic bishops assembled in Carthage, a statue of Hercules, recently restored, had had its golden beard 'shaved' by the action of a Christian mob.[121] The faithful then occupied the church not only to protest against the pagans and their idols, but also to demand the active involvement of the clergy in their struggle against idolatry. To calm their fury, after the failed attempts of Aurelius, the bishop of Carthage, earlier the same day, Augustine had to restate the authority of the people's shepherds against the excessively violent zeal of the mob:

The sentiments and will of the mass of the people for doing everything will have been made plain by these shouts of yours. But the concern of the few on your behalf must be shown not in shouts but in deeds. And so, brothers, since you have fulfilled your part of the business by shouting, please allow us to satisfy you as to whether we are fulfilling our part of the business by acting ... Now far be it from us that, after you have been found worthy, we should be found unworthy. But since both you and we have one and the same will for action in the matters you have been shouting about (though we cannot share the same mode of action), we think, dearly beloved, that your will should be accepted by us, and our plan for carrying out your will should be awaited by you.[122]

Among their many militant words that expressed this 'will', Augustine noted one that revealed well the source of their inspiration: 'As in Rome, so be it in Carthage!'[123] It was therefore the news that circulated about the anti-pagan measures in the capital of the Empire that encouraged the zealous Christians of Carthage to act. This example also reveals how ordinary Christians, through collective deliberation, could indeed and even in opposition to their leaders, develop their own conceptions of what was required in order to achieve the victory of their church.

---

[121] Aug. *Serm.* 24.6 (*CCL* 41: 332). On what follows, see Magalhães de Oliveira 2006, 2012: 227–51; and Shaw 2011: 230–1.

[122] Aug. *Serm.* 24.5 (*CCL* 41: 330): 'Multitudinis animus et voluntas ad quamque rem faciendam istis vocibus poterit apparere. Paucorum autem cura pro vobis, non vocibus, sed rebus debet ostendi. Itaque, Fratres, quoniam iam quod ad vos pertinebat, implestis acclamando, sinite ut probetur vobis, utrum et quod ad nos pertinet impleamus agendo ... Absit a nobis, ut vos inveniamini probi, et nos reprobi. Sed quoniam voluntas agendi de his de quibus acclamastis, una est et nostra et vestra – modus vero agendi par esse non potest – putamus, Carissimi, ideo oportere ut voluntas accipiatur a vobis, consilium implendae voluntatis vestrae exspectetur a nobis. Ut membra Christi non discordent, impleant omnia quae in illius corpore sunt officia sua.'

[123] Aug. *Serm.* 24.6 (*CCL* 41: 332): 'Utique hoc clamastis: "Quomodo Roma, sic et Carthago!"'

Conclusion

To conclude, the plebeian culture of discussion I have attempted to explore in this chapter could be described as an authentic popular culture, in the sense that it actually grew out of the formative experiences of plebeian life. But this is not to say that it was completely autonomous or immune to external influences, especially when the holders of elite culture were constantly attempting to enclose and confine its limits and forms. What is more, over time, plebeian traditions of sociability could be and indeed were used by different actors, and for different purposes. In Late Antiquity, these plebeian traditions were mobilized and energized by a new and more assertive type of church leadership, as we have seen in the case of Augustine (and, through his testimony, of other African churchmen whose texts have not survived). But even when engaged by their leaders, the subaltern classes were never just passive consumers of what was conveyed to them: they were creators, too. As Augustine himself came to realize, no ecclesiastical leader could ever be sure how their messages would be received in popular meetings. In addition, by making the common people a partner in religious disputes, church leaders also risked giving autonomy to the masses. Ordinary Christians could develop their own conceptions of what were their rights and duties, and, sometimes, even take the initiative in religious struggles, in opposition to their own leaders. But in the troubled political conditions of late antique cities and in the context of a sectarian war, church leaders still sensed that the risk was worth taking. This is because their success or failure as leaders depended ultimately on their ability to mobilize the people and their culture.

Bibliography

Abbott, F. F. (1907) 'The theatre as a factor in Roman politics under the Republic', *TAPhS* 38: 49–56.

Adams, C. D. (1905) *Lysias: Selected Speeches.* New York.

Adams, J. N. (1999) 'The poets of Bu Njem: language, culture and the Centurionate', *JRS* 89: 109–34.

Adorno, T. (1991) 'Culture industry reconsidered', in *The Culture Industry: Selected Essays on Mass Culture*, ed. J. M. Bernstein. London, 98–106.

Adorno, T. and Horkheimer, M. (1979) *Dialectic of Enlightenment.* London.

Agier, M. (2010) *Esquisses d'une anthropologie de la ville: Lieux, situations, mouvements.* Leuven.

Akrigg, B. and Tordoff, R. (2013) *Slaves and Slavery in Ancient Greek Comic Drama.* Cambridge.

Albini, U. (1952) 'L'orazione lisiana per l'invalido', *RhM* 95: 328–38.

Aldrete, G. S. (1999) *Gestures and Acclamations in Ancient Rome.* Baltimore, MD, and London.

Aldrin, P. (2005) *Sociologie politique des rumeurs.* Paris.

Alföldi, A. (1966) 'Les cognomina des magistrats de la République romaine', in *Mélanges A. Piganiol.* Paris, 709–22.

Alföldy, G. (1988) *The Social History of Rome*, trans. D. Braund and E. Pollock. London.

Allan, W. and Kelly, A. (2013) 'Listening to many voices: Athenian tragedy as popular art', in *The Author's Voice in Classical and Late Antiquity*, ed. A. Marmadoro and J. Hill. Oxford, 77–122.

Allen, P. (1996) 'The homilist and the congregation: Chrysostom', *Augustinianum* 36: 323–42.

Alston, R. (1995) *Soldier and Society in Roman Egypt: A Social History.* London.

  (1997) 'Houses and households in Roman Egypt', in *Domestic Space in the Roman World: Pompeii and Beyond*, ed. A. Wallace-Hadrill and R. Laurence. Portsmouth, RI, 25–39.

Alston, R. and Alston, R. D. (1997) 'Urbanism and the urban community in Roman Egypt', *JEA* 83: 199–216.

Althusser, L. (1971) 'Ideology and ideological state apparatuses (notes towards an investigation)', in *Lenin and Philosophy and Other Essays*, trans. B. Brewster. London, 127–88.

Andreassi, M. (2001) 'Esopo sulla scene: il mimo della *Moicheutria* e la *Vita Aesopi*', *RhM* 144: 203–25.
Andreau, J. (2001) *Banques et affaires dans le monde romain (IVe siècle av. J.-C. – IIIe siècle apr. J.-C.)*. Paris.
Appadurai, A. (ed.) (1985) *The Social Life of Things: Commodities in Cultural Perspective*. Cambridge.
Arbesmann, R. (1979) 'The "cervuli" and "anniculae" in Caesarius of Arles', *Traditio* 35: 89–118.
Arena, V. (2012) *Libertas and the Practice of Politics in the Late Roman Republic*. Cambridge.
Ariès, P. (1962) *Centuries of Childhood: A Social History of Family Life*, trans. Robert Baldick. New York.
Arnold, C. F. (1894) *Caesarius von Arelate und die gallische Kirche seiner Zeit*. Leipzig.
Arnold, J. (2005) *Belief and Unbelief in Medieval Europe*. London.
Arnold, M. (1960) *Culture and Anarchy*, ed. J. Dover Wilson. Cambridge.
Arnott, W. G. (1971) 'Herodas and the kitchen sink', *G&R* 18: 121–32.
  (2007) *Birds in the Ancient World from A to Z*. London and New York.
Asad, T. (1983) 'Anthropological conceptions of religion: reflections on Geertz', *Man* n.s. 18: 237–59.
Askew, K. (2002) *Performing the Nation: Swahili Music and Cultural Politics in Tanzania*. Chicago.
Assmann, J. (1995) 'Collective memory and cultural identity', *New German Critique* 65: 125–33.
  (2010) *La mémoire culturelle: Écriture, souvenir et imaginaire politique dans les civilisations antiques*. Paris.
Attfield, J. (2000) *Wild Things: The Material Culture of Everyday Life*. Oxford.
Aubert, J.-J. (1994) *Business Managers in Ancient Rome: A Social and Economic Study of Institores, 200 B.C. – A.D. 250*. Leiden, New York and Cologne.
Aune, D. (1980) 'Magic in early Christianity', in *ANRW* II, 23.3: 1507–57. Berlin and New York.
Austin, J. L. (1962) *How to Do Things with Words*. Oxford.
Avery, M. (1941) 'Miniatures of the fables of Bidpai and of the life of Aesop in the Pierpont Morgan Library', *Art Bulletin* 23: 103–16.
Avlamis, P. (2011) 'Isis and the people in the *Life of Aesop*', in *Revelation, Literature, and Community in Late Antiquity*, ed. P. Townsend and M. Vidas. Tübingen, 65–101.
Axtell, H. L. (1915) 'Men's names in the writings of Cicero', *CPh* 10: 386–404.
Bagatti, B. (1971) 'Altre medaglie di Salomone cavaliere e loro origine', *Studii Biblici Franciscani. Liber Annuus* 15: 98–123.
Bagnall, R. S. and Davoli, P. (2011) 'Archaeological work on Hellenistic and Roman Egypt, 2000–2009', *AJA* 115.1: 103–57.

Bagnall, R. S. and Frier, B.W. (2006) *The Demography of Roman Egypt*, 2nd edn. Cambridge.
Bailey, D. (ed.) (1996) *Archaeological Research in Roman Egypt*. Ann Arbor, MI.
Baird, J. (2014) *The Inner Lives of Ancient Houses: An Archaeology of Dura Europos*. Cambridge.
Baird, J. and Pudsey, A. (eds.) (under review) *Between Words and Walls. Material and Textual Approaches to Housing in the Graeco-Roman World*.
Baird, J. and Taylor, C. (eds.) (2011) *Ancient Graffiti in Context*. London.
Bakhtin, M. (1968) *Rabelais and His World*, trans. H. Iswolsky. Cambridge, MA.
  (1981) *The Dialogic Imagination*. Austin, TX.
  (1984) *Problems of Dostoyevsky's Poetics*. Minneapolis, MN.
Balland, A. (2010) *Essais sur la société des Epigrammes de Martial*. Bordeaux.
Ballet, P., Cordier, P. and Dieudonné-Glad, N. (eds.) (2003) *La ville et ses déchets dans le monde romain: Rebuts et recyclages*. Montagnac.
Banniard, M. (1992) 'Latin et communication orale en Gaule franque: le témoignage de la *Vita Eligii*', in *The Seventh Century*, ed. J. Fontaine and J. N. Hillgarth. London, 58–79.
Barb, A. A. (1963) 'The survival of the magical arts', in *The Conflict Between Paganism and Christianity in the Fourth Century*, ed. A. Momigliano. Oxford, 100–25.
Barlow, C. T. (1980) 'The Roman government and the Roman economy, 92–80 BC', *AJPh* 101: 202–19.
Barlow, C. W. (1950) *Martini Episcopi Bracarensis opera omnia*. New Haven, CT, and London.
Barrett, N. (2010) 'Toward an alternative evolutionary theory of religion: looking past computational evolutionary psychology to a wider field of possibilities', *JAAR* 78.3: 583–621.
Bartsch, S. (1989) *Decoding the Ancient Novel: The Reader and the Role of Description in Heliodorus and Achilles Tatius*. Princeton, NJ.
Basanoff, V. (1949) 'L'épisode des joueurs de flutes chez Tite-Live et les Quinquatrus, fête de Minerve', *RIDA* 2: 65–81.
Bastien, J.-L. (2007) *Le triomphe romain et son utilisation politique à Rome aux trois derniers siècles de la République*. Rome.
Baudot, A. (1973) *Les musiciens romains de l'Antiquité*. Montreal.
Baudrillard, J. (1988) *Jean Baudrillard: Selected Writings*, ed. M. Poster. Stanford, CA.
Baudy, D. (1987) '*Strenarum commercium*: über Geschenke und Glückwünsche zum römischen Neujahrsfest', *RhM* 130: 1–28.
Baxter, J. E. (2005) *The Archaeology of Childhood: Children, Gender, and Material Culture*. Walnut Creek, CA.
Beacham, R. C. (1991) *The Roman Theatre and its Audience*. London.
  (2007) 'Playing places: the temporary and the permanent', in *The Cambridge Companion to Greek and Roman Theatre*, ed. M. McDonald and M. Walton. Cambridge, 202–26.

Beard, M. (1991) 'Ancient literacy and the function of the written word in Roman religion', in *Literacy in the Roman World*, ed. John Humphrey, 35–58.
  (2010) 'Fortune-telling, bad breath and stress in Roman society', *TLS* 17 March.
  (2014) *Laughter in Ancient Rome: On Joking, Tickling, and Cracking Up*. Berkeley, CA.
Beard, M., North, J. and Price. S. (1998) *Religions of Rome*, vol. I. Cambridge.
Bearzot, C. (2013) *Come si abbatte una democrazia: Tecniche di colpo di Stato nell'Atene antica*. Rome.
BeDuhn, J. D. (2009) 'Augustine accused: Megalius, Manichaeism, and the inception of the Confessions', *JECS* 17: 85–124.
Beik, W. (1993) 'Debate: The dilemma of popular history', *P&P* 141: 207–15.
Beness, J. L. (1991) 'The urban unpopularity of Lucius Appuleius Saturninus', *Antichthon* 25: 33–62.
Beness, J. L. and Hillard, T. (1990) 'The death of Lucius Equitius on 10 December 100 BC', *CQ* 40: 269–72.
Benjamin, W. (2008) *The Work of Art in the Age of Mechanical Reproduction*, trans. J. A. Underwood. London.
Benner, H. (1987) *Die Politik des P. Clodius Pulcher*. Stuttgart.
Bennett, T. (1980) 'Popular culture: a teaching object', *Screen Education* 34: 17–30.
  (1986) 'Popular culture and the "turn to Gramsci"', in *Popular Culture and Social Relations*, ed. T. Bennett, C. Mercer and J. Woollacott. Buckingham, xi-xix.
Benoist, S. (1999) *La fête à Rome au premier siècle de l'Empire: Recherches sur l'univers festif sous les règnes d'Auguste et des Julio-Claudiens*. Brussels.
Béraud-Sudreau, M. J. (1938–40) 'Céramique gallo-romaine à emblèmes chrétiens provenant de Burdigale', *Bull. arch. du Comité*: 535–60.
Berg, R., Hälikkaä, R., Keltanen, M., Pölönen, J., Setälä, P. and Vuolanto, V. (eds.) (2002) *Women, Wealth and Power in the Roman Empire*. Rome.
Bergamasco, M. (1995) 'Le διδασχαλιχαί nella ricerca attuale', *Aegyptus* 75: 95–167.
Bernstein, F. (1998) *Ludi publici: Untersuchungen zur Entstehung und Entwicklung der öffentlichen Spiele im republikanischen Rom*. Stuttgart.
Bernstein, H. and Byres, T. J. (2001) 'From peasant studies to agrarian change', *Journal of Agrarian Change* 1: 1–56.
Besnier, N. (2009) *Gossip and the Everyday Production of Politics*. Honolulu.
Bianchi Bandinelli, R. (1967) 'Arte plebea', *Dialoghi di Archeologia* 1: 7–19.
  (1970) *Rome the Centre of Power: Roman Art to AD 200*, trans. P. Green. London.
Bierbrier, M. (ed.). (1997) *Portraits and Masks: Burial Customs in Roman Egypt*. London.
Bigsby, C. W. E. (ed.) (1976) *Approaches to Popular Culture*. London.
Binot, C. (2001) 'Le rôle de Scipion Nasica Sérapion dans la crise gracquienne: une relecture', *Pallas* 57: 185–203.

Blandenet, M., Chillet, C. and Courrier, C. (eds.) (2010) *Figures de l'identité: Naissance et destin des modèles communautaires dans la Rome antique.* Lyon.

Bloch, M. L. B. (1966) *French Rural History: An Essay on its Basic Characteristics*, trans. J. Sondheimer. Berkeley and Los Angeles.

Blok, J. (2009) 'Pericles' citizenship law: a new perspective', *Historia* 58: 141–70.

Boak, A. E. R. and Peterson, E. E. (1931) *Karanis: Topographical and Architectural Report of Excavations During the Seasons 1924–1928.* Ann Arbor, MI.

Bober, P. F. (1951) 'Cernunnos: origin and transformation of a Celtic divinity', *AJA* 55: 13–51.

Bodel, J. (2008) 'From columbaria to catacombs: collective burial in pagan and Christian Rome', in *Commemorating the Dead. Texts and Artifacts in Context: Studies of Roman, Jewish, and Christian Burials*, ed. L. Brink and D. Green. Berlin, 177–242.

Boissevain, J. (2013) *Factions, Friends and Feasts: Anthropological Perspectives on the Mediterranean.* Oxford and New York.

Bollinger, T. (1969) *Theatralis licentia: Die Publikumsdemonstrationen an den öffentlichen Spielen im Rom der früheren Kaiserzeit und ihre Bedeutung im politischen Leben.* Winterthur.

Bomgardner, D. L. (2000) *The Story of the Roman Amphitheatre.* London and New York.

Bonifay, M., Raynaud, C. *et al.* (2007) 'Échanges et consommations', *Gallia* 64: 93–161.

Bonner, C. (1944) 'The Philinna papyrus and the gold tablet from the Vigna Codini', *Hesperia* 13: 349–51.

  (1950) *Studies in Magical Amulets, Chiefly Graeco-Egyptian.* Oxford.

Boren, H. C. (1958) 'The urban side of the Gracchan economic crisis', *AHR* 63: 890–902.

Borg, B. (1996) *Mumienporträts: Chronologie und kultureller Kontext.* Mainz.

Botha, P. J. J. (2012) *Orality and Literacy in Early Christianity.* Eugene, OR.

Bourdieu, P. (1973) 'Cultural reproduction and social reproduction', in *Knowledge, Education and Cultural Change*, ed. Richard Brown. London, 71–84.

  (1977) *Outline of a Theory of Practice*, trans. R. Nice. Cambridge.

  (1982) *Ce que parler veut dire: L'économie des échanges linguistiques.* Paris.

  (1984) *Distinction: A Social Critique of the Judgement of Taste*, trans. R. Nice. Cambridge.

Bowes, K. (2008) *Private Worship, Public Values, and Religious Change in Late Antiquity.* Cambridge and New York.

Bowie, E. (1994) 'The readership of Greek novels in the ancient world', in *The Search for the Ancient Novel*, ed. J. Tatum. Baltimore and London, 435–59.

Bowman, A. K. and Rathbone, D.W. (1992) 'Cities and administration in Roman Egypt', *JRS* 82: 107–27.

Bowman, A. K. and Woolf, G. (eds.) (1994) *Literacy and Power in the Ancient World*. Cambridge.

Bradley, K. R. (1991) *Discovering the Roman Family: Studies in Roman Social History*. Oxford.

(2000) 'Animalizing the slave: the truth of fiction', *JRS* 90: 110–25.

Branham, R. B. (2002) *Bakhtin and the Classics*, Evanston, IL.

Bremmer, J. N. (1996) 'The status and symbolic capital of the seer', in *The Role of Religion in the Early Greek Polis*, Proceedings of the Third International Seminar on Ancient Greek Cult, organized by the Swedish Institute at Athens, 16–18 October 1992, ed. R. Hägg. Jonsered, Sweden, 97–109.

(1999) 'The birth of the term "magic"', *ZPE* 126: 1–12.

Bresson, A. (2007) *L'économie de la Grèce des cités*. Paris.

Brett, M. and Fentress, E. (1996) *The Berbers*. Oxford.

Briscoe, J. (1974) 'Supporters and opponents of Tiberius Gracchus', *JRS* 64: 125–35.

Brown, P. (1981) *The Cult of the Saints*. London.

(1992) *Power and Persuasion in Late Antiquity: Towards a Christian Empire*. Madison, WI.

(2000a) *Augustine of Hippo: A Biography*, rev. edn. Berkeley, CA.

(2000b) 'The study of elites in Late Antiquity', *Arethusa* 33: 321–46.

(2002) *Poverty and Leadership in the Later Roman Empire*. Hanover, NH, and London.

(2012) *Through the Eye of a Needle: Wealth, the Fall of Rome, and the Making of Christianity in the West, 350–550 AD*. Princeton, NJ.

Brulé, P. and Vendries, C. (eds.) (2001) *Chanter les dieux: Musique et religion dans l'antiquité grecque et romaine*, Actes du colloque des 16, 17, et 18 décembre 1999. Rennes.

Brunt, P. A. (1966) 'The Roman mob', *P&P* 35: 3–27.

Bruun, C. (1997) 'Acquedotti e condizioni sociali di Roma imperiale: immagini e realtà', in *La Rome impériale. Démographie et logistique*, ed. C. Virlouvet. Rome, 122–55.

(2003) 'Roman emperors in popular jargon: searching for contemporary nicknames (I)', in *The Representation and Perception of Roman Imperial Power*, Proceedings of the Third Workshop of the International Network Impact of Empire, ed. L. Blois and P. Erdkamp. Amsterdam, 69–98.

(2009) 'Civic rituals in imperial Ostia', in *Ritual Dynamics and Religious Change in the Roman Empire*, ed. O. Hekster, S. Schmidt-Hofner and C. Witschel. Leiden and Boston, 123–41.

Bruzza, L. (1875) 'Intorno ad un campanello d'oro trovato sull'Esquilino e all'uso del suono per respingere il fascino', *Annali dell'Istituto di Corrispondenza Archeologica* 47: 50–68.

Buchet, E. (2010–11) 'La grève des tibicines', *Bulletin de l'Association Guillaume Budé*: 174–96.

Burke, P. (1988) 'Bakhtin for historians', *Social History* 13: 85–90.
  (2004) *What is Cultural History?* Cambridge.
  (2009) *Popular Culture in Early Modern Europe*, 3rd edn. Aldershot.
Burkert, W. (2005) 'Signs, commands, and knowledge: ancient divination between enigma and epiphany', in *Mantikê: Studies in Ancient Divination*, ed. S. I. Johnston and P. T. Struck. Leiden, 29–49.
Burrus, V. (2005) *A People's History of Christianity Series*, vol. II: *Late Ancient Christianity*. Minneapolis, MN.
Butler, J. (1997) *Excitable Speech: A Politics of the Performative*. New York.
Calza, G. (1917) 'Un amulet magico con l'effigie di Salomone rinvenuto in Ostia', in *Notizie degli Scavi di Antichità*. Rome, 326–8.
Cameron, A. (1973) *Bread and Circuses: The Roman Emperor and his People*. Inaugural lecture in Latin language and literature at King's College London, 21 May.
  (1976) *Circus Factions: Blues and Greens at Rome and Byzantium*. Oxford.
Camille, M. (1998) *Mirror in Parchment: The Luttrell Psalter and the Making of Medieval England*. London.
Canevaro, M. (2013) *The Documents in the Attic Orators: Laws and Decrees in the Public Speeches of the Demosthenic Corpus*. Oxford.
  (forthcoming 1) 'Demosthenic influences in early rhetorical education: Hellenistic *rhetores* and Athenian imagination', in *The Hellenistic and Early Imperial Greek Reception of Classical Athenian Democracy and Political Thought*, ed. B. Gray and M. Canevaro. Oxford.
  (forthcoming 2) 'Memory, the *rhetors* and the public in Attic oratory', in *Greek Memories: Theories and Practices*, ed. L. Castagnoli and P. Ceccarelli. Cambridge.
Cantarella, E. (1991) 'Moicheia: reconsidering a problem', in *Symposion 1990*, ed. M. Gagarin. Cologne and Vienna, 289–304.
Carandini, A. (2010) *Le case del potere nell'antica Roma*. Rome.
Carey, C. (1990) 'Structure and strategy in Lysias XXIV', *G&R* 37: 44–51.
  (1993) 'Return of the radish or just when you thought it was safe to go back to the kitchen', *LCM* 18.4: 53–5.
  (1995) 'Rape and adultery in Athenian law', *CQ* 45: 407–17.
Carletti, C. (1998) 'Un monogramma tardoantico nell'epigrafia funeraria dei cristiani', in *Domum tuam dilexi: Miscellanea A. Nestori*. Vatican City, 127–42.
Carlsson, S. (2010) *Hellenistic Democracies: Freedom, Independence and Political Procedure in Some East Greek City-States*. Stuttgart.
Carpenter, H. J. (1963) 'Popular Christianity and the theologians in the early centuries', *JThS* 14: 294–310.
Carrié, J.-M. (2002a) 'Antiquité tardive et "democratisation de la culture": un paradigme à géométrie variable', *AntTard* 9: 27–46.

(2002b) 'Les associations professionnelles à l'époque tardive: entre *munus* et convivialité', in *Humana Sapit: Mélanges en l'honneur de Lellia Cracco Ruggini*. Turnhout, 309–32.

Carter, D. M. (2011) 'Plato, drama, and rhetoric', in *Why Athens? A Reappraisal of Tragic Politics*, ed. D. M. Carter. Oxford, 45–67.

Cartledge, P. (1993) 'Classical Greek agriculture: recent work and alternative views', *Journal of Peasant Studies* 21: 127–35.

Caseau, B. (2012) 'Magical protection and stamps in Byzantium', in *Seals and Sealing Practices in the Near East: Developments in Administration and Magic from Prehistory to the Islamic Period*, ed. I. Regulski, K. Duistermaat and P. Verkinderen. Leuven, 115–32.

Cavaggioni, F. (1998) *L. Apuleio Saturnino 'tribunus plebis seditiosus'*. Venice.

Cavallo, D., Coppola, M.-R. and Pavolini, C. (1998) 'Lo scavo del "*Caput Africae*": un contesto stratigrafico altomedievale ricostruibile dai residui', in *I materiali residui nello scavo archeologico*, ed. F. Guidobaldi, C. Pavolini and P. Pergola. Rome, 165–72.

Certeau, M. de (1974) *La culture au pluriel*. Paris.

(1984) *The Practice of Everyday Life*, trans. S. F. Rendall. London and Berkeley, CA.

Chadwick, H. (1996) 'New sermons of St Augustine', *JThS* 47: 69–91

Chambers, E. K. (1903) *The Medieval Stage*, 2 vols. Oxford.

Chaniotis, A. (2005) 'The great inscription, its political and social institutions and the common institutions of the Cretans', in *La grande iscrizione di Gortina: Centoventi anni dopo la scoperta*. Atti del I Convegno internazionale di studi sulla Messarà: Scuola archeologica italiana di Atene, Atene-Haghii Deka, 25–28 maggio 2004, ed. E. Greco, M. Lombardo. Rome: 175–94.

Chartier, R. (1982) 'Stratégies éditoriales et lectures populaires, 1530–1660', in *Histoire de l'édition française*. Paris, 598–602.

(1986) 'Culture populaire', in *Dictionnaire des sciences historiques*, ed. A. Burguière. Paris, 174–9.

(1988) *Cultural History: Between Practices and Representations*, trans. L. Cochrane. Cambridge.

(1991) *The Cultural Origins of the French Revolution*, trans. L. Cochrane. Durham, NC.

(1993) 'Popular culture: a concept revisited', *Intellectual History Newsletter* 15: 3–13.

Chinit, D. E. (2003) *T. S. Eliot and the Cultural Divide*. Chicago.

Choay, F. and Merlin, P. (eds.) (1987) *Dictionnaire de l'urbanisme et de l'aménagement*, Paris.

Christian, W. A. (1981) *Local Religion in Sixteenth-Century Spain*. Princeton, NJ.

Clark, S. (1985) 'The *Annales* historians', in *The Return of Grand Theory in the Human Sciences*, ed. Q. Skinner. Cambridge, 177–98.

Clarke, J. R. (2003) *Art in the Lives of Ordinary Romans: Visual Representation and Non-Elite Viewers in Italy, 100 BC–AD 315*. London.
  (2006) 'High and low: mocking philosophers in the Tavern of the Seven Sages', in *The Art of Citizens, Soldiers and Freedmen in the Roman World*, ed. E. D'Ambra and G. P. R. Métraux. Oxford, 47–57.
  (2007) *Looking at Laughter: Humor, Power, and Transgression in Roman Visual Culture, 100 B.C.–A.D. 250*. Berkeley, CA.
Classen, C. (1993) *Worlds of Sense: Exploring the Senses in History and Across Culture*. London.
  (1997) 'Foundations for an anthropology of the senses', *International Social Sciences Journal* 153: 401–12.
Clavel-Lévêque, M. (1984) *L'Empire en jeux: Espace symbolique et pratique sociale dans le monde romain*. Paris.
Cline, R. H. (2011) 'Archangels, magical amulets, and the defense of late antique Miletus', *JLA* 4:55–78.
Cohen, A. and Rutter, J. (eds.) (2007) *Constructions of Childhood in Ancient Greece and Italy*. Princeton, NJ.
Cohen, D. (1984) 'The Athenian law of adultery', *RIDA* 31: 147–65.
  (1985) 'A note on Aristophanes and the punishment of adultery in Athenian law', *ZRG* 102: 385–7.
  (1991) *Law, Sexuality and Society: The Enforcement of Morals in Classical Athens*. Cambridge.
  (1995) *Law, Violence and Community in Classical Athens*. Cambridge.
Cole, S. G. (1984) 'Greek sanctions against sexual assault', *CPh* 79: 97–113.
Coleman, K. M. (2003) 'Euergetism in its place: where was the amphitheatre in Augustan Rome?' in *Bread and Circuses: Euergetism and Municipal Patronage in Roman Italy*, ed. K. Lomas and T. Cornell. London and New York, 61–88.
  (2011) 'Public entertainments', in *The Oxford Handbook of Social Relations in the Roman World*, ed. M. Peachin. Oxford, 335–57.
Collins, D. (2002) 'Reading the birds: *oiōnomanteia* in early epic', *Colby Quarterly* 38: 17–41.
Connor, W. (1971) *The New Politicians of the Fifth Century*. Princeton, NJ.
Cooper, F. and Morris, S. (1990) 'Dining in round buildings', in *Sympotica: A Symposium on the Symposion*, ed. O. Murray. Oxford, 66–85.
Corbeill, A. (1996) *Controlling Laughter: Political Humor in the Late Roman Republic*. Princeton, NJ.
  (1997) 'Dining deviants in Roman political invective', in *Roman Sexualities*, ed. J. P. Hallett and M. B. Skinner. Princeton, NJ, 99–128.
Corbier, M. (1985) 'Dévaluations et évolution des prix (Ier–IIIe siècles)', *RN* 27: 69–106.
  (1991) 'L'écriture en quête de lecteurs', in *Literacy in the Ancient World*, ed. J. Humphrey. Ann Arbor, MI: 119–31.

Cornell, T. J. (1995) *The Beginnings of Rome: Italy and Rome from the Bronze Age to the Punic Wars (c. 1000–264 BC)*. London and New York.

Courrier, C. (2012) 'De la mémoire du conflit au conflit de mémoire: lutte des ordres et mémoire de la plèbe à la fin de la République romaine', in *La pomme d'Eris: Le conflit et ses représentations dans l'Antiquité*, ed. P. Sauzeau, J.-F. Thomas and H. Ménard. Montpellier, 501–25.

(2014) *La plèbe de Rome et sa culture (fin du IIe s. av. J.-C. – fin du Ier s. ap. J.-C.)*. Rome.

(forthcoming) 'Le peuple de Rome et les ornamenta de la ville: usages et normes. Le cas de la confiscation de l'Apoxyomène de Lysippe par Tibère (Pline, HN, 34.62)', in *La Norme sous la République et le Haut-Empire romains: Élaboration, diffusion et contournements*. Actes du colloque organisé par l'Université de Reims Champagne-Ardenne, 13–15 mars 2014, ed. T. Itgenshorst and P. Le Doze. Bordeaux.

Courtney, E. (1993) *The Fragmentary Latin Poets*. Oxford.

Coy, M. (ed.) (1989) *Apprenticeship: From Theory to Method and Back Again*. New York.

Crawford, M. H. (1970) 'Money and exchange in the Roman world', *JRS* 60: 40–8.

(1996) *Roman Statutes*. London.

Cribiore, R. (2001) *Gymnastics of the Mind: Greek Education in Hellenistic and Roman Egypt*. Princeton, NJ.

Critchley, S. (2002) *On Humour*. London.

Crummy, N. (2010) 'Bears and coins: the iconography of protection in late Roman infant burials', *Britannia* 41: 37–93.

Csapo, E. and Goette, H. R. (2007) 'The men who built the theatres: theatropolai, theatronai, and arkhitektones', in *The Greek Theatre and Festivals: Documentary Studies*, ed. P. Wilson. Oxford, 87–121.

Csapo, E. and Slater, W. J. (1995) *The Context of Ancient Drama*. Ann Arbor, MI.

Cuche, D. (1996) *La notion de culture dans les sciences sociales*. Paris.

Cumont, F. (1897) 'Les Actes de S. Dasius', *AB* 16: 5–15.

Cunningham, M. B. (1986) 'Preaching and community', in *Church and People in Byzantium*, ed. R. Morris. Birmingham, 29–46.

Dalton, O. M. (1901) *Catalogue of the Early Christian Antiquities*. London.

Daly, L. W. (ed.) (1961) *Aesop Without Morals: The Famous Fables and a Life of Aesop*. New York.

D'Ambra, E. and Métraux, G. P. R. (2006) *The Art of Citizens, Soldiers and Freedmen in the Roman World*. Oxford.

Damon, C. (1992) 'Sex. Cloelius, *scriba*', *HSCP* 94: 227–50.

Darkow, A. (1917) *The Spurious Speeches in the Lysianic Corpus*. Bryn Mawr, PA.

Darnton, R. (2003) 'The news in Paris: an early information society', in *George Washington's False Teeth: An Unconventional Guide to the Eighteenth Century*. New York and London, 25–75.

Dasen, V. (2010) 'Archéologie funéraire et histoire de l'enfance: nouveaux enjeux, nouvelles perspectives', in *L'enfant et la mort dans l'Antiquité: Nouvelles recherches dans les nécropoles grecques. Le signalement des tombes d'enfants*. Paris, 19–44.

(2012) 'Cherchez l'enfant! La question de l'identité à partir du matériel funéraire', in *L'enfant et la mort dans l'Antiquité*, vol III: *Le matériel associé aux tombes d'enfants*, ed. A. Hermary and C. Dubois. Paris and Aix-en-Provence, 9–22.

Dasen, V. and Späth, T. (eds.) (2010) *Children, Memory and Family Identity in Roman Culture*. Oxford.

Datema, C. (ed.) (1970) *Asterius of Amasea, Homilies I–XIV: Text, Introduction and Notes*. Leiden.

Davidson, J. N. (1997) *Courtesans and Fishcakes: The Consuming Passions of Classical Athens*. New York.

Davies, J. K. (1971) *Athenian Propertied Families, 600–300 BC*. Oxford.

(1981) *Wealth and the Power of Wealth at Classical Athens*. New York.

(1998) 'Deconstructing Gortyn: when is a code a code?' in *Greek Law in its Political Setting*, ed. L. Foxhall and A. D. E. Lewis. Cambridge, 33–56.

(2005) 'The Gortyn laws', in *The Cambridge Companion to Ancient Greek Law*. Cambridge, 305–27.

Davis, N. Z. (1974) 'Some tasks and themes in the study of popular religion', in *The Pursuit of Holiness in Late Medieval and Renaissance Religion: Papers from the University of Michigan Conference*, ed. C. Trinkhaus and H. A. Oberman. Leiden, 307–36.

(1975) *Society and Culture in Early Modern France*. London.

Dawson, S. (1997) 'The theatrical audience in fifth-century Athens: numbers and status', *Prudentia* 29: 1–14.

De Kleijn, G. (2001) *The Water Supply of Ancient Rome: City Area, Water and Population*. Amsterdam.

De Maria, S., Campagnoli, P., Giorgi, E. and Lepore, G. (2006) *Topografia e urbanistica di Soknopaiou Nesos*, ed. S. Pemigotti and M. Zecchi. Bologna, 23–90.

Depaw, M. (2009) 'Do mothers matter? The emergence of metronymics in early Roman Egypt', in *The Language of the Papyri*, ed. T. V. Evans and D. Obbink. Oxford, 120–39.

De Robertis, F. M. (1955) *Il fenomeno associativo nel mondo romano dai collegi della republica ai corporazioni del Basso Impero*. Naples.

(1963) *Lavoro et lavoratori nel mondo romano*. Bari.

De Rossi, G. B. (1864–7) *Roma sotterranea cristiana*. Rome.

(1888) 'Del *praepositus de via Flaminia*', *Bullettino di Archeologia Cristiana* 1: 53–6.

De Ruyt, C. (1983) *Macellum: marché alimentaire des Romains*. Louvain-la-Neuve.

De Santis, P. (2000) 'Glass vessels as grave goods and grave ornament in the catacombs of Rome: some examples', in *Burial, Society and Context*, ed. R. Pearce, M. Millett and M. Struck. Oxford, 238–43.

De Veer, A. C. (1965) 'L'exploitation du schisme maximianiste par saint Augustin dans sa lutte contre le Donatisme', *RecAug* 3: 219–37.

De Vivo, F. (2007) *Information and Communication in Venice: Rethinking Early Modern Politics*. Oxford.

Delgado, J. A. F., Pordoming, F. and Stramaglia, A. (eds.) (2007) *Escuela y literatura en Grecia antigua*. Cassino.

D'Ercole, M. C. (2014) '*Skutotomos, sutor*: statuts et représentations du métier de cordonnier dans les mondes grecs et romains', in *Les affaires de Monsieur Andreau: Économie et société du monde romain*, ed. C. Apicella, M.-L. Haack and F. Lerouxel. Bordeaux, 234–49.

Dill, S. (1926) *Roman Society in Gaul in the Merovingian Age*. London.

Dillery, J. (2005) 'Chresmologues and *manteis*: independent diviners and the problem of authority', in *Mantikê: Studies in Ancient Divination*, ed. S. I. Johnston and P. T. Struck. Leiden, 167–231.

Dillon, M. P. J. (1995) 'Payments to the disabled at Athens: social justice or fear of aristocratic patronage?', *AncSoc* 26: 27–57.

(1996) '*Oionomanteia* in Greek divination', in *Religion in the Ancient World: New Themes and Approaches*, ed. M. Dillon. Amsterdam, 99–121.

(2001) *Girls and Women in Classical Greek Religion*. London.

Dirks, R. (1988) 'Annual rituals of conflict', *American Anthropologist* 90: 856–70.

Dixon, S. (ed.) (2001) *Childhood, Class and Kin in the Roman World*. London.

Dolansky, F. (2011) 'Celebrating the Saturnalia: religious ritual and Roman domestic life', in *A Companion to Families in the Greek and Roman Worlds*, ed. B. Rawson. Chichester, 488–503.

(2012) 'Playing with gender: girls, dolls, and adult ideals in the Roman world', *ClAnt* 31: 256–92.

Dolbeau, F. (1992) 'Nouveaux sermons de saint Augustin pour la conversion des païens et des donatistes (IV)', *REA* 26: 69–141.

(1995) 'Le sermon 348A de saint Augustin contre Pélage: édition du texte intégral', *RecAug* 28: 37–63.

(1996a) *Augustin d'Hippone: Vingt-six sermons au peuple d'Afrique*. Paris.

(1996b) 'Bède, lecteur des sermons de saint Augustin', *Filologica mediolatina* 3: 105–33.

(1999) 'Un second manuscrit complet du *Sermo contra Pelagium* d'Augustin', *REA* 45: 353–61.

Dolzani, C. (1975) 'Relievo egittizzante nel cimitero di Pretestato (Roma)', *RAC* 51: 97–105.

Dondin-Payre, M. and Tran, N. (eds.) (2012) *Collegia: Le phénomène associatif dans l'Occident romain*. Bordeaux.

Donlan, W. (1980) *The Aristocratic Ideal in Ancient Greece: Attitudes of Superiority from Homer to the End of the Fifth Century*. Lawrence, KS.

Dörpfeld, W. and Reisch, E. (1896) *Das griechische Theater: Beiträge zur Geschichte des Dionysos-Theaters in Athen und anderer griechischer Theater*. Athens.

Dossey, L. (2010) *Peasant and Empire in Christian North Africa*. Berkeley, CA.

Douglas, M. (1999) *Implicit Meanings: Selected Essays in Anthropology*, 2nd edn. London.

Dover, K. J. (1972) *Aristophanic Comedy*. Berkeley and Los Angeles.

(1974) *Greek Popular Morality in the Time of Plato and Aristotle*. Cambridge.

Dowden, K. (trans.) (1998) 'Pseudo-Callisthenes, the Alexander Romance', in *Anthology of Ancient Greek Popular Literature*, ed. W. Hansen. Bloomington, IN, 168–246.

(2009) 'Reading Diktys: the discrete charm of bogosity', in *Readers and Writers in the Ancient Novel*, ed. M. Paschalis, S. Panayotakis and G. Schmeling. Groningen, 155–68.

Driver, M. (2005) 'The cult of martyrs in Asterius of Amaseia's vision of the Christian city', *ChHist* 74: 236–54.

Dufour, J.-M. and Fauquet, H. (1987) *La musique et le pouvoir*. Paris.

Dumézil, G. (1973) *Mythe et épopée: Histoires romaines*. Paris.

Dumont, J.-C. (2009) *L'Antiquité au cinéma: Vérités, légendes et manipulations*. Paris.

Duncan-Jones, R. P. (1982) *The Economy of the Roman Empire: Quantitative Studies*. Cambridge.

Dundes, A., Leach, J. and Özkök, B. (1970) 'The strategy of Turkish boys' verbal dueling rhymes', *Journal of American Folklore* 83: 325–49.

Dupont, A. (2012) *Gratia in Augustine's Sermones ad Populum during the Pelagian Controversy: Do Different Contexts Furnish Different Insights?* Leiden.

Dupré Raventós, X. and Anton Remolà, J. (eds.) (2000) *Sordes vrbis: La eliminación de residuos en la ciudad romana*. Rome.

Eagleton, T. (1981) *Walter Benjamin, or Towards a Revolutionary Criticism*. London.

Eco, U. (2012) *L'antichità: Roma*. Milan.

Edelman, M. (1988) *Constructing the Political Spectacle*. Chicago.

Eidinow, E. (2007) *Oracles, Curses, and Risk among the Ancient Greeks*. Oxford.

(2012) '"What will happen to me if I leave?": ancient Greek oracles, slaves and slave owners', in *Slaves and Religions in Graeco-Roman Antiquity*, ed. S. Hodkinson and D. Geary. Newcastle upon Tyne, 244–78.

Engemann, H. (1990) 'Amuleto', in *Enciclopedia dell'Arte Medievale*, vol. I. Rome, 527–30.

Erdkamp, P. (2002) 'A starving mob has no respect: urban markets and food riots in the Roman world, 100 BC – 400 AD', in *The Transformation of the Economic Life under the Roman Empire*, ed. L. de Blois and J. Rich. Amsterdam, 93–115.

(2005) *The Grain Market of the Roman Empire*. Cambridge.
Espérandieu, E. (1911) *Receuil général des bas-reliefs, statues et bustes de la Gaule romaine*, vol. IV: *Lyonnaise*, part 2. Paris.
Esposito, E. (2010) 'Herodas and the mime', in *A Companion to Hellenistic Literature*, ed. J. J. Clauss and M. Cuypers. Oxford, 266–81.
Evans Grubbs, J. and Parkin, T. G. with Bell, R. (eds.) (2013) *The Oxford Handbook of Children and Education in the Greco-Roman World*. Oxford.
Evans-Pritchard, E. E. (1976) *Witchcraft, Oracles, and Magic among the Azande*. Oxford.
Fagan, G. G. (2011) *The Lure of the Arena: Social Psychology and the Crowd at the Games*. Cambridge.
Fantham, E. (1989) 'Mime: the missing link in Roman literary history', *CW* 82: 153–63.
Faraone, C. A. and Rife, J. L. (2007) 'A Greek curse against a thief from the Koutsongila Cemetery at Roman Kenchreai', *ZPE* 160: 141–57.
Fentress, E. (2006) 'Romanizing the Berbers', *P&P* 190: 3–33.
Ferrua, A. (1940) 'Sopra un'iscrizione del Museo Lateranense', *Epigraphica* 2: 7–20.
   (1957) 'Scoperta di una nuova regione della catacomba di Commodilla. I', *RAC* 33:7–43.
Février, P.-A. (1978) 'Le culte des morts dans les communautés chrétiennes durant le IIIe siècle', in *Atti del IX Congresso Internazionale di Archeologia Cristiana (Roma 21–27 settembre 1975)*, vol. I: *I monumenti preconstantiniani*. Vatican City, 211–74.
   (1980) 'Vera et nova: le poids du passé, les germes de l'avenir, IIIe–VIe siècle', in *Histoire de la France urbaine*, vol. II: *La ville antique des origines au IXe siècle*, ed. P.-A. Février, M. Fixot, C. Goudineau and V. Kruta. Paris, 393–493.
Fickett-Wilbar, D. (2003) 'Cernunnos: looking a different way', *Proceedings of the Harvard Celtic Colloquium* 23: 80–111.
Filotas, B. (2005) *Pagan Survivals, Superstitions and Popular Cultures*. Toronto.
Finkelpearl, E. (2003) 'Lucius and Aesop gain a voice: Apuleius *Met.* 11.1–2 and *Vita Aesopi* 7', in *The Ancient Novel and Beyond*, ed. S. Panayotakis, M. Zimmerman and W. Keulen. Leiden, 37–41.
Fisher, N. R. E. (2000) 'Symposiasts, fish-eaters and flatterers: social mobility and moral concerns', in *The Rivals of Aristophanes: Studies in Athenian Old Comedy*, ed. D. Harvey and J. Wilkins. London, 355–96.
Fitzpatrick, A. P. (1991) 'Celtic (Iron Age) religion – traditional and timeless?', *Scottish Archaeological Review* 8: 123–9.
Flaig, E. (1992) *Den Kaiser herausfordern: die Usurpation im römischen Reich*. Frankfurt am Main.
   (1994) 'Repenser le politique dans la République romaine', *Actes de la recherche en sciences sociales* 105.1: 13–25.
Flambard, J. M. (1977) 'Clodius, les collèges, la plèbe et les esclaves: recherches sur la politique populaire au milieu du Ier siècle', *MEFRA* 89: 115–56.

(1981) '*Collegia compitalicia*: phénomène associatif, cadres territoriaux et cadres civiques dans le monde romain à l'époque républicaine', *Ktèma* 3: 143–66.

Fless, F. (1995) *Opferdiener und Kultmusiker auf stadtrömischen historischen Reliefs*. Mainz.

Fless, F. and Moede, K. (2007) 'Music and dance: forms of representation in pictorial and written sources', in *A Companion to Roman Religion*, ed. J. Rüpke. Malden, MA, and Oxford, 249–62.

Flohr, M. (2007) '*Nec quicquam ingenuum habere potest officina?* Spatial contexts of urban production at Pompeii, AD 79', *BABesch* 82: 129–48.

Flower, H. I. (1995) '*Fabulae praetextatae* in context: when were plays on contemporary subjects performed in republican Rome?' *CQ* 45: 170–90.

(2006) *The Art of Forgetting: Disgrace and Oblivion in Roman Political Culture*. Chapel Hill, NC.

Flower, M. (2008a) *The Seer in Ancient Greece*. Berkeley, CA.

(2008b) 'The Iamidae: a mantic family and its public image', in *Practitioners of the Divine: Greek Priests and Religious Officials from Homer to Heliodorus*, ed. B. Dignas and K. Trampedach. Cambridge, MA, 187–206.

Forsdyke, S. (2012) *Slaves Tell Tales, and Other Episodes in the Politics of Popular Culture in Ancient Greece*. Princeton, NJ.

Foufopoulos, J. and Litinas, N. (2005) 'Crows and ravens in the Mediterranean (the Nile Valley, Greece and Italy) as presented in the ancient and modern proverbial literature', *BASP* 42: 7–39.

Fowler, R. L. (2000) 'Greek magic, Greek religion', in *Oxford Readings in Greek Religion*, ed. R. Buxton. Oxford, 317–43.

Fowler, W. W. (1911) *The Religious Experience of the Roman People from the Earliest Times to the Age of Augustus*. London.

Fox, A. (1997) 'Rumour, news and popular political opinion in Elizabethan and early Stuart England', *Historical Journal* 40: 597–620.

Foxhall, L. (1991). 'Response to Eva Cantarella', in *Symposion 1990*, ed. M. Gagarin. Cologne and Vienna, 297–304.

Frankfurter, D. (1994) 'The magic of writing and the writing of magic', *Helios* 21: 189–221.

(1998) *Religion in Roman Egypt: Assimilation and Resistance*. Princeton, NJ.

(2005) 'Beyond magic and superstition', in *People's History of Christianity*, vol. II: *Late Ancient Christianity*, ed. V. Burrus. Minneapolis, MN, 255–84.

(2010) 'Where the spirits dwell: possession, Christianization, and saints' shrines in late antiquity', *HThR* 103: 27–46.

Franklin, J. L. (1986) 'Games and a lupanar: prosopography of a neighborhood in ancient Pompeii', *CJ* 81: 319–28.

Fraschetti, A. (1990) *Roma e il principe*. Rome and Bari.

Frend, W. (1971) 'Popular religion and Christological controversy in the fifth century', in *Popular Belief and Practice*, ed. G. J. Cuming. Cambridge, 19–28.

Frier, B. W. (1971) 'Sulla's propaganda and the collapse of the Cinnan Republic', *AJP* 92: 585–604.
Funari, P. P. A. (1989) *Cultura popular na Antiguidade Clássica*. São Paulo.
  (1993) 'Graphic caricature and the ethos of ordinary people in Pompeii', *Journal of European Archaeology* 1.2: 133–50.
  (1999) 'Du rire des Grecs au rire des Romains: les inscriptions de Pompéi et le rire', in *Le rire des Grecs: Anthropologie du rire en Grèce ancienne*, ed. M.-L. Desclos. Grenoble, 513–23.
Fusillo, M. (2008) 'Modernity and post-modernity', in *The Cambridge Companion to the Greek and Roman Novel*, ed. T. Whitmarsh. Cambridge, 321–39.
Futre Pinheiro, M. (2009) 'Dialogues between readers and writers in Lucian's *Verae Historiae*', in *Readers and Writers in the Ancient Novel*, ed. M. Paschalis, S. Panayotakis and G. Schmeling. Groningen, 18–35.
Gabrielsen, V. (1994) *Financing the Athenian Fleet: Public Taxation and Social Relations*. Baltimore, MD.
Gaddis, M. (2005) *There is No Crime for Those Who Have Christ: Religious Violence in the Christian Roman Empire*. Berkeley, CA.
Gager, J. (1992) *Curse Tablets and Binding Spells from the Ancient World*. New York.
Gallazzi, C. and Hadji-Minaglou, G. (2000) *Tebtynis I: La reprise des fouilles et le quartier de la chapelle d'Isis-Thermouthis*. Cairo.
Galvão-Sobrinho, C. R. (2012) 'Feasting the dead together: household burials and the social strategies of slaves and freed persons in the early Principate', in *Free at Last! The Impact of Freed Slaves on the Roman Empire*, ed. S. Bell and T. Ramsby. London, 130–76.
  (2013) *Doctrine and Power: Theological Controversy and Christian Leadership in the Later Roman Empire, AD 318-364*. Berkeley, CA.
Garnsey, P. D. A. (1970) *Social Status and Legal Privilege in the Roman Empire*. Oxford.
  (1988) *Famine and Food Supply in the Graeco-Roman World: Responses to Risk and Crisis*. Cambridge
  (1998) *Cities, Peasants and Food in Classical Antiquity: Essays in Social and Economic History*. Cambridge.
Garnsey, P. and Rathbone, D. W. (1985) 'The background of the Grain Law of Caius Gracchus', *JRS* 75: 20–5.
Garraffoni, R. S. and Funari, P. P. A. (2008) 'Reading Pompeii's walls: a social archaeological approach to gladiatorial graffiti', in *Roman Amphitheatres and Spectacula: A 21st Century Approach*, ed. T. Wilmott. Oxford, 185–93.
Garraffoni, R. S. and Laurence, R. (2013) 'Writing in public space from child to adult: the meaning of graffiti', in *Written Space in the Latin West, 200 BC to AD 300*, ed. G. Sears, P. Keegan, and R. Laurence. London, 123–34.
Geddes, A. (1987) 'Rags and riches: the costume of Athenian men in the fifth century', *CQ* 37: 307–31.

Geertz, C. (1973) *The Interpretation of Cultures: Selected Essays*. New York.
Gehl, J. (1987) *Life between Buildings: Using Public Space*. New York.
Gerick, T. (1996) *Der versus quadratus bei Plautus und seine volkstümliche Tradition*. Tübingen.
Gianelli, G. (1993) 'Arx', in *Lexicon Topographicum Urbis Romae*, vol. I, ed. E. M. Steinby. Rome, 127-9.
Gibson, C. A. (2008) *Libanius's Progymnasmata: Model Exercises in Greek Prose Composition and Rhetoric*. Atlanta, GA.
Ginzburg, C. (1980) *The Cheese and the Worms: The Cosmos of a Sixteenth Century Miller*, trans. J. and A. Tedeschi. London.
Girard, J.-L. (1973) 'Minerve et les joueurs de flute', *REL* 51: 36-7.
Girault, A. (1876) 'Notice sur des poteries noires à emblèmes chrétiens du IVe au Ve siècle', *Bull. soc. arch. de Bordeaux* 3: 34-45.
Gleason, M. (1986) 'Festive satire: Julian's *Misopogon* and the New Year at Antioch', *JRS* 76: 106-19.
Gluckman, H. (1954) *Rituals of Rebellion in South-East Africa*. Manchester.
Goette, H. R. (1994) 'Neue attische Felsinschriften', *Klio* 76: 120-34.
  (1995) 'Griechische Theaterbauten der Klassik – Forschungsstand und Fragestellungen', in *Studien zur Bühnendichtung und zum Theaterbau der Antike*, ed. E. Pöhlmann. Frankfurt am Main, 9-48.
Goins, S. E. (1989-90) 'The influence of Old Comedy on the *Vita Aesopi*', *CW* 83: 28-30.
Goldhill, S. (2006) 'The thrill of misplaced laughter', in *Kômôidotragôidia: intersezioni del tragico e del comico nel teatro del V secolo a.C*, ed. E. Medda, M. S. Mirto and M. P. Pattoni. Pisa, 83-102.
Gonfroy, F. (1978) 'Homosexualité et idéologie esclavagiste chez Cicéron', *Dialogues d'histoire ancienne* 4: 219-62.
Goody, E. N. (1989) 'Learning, apprenticeship and the division of labor', in *Apprenticeship: From Theory to Method and Back Again*, ed. M. Coy. New York, 233-56.
Gordon, R. (1990) 'Religion in the Roman Empire: the civic compromise and its limits', in *Pagan Priests*, ed. M. Beard and J. North. London, 233-55.
Gould, J. (1985) 'On making sense of Greek religion', in *Greek Religion and Society*, ed. P. E. Easterling and J. V. Muir. Cambridge, 1-33.
Gowers, E. (2012) *Horace: Satires, Book 1*. Cambridge.
Graesse, T. (1846) *Jacobus de Voragine, Legenda Aurea*. Leipzig.
Graf, F. (1997) *Magic in the Ancient World*, 2nd edn. Cambridge.
  (1998) 'Kalendae Ianuariae', in *Ansichten griechischer Rituale: Geburtstags-Symposion für Walter Burkert*. Stuttgart and Leipzig, 199-216.
  (2005a) 'Satire in a ritual context', in *The Cambridge Companion to Roman Satire*, ed. K. Freudenburg. Cambridge, 192-206.
  (2005b) 'Rolling the dice for an answer', in *Mantikê: Studies in Ancient Divination*, ed. S. I. Johnston and P. T. Struck. Leiden, 51-97.

(2012) 'Fights about festivals: Libanius and John Chrysostom on the *Kalendae Ianuariae* in Antioch', *ARG* 13: 175–86.

(2015) *Roman Festivals in the Greek East*. Cambridge.

Gramsci, A. (1971) *Selections from the Prison Notebooks*, ed. and trans. Q. Hoare and G. Nowell Smith. New York.

Green, M. (1989) *Symbol and Image in Celtic Religious Art*. London.

Greenfield, R. P. H. (1989) 'Saint Sisinnios, the archangel Michael and the female demon Gylou: the typology of the Greek literary stories', *Βυζαντινά* 15: 83–142.

Greer, R. A. and Mitchell, M. M. (2007) *The 'Belly-Myther' of Endor: Interpretations of 1 Kingdoms 28 in the Early Church*. Atlanta, GA.

Gregory, A. P. (1994) 'Powerful images: responses to portraits and the political uses of images in Rome', *JRA* 7: 80–99.

Gregory, T. (1979) *Vox Populi: Popular Opinion and Violence in the Religious Controversies of the Fifth Century A.D.* Columbus, OH.

Grey, C. (2011) *Constructing Communities in the Late Roman Countryside*. Cambridge.

Grieb, V. (2009) *Hellenistische Demokratie: politische Organisation und Struktur in freien griechischen Poleis nach Alexander dem Großen*. Stuttgart.

Grig, L. (2004) *Making Martyrs in Late Antiquity*. London.

(2013a) 'The Bible in popular and non-literary culture', in *The New Cambridge History of the Bible: From the Beginnings to 600*, ed. J. Schaper and J. Carleton Paget. Cambridge, 843–70.

(2013b) 'Approaching popular culture: singing in the Sermons of Caesarius of Arles', *Studia Patristica* 69: 197–204.

Grignon, C. and Passeron, J.-C. (1989) *Le savant et le populaire: Misérabilisme et populisme en sociologie et en littérature*. Paris.

Gros, P. (2001) *L'architecture romaine*, vol. II: *Maisons, palais, villas et tombeaux*. Paris.

Grottanelli, C. (2005) 'Sorte unica pro casibus pluribus enotata: literary texts and lot inscriptions as sources for ancient kleromancy', in *Mantikê: Studies in Ancient Divination*, ed. S. I. Johnston and P. T. Struck. Leiden, 129–46.

Gruen, E. S. (1974) *The Last Generation of the Roman Republic*. Berkeley, CA.

Guidetti, F. (2006) 'Note sull'iconografia di un rilievo funerario da Amiternum: modelli e scelte figurative di un liberto municipale', *ArchClass* 57: 387–401.

Guilhembet, J.-P (2011) *Se loger à Rome: Recherches sur le marché immobilier d'habitation (IIe s. a. C. – IIe s. p. C.)*. Lyon.

Guinan, A. K. (2002) 'A severed head laughed: stories of divinatory interpretation', in *Magic and Divination in the Ancient World*, ed. L. Ciraolo and J. Seidel. Leiden, 7–40.

Guins, R. and Zaragoza Cruz, O. (eds.) (2005) *Popular Culture: A Reader*. London.

Gunderson, E. (1996) 'The ideology of the arena', *ClAnt* 15: 113–51.

Gurevich, A. I. (1988) *Medieval Popular Culture: Problems of Belief and Perception*, trans. J. M. Bak and P. A. Hollingsworth. Cambridge.

Hadji-Minaglou, G. (2007) *Tebtynis IV: Les habitations à l'est du temple de Soknebtynis.* Cairo.
  (2008) 'L'habitat à Tebtynis a la lumière des fouilles récentes Ier s. av.– Ier s. apr. J-C', in *Graeco-Roman Fayum: Texts and Archaeology*, ed. S. Lippert and M. Schentuleit. Wiesbaden, 123–33.
Hägg, T. (1997) 'A professor and his slave: conventions and values in the *Life of Aesop*', in *Conventional Values of the Hellenistic Greeks*, ed. P. Bilde, T. Engberg-Pedersen, L. Hannestad and J. Zahle. Aarhus and Oxford, 177–203.
Hahn, J. (2011) 'Philosophy as a socio-political upbringing', in *The Oxford Handbook of Social Relations in the Roman World*, ed. M. Peachin. Oxford, 19–143.
Hall, E. (2011) 'Playing ball with Zeus: strategies in reading ancient slavery through dreams', in *Reading Ancient Slavery*, ed. R. Alston, E. Hall and L. Proffitt. London, 204–28.
Hall, E. and Wyles, R. (eds.) (2008) *New Directions in Ancient Pantomime.* Oxford.
Hall, S. (1973) 'Encoding and decoding in television discourse', University of Birmingham Centre for Contemporary Cultural Studies. Stencilled paper 7.
  (1981) 'Notes on deconstructing the "popular"', in *People's History and Socialist Theory*, ed. R. Samuel. London, 227–40.
Hällström, G. (1984) *Fides Simpliciorum According to Origen of Alexandria.* Helsinki.
Hano, M. (1986) 'À l'origine du culte impérial: les autels des *lares Augusti*: recherches sur les thèmes iconographiques et leur signification', *ANRW*, 16.3: 2333–81.
Hansen, M. H. (1980) '*Eisangelia* in Athens: a reply', *JHS* 100: 83–95.
  (1985) *Demography and Democracy: The Number of Athenian Citizens in the Fourth Century B.C.* Herning.
  (1989) *The Athenian Ecclesia II: A Collection of Articles, 1983–1989.* Odense.
  (1991) *The Athenian Democracy in the Age of Demosthenes: Structure, Principles, and Ideology.* Oxford.
  (2006) *Polis: An Introduction to the Ancient Greek City-State.* Oxford.
Hansen, W. (ed.) (1998) *Anthology of Ancient Greek Popular Literature.* Bloomington, IN.
Harders, A.-C. (2010) 'Roman patchwork families: surrogate parenting, socialization, and the shaping of tradition', in *Children, Memory and Family Identity in Roman Culture*, ed. V. Dasen and T. Späth. Oxford, 49–72.
Harkins, P. W. (trans.) (1979) *John Chrysostom: Discourses against Judaizing Christians.* Washington DC.
Harlow, M. and Laurence, R. (eds.) (2002) *Growing Up and Growing Old in Ancient Rome.* London.
Harmening, D. (1979) *Superstitio: Überlieferungs- und theoriegeschichtliche Untersuchungen zur kirchlich-theologischen Aberglaubensliteratur des Mittelalters.* Berlin.

Harnack, A. von (1957) *Outlines of the History of Dogma*, trans. E. K. Mitchell. Boston.
Harries, J. (1999) '*Favor populi*: pagans, Christians and public entertainment in late antique Italy', in *Bread and Circuses: Euergetism and Municipal Patronage in Roman Italy*, ed. K. Lomas and T. Cornell. London, 125–41.
Harris, E. M. (2002) 'Workshop, marketplace and household: the nature of technical specialization in classical Athens and its influence on economy and society', in *Money, Labour and Land: Approaches to the Economies of Ancient Greece*, ed. P. Cartledge, E. Cohen and L. Foxhall. London, 67–99.
  (2006) *Democracy and the Rule of Law in Classical Athens: Essays on Law, Society, and Politics*. Cambridge.
  (2013) *The Rule of Law in Action in Democratic Athens*. Oxford.
Harris, M. (2011) *Sacred Folly: A New History of the Feast of Fools*. London.
Harris, W. V. (1989) *Ancient Literacy*. Cambridge, MA.
Harrison, A. R. W. (1968) *The Law of Athens: Family and Property*. Oxford.
Harrison, I. (2008) 'Catiline, Clodius, and popular politics at Rome during the 60s and 50s BCE', *BICS* 51: 95–118.
Harvey, F. D. (1994) 'Lacomica: Aristophanes and the Spartans', in *The Shadow of Sparta*, ed. A. Powell and S. Hodkinson. London and New York, 35–58.
Hawkins, T. (2012) 'Jester for a day, master for a year: Julian's *Misopogon* and the Kalends of 363 CE', *ARG* 13: 161–74.
  (2014) *Iambic Poetics in the Roman Empire*. Cambridge.
Hebdige, D. (1979) 'From culture to hegemony', in *Subculture: The Meaning of Style*. London, 5–19.
Hefele, C. (1829–1912) *A History of the Christian Councils from the Original Documents to the Close of the Council of Nicaea, A.D. 325*, trans. W. R. Clark, 5 vols., 2nd edn. Edinburgh.
Helms, M. W. (1993) *Craft and the Kingly Ideal: Art, Trade, and Power*. Austin, TX.
Hen, Y. (1995) *Culture and Religion in Merovingian Gaul A.D. 481–751*. Leiden, New York, Cologne.
  (2012) 'Le repressione dei pagani nell'agiografia merovingia', in *Agiografia e Culture Populari*, ed. P. Golineli. Bologna, 193–206.
Henderson, Jeffrey (1991) 'Women and the Athenian dramatic festivals', *TAPhA* 121: 133–47.
Henderson, John (1977) 'The homing instinct: Phaedrus, *Appendix* 16', *PCPhS* 23: 17–31.
Hengst, H. (2005) 'Complex interconnections: the global and the local in children's minds and everyday worlds', in *Studies in Modern Childhood: Society, Agency and Culture*, ed. J. Qvortrup. Basingstoke, 21–38.
Herbert-Brown, G. (2009) '*Fasti*: the poet, the prince and the plebs', in *A Companion to Ovid*, ed. P. Knox. Chichester, 120–39.
Hesk, J. (2000) *Deception and Democracy in Classical Athens*. Cambridge.

Hickey, T. M. (2009) 'Writing histories from papyri', in *The Oxford Handbook of Papyrology*, ed. R. S. Bagnall. Oxford, 495–520.

Higgins, R. A. (1967) *Greek Terracottas*. London.

Highmore, B. (2002) *Everyday Life and Cultural Theory: An Introduction*. London.

Hill, E. (trans.) (1997) *Augustine Sermons III/11: Newly Discovered Sermons*. New York.

Hillard, T. (2013) 'Graffiti's engagement: the political graffiti of the Late Roman Republic', in *Written Space in the Latin West, 200 BC to AD 300*, ed. G. Sears, P. Keegan and R. Laurence. London, 105–22.

Hirschfeld, L. A. (2002) 'Why don't anthropologists like children?', *American Anthropologist* 104: 611–27.

Hobden, F. (2013) *The Symposion in Ancient Greek Society and Thought*. Cambridge.

Hofmann, H. (1999) *Latin Fiction: The Latin Novel in Context*. London.

Hoggart, R. (1957) *The Uses of Literacy: Aspects of Working-Class Life*. London.

Holleran, C. (2011) 'The street life of ancient Rome', in *Rome, Ostia, Pompeii: Movement and Space*, ed. R. Laurence and D. J. Newsome. Oxford, 245–61.

Holleran, C. and Pudsey, A. (eds.) (2011) *Demography and Society in the Greek and Roman Worlds: New Insights and Approaches*. Cambridge.

Holloway, S. L. and Valentine, G. (2000) 'Children's geographies and the new social studies of childhood', in *Children's Geographies: Playing, Living, and Learning*, ed. S. L. Holloway and G. Valentine. London, 1–28.

Hölkeskamp, K.-J. (2010) *Reconstructing the Roman Republic: An Ancient Political Culture and Modern Research*, trans. H. Heitmann-Gordon. Princeton, NJ, and Oxford.

Hölscher, T. (2012) '"Präsentativer Stil" im System der römischen Kunst', in *Kunst von unten? Stil und Gesellschaft in der antiken Welt von der "arte plebea" bis heute*, ed. F. de Angelis, J.-A. Dickman, F. Pirson and R. von der Hoff. Wiesbaden, 27–58.

Holzberg, N. (1992) 'Der Äsop-Roman', in *Der Äsop-Roman: Motivgeschichte und Erzählstruktur*, ed. N. Holzberg. Tübingen, 33–75.

Hopkins, K. (1993) 'Novel evidence for Roman slavery', *P&P* 138: 3–27.

Horden, P. and Purcell, N. (2000) *The Corrupting Sea: A Study of Mediterranean History*. Oxford.

Horn, C. B. (2005) 'Children's play as social ritual', in *A People's History of Christianity*, vol. II: *Christianity in the Roman World*, ed. V. Burrus. Augsburg, 95–116.

Horn, C. B. and Phoenix, R. (eds.) (2009) *Children in Late Ancient Christianity*. Tübingen.

Horsfall, N. (1996) 'The cultural horizons of the "Plebs Romana"', *MAAR* 41: 101–19.
  (2003) *The Culture of the Roman Plebs*. London.

Horsley, G. H. R. and Mitchell, S. (eds.) (2000) *The Inscriptions of Central Pisidia*. Bonn.

Howes, D. (2003) *Sensual Relations: Engaging the Senses in Culture and Social Theory*. Ann Arbor, MI.
  (2005) 'Introduction', in *Empire of the Senses: The Sensual Culture Reader*, ed. D. Howes. Oxford and New York, 1–17.
Hugoniot, C. (1992) 'Saint Augustin et les spectacles de l'amphithéâtre de l'Afrique romaine', *Histoire de l'Art* 17–18: 11–21.
Humm, M. (2005) *Appius Claudius Caecus: La République accomplie*. Rome.
Humphrey, J. (ed.) (1991) *Literacy in the Roman World*. Ann Arbor, MI.
Hunink, V. (2011) 'Singing together in church: Augustine's *Psalm against the Donatists*', in *Sacred Words: Orality, Literacy and Religion*, ed. A. P. M. H. Lardinois, J. H. Block and M. G. M. van der Poel. Leiden, 389–403.
Hunt, L. (1989) *The New Cultural History*. Berkeley, CA.
Hunter, R. (2007) 'Isis and the language of Aesop', in *Pastoral Palimpsests: Essays in the Reception of Theocritus and Virgil*, ed. M. Paschalis. Heraklion, 39–58.
  (2008) 'Ancient readers', in *The Cambridge Companion to the Greek and Roman Novel*, ed. T. Whitmarsh. Cambridge, 261–71.
  (2009) 'The curious incident . . .: *polypragmosyne* and the ancient novel', in *Readers and Writers in the Ancient Novel*, ed. M. Paschalis, S. Panayotakis and G. Schmeling. Groningen, 51–63.
Huntley, K. V. (2010) 'Identifying children's graffiti in Roman Campania: a developmental psychological approach', in *Ancient Graffiti in Context*, ed. J. A. Baird and C. Taylor. London, 69–89.
Hurlet, F. (2012) 'Démocratie? Quelle démocratie? En relisant Millar (et Hölkeskamp)', in *Rome, a City and its Empire in Perspective: The Impact of the Roman World through Fergus Millar's Research / Rome, une cité impériale en jeu: L'impact du monde romain selon Fergus Millar*, ed. S. Benoist. Leiden and Boston, 19–43.
Huskinson, J. (2008). 'Pantomime performance and figured scenes on Roman sarcophagi', in *New Directions in Ancient Pantomime*, ed. E. Hall and R. Wyles. Oxford, 87–110.
Ikram, S. (2003) 'Barbering the beardless: a possible explanation for the tufted hairstyle depicted in the "Fayum" portrait of a young boy (J. P. Getty 78. AP.262)', *JEA* 89: 247–51.
Irvine, J. T. (1992) 'Insult and responsibility: verbal abuse in a Wolof village', in *Responsibility and Evidence in Oral Discourse*, ed. J. Hill and J. T. Irvine. Cambridge, 105–34.
James, A. and Prout, A. (1997a) 'A new paradigm for the sociology of childhood? Provenance, promise and problems', in *Constructing and Reconstructing Childhood: Contemporary Issues in the Sociological Study of Childhood*, ed. A. James and A. Prout. London, 7–33.
James, A. and Prout, A. (eds.) (1997b) *Constructing and Reconstructing Childhood: Contemporary Issues in the Sociological Study of Childhood*. London.

James, A., Jenks, C. and Prout, A. (2005) *Theorizing Childhood*, 5th edn. Cambridge.
Jameson, M. H. (1977–8) 'Agriculture and slavery in Classical Athens', *CJ* 73.2: 122–45.
Janowitz, N. (2001) *Magic in the Ancient World: Pagans, Jews, and Christians*. London.
  (2002) *Icons of Power: Ritual Practices in Late Antiquity*. University Park, PA.
Janssen, R. (1996). 'Soft toys from Egypt', in *Archaeological Research in Roman Egypt*, ed. D. Bailey. Ann Arbor, MI, 231–9.
Jebb, R. C. (1893) *The Attic Orators: From Antiphon to Isaeus*, 2nd edn. London.
Jehne, M. (2006) 'Who attended Roman assemblies? Some remarks on political participation in the Roman Republic', in *Repúblicas y ciudadanos: modelos de participación cívica en el mundo antiguo*, ed. F. Marco Simón, F. Pina Polo and J. Remesal Rodríguez. Barcelona, 221–34.
Jennings, V. (2009) 'Borrowed plumes: Phaedrus' fables, Phaedrus' failures', in *Writing Politics in Imperial Rome*, ed. W. J. Dominik, J. Garthwaite and P. A. Roche. Leiden, 225–48.
Johnson, A. C. (1936) *Roman Egypt to the Reign of Diocletian (An Economic Survey of Ancient Rome)*, vol. II, ed. T. Frank. Baltimore and London.
Johnson, M. J. (1997) 'Pagan-Christian burial practices of the fourth century: shared tombs?', *JECS* 5: 37–59.
Johnson, W. A. (2010) *Readers and Reading Culture in the High Roman Empire: A Study of Elite Communities*. Oxford.
Johnson, W. A. and Parker, H. N. (2009) *Ancient Literacies: The Culture of Reading in Greece and Rome*. Oxford and New York.
Johnston, S. I. (2001) 'Charming children: the use of the child in ancient divination', *Arethusa* 34: 97–117.
  (2005) 'Delphi and the dead', in *Mantikê: Studies in Ancient Divination*, ed. S. I. Johnston and P. T. Struck. Leiden, 283–306.
  (2008) *Ancient Greek Divination*. Malden, MA, and Oxford.
Johnston, S. I. and Graf, F. (2013) *Ritual Texts for the Afterlife: Orpheus and the Bacchic Gold Tables*. London.
Jones, A. E. (2009) *Social Mobility in Late Antique Gaul: Strategies and Opportunities for the Non-Elite*. Cambridge.
Jones, A. H. M. (1957) *Athenian Democracy*. Oxford.
Jordan, D. R. (1985) 'The inscribed gold tablet from the Vigna Codini', *AJA* 89: 162–7.
Joshel, S. R. (1992) *Work, Identity and Legal Status at Rome: A Study of the Occupational Inscriptions*. Norman, OK.
Jouanno, C. (2009) 'Novelistic lives and historical biographies: the *Life of Aesop* and the *Alexander Romance* as fringe novels', in *Fiction on the Fringe: Novelistic Writing in the Post-Classical Age*, ed. G. A. Karla. Leiden, 33–48.
Junkelmann, M. (2000) *Das Spiel mit dem Tod*. Mainz.

Kajanto, I. (1965) *The Latin Cognomina*. Helsinki.

Kaldellis, A. (2012) 'The Kalends in Byzantium, 400–1200 AD: a new interpretation', *ARG* 13: 187–203.

Kalifa, D. (2010) 'Culture savante/culture populaire', in *Historiographie: Concepts et débats*, vol. II, ed. C. Delacroix, F. Dosse and P. Garcia. Paris, 994–9.

Kampen, N. B. (1981) *Image and Status: Roman Working Women in Ostia*. Berlin.

(1995) 'On not writing the history of Roman art', *Art Bulletin* 77: 375–8.

Kapferer, J. N. (2013) *Rumors: Uses, Interpretations, and Images*, trans. B. Fink. New Brunswick, NJ.

Kapparis, K. (1995) 'When were the Athenian adultery laws introduced?', *RIDA* 42: 97–122.

(1996) 'Humiliating the adulterer: the law and the practice in Classical Athens', *RIDA* 43: 63–77.

Karla, G. A. (ed.) (2009a) *Fiction on the Fringe: Novelistic Writing in the Post-Classical Age*, ed. G. A. Karla. Leiden.

(2009b) 'Fictional biography vis-à-vis romance: affinity and differentiation', in *Fiction on the Fringe: Novelistic Writing in the Post-Classical Age*, ed. G. A. Karla. Leiden, 13–32.

Kaster, R. A. (2006) *Cicero: Speech on Behalf of Publius Sestius*. Oxford.

Katajala-Peltomaa, S. and Vuolanto, V. (2011) 'Children and agency: religion as socialization in Late Antiquity and the late medieval West', *Childhood in the Past* 4: 79–99.

Kelly, B. (2011) *Petitions, Litigation, and Social Control in Roman Egypt*. Cambridge.

King, H. and Toner, J. (2014) 'Medicine and the sense: humors, potions, and spells', in *A Cultural History of the Senses in Antiquity*, ed. J. Toner. London, 139–61.

Klingshirn, W. (1994) *Caesarius of Arles: The Making of a Christian Community in Late Antique Gaul*. Cambridge.

Knapp, R. C. (2011) *Invisible Romans*. Cambridge, MA.

Kolendo, J. (1981) 'La répartition des places aux spectacles et la stratification sociale dans l'Empire Romain', *Ktèma* 6: 301–15.

Konstan, D. (1985) 'The politics of Aristophanes' *Wasps*', *TAPhA* 115: 27–46.

(2009) 'The active reader and the ancient novel', in *Readers and Writers in the Ancient Novel*, ed. M. Paschalis, S. Panayotakis and G. Schmeling. Groningen, 1–17.

Konstantakos, I. M. (2013) *Ακίχαρος III: Η Διήγηση του Αχικάρ και η Μυθιστορία του Αισώπου*. Athens.

Korres, M. (2002) 'Modell des Dionysos-Theaters', in *Die griechische Klassik – Idee oder Wirklichkeit?* Antikensammlungen Berlin, Staatliche Museen Preußischer Kulturbesitz, exhibition catalogue. Mainz, 540–1.

Koudounaris, P. (2011) *The Empire of Death: A Cultural History of Ossuaries and Charnel Houses*. London.

Krampl, U. and Beck, R. (2013) 'Des sens qui font la ville: pour une histoire sensible du fait urbain', in *Les cinq sens de la ville du Moyen Âge à nos jours*, ed. U. Krampl, R. Beck and E. Retaillaud-Bajac. Tours, 13–25.

Kristensen, K. R. (2004) 'Codification, tradition and innovation in the law code of Gortyn', *Dike* 7: 135–68.

Kroeber, A. L. and Kluckhohn, C. (1952) *Culture: A Critical Review of Concepts and Definitions*. New York.

Kron, G. (2011) 'The distribution of wealth at Athens in comparative perspective', *ZPE* 179: 129–38.

Künzel, F. (1992) 'Paganisme, syncrétisme et culture religieuse populaire au Haut Moyen Age: réflexions de méthode', trans. F. Chevy, *Annales ESC* 47: 1055–69.

Kuper, H. (1944) 'A ritual of kingship among the Swazi', *Africa: Journal of the International African Institute* 14: 230–57.

(1999) *Culture: The Anthropologists' Account*. Cambridge, MA.

Kurke, L. (1999) *Coins, Bodies, Games and Gold: The Politics of Meaning in Archaic Greece*. Princeton, NJ.

(2011) *Aesopic Conversations: Popular Tradition, Cultural Dialogue, and the Invention of Greek Prose*. Princeton, NJ, and Oxford.

Kuttner, A. L. (1999) 'Culture and history at Pompey's museum', *TAPhA* 129: 343–73.

LaCapra, D. (1983) 'Bakhtin, Marxism, and the carnivalesque', in *Rethinking Intellectual History: Texts, Contexts, Language*. Ithaca, NY, and London, 291–324.

Lada-Richards, I. (2003) '"A worthless feminine thing"? Lucian and the "optic intoxication" of pantomime dancing', *Helios* 30: 21–75.

(2004) 'Mythôn Eikôn: pantomime dancing and the figurative arts in imperial and late Antiquity', *Arion* 12: 17–46.

(2007) *Silent Eloquence: Lucian and Pantomime Dancing*. London.

(2008). 'Was pantomime "good to think with" in the ancient world?', in *New Directions in Ancient Pantomime*, ed. E. Hall and R. Wyles. Oxford, 285–313.

Laes, C. (2011) *Children in the Roman Empire: Outsiders Within*. Cambridge.

Laes, C., Mustakallio, K. and Vuolanto, V. (eds.) (2014) *Children and Family in Late Antiquity: Life, Death and Interaction*. Leuven.

Laes, C. and Vuolanto, V. (forthcoming) *Children and Everyday Life in the Roman and Late Antique World*. Abingdon.

Lambot, C. (1935) 'Texte complet et amendé du *Psalmus contra partem Donati* de Saint Augustin', *RBén* 47: 312–30.

Lamont, M. and Lareau, A. (1988) 'Cultural capital: allusions, gaps and glissandos in recent theoretical developments', *Sociological Theory* 6: 153–68.

Lanciani, R. (1892) *Pagan and Christian Rome*. Boston.

Langdon, S. (2013) 'Children as learners and producers in early Greece', in *The Oxford Handbook of Childhood and Education in the Classical World*, ed. J. Evans-Grubbs and T. Parkin with R. Bell. Oxford, 172–94.

La Rocca, E., Parisi Presicce, C., Lo Monaco, A., Giroire, C. and Roger, D. (2013) *Augusto*. Rome.

Laser, G. (1997) *Populo et scaenae serviendum est: die Bedeutung der städtischen Masse in der späten römischen Republik*. Trier.

Laurence, R. (1994a) *Roman Pompeii: Space and Society*. London.

(1994b) 'Rumour and communication in Roman politics', *G&R* 41: 62–74.

(1997) 'Writing the Roman metropolis', in *Roman Urbanism – Beyond the Consumer City*, ed. H. M. Parkins. London and New York, 1–19.

Laurence, R. and Wallace-Hadrill, A. (eds.) (1997) *Domestic Space in the Roman World: Pompeii and Beyond*, Portsmouth, RI.

Lavency, M. (1964) *Aspects de la logographie judiciaire attique*. Louvain.

Lane Fox, R. (1986) *Pagans and Christians*. Harmondsworth.

Lears, T. J. J. (1985) 'The concept of cultural hegemony: problems and possibilities', *AHR* 90.3: 567–93.

Leavis, F. R. (1930) *Mass Civilisation and Minority Culture*. Cambridge.

Le Breton, D. (2007) 'Pour une anthropologie des sens', *Vie sociale et traitements* 96.4: 45–53.

Lech, M. L. (2011) 'Review of D. K. Roselli, Theater of the People: spectators and society in ancient Athens', *BMCR*, available at: http://bmcr.brynmawr.edu/2011/2011-12-19.html.

Ledeen, M. A. (2009) 'Death in Naples'. *First Things* (Aug/Sept). Available at: www.firstthings.com/article/2009/08/death-in-naples.

Leemans, J. (2004) 'Preaching Christian virtue: Basil of Caesarea's panegyrical sermon on Julitta', in *Virtutis Imago: Studies on the Conceptualisation and Transformation of an Ancient Ideal*, ed. G. Partoens, G. Roskam and T. Van Houdt. Paris, 259–85.

Leemans, J., Mayer, W., Allen, P. and Dehandschutter, B. (eds.) (2003) *'Let us Die that We May Live': Greek Homilies on Christian Martyrs from Asia Minor, Palestine and Syria (c. AD 350–AD 450)*. London and New York.

Le Gall, J. (1971) 'Rome: ville de fainéants?', *REL* 49: 266–77.

Le Goff, J. (1977) *Pour un autre moyen âge: Temps, travail et culture en Occident*. Paris; trans. A Goldhammer, as *Time, Work and Culture in the Middle Ages*. London and Chicago, 1986.

Leon, D. W. (2012) 'An *epikrisis* document from Oxyrhynchus (P.Mich.inv. 261)', *BASP* 49: 95–108.

Lepelley, C. (1979) *Les cités de l'Afrique romaine au Bas-Empire*, vol. I. Paris.

(1989) 'Peuplement et richesses de l'Afrique romaine tardive', in *Hommes et richesses dans l'Empire byzantin*, vol. I. Paris, 17–30.

(2001) 'La carrière municipale dans l'Afrique romaine sous l'Empire tardif', in *Aspects de l'Afrique romaine: Les cités, la vie rurale, le christianisme*. Bari, 105–24.

Le Roy Ladurie, E. (1979) *Carnival in Romans*, trans. M. Feeney. New York.
Levine, L. (1988) *Highbrow/Lowbrow: The Emergence of Cultural Hierarchy in America*. Cambridge, MA.
Lévi-Strauss, C. (1966) *The Savage Mind*. Chicago.
Lewis, D. M., Harris, E. M. and Woolmer, M. (2015) *Markets, Households and City-States in the Ancient Greek Economy*. Cambridge.
Lieberman, R. C. (2002) 'Ideas, institutions, and political order: explaining political change', *American Political Science Review* 96.4: 697–712.
Liebeschuetz, J. H. G. W. (2001) *The Decline and Fall of the Roman City*. Oxford.
Lietzmann, H. (1934) 'Ein Gnostiker in der Novatianus Katakombe', *RAC* 11: 359–62.
Lightfoot, J. (2000) 'Sophisticates and solecisms: Greek literature after the classical period', in *Literature in the Greek and Roman Worlds: A New Perspective*, ed. O. Taplin. Oxford, 217–56.
Lillehammer, G. (1989) 'A child is born: the child's world in an archaeological perspective', *Norwegian Archaeological Review* 22.2: 89–105.
  (2000) 'The world of children', in *Children and Material Culture*, ed. J. Sofaer Derevenski. New York, 17–26.
Lim, R. (1995) *Public Disputation, Power and Social Order in Late Antiquity*. Berkeley, CA.
  (1996) 'In the "temple of laughter": visual and literary representations of spectators at Roman games', in *The Art of Ancient Spectacle*, ed. B. Bergmann and C. Kondoleon. Washington, DC, 343–65.
  (1999) 'People as power: games, munificence and contested topography', in *The Transformations of Vrbs Roma in Late Antiquity*, ed. W. V. Harris. Portsmouth, RI, 265–81.
Limberis, V. (2011) *Architects of Piety: The Cappadocian Fathers and the Cult of the Martyrs*. Oxford and New York.
Linderski, J. (1990) 'The surname of M. Antonius Creticus and the cognomina ex victis gentibus', *ZPE* 80: 159–64.
  (2002) 'The pontiff and the tribune: the death of Tiberius Gracchus', *Athenaeum* 90: 339–66.
  (2007) 'A Missing Ponticus', in *Roman Questions*, vol. II, ed. J. Linderski. Stuttgart, 115–23.
Lintott, A. W. (1967) 'P. Clodius Pulcher – Felix Catilina?', *G&R* 14: 157–69.
Lippert, S. and Schentuleit, M. (eds.) (2008) *Graeco-Roman Fayum: Texts and Archaeology*. Wiesbaden.
Lo Cascio, E. (1990) 'Le *professiones* della *Tabula Heracleensis* e le procedure del *census* in età Cesariana', *Athenaeum* 78: 287–318.
  (1997) 'Le procedure di *recensus* dalla tarda Repubblica al tardoantico e il calcolo della popolazione di Roma', in *La Rome impériale: Démographie et logistique*, ed. C. Virlouvet. Rome, 3–76.

(1998) 'Registri dei benificiari e modalità delle distribuzioni nella Roma tardoantica', in *La mémoire perdue: Recherches sur l'administration romaine*, ed. C. Virlouvet and C. Moatti. Rome, 365–85.

(2001) 'La population', *Pallas* 55: 179–98.

(2007), 'Il ruolo dei *vici* e delle *regiones* nel controllo della popolazione e nell'amministrazione di Roma', in *Herrschen und Verwalten: Der Alltag der römischen Administration in der Hohen Kaiserzeit*, ed. R. Haensch and J. Heinrichs. Cologne, Weimar and Vienna, 145–59.

Loomis, W. T. (1998) *Wages, Welfare Costs, and Inflation in Classical Athens*. Ann Arbor, MI.

Lott, J. B. (2004) *The Neighbourhoods of Augustan Rome*. Cambridge.

Lugaresi, L. (2007) '*Regio aliena*: l'attegiamento della chiesa verso i luoghi di spettacolo nella città tardoantica', *AntTard* 15: 21–34.

Lussaut, M. (2003) 'Quartier', in *Dictionnaire de la géographie*, ed. J. Lévy and M. Lussault. Paris, 758–60.

MacCormack, S. (2001) 'The virtue of work: an Augustinian transformation', *AntTard* 9: 219–37.

MacDonald, D. (1957) 'A theory of mass culture', in *Mass Culture: The Popular Arts in America*, ed. B. Rosenberg and D. M. Wright. New York and London, 59–73.

MacDowell, D. M. (1971) *Aristophanes' Wasps*. Oxford.

(1978) *The Law in Classical Athens*. London.

(1995) *Aristophanes and Athens: An Introduction to the Plays*. Oxford.

MacMahon, A. (2003) *The Taberna Structures of Roman Britain*. Oxford.

(2006) 'Fixed-point retail location in the major towns of Roman Britain', *OJA* 25.3: 289–309.

MacMullen, R. (1989) 'The preacher's audience (AD 350–400)', *JThS* 40: 503–11.

(1990) 'The historical role of the masses in Late Antiquity', in *Changes in the Roman Empire: Essays in the Ordinary*. Princeton, NJ, 250–76.

(1997) *Christianity and Paganism in the Fourth to Eighth Centuries*. New Haven, CT.

(2009) *The Second Church: Popular Christianity AD 200–400*. Atlanta, GA.

Madeleine, S. (2008) 'La hauteur des immeubles d'habitation sur la *Forma Vrbis Romae*', in *Roma illustrata: Représentations de la ville*, ed. P. Fleury and O. Desbordes. Caen, 291–316.

Magalhães de Oliveira, J. C. (2006) '"Vt maiores pagani non sint!" Pouvoir, iconoclasme et action populaire à Carthage au début du Ve siècle (Saint Augustin, *Sermons* 24, 279 et Morin 1)', *AntTard* 14: 245–62.

(2012) *Potestas populi: Participation populaire et action collective dans les villes de l'Afrique romaine tardive (vers 300–430 apr. J.-C.)*. Turnhout.

Maier, B. (1997) *Dictionary of Celtic Religion and Culture*, trans. C. Edwards. Woodbridge.

Malaise, M. (1972) *Les conditions de pénétration et de diffusion des cultes égyptiens en Italie.* Leiden.

Mandrou, R. (1964) *De la culture populaire aux XVIIe et XVIIIe siècles: La bibliothèque bleue de Troyes.* Paris.

Manetti, G. (1993) *Theories of the Sign in Classical Antiquity.* Bloomington, IN.

Mann, C. and Scholz, P. (2011) *'Demokratie' im Hellenismus: Von der Herrschaft des Volkes zur Herrschaft der Honoratioren? Die hellenistische Polis als Lebensform.* Berlin.

Manson, M. (1987) 'Le bambole romane antiche', *La Ricerca folklorica* 16: 15–26.
  (1991) 'Jouets et jeux de l'enfance', in *Jouer dans l'Antiquité.* Marseilles, 50–8.
  (1992) 'Les poupées antiques', *Les Dossiers d'archéologie* 168: 48–57.

Mansouri, S. (2002) 'L'agora athénienne ou le lieu de travail, des discussions et des nouvelles politiques: chercher la politique là où elle n'est apparemment pas', *Dialogues d'histoire ancienne* 28.2: 41–63.

March, J. G. and Olsen, J. P. (1984) 'The new institutionalism: organizational factors in political life', *American Political Science Review* 78: 734–49.
  (2006) 'Elaborating the "new institutionalism"', in *The Oxford Handbook of Political Institutions*, ed. R. A. W. Rhodes, S. A. Binder and B. A. Rockman. Oxford, 3–20.

Marchant, E. C. (trans.) (1923) *Xenophon. Memorabilia and Oeconomicus.* London and Cambridge, MA.

Marco Simón, F. and Pina Polo, F. (2000) 'Mario Gratidiano, los compita y la religiosidad popular a fines de la república', *Klio* 82: 154–70.

Marichal, R. (1986) 'La vie et la structure des ateliers de La Graufesenque', in *La terre sigillée gallo-romaine. Lieux de production du Haut-Empire: implantations, produits, relations.* Paris, 16–20.

Markle, M. M. (1985) 'Jury pay and assembly pay at Athens', in *Crux: Essays Presented to G. E. M. de Ste. Croix*, ed. P. Cartledge and F. D. Harvey. London, 265–97.

Markus, R. A. (1990) *The End of Ancient Christianity.* Cambridge.

Marshall, B. A. (1985) *A Historical Commentary on Asconius.* Columbia, MO.

Martin, F. (2003) *L'antiquité au cinéma.* Paris.

Martin-Kilcher, S. (2000) '*Mors immatura* in the Roman world – a mirror of society and tradition', in *Burial, Society and Context in the Roman World*, ed. J. Pearce, M. Millet and M. Struck. Oxford, 63–77.

Marx, K. (1976) *Contribution to the Critique of Political Economy.* Peking.

Marx, K. and Engels, F. (1974) *The German Ideology*, student edn, ed. C. J. Arthur. London.
  (1977) *Selected Letters.* Peking.

Masciadri, M. M. and Montevecchi, O. (1984) *I contratti di baliatico.* Milan.

Massa-Pairault, F.-H. (1985) *Recherches sur l'art et l'artisanat étrusco-italique à l'époque hellénistique.* Rome.

Matthews, S. (2010) *Perfect Martyr: The Stoning of Stephen and the Construction of Christian Identity.* Oxford and New York.

Matthews, V. J. (1973) 'Some puns on Roman cognomina', *G&R* 20: 20–4.

Mattingly, D. J. (2010) *Imperialism, Power and Identity: Experiencing the Roman Empire.* Oxford.

Maxwell, J. (2006) *Christianization and Communication in Late Antiquity: John Chrysostom and his Audience in Antioch.* Cambridge.

Mayer, E. (2012) *The Ancient Middle Classes: Urban Life and Aesthetics in the Roman Empire, 100 BCE – 250 CE.* Cambridge, MA, and London.

Mayer, W. (1998) 'John Chrysostom: extraordinary preacher, ordinary audience', in *Preacher and Audience: Studies in Early Christian and Byzantine Homiletics*, ed. P. Allen and M. B. Cunningham. Leiden, 105–37.

(2000) 'Who came to hear John Chrysostom preach? Recovering a late fourth-century preacher's audience', *Ephemerides Theologicae Lovanienses* 76: 73–87.

Mayer, W. and Neil, B. (eds.) (2006) *The Cult of the Saints: Select Homilies and Letters.* Crestwood, NY.

McCarthy, K. (2000) *Slaves, Masters, and the Art of Authority in Plautine Comedy.* Oxford.

McCartney, E. S. (1919) 'Puns and plays on proper names', *CJ* 14: 343–58.

(1921) 'An animal weather bureau', *CW* 14: 89–93.

McCauley, R. (2012) *Why Religion is Natural and Science is Not.* Oxford and New York.

McGlew, J. F. (1999) 'Politics on the margins: the Athenian *Hetaireiai* in 415 B.C.', *Historia* 48: 1–22.

McKeown, N. (2007) *The Invention of Ancient Slavery?* London.

Melearts, H. and Mooren, L. (2002) *Le rôle et le statut de la femme en Egypte hellénistique, romaine, et byzantine.* Leuven.

Ménard, H. (2004) *Maintenir l'ordre à Rome (IIe–IVe siècles ap. J.-C.).* Seyssel.

Meneghini, R. and Santangeli Valenziani, R. (eds.) (2006) *Formae Urbis Romae: Nuovi frammenti di piante marmoree dallo scavo dei Fori Imperiali.* Rome.

Meslin, M. (1970) *La fête des kalendes de janvier dans l'empire romain: Étude d'un rituel de Nouvel An.* Brussels.

Mikalson, J. D. (1983) *Athenian Popular Religion.* Chapel Hill, NC.

Millar, F. (1983) 'Empire and city, Augustus to Julian: obligations, excuses and status', *JRS* 73: 76–96.

(1995) 'Popular politics at Rome in the Late Republic', originally published in *Leaders and Masses in the Roman World: Studies in Honour of Zvi Yavetz*, ed. I. Malkin and Z. W. Rubinsohn. Leiden, 91–113; reprinted in F. Millar (2002) *The Roman Republic and the Augustan Revolution.* Chapel Hill, NC, 162–82.

(1998) *The Crowd in Rome in the Late Republic.* Ann Arbor, MI.

Miller, M. C. (2010) 'I am Eurymedon: tensions and ambiguities in Athenian war imagery', in *War, Democracy and Culture in Classical Athens*, ed. D. M. Pritchard. Cambridge, 304–37.

Miller, P. (2010) *The Smart Swarm: How Understanding Flocks, Schools, and Colonies can Make us Better at Communicating, Decision Making, and Getting Things Done.* New York.

Miller, P. C. (1994) *Dreams in Late Antiquity: Studies in the Imagination of a Culture.* Princeton, NJ.

Milnor, K. (2009) 'Literary literacy in Roman Pompeii: the case of Virgil's Aeneid', in *Ancient Literacies: The Culture of Reading in Greece and Rome,* ed. W. A. Johnson and H. N. Parker. Oxford and New York, 288–319.

Miranda, E. (1991) 'Una gemma "gnostica" dalle catacomba di S. Gennaro', *RAC* 67: 115–24.

Mirković, M. (2005) 'Child labour and taxes in the agriculture of Roman Egypt: *pais* and *aphelix*', *SCI* 24: 139–49.

Missiou, A. (2011) *Literacy and Democracy in Fifth-Century Athens.* Cambridge.

Molloy, M. E. (1996) *Libanius and the Dancers.* Hildesheim and New York.

Momigliano, A. (1972) 'Popular religious beliefs and the late Roman historians', in *Popular Belief and Practice.* Cambridge, 1–18.

Mommsen, T. (1864) *Römische Forschungen.* Berlin.

Monceaux, P. (1905) *Histoire littéraire de l'Afrique chrétienne depuis les origines jusqu'à l'invasion arabe,* vol. III: *Le IVe siècle d'Arnobe à Victorin.* Paris.

Montanari, E. (2009) *Fumosae imagines: Identità e memoria nell'aristocrazia repubblicana.* Rome.

Monteix, N. (2012), '"Caius Lucretius [...], marchand de couleurs de la rue du fabricant de courroies": réflexions critiques sur les concentrations de métiers à Rome', in *'Quartiers' artisanaux en Grèce ancienne: Une perspective méditerranéenne,* ed. G. Sanidas and A. Esposito. Villeneuve d'Ascq, 333–52.

Montevecchi, O. (1975) 'L'epikrisis dei Greco-egizi', in *Proceedings of the XIV International Congress of Papyrologists.* Oxford, 227–32.

   (1993) 'PSI V 457: Un caso di endogamia o una semplificazione del formulario?', *Aegyptus* 73: 49–55.

Montserrat, D. (1991) '*Mallokouria* and *therapeuteria*: rituals of transition in a mixed society?', *BASP* 28: 43–9.

   (1993) 'The representation of young males in "Fayum portraits"', *JEA* 79: 215–25.

Moore, J. and Scott, E. (eds.) (1997) *Invisible People and Processes: Writing Gender and Childhood into European Archaeology.* Leicester, 248–50.

Moreau, P. (1980) 'Cicéron, Clodius et la publication du Pro Murena', *REL*: 220–37.

Morgan, J. D. (1990) 'The death of Cinna the poet', *CQ* 40: 558–9.

Morgan, T. (2007) *Popular Morality in the Early Roman Empire.* Cambridge.

Morstein-Marx, R. (2004) *Mass Oratory and Political Power in the Late Roman Republic.* Cambridge.

(2013) '"Cultural hegemony" and the communicative power of the Roman elite', in *Commmunity and Communication: Oratory and Politics in Republican Rome*, ed. C. Steel and H. van der Blom. Cambridge, 29–47.

Mouritsen H. (2001) *Plebs and Politics in the Late Roman Republic*. Cambridge.

Mühlenberg, E. (2012) 'Gregor von Nyssa über die Vierzig und den ersten Märtyrer Stephanus)', in *Christian Martyrdom in Late Antiquity (300–450 AD)*, ed. P. Gemeinhardt and J. Leemans. Berlin, 115–32.

Muir, E. (1991) 'Introduction: observing trifles', in *Microhistory and the Lost Peoples of Europe*, ed. E. Muir and G. Ruggiero. Baltimore, MD, 1–10.

Muir, S. (2011) 'Religion on the road in ancient Greece and Rome', in *Travel and Religion in Antiquity*, ed. P. A. Harland. Waterloo, Ont., 29–47.

Müller, N. (1915) 'Il cimitero degli ebrei posto sulla via Portuense', *Rendiconti della Pontificia Accademia Romana di Archeologia* 2.12: 205–318.

Murray, O. (1990) 'The affair of the Mysteries: democracy and the drinking group', in *Sympotica: A Symposium on the Symposion*, ed. O. Murray. Oxford, 149–61.

(1993) *Early Greece*, 2nd edn. Cambridge, MA.

Mustakallio, K., Hanska, J., Sainio, H. L. and Vuolanto, V. (eds) (2005) *Hoping for Continuity: Childhood, Education and Death in Antiquity and the Middle Ages*. Rome.

Musurillo, H. (1972) *Acts of the Christian Martyrs*. Oxford.

Nafissi, M. (2009) 'Sparta', in *A Companion to Archaic Greece*, ed. K. A. Raaflaub and H. van Wees. Chichester, 117–37.

Nagy, G. (1979) *The Best of the Achaeans: Concepts of the Hero in Archaic Greek Poetry*. Baltimore, MD.

Nelson, C. (2002) 'Status declarations in Roman Egypt', in *Le rôle et le statut de la femme en Egypte hellénistique, romaine, et byzantine*, ed. H. Melearts and L. Mooren. Leuven, 337–53.

Nelson, H. (1950) 'Cato the Younger as a stoic orator', *Classical Weekly* 44: 65–9.

Neu, J. (2009) *Sticks and Stones: The Philosophy of Insult*. Cambridge.

Newlands, C. (2002) *Statius' Silvae and the Poetics of Empire*. Cambridge.

Newsome, D. J. (2010) 'The forum and the city: rethinking centrality in Rome and Pompeii (3rd century BC – 2nd century AD)'. Unpublished PhD thesis, University of Birmingham.

Nicolet, C. (1976) *Le métier du citoyen dans la Rome républicaine*. Paris.

(1977) 'L'onomastique des groupes dirigeants sous la République', in *L'onomastique latine*. Actes du colloque international, 13–15 octobre 1975. Paris, 45–61.

(1985) 'Plèbe et tribus: les statues de Lucius Antonius et le testament d'Auguste', *MEFRA* 97: 799–839.

Nilsson, M. P. (1916–19) 'Studien zur Vorgeschichte des Weihnachtsfestes', *ARW* 19: 50–150.

Nippel, W. (1995) *Public Order in Ancient Rome*. Cambridge.

Nodes, D. J. (2009) 'The organization of Augustine's Psalmus contra Partem Donati,' *VChr* 63: 390–408.

Nongbri, B. (2013) *Before Religion: The History of a Modern Concept*. New Haven, CT.

North, J. (1990a) 'Democratic politics in Republican Rome', *P&P* 126: 3–21.

(1990b) 'Diviners and divination at Rome', in *Pagan Priests: Religion and Power in the Ancient World*, ed. M. Beard and J. North. Ithaca, NY, 49–71.

Nuzzo, D. (2000) 'Amulet and grave in late antiquity: some examples from Roman cemeteries', in *Burial, Society and Context*, ed. R. Pearce, M. Millett and M. Struck. Oxford, 249–56.

Obelkevich, J. (1987) 'Proverbs and social history', in *The Social History of Language*, ed. P. Burke and R. Porter. Cambridge, 43–72.

Ober, J. (1989) *Mass and Elite in Democratic Athens: Rhetoric, Ideology, and the Power of the People*. Princeton, NJ.

(1998) *Political Dissent in Democratic Athens: Intellectual Critics of Popular Rule*. Princeton, NJ.

(2010) 'Wealthy Hellas', *TAPhA* 140: 241–86.

(2015) *The Rise and Fall of Classical Greece*. Princeton, NJ.

Oehler, F. (1856) *Corpus haeresiologicum I*. Berlin.

Ogden, D. (2001) *Greek and Roman Necromancy*. Princeton, NJ.

Olson, S. D. (1996) 'Politics and poetry in Aristophanes' *Wasps*', *TAPhA* 126: 129–50.

(ed.) (1998) *Aristophanes' Peace*. Oxford and New York.

(ed.) (2002) *Aristophanes' Acharnians*. Oxford and New York.

O'Neill, P. (2001) 'A culture of sociability: popular speech in Ancient Rome'. Unpublished PhD thesis, University of Southern California.

(2003) 'Going round in circles: popular speech in ancient Rome', *ClAnt* 22: 135–76.

Orsi, R. (1997) 'Everyday miracles', in *Lived Religion in America: Toward a Theory of Practice*, ed. David Hall. Princeton, NJ, 3–21.

Osborne, R. (1985) 'Law in action in classical Athens', *JHS* 105: 40–58.

Ostwald, M. (1986) *From Popular Sovereignty to the Sovereignty of Law*. Berkeley and Los Angeles.

O'Sullivan, T. M. (2011) *Walking in Roman Culture*. Cambridge.

Packer, J. E. (1968–9) 'La casa di via Giulio Romano', *BCAR* 81: 127–48.

(1971) *The Insulae of Imperial Ostia*. Rome.

Pagliai, V. (2009) 'The art of dueling with words: toward a new understanding of verbal duels across the world', *Oral Tradition* 24: 61–88.

Pailler, J.-M. (2001) 'Et les aulètes refusèrent de chanter les dieux ... (Plutarque, Questions romaines, 55)', in *Chanter les dieux: Musique et religion dans l'antiquité grecque et romaine. Actes du colloque des 16, 17, et 18 décembre 1999*, ed. P. Brulé and C. Vendries. Rennes, 307–38.

Palardy, W. B. (2005) *St Peter Chrysologus: Selected Sermons*, vol. III. Washington, DC.

Palazzo, E. (2012) 'Les cinq sens au Moyen Âge: état de la question et perspectives de recherche', *Cahiers de civilisation médiévale* 55: 339–66.

Palmer, R. (1965) 'The censors of 312 B.C. and the state religion', *Historia* 14: 293–324.

Panayotakis, C. (2005) 'Comedy, Atellane farce, and mime', in *A Companion to Latin Literature*, ed. S. J. Harrison. Oxford, 130–47.

(2008) 'Virgil on the popular stage', in *New Directions in Ancient Pantomime*, ed. E. Hall and R. Wyles. Oxford, 185–97.

Paoli, U. E. (1950) 'Il reato di adulterio (moicheia) in diritto attico', *SDHI* 16: 123–82.

Papaconstantinou, A. and Talbot, M.-A. (eds.) (2009) *Becoming Byzantine: Children and Childhood in Byzantium*. Washington DC.

Papi, E. (2002) 'La "turba inpia": artigiani e commercianti del Foro Romano e dintorni (I sec. a. C.–64 d. C.)', *JRA* 15: 45–62.

Parenti, M. (2003) *The Assassination of Julius Caesar: A People's History of Ancient Rome*. New York.

Parker, G. (2008) *The Making of Roman India*. Cambridge.

Parker, H. N. (1999) 'The observed of all observers: spectacle, applause, and cultural poetics in the Roman theatre audience', in *The Art of Ancient Spectacle*, ed. B. Bergmann and C. Kondoleon. New Haven, CT, and London, 163–79.

(2011) 'Toward a definition of popular culture', *History and Theory* 50: 147–70.

Parker, R. (2000) 'Greek states and Greek oracles', in *Oxford Readings in Greek Religion*, ed. R. Buxton. Oxford, 76–108.

(2011) *On Greek Religion*. Ithaca, NY.

Parkin, T. G. (2013) 'The demography of infancy and early childhood in the ancient world', in *The Oxford Handbook of Childhood and Education in the Classical World*, ed. J. Evans-Grubbs and T. Parkin with R. Bell. Oxford, 40–62.

Parlasca, K. (1966) *Mumienporträts und verwandte Denkmäler*. Wiesbaden.

Parsons. P. (2007) *City of the Sharp-Nosed Fish: Greek Lives in Roman Egypt*. London.

Patera, M. (2011) 'Le corbeau: un signe dans le monde grec', in *La raison des signes: présages, rites, destin dans les sociétés de la Méditerranée ancienne*, ed. S. Georgoudi, R. Koch Piettre and F. Schmidt. Leiden, 157–75.

Peachin, M. (2011) *The Oxford Handbook of Social Relations in the Roman World*. Oxford.

Pedroni, L. (1992) 'Per una lettura verticale della *Forma Vrbis Marmorea*', *Ostraka*, 2: 223–30.

Peirano, I. (2012) *The Rhetoric of the Roman Fake: Latin Pseudepigrapha in Context*. Cambridge.

Pelikan, J. (1993) *Christianity and Classical Culture: The Metamorphosis of Natural Theology in the Christian Encounter with Hellenism*. New Haven, CT.

Perkins, J. (1995) *The Suffering Self: Pain and Narrative Representation in the Early Christian Era*. London.

Perlman, P. J. (1992) 'One Hundred-Citied Crete and the Cretan *Politeia*', *CP* 87: 193–205.

Perry, B. E. (1939) 'Some addenda to Liddell and Scott', *AJPh* 60: 29–40.

(1967) *The Ancient Romances: A Literary-Historical Account of their Origin*. Berkeley, CA.

Pervo, R. I. (1998) 'A nihilist fable: introducing *The Life of Aesop*', in *Ancient Fiction and Early Christian Narrative*, ed. R. F. Hock, J. B. Chance and J. Perkins. Atlanta, GA, 77–120.

Petersen, L. H. (2003) 'The baker, his tomb, his wife, and her breadbasket: the monument of Eurysaces in Rome', *Art Bulletin* 85: 230–57.

(2006) *The Freedman in Roman Art and Art History*. New York.

Pettinau, B. (1996) 'Le *insulae*: aspetti di un quartiere di Roma antica', in *Antiche stanze: Un quartiere di Roma imperiale nella zona di Termini*. Milan, 179–90.

Pickard-Cambridge, A. (1988) *The Dramatic Festivals of Athens*, ed. J. Gould and D. M. Lewis, 2nd rev. edn. Oxford.

Piganiol, A. (1923) *Recherches sur les jeux romains*. Strasbourg.

Pighi, G. B. (1965) *De ludis saecularibus populi Romani Quiritium*. Amsterdam.

Pillinger, R. (ed. and trans.) (1988) *Das Martyrium des Heiligen Dasisus*. Vienna.

Pina Polo, F. (1991) 'Cicerón contra Clodio: el lenguaje de la invectiva', *Gerión* 9: 131–50.

(1996) *Contra arma verbis: Der Redner vor dem Volk in der späten römischen Republik*. Stuttgart.

(2006) 'The tyrant must die: preventive tyrannicide in Roman political thought', in *Repúblicas y ciudadanos: modelos de participación cívica en el mundo antiguo*, ed. F. Marco Simón, F. Pina Polo and J. Remesal Rodríguez. Barcelona, 71–101.

(2010) '*Frigidus rumor*: the creation of a (negative) public image in Rome', in *Private and Public Lies: The Discourse of Despotism and Deceit in the Graeco-Roman World*, ed. A. J. Turner, K. O. Chong-Gossard and F. J. Vervaet. Leiden, 75–90.

(2013) 'The political role of the *consules designati* at Rome', *Historia* 62: 420–52.

(2014) 'Impostores populares y fraudes legales en la Roma tardorrepublicana', in *Fraude y engaño en el mundo antiguo*, ed. F. Marco Simón, F. Pina Polo and J. Remesal Rodríguez. Barcelona, 9–26.

(forthcoming) 'How much history did the Romans know? Historical references in Cicero's speeches to the people', in *Omnium annalium monumenta:*

Annals, Epic and Drama in Republican Rome, ed. K. Sandberg and C. Smith. Stuttgart.

Platter, C. (2007) *Aristophanes and the Carnival of Genres*. Baltimore, MD.

Pleket, H. W. (1993) 'Rome: A pre-industrial megalopolis', in *Megalopolis: The Giant City in History*, ed. T. Barker and T. Sutcliffe. London, 14–35.

Podini, M. (2004) 'Musica e musicisti nel rilievo storico romano: la dialettica fra immagine e significato', *Ocnus* 12: 223–46.

Pöhlmann, E. and West, M. L. (2001) *Documents of Ancient Greek Music*. Oxford.

Pomeroy, A. J. (1991) 'Status anxiety in the Greco-Roman dream books', *AncSoc* 22: 51–74.

Pope, M. (1986) 'Athenian festival judges – seven, five, or however many', *CQ* 36: 322–6.

Potter, D. S. (1994) *Prophets and Emperors: Human and Divine Authority from Augustus to Theodosius*. Cambridge, MA.

Prescendi, F. (2007) *Décrire et comprendre le sacrifice: Les réflexions des Romains sur leur propre religion à partir de la littérature antiquaire*. Stuttgart.

(2010) 'Children and the transmission of religious knowledge', in *Children, Memory and Family Identity in Roman Culture*, ed. V. Dasen and T. Späth. Oxford, 73–93.

Priester, S. (2002) *Ad summas tegulas: Untersuchungen zu vielgeschossigen Gebäudeblöcken mit Wohneinheiten und Insulae im kaiserzeitlichen Rom*. Rome.

Pritchard, D. (2012) 'Aristophanes and de Ste. Croix: the value of Old Comedy as evidence for Athenian popular culture', *Antichthon* 46: 14–51.

Pudsey, A. (2011) 'Nuptiality and the demographic life cycles of families in Roman Egypt', in *Demography and Society in the Greek and Roman Worlds: New Insights and Approaches*, ed. C. Holleran and A. Pudsey. Cambridge, 60–98.

(2013) 'Children and families in Roman Egypt', in *The Oxford Handbook of Childhood and Education in the Classical World*, ed. J. Evans-Grubbs and T. Parkin with R. Bell. Oxford, 484–509.

(2015) 'Children in late Roman Egypt: family and everyday life in monastic contexts', in *Children and Family in Late Antiquity: Life, Death and Interaction*, ed. C. Laes, K. Mustakallio and V. Vuolanto. Leuven, 215–34

(under review) 'House as community: structures in kinship and housing in Roman Tebtynis', in *Between Words and Walls: Material and Textual Approaches to Housing in the Graeco-Roman World*, ed. J. Baird and A. Pudsey.

Pudsey, A. and Vuolanto, V. (forthcoming) 'Being a niece or a nephew in an ancient city: children's social environment in Oxyrhynchus', in *Children and Everyday Life in the Roman and Late Antique World*, ed. R. C. Laes and V. Vuolanto. London.

Purcell, N. (1994) 'The city of Rome and the *plebs urbana* in the late Republic', in *The Cambridge Ancient History*, vol. IX: *The Last Age of the Roman Republic, 146–43 BC*, ed. J. A. Crook, A. Lintott and E. Rawson. Cambridge, 644–88.

(1995) 'Literate games: Roman urban society and the game of alea', *P&P* 147: 3–37.

(1996) 'Rome and its development under Augustus and his successors', in *The Cambridge Ancient History*, vol. X: *The Augustan Empire, 43 B.C.–A.D. 79*, ed. A. Bowman, E. Champlin and A. Lintott. Cambridge, 782–811.

(1999) 'The populace of Rome in late antiquity: problems of classification and historical description', in *The Transformations of Vrbs Roma in Late Antiquity*, ed. W. V. Harris. Portsmouth, RI, 135–61.

Pütz, B. (2003) *The Symposium and Komos in Aristophanes*. Stuttgart.

Qvortrup, J. (1994) 'Childhood matters: an introduction', in *Childhood Matters: Social Theory, Practice and Politics*, ed. J. Qvortrup *et al.* Aldershot, 21–33.

Qvortrup, J., Bardy, M., Sgritta, G. and Wintersberger, H. (eds.) (1994) *Childhood Matters: Social Theory, Practice and Politics*. Aldershot.

Rathbone, D. W. (1991) *Economic Rationalism and Rural Society in Third-Century A.D. Egypt: The Heroninos Archive and the Appianus Estate*. Cambridge.

Rawson, B. (2003) *Children and Childhood in Roman Italy*. Oxford.

Rawson, E. (1977) 'More on the *clientelae* of the patrician Claudii', *Historia* 26: 340–57.

(1985) *Intellectual Life in the Late Roman Republic*. London.

(1987) '*Discrimina ordinum*: The *Lex Julia Theatralis*', *PBSR* 55: 83–114.

Rebillard, E. (2009) *The Care of the Dead in Late Antiquity*, trans. E. Trapnell Rawlings and J. Routier-Pucci. Ithaca, NY.

Redfield, R. (1956) *Peasant Society and Culture: An Anthropological Approach to Civilisation*. Chicago.

Revell, L. (2010) 'Geography and the environment', in *A Cultural History of Childhood and Family in Antiquity*, vol. I, ed. M. Harlow and R. Laurence. Oxford, 61–78.

Revermann, M. (2006a) *Comic Business: Theatricality, Dramatic Technique, and Performance Contexts of Aristophanic Comedy*. Oxford and New York.

(2006b) 'The competence of theatre audiences in fifth- and fourth-century Athens', *JHS* 126: 99–124.

Reynolds, D. W. (1996) *Forma Urbis Romae: The Severan Marble Plan and the Urban Form of Ancient Rome*. Ann Arbor, MI.

Rhodes, P. J. (1972) *The Athenian Boule*. Oxford.

(1980) '*Ephebi, bouleutae* and the population of Athens', *ZPE* 38: 191–201.

(1981) *A Commentary on the Aristotelian Athenaion Politeia*. Oxford.

(1982) 'Problems in Athenian *eisphora* and liturgies', *AJAH* 7: 1–19.

(1984) 'Members serving in the Athenian Boule and the population of Athens again', *ZPE* 57: 200–2.

(2006) *A History of the Classical Greek World*. Oxford.

Richlin, A. (1983) *The Garden of Priapus: Sexuality and Aggression in Roman Humor*. New Haven, CT.

Rickman, G. (1980) *The Corn Supply of Ancient Rome*. Oxford.

Riggs, C. (2002) 'Facing the dead: recent research on the funerary art of Ptolemaic and Roman Egypt' *AJA* 116: 85–101.
  (2005) *The Beautiful Burial in Roman Egypt: Art, Identity, and Funerary Religion*. Oxford.
Rigoir. J. (1960) 'La céramique sigillée grise paléo-chrétienne', *Prov. Hist.* 10: 1–93.
Rigoir, J., Rigoir Y. and Meffre, J. F. (1973) 'Les dérivées des sigillés paléochrétiennes du groupe atlantique', *Gallia* 31: 207–63.
Ripat, P. (2006) 'Roman omens, Roman audiences, and Roman history', *G&R* 53: 155–74.
Ristuccia, N. J. (2013) 'The rise of the Spurcalia: medieval festival and modern myth', *Comitatus* 44: 55–76.
Rivière, C.-A. (2004) 'La spécificité française de la construction sociologique du concept de sociabilité', *Réseaux* 123.1: 207–31.
Robinson, E. W. (1997) *The First Democracies: Early Popular Government Outside Athens*. Stuttgart.
  (2011) *Democracy Beyond Athens: Popular Government in the Greek Classical Age*. Cambridge.
Robson J. (2006) *Humour, Obscenity and Aristophanes*. Tübingen.
  (2015) 'Fantastic sex: fantasies of sexual assault in Aristophanes', in *Sex in Antiquity: Reconsidering Gender and Sexuality in the Ancient World*, ed. M. Masterson, N. S. Rabinowitz and J. Robson. Abingdon and New York, 315–31.
Roche, D. (1981) *Le peuple de Paris*. Paris.
Rodenwaldt, G. (1940) 'Römische Reliefs: Vorstufen zur Spätantike', *JDAI* 55: 12–43.
Roman, D. and Roman, Y. (2007) *Aux miroirs de la ville: Images et discours identitaires romains (IIIe s. avant J.-C. – IIIe s. après J.-C.)*. Brussels.
Ronke, J. (1987) *Magistratische Repräsentation im römischen Relief: Studien zu standes- und statusbezeichnenden Szenen*. Oxford.
Rose, J. (2001) *The Intellectual Life of the British Working Classes*. London and New Haven, CT.
Roselli, D. K. (2011) *Theatre of the People: Spectators and Society in Ancient Athens*. Austin, TX.
Rosen, R. M. (1984) 'The Ionian at Aristophanes *Peace* 46', *GRBS* 25: 389–96.
  (2007) *Making Mockery: The Poetics of Ancient Satire*. Oxford.
Rosillo-López, C. (2007) 'Temo a los troyanos: rumores y habladurías en la Roma tardorrepublicana', *Polis* 9: 113–34.
  (forthcoming) *Public Opinion and Politics in the Late Roman Republic*. Cambridge.
Rostovtzeff, M. (1957) *The Social and Economic History of the Roman Empire*. Oxford.
Rothwell, K. S. (1995) 'Aristophanes' "Wasps" and the sociopolitics of Aesop's fables', *CJ* 90.3: 233–54.

Roueché, C. (1993) *Performers and Partisans at Aphrodisias in the Roman and Late Roman Periods*. London.
Rouland, N. (1979) *Pouvoir politique et dépendance personnelle dans l'Antiquité romaine: Genèse et rôle des rapports de clientèle*. Brussels.
Roussel, L. (1966) *Pseudo-Lysias: L'invalide*. Paris.
Rowlandson, J. (ed.) (1998) *Women in Graeco-Roman Egypt: A Sourcebook*. London.
Roy, J. (1991) 'Traditional jokes about the punishment of adulterers in ancient Greek Literature', *LCM* 16: 73–6.
Rubinstein, L. (2000) *Litigation and Cooperation: Supporting Speakers in the Courts of Classical Athens*. Stuttgart.
Rudhardt, J. (1988) 'Remarques sur le geste rituel, le sens qu'il paraît impliquer et les explications que l'on en donne', in *Essais sur le rituel*, vol. I, ed. A.-M. Blondeau and K. Schipper. Paris, 1–14.
Ruffell, I. (2003) 'Beyond satire: Horace, popular invective and the segregation of literature', *JRS* 93: 35–65.
Ruffini, G. (2006) 'Genealogy and the gymnasium', *BASP* 43: 71–99.
Rusten, J. (ed.) (2011) *The Birth of Comedy: Texts, Documents, and Art from Athenian Comic Competitions, 486–280*, trans. J. Henderson, D. Konstan, R. Rosen, J. Rusten and N. W. Slater. Baltimore, MD.
Ryberg, I. S. (1955) *Rites of the State Religion in Roman Art*. Rome.
Rylaarsdam, D. (2014) *John Chrysostom on Divine Pedagogy: The Coherence of his Theology and Preaching*. Cambridge.
Salamito, J.-M. (2005) *Les virtuoses et la multitude: Aspects sociaux de la controverse entre Augustin et les pélagiens*. Grenoble.
Salomies, O. (2008) 'Choosing a cognomen in Rome: some aspects', in *A Roman Miscellany: Essays in Honour of Anthony R. Birley on his Seventieth Birthday*, ed. H. M. Schellenberg, V.-E. Hirschmann and A. Krieckhaus. Gdansk, 79–91.
Salway, B. (1994) 'What's in a name? A survey of Roman onomastic practice from c. 700 BC to AD 700', *JRS* 84: 125–45.
Salzman, M. (1990) *On Roman Time: The Codex-Calendar of 354 and the Rhythms of Urban Life in Late Antiquity*. Berkeley, CA.
Sartori, F. (1967) *Le eterie nella vita politica ateniese del VI e V secolo a.C.* Rome.
Sauron, G. (2000) *L'histoire végétalisée: Ornement et politique à Rome*. Paris.
Schaff, P. and Wace, P. (1899) *The Seven Ecumenical Councils*. Edinburgh.
Scheid, J. (2003) 'Communauté et communauté: réflexions sur quelques ambiguïtés d'après l'exemple des thiases de l'Égypte romaine', in *Les communautés religieuses dans le monde gréco-romain: Essais de définition*, ed. N. Belayche and S. C. Mimouni. Turnhout, 61–74.
  (2005) *Quand faire c'est croire: Les rites sacrificiels des Romains*. Paris.

(2013) *Les dieux, l'État et l'individu: Réflexions sur la religion civique à Rome*. Paris.
Scheidel, W. (2003) 'Germs for Rome', in *Rome the Cosmopolis*, ed. C. Edwards and G. Woolf. Cambridge, 158–76.
 (2010) 'Real wages in early economies: evidence for living standards from 1800 BCE to 1300 CE', *Journal of the Social and Economic History of the Orient* 53: 425–62.
 (2014) '"Germs for Rome". Ten years after', in *Les affaires de Monsieur Andreau: Économie et société du monde romain*, ed. C. Apicella, M.-L. Haack and F. Lerouxel. Bordeaux, 311–15.
Scheidel, W. and Friesen, S. J. (2009) 'The size of the economy and the distribution of income in the Roman Empire', *JRS* 99: 61–91.
Schmidt, G. (2002) *Rabe und Krähe in der Antike: Studien zur archäologischen und literarischen Überlieferung*. Wiesbaden.
Schmidt, V. A. (2008) 'Discursive institutionalism: the explanatory power of ideas and discourse', *Annual Review of Political Science* 11: 303–26.
 (2010) 'Taking ideas and discourse seriously: explaining change through discursive institutionalism as the fourth "new institutionalism"', *European Political Science Review* 2.1: 1–25.
 (2011) 'Speaking of change: why discourse is key to the dynamics of policy transformation', *Critical Policy Studies* 5.2: 106–26.
Schmitt, J.-C. (1976) '"Religion populaire" et culture folklorique', *Annales: ESC* 31: 951–3.
Schmitz, W. N. (2004) *Nachbarschaft und Dorfgemeinschaft im archaischen und klassischen Griechenland*. Berlin.
Schnegg-Köhler, B. (2002) *Die augusteischen Säkularspiele*. Leipzig.
Schwartz, H. (2011) *Making Noise: From Babel to the Big Bang and Beyond*. New York.
Schweitzer, A. (1998) 'L'évolution stylistique et iconographique des parures de cartonnage d'Akhmîm du début de l'époque ptolémaique à l'époque romain', *BIAO* 98: 325–52.
Scobie, A. (1986) 'Slums, sanitation, and mortality in the Roman world', *Klio* 68: 399–433.
Scott, J. C. (1976) *The Moral Economy of the Peasant: Rebellion and Subsistence in Southeast Asia*. London.
 (1985) *Weapons of the Weak: Everyday Forms of Peasant Resistance*. London.
 (1990) *Domination and the Arts of Resistance: Hidden Transcripts*. New Haven, CT.
Scribner, R. W. (1987) *Popular Culture and Popular Movements in Reformation Germany*. London.
Scullard, H. H. (1981) *Festivals and Ceremonies of the Roman Republic*. London.
Scullion, S. (1994) *Three Studies in Athenian Dramaturgy*. Stuttgart and Leipzig.
Shackleton Bailey, D. R. (1960) 'Sex. Clodius–Sex. Cloelius', *CQ* 10: 41–2.

(1977) *Cicero: Epistulae ad Familiares*, vol. II: *47–43 BC*. Cambridge.
(1979) 'On Cicero's speeches', *HSPh* 83: 237–85.
Shaked, S., Ford, N. J. and Bhayro, S. (2013) *Aramaic Bowl Spells*. Leiden.
Shaw, B. (1996) 'Seasons of death: aspects of mortality in imperial Rome', *JRS* 86: 100–38.
(2011) *Sacred Violence: African Christians and Sectarian Hatred in the Age of Augustine*. Cambridge.
Shibutani, T. (1966) *Improvised News: A Sociological Study of Rumor*. Indianapolis and New York.
Shiner, W. (1998) 'Creating plot in episodic narratives: *The Life of Aesop* and the Gospel of Mark', in *Ancient Fiction and Early Christian Narrative*, ed. R. F. Hock, J. B. Chance and J. Perkins. Atlanta, GA, 155–76.
Sijpesteijn, P. (1976) 'Some remarks on the *Epicrisis* of οἱ ἀπὸ γυμνασίου in Oxyrhynchus', *BASP* 13: 181–90.
Silk, M. S. (2000) *Aristophanes and the Definition of Comedy*. Oxford and New York.
Sivan, H. (2008) *Palestine in Late Antiquity*. Oxford.
Slater, N. W. (1997) 'Bringing up father: *paideia* and *ephebeia* in the *Wasps*', in *Education in Greek Fiction*, ed. A. H. Sommerstein and C. Atherton. Bari, 27–52.
(1999) 'Making the Aristophanic audience', *AJP* 120: 351–68.
Slater, W. J. (1996) 'Sorting out pantomime (and mime) from top to bottom', in *Roman Theater and Society*, ed. W. J. Slater. Ann Arbor, MI, 533–41.
Smelik, K. A. D. (1979) 'The witch of Endor: 1 Samuel 28 in Rabbinic and Christian exegesis till 800 A.D.', *VChr* 33: 160–79.
Smith, D. G. (2013) 'A regional performance culture? The case of Syracuse', in *Regionalism and Globalism in Antiquity: Exploring their Limits*, ed. F. de Angelis. Leuven, Paris and Walpole, MA, 127–42.
Smith, M. M. (2007) *Sensory History*. Oxford.
Smith, R. M. (2008) 'Historical institutionalism and the study of law', in *The Oxford Handbook of Law and Politics*, ed. K. E. Whittington, R. D. Kelemen and G. A. Caldeira. Oxford, 46–59.
Snowden, F. M. (1983) *Before Color Prejudice*. Cambridge, MA.
Sofaer Derevenski, J. (1997) 'Engendering children, engendering archaeology', in *Invisible People and Processes: Writing Gender and Children in European Archaeology*, ed. J. Moore and E. Scott. London, 192–202.
(2000) 'Material culture shock: confronting expectations in the material culture of children', in *Children and Material Culture*, ed. J. Sofaer Derevenski. New York, 3–16.
Sommerstein, A. H. (1981) *The Comedies of Aristophanes*, vol. II: *Knights*. Warminster.
(1982) *The Comedies of Aristophanes*, vol. III: *Clouds*. Warminster.
(1985) *The Comedies of Aristophanes*, vol. V: *Peace*. Warminster.

(1990) *The Comedies of Aristophanes*, vol. VII: *Lysistrata*. Warminster.

(1996) 'How to avoid being a *Komodoumenos*', *CQ* 46: 327–56.

(1997) 'The theatre audience, the *dēmos* and the Suppliants of Aeschylus', in *Greek Tragedy and the Historian*, ed. C. Pelling. Oxford, 63–79.

(1998a) *The Comedies of Aristophanes*, vol. X: *Ecclesiazusae*. Warminster.

(1998b) 'The theatre audience and the *dēmos*', in *La comedia griega y su influencia en la literatura española*, ed. J. A. López Férez, Madrid, 43–62.

(2001) *The Comedies of Aristophanes*, vol. XI: *Wealth*. Warminster.

Stallybrass, P. and White, A. (1986) *The Politics and Poetics of Transgression*. London.

Staszak, J.-F. (2003) 'Espace vécu', in *Dictionnaire de la géographie*, ed. J. Lévy and M. Lussault. Paris, 341–2.

Ste. Croix, G. E. M. de (1972) *Origins of the Peloponnesian War*. London.

(1981) *The Class Struggle in the Ancient Greek World from the Archaic Age to the Arab Conquests*. London.

Stearns, P. N. (1976) 'Social history today ... and tomorrow', *Journal of Social History* 10: 129–55.

Steiner, A. (2002) 'Private and public: links between *Symposion* and *Syssition* in Fifth-Century Athens', *ClAnt* 21: 347–79.

Stephens, S. A. (1994) 'Who read ancient novels?', in *The Search for the Ancient Novel*, ed. J. Tatum. Baltimore, MD, and London, 405–18.

(2008) 'Cultural identity', in *The Cambridge Companion to the Greek and Roman Novel*, ed. T. Whitmarsh. Cambridge, 56–71.

Stern, K. (2013) 'Graffiti as gift: mortuary and devotional graffiti in the late ancient Levant', in *The Gift in Antiquity*, ed. M. Satlow. Malden, MA, 137–57.

Stewart, P. (2008) *The Social History of Roman Art*. Cambridge.

Stiaffini, D. (1993) 'The presence of glass in funerary contexts in Italy (4th–7th centuries)', in *Annales du 12 Congrès de l'Association Internationale pour l'Histoire du Verre (Wien 26–31 Août 1991)*, vol. I. Amsterdam, 177–85.

Stone, L. M. (1984) *Costume in Aristophanic Comedy*. Salem, MA.

Storchi Marino, A. (1979) 'Artigiani e rituali religiosi nella Roma arcaica', *RAAN*, n.s. 54: 333–57.

Storey, J. (2006) *Cultural Theory and Popular Culture: An Introduction*, 4th edn. London.

(2008) *Cultural Theory and Popular Culture: A Reader*, 4th edn. London.

Stowers, S. (2008) 'Theorizing the religion of ancient households and families', in *Household and Family Religion in Antiquity*, ed. J. Bodel and S. Olyan. Oxford, 5–19.

Stratton, K. (2014) 'Magic, abjection, and gender in Greek and Roman literature', in *Daughters of Hecate*, ed. D. Kalleres and K. Stratton. Oxford, 152–80.

Strinati, D. (2004) *An Introduction to Theories of Popular Culture*, 2nd edn. London.

Struck, P. T. (2005) 'Divination and literary criticism', in *Mantikê: Studies in Ancient Divination*, ed. S. I. Johnston and P. T. Struck. Leiden, 147–65.
Swift, L. A. (2010) *The Hidden Chorus: Echoes of Genre in Tragic Lyric*. Oxford and New York.
Syme, R. (1939) *The Roman Revolution*. Oxford.
Takács, S. (1995) *Isis and Sarapis in the Roman World*. Leiden.
Tandy, D. (1997) *Warriors into Traders: The Power of the Market in Early Greece*. Berkeley, CA.
Tarpin, M. (2008) 'Les *vici* de Rome, entre sociabilité de voisinage et organisation administrative', in *'Rome des quartiers': des vici aux rioni. Cadres institutionnels, pratiques sociales et requalifications entre Antiquité et époque moderne*, ed. M. Royo, É. Hubert and A. Bérenger. Paris, 35–64.
Tatum. J. (ed.) (1994) *The Search For the Ancient Novel*. Baltimore, MD.
Tatum, W. J. (1999) *The Patrician Tribune: Publius Clodius Pulcher*. Chapel Hill, NC.
  (2008) *Always I am Caesar*. Malden, MA, and Oxford.
Taylor, L. R. (1960) *Voting Districts of the Roman Republic: The Thirty-Five Urban and Rural Tribes*. Rome.
Temin, P. (2006) 'The economy of the early Roman Empire', *Journal of Economic Perspectives* 20: 133–51.
Testini, P. (1966) *Le catacombe e gli antichi cimiteri cristiani in Roma*. Bologna.
Thomas, C. M. (1998) 'Stories without texts and without authors: the problem of fluidity in ancient novelistic texts and early Christian literature', in *Ancient Fiction and Early Christian Narrative*, ed. R. F. Hock, J. B. Chance and J. Perkins. Atlanta, GA, 273–91.
Thomas, R. (1989) *Oral Tradition and Written Record in Classical Athens*. Cambridge.
  (1992) *Literacy and Orality in Ancient Greece*. Cambridge.
  (2009) 'Writing, reading, public and private "literacies"', in *Ancient Literacies: The Culture of Reading in Greece and Rome*, ed. W. A. Johnson and H. N. Parker. Oxford and New York, 13–45.
Thompson, E. P. (1963) *The Making of the English Working Class*. London.
  (1971) 'The moral economy of the English crowd in the eighteenth century', *P&P* 50: 76–136.
  (1991) *Customs in Common*. London.
Tilly, C. (1978) *From Mobilization to Revolution*. New York.
  (1979) 'Repertoires of contention in America and Britain', in *The Dynamics of Social Movements: Resource Mobilization, Social Control and Tactics*, ed. M. N. Zald and J. McCarthy. Cambridge, 126–55.
  (1986) *La France conteste: de 1600 à nos jours*. Paris.
  (1995) *Popular Contention in Great Britain 1758–1834*. Cambridge.
Todd, S. C. (1990) '*Lady Chatterley's Lover* and the Attic orators: the social composition of the Athenian jury', *JHS* 110: 146–73.
  (1993) *The Shape of Athenian Law*. Oxford.

(2000) *Lysias*. Austin, TX.

(2007) *A Commentary on Lysias, Speeches 1–11*. Oxford.

Toner, J. (1995) *Leisure and Ancient Rome*. Cambridge.

(2009) *Popular Culture in Ancient Rome*. Cambridge.

(ed.) (2014) *A Cultural History of the Senses in Antiquity*. London.

(2015) 'Barbers, barbershops and searching for Roman popular culture', *PBSR* 83: 91–109.

Tram Tam Tinh, V. (1964) *Le culte d'Isis à Pompéi*. Paris.

Trampedach, K. (2008) 'Authority disputed: the seer in Homeric epic', in *Practitioners of the Divine: Greek Priests and Religious Officials from Homer to Heliodorus*, ed. B. Dignas and K. Trampedach. Cambridge, MA, 207–30.

Tran, N. (2006) *Les membres des associations romaines: Le rang social des collegiati en Italie et en Gaules, sous le Haut-Empire*. Rome.

(2011) 'Les gens de métier romains: savoirs professionnels et supériorités plébéiennes', in *Les savoirs professionnels des gens de métier: Études sur le monde du travail dans les sociétés urbaines de l'empire romain*, ed. N. Monteix and N. Tran. Naples, 119–33.

(2013) *Dominus tabernae: Le statut de travail des artisans et des commerçants de l'Occident romain (Ier siècle av. J.-C. – IIIe siècle ap. J.-C.)*. Rome.

Treggiari, S. (2002) *Roman Social History*. London.

Trisciuoglio, A. (1998) *'Sarta tecta, ultrotributa, opus publicum faciendum locare': Sugli appalti relativi alle opere pubbliche nell'età repubblicana e Augustea*. Naples.

Truax, B. (1984) *Acoustic Communication*. Norwood, NJ.

Twycross, M. and Carpenter, S. (2002) *Masks and Masking in Medieval and Early Tudor England*. Aldershot.

Tylor, E. B. (1871) *Primitive Culture: Researches in the Development of Mythology*, vol. I. London.

Usher, S. (1965) 'Individual characterization in Lysias', *Eranos* 63: 99–119.

Van Dam, R. (2003) *Becoming Christian: The Conversion of Roman Cappadocia*. Philadelphia, PA.

Van der Blom, H. (2010) *Cicero's Role Models: The Political Strategy of a Newcomer*. Oxford.

Vanderbroeck, P. J. J. (1987) *Popular Leadership and Collective Behavior in the Late Roman Republic (ca. 80–50 BC)*. Amsterdam.

Van Nijf, O. M. (1997) *The Civic World of Professional Associations in the Roman East*. Amsterdam.

Van Wees, H. (2011) 'Demetrius and Draco: Athens' property classes and population in and before 317 BC', *JHS* 131: 95–114.

Veblen, T. (1899) *The Theory of the Leisure Class: An Economic Study of Institutions*. London.

Vendries, C. (2007) 'La trompe de Neuvy: anatomie d'un objet sonore', in *Le cheval et la danseuse: À la redécouverte du trésor de Neuvy-en-Sullias*. Orléans, 120–45.

Vernant, J.-P. (1991) 'Speech and mute signs', in *Mortals and Immortals: Collected Essays*, ed. F. Zeitlin. Princeton, NJ, 303–17.

Versnel, H. S. (1994) *Inconsistencies in Greek and Roman Religion*, vol. II: *Transition and Reversal in Myth and Ritual*, 2nd edn. Leiden, New York and Cologne.

Veyne, P. (2002) 'Lisibilité des images, propagande et apparat monarchique dans l'Empire romain', *Revue historique* 304.1: 3–30.

(2005) 'Existait-il une classe moyenne en ces temps lointains?', in *L'Empire gréco-romain*, ed. P. Veyne. Paris: 117–61.

Vikan, G. (1984) 'Art, medicine, and magic in Early Byzantium', *DOP* 38: 65–86.

Villeneuve, F. (2001) *Satires / Horace*. Paris.

Vincent, A. (2013) 'La musique du sacrifice: le cas des autels compitalices d'époque augustéenne', *Bulletin de l'Association Suisse d'Archéologie Classique*: 54–8.

(2016) *Jouer pour la cité: Une histoire sociale et politique des musiciens professionnels de l'Occident romain*. Rome.

Virlouvet, C. (1985) *Famines et émeutes à Rome des origines de la République à la mort de Néron*. Rome.

(1994) 'Les lois frumentaires d'époque républicaine', in *Le ravitaillement en blé de Rome et des centres urbains des débuts de la République jusqu'au Haut-Empire*. Rome and Naples, 11–29.

(1995) *Tessera frumentaria: Les procédures de la distribution du blé public à Rome à la fin de la République et au début de l'Empire*. Rome.

(2006) 'Encore à propos des *horrea Galbana* de Rome', *CCG* 17: 23–60.

(2009) *La plèbe frumentaire dans les témoignages épigraphiques: Essai d'histoire sociale et administrative du peuple de Rome antique*. Rome.

Vuolanto, V. (2014) 'Children in the Roman world: cultural and social perspectives. A review article', *Arctos* 48: 435–50.

(2015) 'Children and work: family strategies and socialization in Roman and late antique Egypt', in *Agents and Objects: Children in Pre-Modern Europe*, ed. K. Mustakallio and J. Hanska. Rome, 97–112.

Wald, E. (2012) *The Dozens: A History of Rap's Mama*. Oxford.

Walin, D. (2009) 'An Aristophanic slave: *Peace* 819–1126', *CQ* n.s. 59.1: 30–45.

Walker, S. and Bierbrier, M. (1997) *Ancient Faces: Mummy Portraits from Roman Egypt*. London.

Wallace-Hadrill, A. (1994) *Houses and Society in Pompeii and Herculaneum*. Princeton, NJ.

(2000) 'Case e abitanti a Roma', in *Roma Imperiale: una metropoli antica*, ed. E. Lo Cascio. Rome, 173–220.

(2008) *Rome's Cultural Revolution*. Cambridge.

Ward-Perkins, B. (1998) 'The cities', in *The Cambridge Ancient History*, vol. XI: *The Late Empire, A.D. 337–425*, ed. Av. Cameron and P. Garnsey. Cambridge, 371–410.

(2005) *The Fall of Rome and the End of Civilization*. Oxford.

Ware, K. (1993) *The Orthodox Church*. London and New York.

Weaver, P. R. C. (1972) *Familia Caesaris: A Social Study of the Emperor's Freedmen and Slaves*. Cambridge.
Webb, R. (2008a) *Demons and Dancers: Performance in Late Antiquity*. Cambridge, MA.
  (2008b) 'Behind the mask: pantomime from the performer's perspective', in *New Directions in Ancient Pantomime*, ed. E. Hall and R. Wyles. Oxford, 43–60.
  (2013) 'Mime and the romance', in *The Romance between Greece and the East*, ed. T. Whitmarsh and S. Thomson. Cambridge, 285–99.
Weinberger, Y. B. and Rosenschein, J. S. (2004) 'Passive threats among agents in state oriented domains', in *Proceedings of the 16th European Conference on Artificial Intelligence*, ed. R. López de Mántaras and L. Saitta. Valencia, 89–96.
Weinstock, S. (1964) 'Saturnalien und Neujahrsfest in den Märtyreracten', in *Mullus: Festschrift Theodor Klauser*, ed. A. Stuiber and A. Hermann. Münster, 391–400.
Wecowski, M. (2014) *The Rise of the Greek Aristocratic Banquet*. Oxford.
Welch, K. (1998) 'Caesar and his officers in the Gallic War Commentaries', in *Julius Caesar as Artful Reporter: The War Commentaries as Political Instruments*, ed. K. Welch and A. Powell. London, 85–110.
  (2007) *The Roman Amphitheatre from its Origins to the Colosseum*. Cambridge.
Whitehead, D. (1977) *The Ideology of the Athenian Metic*. Cambridge.
Whitmarsh, T. (2008a) *The Cambridge Companion to the Greek and Roman Novel*. Cambridge.
  (2008b) 'Introduction', in *The Cambridge Companion to the Greek and Roman Novel*, ed. T. Whitmarsh. Cambridge, 1–14.
  (2008c) 'Class', in *The Cambridge Companion to the Greek and Roman Novel*, ed. T. Whitmarsh. Cambridge, 72–87.
  (2011) 'Crashing the Delphic party', *LRB* 33.12: 37–8.
Whitmarsh, T. and Bartsch, S. (2008) 'Narrative', in *The Cambridge Companion to the Greek and Roman Novel*, ed. T. Whitmarsh. Cambridge, 237–57.
Whitmarsh, T. and Thomson, S. (2013) *The Romance Between Greece and the East*. Cambridge, 261–84.
Whittaker, C. R. (1992) 'Le pauvre', in *L'homme romain*, ed. A. Giardina. Paris, 335–70.
Whittow, M. (1990) 'Ruling the late Roman and early Byzantine city: a continuous history', *P&P* 129: 3–29.
Wickham, C. (2005) *Framing the Early Middle Ages: Europe and the Mediterranean, 400–800*. Oxford.
Wilkie, L. (2000) 'Not merely child's play: creating a historical archaeology of children and childhood', in *Children and Material Culture*, ed. J. Sofaer Derevenski. New York, 100–14.
Wille, G. (1967) *Musica Romana: Die Bedeutung der Musik im Leben der Römer*. Amsterdam.
Willetts, R. F. (1967) *The Law Code of Gortyn*. Berlin.
Williams, R. (1976) *Keywords: A Vocabulary of Culture and Society*. London.

Wilson, A. (2002) 'Urban production in the Roman world: the view from North Africa', *PBSR* 70: 231–73.

Wilson, P. (2000) *The Athenian Institution of the Khoregia: The Chorus, the City and the Stage*. Cambridge.

(2011) 'The glue of democracy? Tragedy, structure and finance', in *Why Athens? A Reappraisal of Tragic Politics*, ed. D. M. Carter. Oxford, 18–43.

Wirszubski, C. (1950) *Libertas as a Political Idea at Rome during the Late Republic and Early Principate*. Cambridge.

Wiseman, T. P. (1995) *Remus: A Roman Myth*. Cambridge.

(2009) *Remembering the Roman People: Essays on Late-Republican Politics and Literature*. Oxford.

Witt, R. E. (1971) *Isis in the Graeco-Roman World*. London.

Wolpert, A. and Kapparis, K. (2011) *Legal Speeches of Democratic Athens: Sources for Athenian History*. Indianapolis, IN.

Wood, E. M. (1988) *Peasant-Citizen and Slave: The Foundations of Athenian Democracy*. London.

Woolf, G. (1998) *Becoming Roman: The Origins of Provincial Civilization in Gaul*. Cambridge.

(2009) 'Literacy or literacies in Rome?', in *Ancient Literacies: The Culture of Reading in Greece and Rome*, ed. W. A. Johnson and H. N. Parker. Oxford and New York, 46–68.

(2000) 'Literacy', in *The Cambridge Ancient History*, vol. XI: *The High Empire, AD 70–192*, ed. A. K. Bowman, P. Garnsey and D. Rathbone. Cambridge, 875–97.

Wright, M. E. (2012) *The Comedian as Critic: Greek Old Comedy and Poetics*. London.

Wyles, R. (2008) 'The symbolism of costume in ancient pantomime', in *New Directions in Ancient Pantomime*, ed. E. Hall and R. Wyles. Oxford, 61–86.

Yakobson, A. (1999) *Elections and Electioneering in Rome: A Study in the Political System of the Late Republic*. Stuttgart.

Yavetz, Z. (1969) *Plebs and Princeps*. Oxford.

Yiftach-Firanko, U. (2010) 'A gymnasial registration report from Oxyrhynchus', *BASP* 47: 45–65.

Zanker, P. (1975) 'Grabreliefs römischer Freigelassener', *JDAI* 90: 257–315.

(1988) *The Power of Images in the Age of Augustus*, trans. A. Shapiro. Ann Arbor, MI.

(1998) *Pompeii: Public and Private Life*, trans. D. L. Schneider. Cambridge.

Zeitlyn, D. (1995) 'Divination as dialogue: the negotiation of meaning with random responses', in *Social Intelligence and Interaction*, ed. E. N. Goody. Cambridge, 189–205.

Zweig, B. (1992) 'The mute nude female characters in Aristophanes' plays', in *Pornography and Representation in Greece and Rome*, ed. A. Richlin. New York and Oxford, 73–89.

Index

Abzou 259
Aeneas 30, 305
Aeschines 51–2, 131
Aesop 16, 60
   Life of Aesop 16, 28, 34, 189–207
      audience of 199–200
      see also fables
Agrippa, Marcus 126
aischrologia 27, 30 *see also* insults; invective
Alexander Romance 28, 189, 197
Alexandria 23n137, 144, 229n84, 282, 285
Althusser, Louis 6–7
Ammianus Marcellinus 185, 307
amulets 232, 259–60, 263, 264, 267n41, 268, 269
Antioch 145, 238, 246, 307
Apollo 198–9, 204–5
apotropaic objects 264–9 *see also* amulets
   practices 135n15, 136n21, 244
apprenticeship 214–20
Apuleius 167, 179, 261
Aristophanes 27, 39, 66–87
   discussions of comedy 82–5
   make-up of audience 51, 69–74
   see also comedy; jokes; laughter
Aristotle 17, 66, 85n66, 86, 131, 211n11
Arnold, Matthew 4–5
art
   and popular culture 31–3
   'popular art' 32, 171
Asinius Pollio 129
Assmann, Jan 151, 160
Asterius of Amasea 241n30, 242, 243, 253, 292–3
astrologers 144, 259
Athanasius, bishop 264n27, 272
audiences
   cultural understanding 51–2, 82–6, 180–3
   psychology of 137
   social divisions 130–1
   see also Aristophanes; comedy; mime; pantomime; Spectacles

Augustine of Hippo 240, 243–4, 259, 304–16
Augustus 129, 136–7, 146, 162

Babrius 198, 204n93, 205n96
Baccus 262
Bakhtin, Mikhail 11–12, 14, 27, 28, 41, 67n7, 108, 167
   'lower bodily stratum' 167
   on ancient novels 12, 28, 192–3
   see also carnival
barbers 95, 178, 218–19, 299n16
Basil of Caesarea 289
baths 116, 126, 273
birds 195–6, 197, 201–6
board games 183–6 *see also* dice; gambling
Bourdieu, Pierre 9, 32n196, 39n3, 151n9, 180, 297
bricolage 8
Brown, Peter 24–5, 275, 278, 303
Burke, Peter 4, 10, 12–13, 33, 56

Caesarius of Arles 14, 237–8, 242–3, 244, 246–7, 253
Caligula 126, 142, 184
Caracalla 19, 145n50
carnival and carnivalesque 11–12, 16, 27, 33, 145, 167, 240, 254
Carthage 304–5, 306, 309, 311n94, 316
Catullus 132–3, 134n14, 135n15
Certeau, Michel de 8, 145–6, 297
chance 192, 195, 241n33
charioteers 300, 305
Chartier, Roger 108–9, 296
children 208–34
   as a sub-category of popular culture 208–12
   as audience 85n66, 171–2
   as transmitters of culture 226–32
   children's culture 221–6
   tombs 231–2, 263, 266–7
   see also apprenticeship; toys
Christianity
   and popular religion 24–5
   as a two-tier religion 278

365

Christianity (cont.)
   'ordinary Christianity' 258–9
   see also magic; religion; ritual
church *see* Christianity; magic; religion; ritual
Cicero 98–106
circuli 93, 302, 307–8, 309
citizenship 19, 40n6, 69, 78, 123, 145n50, 155
class 32
   and popular culture 6, 8–9
   class struggle 297
   in classical Athens 17–18, 67–8
   in the Roman world 18–19
   see also elites; non-elite/s; social status; work
Claudius 142, 146, 147, 184
Cleon 75
Clodius 35, 100, 101–2, 103, 104–6, 121, 124
cognomina 96–7 *see also* nicknames
collegia 35, 114, 300, 302, 306
comedy 27 *see also* Aristophanes; humour and popular culture
Commodus 135n15, 141n45, 142
Compitalia 114, 239, 240
Constantinople 142–3, 239
contiones 35, 92
craftsmen 31n187, 79, 80, 121–2 see also *collegia*; work
cross-dressing *see* dress; gender
crossroads (*compita*) 93–4, 97, 307 *see also* Compitalia
crowds 121, 122 *see also* audience; popular politics; riots; Spectacles
cultural capital 9, 39, 151n9 *see also* Bourdieu
cultural hegemony 7, 35n217 *see also* Gramsci
cultural history 10 *see also* Burke
culture
   as 'high culture' 4–5
   definitions of 3–4, 10
   see also elite culture; folk culture; mass culture; popular culture
curses 269–71
curse tablets 193, 270–1

dance
   and popular culture 15
   at festivals 241, 250–1, 286
   dancers fig. 11.3, fig, 11.4, 250–1
   as term of abuse 94, 98
   pantomime dancers 179–82 *see also* pantomime
defixiones see curse tablets
Demosthenes 47, 49, 131–2
dice 184, 240, 241 *see also* board games; gambling; oracles

   in tombs 265
divination 193–207 *see also* omens; oracles
Domitian 126, 142, 240n25
Donatists 310–14
dolls 222–4, 266
dreams 192–3, 194, 204, 258, 272
dress
   and identity 60, 231–2
   dressing up 246–7, 253–5
      as animals 247, 250–1
      cross-dressing 242–3, 253–5
drinking 241, 286, 307

Egypt 211–34
elite culture
   as authorized culture 39–41
   as the subject of 'Classics' 1
   as unofficial culture 57–63, 65
elites
   and popular culture 12–13
   definition 17, 18, 24, 131
   see also elite culture
Ephesus 285, 301–2
epigraphy 159
   inscriptions 29, 48, 158–9, 172n16, 267
epitaphs 116, 117, 118, 119, 172n16, 209

fables 33, 60, 172–6, 198 *see also* Aesop; Phaedrus
farmers 18, 50n44, 79, 80, 87, 173, 197 *see also* peasants
Fayum 213, 216, 232
Fescennine verses 129, 130, 136
festivals 26–7, 40 *see also* carnival; Kalends; martyrs; ritual; Saturnalia
figurines 31, 225, 231n96, 263, 264n23 *see also* dolls
folk culture 4, 20
Forsdyke, Sara 16–17, 41–2, 52–3, 55, 60
fortune-telling 177, 193, 197n59
fountains 92, 93–4
Frankfurter, David 25, 26n154, 272, 273, 278
freedmen/women 14, 22, 229
freedom of speech 92 *see also* licence
frumentationes see grain, dole
fullers 18n104, 30

gambling 183–6, 188, 241, 300 *see also* board games; dice
Games, Roman *see* Spectacles
Geertz, Clifford 10, 170, 183
gender
   socialization 213n15, 222, 223, 233

transgression 27, 134–5, 242–3 *see also* dress
Ginzburg, Carlo 42–3, 109n12
gladiators 125, 129, 137, 146, 267, 300
gossip 92, 93, 95 *see also* rumour
Gracchi brothers 35n215, 94, 98, 105, 106
graffiti 30, 93, 169, 210n7, 267, 302
grain
    dole 111–13, 124
    supply 101–3
Gramsci, Antonio 6–7, 296–7
Gregory of Nazianzus 284
Gregory of Nyssa 284, 289, 294
Gurevich, Aaron 13–14

Hall, Stuart 7–8, 297
Harris, William 28–9
Hecate 262
Herodas 1, 190n12 *see also* mime
'hidden transcripts' 7, 33, 64n94, 91n1, 176
Hoggart, Richard 108
Homer 51–2, 178, 189, 195
Horace 94, 97, 107, 132, 133, 261
Horsfall, Nicholas 14–15, 19n112, 30, 150, 169, 172n16
humiliation, rituals of 53–4, 313
humour and popular culture 176, 185, 197n59 *see also* Aristophanes; comedy; jokes; laughter

iambics 73n34, 134n14
ideology and popular culture, 5–9, 33–4 *see also* Althusser; cultural hegemony; Hall; Marxist theory; mass culture
illiteracy 169 *see also* literacy
inscriptions *see* epigraphy; epitaphs
insults 132–4 *see also* invective; nicknames
invective 129–48 *see also* iambics; insult
Isis and Serapis 22, 198, 204, 231, 232, 262, 264, 269

John Chrysostom 259, 287, 289–91, 293–4
jokes 133, 177–8 *see also* Aristophanes; comedy; humour; *Philogelos*
Julian 135n15, 145, 290n49
Julius Caesar 134–5
Justinian 142
Juvenal 36, 95, 111, 125, 147n57, 152

Kalends of January 26 132, 145, 237–56
Karanis 213, 214–15, 216, 225, 231

Kronia, *see* Saturnalia
Kurke, Leslie 15–16, 183

laughter 11, 82–5 *see also* carnival; comedy; humour and popular culture
lawcourt, as a popular site 49–52, 120
Libanius 181, 238n7, 241n34, 241n36, 242, 244n55
licence 11, 241–2
    theatralis licentia 137, 139n36, 147, 301
literacy 28–9, 168–9, 312–13 *see also* orality
Lucian 132, 180–2, 190n10
Lucilius 134n14
Ludi see Spectacles
Lysias 43–7, 61

MacMullen, Ramsay 24, 255, 281, 283, 285, 286n34
Macrobius 119, 129n1
magic 23–4, 184, 257–76 *see also* Christianity; religion; ritual; superstition
Marcus Aurelius 145, 146
Marius 123, 143
martyrs, cult of 24, 278
    festivals 279–80, 286–7, 294–5, 308
    shrines 272–3
Marxist theory 5–6
masks 180, 246, 252
mass culture 5 *see also* popular culture, and mass culture
memory
    cultural/popular memory 91, 106, 111, 113, 160, 226
metics 40, 68, 73, 74, 79
middle classes 17, 18n107, 107n6 *see also* plebs, *plebs media*
mime 27, 182, 190
music, musicians 149–64, 179, 250, fig.11.3 *see also* songs and singing
myth 171–2, 179

Naples 257–8, 267n41
necromancy 261, 271–2 *see also* magic
Nero 141–2, 145
nicknames 91–106 *see also* insults
non-elite/s, definition of 17, 109 *see also* elites; plebeian; plebs; social status
novels, ancient 1, 27–8, 192–3
numeracy 183

Octavian, *see* Augustus
Old Comedy *see* Aristophanes; comedy

omens 94, 193, 195, 196, 201–2, *see also* birds; divination; oracles
oracles
  dice/lot oracles 26, 186–7, 194, 196n50, 206, 207 *see also* dice
  octopus oracles 194n36
  oracles of Astrampsychus 197
  saints' oracles 272
  skull oracles 257–8, 272, 275
  see also divination
orality, oral tradition 28–30, 169, 190 *see also* literacy
Ostia 30, 95, 114, 115–16, 161, 176
Oxyrhynchus, 214, 217–18, 221, 223–4, 227, 228–9, 230, 232

pantomime 178–83
papyri 26, 28, 211, 232
Parker, H. N. 3, 8–9, 39–40, 277n1
peasants 18, 19, 20 *see also* farmers
Peter Chrysologus 245, 246, 254n94
Petronius 131, 172n16, 174
Phaedrus 174, 175n41, 197, 199
Philogelos 177–8, 190
philosophy
  as an activity for the elite 167–8
  mocked 30–1, 176–7
  popular 171–6
phylacteries, *see* amulets
Plautus 27n161, 93, 95
plebeian
  as a synonym/alternative for 'popular' 32n191, 107–28
plebs
  and the emperor 125–7, 140–7
  definition 107–8
  political activity 34–5, 92, 120–7 *see also* popular politics
  plebs frumentaria 111–12
  plebs media 107, 118n64
politics *see* popular politics
Pompeii 22, 32–3, 94, 95, 169
popular culture
  and the church 245, 304–16
  and elite culture 42, 63–5, 188, 278–9
  and mass culture 6, 8n35 *see also* Parker, Holt
  and poverty 110–13, 121, 174, 185, 306
  and power relations 173–4, 206–7, 296–7
  and resistance 7–8, 33, 119–20, 255–6
  as 'trickle down' 32–3, 287
  comparative approaches 13, 16, 41
  definitions 3, 36, 39, 108–9

history of scholarship of 4–17, 108–9
interpenetration by high culture 12, 27, 66–7, 86–7, 198–9 *see also* Bakhtin; graffiti
rural versus urban 19–20
popular justice 53–5
popular literature 27–8, 189–91 *see also* Aesop; fables; novels, ancient
popular morality 172–5, 278–9 *see also* fables; philosophy
popular politics 34–6 *see also* plebs, political activity; popular culture, and resistance; protests
populus Romanus 34, 141 *see also* plebs
poverty *see* class; popular culture, and poverty
protests 125–6, 154, 302–3
proverbs 172–5

Rabelais *see* Bakhtin
Ravenna 246
Redfield, Robert 12, 25
religion
  'lived religion' 26, 258
  popular religion 21–6, 191–3, 277–9, 280–1
  see also Christianity; divination; magic; ritual; sacrifice; superstition; theology
riots 101–3, 122, 142, 283, 315–16
risk management 185–7, 193
ritual
  and cultural memory 160–1
  and insult/invective 132, 136
  see also apotropaic, practices; festivals; magic; popular justice; religion; sacrifice
Rome
  Arx 156
  Catacombs 260–73
  Forum Romanum 93, 121, 144, 156–7
  Theatre of Pompey 138–40
rumour 92, 94, 302, 308, 314–15 *see also* gossip

sacrifice 153–4, 161 *see also* ritual
saints *see* martyrs
Saturnalia 26–7, 199, 239–40, 241–2
Scott, James C. 7, 64, 176, 240n23, 303n42 *see also* 'hidden transcripts'
senses, history of 20, 150, 163
shops 95, 114–15, 121 see also *tabernae*
slaves
  and fables 174, 175
  and popular culture 40, 192n21
  and Saturnalia/Kalends 241

child slaves 213–15, 219, 228–9
ownership by non-elite 18, 45
religion 22
subjectivity 33–4
see also Aesop; fables
sociabilité 298
social mobility 184, 196, 198
social status *see* class; elites; non-elite/s
soldiers 144–5, 156–7, 225, 242–3
songs and singing 243–4, 305, 306, 310–11 *see also* music
Spectacles
   expression of public opinion at 94, 125–7 *see also* licence; plebs, and the emperor
   in Late Antiquity 304–5
   music at 152
   organization of 152–3
   Secular Games 158–9
   see also audience; mime; pantomime; theatre
subaltern studies 7
superstition 22–4, 194 *see also* Christianity; magic; religion, *esp.* popular religion

tabernae 114, 299 *see also* shops
taverns 95, 114–15, 306–7
theatre *see* Aristophanes; audiences; comedy; mime; pantomime; Spectacles; tragedy
theology 277–95
Thompson, E. P. 9–10, 33n203, 297
Tiberius, emperor 126, 143–4, 240n29
Toner, Jerry 15, 17, 164, 240
toys 222–6
tragedy 50, 85n66
triumph, Roman 134–5, 144n49, 153

Vespasian 144
violence 184, 307, 311, 313–14
   see also riots
Virgil 30, 169, 304–5

wages 43–4, 111–12, 215
Williams, Raymond 3–4
Wiseman, Peter 29–30, 33n205
witches 23 *see also* magic; necromancy
work
   and non-elite identity 117–19
   children and 215–20